W9-AAG-568

CompTIA

Network+

Exam N10-002

Drew Bird
Mike Harwood

Training Guide

NETWORK+ TRAINING GUIDE

International Standard Book Number: 0-7897-2830-3

Library of Congress Catalog Card Number: 2002108936

Printed in the United States of America

First Printing: August 2002

07   06   7

Trademarks

Warning and Disclaimer

PUBLISHER
Paul Boger

ACQUISITIONS EDITOR
Jeff Riley

DEVELOPMENT EDITOR
Ginny Bess Munroe

MANAGING EDITOR
Thomas F. Hayes

PROJECT EDITOR
Tonya Simpson

COPY EDITOR
Kitty Wilson Jarrett

INDEXER
Ginny Bess Munroe

PROOFREADER
Juli Cook

TECHNICAL EDITORS
Dave Bixler
Bill Ferguson

TEAM COORDINATOR
Rosemary Lewis

MULTIMEDIA DEVELOPER
Michael Hunter

INTERIOR DESIGNER
Louisa Klucznik

COVER DESIGNER
Charis Ann Santille

PAGE LAYOUT
Cheryl Lynch

Contents at a Glance

Introduction *1*

PART I Exam Preparation

1 Introduction to Networking 15
2 Cabling and Connectors 59
3 Networking Components and Devices 101
4 The OSI Model 149
5 Overview of Network Protocols 171
6 Working with TCP/IP 201
7 WAN Technologies 257
8 Remote Access and Security Protocols 289
9 Network Operating Systems and Clients 315
10 Fault Tolerance, Disaster Recovery, VLANs, and NAS 383
11 Configuring Network Connectivity 423
12 Securing the Network 459
13 Troubleshooting Connectivity 497
14 Troubleshooting Tools and Utilities 547
15 Troubleshooting Procedures and Best Practices 581

PART II Final Review

Fast Facts 627
Study and Exam Preparation Tips 647
Practice Exam 653

PART III Appendixes

A Glossary 675

B Overview of the Certification Process 703

C What's on the CD-ROM 705

D Using the *PrepLogic Practice Tests, Preview Edition* Software 707

Index 713

Table of Contents

PART I: Exam Preparation

1 Introduction to Networking   **15**

Introduction 18

What Is a Network? 18
    The Functions of a Network 19

Peer-to-Peer Versus Client/Server Networks 20
    The Peer-to-Peer Networking Model 21
    The Client/Server Networking Model 23
    Distributed and Centralized Computing 26

LANs, WANs, and MANs 26
    LANs 27
    WANs 27
    MANs 28

LAN Topologies 28
    Physical and Logical Topologies 29
    The Bus Topology 29
    The Star Topology 31
    The Ring Topology 32
    Mesh Topology 33
    Wireless Topology 34

The IEEE and Networking Standards 36
    Characteristics Specified in the IEEE 802 Standards ... 38
    The IEEE 802 Standards 45
    Exercises 52
    Exam Questions 53
    Answers to Review Questions 56

2 Cabling and Connectors   **59**

Introduction 62

Media Considerations 62
    Media Interference 62
    Bandwidth 63

Media Length 64

Security 65

Installation and Repair 65

Baseband Versus Broadband Signaling 65

Baseband 66

Broadband 66

Simplex, Half-Duplex, and Full-Duplex 66

Common Network Cable 68

Cable Media 68

Cable Summary 73

Wireless Media 74

Media Connectors 78

D-shell Connectors 78

RJ Connectors 81

BNCs 82

Fiber Connectors 82

Centronic Connectors 83

Features and Characteristics of Ethernet 802.3 Standards ... 84

10Base2 84

10Base5 86

10BaseT 87

Fast Ethernet: 100BaseX 89

Gigabit Ethernet: 1000BaseX 90

Choosing the Appropriate Media Connector for Adding Clients to an
Existing Network 92

Exercises 95

Exam Questions 95

Answers to Exam Questions 98

3 Networking Components and Devices   101

Introduction 104

Hubs 104

Switches 106

Switching Methods 108

Working with Hubs and Switches 109

Hub and Switch Ports 110

Cables Connecting Hubs and Switches 111

Hub and Switch Indicator Lights 112

Rack Mount, Stackable, and Freestanding Devices 113

Managed Hubs and Switches 113

Bridges 114

Bridge Implementation Considerations 114

Types of Bridges 115

Routers 116

Routable Protocols and Routing Protocols 118

Dedicated Hardware Versus Server-Based Routers 123

Gateways 124

CSUs/DSUs 125

Wireless Access Point (WAPs) 126

Modems 126

Modem Connection Speeds 127

Network Cards (NICs) 129

Types of Network Interfaces 130

Installing Network Cards 133

ISDN Terminal Adapters 135

System Area Network Cards 137

Network Devices Summary 137

Identifying MAC Addresses 138

Exercises 142

Exam Questions 142

Answers to Exam Questions 145

4 The OSI Model   149

Introduction 151

Why Do We Need a Network Model? 151

OSI Reference Model 101 151

Layer 1: The Physical Layer 153

Layer 2: The Data-Link Layer 154

Layer 3: The Network Layer 155

Layer 4: The Transport Layer 157

Layer 5: The Session Layer 159

Layer 6: The Presentation Layer 159

Layer 7: The Application Layer 160

OSI Model Summary 161

The Layers at Which Devices Operate 162
   Hubs 162
   Switches 162
   Bridges 163
   Routers 163
   NICs 163
   Summary of the Layers at Which Devices Operate 164
   Exercises 166
   Exam Questions 166
   Answers to Exam Questions 169

5 **Overview of Network Protocols**   **171**

   Introduction 174
   Introduction to Protocols 174
      The Function of Protocols 175
      Mapping Protocols to the OSI Model 177
   Transmission Control Protocol/Internet Protocol (TCP/IP) 179
      A Brief History of TCP/IP 179
      The TCP/IP Protocol Suite 180
      TCP/IP Standards 180
      TCP/IP Addressing 181
      TCP/IP Interoperability 182
      TCP/IP Naming 182
      TCP/IP Routing Protocols 183
      Mapping TCP/IP to the OSI Model 183
   Internetwork Packet Exchange/Sequenced Packet Exchange (IPX/SPX) 183
      The IPX/SPX Protocol Suite 184
      IPX Addressing 186
      Mapping IPX/SPX to the OSI Model 187
      IPX/SPX Interoperability 187
      IPX/SPX Naming 187
   AppleTalk 188
      AppleTalk Addressing 189
      Mapping AppleTalk to the OSI Model 190
      AppleTalk Interoperability 190
      AppleTalk Routing 191
      AppleTalk Naming 191
   NetBEUI 191
      Mapping NetBEUI to the OSI Model 191
      NetBEUI Addressing 325 192

Protocol Overview and Comparison 192
    Exercises 195
    Exam Questions 196
    Answers to Exam Questions 198

6 Working with TCP/IP   201

Introduction 205
TCP/IP Protocols 205
    Internet Protocol (IP) 205
    Transmission Control Protocol (TCP) 206
    User Datagram Protocol (UDP) 206
    File Transfer Protocol (FTP) 207
    Trivial File Transfer Protocol (TFTP) 209
    Simple Mail Transfer Protocol (SMTP) 209
    Hypertext Transfer Protocol (HTTP) 209
    Hypertext Transfer Protocol Secure (HTTPS) 210
    Post Office Protocol/Internet Message Access Protocol (POP/IMAP) 210
    Telnet 211
    Internet Control Message Protocol (ICMP) 211
    Address Resolution Protocol (ARP) 212
    Network Time Protocol (NTP) 213
    TCP/IP Protocol Suite Summary 213
TCP/UDP Ports 214
TCP/IP-Based Network Services 216
    Dynamic Host Configuration Protocol (DHCP) 217
    BOOT Protocol (BOOTP) 220
    Domain Name System (DNS) 220
    Network Address Translation (NAT) and Internet Connection
        Sharing (ICS) 224
    Simple Network Management Protocol (SNMP) 226
    SNMP Communities 230
    Windows Internet Name Service (WINS) 230
    TCP/IP Service Summary 232
IP Addressing 233
    General IP Addressing Principles 233
    IPv4 234
    IP Address Classes 235
    Subnet Mask Assignment 236
    IPv6 237

Subnetting 238

Reasons to Subnet 241

Default Gateways 241

Identifying the Differences Between Public and Private Networks 242

    Private Address Ranges 244

    Practical Uses of Public and Private IP Addressing 245

    Exercises 247

    Exam Questions 250

    Answers to Exam Questions 253

7 WAN Technologies   257

Introduction 260

Introduction to WAN Technologies 260

    Public Networks 261

    Private Networks 263

    Switching Methods 264

    Packet Switching 265

    Circuit Switching 267

    Message Switching 268

    Switching Methods Comparison 268

WAN Technologies 269

    Dial-up Modem Connections 270

    Integrated Services Digital Network (ISDN) 270

    T-carrier Lines 272

    Fiber Distributed Data Interface (FDDI) 274

    Asynchronous Transfer Mode (ATM) 277

    X.25 278

    Frame Relay 278

    SONET/OC*x* 279

    WAN Technology Summary 280

    Exercises 282

    Exam Questions 282

    Answers to Exam Questions 285

8 Remote Access and Security Protocols   289

Introduction 291

Remote Access Protocols and Services 292

    Remote Access Service (RAS) 292

    Serial Line Internet Protocol (SLIP) 294

Point-to-Point Protocol (PPP) 295
PPTP 297
Independent Computing Architecture (ICA) 298

Security Protocols 299
IPSec 300
L2F 301
Layer Two Tunneling Protocol (L2TP) 301
Secure Sockets Layer (SSL) 302
Kerberos 303
SSH 303
Remote Authentication Dial-In User Service (RADIUS) 304

Types of Remote Access 304
Dial-up Remote Access 305
Virtual Private Networks 305
Exercises 307
Exam Questions 310
Answers to Exam Questions 312

9 Network Operating Systems and Clients **315**

Introduction 319

Introduction to Network Operating Systems 319
Choosing a Network Operating System 320
Which Network Operating System Is Best? 321

Windows NT 4 324
Domains and Workgroups 325
Windows NT 4 System Requirements 327
Windows NT 4 File Systems 327
Windows NT 4 Monitoring and Performance Tools 328
Windows NT 4 User Management Basics 331
Verifying Network Settings in Windows NT 4 332
Windows NT 4 Authentication 333
Windows NT 4 File and Print Services 333
Windows NT 4 Application Support 334
Windows NT 4 Security 334

Windows 2000 335
Windows 2000 Active Directory and Domains 335
Windows 2000 System Requirements 336
Windows 2000 File Systems 337
Windows 2000 Monitoring and Performance Tools 337

Managing Windows 2000 Disk Drives 341
Windows 2000 User Management Basics 342
Windows 2000 Authentication 342
Windows 2000 File and Print Services 343
Windows 2000 Application Support 344
Windows 2000 Security 344

Novell NetWare 344
NetWare System Requirements 345
NetWare File Systems 345
NetWare Performance-Monitoring Tools 346
NetWare User Administration 347
NetWare Server Configuration 348
Viewing and Changing a NetWare Network Configuration 349
NetWare Authentication 350
NetWare File and Print Services 351
NetWare Application Support 351
NetWare Security 352

Linux 353
Linux System Requirements 355
Linux File Systems 355
Linux Monitoring and Performance Tools 356
Managing Linux Disk Drives 358
Linux User Management Basics 358
Verifying Linux Network Settings 360
Linux Authentication 360
Linux File and Print Services 360
Linux Application Support 361
Linux Security 362

Operating System Interoperability 363
Using Windows with NetWare 364
Using Windows and Linux Servers 364
Using NetWare and Linux Servers 365

Operating System Client Support 365
Windows Server Client Support 365
NetWare Server Client Support 366
Linux Server Client Support 366

Client Operating Systems 367
Windows 95, Windows 98, and Windows Me 367
Windows NT Workstation, Windows 2000 Professional, and
    Windows XP Professional 369

Linux 370

Macintosh 372

Exercises 375

Exam Questions 377

Answers to Exam Questions 380

10 Fault Tolerance, Disaster Recovery, VLANs, and NAS   383

Introduction 386

Understanding Fault Tolerance 386

RAID 388

Other Fault-Tolerance Measures 398

Disaster Recovery 403

Backup Methods 403

A Comparison of Backup Methods 405

Backup Rotation Schedules 406

Backup Best Practices 407

VLANs 408

VLAN Membership 409

Network Storage 411

Traditional File Server Storage 411

Network Attached Storage (NAS) 412

SANs 413

Exercise 416

Exam Questions 417

Answers to Exam Questions 419

11 Configuring Network Connectivity   423

Introduction 426

Configuring Remote Connectivity 426

Physical Connections 427

Protocols 428

Software 429

Dial-up Access 430

Security 432

Selecting an NIC and Network Configuration Settings 432

Choosing an NIC 433

Installing an NIC 433

Connecting the PC to the Network 435

Testing and Troubleshooting the NIC 436

Configuring the NIC Settings 437
Using DHCP 442

Configuring Clients to Access Servers 443
Configuring Microsoft Windows Clients 443
Novell Client Software 444
Unix/Linux Client Software 446

Adding, Modifying, or Removing Network Services 446
Adding, Modifying, or Removing DHCP 447
Adding, Modifying, or Removing WINS 448
Adding, Modifying, or Removing DNS 449
Exercises 451
Exam Questions 452
Answers to Exam Questions 455

12 Securing the Network **459**

Introduction 462

Threats to Security 462
Security Responsibilities of a Network Administrator ... 464

Physical and Logical Security 465
Physical Security 465
Logical Security 466

Firewalls 475
The Purpose and Function of a Firewall 476
Demilitarized Zones 478

Proxy Servers 479
Caching Proxy Servers 480
Using a Proxy Server 482

Understanding How Security Affects a Network 482
Blocking Port Numbers 483
Encryption 484
Auditing 487
Exercises 489
Exam Questions 491
Answers to Exam Questions 493

13 Troubleshooting Connectivity **497**

Introduction 500

Troubleshooting Tools 500
The ping Utility 501
The Trace Route Utility 504

The arp Utility 506

The netstat Utility 507

The nbtstat Utility 509

The ipconfig and ifconfig Utilities 511

The winipcfg Utility 512

The nslookup Utility 513

The route Utility 515

Troubleshooting in a Small Office/Home Office Environment 516

DSL Internet Access 520

Cable Internet Access 523

Home Satellite Internet Access 525

Wireless Internet Access 526

POTS Internet Access 528

Calling Technical Support 533

Troubleshooting Remote Connectivity Errors 534

Troubleshooting Authentication Failure 534

Troubleshooting Physical Connectivity Problems 535

Troubleshooting Protocol Configuration Problems 536

Exercises 539

Exam Questions 540

Answers to Exam Questions 544

14 Troubleshooting Tools and Utilities   547

Introduction 549

Selecting the Appropriate Tool for Wiring 549

Wire Crimpers 550

Punchdown Tools 550

Tone Generators 551

Media Testers 552

Hardware Loopback Connectors 553

Interpreting Visual Indicators 553

LEDs on Networking Devices 554

LEDs on NICs and Other Devices 555

Using Diagnostic Utilities 557

ping 557

The tracert Command 560

The netstat Command 563

The ipconfig Command 568

The winipcfg Command 570

Exercises 572
Exam Questions 573
Answers to Exam Questions 577

15 Troubleshooting Procedures and Best Practices   581

Introduction 584
Troubleshooting Basics 584
Troubleshooting Servers and Workstations 585
General Troubleshooting Considerations 586
The Art of Troubleshooting 588
Establishing What the Symptoms Are 589
Identifying the Affected Area 592
Establishing What Has Changed 592
Selecting the Most Probable Cause of the Problem 594
Implementing a Solution 595
Testing the Results 596
Recognizing the Potential Effects of the Solution 596
Documenting the Solution 597
Troubleshooting Topology Errors 598
Bus Network Errors 598
Star Network Errors 599
Ring Network Errors 601
Mesh Network Errors 601
Wireless Network Errors 602
Troubleshooting Client Connectivity Errors 602
Protocol Errors 603
Authentication 604
Permissions Errors 605
Physical Connectivity Errors 606
Troubleshooting Wiring- and Infrastructure-Related Problems 607
Troubleshooting Wiring 608
Troubleshooting the Infrastructure 609
Troubleshooting Checklists 611
Troubleshooting Cable Problems 611
Troubleshooting Network Connectivity 612
Troubleshooting Network Printing 613
Troubleshooting Data Access 613
Troubleshooting NICs 614
Exercises 617
Exam Questions 617
Answers to Exam Questions 621

PART II: Final Review

Fast Facts   **627**

1.0—Media and Topologies 627
    Network Types and Physical and Logical Topologies 628
    Standards and Access Methods 630
    Media Considerations and Limitations 631
    Dialog Modes 632
    Network Media 632
    10BaseX, 100BaseX, and 1000BaseX Standards 633
    Network Devices 634

2.0—Protocols and Standards 637
    OSI Model 637
    TCP/IP 639
    Public Versus Private Networks 640
    WAN Technologies 640
    Remote Access and Security Protocols 641

3.0—Network Implementation 642
    Backups 642
    LANs and NAS 643
    Client Connectivity 643
    Security: Physical, Logical, Passwords, and Firewalls 643
    Proxy Servers 644
    Port Blocking 644

4.0—Network Support 644
    TCP/IP Utilities 644
    DSL 645
    Media Tools and LEDs 645
    Troubleshooting Steps 645

Study and Exam Prep Tips   **647**

Learning As a Process 647

Study Tips 648
    Study Strategies 648
    Pretesting Yourself 649

Exam Prep Tips 649
    More Exam Prep Tips 650
    Tips for During the Exam Session 650

Practice Exam   **653**

Answers to Exam Questions 664

PART III: Appendixes

A Glossary   **675**

B Overview of the Certification Process   **703**

Description of the Path to Certification 703

About the Network+ Certification Program 703

C What's on the CD-ROM   **705**

PrepLogic Practice Tests, Preview Edition 705

D Using the *PrepLogic Practice Tests, Preview Edition* Software   **707**

Exam Simulation 707

Question Quality 707

Interface Design 707

Effective Learning Environment 707

Software Requirements 708

Installing *PrepLogic Practice Tests, Preview Edition* 708

   Removing *PrepLogic Practice Tests, Preview Edition* from Your Computer 708

Using *PrepLogic Practice Tests, Preview Edition* 708

   Starting a Practice Test Mode Session 709

   Starting a Flash Review Mode Session 709

   Standard *PrepLogic Practice Tests, Preview Edition* Options 709

   Time Remaining 710

   Your Examination Score Report 710

   Review Your Exam 710

Get More Exams 710

   Contacting PrepLogic 711

Customer Service 711

   Product Suggestions and Comments 711

   License Agreement 711

Index   **713**

About the Authors

Mike Harwood (MCSE, A+, Network+, Server+, Linux+) is the manager of a multisite network and co-author of numerous computer books. When he's not working, Mike entertains his two daughters, Paige and Breanna, with stories of magical lands where networks configure themselves and users are always friendly.

Drew Bird (CNI, MCNE, MCP, Network+, Server+, Linux+) has been working in the IT industry since 1988. In addition to authoring a number of computer books and performing training and consultancy assignments, Drew is the managing editor of the Internet.com-owned Web sites EnterpriseStorageForum.com and IntranetJournal.com. Drew lives with his wife, Zoë, and their dog, Merlin, in the hills outside Kelowna, British Columbia, Canada. When he's not working, Drew enjoys most outdoor activities, including snowboarding, camping, and kayaking.

About the Technical Reviewers

Bill Ferguson (MCT, MCSE, MCP+I, A+, Network+) has been in the computer industry for more than 15 years. Originally in technical sales and sales management with Sprint, Bill made his transition to Certified Technical Trainer in 1997, with ExecuTrain. Bill now runs his own company as an independent contractor in Birmingham, Alabama, teaching classes for most of the national training companies and some regional training companies. In addition, Bill writes and produces technical training videos for Virtual Training Company, Inc. He currently has certifications in A+, Network+, Windows 2000 management, Windows XP management, and Windows 2000 security. Bill keeps his skills sharp by reviewing books and sample tests. He says, "My job is to understand the material so well that I can make it easier for my students to learn than it was for me to learn."

Dave Bixler (MCSE, MCNE, PSE, CCSE) is the technology services manager for one of the largest systems integrators in the United States. He has been working in the industry for the past 15 years, working on network designs, server implementations, and network management. Dave has focused on Internet technologies, including DNS and Web servers, information security, firewalls, and Windows 2000. Dave has also worked on a number of titles as an author, a technical editor, or a book reviewer. Dave's industry certifications include Microsoft's MCPS and MCSE, as well as Novell's CNE for NetWare versions 3.x, 4.x, and IntranetWare, ECNE, and MCNE. Dave lives in Cincinnati, Ohio, with his wife, Sarah, and his sons, Marty and Nicholas.

Dedication

This book is dedicated to camping trips, Chinese food, Bruce Springsteen, Eric Clapton, and Homer Simpson. Without these, this book would not have been possible. :)

Acknowledgments

We would like to thank our family and friends for putting up with the long hours required to complete this project—twice!

We also would like to say a huge thanks our new friends at Que Publishing, Ginny Bess and Tonya Simpson, who had the daunting task of reshaping and formatting this book on a seemingly impossible time line. How they managed to do it we will never know. Thanks to Kitty ("Edits here ok?") Jarrett, for her thorough copy edits and for spotting our mistakes.

We can't forget the technical editors, Dave Bixler and Bill Ferguson, who kept us on track technically. And finally, thanks to Jeff Riley for overseeing the project and giving us a chance in the first place.

We Want to Hear from You!

As the reader of this book, *you* are our most important critic and commentator. We value your opinion and want to know what we're doing right, what we could do better, what areas you'd like to see us publish in, and any other words of wisdom you're willing to pass our way.

As an executive editor for Que, I welcome your comments. You can email or write me directly to let me know what you did or didn't like about this book—as well as what we can do to make our books better.

Please note that I cannot help you with technical problems related to the *topic* of this book. We do have a User Services group, however, where I will forward specific technical questions related to the book.

When you write, please be sure to include this book's title and author as well as your name, email address, and phone number. I will carefully review your comments and share them with the author and editors who worked on the book.

Email: feedback@quepublishing.com

Mail: Jeff Riley
            Que Certification
            800 East 96th Street
            Indianapolis, IN 46240 USA

For more information about this book or another Que title, visit our Web site at www.quepublishing.com. Type the ISBN (excluding hyphens) or the title of a book in the Search field to find the page you're looking for.

Introduction

The CompTIA Network+ exam has become the leading introductory-level network certification available today. Network+ is recognized by both employers and industry giants such as Microsoft and Novell as providing candidates with a solid foundation of networking concepts, terminology, and skills. The Network+ exam covers a broad range of networking concepts, to prepare candidates for the technologies that they are likely to be working with in today's network environments.

This book is your one-stop shop. Everything you need to know to pass the exam is in here. You do not have to take a class in addition to buying this book in order to pass the exam. However, depending on your personal study habits or learning style, you might benefit from buying this book *and* taking a class.

Training guides are meticulously crafted to give you the best possible learning experience for the particular characteristics of the technology covered and the actual certification exam. The instructional design that is implemented in the training guides reflects the task- and experience-based nature of CompTIA certification exams. The training guides provide you with the factual knowledge base you need for the exams, but then take it to the next level, with exercises and exam questions that require you to engage in the analytic thinking that is needed to pass the Network+ exam.

CompTIA recommends that the typical candidate for this exam have a minimum of nine months' experience in network support and administration. In addition, CompTIA recommends that candidates have preexisting hardware knowledge such as CompTIA A+ certification.

HOW THIS BOOK HELPS YOU

This book takes you on a self-guided tour of all the areas covered by the Network+ exam and teaches you the specific skills you need in order to achieve your certification. The book also contains helpful hints, tips, real-world examples, and exercises, as well as references to additional study materials. Specifically, this book is set up to help you in the following ways:

◆ **Organization**—This book is organized by individual exam objectives. Every objective you need to know for the Network+ exam is covered in this book. We have attempted to present the objectives in an order that is as close as possible to that listed by CompTIA. However, we have not hesitated to reorganize them where needed to make the material as easy as possible for you to learn. We have also attempted to make the information accessible in the following ways:

  • The full list of exam units and objectives is included in this introduction.

  • Each chapter begins with a list of the objectives to be covered.

  • Each chapter also begins with an outline that provides you with an overview of the material and the page numbers where particular topics can be found.

  • The objectives are repeated where the material most directly relevant to it is covered.

◆ **Instructional features**—This book has been designed to provide you with multiple ways to learn and reinforce the exam material. Following are some of the helpful methods:

- *Objective explanations*—As mentioned previously, each chapter begins with a list of the objectives covered in the chapter. In addition, immediately following each objective is an explanation of the objective, in a context that defines it meaningfully.

- *Study strategies*—The beginning of each chapter also includes strategies for approaching the studying and retention of the material in the chapter, particularly as it is addressed on the exam, but also in ways that will benefit you on the job.

- *Exam tips*—Exam tips provide specific exam-related advice. Such tips might address what material is covered (or not covered) on the exam, how it is covered, mnemonic devices, or particular quirks of that exam.

- *Review breaks and summaries*—Crucial information is summarized at various points in the book in lists or tables. Each chapter ends with a summary as well.

- *Key terms*—A list of key terms appears at the end of each chapter.

- *Notes*—Notes contain various kinds of useful or practical information such as tips on technology or administrative practices, historical background on terms and technologies, or side commentary on industry issues.

- *Warnings*—When using sophisticated information technology, there is always the potential for mistakes or even catastrophes to occur because of improper application of the technology. Warnings alert you to such potential problems.

- *In the Field sidebars*—These relatively extensive discussions cover material that might not be directly relevant to the exam but that is useful as reference material or in everyday practice. In the Field sidebars also provide useful background or contextual information that is necessary for understanding the larger topic under consideration.

- *Exercises*—Found at the end of the chapters in the "Apply Your Knowledge" section, exercises are performance-based opportunities for you to learn and assess your knowledge.

◆ **Extensive practice test options**—The book provides numerous opportunities for you to assess your knowledge and practice for the exam. The practice options include the following:

- *Exam questions*—These questions appear in the "Apply Your Knowledge" section. You can use them to help determine what you know and what you need to review or study further. Answers and explanations for these questions are provided in a separate section, titled "Answers to Exam Questions."

- *Practice exam*—A practice exam is included in the "Final Review" section of the book. The "Final Review" section and the practice exam are discussed below.

- *PrepLogic.* The *PrepLogic, Preview Edition* software included on the CD-ROM provides further practice questions.

NOTE

PrepLogic, Preview Edition Software
For a complete description of the PrepLogic test engine, please see Appendix D, "*Using the PrepLogic Practice Tests, Preview Edition Software.*"

◆ **Final Review**—This part of the book provides three valuable tools for preparing for the exam:

- *Fast Facts*—This condensed version of the information contained in the book is extremely useful for last-minute review.

- *Study and Exam Tips*—You should read this section early on, to help develop study strategies. This section also provides you with valuable exam-day tips and information on exam/question formats such as adaptive tests and case study–based questions.

- *Practice exam*—A practice test is included. Questions on this practice exam are written in styles similar to those used on the actual exam. You should use the practice exam to assess your readiness for the real thing. Use the extensive answer explanations to improve your retention and understanding of the material.

The book includes several other features, such as a section titled "Suggested Readings and Resources" at the end of each chapter that directs you to additional information that can aid you in your exam preparation and your real-life work. There are valuable appendixes as well, including a glossary (Appendix A), an overview of the certification process (Appendix B), a description of what is on the CD-ROM (Appendix C), and a discussion of the *PrepLogic, Preview Edition* software (Appendix D).

For more information about the exam or the certification process, refer to the CompTIA Web site, at www.comptia.org/certification.

What the Network+ Certification (N10-002) Exam Covers

The CompTIA Network+ exam covers a broad range of networking technologies and concepts. The objectives for the exam are classified into four networking domains:

◆ Media and topologies

◆ Protocols and standards

◆ Network implementation

◆ Network support

Each of these domains is broken down into specific exam objectives. Before taking the exam, you should be proficient in each of the objectives within each domain. These objectives and subobjectives are described in the following sections.

Recognize the following logical or physical topologies, given a schematic diagram or description:

◆ Star/hierarchical

◆ Bus

◆ Mesh

◆ Ring

◆ Wireless

Specify the main features of the 802.2 (LLC), 802.3 (Ethernet), 802.5 (Token Ring), 802.11b (wireless), and FDDI networking technologies, including the following:

◆ Speed

◆ Access method

◆ Topology

◆ Media

Specify the characteristics (for example, speed, length, topology, cable type) of the following IEEE 802.3 (Ethernet) standards:

◆ 10BaseT

◆ 10BaseTX

◆ 10Base2

◆ 10Base5

◆ 100BaseFX

◆ Gigabit Ethernet

Recognize the following media connectors and describe their uses:

◆ RJ-11

◆ RJ-45

◆ AUI

◆ BNC

◆ ST

◆ SC

Choose the appropriate media type and connectors to add a client to an existing network.

Identify the purpose, features, and functions of the following network components:

◆ Hubs

◆ Switches

◆ Bridges

◆ Routers

◆ Gateways

◆ CSU/DSU

◆ Network interface cards/ISDN adapters/system area network cards

◆ Wireless access points

◆ Modems

Given an example, identify a MAC address.

Identify the seven layers of the OSI model and their functions.

Differentiate between the following network protocols in terms of routing, addressing schemes, interoperability, and naming conventions:

- ◆ TCP/IP
- ◆ IPX/SPX
- ◆ NetBEUI
- ◆ AppleTalk

Identify the OSI layers at which the following network components operate

- ◆ Hubs
- ◆ Switches
- ◆ Bridges
- ◆ Routers
- ◆ Network interface cards

Define the purpose, function, and/ or use of the following protocols within TCP/IP:

- ◆ IP
- ◆ TCP
- ◆ UDP
- ◆ FTP
- ◆ TFTP
- ◆ SMTP
- ◆ HTTP
- ◆ HTTPS
- ◆ POP3/IMAP4

- ◆ Telnet
- ◆ ICMP
- ◆ ARP
- ◆ NTP

Define the function of TCP/UDP ports. Identify well-known ports.

Identify the purpose of the following network services (e.g. DHCP/ bootp, DNS, NAT/ICS, WINS, and SNMP).

Identify IP addresses (IPv4, IPv6) and their default subnet masks.

Identify the purpose of subnetting and default gateways.

Identify the differences between public vs. private networks.

Identify the basic characteristics (e.g., speed, capacity, media) of the following WAN technologies:

- ◆ Packet switching vs. circuit switching
- ◆ ISDN
- ◆ FDDI
- ◆ ATM
- ◆ Frame Relay
- ◆ Sonet/SDH
- ◆ T1/E1
- ◆ T3/E3
- ◆ OCX

Define the function of the following remote access protocols and services:

- ◆ RAS
- ◆ PPP
- ◆ PPTP
- ◆ ICA

Identify the following security protocols and describe their purpose and function:

- ◆ IPSec
- ◆ L2TP
- ◆ SSL
- ◆ Kerberos

Identify the basic capabilities (i.e. client support, interoperability, authentication, file and print services, application support, and security) of the following server operating systems:

- ◆ Unix/Linux
- ◆ NetWare
- ◆ Windows
- ◆ Macintosh

Identify the basic capabilities of client workstations (i.e., client connectivity, local security mechanisms, and authentication).

Identify the main characteristics of VLANs.

Identify the main characteristics of network attached storage.

Identify the purpose and characteristics of fault tolerance.

Identify the purpose and characteristics of disaster recovery.

Given a remote connectivity scenario (e.g., IP, IPX, dial-up, PPPoE, authentication, physical connectivity etc.), configure the connection.

Identify the purpose, benefits, and characteristics of using a firewall.

Identify the purpose, benefits, and characteristics of using a proxy.

Given a scenario, predict the impact of a particular security implementation on network functionality (e.g. blocking port numbers, encryption, etc.).

Given a network configuration, select the appropriate NIC and network configuration settings (DHCP, DNS, WINS, protocols, NETBIOS/ host name, etc.).

Given a troubleshooting scenario, select the appropriate TCP/IP utility from among the following:

- ◆ tracert
- ◆ ping
- ◆ arp
- ◆ netstat
- ◆ nbtstat
- ◆ ipconfig/ifconfig
- ◆ winipcfg
- ◆ nslookup

Given a troubleshooting scenario involving a small office/home office network failure (e.g., xDSL, cable, home satellite, wireless, POTS), identify the cause of the failure.

Given a troubleshooting scenario involving a remote connectivity problem (e.g., authentication failure, protocol configuration, physical connectivity) identify the cause of the problem.

Given specific parameters, configure a client to connect to the following servers:

- ◆ Unix/Linux
- ◆ NetWare
- ◆ Windows
- ◆ Macintosh

Given a wiring task, select the appropriate tool (e.g., wire crimper, media tester/certifier, punch down tool, tone generator, optical tester, etc.).

Given a network scenario, interpret visual indicators (e.g., link lights, collision lights, etc.) to determine the nature of the problem.

Given output from a diagnostic utility (e.g. `tracert`, `ping`, `ipconfig`, etc.), identify the utility and interpret the output.

Given a scenario, predict the impact of modifying, adding, or removing network services (e.g., DHCP, DNS, WINS, etc.) on network resources and users.

Given a network problem scenario, select an appropriate course of action based on a general troubleshooting strategy. This strategy includes the following steps:

- ◆ Establish the symptoms
- ◆ Identify the affected area
- ◆ Establish what has changed
- ◆ Select the most probable cause
- ◆ Implement a solution
- ◆ Test the result
- ◆ Recognize the potential effects of the solution
- ◆ Document the solution

Given a troubleshooting scenario involving a network with a particular physical topology (i.e., bus, star/hierarchical, mesh, ring, and wireless) and including a network diagram, identify the network area affected and the cause of the problem.

Given a network troubleshooting scenario involving a client connectivity problem (e.g., incorrect protocol/client software/authentication configuration, or insufficient rights/permission), identify the cause of the problem.

Given a network troubleshooting scenario involving a wiring/infrastructure problem, identify the cause of the problem (e.g., bad media, interference, network hardware).

NETWORK HARDWARE AND SOFTWARE REQUIREMENTS

As a self-paced study guide, *Network+ Certification Training Guide* is meant to help you understand concepts that must be refined through hands-on experience. To make the most of your studying, you need to have as much background on and experience with both common operating systems and networks environments as possible. The best way to do this is to combine studying with work on actual networks. These networks need not be complex; the concepts involved in configuring a network with only a few computers follow the same principles as those involved in configuring a network that has hundreds of connected systems. This section describes the recommended requirements you need to form a solid practice environment.

To fully practice some of the exam objectives, you need to create a network with two (or more) computers networked together. To do this, you need an operating system. CompTIA maintains that the exam is vendor neutral, and for the most part it appears to be. However, if there were a slight tilt in the exam questions, it would be toward Microsoft Windows. Therefore, you would do well to set up a small network using a Microsoft server platform such as Windows 2000 server. In addition, you need clients with operating systems such as Windows 98/Me, Linux, or Mac. When you really get into it, you might want to install a Linux server as well because you are most certainly going to be working with them in the real world. The following is a detailed list of the hardware and software requirements needed to set up your network:

- ◆ A network operating system such as Windows 2000 Server or Linux.

- ◆ Client operating system software such as Windows 98/Me.

- ◆ A Pentium 233MHz (or better). (Pentium 300 MHz is recommended.)

- ◆ A minimum 1.5GB of free disk space.

- ◆ Super VGA (800×600) or higher resolution video adapter and monitor.

- ◆ A mouse or an equivalent pointing device.

- ◆ A CD-ROM or DVD drive.

- ◆ A network interface card (NIC) for each computer system.

- ◆ Network cabling such as Category 5 unshielded twisted-pair.

- ◆ A two-port (or more) miniport hub to create a test network.

- ◆ 128MB of RAM or higher (64MB minimum).

It's easy to obtain access to the necessary computer hardware and software in a corporate business environment. It can be difficult, however, to allocate enough time within the busy workday to complete a self-study program. Most of your study time will occur after normal working hours, away from the everyday interruptions and pressures of your regular job.

ADVICE ON TAKING THE EXAM

More extensive tips are found in the "Study and Exam Prep Tips" section, but keep this advice in mind as you study:

◆ **Read all the material**—CompTIA has been known to include material that is not expressly specified in the objectives. This book includes additional information that is not reflected in the objectives, in an effort to give you the best possible preparation for the examination—and for your real-world experiences to come.

◆ **Complete the exercises in each chapter**—They will help you gain experience in using the specified methodology or approach. CompTIA exams may require task- and experienced-based knowledge and require you to have an understanding of how certain network procedures are accomplished.

◆ **Use the exam questions to assess your knowledge**—Don't just read the chapter content; use the exam questions to find out what you know and what you don't know. If you are struggling, study some more, review, and then assess your knowledge again.

◆ **Review the objectives**—Develop your own questions and examples for each objective listed. If you can develop and answer several questions for each objective, you should not find it difficult to pass the exam.

> **NOTE**
>
> **Exam-Taking Advice** Although this book is designed to prepare you to take and pass the Network+ certification exam, there are no guarantees. Read this book, work through the questions and exercises, and when you feel confident, take the practice exam and additional exams provided in the *PrepLogic, Preview Edition* software. Your results should tell you whether you are ready for the real thing.
>
> When taking the actual certification exam, make sure you answer all the questions before your time limit expires. Do not spend too much time on any one question. If you are unsure about the answer to a question, answer it as best as you can; then mark it for review when you have finished the rest of the questions. Note that this advice does not apply if you are taking an adaptive exam. In that case, you should take your time on each question because there is no opportunity to go back to a question.

Remember that the primary object is not to pass the exam, but to understand the material. When you understand the material, passing the exam should be simple. Knowledge is a pyramid; to build upward, you need a solid foundation. This book and the Network+ certification are designed to ensure that you have that solid foundation.

Good luck!

EXAM PREPARATION

1 Introduction to Networking

2 Cabling and Connectors

3 Networking Components and Devices

4 The OSI Model

5 Overview of Network Protocols

6 Working with TCP/IP

7 WAN Technologies

8 Remote Access and Security Protocols

9 Network Operating Systems and Clients

10 Fault Tolerance, Disaster Recovery, VLANs, and NAS

11 Configuring Network Connectivity

12 Securing the Network

13 Troubleshooting Connectivity

14 Troubleshooting Tools and Utilities

15 Troubleshooting Procedures and Best Practices

This chapter covers the following CompTIA-specified objectives for the "Media and Topologies" section of the Network+ exam.

Recognize the following logical or physical topologies, given a schematic diagram or description:

- **Star/hierarchical**
- **Bus**
- **Mesh**
- **Ring**
- **Wireless**

▶ One of the fundamental network concepts that must be understood by all network administrators is topologies. A handful of topologies are currently defined and in use, and you will be expected to know the characteristics of each one.

Specify the main features of the 802.2 (LLC), 802.3 (Ethernet), 802.5 (Token Ring), 802.11b (wireless), and FDDI networking technologies, including the following:

- **Speed**
- **Access method**
- **Topology**
- **Media**

▶ Standards enable network components from different manufacturers to work together on the same network. It is important that network administrators understand the characteristics of commonly implemented standards.

CHAPTER 1

Introduction to Networking

OUTLINE

Introduction   **18**

What Is a Network?   **18**

    The Functions of a Network   19

Peer-to-Peer Versus Client/Server Networks   **20**

    The Peer-to-Peer Networking Model   21
        Advantages of Peer-to-Peer Networks   22
        Disadvantages of Peer-to-Peer
        Networks   22
    The Client/Server Networking Model   23
        Servers   23
        Client Computers   24
        Advantages of Client/Server
        Networking   24
        Disadvantages of Client/Server
        Networking   25
    Distributed and Centralized Computing   26

LANs, WANs, and MANs   **26**

    LANs   27
    WANs   27
    MANs   28

LAN Topologies   **28**

    Physical and Logical Topologies   29
    The Bus Topology   29
    The Star Topology   31
    The Ring Topology   32
    Mesh Topology   33
    Wireless Topology   34

The IEEE and Networking Standards   **36**

    Characteristics Specified in the IEEE 802
    Standards   38
        Speed   38
        Access Methods   39
        Topology   44
        Media   44
    The IEEE 802 Standards   45
        802.2: The LLC Sublayer   45
        802.3: Ethernet   45
        802.5: Token Ring   47
        802.11b: Wireless   48
        FDDI   49

Chapter Summary   **50**

Apply Your Knowledge   **52**

STUDY STRATEGIES

▶ Read the objectives at the beginning of the chapter.

▶ Study the information in the chapter, paying special attention to the tables, which summarize.

▶ Review the objectives again.

▶ Answer the exam questions at the end of the chapter and check your results.

▶ Use the ExamGear test on the CD-ROM that accompanies this book to answer additional exam questions concerning this material.

▶ Review the notes, tips, and exam tips in this chapter. Be sure you understand the information in the exam tips. If you don't understand the topic referenced in an exam tip, refer to the information in the chapter text and then read the exam tip again.

INTRODUCTION

By itself, the computer sitting on your desk is a powerful personal and business tool. Link that system with 1, 2, or even 1,000 other computers, and the possibilities and potential of your system become almost endless. That is the nature of networking.

Companies of all sizes depend on a collection of interconnected computers to conduct business. These computer networks make possible most of the applications and services used in corporate and home environments. Email, printing, real-time communication, file sharing, and videoconferencing would all be unavailable (or pointless) without networks.

The CompTIA Network+ exam is designed to prepare people to work with and around computer networks. The CompTIA objectives introduce basic networking concepts and design, laying the foundation for a solid, comprehensive understanding of networking fundamentals. This book closely follows the CompTIA objectives, clearly explaining each objective and highlighting the important concepts that are most likely to appear on the exam.

This chapter examines some of the fundamental principles that affect modern networking. These include a discussion about peer-to-peer and client/server computing, a discussion of the differences between local area networks (LANs), wide area networks (WANs), and metropolitan area networks (MANs). This chapter also looks at network topologies and how they can affect the basic layout and makeup of a network.

WHAT IS A NETWORK?

By definition, a *network* is a group of connected computers. The group can be as small and simple as two computers and a printer set up in a house or as large and complex as a multisite network that supports thousands of computers and hundreds of printers and other devices. Regardless of the size and complexity of a network, its fundamental function is to allow you to communicate and share data and resources.

Although the basic purpose of a network has not changed since the first network was created, the way in which we build and use networks has evolved in an amazing way. What was once a luxury that only the largest companies and governments could afford has become a vital business tool that hundreds of millions of people rely on every day.

The operation of a network should be transparent to the people who use it. Users should, for example, be able to print to a printer connected to the network just as easily as if it were attached to their own PCs. They should also be able to access files this easily. The degree of transparency of a network depends on how good the network's structure is and, to a certain extent, how well the network is managed. (But no matter how well a network is managed, problems will occasionally crop up.)

The Functions of a Network

If the purpose of a network is to share resources among computer systems, what types of information and services are shared on a network—and why? All networks, regardless of their design or size, perform one or all of a number of network functions. The following are some common reasons for implementing a network:

◆ **Communication**—Increased communication is one of the primary purposes of a network. Networks allow a variety of communications, including videoconferencing, real-time chats, and email. Many organizations have grown so dependent on network communications that without it, they cannot function.

◆ **Sharing hardware**—Printing is the best example of hardware sharing. Without a network, each computer that requires printing capabilities would need a printer connected directly to it—and that would be impractical and costly. Although printers are almost certainly the most popular devices shared on networks, other devices are often shared as well, including scanners, CD-ROM drives, tape drives, and other removable media.

◆ **Data sharing**—Linking users on the same system makes it easy for them to share files with others on the network.

NOTE

The Internet   It might seem as though a small network in your house is very different from a network such as the Internet, but you would be surprised how much the two have in common. For example, the PCs on a home network most likely communicate in the same way as systems on the Internet. Also, the Internet has clients and servers just like a small network might have. The Internet uses certain devices, such as network routers, that you might not find on a home network, but the basic building blocks of both networks are the same. In fact, the term *Internet* is derived from the term *internetwork*, which is used to describe a group of connected networks.

However, because people can access the data across the network, access to both the data and the network must be carefully controlled. Fortunately, network operating systems provide mechanisms that allow you to secure data so that access can be controlled.

◆ **Application sharing**—Networking makes it possible for numerous users to share a single application. This makes it unnecessary to install the same application on several computer systems; instead, the application can be run from a central location. Such a strategy is often used on medium to large networks, where it is difficult and time-consuming to install and maintain applications on numerous individual systems. Application sharing is also important for centralized systems such as databases; users rely on networks to access and use such systems.

◆ **Data backup and retrieval**—A network makes it possible to store data in a central location. When the data is in a central location, it is easier to back up and retrieve. The importance of this benefit cannot be overstated. No matter how much money is invested in a computer network, the data that travels on it has the most value.

Because of these network functions, the majority of businesses and increasing numbers of home users have networks. Given such advantages, the real decision often is not whether to set up a network but what type of network to create. This chapter explores some of the options.

PEER-TO-PEER VERSUS CLIENT/SERVER NETWORKS

Networks use two basic models: peer-to-peer and client/server. The model used by an organization depends on the role of the network and what the users require from it. You will probably encounter both network models; therefore, you need to understand how these models work as well as their strengths and weaknesses.

The Peer-to-Peer Networking Model

Peer-to-peer networking is a low-cost, easily implemented network solution that is generally used in small network environments that need to share a few files and maybe some hardware, such as printers. As its name suggests, on a peer-to-peer network all systems are equal, or *peers*. Each system can share hardware or files and access the same things on other systems.

A peer-to-peer network offers no centralized data storage or centralized control over the sharing of files or resources. In a sense, everyone on a peer-to-peer network is a network administrator and can share resources as they see fit. They have the option to grant all users on the network complete access to their computers, including printers and files, or they can choose not to share anything. Figure 1.1 shows an example of a peer-to-peer network.

NOTE

Peer-to-Peer Home Networks Peer-to-peer networks are often seen in residential settings, where home computers are linked together to share an Internet connection, printers, or files. All popular workstation PC operating systems offer peer-to-peer network functionality.

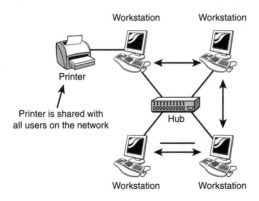

FIGURE 1.1
An example of a peer-to-peer network.

Resources of each system are made available to other systems on the network

The peer-to-peer model works quite well on networks that have 10 or fewer computers, but as a network grows, it becomes more complicated. Peer-to-peer networking is often referred to as *decentralized networking* because the network files, data, and administration are not handled from a central location. This arrangement can lead to huge problems, especially in large networks. For example, locating specific files can become difficult because the files might be on multiple computers. Data backup cannot be performed from a central location; each computer must be backed up individually. Decentralized computing can also be difficult in terms of network security because security is controlled by individual computer users rather than being administered from a central location. This decentralized security model requires that each user have a user ID and password defined on each and every system that he or she will access. With no way of synchronizing passwords between the systems, this can quickly become a problem. Many users have problems remembering just one or two passwords—let alone a dozen.

Given the complexity and drawbacks of using peer-to-peer networking, you might wonder why anyone would use it. Many small companies begin with a peer-to-peer network because it's the easiest and least expensive type to install. After the networks grow too big, they switch to the client/server model, which is discussed in the next section.

Advantages of Peer-to-Peer Networks

The following are some of the advantages of using the peer-to-peer networking model:

◆ **Cost**—Because peer-to-peer networking does not require a dedicated server, such networks are very cost-effective. This makes them an attractive option in environments where money is tight.

◆ **Ease of installation**—The built-in support for peer-to-peer networking in modern operating systems makes installing and configuring a peer-to-peer network a straightforward process.

Disadvantages of Peer-to-Peer Networks

The following are some of the disadvantages of using the peer-to-peer networking model:

◆ **Security**—In a decentralized model, a networkwide security policy cannot be enforced from a server; rather, security needs to be applied to each computer and resource individually.

◆ **Data backup**—Because files and data are located on individual computers, each system must have its data backed up individually.

◆ **Resource access**—In a decentralized approach, it can be difficult to locate resources on the network. Printers and files may be distributed among numerous computer systems.

NOTE

Peer-to-Peer Network Size A peer-to-peer network can link an unlimited number of PCs; no standards define a maximum. The only limits are the practicality of managing multiple systems in a peer-to-peer model and the restrictions of the operating system being used on the workstations.

◆ **Limited numbers of computers**—Peer-to-peer networking is effective only on small networks (fewer than 10 computers).

As you can see, the disadvantages of peer-to-peer networking outweigh the advantages. Therefore, client/server networks are far more popular in corporate or business environments than peer-to-peer networks.

The Client/Server Networking Model

Client/server networking—or *server-based networking*, as it is commonly called—is the network model you are most likely to see in the corporate world. The server-based network model is completely scalable, allowing additional computers or other networked devices to be added with little difficulty. Perhaps the greatest benefit of this model is that it allows for centralized management of all network services, security, and streamlined backup procedures. Figure 1.2 shows an example of a client/server network.

As you may have gathered, two different types of computers are required for the server-based model: the client and the server. Figure 1.3 shows the relationship between client and server computers. These two computer systems are often very different from each other, and each plays a unique role on a network.

Servers

Servers are the workhorses of the network. They spend their time responding to the numerous requests that come from client computers, such as requests for files, network authentication, and access to shared hardware resources. Network administration—including network security, backups, and network monitoring—is done from the server.

To be able perform their functions, server computers require additional resources and computing power. Server systems often use specialized hardware and software in fault-tolerant configurations to ensure that they remain operational. When a server fails and goes offline, it is unable to respond to requests from client systems and its functions are unavailable. This situation can be frustrating for users and very costly for an organization.

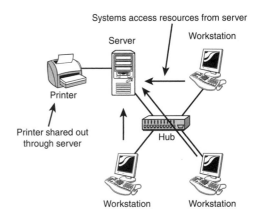

FIGURE 1.2
An example of a client/server network.

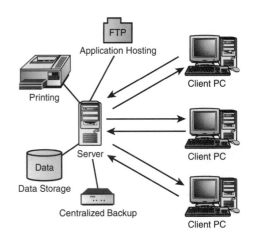

FIGURE 1.3
The relationship between client and server computers.

In addition to requiring specific hardware, servers also require a network operating system. A network operating system stands above ordinary desktop operating systems; it has unique features and functions that allow an administrator to manage, monitor, and administer the data and resources of the server as well as the users who connect to it. In addition, network operating systems are designed to be resilient in case of the kind of downtime discussed earlier. The most common network operating systems used today are the Microsoft Windows network operating systems (including Windows NT, Windows 2000, and Windows XP/Windows .Net), Unix, Linux, and Novell NetWare. Knowledge of these operating systems is an important element of the Network+ exam, so detailed coverage of them is provided in Chapter 9, "Network Operating Systems and Clients."

A network may have a single server that offers more than one network service or hundreds of servers, each performing a dedicated task. For instance, one server might be used only to authenticate users and another might be used to store an applications database. Some of the most common roles for dedicated servers include acting as file and print servers, application servers, Web servers, database servers, firewall servers, and proxy servers.

Client Computers

Client computers are the other half of the client/server model. Client computers connect to the network and access the resources of the server. Software is needed to allow the client to connect to the network, although the need for networking has become so fundamental that the client software functionality is now built in to desktop operating systems. More coverage of the role and requirements of client computers is provided in Chapter 9.

Advantages of Client/Server Networking

The following are some of the advantages of the client/server networking model:

◆ **Centralized management and security**—The ability to manage the network from a single location is the biggest advantage of the client/server model. From a server, you can perform backups of all data, share resources and control access to those resources, manage user accounts, and monitor network activity.

◆ **Scalability**—In a server-based network administrators can easily add computers and devices. In addition, the network is not restricted to a small number of computers. In a client/server network, the number of clients is limited by factors such as licensing and network capacity rather than by the operating system's ability to support them.

◆ **Simplified backups**—On server-based networks, files and folders typically reside in a single location or a small number of locations and are therefore easier to back up than the files on a peer-to-peer network. Scheduling backups to occur at regular intervals is simple.

Disadvantages of Client/Server Networking

The following are some of the disadvantages of the client/server networking model:

◆ **High cost**—A server-based network requires additional hardware and software, so it can be a costly venture. The costs of the client/server model include the costs of the network operating system and at least one server system, replete with specialized server hardware. Also, because the client/server model can support far more systems than the peer-to-peer model, networking devices such as hubs, routers, and switches are often needed.

◆ **Administration requirements**—Client/server networks require additional administrative skills over those required on a peer-to-peer network. In particular, the technical capabilities of the administrator need to be greater. Organizations that use the server-based model often need technically skilled people to manage and maintain the network and the servers.

◆ **Single points of failure**—In a client/server model, the client systems depend on servers to provide network services. If the server fails, the clients can't access the services that reside on the server. Great effort and expense are needed to ensure the high availability of network servers.

Given the limitations of the peer-to-peer network design, such networks are used in only a few situations. On the other hand, the client/server networking model is versatile, and its shortcomings are overshadowed by its capabilities and advantages. You will spend most of your time working with server-based networks of all shapes and sizes.

NOTE

Combination Networks The distinction between networks that use a peer-to-peer design and those that use a client/server design is not always clear. Today's operating systems let client computers share resources with other systems in a peer-to-peer configuration and also be connected to a server. Such an arrangement is sometimes referred to as a *combination network*. Although this model takes advantage of the benefits of both network models, it is also susceptible to their combined shortcomings.

Distributed and Centralized Computing

Although they're less of an issue than in the past, you need to be familiar with two important networking concepts: distributed and centralized computing. These concepts are not directly related to the server-based/peer-to-peer discussion, although by definition a peer-to-peer system is a distributed computing model.

The terms *distributed* and *centralized computing* describe the location on a network where the processing takes place. In an environment such as a mainframe, the processing is performed on a centralized system that also stores all the data. In such a model, no data processing or data storage occurs on the client computer. In contrast, in a distributed processing environment, processing is performed in more than one place. If a network has servers and workstations, processing can take place on the server or on the client.

It is relatively unusual for a company to have just a centralized computing environment. A company is far more likely to have a server-based network, which would fall under the banner of distributed computing, and perhaps a mainframe that is accessed from the same PCs as the server-based network, which would fall under the banner of centralized computing. A good example of such an environment might be a company that books hotel reservations for customers, in which the booking system is held on a mainframe but the email system used to correspond with clients is held on a PC-based server and accessed through client software on the PCs.

Regardless of whether a network uses a centralized or distributed model, networks can be placed into categories that define the geographic location over which they are spread. The three accepted terms for these categories are LAN, WAN, and MAN.

LANs, WANs, and MANs

Networks are categorized according to how many locations they span. A network that is confined to a single location is known as a LAN. Networks that span multiple geographic locations are known as WANs. There is also another category, called a MAN, which is used to classify networks that fall somewhere between LANs and WANs. The following sections examine the characteristics of these types of networks.

LANs

A LAN is confined to a single geographic location, such as a single building, office, or school. LANs are created with networking media that are very fast but that can cover a limited distance. Figure 1.4 shows an example of a LAN.

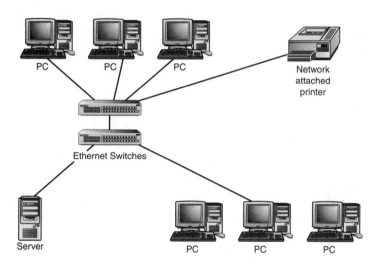

Ethernet Switches

Server

PC   PC   PC

FIGURE 1.4
An example of a LAN.

EXAM TIP

LAN/WAN Technologies   An understanding of the technologies used in both LANs and WANs is required for the Network+ test. These technologies are covered in detail throughout the rest of this book.

NOTE

When Does a LAN Become a WAN? Technically, a LAN never becomes a WAN. If the definitions of LAN and WAN were taken literally and applied to a working model that had three connected sites, the portions of the network confined within each site would be LANs and the network elements connecting the sites together would be called the WAN. You should avoid the temptation to refer to the entire internetwork as a WAN because WANs and LANs employ some very different technologies.

WANs

A WAN is a network that spans multiple geographic locations. WANs are generally slower than LANs and are considerably more expensive to run. WANs are all about bandwidth, and the more bandwidth you are willing to pay for, the more speed you can get. WANs connect LANs together to create an *internetwork*. Figure 1.5 shows an example of a WAN.

WANs often use different technologies from LANs. WAN technologies are discussed in Chapter 7, "WAN Technologies."

FIGURE 1.5
An example of a WAN.

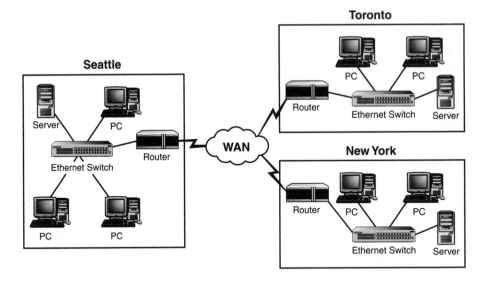

MANs

A MAN is confined to a certain geographic area such as a university campus or a city. No formal guidelines dictate the differences between a MAN and a WAN; technically, a MAN is a WAN. Perhaps for this reason, the term *MAN* is used less frequently than *WAN*. If any distinction exists, it's that a MAN is smaller than a WAN.

Having established the purpose and function of networks and how networks are classified based on size, the following section looks at the specific features of a network, beginning with LAN topologies.

LAN TOPOLOGIES

▶ Recognize the following logical or physical topologies, given a schematic diagram or description:
  - Star/hierarchical
  - Bus
  - Mesh
  - Ring
  - Wireless

The term *network topology* refers to the layout of a network. The type of topology affects what networking method is used, as well as what cable types and network devices are required. Topologies are very important, and they serve as the foundation for the information you'll learn in the following sections. You will certainly be asked about topologies on the Network+ exam.

Before we look at the different types of topologies, we must first examine one of the most confusing networking principles: the difference between physical and logical topologies. Then we'll examine the specific physical LAN topologies in use today: bus, star, ring, mesh, and wireless.

Physical and Logical Topologies

Network topologies can be defined on a physical level or on a logical level. The *physical topology* refers to how a network is physically constructed—that is, how it actually looks. The *logical topology* refers to how a network looks to the devices that use it—in other words, how it actually functions. In a number of commonly implemented network models, the physical topology differs from the logical topology. It can be difficult to appreciate what that means, so let's use an example.

The most commonly implemented network model is a physical star/logical bus topology. In this configuration, computers are connected to a central device, called a *hub* or *switch*, which gives the network the appearance of a star (or a reasonable facsimile thereof). However, the devices attached to the star see the network as a linear bus topology and use the topology based on its logical characteristics.

The Bus Topology

The bus network topology is also known as a *linear bus* because the computers in such a network are linked together using a single cable called a *trunk,* or *backbone.* Computers are connected to this backbone as shown in Figure 1.6.

EXAM TIP

Network Topologies
Understanding network topologies and their characteristics is an objective for the Network+ exam. Therefore, you should ensure that you understand the concept of topologies.

NOTE

How Did We Get Here? The physical/logical topology discussion can be confusing, so let's examine its background. When networks were first created, they followed a simple path. For example, the first Ethernet network was a physical and logical bus (single length of cable). As you will see in upcoming sections, however, this physical bus approach has a number of disadvantages; therefore, alternatives were sought. In this case, the solution was to move away from the single cable segment approach and instead use different types of cable on a physical star. The media access method and the networking system remained the same, however, resulting in a physical star/logical bus topology.

FIGURE 1.6
An example of the bus topology.

EXAM TIP

BUS Topology You should be pre-pared to identify the bus topology on the Network+ exam.

NOTE

Ethernet Standards The most common implementation of a linear bus is the Institute of Electrical and Electronics Engineers (IEEE) 802.3 standard, 10Base2, which is an Ethernet standard. Ethernet standards are covered later in this chapter.

EXAM TIP

Bus Topology Advantages/ Disadvantages For the Network+ exam, be sure you understand the advantages and disadvantages of the bus topology.

The computers can be connected to the backbone by a cable, known as a *drop cable*, or, more commonly, directly to the backbone, via T connectors. At each end of the cable, terminators prevent the signal from bouncing back down the cable. In addition, one end of the cable should be grounded. More information on the specific connectors and connections used in different networks is provided in Chapter 2, "Cabling and Connectors."

Bus topologies are easy and inexpensive to implement because a single-segment bus topology doesn't require any special networking equipment. However, they are notoriously difficult to troubleshoot, and a single break in the network cable renders the entire segment useless. For this and a number other reasons, such as limited speed capacity, bus topologies have been largely replaced with the physical star topology. The main features, advantages, and disadvantages of bus topologies are provided in Table 1.1.

TABLE 1.1

FEATURES, ADVANTAGES, AND DISADVANTAGES OF THE LINEAR BUS TOPOLOGY

Features	Advantages	Disadvantages
Uses a single length of cable.	It is inexpensive and easy to implement.	It cannot be expanded easily. Doing so may render the network inaccessible while the expansion is performed.
Devices connect directly to the cable.	It doesn't require special equipment.	A break in the cable renders the entire segment unusable.
The cable must be terminated at both ends.	It requires less cable than other topologies.	It is difficult to troubleshoot.

The Star Topology

In a star topology, each device on the network connects to a centralized device via a single cable. This arrangement creates a point-to-point network connection between the two devices and overall gives the appearance of a star. Figure 1.7 shows an example of the star topology.

Because each device must have its own cable, a star topology requires far more cable than other topologies such as a physical linear bus. In addition, special equipment is required to create the hub of the star layout, adding to the cost of implementing a star topology. (Chapter 3, "Networking Components and Devices," explains the function of network devices such as hubs and switches that are used in a star topology.)

Multiple stars can be combined into a tree-like structure known as a *hierarchical star*. The hierarchical star allows for high levels of flexibility and expandability. Depending on the networking equipment used, it also makes it possible to manage traffic and isolate high-traffic areas of the network. Figure 1.8 shows an example of a hierarchical star topology.

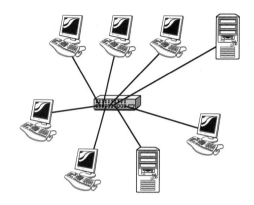

FIGURE 1.7
An example of the star topology.

> **EXAM TIP**
>
> **Star Topology** You should be prepared to identify the star topology on the Network+ exam.

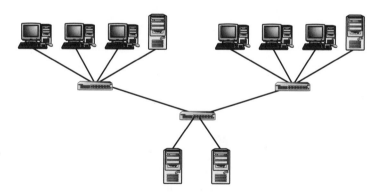

FIGURE 1.8
An example of the hierarchical star topology.

One of the biggest advantages of the star topology is that computers can be connected to and disconnected from the network without affecting any other systems. Thus it's very easy to add systems to or remove systems from the network. In addition, the failure of a system or the cable it uses to attach likewise generally has no effect on other stations on the network. However, in the star topology, all devices on the network connect to a central device, and this central device creates a single point of failure on the network.

> **EXAM TIP**
>
> **Hierarchical Star Topology** You should be prepared to identify a hierarchical star topology on the Network+ exam.

The Ethernet 10BaseT Standard
The most common implementation of
the physical star topology is the
Ethernet 10BaseT standard.

**Star Topology Advantages/
Disadvantages**   For the Network+
exam, be sure you understand the
advantages and disadvantages of
the star topology.

The star topology is the most widely implemented network design
in use today; you will definitely encounter it in the real world.
Working with and troubleshooting a star topology can be a tricky
matter, however, and you need to know what to look for and where
to look. For more information on troubleshooting star networks and
other specific network topology errors, see Chapter 15, "
Troubleshooting Procedures and Best Practices."

The features, advantages, and disadvantages of the physical star
topology are provided in Table 1.2.

TABLE 1.2

**FEATURES, ADVANTAGES, AND DISADVANTAGES OF THE
PHYSICAL STAR TOPOLOGY**

Features	*Advantages*	*Disadvantages*
Devices connect to a central point.	It can be easily expanded without disruption to existing systems.	It requires additional networking equipment to create the network layout.
Each system uses an individual cable to attach.	A cable failure affects only a single system.	It requires considerably more cable than other topologies, such as the linear bus.
Multiple stars can be combined to create a hierarchical star.	It is easy to troubleshoot.	Centralized devices create a single point of failure.

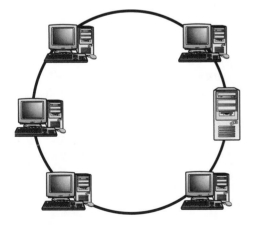

FIGURE 1.9
An example of the ring topology.

The Ring Topology

In the ring topology, the network layout forms a complete ring.
Computers connect to the network cable directly or, far more commonly, through a specialized network device.

On a ring network, data travels in one direction, passing from one
computer to the next until it reaches the intended destination.
Figure 1.9 shows an example of the ring topology.

Ring topologies are more difficult to install and configure than other
topologies because breaking the loop disrupts the entire network.
Even if network devices are used to create the ring, the ring must
still be broken if a fault occurs or the network needs to be expanded.

Ring topologies are relatively uncommon; the physical star layout is by far the most popular topology. For this reason, you are unlikely to actually install a ring topology. Table 1.3 shows the features, advantages, and disadvantages of the ring topology.

EXAM TIP

Ring Topology   You should be prepared to identify the ring topology on the Network+ exam.

TABLE 1.3

FEATURES, ADVANTAGES, AND DISADVANTAGES OF THE RING TOPOLOGY

Features	Advantages	Disadvantages
Devices are connected in a closed loop or ring.	It is easy to troubleshoot.	A cable break can disrupt the entire network.
Dual-ring configuration can be used for fault tolerance.	Can be implemented in a fault tolerant configuration.	Network expansion creates network disruption.

NOTE

Dual Rings   To negate the problem of a broken ring making the network unavailable, you can configure dual rings so that one ring can be used if the other fails. One ring topology that employs this strategy is FDDI, which is discussed in Chapter 7.

Mesh Topology

The mesh topology is unique: It requires each computer on the network to be individually connected to every other device. This configuration provides maximum reliability and redundancy for the network. If one cable or link fails, the data can use an alternate path to get to its destination. Figure 1.10 shows an example of the mesh topology.

EXAM TIP

Ring Topology Advantages/ Disadvantages   For the Network+ exam, you should be sure you understand the advantages and disadvantages of the ring topology.

EXAM TIP

Mesh Topology   You should be prepared to identify the mesh topology on the Network+ exam.

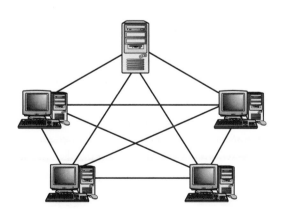

FIGURE 1.10
An example of the mesh topology.

NOTE

Fault Tolerance   Although it is impractical to implement, the mesh layout is the most fault tolerant of all the network topologies. Redundant links exist between all nodes, and the failure of a single link does not affect the overall functionality of the network.

NOTE

Hybrid Mesh Networks   The term *hybrid mesh* is sometimes used to refer to a mesh network that has direct links between some systems but not all. Again, such a configuration is more likely to be seen in a WAN configuration than in a LAN.

EXAM TIP

Mesh Topology Advantages/ Disadvantages   For the Network+ exam, you should be sure you understand the advantages and disadvantages of the mesh topology.

Given the relative ease with which the other topologies can be created and the complexity of the mesh layout, you should not be surprised to learn that networks using the mesh layout are few and far between. In fact, you are extremely unlikely to see a mesh layout in a LAN setting. The mesh topology is sometimes adopted in WAN configurations that require direct connections between each and every geographic site.

However unlikely you are to see a mesh topology, it is mentioned in the Network+ exam objectives, so be sure you can identify a mesh layout should the need arise. Table 1.4 lists the features, advantages, and disadvantages of the mesh topology.

TABLE 1.4

FEATURES, ADVANTAGES, AND DISADVANTAGES OF THE MESH TOPOLOGY

Features	Advantages	Disadvantages
A true mesh uses point-to-point connectivity between all devices.	Multiple links provide fault tolerance and redundancy.	It is difficult to implement.
A hybrid mesh uses point-to-point connectivity between certain devices, but not all of them.	The network can be expanded with minimal or no disruption.	It can be expensive because it requires specialized hardware and cable.

Wireless Topology

The wireless topology is the newest type of network layout. The wireless topology is hard to define because, as the name implies, it uses no wires.

There are many types of wireless networks, but this section focuses on the kind found in a LAN. These systems, which are relative newcomers to the networking scene, use a centralized device known as a *wireless access point* (*WAP*) that transmits signals to devices with wireless NICs installed in them. Figure 1.11 shows an example of such a layout.

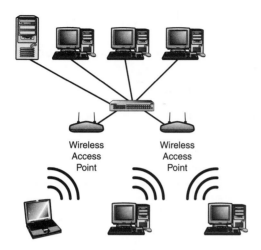

FIGURE 1.11
An example of the wireless topology.

Wireless
Access
Point

Wireless
Access
Point

Computer

Wireless networking has advantages such as the ability to move around without worrying about physical cable access points on the network. This flexibility can be seen in many real-world scenarios. For example, on a university campus, students using laptops can move from classroom to classroom without disconnecting from the network or worrying about network connection points. In a hospital, doctors can do rounds and have real-time access to medical records. These examples make it clear why wireless networking is sure to become increasingly popular.

From an installation and troubleshooting perspective, wireless networks have some unique advantages over standard wired topologies. No cables means no faulty cables or cable breaks. Although the WAPs represent central points of failure, if a WAP develops a fault, systems connected to that WAP can simply relocate to another area to access a different WAP.

Wireless networking is not without drawbacks, though. Wireless networks are currently slower than conventional cable-based networks. In addition, security concerns discourage many people from using wireless networking, although many of these issues have now been addressed. Table 1.5 outlines the features, advantages, and disadvantages of wireless topologies.

EXAM TIP

Wireless Topology   You should be prepared to identify the wireless topology on the Network+ exam.

TABLE 1.5

FEATURES, ADVANTAGES, AND DISADVANTAGES OF THE WIRELESS TOPOLOGY

Features	Advantages	Disadvantages
No physical connections are required.	It provides flexible network access.	It is still relatively new and expensive.
It can be used in LAN or WAN environments.	It can be used in environments where physical access is not possible.	It has potential security issues. Speed is limited in certain implementations.

THE IEEE AND NETWORKING STANDARDS

▶ Specify the main features of the 802.2 (LLC), 802.3 (Ethernet), 802.5 (Token Ring), 802.11b (wireless), and FDDI networking technologies, including the following:

- Speed
- Access method
- Topology
- Media

Whereas a topology defines the structure of a network, network standards define how it works. As early as the 1970s, it was apparent that networks were going to play a large role in future corporate environments. Many manufacturers saw the computing and network trend and became increasingly active in network component development. These companies realized that in order for their products to work together, standards would be necessary to ensure compatibility. The task of producing the standards fell to an international body called the IEEE.

The IEEE developed a set of standards called the 802 project. These standards are still used today, although there have been many changes and additions along the way. By using the standards defined by the IEEE, manufacturers can be sure that their products will work with products from other companies that adhere to the standards.

Some of the IEEE 802 standards define only certain technologies, whereas others, such as the 802.3 standard, define entire networking systems. The following are some of the most important IEEE 802 standards:

◆ **802.1, internetworking**—Defines internetwork communications standards between devices and includes specifications for routing and bridging.

◆ **802.2, the LLC sublayer**—Defines specifications for the Logical Link Control (LLC) sublayer in the 802 standard series.

◆ **802.3, CSMA/CD**—Defines the carrier-sense multiple-access with collision detection (CSMA/CD) media access method used in Ethernet networks. This is the most popular networking standard used today.

◆ **802.4, a token passing bus (rarely used)**—Defines the use of a token-passing system on a linear bus topology.

◆ **802.5, Token Ring networks**—Defines Token Ring networking.

◆ **802.6, metropolitan area network (MAN)**—Defines a data transmission method called distributed queue dual bus (DQDB), which is designed to carry voice and data on a single link.

◆ **802.7, Broadband Technical Advisory Group**—Defines the standards and specifications of broadband communications methods.

◆ **802.8, Fiber-Optic Technical Advisory Group**—Provides assistance to other IEEE 802 committees on subjects related to the use of fiber-optics.

◆ **802.9, Integrated Voice and Data Networks Group**—Works on the advancement of integrated voice and data networks.

◆ **802.10, network security**—Defines security standards that make it possible to safely and securely transmit and exchange data.

◆ **802.11, wireless networks**—Defines standards for wireless LAN communication.

◆ **802.12, 100BaseVG-AnyLAN**—Defines standards for high-speed LAN technologies.

For the Network+ exam and day-to-day real-life networking, some of these standards are more important than others. The Network+ exam focuses on the LAN standards: 802.2, 802.3, 802.5, and 802.11. These IEEE standards specify the characteristics of the networking systems, including the cable types used, access methods, speeds, and topologies. Although you don't need detailed knowledge of all these IEEE standards in real-world applications, a general understanding of these standards will be an asset.

Characteristics Specified in the IEEE 802 Standards

Let's review some of the characteristics that are specified within each standard: speed, access methods, topology, and media.

Speed

Many factors contribute to the speed of a network. The standard defines the maximum speed of a networking system. The speed normally is measured in megabits per second (Mbps), although some faster network systems use gigabits per second (that is, Gbps, where 1Gbps is equivalent to 1000Mbps).

A maximum speed of 1Gbps might seem very fast, but in standard computing terms, it is quite slow. Roughly translated, 1Gbps is 1MBps. That means it would take 10 seconds to transfer a 10MB file across a link, assuming (which you can't do) that you could access 100% of the bandwidth. Even the slowest Small Computer Systems Interface (SCSI) standard is 5 times faster than this; the newest standard, Ultra320, is (as you might have guessed) 320 times faster. As you can see, although a 1Gbps network connection might be fast in networking terms, it is still considered the weakest link in the data communications path between two devices.

Some networks are faster than others. For example, a Token Ring (802.5) network has a maximum speed of 16Mbps. Many Ethernet networks (802.3x) now operate at 100Mbps. As you will see later in this chapter, when we discuss networking components, it is possible to further increase these figures. However, the maximum speed attainable on a network can be affected by many factors. Networks that achieve 100% of their potential bandwidth are few and far between.

> **NOTE**
>
> **Bandwidth** The term *bandwidth* describes the amount of data that can travel over a network connection in a given time period. Generally speaking, WAN network links have a lower bandwidth than LAN connections.

Access Methods

Access methods govern the way in which systems access the network media and send data. Access methods are necessary to ensure that systems on the network can communicate with each other. Without an access method, it would be possible for two systems to communicate at the exclusion of every other system. Access methods ensure that everyone gets an opportunity to use the network.

Several access methods are used in networks; the most popular are CSMA/CD and token passing. Other methods, such as demand priority and contention, are also used. We'll look at each of these access methods separately.

CSMA/CD

CSMA/CD, which is defined in the IEEE 802.3 standard, is the most popular media access method because it is associated with Ethernet networking, which is by far the most popular networking system.

On a network that uses CSMA/CD, when a system wants to send data to another system, it first checks to see if the network media is free. It must do this because each piece of network media used in a LAN can carry only one signal at a time. If the sending node detects that the media is free, it transmits, and the data is sent to the destination. It seems simple.

Now, if it always worked like this, you wouldn't need the CD part of CSMA/CD. Unfortunately, in networking, as in life, things do not always go as a planned. The problem arises when two systems attempt to transmit at exactly the same time. It might seem like a long shot that two systems will pick the same moment to send data, but we are dealing with communications that occur many times in a single second—and most networks have more than two machines.

> **NOTE**
>
> **Nodes** A *node* is any device that is connected to the network. A node might be a client computer, server computer, printer, router, or gateway.

Contention   CSMA/CD is known as a *contention media access method* because systems contend for access to the media.

Equal Access   On a network that uses CSMA/CD, every node has equal access to the network media.

A Variation on a Theme   A variation of CSMA/CD (or the other way around, depending on your point of view) is carrier-sense multiple-access with collision avoidance (CSMA/CA). Computer systems that use CSMA/CA send a special signal to notify other computers on the network that they are going to send data. This way, data is sent only when the media is clear, thereby avoiding collisions. Although this system may seem safer than CSMA/CD, it's also slower, due to the overhead associated with systems broadcasting their intent to transmit.

Imagine that 200 people are in a room. The room is silent, but then two people decide to say something at exactly the same time. Before they start to speak, they check (listen) to see if someone else is speaking; because no one else is speaking, they begin to talk. The result is two people speaking at the same time, which is similar to a network collision.

Collision detection works by detecting fragments of the transmission on the network media that result when two systems try to talk at the same time. The two systems wait for a randomly calculated amount of time before attempting to transmit again. This amount of time—a matter of milliseconds—is known as the *backoff*.

When the backoff period has elapsed, the system attempts to transmit again. If the system doesn't succeed on the second attempt, it keeps retrying until it gives up and reports an error.

The upside of CSMA/CD is that it has relatively low overhead, meaning that not much is involved in the workings of the system. The downside is that as more systems are added to the network, more collisions occur and the network becomes slower. The performance of a network that uses CSMA/CD degrades exponentially as more systems are added. Its low overhead means that CSMA/CD systems theoretically can achieve greater speeds than high-overhead systems, such as token passing. However, because collisions take place, the chances of all that speed translating into usable bandwidth are relatively low.

Despite its problems, CSMA/CD is a very efficient system. As a result, rather than replace it with some other technology, workarounds have been created that reduce the likelihood of collisions. One such strategy is the use of network switches that create multiple collision domains and therefore reduce the impact of collisions on performance. Chapter 3 provides more information about using switches.

Table 1.6 summarizes the advantages and disadvantages of the CSMA/CD access method.

TABLE 1.6

ADVANTAGES AND DISADVANTAGES OF CSMA/CD

Advantages	*Disadvantages*
It has low overhead.	Collisions degrade network performance.
Able to utilize all available bandwidth when possible.	Priorities cannot be assigned to certain nodes. Performance degrades exponentially as devices are added.

Token Passing

Although token passing, which is specified in IEEE 802.5, is the second most popular media access method, the domination of Ethernet networking makes it second by a considerable margin. However, it might not be popular, but it is clever.

On a token-passing network, a special packet called a *token* is passed among the systems on the network. The network has only one token, and a system can send data only when it has possession of the token.

When the data arrives, the receiving computer sends a verification message to the sending computer. The sender then creates a new token, and the process begins again. Standards dictate how long a system can have control over the token. Figure 1.12 shows how data is sent on a token-passing network.

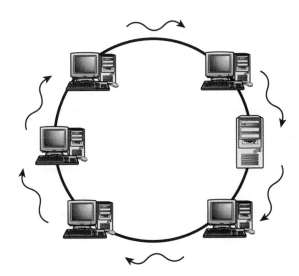

FIGURE 1.12
Data travel on a token-passing network.

One of the big advantages of the token-passing access method is the lack of collisions. Because a system can transmit only when it has the token, there is no contention. Even under heavy load conditions, the speed of a token-passing system does not degrade in the same way as a contention-based method such as CSMA/CD. In a practical scenario, this fact makes token passing more suitable than other access methods for applications such as videoconferencing.

However, token passing does have drawbacks. The creation and passing of the token generate overhead on the network, which reduces the maximum speed. In addition, the software and hardware requirements of token-passing network technologies are more complex—and therefore more costly—than those of other media access methods.

IN THE FIELD

TOKEN BUS

Token passing is most commonly associated with Token Ring networks. However, the IEEE's 802.4 standard defines a token-passing system implemented on a physical bus rather than a ring. Given that Token Ring is not one of the most commonly used LAN technologies and that token bus didn't catch on even as well as Token Ring, you probably won't ever see a token bus network. Still, it's nice to know that such networks exist—you never know when someone might challenge your networking knowledge.

EXAM TIP

RI and RO Ports on MSAU Be sure you understand the function and purpose of the RI and RO ports on an MSAU for the Network+ exam. Also make sure you understand how the cables should be connected between MSAUs and the consequences of not connecting them correctly (that is, most likely none of the systems on the ring will be able to communicate).

NOTE

MSAU Versus MAU MSAU is sometimes, incorrectly, shortened to MAU. A media access unit (MAU) is a device used in Ethernet networks to provide a connection between certain types of network interfaces and the network media.

You might have difficulty grasping the difference between the physical and the logical topologies of ring networks. For example, a common implementation of the token-passing method is Token Ring. A Token Ring network operates and passes data around the network in a logical ring, as shown in Figure 1.12. The physical layout of a ring network is altogether different from this. Ring networks are most commonly wired in a star configuration. In a Token Ring network, a multistation access unit (MSAU) is equivalent to a hub or switch on an Ethernet network. The MSAU performs the token circulation internally. To create the complete ring, the Ring In (RI) port on each MSAU is connected to the Ring Out (RO) port on another MSAU. The last MSAU in the ring is then connected to the first, to complete the ring. Figure 1.13 shows how this works.

Table 1.7 summarizes the advantages and disadvantages of the token-passing access method.

TABLE 1.7

ADVANTAGES AND DISADVANTAGES OF TOKEN PASSING

Advantages	Disadvantages
No collisions means more consistent performance in high-load configurations.	The generation of a token creates network overhead.
Performance is consistently predictable, making it suitable for time-sensitive applications.	Network hardware is more complex and expensive than that used with other access methods.
	The maximum speed is limited due to the overhead of passing and token regeneration.

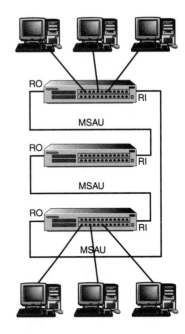

FIGURE 1.13
The physical topology of a Token Ring network.

> **NOTE**
> **100VG-AnyLAN**   Even though 100VG-AnyLAN is based on an Ethernet standard, it is defined in its own IEEE standard (802.12) because it uses demand priority as an access method instead of CSMA/CD.

Demand Priority

Demand priority was developed for use on an Ethernet standard known as 100VG-AnyLAN.

On a demand priority network, a special hub queries each computer connected to it, trying to find one that has data to send. When a computer is found that has information to send, the hub opens a connection for that computer, and no other computer is allowed to transmit. This eliminates the possibility of collisions and therefore provides for very high access speeds and controlled media access.

Demand priority lets the administrator assign a priority to requests for media access. If there is contention for media access, the link with the highest priority wins, making the demand priority system good for time-sensitive applications.

Networks that use demand priority require specialized network devices to manage access. Thus demand priority implementations are more expensive than alternatives such as CSMA/CD. The polling process and evaluation of priorities also add to the network traffic and so create more overhead than is experienced with other networking systems.

Table 1.8 summarizes the advantages and disadvantages of the demand priority access method.

TABLE 1.8

ADVANTAGES AND DISADVANTAGES OF DEMAND PRIORITY

Advantages	*Disadvantages*
Applications can be assigned higher priorities, resulting in faster access to the network.	It has more overhead than other access methods.
No collisions means 100% access to the network bandwidth.	Extra overhead results from determination of priority.
Centralized access makes for easier network management.	Demand priority equipment is expensive compared to the equipment used with other access methods.

Topology

As discussed earlier in this chapter, topologies dictate both the physical and logical layouts of the network. Remember that topologies include bus, star, ring, mesh, and wireless. Each of the IEEE LAN standards can be implemented by using the topology specified within the standard. Some standards, such as 802.3 (Ethernet), have multiple physical topologies, but always use the same logical topology. Token Ring has two possible physical topologies and a single logical topology. We'll talk more about the different topologies in the sections about their respective standards, which is discussed in the next section.

Media

Each IEEE specification defines what media are available to transport the signal around the network. The term *media*, which is the plural of *medium*, generically describes the methods by which data is transported from one point to another. Common network media types include twisted-pair cable, coaxial cable, and fiber-optic cable. Wireless media include infrared, microwave, and radio waves. Chapter 2 provides a detailed discussion of media types.

The IEEE 802 Standards

Now that we have looked at some of the characteristics defined by the IEEE standards, let's examine the standards themselves. Be sure you are completely familiar with the information provided in each of the following sections before you take the Network+ exam.

802.2: The LLC Sublayer

The IEEE 802.2 standard, often referred to as LLC sublayer, is different from the other IEEE 802 networking standards because it does not define a complete networking model. Instead, it defines the standards for controlling the data received and sent by a system. Specifically, it specifies protocols and technologies that perform data flow control and error-checking functions. These control functions form the foundation for the other IEEE 802 networking standards. You can think of 802.2 as an enabler for the other standards. More information on the function of the 802.2 standard can be found in Chapter 4, "The OSI Model," which discusses the Open System Interconnect (OSI) model.

802.3: Ethernet

The Ethernet standard, IEEE 802.3, is by far the most common networking standard in use today, due in part to its flexibility and ease of implementation. Similar to the other IEEE standards, the 802.3 standard specifies the key characteristics of the network model. In addition to the original standard, a number of other standards are based on 802.3. These standards are assigned a designator, such as 802.3u for Fast Ethernet. Collectively, they are often referred to as the *802.3x* standards.

Different implementations of Ethernet accommodate different physical topologies. For example, the 802.3 standard accommodates physical bus and physical star configurations. Other Ethernet standards support only the physical star topology. The logical topology for Ethernet is the linear bus, regardless of the physical topology used.

Table 1.9 provides a summary of the original Ethernet (802.3) standard.

EXAM TIP

Ehternet Ethernet is far and away the most popular LAN networking system, and its coverage in the Network+ objectives is much more detailed than the coverage of the other networking systems. The information presented here is intended as a means for comparison with the other networking standards rather than a full tutorial on the subject. That is left to Chapter 2.

TABLE 1.9

CHARACTERISTICS OF ETHERNET

Characteristic	Description
Specification	IEEE 802.3
Physical topologies	Bus, star
Access method	CSMA/CD
Media	Twisted-pair cable, thick coaxial cable, thin coaxial cable, fiber-optic cable
Speed	10Mbps

802.3u: Fast Ethernet

In networking, speed is everything. At 10Mbps, the original Ethernet standard is too slow for modern implementations. An improved version of the standard, known as 100BaseT, or Fast Ethernet, transmits data at 100Mbps and higher. Fast Ethernet, which is defined in IEEE 802.3u, is available only over twisted-pair and fiber-optic cable.

Table 1.10 summarizes the characteristics of Fast Ethernet (100BaseT).

TABLE 1.10

CHARACTERISTICS OF FAST ETHERNET (100BaseT)

Characteristic	Description
Specification	IEEE 802.3u
Physical topology	Star
Access method	CSMA/CD
Media	Twisted-pair cable, fiber-optic cable
Speed	100Mbps and higher

802.3z: Gigabit Ethernet

Gigabit Ethernet (1000BaseX) is another extension of the 802.3 Ethernet standard. Gigabit Ethernet, which is defined in IEEE 802.3z, can transmit data at 1Gbps (that is 1000Mbps) and can be used with Ethernet and Fast Ethernet devices. Gigabit Ethernet has the same characteristics as the original standard and is backward compatible with older Ethernet technologies such as 10BaseT and 100BaseT. Table 1.11 summarizes the characteristics of Gigabit Ethernet.

TABLE 1.11

CHARACTERISTICS OF GIGABIT ETHERNET

Characteristic	Description
Specification	IEEE 802.3z
Topology	Star
Access method	CSMA/CD
Media	Twisted-pair cable, fiber-optic cable
Speed	1Gbps

NOTE **100VG-AnyLAN** As mentioned earlier in this chapter, the 100VG-AnyLAN standard is based on the Ethernet standard but uses the demand priority access method instead of CSMA/CD. The 100VG-AnyLAN standard defines a physical star networking system over twisted-pair or fiber-optic cable at 100Mbps. 100VG-AnyLAN is defined by the IEEE 802.12 standard.

802.5: Token Ring

Token Ring was introduced by IBM in the mid-1980s and quickly became the network topology of choice—that is, until the rise in popularity of Ethernet. Token Ring is defined for physical and logical ring topologies as well as the physical star topology. Token Ring is defined in the 802.5 specification. Table 1.12 summarizes the characteristics of the Token Ring standard.

NOTE **Ethernet Versus Token Ring** Some people compare Token Ring and Ethernet to Betamax and VHS. Although this comparison may be a little too harsh, it's not far from the truth. Some sources put the ratio of Ethernet networks to Token Ring networks as high as 99 to 1.

TABLE 1.12

CHARACTERISTICS OF TOKEN RING

Characteristic	Description
Specification	IEEE 802.5
Topology	Physical star, physical ring logical ring*
Access method	Token passing
Media	Twisted-pair cable*
Speed	4Mbps or 16Mbps

*The 802.5 standard does not mandate these characteristics, but Token Ring networks are most commonly implemented using these specifications.

Token Ring   This is the one and only section of the Network+ objectives that mentions Token Ring. Concentrate on the basic information provided here, and you should be able to tackle any Token Ring–related questions on the exam.

War Driving   The advent of wireless networking has led to a new phenomenon: *war driving*. Armed with a Global Positioning System (GPS) receiver and a laptop with an 802.11b wireless NIC, hackers drive around metropolitan areas seeking out wireless networks. Once they find one, the hackers attempt to gain access to the network just as if they were connected to the network through a physical link. Such practices are illegal, although little can be done to prevent them other than using the built-in security features of 802.11b. The problem is, not many installations use these features. If you are responsible for a network that has a wireless element, be sure to implement all the security features available. Not doing so is tantamount to letting a hacker into your building and letting him use one of your PCs to access the server.

As you can see from Table 1.12, Token Ring networks can operate at 4Mbps *or* 16Mbps. The key word here is *or*. All devices on the ring must operate at the same speed. Placing a system on the network without configuring the speed correctly will make it unable to participate on the ring. The maximum length of the ring depends on the cable type being used.

Although Token Ring is a very good networking system, the simplicity of Ethernet networking and the low cost of Ethernet equipment has all but eliminated Token Ring from the networking market. Some organizations still use it, mainly for historical reasons, but you are unlikely to see new Token Ring implementations.

802.11b: Wireless

Today we have untethered high-speed networking at our fingertips. The IEEE 802.11b standard defines wireless Ethernet networking for use in LANs.

The 802.11b standard can be implemented many different ways, but the most common is to have special devices called *wireless access points* that allow multiple wireless devices to communicate with each other. In addition, these wireless access points can be connected to wired networks to create wireless portions of entire networks. Wireless access points can cover distances up to several hundred feet, but the actual range depends on the location of the receiver and the local conditions.

Wireless network access now makes it possible to provide network access in any environment, from a coffee shop to an airport and everywhere in between.

The 802.11b standard provides for a maximum transmission speed of 11Mbps. However, devices are designed to be backward compatible with previous standards that provided for speeds of 1-, 2-, and 5.5Mbps. Table 1.14 defines the characteristics of the 802.11b standard.

TABLE 1.14	
CHARACTERISTICS OF THE 802.11B STANDARD	
Characteristic	*Description*
Specification	802.11b
Topology	Wireless
Access method	CSMA/CA
Media	2.4GHz radio waves
Speed	11Mbps

EXAM TIP

WiFi Standards aside, there are no guarantees that one manufacturer's wireless products will work with another's. For that reason, the Wireless Ethernet Compatibility Alliance has a Wireless Fidelity (WiFi) certification program that guarantees compatibility between products. When you're specifying or buying wireless networking equipment, look for WiFi approval.

Although the popularity of 802.11b is still relatively low, it is sure to become a major feature of the networking landscape in coming years. As speeds rise and the cost of wireless networking equipment falls, wireless is likely to become the networking method of choice, particularly because new standards that provide for much faster transmissions are being developed at a rapid rate.

FDDI

FDDI was developed by the American National Standards Institute (ANSI) in the mid-1980s, to meet the growing need for reliable, fast network transmissions to accommodate distributed applications. In particular, FDDI was intended for use in specific applications such as backbones.

FDDI is a 100Mbps token-passing network standard. FDDI uses fiber-optic cable as its main transmission media, but it can also work over copper wire (in which case it is called Copper Distributed Data Interface [CDDI]).

Although FDDI is a ring topology, it does not suffer from the fault-tolerance issues inherent in the IEEE 802.5 standard. To avoid a single break in the ring that could disrupt network connectivity, FDDI uses a dual-ring configuration. If one computer or cable is damaged, the other ring will form a single ring topology, and the data signals can continue to travel around the network. Devices that must remain available in the event of a media failure can be attached to both rings. Less important systems can be connected to just the primary ring. Figure 1.14 shows the dual-ring configuration of FDDI.

NOTE

CDDI It is possible to use the FDDI protocols over copper wire; this is called CDDI. Like FDDI, CDDI uses a dual-ring configuration and has transfer rates of 100Mbps.

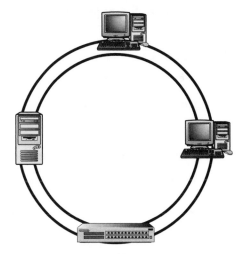

FIGURE 1.14
An example of a FDDI dual-ring configuration.

In many ways, FDDI is similar to Token Ring. It uses a logical ring and a physical star topology, and it uses token passing as a media access method. However, FDDI has much faster data transmission rates than Token Ring, so is better suited to today's high-bandwidth applications. Table 1.15 summarizes the characteristics of FDDI.

TABLE 1.15

CHARACTERISTICS OF FDDI

Characteristic	Description
Specification	ANSI X3T9.5
Topology	Dual ring
Access method	Token passing
Media	Fiber-optic (Shielded Twisted Pair [STP] or Unshielded Twisted Pair [UTP] is CDDI)
Speed	100Mbps

For more information on FDDI, see Chapter 7, "WAN Technologies."

CHAPTER SUMMARY

KEY TERMS

- peer-to-peer networking
- client/server networking
- distributed computing
- centralized computing
- LAN
- WAN

This chapter provides an overview of the functions and purposes of computer networks. Key among the functions of the network are increased communication, both in real-time and via email, sharing of hardware between multiple users, reduction in overall cost and support of multiple devices, and the ability to share files.

Two network models are identified in this chapter: peer-to-peer networking and client/server networking. Peer-to-peer networking is restricted to networks with few users and does not use a centralized server. Peer-to-peer networks are most commonly seen in home network environments and in small offices.

CHAPTER SUMMARY

The client/server model is more common and familiar than the peer-to-peer model, especially in larger networks. The client/server model uses a dedicated server and offers many advantages over the peer-to-peer network model. Perhaps most notable of these advantages is the ability to centrally manage the network, although the cost and administration requirements are higher than those of peer-to-peer networks.

Networks have both physical and logical topologies. The physical topology refers to the way the network is physically laid out, including media, computers, and other networking devices such as hubs or MSAUs. The logical topology refers to how data is transmitted around the network. Common network topologies include star, ring, bus, and mesh. Each of these topologies offers distinct advantages and disadvantages and various levels of fault tolerance.

Access methods are the methods by which data is sent onto the network. Two of the most common access methods are CSMA/CD, which uses a collision detection and contention method, and token passing.

The IEEE defines several LAN standards, including 802.2 (the LLC layer), 802.3 (Ethernet), 802.5 (Token Ring), and 802.11b (wireless). Each of these standards identifies specific characteristics, including the network's media, speed, access method, and topology.

KEY TERMS
- physical topology
- logical topology
- bus topology
- star topology
- ring topology
- mesh topology
- wireless topology
- IEEE
- 802.x standards
- CSMA/CD
- token passing
- MSAU
- demand priority
- media
- Fast Ethernet
- Gigabit Ethernet
- Token Ring
- 802.11b wireless
- FDDI

APPLY YOUR KNOWLEDGE

Exercises

1.1   Enabling File and Print Sharing on Windows Me

After just three months working as a freelance accountant, you find yourself unable to cope with your workload. As a result, you decide to recruit an assistant to help you. Up to this point, you have had only a single PC for your business, but you now realize that you need an additional PC, so you can share data with your new assistant. You buy an additional PC with a small workgroup hub. After unpacking and connecting the new PC and connecting the new hub, you are ready to share data from your PC, which is running Microsoft Windows Me, with the other PC.

This exercise shows how you can enable file and print sharing. (This exercise assumes that you are running Windows Me.)

Estimated time: 10 minutes

1. In Windows Me, right-click My Network Places and then select Properties. The Network dialog box appears.

2. Click the File and Print Sharing button. The File and Print Sharing dialog box appears.

3. Select the option to share your files and then click OK.

> **WARNING**
>
> **Warning**   If you have a connection to the Internet, allowing others to access your hard disk presents security risks. Be cautious in sharing your disk. If in doubt, disable file and print sharing before connecting to the Internet.

4. If you're prompted to supply Windows files, input the correct location of your files. After the files have been copied, you will be prompted to reboot.

5. Navigate to the folder you want to share. Right-click the folder and select Sharing from the drop-down menu. If the Sharing option does not appear, make sure you completed step 4 as described.

6. In the Properties dialog box, select the Shared As option and enter the name you want to use for this share. If you want, you can add a password that users must supply when accessing the folder. Click OK.

7. If the sharing process is successful, a blue hand appears under the folder, indicating that it is now shared and accessible to the network.

1.2   Connecting to Mapped Drives Through Windows 2000

After you enable file sharing in Exercise 1.1, you turn your attention to configuring your new PC to connect to the newly shared folder. The new PC came preloaded with Windows 2000 Professional, and although you have not used this version of Windows before, you have heard that the process of mapping network drives in Windows 2000 is similar to doing so on all other versions of Windows.

This exercise shows how you must connect to a mapped drive through Windows 2000. This exercise assumes that you have a PC running Windows 2000, that you are connected to a network on which at least one other system has a shared folder, and that you have the necessary rights to access that folder. You might also need a valid user ID and password for the target system.

APPLY YOUR KNOWLEDGE

Estimated time: 5 minutes

1. In Windows 2000, right-click My Computer and select Map Network Drive from the menu. The Map Network Drive dialog box appears.

2. Click the Browse button. The Browse for Folder dialog box appears.

3. Expand the browse tree as necessary to locate another system that is sharing folders.

4. When you have located a shared folder to connect to, double-click it. You are returned to the Map Network Drive dialog box.

5. If you want, you can clear the Reconnect at Logon check box. Then click Finish. Depending on the configuration of the shared folder, you might be asked for a password.

6. The contents of the folder you connected to appear in Windows Explorer.

Exam Questions

1. Which of the following is a disadvantage of the physical bus topology?

   a. Has complex cabling requirements

   b. Is prone to cable faults

   c. Requires a dedicated server

   d. Requires a dedicated hub

2. Which of the following are IEEE standards that define LAN networking systems? (Choose the three best answers.)

   a. 802.3

   b. 802.4

   c. 802.5

   d. 802.10

3. Which of the following IEEE standards provides the specifications for a Token Ring LAN?

   a. 802.3

   b. 802.4

   c. 803.3

   d. 802.5

4. Which of the following topologies offers the greatest level of redundancy?

   a. Mesh

   b. Star

   c. Bus

   d. Ring

5. Which of the following IEEE specifications does CSMA/CD relate to?

   a. 802.2

   b. 802.3

   c. 802.4

   d. 802.5

6. As a network administrator, you have been called to replace an NIC on a computer in a Token Ring network. After you replace the NIC and connect the cable, the computer cannot communicate on the network. Which of the following is the most likely problem?

   a. The NIC is configured for the wrong speed.

   b. A token must be created for the newly installed card.

   c. The card's address must be added to the token list.

   d. The computer must be inserted into the ring.

7. Which of the following IEEE standards specifies a physical star/logical ring topology and a token-passing access method?

   a. 802.1

   b. 803.2

   c. 802.5

   d. 802.2

8. Which network topology is represented in the following diagram?

   a. Bus

   b. Star

   c. Logical ring

   d. Mesh

9. Part of your responsibility as network administrator is to design your company's new network. You have been asked to implement a network in which each computer must have guaranteed and equal access to the network. Which of the following would best suit your company's needs?

   a. Token Ring

   b. Mesh topology

   c. Ethernet

   d. CSMA/CD

10. Which of the following topologies has a single connection between each node on the network and a centralized device?

   a. Ring

   b. Mesh

   c. Star

   d. Bus

11. Which of the following devices is associated with a Token Ring network?

   a. Switch

   b. Hub

   c. MSAU

   d. CSMA/CD

12. As a network administrator, you are called in to correct a problem associated with the network's MSAU. What physical topology are you troubleshooting?

   a. Star topology

   b. Ring topology

   c. Mesh topology

   d. Bus topology

13. What is the name for a network that connects two geographic locations?

   a. PAN

   b. LAN

   c. DAN

   d. WAN

APPLY YOUR KNOWLEDGE

14. Which network topology is represented in the following diagram?

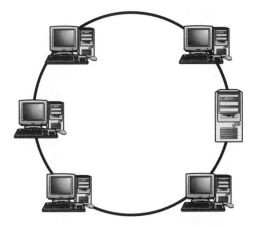

a. Bus

b. Star

c. Mesh

d. Ring

15. Which of the following is a feature of the physical star topology?

a. It requires less cable than other physical topologies.

b. The network is very easy to expand.

c. Apart from the cable and connectors, no other equipment is required to create the network.

d. There is no single point of failure.

16. The 802.11b standard describes what kind of network?

a. Token passing

b. Contention

c. Wireless

d. Token bus

17. A mainframe is an example of what computing model?

a. Segregated

b. Distributed

c. Centralized

d. Decentralized

18. What kind of access method is CSMA/CD?

a. Contention

b. Demand priority

c. Collision avoidance

d. Token passing

19. Which network topology is represented in the following diagram?

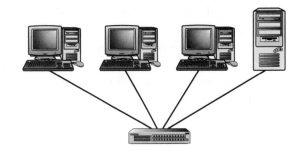

a. Star

b. Bus

c. Mesh

d. Ring

APPLY YOUR KNOWLEDGE

20. What is the maximum network speed defined by the 802.11b standard?

    a. 100Mbps

    b. 5.5Mbps

    c. 11Mbps

    d. 10Mbps

Answers to Review Questions

1. **b.** One of the disadvantages of the physical bus topology is that it's prone to cable faults. In addition, a fault on the cable can render the entire network unusable. The advantages of the physical bus topology are that the cabling is simple and no additional network hardware is required to create the network. For more information, see the section "LAN Topologies," in this chapter.

2. **a, b, c.** The IEEE 802.3 standard defines Ethernet, the 802.4 standard defines token bus, and the 802.5 standard defines Token Ring. The IEEE 802.10 defines security standards that make it possible to safely and securely transmit and exchange data. For more information, see the section "The IEEE 802 Standards," in this chapter.

3. **d.** The IEEE 802.5 standard defines Token Ring networking. The 802.3 standard defines Ethernet. 802.4 defines the use of a token-passing system on a linear bus topology. 803.3 is not a LAN standard. For more information, see the section "The IEEE 802 Standards," in this chapter.

4. **a.** In a mesh topology, each device is connected directly to every other device. If there is a break in the connection between two devices, alternate paths between the two systems are available. None of the other topologies provide this level of redundancy. For more information, see the section "LAN Topologies," in this chapter.

5. **b.** The IEEE 802.3 standard defines the Ethernet networking system, which uses CSMA/CD as its media access method. 802.2 defines specifications for the LLC sublayer of the 802 standard series. 802.4 defines the use of a token-passing system on a linear bus topology. 802.5 defines Token Ring networking. For more information, see the section "The IEEE 802 Standards," in this chapter.

6. **a.** On a Token Ring network, all devices must be configured to run at the same speed. If a device is connected to the network and not configured for the correct speed, it will not work. None of the other answers are valid. For more information, see the section "The IEEE 802 Standards," in this chapter.

7. **c.** The IEEE 802.5 standard defines Token Ring, a physical star/logical ring topology that uses token passing as a media access method. The 802.1 standard defines internetwork communications standards between devices and includes specifications for routing and bridging. 803.2 is not a LAN standard. 802.2 defines specifications for the LLC sublayer of the 802 standard series. For more information, see the section "The IEEE 802 Standards," in this chapter.

8. **a.** The diagram shows the physical bus topology. None of the other answers are valid. For more information, see the section "LAN Topologies," in this chapter.

9. **a.** Token Ring uses a token-passing media access method that provides guaranteed and equal access

APPLY YOUR KNOWLEDGE

to the network media. Ethernet, the only other reasonable answer, uses CSMA/CD to govern media access. For more information, see the section "The IEEE and Networking Standards," in this chapter.

10. **c.** A star topology is created when each node on the network is connected to a central device. None of the other answers are valid. For more information, see the section "LAN Topologies," in this chapter.

11. **c.** An MSAU is used on Token Ring networks to connect systems to the network. Switches and hubs are used on Ethernet networks. CSMA/CD is a media access method, not a networking device. For more information, see the section "The IEEE 802 Standards," in this chapter.

12. **a.** Because MSAUs are being used, the network system in use is Token Ring. The use of MSAUs on a Token Ring network creates a physical star configuration. Star topologies are most commonly associated with Ethernet networks. Mesh topologies do not use MSAUs. Token passing, not Token Ring, can be implemented on a bus network, per the IEEE 802.4 standard, though such a configuration would not use MSAUs; therefore, Answer d is incorrect. For more information, see the section "The IEEE 802 Standards," in this chapter.

13. **d.** The term *WAN* describes a network that spans more than one geographic location. The only other valid term for a type of network is *LAN*, but a LAN is a network that is confined to a single location. None of the other answers are recognized terms for describing a network. For more information, see the section "LANs, WANs, and MANs," in this chapter.

14. **d.** The diagram shows a physical ring topology. All the other answers are incorrect. For more information, see the section "LAN Topologies," in this chapter.

15. **b.** Physical star networks use centralized devices to connect nodes on the network. Because devices can be plugged and unplugged from these devices without affecting any other systems on the network, star configurations are very easy to expand. The disadvantages of a physical star network are that they require more cable than other topologies, they require additional networking equipment, and they create a single point of failure. For more information, see the section "LAN Topologies," in this chapter.

16. **c.** The IEEE 802.11b standard defines wireless networking architectures. Token passing and contention are media access methods, and token bus is an implementation of token-passing media access on a physical bus topology. For more information, see the section "The IEEE and Networking Standards," in this chapter.

17. **c.** A mainframe is an example of a centralized computing model. All the other answers are incorrect. For more information, see the section "Peer-to-Peer Versus Client/Server Networks," in this chapter.

18. **a.** CSMA/CD is described as a contention-based media access method because devices contend for access. All the other answers are incorrect. For more information, see the section "The IEEE and Networking Standards," in this chapter.

19. **a.** A star topology is shown in the diagram. All the other answers are incorrect. For more information, see the section "LAN Topologies," in this chapter.

APPLY YOUR KNOWLEDGE

20. **c.** The IEEE 802.11b standard for wireless networks defines a maximum speed of 11Mbps. 100Mbps is the defined speed for Fast Ethernet. 5.5Mbps is the speed specified in earlier wireless networking standards. 10Mbps is the maximum speed of standard Ethernet. For more information, see the section "The IEEE and Networking Standards," in this chapter.

Suggested Readings and Resources

1. Sloan Joseph D. *Network Troubleshooting Tools (O'Reilly System Administration).* O'Reilly & Associates, 2001.

2. Habraken, Joe. *Absolute Beginner's Guide to Networking,* third edition. Que Publishing, 2001.

3. Haugdahl, J. Scott. *Network Analysis and Troubleshooting.* Addison-Wesley, 2000.

4. Cisco Systems Inc. *Internetworking Troubleshooting Handbook,* second edition. Cisco Press, 2001.

5. Computer networking products and testing tools, `www.trendware.com`.

6. Network cable information, `www.techfest.com/networking/cabling.htm`.

7. Computer networking tutorials and advice, `compnetworking.about.com`.

8. "TechEncyclopedia," `www.techencyclopedia.com`.

9. Networking technology information from Cisco, `www.cisco.com/public/products_tech.shtml`.

10. "Network Cabling Help," `www.datacottage.com`.

This chapter covers the following CompTIA-specified objectives for the "Media and Topologies" section of the Network+ certification exam:

Recognize the following media connectors and describe their uses:

- **RJ-11**
- **RJ-45**
- **AUI**
- **BNC**
- **ST**
- **SC**

▶ Specific cable types use one or more types of connectors. Being able to identify which connector is associated with which cable is an important skill for a network administrator.

Specify the characteristics (e.g., speed, length, topology, cable type, etc.) of the following 802.3 (Ethernet) standards:

- **10BaseT**
- **10BaseTX**
- **10Base2**
- **10Base5**
- **100BaseFX**
- **Gigabit Ethernet**

▶ A wide variety of network media are used in networking. To pass the Network+ exam, you will need to understand the various media types and their characteristics.

CHAPTER 2

Cabling and Connectors

OBJECTIVES

Choose the appropriate media type and connectors to add a client to an existing network.

▶ As a network administrator, you will work in a range of environments. Understanding the requirements to connect systems to the network is a key skill.

OUTLINE

Introduction   **62**

Media Considerations   **62**

    Media Interference   62
    Bandwidth   63
    Media Length   64
    Security   65
    Installation and Repair   65

Baseband Versus Broadband Signaling   **65**

    Baseband   66
    Broadband   66

Simplex, Half-Duplex, and Full-Duplex   **66**

Common Network Cable   **68**

    Cable Media   68
      Coaxial Cable   68
      Twisted-Pair   70
      Fiber-optic Cable   72
    Cable Summary   73
    Wireless Media   74
      Radio   74
      Microwave   76
      Infrared Wireless Networking   77

OUTLINE

Media Connectors	**78**
D-shell Connectors	78
Attachment Unit Interface Connectors	78
External SCSI Connectors	79
Serial (RS-232) Connectors	80
Parallel Connectors	81
RJ Connectors	81
BNCs	82
Fiber Connectors	82
Centronic Connectors	83
Features and Characteristics of Ethernet 802.3 Standards	**84**
10Base2	84
10Base5	86
10BaseT	87
Fast Ethernet: 100BaseX	89
100BaseTX	89
100BaseT4	89
100BaseFX	89
Fast Ethernet Comparison	90
Gigabit Ethernet: 1000BaseX	90
1000BaseT	91
Choosing the Appropriate Media Connector for Adding Clients to an Existing Network	**92**
Chapter Summary	**93**
Apply Your Knowledge	**95**

STUDY STRATEGIES

▶ Read the objectives at the beginning of the chapter.

▶ Study the information in the chapter, paying special attention to the tables that summarize key information.

▶ Review the objectives again.

▶ Answer the exam questions at the end of the chapter and check your results.

▶ Use the ExamGear test on the CD-ROM that accompanies this book to answer additional exam questions concerning this material.

▶ Review the notes, tips, and exam tips in this chapter. Be sure you understand the information in the exam tips. If you don't understand the topic referenced in an exam tip, refer to the information in the chapter text, and then read the exam tip again.

INTRODUCTION

As identified in Chapter 1, "Introduction to Networking," a *network* is simply a group of connected computers. The computers on a traditional local area network (LAN) are connected by network media. Many types of media are used to connect network devices, and each type offers unique characteristics that you must understand in order to determine the media's suitability for a given network environment.

In addition to these characteristics, network media requires specific connector types to attach media to networking devices such as network cards or hubs. This chapter helps you identify and understand the characteristics and connectors used by the different types of network media and with this knowledge, you'll be able to implement the correct media for a given network design.

Before discussing the various network media, let's identify some of the terms and general considerations that are relevant to network media.

MEDIA CONSIDERATIONS

Managing a network involves many factors, from configuring the operating system and protocols to monitoring users and network performance. Despite the complexity of networks, it is important not to forget about one of the basics components of a network—the network media.

Choosing the correct network media is an important consideration because the media form the foundation for the entire network. When you're working with any media, you must be aware of the factors that influence its suitability for a given network implementation. Some of the most common media considerations are discussed in the following sections.

> **NOTE**
>
> **Media** Because not all networks use traditional cable, the term *media* is used. This term encompasses copper-based and fiber-optic cable as well as wireless media types.

Media Interference

As a data signal travels through a specific media, it may be subjected to a type of interference known as *electromagnetic interference* (*EMI*).

Many different things cause EMI; common sources include computer monitors and fluorescent lighting fixtures—basically, anything that creates an electromagnetic field. If a network cable is too close to such devices, the signal within the cable can become corrupted. As you might expect, some network media are more susceptible than others to the effects of EMI. Copper-based media are prone to EMI, whereas fiber-optic cable is completely resistant to it.

In most networks, standard cable provides sufficient resistance that EMI isn't a problem. However, you might work in some environments in which interference is a concern. In such environments, it becomes important to understand which media offer the greatest resistance to EMI.

EMI is just one of the threats to network transmissions. Data signals may also be subjected to something commonly referred to as *crosstalk*, which occurs when signals from two cables in close proximity to one another interfere with each other. As a result, the signals on both cables may become corrupted. When you're troubleshooting intermittent network problems, it might be worth your time to confirm that crosstalk or EMI is not at the root of your problems.

> **NOTE**
>
> **EMI-Resistant Cable Cost**   Cables designed for greater resistance to EMI cost more than those that aren't.

Bandwidth

The term *bandwidth* is tossed around a lot in the network world, and rightly so—it is a very important consideration. *Bandwidth* is the transmission capacity of a media or, in other words, the amount of data that a media can carry. Data throughput is measured in bits per second (bps). The speed of modern networks is measured in megabits per second (Mbps) and gigabits per second (Gbps).

The different types of network media vary in the amount of bandwidth they can accommodate. If you're working on a network that accommodates huge amounts of data, then bandwidth is a crucial consideration. In contrast, many older networks in small offices may only occasionally share files and maybe a printer. In such an environment, bandwidth is not a very big issue.

Two rules apply to bandwidth:

◆ **Bigger is better**—It seems that there is never enough bandwidth to accommodate the demand placed on networks by many applications.

◆ **You have to pay to play**—Understandably, everybody would like more bandwidth, but it can be costly. For organizations that need to surpass the 100Mbps mark, the price can climb quickly.

Media Length

Not all networks have the same design. Some are isolated to a single office building, and others span large distances. For large network implementations, *media length* (that is, the maximum distance over which a certain type of media can be used) may be a factor in the network administrator's choice of network media. Each media has a recommended maximum length, and surpassing these recommendations can cause unusual network problems that are often difficult to troubleshoot. In some cases, the network simply will not work.

Media have maximum lengths because a signal weakens as it travels farther from its point of origin. If the signal travels far enough, it can weaken so much that it becomes unusable. The weakening of data signals as they traverse the media is referred to as *attenuation*.

All media are susceptible to attenuation, although each media offers some degree of resistance to weakening signals. Some physical media use a special shielding inside the cable, which increases the distance the signal travels. Another strategy that is commonly employed to compensate for attenuation is *signal regeneration*. The cable itself does not perform the regeneration process; rather, network devices such as switches or repeaters handle signal regeneration. These devices strengthen the signal as it passes and in doing so, they increase the distance the signal can travel. Network devices, such as hubs, routers, and switches, are covered in Chapter 3, "Networking Components and Devices."

Some cable types, such as fiber-optic, offer very long media distances; other types, such as twisted-pair, offer very short distances (a fraction of the distance of fiber). Some unbound media (wireless media), don't have an exact figure for the allowable distance because there are so many variables. The next section reviews the different types of network media and compares them according to their resistance to attenuation.

EXAM TIP

Attenuation For the Network+ exam, you will be expected to know what attenuation is and how it affects a network.

Security

Physical media provide relatively secure transmission because to gain access to the signal on the cable, a person must be able to physically access it—that is, he or she must be able to tap into the cable. Fiber-optic cable is even more difficult to access than other cable types because the light transmissions and glass cable used for fiber make it particularly difficult to tap into.

Wireless media, on the other hand, can be insecure; tapping into, or *eavesdropping* on, signals is a relatively easy process. For organizations that transmit sensitive data, using wireless media can be a security risk. However, a number of security measures can be employed to secure data as it travels across wireless links.

Installation and Repair

Some network media are easier to manage and install than others. This might seem like a minor consideration, but in real-world applications, it can be very important. For example, fiber-optic cable is far more complex to install and troubleshoot than twisted-pair. It's so complicated, in fact, that special tools and training are often needed to install a fiber network.

Each media has a certain level of handling difficulty. It is important to be aware of what you are in for when it's time to implement or repair the network media.

In addition to the factors already discussed, you need to understand some important concepts before we examine the specific media types; you need to understand baseband and broadband signaling, physical media terminology, and duplexing.

BASEBAND VERSUS BROADBAND SIGNALING

Two types of signaling methods are used to transmit information over network media: baseband and broadband.

NOTE

Plenum Cables *Plenum* is the mysterious space that resides between the false, or drop, ceiling and the true ceiling. This space is typically used for the air conditioning or heating ducts. It might also hold a myriad of cables, including telephone, electrical, and network cables. The cables that occupy this space must be plenum rated. Plenum cables are coated with a nonflammable material, often Teflon or Kynar, and do not give off toxic fumes if they catch fire. As you might imagine, plenum-rated cables cost more than regular cables, but they are mandatory when cables are not run through a conduit. As an added bonus, plenum-rated cables suffer from less attenuation than nonplenum cables.

EXAM TIP

Baseband and Broadband Be prepared to identify the characteristics of baseband and broadband for the Network+ exam.

Baseband

Baseband transmissions typically use digital signaling over a single wire; the transmissions themselves take the form of either electrical pulses or light. The digital signal used in baseband transmission occupies the entire bandwidth of the network media to transmit a single data signal. Baseband communication is bidirectional, allowing computers to both send and receive data using a single cable; however, the sending and receiving cannot occur at the same time.

Using baseband transmissions, it is possible to transmit multiple signals on a single cable by using a process known as *multiplexing*. Baseband uses Time-Division Multiplexing (TDM), which divides a single channel into time slots. The key thing about TDM is that it doesn't change how baseband transmission works—only the way data is placed on the cable.

Broadband

Whereas baseband uses digital signaling, broadband uses analog signals in the form of optical or electromagnetic waves over multiple transmission frequencies. For signals to be both sent and received, the transmission media must be split into two channels. Alternatively, two cables can be used—one to send and one to receive transmissions.

Multiple channels are created in a broadband system by using a multiplexing technique known as *Frequency-Division Multiplexing (FDM)*. FDM allows broadband media to accommodate traffic going in different directions on a single media at the same time.

SIMPLEX, HALF-DUPLEX, AND FULL-DUPLEX

Those who do not know about duplexing might assume that network transmissions travel in any direction through the media. In fact, specific dialog control modes determine the direction in which data can flow through the network media. The three dialog modes are simplex, half-duplex, and full-duplex.

The *simplex* mode allows only one-way communication through the media. A good example of simplex is a radio or television signal: There is only one transmitting device, and all other devices are receiving devices. A simplex dialog mode uses the full bandwidth of the media for transmitting the signal. The advantages of the simplex dialog mode can be seen in many applications, but networks are not among them.

Half-duplex allows each device to both transmit and receive, but only one of these processes can occur at one time. Many networks are configured for and support only half-duplex communication. A good example of half-duplex transmission is a modem that can either transmit or receive but not do both simultaneously. The transmitting device can use the entire bandwidth of the media.

If at all possible, the preferred method of communication on networks is full-duplex mode. *Full-duplex* allows devices to receive and transmit simultaneously. On a network, network cards that can use full-duplexing can double their transfer rates. For instance, a 100Mbps network card in full-duplex mode can operate at 200Mbps and therefore significantly increases the speed on the network. An example of full-duplex is a telephone conversation, where both parties are able to talk (send) and listen (receive) simultaneously.

> **EXAM TIP**
>
> **Simplex Transmission**   A broadcast messages—that is, one that is sent to all nodes on the network— is a good example of a simplex transmission. Remember this for the exam.

> **EXAM TIP**
>
> **Know the Difference**   Half-duplex allows two-way communication over a single channel. Full-duplex provides two-way communication by using different channels for sending and receiving signals. For the exam, know the difference.

IN THE FIELD

NETWORKING TERMINOLOGY

The term *segment* is used extensively in discussions of network media. However, what *segment* means appears to be open to some interpretation. Technically speaking, a segment is simply a section of a larger entity. In networking, a segment is a part of the network or a single length of cable. You can just as easily say that one computer is on the same segment as another as you can say that each computer is on its own segment. In this case, the cable type affects the definition of *segment*. The first statement is correct if you're using coaxial cable; the second is correct if you're using twisted-pair.

COMMON NETWORK CABLE

Having now examined some of the general considerations that surround network media, the next step is to look at the different types of media available. The network media are not the most glamorous part of computer networking, but they are important both for the Network+ exam and the real world. Besides, who said networking was glamorous?

Network media can be divided into two distinct categories: cable and wireless, sometimes referred to as *bound* and *unbound* media. Cable media come in three common types: twisted-pair, coaxial, and fiber-optic. Wireless media has another range. The following sections identify the characteristic of each type of media.

Cable Media

Working with today's networks, you are more likely to be working with cable media than with any wireless alternative. Cable media provides a physical connection between networked devices—for example, a copper cable running from a desktop computer to a hub in the server room. Data transmissions pass through the cable to their destination.

There are two types of cable media: metal and optical-based cable. Copper-based cable is widely used to connect LANs and wide area networks (WANs), and optical cable is mainly used for large-scale network implementations. The following sections review the various types of cable media and the networks on which they are used.

Coaxial Cable

At one time, almost all networks used coaxial cable. Times have changed, and coax has fallen out of favor, giving way to faster and more durable cable options. That is not to say that you won't be working with coax at some point. Many environments have been using coax and continue to do so because their network needs do not require an upgrade to another media—at least not yet. Many small offices continue to use coax on their networks, so we'll include it in our discussion.

Coaxial cable resembles standard TV cable and is constructed using an outside insulation cover, braided metal shielding, and a copper wire at the center. The shielding and insulation help combat attenuation, crosstalk, and EMI. Some coax is available with dual and even quad shielding.

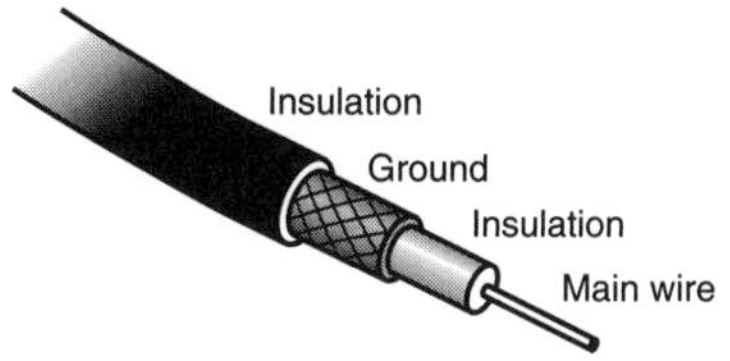

Two types of coax are used in networking: thin coax and thick coax. Neither is particularly popular anymore, but you are most likely to encounter thin coax. Figure 2.1 shows the construction of a standard coaxial cable.

FIGURE 2.1
Coaxial cable construction.

Thin Coax

Thin coax is by far the most widely used type of coax. As the name suggests, it is thin—at least compared to other forms of available coax. Thin coax, also called Thinnet, is only .25 inches in diameter, making it fairly easy to install; it has a maximum cable length of 185 meters (that is, just over 600 feet). If longer lengths of thin coax are used, data signals sent along the cable will suffer from attenuation, compromising data integrity. Table 2.1 summarizes the types of thin coax cable.

TABLE 2.1

THIN COAX TYPES

Cable Type	Description
RG-58 /U	Has a solid copper core
RG-58 A/U	Has a stranded wire core
RG-58 C/U	Used for military specifications
RG-59	Often used for cable TV and cable modems
RG-62	Used for ARCnet specifications

Thin coax typically runs from computer to computer and uses British Naval connectors (BNCs) to connect to network devices. Figure 2.2 shows BNC T connectors and terminators, which are often used with thin coax.

NOTE

Cable and Standards Thin and thick coax cable are used for the Institute of Electrical and Electronics Engineers (IEEE) network standards 10Base2 and 10Base5, respectively. More details on these standards are presented later in this chapter.

FIGURE 2.2
BNC T connectors and terminators.

Thick Coax

Thick coax is indeed thicker than thin coax. The popularity of thick coax has fallen due to its implementation difficulty and low network speeds. In its day, thick coax found its niche as a backbone for network environments because of its better-than-average resistance to attenuation and EMI.

Unlike thin coax, which connects to individual network devices via BNCs, thick coax requires an extra length of cable that runs from it to the networked system. Thick coax networks use a device called a *tap* to connect a smaller cable to the thick coax backbone. Taps are simple devices that penetrate the outer insulation and create a connection directly to the inside wire.

It is unlikely that you will be involved in designing and implementing a network with thick coax. However, you might work with a network that has an existing thick coax infrastructure.

Twisted-Pair

Now and for the foreseeable future, twisted-pair cable is the network media of choice. It is relatively inexpensive, easy to work with, and well suited to the needs of the modern network. There are two distinct types of twisted-pair cable: unshielded twisted-pair (UTP) and shielded twisted-pair (STP). UTP is the most common implementation of twisted-pair cable, and it is used for both telephone systems and computer networks.

STP, as its name implies, adds extra shielding within the casing, so it copes with interference and attenuation better than regular UTP. Because of this shielding, cable distances for STP can be greater than for UTP; but, unfortunately, the additional shielding also makes STP considerably more costly than regular UTP.

The Electronic Industries Association/Telecommunications Industry Association (EIA/TIA) has specified five categories of twisted-pair cable:

◆ **Category 1**—Voice-grade UTP telephone cable. Due to its susceptibility to interference and attenuation and its low bandwidth capability, Category 1 UTP is not practical for network applications.

◆ **Category 2**—Data-grade cable that is capable of transmitting data up to 4Mbps. Category 2 cable is, of course, too slow for networks. It is unlikely that you will encounter Category 2 used on any network today.

◆ **Category 3**—Data-grade cable that is capable of transmitting data up to 10Mbps. A few years ago, Category 3 was the cable of choice for twisted-pair networks. As network speeds pushed the 100Mbps speed limit, Category 3 became ineffective.

◆ **Category 4**—Data-grade cable that has potential bandwidth of 16Mbps. Category 4 cable was often implemented in the IBM Token Ring networks.

◆ **Category 5**—Data-grade cable that is capable of transmitting data at 100Mbps. Category 5 is the cable of choice on twisted-pair networks and is associated with Fast Ethernet technologies.

To keep pace with today's faster network speeds, twisted-pair categories beyond 5 have been developed. Because not all Category 5 cable is suitable for Gigabit Ethernet applications, an enhanced version of Category 5 has been developed: Category 5e. Category 6 supports data throughput up to three times greater than that of Category 5, but it costs considerably more. In fact, the price of Category 6 might be close enough to fiber that companies will probably choose fiber-optic cable instead. Stay tuned for further developments.

EXAM TIP

Another Name for STP STP cable is sometimes called IBM-type cable. You should know this for the exam.

NOTE

What's with the Twist? Ever wonder why twisted-pair is twisted? In the ongoing battle with interference and attenuation, it was discovered that twisting the wires within a cable resulted in greater signal integrity than running the wires parallel to one another. UTP cable is particularly susceptible to crosstalk, and increasing the number of twists per foot in the wire achieves greater resistance against interference. The technique of twisting wires together is not limited to network cable; some internal and external SCSI cable employs a similar strategy.

EXAM TIP

Determining Cable Categories If you're working on an existing network that is a few years old, you might need to determine which category of cable is used on the network. The easiest way to do this is to simply read the cable. The category number should be clearly printed on it.

Fiber-optic Cable

Fiber-optic cable is a newcomer on the networking scene compared to the other network cable media, and it is perhaps the most interesting. Unlike standard networking cables, which use electric signals to send data transmissions, fiber uses light. As a result, fiber-optic transmissions are not susceptible to EMI or crosstalk, giving fiber cable an obvious advantage over copper-based media. In addition, fiber-optic cable is highly resistant to attenuation, allowing data signals to travel distances measured in kilometers rather than meters, as with copper-based media. Further advantages of fiber cable include the fact that it's small in diameter, it's lightweight, and it offers significantly faster transmission speeds than other cable media. Quite simply, fiber beats twisted-pair from almost every angle. So, why aren't all networks using fiber cable? The same reason we don't all drive Porsches: cost.

A few things will continue to ensure that there is room for twisted-pair and copper-based media in network environments. First, a fiber solution is very costly, eliminating it from many small- to mid-sized companies that simply do not have the budget to support a fiber-optic solution. The second drawback of fiber is the complexity of its installation and maintenance. Working with fiber-optic cable often requires trained professionals and specialized tools. Third, fiber technology is incompatible with much of the existing electronic network infrastructure, meaning that to use fiber-optic cable, much of the current network hardware needs to be retrofitted or upgraded, and that can be a very costly commitment.

A fiber-optic cable consists of several components, including the optic core at the center, an optic cladding, insulation, and an outer jacket. The optic core is responsible for carrying the light signal and is commonly constructed of plastic or glass. Figure 2.3 shows an example of the components of a fiber-optic cable.

Two types of optical fiber are available: single-mode and multimode. Multimode fiber has a larger core than single-mode. This larger core allows hundreds of light rays to flow through the fiber simultaneously. Single-mode fiber, on the other hand, has a small core that allows only a single light beam to pass. The light transmissions in single-mode fiber pass through the core in a direct line, like a flashlight beam. The numerous light beams in multimode fiber bounce around inside the core, inching toward their destination. Because light beams bounce within the core, the light beams slow down, reduce in strength, and take some time to travel along the cable.

For this reason, single-mode fiber's speed and distance are superior to those of multimode.

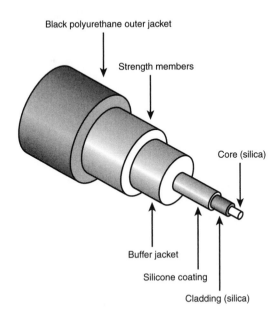

FIGURE 2.3
Fiber-optic cable.

Fiber cable can also have a variety of internal compositions (glass or plastic core), and the size of the core inside the cable, measured in microns, can vary. Some of the common types of fiber-optic cable include the following:

◆ 62.5 micron core/125 micron cladding multimode

◆ 50 micron core/125 micron cladding multimode

◆ 100 micron core/140 micron cladding multimode

◆ 8.3 micron core/125 micron cladding single mode

> **NOTE**
> **Fiber-Optic Cable Transmission Rates**
> The rate at which fiber-optic cable can transmit data is determined by the mode used and whether the fiber core is glass or plastic.

REVIEW BREAK

Cable Summary

Be prepared: The CompTIA Network+ exam will require you to identify the basic characteristics of each cable type discussed in this section. In particular, you will be expected to know which cables offer the greatest resistance to interference and attenuation, and you must be able to identify which type of cable is best suited for a particular network environment. Table 2.2 summarizes the characteristics of the various cable media.

TABLE 2.2
CABLE MEDIA CHARACTERISTICS

Media	Resistance to Attenuation	Resistance to EMI/Crosstalk	Cost of Implementation	Difficulty of Implementation
Thin coax	Moderate	Moderate	Low	Low
Thick coax	High	High	Moderate	Moderate
UTP	Low	Low	Low	Low
STP	Moderate	Moderate	Moderate	Low
Fiber-optic	Very high	Very high	Very high	Extremely difficult

Wireless Media

If you looked at the back of your computer right now, you'd no doubt see wires of all shapes and sizes coming out in all directions. Wouldn't it be nice if these unsightly and cumbersome cables were not needed? It is the goal of wireless communications to one day make this possible. As far as networking is concerned, it is possible to have at least one fewer cable hanging from your system.

Wireless is the alternative to cable-based media. Wireless networks do not use standard cable per se, but they still require a media for signal transmission. Wireless communications connect sending and receiving devices by transmitting signals through the atmosphere. These signals take the form of waves inside the electromagnetic spectrum. Located in this electromagnetic spectrum are the frequency ranges, or *bands*, commonly associated with wireless data transmissions. These include radio, microwave, and infrared.

Radio

Radio frequency (RF) sits somewhere between 10KHz and 1GHz on the electromagnetic spectrum. Networks can take advantage of radio transmissions within this range to send and receive data. Three types of RF transmissions can be used: single-frequency low-power RF, single-frequency high-power RF, and spread-spectrum.

Single-frequency low-power RF transmissions are used where the data has to travel a limited distance. Single-frequency RF transmissions do not require a line of sight between communicating devices;

however, structures such as walls or buildings can completely or partially block signals between the sending and receiving devices.

The downside of single-frequency low-power RF transmissions is that the distance a signal can travel is very limited. The distance depends on many factors, but 50 to 70 meters is generally the maximum distance. A second drawback is that the speeds of single-frequency low-power RF signal transmission hover between 1Mbps and 10Mbps. This might be fine to transmit small files, but as the amount of data transmitted increases, transmission slows down—it's akin to trying to download MP3s using a 14.4Kbps modem.

A final, and perhaps most important, consideration that affects RF transmissions (and any other wireless broadcast transmission, for that matter) is the security risk involved. Interrupting or intercepting transmissions is possible, so any sensitive data being transmitted is potentially at risk. Because the signals do not travel far for single-frequency low-power RF, eavesdropping on the transmission must be done from close range.

Single-frequency high-power RF transmissions can be transmitted significantly farther than can single-frequency low-power RF. The devices required to create the increased distance capability also increase the cost, making the single-frequency high-power RF much more expensive than the single-frequency low-power RF. High-power RF is also much more complicated than low-power RF; skilled technicians are often required to install and configure it. Like the low-power RF, high-power RF is susceptible to eavesdropping, and because the signals travel so much farther than low-power RF signals, the signal can be tampered with from far away.

High-power RF maintains the same transmission rates as low-power RF: 1Mbps to 10Mbps.

Spread-spectrum is an improvement over the single-frequency transmissions because it uses multiple frequencies simultaneously. This strategy makes transmissions more reliable, decreases the potential of eavesdropping, and reduces the susceptibility to interference. All this is accomplished by using two kinds of spread-spectrum communication: frequency hopping and direct sequence modulation.

Frequency hopping is the technique of switching data between multiple frequencies. *Direct sequence modulation* breaks data into segments called *chips* and sends the chips on multiple frequencies.

NOTE

Controlling the Air   Most radio frequencies are controlled and regulated by government agencies, such as the Federal Communications Commission (FCC) in the United States and the Canadian Radio-Television and Telecommunications Commission in Canada. To obtain exclusive use of any specific frequencies, interested parties must go through a costly and lengthy process of appealing to such government agencies for approval. This does not mean that anyone wanting to establish a wireless connection or even use a remote control car need apply to the FCC. To accommodate the average user, the FCC sets aside frequencies for unregulated use. Both low-power RF and high-power RF use these unregistered frequencies.

Frequency hopping is perhaps the most cost-effective type of wireless LAN media to deploy—that is, if you can live with network speeds of 2Mbps or less. Direct sequence provides increased data rates and may be worth the cost for a network that uses bandwidth-intensive applications.

Table 2.3 compares the various RF transmission methods.

TABLE 2.3

COMPARISON OF RF TRANSMISSION METHODS

Characteristic	Low-Power Single-Frequency RF	High-Power Single-Frequency RF	Spread-spectrum
Distance	Short distances; 50 to 70 meters	Very long distances; often several miles	N/A
Bandwidth	1Mbps to 10Mbps	1Mbps to 10Mbps	1Mbps to2Mbps for frequency hopping, 2Mbps to6Mbps for direct sequence
Installation	Easy	Difficult; requires trained technicians	Moderate to difficult
Interference	Highly susceptible to interference	Highly susceptible to interference	Moderately resistant to interference
Cost	Moderate compared to other technologies	Very expensive	Moderate
Security	Eavesdropping possible from within close within close	Eavesdropping possible from close and distant sources	Highly resistant to eavesdropping

---

Microwave

Unlike the RF wireless communications, microwave requires a line of sight between the sending and receiving devices. Microwave communication is typically able to reach higher transmission speeds on average than its RF counterparts, but the associated costs, including that of licensing frequencies, are higher as well. Microwave data communication is available in two types: terrestrial (earth-based) and satellite systems. Each of these is discussed in the following sections.

Terrestrial Microwave

Terrestrial microwave transmissions are line-of-sight transmissions between microwave towers or microwave transmitters. Microwave transmitters are typically mounted in high locations such as mountaintops or tall buildings, to help ensure a clean line of sight between the transmitters.

Terrestrial microwave is commonly implemented to connect buildings where traditional cable would be too complicated or costly to set up. The cost of a microwave solution depends largely on the distance required for transmission. Microwave solutions for limited distances, usually only a few hundred meters, are comparatively inexpensive. Microwave solutions requiring data transmission distances measured in kilometers are very costly.

As with radio wave transmissions, data transfer speeds for terrestrial microwave are limited (somewhere between 1Mbps and 10Mbps), and transmissions are susceptible to interference and eavesdropping. Attenuation in microwave transmissions is more of an issue for long distances than for short distances.

EXAM TIP	**Licensing** Terrestrial microwave installations often require licensing approval.

Satellite Microwave

Satellite transmissions require a device on earth and a geosynchronous orbiting satellite. These satellites hover some 23,000 miles above the earth, so you can expect transmission delays with satellite microwave. These delays typically range between .5 and 5 seconds; given the distance the signal is traveling, that delay is definitely acceptable.

Very few companies and fewer individuals can afford to launch their own satellite to send and receive data; rather, satellite services can be purchased from vendors. Satellite microwave solutions have transfer speeds comparable to those of terrestrial microwave and are also susceptible to atmospheric interference and eavesdropping. Installing a satellite microwave system requires exact configurations on the earth-bound system; but, thankfully, you are not required to launch into space to configure things at the other end.

Infrared Wireless Networking

Infrared wireless networking uses infrared beams to send data transmissions between devices. Infrared wireless networking offers higher transmission rates than the other wireless technologies, reaching 10Mbps to 16Mbps.

There are two types of infrared transmissions: broadcast and point-to-point. The broadcast method disperses the infrared beam in a wider area. Point-to-point infrared transmissions use a more focused beam between devices. Point-to-point infrared transmissions offer higher transfer speeds and are less susceptible to interference.

However, point-to-point is harder to configure than broadcast because it requires a much more finely tuned line-of-sight configuration than broadcast.

MEDIA CONNECTORS

▶ Recognize the following media connectors and describe their uses:
  - RJ-11
  - RJ-45
  - AUI
  - BNC
  - ST
  - SC

EXAM TIP

Know the Connectors   You will be expected to identify the various media connectors and know which connectors are associated with which cable.

All forms of network media need to be physically attached to the networked devices in some way. Media connectors provide the interface between the cables and the devices to which they attach (similar to the way an electrical cord connects a television and an electrical outlet). This section explores the common connectors and adapters you are likely to encounter in your work and, perhaps more importantly, on the Network+ exam.

D-shell Connectors

EXAM TIP

Know the D-shell Connectors   You will be expected to identify a few D-shell connectors on the Network+ exam.

D-shell connectors, which physically resemble a capital letter *D*, are perhaps the most common of all connector types. D-shell connectors use pins and sockets to connect devices; the number of pins used in a D-shell connector is reflected in the name of the specific connector. For example, a DB-15 uses 15 pins. D-shell connectors are used in everything from parallel ports to serial ports, joysticks, and video adapters.

Attachment Unit Interface Connectors

Attachment unit interface (AUI) ports are network interface ports that are often associated with thick coax (that is, 10Base5) networks. The AUI port is a 15-pin socket to which a transceiver is connected.

AUI ports also commonly appear on hubs and routers, and they are used for a variety of reasons. You are not likely to see AUI ports today, as 10Base5 networks are rarely used. You can expect to see AUI when you work with hubs. Figure 2.4 shows the AUI ports on the back of a network router; Figure 2.5 shows an AUI port and a BNC connector on the front of a network hub.

FIGURE 2.4
AUI ports on the back of a network router.

FIGURE 2.5
AUI ports and a BNC connectors on hubs.

External SCSI Connectors

Some external SCSI connectors use D-shell connectors. The original SCSI standard, SCSI-1, used a 50-pin D-shell connector. That connector is no longer used, and you are unlikely to see 50-pin D-shell connectors in real-world environments. The newer external SCSI connectors use an improved version of D-shell connectors known as *high-density external D-shell connectors*. The spacing between the pins has been reduced in these connectors, making the cable less expensive and easier to use. High-density external SCSI cables come in 50-pin and 68-pin varieties and are in common use today.

Another external SCSI connector you might encounter is the very high-density cable interconnect (VHDCI) connector. VHDCI connectors are available in a 68-pin variety only. Figure 2.6 shows an external VHCDI SCSI connector.

FIGURE 2.6
An external SCSI VHDCI connector.

Serial (RS-232) Connectors

Serial ports are familiar to those who have spent time around computers and have connected peripheral devices. Serial connectors, most commonly DB-9 or DB-25 pin varieties, are used for connecting devices such as mouse pointers, modems, handhelds, and scanners. In the network world, serial connectors are sometimes used to connect two computers together, although the transmission speed between those two computers is very slow compared to the speed you would get by using normal networking methods.

In addition, some managed network devices, such as hubs, switches, and routers, have serial ports that can be used to connect to the devices and manage them.

Parallel Connectors

Parallel ports are most often associated with printing and use a standard DB-25 connector. Sometimes, as with the serial port, the parallel port can be used to network two computer systems together. The short transfer distance of the parallel cable and the slow data transmission speeds make this a very impractical solution. But in some fairly unique environments you might encounter this configuration.

RJ Connectors

The connector you are most likely to encounter on modern networks is the RJ-45 (registered jack) connector. RJ-45 connectors bear a passing resemblance to the familiar RJ-11 connectors used with common phone connections. The difference between the two connectors is that the standard phone connector uses four wires, whereas the RJ-45 network connector uses eight. RJ-45 connectors are associated with twisted-pair cable. Figure 2.7 shows RJ-45 connectors.

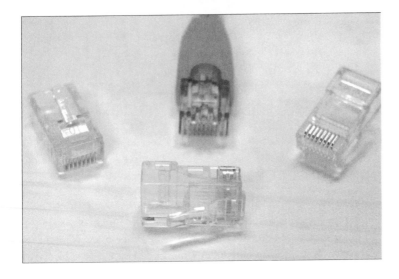

FIGURE 2.7
RJ-45 connectors.

BNCs

BNCs are commonly associated with Ethernet networks—more specifically, with Thinnet (that is, 10Base2) networks. BNCs are rarely used anymore; RJ-45 connectors are more prevalent because twisted-pair cable has almost completely replaced coaxial cable. However, if you find yourself working on an existing network or with legacy network cards, you might encounter BNCs. Many older 10Mbps network cards accommodate both BNCs and RJ-45 connectors, and some really old network cards even have BNC, RJ-45, and AUI connectors. These cards—or any other cards with more than one type of connector—are often referred to as *combo cards*. Figure 2.8 shows a network card with (from left to right) a BNC connector, an AUI connector, and an RJ-45 connector.

FIGURE 2.8

A network card with BNC, RJ-45, and AUI ports.

EXAM TIP

Fiber-Optic Connectors You will be expected to identify the various fiber-optic connectors for the Network+ exam.

Fiber Connectors

Several types of connectors are associated with fiber-optic cable. Which one is used is determined by the fiber implementation. Figure 2.9 shows some of the different fiber connectors you might encounter when working with fiber networks.

ST

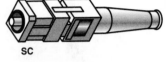

SC

SMA Type 906

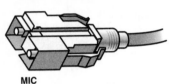

MIC

FC

Fiber Jack

FIGURE 2.9

Fiber connectors. (Reproduced with permission from Computer Desktop Encyclopedia © 1981–2001 The Computer Language Co. Inc., www.computerlanguage.com.)

All fiber-optic connectors use ferrules to hold the ends of the fiber and keep them properly aligned.

The ST connector uses a haof-twist bayonet type of lock, while SMA and FC use threaded connections.

The SC uses a push-pull connector similar to common audio and video plugs and sockets.

The MIC is the standard FDDI connector.

The Fiber Jack connector attaches two fibers is a snap lock connector similar in size and ease of use as an RJ-45 connector.

Centronic Connectors

Unlike other connector types that often use rows of pins, a Centronic connector uses two rows of flat contacts. The most common place to see Centronic connectors is with standard printers, where the data cable plugs into the printer.

External SCSI Centronic connectors use the same design as connectors used with printers, but they use a wider row of contacts, typically 50 pins. Centronic connectors have latches on either side of the cable to help hold it in place. Figure 2.10 shows an external SCSI Centronic connector.

FIGURE 2.10
An external SCSI Centronic connector.

FEATURES AND CHARACTERISTICS OF ETHERNET 802.3 STANDARDS

▶ Specify the characteristics (e.g., speed, length, topology, cable type, etc.) of the following 802.3 (Ethernet) standards:

  · 10BaseT

  · 10BaseTX

  · 10Base2

  · 10Base5

  · 100BaseFX

  · Gigabit Ethernet

As outlined in Chapter 1, the IEEE 802 standards specify the characteristics of LAN systems. Of all the standards detailed by the IEEE, the most widely implemented is the 802.3 standard. Since the introduction of the original 802.3 standards, many substandards have been developed, each of which has its own specifications.

Each 802.3 standard specifies the signaling mode (baseband or broadband), topology, data rates, and media type used. The following sections describe the characteristics of the 802.3 standards.

10Base2

10Base2, sometimes called Thinnet or Thin Ethernet, is the 802.3 specification for a network that uses thin coaxial cable (that is,

EXAM TIP

The 802.3 Standards   Pay special attention to the 802.3 standards. You can expect a question regarding the characteristics of the various standards on the Network+ exam.

RG-58 cable). 10Base2 specifies a maximum speed of 10Mbps; although 10Mbps has been sufficient in the past, it is now considered too slow for many network implementations. Because it uses thin coaxial cable, 10Base2 specifies BNC barrel and BNC T-connectors to connect the cable and computers. At the physical ends of each cable segment, a 50-ohm terminator absorbs the signal, thus preventing signal reflection. One of the terminators must be grounded. Figure 2.11 shows the basic layout of a 10Base2 network.

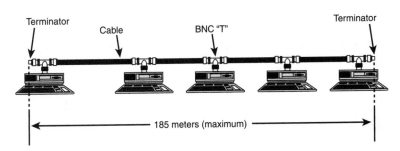

FIGURE 2.11
10Base2 network design.

The 10Base2 standard specifies a limit of 185 meters per segment (that is, approximately 600 feet). Thinnet cable is prone to breaks, and a break anywhere in the cable renders the entire network unusable. For this reason, and due to speed and distance limitations, 10Base2 networks have largely been replaced. You may find an existing 10Base2 network, but you are unlikely to install one. Regardless of its low profile in the networking arena, you will be expected to know the characteristics of 10Base2 for the Network+ exam and be able to identify why such a network may be used.

In a 10Base2 network, only 30 networked devices can be attached to a single segment. A maximum of 3 segments can have network devices connected, or *populated* (although the network can have a total of 5 segments). This means that a 10Base2 network can have a maximum of 90 computers attached, but you can extend this limit if you use repeaters. The minimum distance between two devices on a 10Base2 network is .5 meters.

Table 2.4 summarizes the features of 10Base2.

EXAM TIP

10Base2 Networks For the Network+ exam, remember that 10Base2 networks can have a total of five segments, and only three of those segments can be populated.

TABLE 2.4

SUMMARY OF 10BASE2 CHARACTERISTICS

Characteristic	Description
Transmission method	Baseband
Speed	10Mbps
Total distance	185 meters
Cable type	Thin coax
Number of systems/segment	30
Min. distance between nodes	.5 meter

10Base5

10Base5 networks use thick coaxial cable (that is, RG-8 cable), also known as Thicknet or Thick Ethernet, and devices attach to it by using external transceivers and AUI ports. The transceivers attach to the thick coax cable via *vampire taps*, which penetrate the outer sheath of the cable and make a connection to the inside core.

10Base5 uses baseband transmission, has a maximum transfer rate of 10Mbps, and has a cable distance of 500 meters per segment (that is, about 1,600 feet). A maximum of 100 devices can be attached per segment, and the total number of populated segments allowed is 3. The minimum distance between each vampire tap on the network must be no less than 2.5 meters, and the maximum allowed distance between the tap and the networked device is 5 meters. As with 10Base2, each end of the cable must be terminated with a 50-ohm terminator. Figure 2.12 shows an example of a 10Base5 network.

FIGURE 2.12
10Base5 network design.

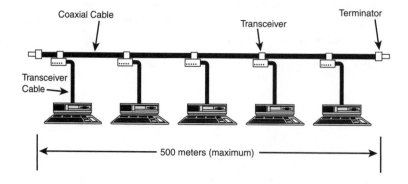

At one time, because of the distances 10Base5 allowed, it was relatively popular; however, today it is rarely used. Its transfer speeds and implementation difficulty exclude 10Base5 from being a viable network solution. Table 2.5 summarizes the characteristics of the 10Base5 specification.

EXAM TIP

Know the Standards For the Network+ exam, be prepared to recognize these standards by all their names. 10Base2 may be referred to as *Thinnet*; *10Base5* and *Thicknet* may also be used interchangeably.

TABLE 2.5

SUMMARY OF 10BASE5 CHARACTERISTICS

Characteristic	Description
Transmission Method	Baseband
Speed	10Mbps
Total distance	500 meters
Cable type	Thick coax
Number of systems/segment	100
Min. distance between nodes	2.5 meters

EXAM TIP

The 5-4-3 Rule When you're working with coaxial or studying for the Network+ exam, you might hear about the 5-4-3 rule for Ethernet coaxial implementations. This rule dictates that there can be a maximum of five segments on the network connected by four repeaters, and that only three of the segments can be populated.

10BaseT

The 10BaseT LAN standard specifies an Ethernet network that commonly uses UTP cable; however, in some implementations that require a greater resistance to interference and attenuation, STP can be used. Remember from the section "Twisted-Pair," earlier in this chapter, that STP has extra shielding to combat interference.

10BaseT uses baseband transmission and has a maximum segment length of 100 meters. As with the coaxial standards, repeaters are sometimes used to extend the maximum segment length, although the repeating capability is now often built in to networking devices used in twisted-pair networks. 10BaseT specifies transmission speeds of 10Mbps and can use several categories of UTP cable, including Categories 3, 4, and 5 (all of which use RJ-45 connectors). 10BaseT takes advantage of the multiple wires inside twisted-pair cable to create independent transmit and receive paths, which means that a full-duplex mode can be optionally supported. The maximum number of computers supported on a 10BaseT network is 1,024.

NOTE

Crossover Cable   You can link two 10BaseT computer systems directly, without the use of a hub, by using a specially constructed crossover cable.

NOTE

The 5-4-3 Rule and Ethernet Networks   The 5-4-3 rule sort of applies to Ethernet networks that use twisted-pair cable. A total of five segments can be used per network, with no more than four hubs or repeaters used. Thus, in the case of Ethernet networks, it is the 5-4 rule.

All 10BaseT networks use a point-to-point network design, with one end of the connection attaching to the network card and the other to a hub or switch. These point-to-point connections result in a physical star topology. Chapter 3 provides more information on the devices used in twisted-pair networks.

Table 2.6 summarizes the characteristics of the 10BaseT standard.

TABLE 2.6

SUMMARY OF 10BASET CHARACTERISTICS

Characteristic	Description
Transmission Method	Baseband
Speed	10Mbps
Total distance/segment	100 meters
Cable type	Category 3, 4, or 5 UTP or STP
Connector	RJ-45

IN THE FIELD

MAKE OR BUY?

During your networking career, you will most certainly encounter the debate about whether to crimp your own RJ-45 network cables or buy them. The arguments for making cables always seems to hinge on cost savings. The arguments against crimping cable are often much more solid. Purchasing cables from a reputable maker ensures that the cables you install will work every time. The same cannot be said of homemade cables. In addition, when you factor in the time it takes to make a cable or troubleshoot a poorly made one, the cost savings are lessened. However, in some instances you'll have no choice but to make cables—for instance, when special-distance cables are required or when your local Cables-R-Us is closed.

Fast Ethernet: 100BaseX

Many networks demand more bandwidth than is available with 10Mbps network solutions. For such networks, Fast Ethernet is the most commonly used network design. Fast Ethernet standards are specified in the IEEE 802.3u standard. Three standards are defined by 802.3u: 100BaseTX, 100BaseT4, and 100BaseFX.

100BaseTX

100BaseTX is a Fast Ethernet networking design and is one of three 802.3u standards. As its name suggests, 100BaseTX transmits network data at speeds up to 100Mbps, the speeds at which most LANs operate today. 100BaseTX is most often implemented with UTP cable, but it can use STP; therefore, it suffers from the same 100 meter distance limitations as other UTP-based networks. 100BaseTX uses Category 5 UTP cable and, like 10BaseT, it uses independent transmit and receive paths and can therefore support full-duplex operation. 100BaseTX is without question the most common Fast Ethernet standard.

100BaseT4

100BaseT4 is the second Fast Ethernet standard specified under 802.3u. It can use Category 3, 4, and 5 UTP cable, and it uses all four of the available pairs of wires within the cable, limiting full-duplex transfer. 100BaseT4 is similar in other respects to 100BaseTX: Its cable distance is limited to 100 meters, and its maximum transfer speed is 100Mbps. 100BaseT4 is not widely implemented, but it is sometimes used in environments where existing cable, such as Category 3 cable, exists. In such a situation, you can use 100BaseT4 instead of replacing the Category 3 cable with Category 5 UTP.

100BaseFX

100BaseFX is the IEEE standard for running Fast Ethernet over fiber-optic cable. Due to the expense of fiber implementations, 100BaseFX is largely limited to use as a network backbone.

EXAM TIP
Fast Ethernet Lingo   Fast Ethernet is often referred to as 100BaseX, which also refers collectively to the 100BaseTX, 100BaseT4, and 100BaseFX standards.

EXAM TIP
Repeaters   Fast Ethernet repeaters are sometimes needed when you connect segments that use 100BaseTX, 100BaseT4, or 100BaseFX.

NOTE
100BaseVG-AnyLAN   Another member of the 100Mbps club is the 100BaseVG-AnyLAN IEEE 802.12 specification. 100BaseVG-AnyLAN allows data transmissions of up to 100Mbps over Category 3 UTP cable, using four pairs of wires, but it can also use Category 4 and 5 with two pairs of wires. 100BaseVG-AnyLAN is not included in the 802.3 specification because it does not use the CSMA/CD access method; instead, it uses a demand priority access method. For more information on CSMA/CD, refer to Chapter 1.

100BaseFX can use two-strand multimode fiber or single-mode fiber media. The maximum segment length for half-duplex multimode fiber is 412 meters, but this maximum increases to an impressive 10,000 meters for full-duplex single-mode fiber. 100BaseFX often uses SC or MIC fiber connectors. To see where 100BaseFX compares with other 100Base technologies refer to Table 2.7.

R E V I E W   B R E A K

Fast Ethernet Comparison

Table 2.7 summarizes the characteristics of the 802.3u Fast Ethernet specifications.

TABLE 2.7
SUMMARY OF 802.3U FAST ETHERNET CHARACTERISTICS

	100BaseTX	*100BaseT4*	*100BaseFX*
Transmission Method	Baseband	Baseband	Baseband
Speed	100Mbps	100Mbps	100Mbps
Distance	100 meters	100 meters	412 meters (multimode, half-duplex); 10,000 meters (single-mode, full-duplex)
Cable Type	Category 5 UTP, STP	Category 3, 4, 5	Fiber-optic
Connector Type	RJ-45	RJ-45	SC, MIC

Gigabit Ethernet: 1000BaseX

Gigabit Ethernet, 1000BaseX, is another variation on the 802.3 standard and is given its own identifier: 802.3z. Gigabit Ethernet offers transfer rates of up to 1000Mbps and is most often associated with fiber cable. 1000BaseX refers collectively to three distinct standards: 1000BaseLX, 1000BaseSX, and 1000BaseCX.

Both 1000BaseSX and 1000BaseLX are laser standards used over fiber. *LX* refers to *long wavelength laser,* and *SX* refers to *short wavelength laser.* Both the SX and LX wave lasers can be supported over two types of multimode fiber: fibers of 62.5 micron and 50 micron diameters. Only LX wave lasers support the use of single-mode fiber.

At the end of the day, the differences between 1000BaseLX and the 1000BaseSX have to do with cost and transmission distance. 1000BaseLX can transmit over 316 meters in half-duplex for both multimode fiber and single-mode fiber, 550 meters for full-duplex multimode fiber, and 5,000 meters for full-duplex single-mode fiber. Although 1000BaseSX is less expensive than 1000BaseLX, it cannot match the distances achieved by 1000BaseLX.

1000BaseCX moves away from the fiber cable and uses shielded copper wire. Segment lengths in 1000BaseCX are severely restricted; the maximum cable distance is 25 meters. Because of the restricted cable lengths, 1000BaseCX networks are not widely implemented. Table 2.8 summarizes the characteristics of Gigabit Ethernet 802.3z standards.

TABLE 2.8

SUMMARY OF IEEE 802.3Z GIGABIT ETHERNET CHARACTERISTICS

	1000BaseSX	*1000BaseLX*	*1000BaseCX*
Transmission Method	Baseband	Baseband	Baseband
Speed	1000Mbps	1000Mbps	1000Mbps
Distance	Half-duplex 275 (62.5 micron multimode fiber); half-duplex 316 (50 micronl8u multimode fiber); full-duplex 275 (62.5 micron multimode fiber); full-duplex 550 (50 micron multimode fiber)	Half-duplex 316 (multimode and single-mode fiber); full-duplex 550 (multimode fiber); full-duplex 5000 (single-mode fiber)	25 meters for both full-duplex and half-duplex operations
Cable Type	62.5/125 and 50/125 multimode fiber	62.5/125 and 50/125 multimode fiber; two 10-micron single-mode optical fibers	Shielded copper cable
Connector Type	SC connector	SC connector	9-pin shielded connector, 8-pin fiber channel type 2 connector

1000BaseT

1000BaseT is another Gigabit Ethernet standard, and it is given the IEEE 802.3ab designation. The 802.3ab standard specifies Gigabit Ethernet over Category 5 UTP cable. The standard allows for full-duplex transmission using the four pairs of twisted cable.

To reach speeds of 1000Mbps over copper, a data transmission speed of 250Mbps is achieved over each pair of twisted-pair cable. Table 2.9 summarizes the characteristics of 1000BaseT.

TABLE 2.9

SUMMARY OF 1000BaseT CHARACTERISTICS

Characteristic	Description
Transmission method	Baseband
Speed	1000Mbps
Total distance/segment	100 meters
Cable type	Category 5 or better
Connector type	RJ-45

CHOOSING THE APPROPRIATE MEDIA CONNECTOR FOR ADDING CLIENTS TO AN EXISTING NETWORK

▶ Choose the appropriate media type and connectors to add a client to an existing network.

In most network jobs, you will find yourself modifying and adding clients to existing networks rather than installing a new network from scratch. Therefore, you should be able to identify the network infrastructure that is in place so you can successfully add clients to the network.

Identifying the network media and connectors in a network is as simple as looking at the backs of computers to identify what is being used. If you find coax cable connected to the computer with BNCs, you are probably working with an older 10Base2 network. If you find RJ-45 connectors, you might need to look at the cable to see which type of cable is being used. It could be either Category 3 UTP or Category 5. Adding clients to the network requires knowledge of the exact cable being used.

When you're adding clients to an existing network, you might be able to locate documentation created when the network was initially implemented. Of course, on some networks, especially small networks, such documentation may be nonexistent.

CHAPTER SUMMARY

Networks are often complex in design, maintenance, and implementation, and the basics—such as network media—are often forgotten. But network media are a foundation block of a network; as a network administrator, you will be required to understand the characteristics of the media commonly used in networks.

Several key characteristics and considerations determine a media's suitability for a specific network environment. These considerations include crosstalk, attenuation, EMI, bandwidth, installation and repair, and security. You need to understand each of these to determine the appropriate media for a network.

Networks use dialog modes to determine the direction that transmissions flow over the network media. Three dialog modes are used: simplex, half-duplex, and full-duplex. Simplex allows only one-way communication; half-duplex allows two-way communication, but devices cannot send and receive simultaneously; and full-duplex allows devices to simultaneously receive and transmit.

Several different types of cable are used on modern networks, including coaxial, twisted-pair, and fiber-optic cable. Each cable has different strengths and weaknesses, making some types of cable more suitable than others in a given network environment. Part of the role of the network administrator is to be able to identify the characteristics of the various cable types and to know how to troubleshoot them when required.

Each of these different cable types requires the appropriate connector. By far the most commonly used connector type today is the RJ-45 connector, which is used with twisted-pair cable. Other connector types include SC and MIC connectors for fiber-optic cable and BNCs for thin coax cable.

KEY TERMS

- media
- topology
- 802.3
- 10BaseT
- 10BaseTX
- 10Base2
- 10Base5
- 10BaseFX
- Fast Ethernet
- Gigabit Ethernet
- RJ-11
- RJ-45
- AUI
- BNC
- ST
- SC

CHAPTER SUMMARY

The IEEE 802.3 standard specifies Ethernet networking and uses the various cable media discussed in this chapter. The 802.3 LAN standards include 10Base2, 10Base5, 10BaseT, 100BaseT, and 1000BaseX network standards. Each of these standards specifies numerous networking characteristics, including network speed, cable type, topology, transmission method, and cable distance.

To be able to add clients to an existing network, you need to identify the connectors and cables that are already in use on the network. By using observation techniques—examining the cables and connectors already in use—you can find out what you need to know to correctly add computers to the network.

APPLY YOUR KNOWLEDGE

Exercises

2.1   Identifying Cable Costs

In this project, you use the Internet to identify cable characteristics and associated costs.

This chapter focuses on network media, connectors, and standards—all of which are essential to networks. As a network administrator, you will need to have a detailed knowledge of network media and their associated connectors. When you are called upon to troubleshoot or implement a network, this knowledge will prove invaluable.

A common task for network administrators is to source out the costs of cable and connectors. Consider the following scenario: You have been contracted by BootCo, a maker of snowshoes and toques, to begin the process of implementing a network. BootCo requires a network of 25 systems and needs to know the costs associated with the media for the network. The network will require both UTP and 20 feet of STP cable.

Estimated time: 20 minutes

1. Get on the Internet and from a search engine, look for a company that sells network cable. The search is likely to return many results, and it may be necessary to restrict your search to local vendors.

2. Browse a vendor's Web site and locate UTP Category 5/5e and STP cable.

3. To connect 25 systems with UTP cable, you need 25 patch cables. To connect other network devices, you need additional cables.

4. Continue to search the site for the costs for the STP cable. To get a better idea of costs, it might be necessary to find information from several vendors.

5. Compare the cost of buying bulk cable and connectors to the cost of buying premade cables and connectors.

Exam Questions

1. Which of the following connectors are associated with external SCSI? (Choose the two best answers.)

   a. 68-pin D-shell connector

   b. 36-pin Centronic connector

   c. 50-pin Centronic connector

   d. 39-pin female connector

2. You have been asked to support a network installation, and you are required to identify a network media that can connect two remote servers that are 1.5 km apart. The network cable should not be dependent on network devices to help regenerate the signal. Which of the following cables best suits the company's needs?

   a. Fiber-optic

   b. Category 3

   c. Category 5 STP

   d. Category 5 UTP

3. What is the transmission speed you can expect when working with low- and high-frequency radio wave transmissions?

   a. 100Mbps to 500Mbps

   b. 10Mbps to 20Mbps

   c. 1Mbps to 10Mpbs

   d. 1Gbps to 100Gbps

APPLY YOUR KNOWLEDGE

4. You need to connect two servers that are located 600 meters apart. You require a direct connection without the use of signal regeneration. Which of the following Ethernet standards would you employ?

   a. 10BaseT

   b. 100BaseT

   c. 10Base5

   d. 100BaseFX

5. You are working on an older network and are required to add a client. The network is using Category 5 UTP cable. Which connector should you use?

   a. BNC

   b. Transceiver

   c. RJ-45

   d. RJ-11

6. Which of the following is associated with FDM?

   a. Baseband

   b. Broadband

   c. 100BaseFX

   d. 100BaseT

7. Which of the following wireless media does not require a direct line of sight? (Choose the two best answers.)

   a. Low-frequency RF

   b. Terrestrial microwave

   c. Infrared

   d. High-frequency RF

8. What is the maximum cable length specified in the IEEE 802.3 10Base2 standard?

   a. 185 meters

   b. 500 meters

   c. 100 meters

   d. 250 meters

9. As a network administrator, you have been asked to recommend a networking standard that can support data transfers of up to 100Mbps, using the existing Category 3 cable and the CSMA/CD access method. Which of the following best suits your needs?

   a. 100BaseTX

   b. 100BaseFX

   c. 100BaseVG-AnyLAN

   d. 100BaseT4

10. What is the maximum distance a signal can travel over multimode fiber?

    a. 10,000 meters

    b. 412 meters

    c. 500 meters

    d. 100 meters

11. Which of the following are associated with IEEE 802.3z? (Choose the three best answers.)

    a. 1000BaseLX

    b. 1000BaseCX

    c. 1000BaseBX

    d. 1000BaseSX

APPLY YOUR KNOWLEDGE

12. Which of the following media types offers the greatest resistance to interference?

    a. STP

    b. Thick coax

    c. Fiber-optic

    d. Thin coax

13. What is the maximum transfer distance of 1000BaseT?

    a. 100 meters

    b. 412 meters

    c. 1,000 meters

    d. 550 meters

14. Which of the following uses twisted-pair cable and has a maximum transfer speed of 10Mbps?

    a. 10BaseT

    b. 10Base5

    c. 10Base2

    d. Thinnet

15. You have been asked to install a client computer on an existing network. Upon inspection of the cable, you identify that it is connected by using BNC connectors. Which of the following network standards is in use?

    a. 10BaseT

    b. 10Base2

    c. 100BaseTX

    d. Fast Ethernet

16. Which of the following terms identifies the loss in signal strength as a signal travels through a media?

    a. Crosstalk

    b. EMI

    c. Plenum

    d. Attenuation

17. You are a network administrator for a large company. Transfer speeds have been too slow, and you have been asked to recommend a 1000Mbps network solution. The network requires a transfer distance of 3,500 meters. Which of the following would you recommend?

    a. 1000BaseCX

    b. 1000BaseLX

    c. 1000BaseBX

    d. 1000BaseSX

18. Which fiber-optic mode allows the fastest transfer rates?

    a. SC

    b. ST

    c. Single-mode

    d. Multimode

19. A company that transfers very sensitive data has asked you to install a media that is highly resistant to eavesdropping and signal tampering. Which of the following media would you recommend?

    a. STP

    b. UTP

APPLY YOUR KNOWLEDGE

c. Coaxial

d. Fiber

20. Baseband sends transmissions in which of the following forms?

a. Digital

b. Analog

c. Digital and analog

d. RF

Answers to Exam Questions

1. **a, c.** The SCSI interface uses both 68-pin D-shell connectors and 50-pin Centronic connectors. It may also use 50-pin external connectors. The other connector types are not valid SCSI connectors. For more information, see the section "Media Connectors," in this chapter.

2. **a.** Fiber-optic cable uses light transmission, making it less susceptible to interference and attenuation. Therefore, data signals can travel significant distances. In this case, only fiber-optic cable meets the distance requirements. All the other cables listed in the answer are limited to much shorter distances than fiber-optic. For more information, see the section "Common Network Media," in this chapter.

3. **c.** Wireless radio wave transmissions do not offer fast data transfer speeds. Speeds are usually between 1Mbps and 10Mbps. For more information, see the section "Common Network Media," in this chapter.

4. **d.** 100BaseFX has the potential to transmit distances that exceed 600 meters. However, to reach

distances of 600 meters, you'd need to use single-mode fiber. Of the other standards, 10Base5 has the greatest transmission distance, but it is limited to 500 meters. For more information, see the section "Common Network Media," in this chapter.

5. **c.** To add a client to an existing network that is using Category 5 UTP, you would work with RJ-45 connectors. BNCs are used with coaxial cable, and RJ-11 is the connector type associated with telephone cable. For more information, see the section "Media Connectors," in this chapter.

6. **b.** FDM is a technique that is used with broadband systems to allow data flow in different directions on the cable. All the other standards mentioned are baseband transmission media and so do not use multiplexing. For more information, see the section "Media Considerations," in this chapter.

7. **a, d.** Neither low-frequency RF nor high-frequency RF requires a direct point-to-point line of sight between sending and receiving devices. Microwave and infrared data transmissions do require a direct line of sight. For more information, see the section "Common Network Media," in this chapter.

8. **a.** The 10Base2 standard specifies thin coax cable that has a maximum segment length of 185 meters. If that length is exceeded, the signals on the cable may weaken and become unusable. For more information, see the section "Features and Characteristics of Ethernet 802.3 Standards," in this chapter.

9. **d.** 100BaseT4 is a Fast Ethernet standard that can use existing Category 3 cable and have transmission speeds of up to 100Mbps.

100BaseVG-AnyLAN can also use Category 3 cable, but it uses a demand priority access method. 100Base- requires Category 5 cable and 100BaseFX uses fiber-optic cable. For more information, see the section "Features and Characteristics of Ethernet 802.3 Standards," in this chapter.

10. **b.** The maximum distance for multimode fiber is 412 meters. Single-mode fiber increases the distance to 10,000 meters. Answers c and d are not valid. For more information, see the section "Features and Characteristics of Ethernet 802.3 Standards," in this chapter.

11. **a, b, d.** Three standards are associated with 802.3z: 1000BaseLX, 1000BaseSX, and 1000BaseCX. 100BaseBX is not a valid standard. For more information, see the section "Features and Characteristics of Ethernet 802.3 Standards," in this chapter.

12. **c.** Because fiber uses light to transmit data, it is not susceptible to EMI and crosstalk. It is the media of choice in high-interference network environments. All the other cable types mentioned are copper based and are therefore susceptible, to varying degrees, to EMI and crosstalk. For more information, see the section "Common Network Media," in this chapter.

13. **a.** The 1000BaseT standard uses copper cable and has a segment maximum of 100 meters. For more information, see the section "Features and Characteristics of Ethernet 802.3 Standards," in this chapter.

14. **a.** The 10BaseT standard uses twisted-pair cable with a maximum transfer rate of 10Mbps. Of the other standards, 10Base5 uses thick coaxial cable,

10Base2 uses thin coaxial cable, and thinnet is a term used to refer to 10Base2. For more information, see the section "Features and Characteristics of Ethernet 802.3 Standards," in this chapter.

15. **b.** The 10Base2 standard specifies coaxial cable that uses BNCs to add clients to existing networks. 10BaseT and 100BaseTX both use RJ-45 connectors. For more information, see the section "Features and Characteristics of Ethernet 802.3 Standards," in this chapter.

16. **d.** *Attenuation* refers to signal degradation as it travels through media. *Crosstalk* is the term used to refer to interference from other cables; *EMI* is a condition created by electronic or mechanical equipment. *Plenum* is not a type of interference; it is the term used to classify cables that are suitable for installation in suspended ceilings and other enclosed areas. For more information, see the section "Media Considerations," in this chapter.

17. **b.** 1000BaseLX can transmit up to 5,000 meters, using single-mode fiber. The other standards listed operate over much shorter distances. For more information, see the section "Features and Characteristics of Ethernet 802.3 Standards," in this chapter.

18. **c.** Single-mode fiber allows faster transfer rates than multimode fiber and supports longer data transmissions. SC and ST are types of fiber connectors, not types of cable. For more information, see the section "Common Network Media," in this chapter.

19. **d.** Because of the construction of fiber cable and the fact that it uses light transmission instead of electronic signals, it is very resistant to tampering

APPLY YOUR KNOWLEDGE

and eavesdropping. All the other cable types listed are copper based and are therefore less secure than fiber-based media. For more information, see the section "Common Network Media," in this chapter.

20. **a.** Baseband transmissions use digital signaling. Analog signaling is associated with broadband. For more information, see the section "Baseband Versus Broadband Signaling," in this chapter.

Suggested Readings and Resources

1. Groth, David, Jim McBee. *Cabling: The Complete Guide to Network Cabling.* Sybex, 2000.

2. Habraken, Joe. *Absolute Beginner's Guide to Networking,* third edition. Que Publishing, 2001.

3. Vacca, John R. *The Cabling Handbook,* second edition. Prentice Hall, 2000.

4. Cisco Systems, Inc. *Internetworking Troubleshooting Handbook,* second edition. Cisco Press, 2001.

5. Network Cabling Information, `www.techfest.com/networking/cabling.htm`.

6. "Computer Networking Tutorials and Advice," `compnetworking.about.com`.

7. "TechEncyclopedia," `www.techencyclopedia.com`.

8. Networking technology information, `www.cisco.com/public/products_tech.shtml`.

9. "Network Cabling Help," `www.datacottage.com`.

This chapter covers the following CompTIA-specified objectives for the "Media and Topologies" and "Protocols and Standards" sections of the Network+ exam:

Identify the purpose, features, and functions of the following network components:

- **Hubs**
- **Switches**
- **Bridges**
- **Routers**
- **Gateways**
- **CSU/DSU**
- **Network interface cards (NICs), ISDN adapters, and system area network cards**
- **Wireless access points (WAPs)**
- **Modems**

▶ A wide range of devices are used in modern networking. As a Network+ certified technician, you will need to have a good understanding of commonly used devices.

Given an example, identify a Media Access Control (MAC) address.

▶ MAC addresses are the means by which systems communicate at a base level. As a network administrator, you will need to understand the purpose, function, and expression of MAC addresses.

CHAPTER 3

Networking Components and Devices

OUTLINE

Introduction   104

Hubs   104

Switches   106
    Switching Methods   108

Working with Hubs and Switches   109
    Hub and Switch Ports   110
    Cables Connecting Hubs and Switches   111
    Hub and Switch Indicator Lights   112
    Rack Mount, Stackable, and Freestanding
    Devices   113
    Managed Hubs and Switches   113

Bridges   114
    Bridge Implementation Considerations   114
    Types of Bridges   115

Routers   116
    Routable Protocols and Routing Protocols   118
      Routable Protocols   118
      Routing Protocols   119
    Dedicated Hardware Versus Server-Based
    Routers   123

Gateways   124

CSUs/DSUs   125

Wireless Access Point (WAPs)   126

Modems   126
    Modem Connection Speeds   127

Network Cards (NICs)   129
    Types of Network Interfaces   130
    Installing Network Cards   133

ISDN Terminal Adapters   135

System Area Network Cards   137
    Network Devices Summary   137

Identifying MAC Addresses   138

Chapter Summary   140

Apply Your Knowledge   142

STUDY STRATEGIES

▶ Read the objectives at the beginning of the chapter.

▶ Study the information in this chapter, paying special attention to the tables, which summarize key information.

▶ Review the objectives again.

▶ Answer the exam questions at the end of the chapter and check your results.

▶ Use the ExamGear test on the CD-ROM that accompanies this book to answer additional exam questions concerning this material.

▶ Review the notes, tips, and exam tips in this chapter. Make sure you understand the information in the exam tips. If you don't understand the topic referenced in an exam tip, refer to the information in the chapter text and then read the exam tip again.

INTRODUCTION

So far this book has examined topologies, media access methods, networking standards, and cable types and connectors. To complete our examination of networking on a physical level, this chapter looks at the network devices that are used to create networks.

▶ Identify the purpose, features, and functions of the following network components:

- Hubs
- Switches
- Bridges
- Routers
- Gateways
- CSU/DSU
- Network interface cards (NICs), ISDN adapters, and system area network cards
- Wireless access points (WAPs)
- Modems

Each of these devices fulfills a specific role in a network; however, only the largest and most complex environments use all of them. We'll begin our discussion of networking devices with perhaps the most simple and common network device used today: the hub.

HUBS

Hubs are the simplest network devices, and their simplicity is reflected in their low cost. Small hubs with four or five ports (often referred to as *workgroup hubs*) cost less than $50; with the requisite cables, they provide everything needed to create a small network. Hubs with more ports are available for networks that require greater capacity. Figure 3.1 shows an example of a workgroup hub, and Figure 3.2 shows an example of the type of hub you might see on a corporate network.

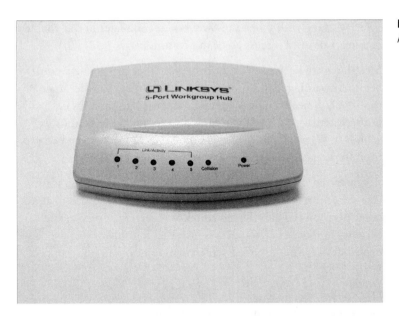

FIGURE 3.1
A workgroup hub.

FIGURE 3.2
A high-capacity, or high-density, hub.

Computers connect to a hub via a length of twisted-pair cabling. In addition to ports for connecting computers, even a very inexpensive hub generally has a port designated as an uplink port that enables the hub to be connected to another hub to create larger networks.

Token Ring and MSAUs   Both hubs and switches are used in Ethernet networks. Token Ring networks, which are few and far between, use special devices called multistation access units (MSAUs) to create the network. In some cases, MSAUs are referred to as *Token Ring switches*; but because of the way Token Ring operates, these devices perform a very different function from the hubs and switches discussed in this section.

NOTE

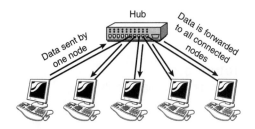

FIGURE 3.3
How a hub works.

FIGURE 3.4
A 32-port Ethernet switch. (Photo courtesy TRENDware International, www.trendware.com.)

The "Working with Hubs and Switches" section later in this chapter presents a detailed discussion of this feature.

Most hubs are referred to as *active* because they regenerate a signal before forwarding it to all the ports on the device. In order to do this, the hub needs a power supply; small workgroup hubs normally use an external power adapter, but on larger units the power supply is built in. Passive hubs (which are rare) do not need power because they don't regenerate the signal.

Regeneration of the signal aside, the basic function of a hub is to take data from one of the connected devices and forward it to all the other ports on the hub. This method of operation is very inefficient because, in most cases, the data is intended for only one of the connected devices. You can see a representation of how a hub works in Figure 3.3.

Due to the inefficiencies of the hub system and the constantly increasing demand for more bandwidth, hubs are slowly but surely being replaced with switches. As you will see in the next section, switches offer distinct advantages over hubs.

SWITCHES

On the surface, a switch looks much like a hub, although the price tag might be a giveaway—switches are considerably more expensive than hubs. The main reason for the price disparity is that switches can do much more and offer many more advantages than hubs. Figure 3.4 shows an example of a 32-port Ethernet switch. If you refer to Figure 3.2, you'll notice few differences in the appearance of the high-density hub and this switch.

As with a hub, computers connect to a switch via a length of twisted-pair cable. Multiple switches can be used, like hubs, to create larger networks. Despite their similarity in appearance and their identical physical connections to computers, switches offer significant operational advantages over hubs.

As discussed earlier in the chapter, on a hub, data is forwarded to all ports, regardless of whether the data is intended for the system connected to the port. This arrangement is very inefficient; however, it requires very little intelligence on the part of the hub, which is why hubs are inexpensive.

Rather than forwarding data to all the connected ports, a switch forwards data only to the port on which the destination system is connected. It looks at the Media Access Control (MAC) addresses of the devices connected to it to determine the correct port. A *MAC address* is a unique number that is programmed into every NIC. By forwarding data only to the system to which the data is addressed, the switch decreases the amount of traffic on each network link dramatically. In effect, the switch literally channels (or *switches,* if you prefer) data between the ports. Figure 3.5 illustrates how a switch works.

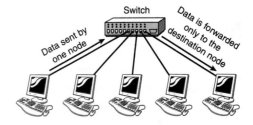

FIGURE 3.5
How a switch works.

You might recall from our the discussions of Ethernet networking in Chapter 2, "Cabling and Connectors," that collisions occur on the network when two devices attempt to transmit at the same time. Such collisions cause the performance of the network to degrade. By channeling data only to the connections that should receive it, switches reduce the number of collisions that occur on the network. As a result, switches provide significant performance improvements over hubs.

Switches can also further improve performance over the performance of hubs by using a mechanism called *full-duplex.* On a standard network connection, the communication between the system and the switch or hub is said to be *half-duplex.* In a half-duplex connection, data can be either sent or received on the wire, but not at the same time. Because switches manage the data flow on the connection, a switch can operate in full-duplex mode—it can send and receive data on the connection at the same time. In a full-duplex connection, the maximum bandwidth is double that for a half-duplex connection—for example, 10Mbps becomes 20Mbps and 100Mbps becomes 200Mbps. As you can imagine, the difference in performance between a 100Mbps network connection and a 200Mbps connection is considerable.

EXAM TIP

Half-Duplex   It's important to remember that a full-duplex connection has a maximum data rate of double the standard speed, and a half-duplex connection is the standard speed. The term *half-duplex* can sometimes lead people to believe that the connection speed is half of the standard, which is not the case. A simple way to remember this is to think of the half-duplex figure as half the full-duplex figure, not half the standard figure.

NOTE

Microsegmentation   The process that switches perform is referred to as *microsegmentation*.

EXAM TIP

Troubleshooting Network Connection Speed   Most NICs can automatically detect the speed of the network connection they are connected to. However, although the detection process is normally reliable, on some occasions it may not work correctly. If you are troubleshooting a network connection and the autodetect feature is turned on, try setting the speed manually (preferably to a low speed) and then give it another go. If you are using a managed switch, which is discussed later in this chapter, you might have to do the same thing at the switch end of the connection.

The secret of full-duplex lies in the switch. As discussed previously in this section, switches can isolate each port and effectively create a single segment for each port on the switch. Because there are only two devices on each segment (the system and the switch), and because the switch is calling the shots, there are no collisions. No collisions means no need to detect collisions—thus, a collision-detection system is not needed with switches. The switch drops the conventional carrier-sense multiple-access with collision detection (CSMA/CD) media access method and adopts a far more selfish (and therefore efficient) communication method.

To use a full-duplex connection, you basically need three things: a switch, the appropriate cable, and an NIC (and driver) that supports full-duplex communication. Given these requirements, and the fact that most modern NICs are full-duplex-ready, you might think everyone would be using full-duplex connections. However, the reality is a little different. In some cases, the NIC is simply not configured to make use of the driver. For example, NetWare 4 required that a parameter be passed when the driver was loaded to take advantage of a full-duplex connection.

IN THE FIELD

ALL SWITCHES ARE NOT CREATED EQUAL

Having learned the advantages of using a switch and looked at the speeds associated with the network connections on the switch, you could assume that one switch is just as good as another. This is not the case. Switches are rated by the number of packets per second (pps) they can handle. Good-quality, high-end switches can accommodate 90 million pps and higher. When you're buying network switches, be sure to look at the pps figures before making a decision.

Switching Methods

Switches use three methods to deal with data as it arrives:

◆ **Cut-through**—In a cut-through configuration, the switch begins to forward the packet as soon as it is received. No error checking is performed on the packet, so the packet is moved through very quickly. The downside of cut-through is that because the integrity of the packet is not checked, the switch can propagate errors.

◆ **Store-and-forward**—In a store-and-forward configuration, the switch waits to receive the entire packet before beginning to forward it. It also performs basic error checking.

◆ **Fragment-free**—Building on the speed advantages of cut-through switching, fragment-free switching works by reading only the part of the packet that enables it to identify fragments of a transmission.

As you might expect, the store-and-forward process takes longer than the cut-through method, but it is more reliable. In addition, the delay caused by store-and-forward switching increases with the packet size. The delay caused by cut-through switching is always the same—only the address portion of the packet is read, and this is always the same size, regardless of the size of the data packet. The difference in delay between the two protocols is very high. On average, cut-through switching is 30 times faster than store-and-forward switching.

> **NOTE** **Latency** The time it takes for data to travel between two locations is known as the *latency*. The higher the latency, the bigger the delay in sending the data.

It might seem that cut-through switching is the obvious choice, but today's switches are fast enough to be able to use store-and-forward switching and still deliver high performance levels. On some managed switches, you can select the switching method you want to use.

WORKING WITH HUBS AND SWITCHES

As switches become more commonplace and the technology becomes less expensive, you can expect the use of switches to all but eliminate hubs. However, the reliable nature of networking devices means you are likely to see hubs installed in networks for a long time to come. Therefore, it is important to know how to work with hubs and switches, sometimes in the same environment.

You must be aware of some of the aspects of hubs and switches when working with them. This is very important because you're likely to work with both hubs and switches in a production environment.

> **NOTE** **Production Environments** The term *production* is used to describe a working, or live, computing environment.

Hub and Switch Ports

Hubs and switches have two types of ports: medium dependent interface (MDI) and medium dependent interface crossed (MDI-X). The two types of ports differ in their wiring. As the *X* implies, an MDI-X port's wiring is crossed; this is because the transmit wire from the connected device must be wired to the receive line on the other. Rather than use a crossover cable (which is discussed in the next section, "Cables Connecting Hubs and Switches"), you can use the more simple straight-through cable (also discussed in the next section) to connect systems to the switch or hub.

On most modern hubs and switches, a special port called the *uplink port* allows you to connect two hubs and switches together to create larger networks. Because the aim of this type of network connection is to make each hub or switch think that it is simply part of a larger network, the connection for the port is not crossed; a straight-through network cable is used to connect the two hubs or switches together. Figure 3.6 shows the uplink port on an Ethernet switch.

FIGURE 3.6
The uplink port on an Ethernet switch.

NOTE

Hub Ports Rather than having a dedicated uplink port, some switches and hubs have a port that you can change between MDI and MDI-X by pushing a button. If you are using the port to connect a computer, you should make sure it is set to MDI-X. If you're connecting to another hub or switch, you should make sure it's set to MDI.

In the absence of an uplink port, you can connect two hubs or switches together by using MDI-X ports, but you must use a crossover cable to do so.

Cables Connecting Hubs and Switches

Two types of cables are used to connect devices to hubs and switches: crossover cables and straight-through cables. The difference between the two types is that in a crossover cable, two of the wires are crossed; in a straight-through cable, all the wires run straight through.

Specifically, in a crossover cable, Wires 1 and 3 and Wires 2 and 6 are crossed: Wire 1 at one end becomes Wire 3 at the other end, Wire 2 at one end becomes Wire 6 at the other end, and vice versa in both cases. You can see the differences between the two cables in Figures 3.7 and 3.8. Figure 3.7 shows the pinouts for a straight-through cable, and Figure 3.8 shows the pinouts for a crossover cable.

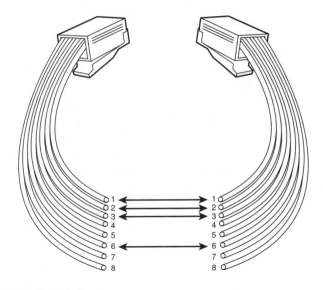

FIGURE 3.7
Pinouts for a straight-through twisted-pair cable.

IN THE FIELD

HOW MANY IS TOO MANY?

Although Ethernet standards state that you can have as many as 1,024 nodes on a network, the practical maximum may be much lower. The number of nodes you can accommodate depends on a number of factors. Using switches instead of hubs makes a *huge* difference, particularly if you are using the full-duplex features of these devices. The amount of traffic generated by clients also has a significant effect, as does the type of traffic. On a more subtle level, you must consider the quality of the networking components and devices you use.

FIGURE 3.8
Pinouts for a crossover twisted-pair cable.

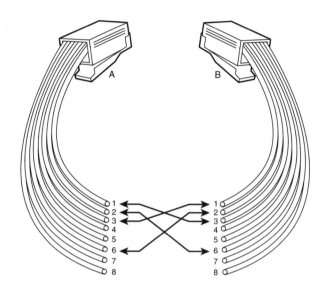

Switches—Read the Label   Switches are often labeled as being 10/100 switches. This label normally means that the ports on the switch are capable of operating at 10Mbps or 100Mbps. Don't take it for granted, though. Some older switches have 10Mbps ports for connecting systems and 100Mbps ports for uplinking. Because there are no guidelines for labeling devices, some of those older switches are referred to as 10/100 switches. Always check the specifications before buying a switch.

Hubs and switches are sometimes equipped with a network connection for another cable type, such as coaxial. Other higher-end devices simply have empty sockets into which you can plug connectivity modules of choice. This approach lets you create very fast networks. For example, three 24-port 10/100 Ethernet switches could be connected to each other by a Gigabit Ethernet fiber-optic connection. This would create a very fast network structure in which switch-to-system communication can occur at 200Mbps (in full-duplex mode) and switch-to-switch communication can occur at Gigabit Ethernet speeds. The result is a very fast local area network (LAN).

Hub and Switch Indicator Lights

Both hubs and switches use light-emitting diodes (LEDs) to indicate certain connection conditions. At the very least, a link light on the hub will indicate the existence of a live connection. On higher-end devices, additional lights might indicate activity, the speed of the connection, whether the connection is at half- or full-duplex, and sometimes errors or collisions. The LEDs provide an immediate visual indicator about the status of the device, so familiarizing yourself with their function is a worthwhile exercise. There is a further discussion of hub and switch LEDs in Chapter 14, "Troubleshooting Tools and Utilities."

Rack Mount, Stackable, and Freestanding Devices

Some hubs and switches, as well as many other networking devices, are designed to be placed in a rack, whereas others are labeled as stackable or freestanding. Rack-mount devices are designed for placement into equipment racks, which are a common sight in computer rooms. The racks are approximately 19 inches wide; devices that are designed to be rack-mounted are slightly smaller than freestanding devices, so they can fit in the racks. Small metal brackets are screwed to the sides of the devices to allow them to be fitted into the racks.

If you don't have racks, you need to use stackable or freestanding devices. These devices can literally be placed on top of one another. Many network equipment manufacturers realize that not everyone has racks, and so they make their equipment usable in either a rack or a freestanding configuration.

Managed Hubs and Switches

Both hubs and switches come in managed and unmanaged versions. A managed device has an interface through which it can be configured to perform certain special functions. For example, it may allow for port mirroring, which can be useful for network monitoring, or allow ports to be specified to operate at a certain speed. Because of the extra functionality of a managed device, and because of the additional components required to achieve it, managed devices are considerably more expensive than unmanaged devices. When you're specifying switches or hubs, consider the need for manageability carefully. If a switch will be used to connect servers to the network, a managed device might make the most sense—the extra functionality might come in handy. On parts of the network that accommodate client computers, nonmanaged devices generally suffice.

At the time of this writing, switches are still quite a bit more expensive than hubs with equivalent capacity, but the gap is narrowing quickly. Some manufacturers have stopped producing hubs and instead are putting all their efforts into developing switches. This would seem to be a sound strategy. In all but the smallest networks or companies with the most restrictive budgets, hubs are rapidly being replaced by switches. In new implementations, hubs are very unlikely to be specified and installed.

> **NOTE**
>
> **Port Density** Excluding the small workgroup hubs, hubs and switches normally have 8, 16, 24, or 32 ports each, although variations are available. To help you compare prices between devices, manufacturers often quote a price per port. In some cases, a higher-density device with more ports may cost significantly less than a device with fewer ports. Typically, the more ports on a device, the lower the price per port.

BRIDGES

Bridges are networking devices that divide up networks. In the days before routers and switches became popular, bridges were used to divide up networks and thus reduce the amount of traffic on each network. Network switches have largely replaced them.

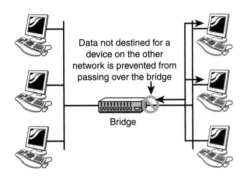

Data not destined for a device on the other network is prevented from passing over the bridge

Bridge

FIGURE 3.9
How a bridge works.

A bridge functions by blocking or forwarding data, based on the destination MAC address written into each frame of data. If the bridge believes the destination address is on a network other than that from which the data was received, it can forward the data to the other networks to which it is connected. If the address is not on the other side of the bridge, the data is blocked from passing. Bridges "learn" the MAC addresses of devices on connected networks by "listening" to network traffic and recording the network from which the traffic originates. Figure 3.9 shows a representation of a bridge.

The advantages of bridges are simple and significant. By preventing unnecessary traffic from crossing onto other network segments, a bridge can dramatically reduce the amount of network traffic on a segment. Bridges also make it possible to isolate a busy network from a not-so-busy one, thereby preventing pollution from busy nodes.

> **NOTE**
>
> **Manual Bridge Configuration** Some early bridge implementations required you to enter the information for each device on the network manually. Fortunately, bridges are now of the learning variety, and manual configuration is no longer necessary.

Bridge Implementation Considerations

Although implementing bridges can offer huge improvements in performance, you must factor in a number of considerations. The first is bridge placement. Generally, you should follow the 80/20 rule for bridge placement: 80% of the traffic should not cross the bridge, and 20% of the traffic should be on the other side of the bridge. The rule is easy to understand, but accurately determining the correct location for the bridge to accommodate the rule is another matter.

Another, potentially more serious, consideration is bridging loops, which can be created when more than one bridge is used on a network. Multiple bridges can provide fault tolerance or improve performance. Bridging loops occur when multiple bridges become confused about where devices are on the network.

As an example of bridging loops, imagine that you have a network with two bridges, as depicted in Figure 3.10. During the learning process, the north bridge receives a packet from Interface A (step 1 in Figure 3.11) and determines that it is for a system that is not on Network Z; therefore, the bridge forwards the packet to Network X (step 2 in Figure 3.11). Now, the south bridge sees a packet originating on Network X on Interface C (step 3 in Figure 3.11); because it thinks the destination system is not on Network X, it forwards the packet to Network Z (step 4 in Figure 3.11), where the north bridge picks it up (step 5 in Figure 3.11). The north bridge determines that the destination system is not on Network Z, so it forwards the packet to Network X—and the whole process begins again.

You can work around the looping problem by using the Spanning Tree Algorithm (STA). When STA is used, each interface on a bridge is assigned a value. As the bridge forwards the data, the value is attached to the packet. When another bridge sees the data, if the STA value for the interface is higher than that assigned to its interfaces, the bridge doesn't forward the data, thus eliminating the possibility of a bridging loop. STA eliminates the bridging loop but still provides the fault tolerance of having more than one bridge in place. If the bridge with the higher STA value (sometimes referred to as the *primary bridge*) fails, the other bridge continues functioning because it becomes the bridge with the higher STA value. All this is achieved by the Spanning Tree Protocol (STP).

Types of Bridges

Three types of bridges are used in networks. You don't need detailed knowledge of how each bridge works, but you should have an overview:

◆ **Transparent bridge**—A transparent bridge is invisible to the other devices on the network. Transparent bridges only perform the function of blocking or forwarding data based on the MAC address; the devices on the network are oblivious to these bridges' existence. Transparent bridges are by far the most popular types of bridges.

◆ **Translational bridge**—A translational bridge can convert from one networking system to another. As you might have guessed, it translates the data it receives. Translational bridges

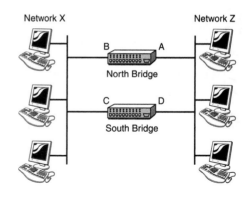

FIGURE 3.10
A network with two bridges.

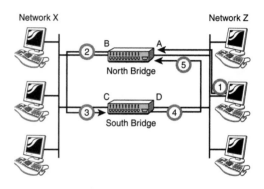

FIGURE 3.11
A bridging loop.

> **NOTE**
>
> **STP** STP is defined in the IEEE 802.1d standard.

are useful for connecting two different networks, such as Ethernet and Token Ring networks. Depending on the direction of travel, a translational bridge can add or remove information and fields from the frame as needed.

◆ **Source-route bridge**—Source-route bridges were designed by IBM for use on Token Ring networks. The source-route bridge derives its name from the fact that the entire route of the frame is embedded within the frame. This allows the bridge to make specific decisions about how the frame should be forwarded through the network. The diminishing popularity of Token Ring makes the chances that you'll work with a source-route bridge very slim.

As switches become ever cheaper, bridges have been overtaken by switches in terms of both functionality and performance. You should expect to be working with switches more often than with bridges.

ROUTERS

Routers are an increasingly common sight in any network environment, from a small home office that uses one to connect to an Internet service provider (ISP) to a corporate IT environment where racks of routers manage data communication with disparate remote sites. Routers make internetworking possible, and in view of this, they warrant detailed attention.

Routers are network devices that literally route data around the network. By examining data as it arrives, the router is able to determine the destination address for the data; then, by using tables of defined routes, the router determines the best way for the data to continue its journey. Unlike bridges and switches, which use the hardware-configured MAC address to determine the destination of the data, routers use the software-configured network address to make decisions. This approach makes routers more functional than bridges or switches, and it also makes them more complex because they have to work harder to determine the information. Figure 3.12 shows basically how a router functions.

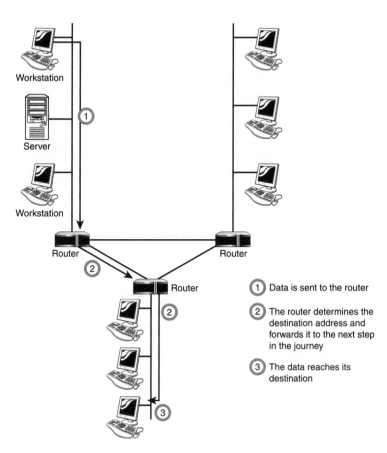

FIGURE 3.12
The basic function of a router.

The basic requirement for a router is that it must have at least two network interfaces. If they are LAN interfaces, then the router can manage and route the information between two LAN segments. More commonly, a router is used to provide connectivity across wide area network (WAN) links. Figure 3.13 shows a router with two LAN ports (marked AUI 0 and AUI 1) and two WAN ports (marked Serial 0 and Serial 1). This router is capable of routing data between two LAN segments and two WAN segments.

FIGURE 3.13
A router with two LAN ports and two WAN ports.

FIGURE 3.13
A router with two LAN ports and two WAN ports.

Routable Protocols and Routing Protocols

Routers rely on two types of network protocols to make the routing magic happen: routable protocols and routing protocols. We'll examine them separately in the next sections.

Routable Protocols

Large internetworks need protocols that allow systems to be identified by the address of the network to which they are attached and by an address that uniquely identifies them on that network. Network protocols that provide both of these features are said to be *routable*. Two routable network protocols are used commonly today:

◆ **Transmission Control Protocol/Internet Protocol (TCP/IP)**—TCP/IP was developed in the 1970s by the Department of Defense, which needed a protocol to use on its WAN. TCP/IP's flexibility, durability, and functionality meant that it soon became the WAN protocol of choice and also became the standard for LANs. Today, most networks use TCP/IP in some fashion, even if the main LAN protocol is something other than TCP/IP. TCP/IP is a huge topic, and anyone in networking must understand it. The Network+

exam dedicates an entire exam objective to it. Chapter 6, "Working with TCP/IP," provides complete coverage of TCP/IP.

◆ **Internetwork Packet Exchange/Sequenced Packet Exchange (IPX/SPX)**—Created by Novell for use on NetWare networks, IPX/SPX is a routable protocol that was popular for many years. Today, even Novell acknowledges that TCP/IP is the network protocol of choice and so has moved away from IPX/SPX and toward a pure TCP/IP environment. In fact, the last few versions of Novell NetWare have used TCP/IP as the default protocol and allowed IPX/SPX to be enabled if needed.

> **NOTE**
>
> **AppleTalk** Another routable protocol, AppleTalk, was developed for use in Apple-based networks. Although it was popular for a time, it has now been largely replaced by TCP/IP.

Some routers are capable of routing more than one protocol at a time, a feature known as *multiprotocol routing*. Multiprotocol routing brings with it a number of considerations, not the least of which is the fact that a multiprotocol router may have to work considerably harder than a router working with only a single protocol. This is the case not only because there is more than one protocol but because there may also be multiple routing protocols.

Routing Protocols

Routing protocols are the means by which routers communicate with each other. This communication is necessary so that routers can learn the network topology and changes that occur in it.

The two types of routing protocols are distance-vector and link-state protocols. Each has a very different strategy for dealing with router-to-router communication.

Distance-Vector Protocols

With distance-vector routing protocols, each router communicates all the routes it knows about to all other routers to which it is directly attached (that is, its *neighbors*). Because each router in the network knows only about the routers to which it is attached, it doesn't know how to complete the entire journey; instead, it only knows how to make the next hop. *Hops* are the means by which distance-vector routing protocols determine the shortest way to reach a given destination. Each router constitutes one hop; so if a router is four hops away from another router, there are three routers, or hops,

> **NOTE**
>
> **Static Routing** The alternative to using routing protocols is *static routing*, which means that route information must be manually entered by the administrator. There are two main disadvantages of this approach: First, manually entering routes is time-consuming and susceptible to human error. Second, if the topology of the network changes, the routers must be manually reconfigured. Therefore, static routing is generally used only in the smallest of environments. In environments with more than a handful of routers, dynamic routing is the preferred option.

Metrics   In routing, the term *metric* describes the "cost" of a certain route. The metric can be a combination of factors, including the number of routers between a router's position and the destination, the time it takes to complete the journey, and even a value that can be assigned by an administrator to discourage use of a certain route. Under normal circumstances, routers choose the route with the lowest metric.

between itself and the destination. Distance-vector protocols can also use a time value known as a *tick*, which enables the router to make a decision about which path is quickest if given the choice of more than one (a common situation on networks with redundant links).

The frequency with which routers send route updates depends on the routing protocol being used, but it is usually between 10 and 60 seconds. At each update, the entire routing table of the sender is sent to the other connected routers. When the other routers receive the information, they check it against the existing information; if there are any changes, they alter their routing tables accordingly.

This constant update cycle is one of the problems of distance-vector routing protocols because it can lead to large amounts of network traffic. Furthermore, after the initial learning period, the updates should (hopefully) be irrelevant—the chances of the network topology changing every 30 seconds or so are slim, and if you do have such a network, some troubleshooting may be in order.

When a change does occur on the network, it may take some time for all the routers to learn of the change. The process of each router learning about the change and updating its routing tables is known as *convergence*. In a small network, convergence might not take long; but in larger networks, those with, say, more than 20 routers, it might take some time to complete. Rather than cause the routers to wait for the updates, you can configure *triggered updates*, which are sent when a topology change is detected. Using triggered updates can significantly improve the convergence speed of distance-vector–based networks.

You can also use *hold-down timers* to improve convergence. A hold-down timer prevents a router from trying to make too many changes too quickly. When a router receives a change about a route, it makes the change and then applies a hold-down timer to the change. The hold-down timer prevents further changes from being made to that route within the defined time period. Hold-down timers are particularly useful when an unreliable router keeps going on and off the network. If hold-down timers are not applied, updates to the routing tables on routers would continually be changing, and the network might never converge.

In some configurations, distance-vector routing protocols can lead to routing loops. *Routing loops* occur when a router tells another router about a route that it heard about from the same router. For example, consider the router layout in Figure 3.14. If Router C becomes unable to access Router D through Network 1, it removes the route from its table and sends the update to Router B; Router B removes the route. But if Router B receives an update from Router A before it sends an update to Router A, the route is reinstated because according to Router A, it can still access Network 1. Now Router B begins to send anything destined for Network 1 back to Router A, which duly sends it back to Router B, and so on, thus creating a routing loop. Each time the route is added to the table, the hop count for the route increases—a problem known as the *count to infinity*.

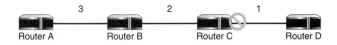

FIGURE 3.14
How routing loops occur.

You can use two strategies to prevent routing loops when using distance-vector routing protocols:

◆ **Split horizon**—The split horizon algorithm addresses the problem of routing loops by not advertising routes back on the interface from which they are learned. In other words, using Figure 3.14 as an example, Router C would not advertise back to Router B any route that it learned from Router B. Basically, Router C figures that, because it learned about the route from Router B, Router B must be nearer to the destination than it is.

◆ **Split horizon with poison reverse**—With this strategy, also known simply as poison reverse, routers do advertise routes back on the interfaces from which they were learned, but they do so with a hop count of infinity. The value used for infinity (which seems like an impossible situation) depends on the routing protocol being used. Again using the example from Figure 3.14, Router C would advertise to Router B the routes it learned from Router B, but it would also add the infinite hop count. In other words, Router C would say, "I know about Router A, but I can't reach it myself." This way, Router B would never try to add the route to Router A through Router C, because according to Router C, it can't reach Router A.

The most popular distance-vector routing protocols are both called Routing Information Protocol (RIP). The distance-vector routing protocol for TCP/IP is called RIP, as is the one for IPX/SPX. To set the two apart, the IPX version is often called IPX RIP.

Link-State Protocols

A router that uses a link-state protocol differs from a router that uses a distance-vector protocol because it builds a map of the entire network and then holds that map in memory. On a network that uses a link-state protocol, routers send out link state advertisements (LSAs) that contain information about what networks they are connected to. The LSAs are sent to every router on the network, thus enabling the routers to build their network maps.

When the network maps on each router are complete, the routers update each other at a given time, just like with a distance-vector protocol, but the updates occur much less frequently with link-state protocols than with distance-vector protocols. The only other circumstance under which updates are sent is if a change in the topology is detected, at which point the routers use LSAs to detect the change and update their routing tables. This mechanism, combined with the fact that routers hold maps of the entire network, makes convergence on a link-state–based network occur very quickly.

Although it might seem like link-state protocols are an obvious choice over distance-vector protocols, routers on a link-state–based network require more powerful hardware and more RAM than those on a distance-vector–based network. Not only do the routing tables have to be calculated, but they must also be stored. A router that uses distance-vector protocols need only maintain a small database of the routes accessible by the routers to which it is directly connected. A router that uses link-state protocols must maintain a database of the routers in the entire network.

Two of the most popular link-state routing protocols are Open Shortest Path First (OSPF) and NetWare Link State Protocol (NLSP). The former is used on TCP/IP networks, and the latter is used on networks that use IPX/SPX.

EXAM TIP

Identify the Protocols Be prepared to identify both the link-state and distance-vector routing protocols used on both TCP/IP and IPX/SPX networks.

NOTE

Multiprotocol Routing In this section and the previous section, we have discussed routing protocols as they apply to single protocols. But remember that one router may be routing more than one protocol; it may, for example, use OSPF and NLSP.

Dedicated Hardware Versus Server-Based Routers

A router can be either a dedicated hardware device or a server system that has at least two network interfaces installed in it. All common network operating systems offer the capability to act as routers as part of their functionality.

Dedicated hardware routers offer greater performance levels than server-based solutions, but they have the disadvantage of offering a limited range of features for their cost. However, the attraction of a dedicated hardware device often outweighs this factor.

The following are some of the advantages of dedicated hardware routers:

◆ Typically faster than server-based routers

◆ Generally more reliable than server-based routers

◆ Easier to harden against attacks than server-based routing solutions

The following are some of the disadvantages of dedicated hardware routers:

◆ More expensive than server-based router solutions; extra functionality may have to be purchased

◆ Often require specialized skills and knowledge to manage them

◆ Limited to a small range of possible uses

The capabilities of a router depend on the features it has installed. A basic router may route only one protocol between two network interfaces of the same type. A more advanced router may act as a gateway between two networks and two protocols. In addition, it may offer firewall services, security and authentication, or remote access functionality such as virtual private networking.

The topic of routing is complex, and the routing information provided in this chapter is the most basic of tutorials. Although we've told you what you need to know for the exam, if you're working with routers on a daily basis, you will want to seek out further sources of information—and there is no shortage of such sources.

> **NOTE**
>
> **Brouters**   A *brouter* is a device that can route anything that can be routed and bridge anything that cannot be routed. As bridges have been replaced by the more flexible routers, brouters have also fallen out of favor. In today's networking world, routers rule. Just ask Cisco.

GATEWAYS

The term *gateway* is applied to any device, system, or software application that can perform the function of translating data from one format to another. The key feature of a gateway is that it converts the format of the data, not the data itself.

You can use gateway functionality in many ways. For example, a router that can route data from an IPX network to an IP network is, technically, a gateway. The same can be said of a translational bridge that, as described earlier in this chapter, converts from an Ethernet network to a Token Ring network and back again.

Software gateways can be found everywhere. Many companies use an email system such as Microsoft Exchange or Novell GroupWise. These systems transmit mail internally in a certain format. When email needs to be sent across the Internet to users using a different email system, the email must be converted to another format, usually to Simple Mail Transfer Protocol (SMTP). This conversion process is performed by a software gateway.

Another good (and often used) example of a gateway involves the Systems Network Architecture (SNA) gateway, which converts the data format used on a PC to that used on an IBM mainframe or minicomputer. A system that acts as an SNA gateway sits between the client PC and the mainframe and translates requests and replies from both directions. Figure 3.15 shows how this would work in a practical implementation.

FIGURE 3.15
An SNA gateway.

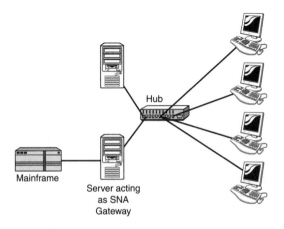

If it seems from the text in this section that we are being vague about what a gateway is, it's because there is no definite answer. The function of a gateway is very specific, but how the gateway functionality is implemented is not.

No matter what their use, gateways slow the flow of data and can therefore potentially become bottlenecks. The conversion from one data format to another takes time, and so the flow of data through a gateway is always slower than the flow of data without one.

CSUs/DSUs

A CSU/DSU acts as a translator between the LAN data format and the WAN data format. Such a conversion is necessary because the technologies used on WAN links are different from those used on LANs. In reality, you can think of a CSU/DSU as a digital modem; but unlike a normal modem, which changes the signal from digital to analog, a CSU/DSU changes the signal from one digital format to another. Figure 3.16 shows how a CSU/DSU might fit into a network.

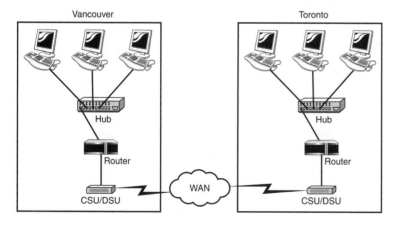

FIGURE 3.16
How a CSU/DSU is used in a network.

A CSU/DSU has physical connections for the LAN equipment, normally via a serial interface, and another connection for a WAN. Traditionally, the CSU/DSU has been in a separate box from other networking equipment; however, the increasing use of WAN links means that some router manufacturers are now including the CSU/DSU functionality in routers or are providing the expansion capability to do so.

NOTE

Is a CSU/DSU a Gateway? A CSU/DSU is in a sense a gateway device because it translates data from one format (that used on the LAN) to another (that used on the WAN). The same can be said of a normal modem.

NOTE

Wired Access Points When a WAP connects to a wired network, it is often referred to as a *wired access point* because it joins the wireless portion of the network with the wired portion.

NOTE

A WAP for All Seasons Because wireless networks are sometimes deployed in environments other than inside a warm, dry building, some manufacturers offer rugged versions of WAPs. These devices are sealed against the elements, making them suitable for placement in locations where nonrugged devices would not survive. If you are implementing a wireless network, you should consider whether using these rugged devices may be warranted.

WIRELESS ACCESS POINT (WAPs)

Wireless network devices gain access to the network via WAPs. WAPs are typically deployed as part of a larger network infrastructure, but in some environments, such as small businesses or home offices, they can operate completely independently of a normal network.

WAPs are fairly innocuous, hub-like devices; the only giveaway to their function is the antennae that protrude from the box. Because WAPs process signals and are often connected into a wired network, they require power, which is supplied through an external AC power adapter or a built-in power supply.

MODEMS

Modem is a contraction of the terms *modulator* and *demodulator*. Modems perform a simple function: They translate digital signals from a computer into analog signals that can travel across conventional phone lines. The modem modulates the signal at the sending end and demodulates at the receiving end.

Modems provide a relatively slow method of communication. In fact, the fastest modem available on the market today has a maximum speed of 56Kbps. Compare that to the speed of a 10Mbps network connection, and you'll find that the modem is approximately 180 times slower. That makes modems okay for browsing Web pages or occasionally downloading small files but wholly unsuitable for downloading large files. As a result, many people prefer to use other remote access methods, including ISDN (which is discussed later in this chapter, in the section "ISDN Terminal Adapters") and cable/DSL access.

Modems are available as internal devices that plug into expansion slots in a system; external devices that plug into serial or USB ports; PCMCIA cards designed for use in laptops; and specialized devices designed for use in systems such as handheld computers. In addition, many laptops now come with integrated modems. For large-scale modem implementations, such as at an ISP, rack-mounted modems are also available. Figure 3.17 shows an internal modem and a PCMCIA modem.

FIGURE 3.17
An internal modem (left) and a PCMCIA modem (right).

Modems are controlled through a series of commands known as the Hayes AT command set. Hayes was a company that, for many years, led the field in the development of modems and modem technology. The AT commands allow you to control a modem as well as configure and diagnose it. Some of the most commonly used AT commands are provided in Table 3.1.

EXAM TIP	**Know the AT Command** On the Network+ exam, you might be asked to identify the correct AT command to be used in a given situation.

TABLE 3.1

COMMONLY USED AT MODEM COMMANDS

Command	Result
ATA	Answers an incoming call
ATH	Hangs up the current connection
ATZ	Resets the modem
ATI3	Displays modem identification information

Modem Connection Speeds

The actual speed you obtain on a modem connection depends on a variety of factors, including the quality of the line you are using and the speed of the modem. For example, you might find (as we often do) that even with a 56Kbps modem, the most you can get on a certain connection is 49Kbps. If you try the same connection again on a different phone line, you might get a higher or lower rate. Quality of the connection aside, two factors govern the maximum speed attainable by your modem: the speed of the Universal Asynchronous Receiver/Transmitter (UART) chip in your system (which controls the serial ports) and the speed of the modem itself.

In older systems, the UART chips were capable of only slow speeds, making them unable to keep up with fast modems. Today, most systems have UART chips that are capable of speeds well in excess of those offered by modems. Now the modem, not the UART chip, is the bottleneck. The types of commonly used UART chips and their associated speeds are provided in Table 3.2.

TABLE 3.2

UART CHIPS AND THEIR ASSOCIATED SPEEDS

UART Chip	Speed (bps)
8250	9,600
16450	115,200
16550	115,200
16650	430,800
16750	921,600
16950	921,600

EXAM TIP

Know the UART Speed   On the Network+ exam, you might be asked to identify the maximum speed of a given UART chip.

Modem speeds can be expressed in either baud rate or bits per second (bps). The *baud rate* refers to the number of times a signal changes in each second, and the *bps rate* is the number of bits of data that can be sent or received in a second. Although the figures are identical in some modems, in others the bps rate is higher than the baud rate. The baud rate is actually quite meaningless, and the higher the bps figure, the better. Most modern modems offer bps rates far greater than the baud rate.

To make it easier to compare modems, standards have been created that define the speed of the modem and what features it provides.

These are sometimes referred to as the *V standards*, and you can use them when buying a modem to determine the modem's capabilities.

NETWORK CARDS (NICs)

NICs—sometimes called network cards—are the mechanisms by which computers connect to a network. NICs come in all shapes and sizes, and they come in prices to suit all budgets. You need to consider the following when buying an NIC:

> **NOTE**
>
> **NIC Terminology**   Many different terms are used to refer to NICs, such as network card, network adapter, and LAN adapter. All refer to the same thing.

◆ **Network compatibility**—Perhaps this is a little obvious, but sometimes people order the wrong type of NIC for the network. Given the prevalence of Ethernet networks, you are likely to have to specify network compatibility only when buying an NIC for another networking system.

◆ **Bus compatibility**—Newly purchased NICs will almost certainly use the Peripheral Component Interconnect (PCI) bus, although if you are replacing a card in an older system, you might have to specify an Industry Standard Architecture (ISA) bus card instead. If the card you are buying is PCI, you should check to see what kind of PCI interface is being used. Many high-end server systems now come with 64-bit PCI slots; if you have them, it is definitely worth taking advantage of the extra performance they offer. Such 64-bit PCI slots can be easily identified because they are the same color and width as 32-bit PCI slots, but are longer. Figure 3.18 shows 32-bit PCI slots on a system board.

◆ **Port compatibility**—Generally an NIC has only one port, for twisted-pair cabling. If you want some other connectivity, you need to be sure to specify your card accordingly; for example, you might need a fiber-optic or coaxial cable port.

> **NOTE**
>
> **Combo Cards**   Sometimes an NIC has a twisted-pair socket, a coaxial connector, and an attachment unit interface (AUI) port. These cards are referred to as *combo* cards. Today, the dominance of twisted-pair cabling means that most NICs have only a twisted-pair connection.

◆ **Hardware compatibility**—Before installing a network card into a system, you must verify compatibility between the network card and the operating system on the PC in which you are installing the NIC. If you are using good-quality network cards from a recognized manufacturer, such verification should be little more than a formality.

FIGURE 3.18
32-bit PCI slots on a system board. (Photo copyright © 2001, Intel Corporation.)

Types of Network Interfaces

Network interfaces come as add-in expansion cards or as PCMCIA cards used in laptop systems. In some cases, rather than have an add-in NIC, the network interface is embedded into the motherboard. Figure 3.19 shows an example of an add-in NIC, Figure 3.20 shows a PCMCIA network card, and Figure 3.21 shows a built-in network interface in a laptop system.

IN THE FIELD

THE FALSE ECONOMY OF NICS

The difference between an inexpensive network card and an expensive one is less than you might think; but even so, people are tempted to go for the low-cost option. In many cases, this turns out to be a false economy. Not only do higher-end cards tend to be easier to install, they are generally easier to troubleshoot as well. An hour trying to troubleshoot a misbehaving inexpensive network card can negate any cost savings from the purchase. This is particularly relevant on server systems, where a problem network card will not only cause you frustration, but will most likely cause the users of the server problems. In fact, if you are working on server systems, it's worth investigating fault-tolerant network card configurations, such as adapter teaming.

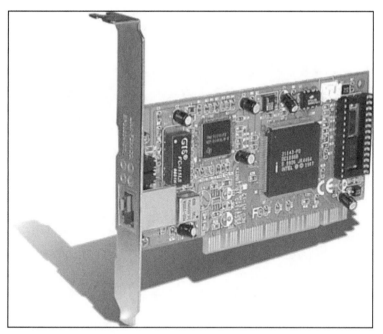

FIGURE 3.19
An expansion NIC. (Photo courtesy TRENDware International, www.trendware.com.)

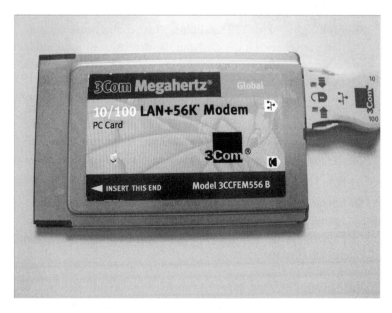

FIGURE 3.20
A PCMCIA NIC.

PCMCI Amazing You might notice that the modem in Figure 3.20 is the same card used in Figure 3.17. No, it's not a mistake: This PCMCIA card is a network card and a modem. Clever, eh?

FIGURE 3.21
A built-in network interface on a laptop system.

A network interface typically has at least two LEDs that indicate certain conditions:

◆ **Link light**—This LED indicates whether a network connection exists between the card and the network. An unlit link light is an indicator that something is awry with the network cable or connection.

◆ **Activity light**—This LED indicates network activity. Under normal conditions, the light should flicker sporadically and often. Constant flickering may indicate a very busy network or a problem somewhere on the network that is worth investigating.

◆ **Speed light**—This LED indicates that the interface is connected at a certain speed. This feature is normally found on Ethernet NICs that operate at 10Mbps/100Mbps—and then only on certain cards.

Some network cards combine the functions of certain lights by using dual-color LEDs. PCMCIA cards sometimes have no lights, or the lights are incorporated into the media adapter that comes with the card. You can see an example in Figure 3.22.

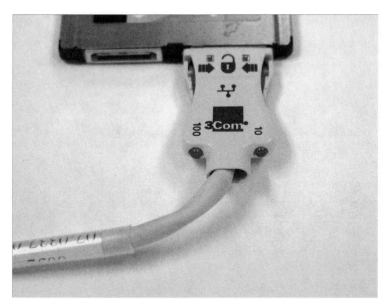

FIGURE 3.22
Indicator lights on a media adapter for a PCMCIA NIC.

Installing Network Cards

At some point in your networking career, it is very likely that you will have to install an NIC into a system. For that reason, an understanding of the procedures and considerations related to NIC installations is useful. Here are some of the main things you should consider:

♦ **Drivers** Almost every NIC is supplied with a driver disk, but the likelihood of the drivers on the disk being the latest drivers is slim. You should always ensure that you have the latest drivers by visiting the Web site of the NIC manufacturer. The drivers play a very important role in the correct functioning of the NIC, so spend a few extra minutes to make sure the drivers are installed and configured correctly.

♦ **NIC configuration utilities**—In days gone by, NICs were configured with small groups of pins known as *jumpers*, or with small plastic blocks of switches known as *dip switches*. Figure 3.23 shows an example of jumpers. Unless you are working with very old equipment, you are unlikely to encounter dip switches.

EXAM TIP

Avoid ESD When installing any component in a system, you need to observe proper and correct procedures to guard against electrostatic discharge (ESD). ESD into a computer component can cause it to fail immediately or degrade so that it fails at some point in the future. Proper ESD precautions include wearing an antistatic wrist strap and properly grounding yourself.

FIGURE 3.23
A block of jumpers.

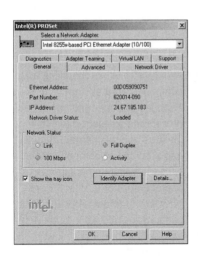

FIGURE 3.24
The Intel PROSet utility.

Although these methods were efficient and easy to use, they have now largely been abandoned in favor of software configuration utilities, which allow you to configure the settings for the card (if any) and to test whether the card is working properly. Other utilities can be used through the operating system to obtain statistical information, help, and a range of other features. Figure 3.24 shows an example of one such utility, called PROSet, for the Intel 8255x series of NICs.

◆ **System resources**—In order to function correctly, NICs must have certain system resources allocated to them: the interrupt request (IRQ) and memory addresses. In some cases, you might need to assign the values for these manually. In most cases, you can rely on plug-and-play, which assigns resources for devices automatically.

◆ **Physical slot availability**—Most modern PCs have at least three or four usable expansion slots. Not only that, but the increasing trend toward component integration on the motherboard means that devices such as serial and parallel ports and sound cards are now built into the system board and therefore don't use up valuable slots. If you're working on older systems or systems that have a lot of add-in hardware, you might be short of slots. You should check to ensure that a slot is available before you begin.

◆ **Built-in network interfaces**—A built-in network interface is
a double-edged sword. The upsides are that it doesn't occupy
an expansion slot and hardware compatibility with the rest of
the system is almost guaranteed. The downside is that a built-
in component is not upgradable. For this reason, you might
find yourself installing an add-in NIC and at the same time
disabling the on-board network interface. Disabling the on-
board interface is normally a straightforward process, achieved
by going into the BIOS setup screen or, on some systems, a
system configuration utility. In either case, you should consult
the documentation that came with the system or look for
information on the manufacturer's Web site.

As time goes on, NIC and operating system manufacturers are
making it increasingly easy to install NICs in systems of all sorts and
sizes. By understanding the requirements of the card and the correct
installation procedure, you should be able to install cards simply and
efficiently.

ISDN TERMINAL ADAPTERS

When the speed provided by a modem just isn't enough, you must
seek alternatives. One of the speedier options available is an ISDN
link. ISDN is a digital communication method that can be used over
a conventional phone line, although certain criteria must be met for
an ISDN line to be available (such as the availability of the service
and the proximity of your location to the telco's site). (The information in this section is intended only to cover ISDN terminal adapters,
not ISDN as a system. Detailed coverage of ISDN is provided in
Chapter 7, "WAN Technologies," which covers WAN topics.)

To use ISDN, you need a device called an *ISDN terminal adapter*.
ISDN terminal adapters are available as add-in expansion cards that
are installed into computers, external devices that connect to the serial interfaces of PC systems, or modules in a router. You can think of
an ISDN terminal adapter as a kind of digital modem—but don't
call it that, or you might find yourself being corrected by another
techie. (Remember that a modem converts a signal from digital to
analog and vice versa. An ISDN terminal adapter translates the
signal between two digital formats.) Figure 3.25 shows an external

ISDN terminal adapter, and Figure 3.26 shows an example of an internal ISDN adapter. Notice that an ISDN terminal adapter is very similar in appearance to a standard NIC.

FIGURE 3.25
An external ISDN adapter.

FIGURE 3.26
An internal ISDN adapter.

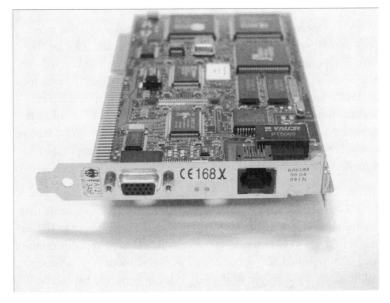

Installing an external ISDN adapter is very simple because, like an external modem, an external ISDN adapter plugs into the serial port of the system and thus uses its resources. You need drivers for the an ISDN terminal adapter, so you should be sure to visit the manufacturer's Web site and download the latest drivers that are available. An internal ISDN terminal adapter requires a little more effort: You must make sure you have physical and logical system resources to accommodate it. As far as the physical installation goes, consider the information provided in the section "Installing NICs," earlier in this chapter; much of it applies to the installation of internal ISDN terminal adapters.

SYSTEM AREA NETWORK CARDS

As processing needs become ever greater and demands on server availability increase, single-server systems are giving way to server clusters. In a *server cluster,* systems can share storage and processing power and are fault tolerant; that is, if a system in the cluster fails, one of the other systems in the cluster can take over for it and continue processing.

This level of functionality requires many things. It needs operating systems that are capable of being clustered and applications that can do the same. It also requires that the systems in the cluster be able to talk to each other. That's where system area network cards come in.

System area network cards are used in clustered systems to facilitate communication between the devices in the cluster. Figure 3.27 shows how system area network cards are used.

If only two systems are in the cluster, they can be connected directly by a cable. If the cluster has more than two systems, a specialized hub is required.

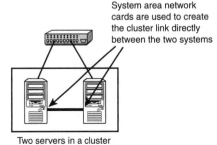

FIGURE 3.27
How system area network cards are used.

REVIEW BREAK

Network Devices Summary

The information in this chapter is very important for the Network+ exam. To summarize our coverage of network devices, we have placed some of the key points about each device in Table 3.3. You should learn this information well.

TABLE 3.3
NETWORK DEVICES SUMMARY

Device	Function/Purpose	Key Points
Hub	Connects devices on a twisted-pair network.	A hub does not perform any tasks besides signal regeneration.
Switch	Connects devices on a twisted-pair network.	A switch forwards data to its destination by using the MAC address embedded in each packet.
Bridge	Divides networks to reduce overall network traffic.	A bridge allows or prevents data from passing through it by reading the MAC address.
Router	Connects networks together.	A router uses the software-configured network address to make forwarding decisions.
Gateway	Translates from one data format to another.	Gateways can be hardware or software based. Any device that translates data formats is called a gateway.
CSU/DSU	Translates digital signals used on a LAN to those used on a WAN.	CSU/DSU functionality is sometimes incorporated into other devices, such as a router with a WAN connection.
Network card	Enables systems to connect to the network.	Network interfaces can be add-in expansion cards, PCMCIA cards, or built-in interfaces.
ISDN terminal adapter	Connects devices to ISDN lines.	ISDN is a digital WAN technology often used in place of slower modem links. ISDN terminal adapters are required to reformat the data format for transmission on ISDN links.
System area network card	Used in server clusters to provide connectivity between nodes.	System area network cards are high-performance devices capable of coping with the demands of clustering applications.
WAP	Provides network capabilities to wireless network devices.	A WAP is often used to connect to a wired network, thereby acting as a link between wired and wireless portions of the network.
Modem	Provides serial communication capabilities across phone lines.	Modems modulate the digital signal into analog at the sending end and perform the reverse function at the receiving end.

IDENTIFYING MAC ADDRESSES

▶ Given an example, identify a Media Access Control (MAC) address.

This chapter many times refers to MAC addresses and how certain devices use them. However, it has not yet discussed why MAC addresses exist, how they are assigned, and what they consist of. Let's do that now.

A MAC address is a 6-byte address that allows an NIC to be uniquely identified on the network. The MAC address forms the basis of network communication, regardless of the protocol used to achieve network connection. Because the MAC address is so fundamental to network communication, mechanisms are in place to ensure that there is no possibility of duplicate addresses being used.

To combat the possibility of duplicate MAC addresses being assigned, the Institute of Electrical and Electronics Engineers (IEEE) took over the assignment of MAC addresses. But rather than be burdened with assigning individual addresses, the IEEE instead decided to assign each manufacturer an ID and then let the manufacturer further allocate IDs. The result is that in a MAC address, the first three bytes define the manufacturer and the last three are assigned by the manufacturer.

For example, consider the MAC address of the computer on which this book is being written: 00:D0:59:09:07:51. The first three bytes (00:D0:59) identify the manufacturer of the card; because only this manufacturer can use this address, it is known as the organizationally unique identifier (OUI). The last three bytes (09:07:51) are then referred to as the Universal LAN MAC address: They make this interface unique. You can find a complete listing of organizational MAC address assignments at `http://standards.ieee.org/regauth/oui/oui.txt`.

You can discover the MAC address of the NIC in various ways, depending on what system or platform you are working on. Table 3.4 defines various platforms and the method you can use to view the MAC address of an interface.

> **EXAM TIP**
>
> **A MAC Address Is the Physical Address** A MAC address is sometimes referred to as a *physical address* because it is physically embedded in the interface. Sometimes it is also referred to as a *network address*, which is incorrect. A *network address* is the logical protocol address assigned to the network to which the interface is connected.

> **EXAM TIP**
>
> **MAC Address Tip** Because MAC addresses are expressed in hexadecimal, only the numbers 0 through 9 and the letters A through F can be used in them. If you get a Network+ exam question about identifying a MAC address and some of the answers contain letters and numbers other than 0 through 9 and the letters A through F, you can discount those answers immediately.

TABLE 3.4

METHODS OF VIEWING THE MAC ADDRESSES OF NICS

Platform	Method
Windows 95/98/Me	Run the `winipcfg` utility
Windows NT/2000	Run `ipconfig /all` from a command prompt
Linux/some Unix	Run the `ifconfig -a` command
Novell NetWare	Run the `config` command
Cisco router	Run the `sh int <interface name>` command

Figure 3.28 shows the `ipconfig /all` command run on a Windows 2000 system. The MAC address is defined on the Physical Address line of the output.

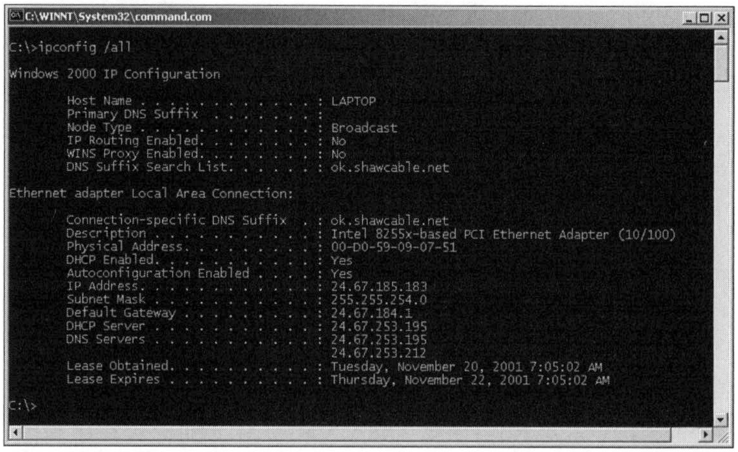

FIGURE 3.28
The output from the `ipconfig /all` command on a Windows 2000 system.

CHAPTER SUMMARY

KEY TERMS

- hub
- switch
- bridge
- router
- gateway
- CSU/DSU
- NIC
- ISDN adapter
- WAP
- modem
- MAC address
- cut-through

Many devices are used to create networks. Every network except the simplest, single-segment coaxial networks uses one or more of these devices. Knowledge of the purpose of the devices discussed in this chapter is vital for the Network+ exam, as well as for the real world.

Hubs and switches provide a mechanism to connect devices to a network that is created with twisted-pair cabling. Switches offer a speed advantage over hubs because they can use full-duplex communications. They also create dedicated paths between devices, reducing the number of collisions that occur. Both hubs and switches are available in managed and nonmanaged varieties.

Bridges allow network traffic to be confined to certain network segments, thereby reducing the amount of network traffic. On Ethernet networks, an additional benefit is reduced collisions.

Routers are devices that connect networks and thereby create internetworks. Because routers use software-configured network addresses instead of hardware-defined MAC addresses, they can provide more functionality than bridges. Routers can be either dedicated hardware devices or implemented through software on server systems.

CHAPTER SUMMARY

A gateway is a device that translates from one data format to another; it can be a hardware device or a software application. A CSU/DSU is an example of a gateway: CSUs/DSUs translate from the data format used on LANs to that used on WANs. A modem, which translates a signal from digital to analog so that it can be transmitted across a conventional phone line, is another example of a gateway.

WAPs are a relative newcomer to the networking equipment field. Wireless network clients use WAPs to connect to the network. WAPs also generally have a connection point that lets them connect to a wired network infrastructure.

NICs are the point of connectivity between devices and the network. NICs can be add-in expansion cards, PCMCIA devices for laptops, or devices that are built into the system board. When you install NICs, you must observe ESD best practices and also pay attention to hardware compatibility and bus compatibility issues.

In addition to NICs used to connect to a LAN, ISDN terminal adapters are sometimes used for remote connectivity.

When you're using clustering, a special system-area NIC is applied to network interfaces used to communicate clustering information between servers.

On a network, each NIC is identified by a unique MAC address. MAC addresses are assigned by the manufacturers that produce the devices, although the high-level assignment of addresses is managed and carried out by the IEEE.

If you get a chance to use all the hardware devices discussed in this chapter, count yourself lucky. Almost every environment will use some of them, but very few use them all.

KEY TERMS

- store-and-forward
- fragment-free
- MDI
- MDI-X
- uplink port
- rack mounting
- 80/20 rule
- STA
- STP
- transparent bridge
- translational bridge
- source-route bridge
- TCP/IP
- IPX/SPX
- multiprotocol routing
- distance-vector protocols
- split horizon
- split horizon with poison reverse
- RIP
- link-state protocol
- AT modem commands
- UART chips

APPLY YOUR KNOWLEDGE

Exercises

3.1   Determining MAC Addresses for Network Cards

This chapter identifies the characteristics and functions of network devices. In an ideal world, this project would require hands-on experience with these devices, but this is not an ideal world, and access to this equipment is not always easy. Therefore, we will include two exercises that you might be required to perform if such devices are used on your network.

This project assumes that you are using Windows 2000.

Estimated time: 20 minutes

1. Open a command window by selecting Start, Run. In the command box, type **command** and then click OK.

2. At the command prompt, type **ipconfig /all**. The MAC address of your NIC is displayed in the Physical Address line.

3. Open a Web browser and go to the following Web site: http://standards.ieee.org/regauth/oui/oui.txt.

4. Using the Find functionality in your Web browser, locate the entry that corresponds with the address of your NIC. Is the manufacturer of your NIC the company you expected it to be? Some NIC manufacturers re-brand cards manufactured by another company. For that reason, the MAC address may correspond to a manufacturer that is different from the brand name of the card.

3.2   Using the tracert Utility to View the Path to an Internet Destination

One of the tools network administrators have at their disposal is the tracert utility. tracert allows you to see the hops a network packet takes to get to its destination. At each point along the way, the packet gives information about the route it is taking, along with details of the routers it crosses. More information on the tracert utility is provided in Chapter 13, "Troubleshooting Connectivity."

NOTE

Firewalls If you are using a system that is protected by a firewall system, this exercise might not work because firewalls are commonly configured to block tracert traffic.

In this exercise, you will use the tracert utility to view the path to an Internet destination. This project assumes that you are using Windows 2000.

Estimated time: 5 minutes

1. Open a command window by selecting Start, Run. In the command box, type **cmd.exe** and then click OK.

2. At the command prompt, type **tracert www.comptia.org**. The route to the CompTIA Web server is displayed.

3. How many hops are you from the destination?

Exam Questions

1. You have configured a 100Mbps network connection between your computer and the switch as half-duplex. What will be the maximum speed of the connection?

   a. 50Mbps

   b. 100Mbps

APPLY YOUR KNOWLEDGE

    c. 100MBps

    d. 200Mbps

2. You want to create a larger network by connecting two switches together. One of the switches has a port that can be switched from MDI to MDI-X as needed. The other switch doesn't have such a port or a dedicated uplink port. Which type of cable should you use, and how should you configure the switchable port to create the larger network?

    a. Use a straight-through cable and set the port to MDI

    b. Use a crossover cable and set the port to MDI-X

    c. Use a straight-through cable and set the port to MDI-X

    d. Use a crossover cable and set the port to MDI

3. Of the following, which represents a valid MAC address?

    a. 00:D0:59:09:07:51

    b. 000:D00:599:099:071:512

    c. 00:D0:59:09:07:51:C4:56

    d. 00:H0:59:09:07:51

4. A bridge makes forwarding decisions based on what information?

    a. IP address

    b. MAC address

    c. Binary address

    d. Frame address

5. What information does a switch use to determine the port to which data should be sent?

    a. The IP address of the connected device

    b. The priority of the connected device

    c. The MAC address of the connected device

    d. The Ethernet address of the connected device

6. Which of the following is a link-state routing protocol used on TCP/IP networks?

    a. RIP

    b. ARP

    c. OSPF

    d. NLSP

7. On a Windows 2000 system, what command would you use to view the MAC address?

    a. `ifconfig -a`

    b. `ipconfig /all`

    c. `ipconfig`

    d. `config /all`

8. What is the purpose of the uplink port on a hub or switch?

    a. It allows for satellite connections.

    b. It allows hubs or switches to be connected together.

    c. It allows computers to connect to the device.

    d. It provides a spare port, which can be used if another port fails.

APPLY YOUR KNOWLEDGE

9. By what method does a router determine the destination address for a packet?

    a. It looks at the MAC address of the sender.

    b. It looks for the MAC address of the destination.

    c. It looks for the software-configured network address for the destination.

    d. It looks at the FCS field of the packet.

10. Which of the following statements best describes split horizon?

    a. Routes are advertised back on the interface from which they were learned, with a metric of 16.

    b. Routes are advertised back on the interface from which they were learned, with a metric of 0.

    c. Routes are not advertised back on the interface from which they were learned.

    d. Routes are advertised back on the interface from which they were learned, with a metric of 16, and on all other interfaces they are advertised back on the interface from which they were learned, with a metric of 0.

11. In a network that uses distance-vector routing protocols, what information is included in the update that is sent out by each router?

    a. Details of the routers to which it is directly connected

    b. A map of the entire network, with hop counts valued from its current position

    c. Details of all the routers it knows about

    d. Details of its own configuration

12. What is the difference between an active hub and a passive hub?

    a. An active hub has management capabilities.

    b. An active hub forwards the data only to the ports that need it.

    c. An active hub channels bandwidth to a given connection if the connection becomes too slow.

    d. An active hub regenerates the signal before forwarding it.

13. What condition can arise if routers advertise a route back to the router from which it was learned?

    a. Count to infinity

    b. Road to nowhere

    c. Loop de loop

    d. Count to 16

14. What term is used by routers to describe each step necessary to reach a destination?

    a. Hop

    b. Jump

    c. Skip

    d. Leap

15. What is the maximum speed of a 16550 UART chip?

    a. 64,000bps

    b. 115,200bps

    c. 430,800bps

    d. 921,600bps

APPLY YOUR KNOWLEDGE

16. What is the name of the bridging method used to segregate Ethernet networks?

    a. Source-route

    b. Invisible

    c. Cut-through

    d. Transparent

17. Which of the following is a distance-vector routing protocol used on TCP/IP networks?

    a. ARP

    b. NLSP

    c. OSPF

    d. RIP

18. A CSU/DSU is used in which of the following network configurations?

    a. When converting from a Token Ring network to an Ethernet network

    b. When converting a digital signal to an analog signal

    c. When converting from the digital signals used on a LAN to the digital signals used on a WAN

    d. When converting from the digital signal format used on a LAN to the analog signal format used on a WAN

19. A router makes its forwarding decisions based on which of the following information?

    a. IP address

    b. ARP address

    c. Binary address

    d. Frame address

20. You are tasked with upgrading a new NIC in the company file and print server. Which of the following should you determine before buying a replacement card? (Choose the three best answers.)

    a. Bus compatibility

    b. Network compatibility

    c. Hardware compatibility

    d. Cooling requirements

Answers to Exam Questions

1. **b.** A half-duplex connection operates at the normal speed of the link. Thus, a 100Mbps network connection in a half-duplex configuration would operate at a maximum of 100Mbps. All the other answers are invalid. For more information, see the section "Working with Hubs and Switches," in this chapter.

2. **b.** Because one of the switches does not have MDI capability, the switchable port should be set to MDI-X. Then, a crossover cable should be used to cancel out the crossing between the two devices. None of the other options would result in a successful connection. For more information, see the section "Working with Hubs and Switches," in this chapter.

3. **a.** A MAC address comprises 6 bytes presented in a hexadecimal format. The letters A through F and numbers 0 through 9 are the only valid characters. Therefore, all the other answers provided are incorrect. For more information, see the section "Identifying MAC Addresses," in this chapter.

APPLY YOUR KNOWLEDGE

4. **b.** Bridges make forwarding decisions based on the destination MAC address embedded in each packet. Routers use software addresses, such as IP addresses, to make forwarding decisions. Answers c and d are not valid. For more information, see the section "Bridges," in this chapter.

5. **c.** A switch uses the MAC address of the connected device to determine the port to which data is forwarded. Routers use software addresses, such as IP addresses, to make forwarding decisions. Answer b is not valid. Although there are many addressing schemes used on networks, *Ethernet address* is not a valid term. Therefore, Answer d is incorrect. For more information, see the section "Switches," in this chapter.

6. **c.** OSPF is a link-state routing protocol used on TCP/IP networks. RIP is a distance-vector routing protocol used on both TCP/IP and IPX/SPX networks, ARP is a component of the TCP/IP protocol suite. NLSP is a link-state routing protocol used on IPX/SPX networks. For more information, see the section "Routers," in this chapter.

7. **b.** The ipconfig /all command shows a range of network-related information, including the MAC addresses of any installed NICs. None of the other answers are valid. For more information, see the section "Identifying MAC Addresses," in this chapter.

8. **b.** The uplink port can be used to connect hubs and switches together, using a standard twisted-pair cable. All the other answers are invalid. For more information, see the section "Working with Hubs and Switches," in this chapter.

9. **c.** Routers use the software-configured network address to make routing decisions. Bridges use MAC addresses to make decisions. Answer d is not valid. The FCS (that is, frame checksum) field is used for error detection. For more information, see the section "Routers," in this chapter.

10. **c.** Split horizon is a routing algorithm which dictates that routes are not advertised back on the interface from which they were learned. Answer a describes the operation of the split horizon with poison reverse algorithm. None of the other answers are valid. For more information, see the section "Routers," in this chapter.

11. **c.** In a network that uses distance-vector routing protocols, routers advertise details of the routers they know about. These updates are sent to all the neighbor routers. Answer a describes the actions on a link-state-based network. Answers b and d are invalid. For more information, see the section "Routers," in this chapter.

12. **d.** An active hub regenerates the data signal before forwarding it to all connected devices. Active hubs come in both managed and unmanaged varieties. Answer b describes the action of a switch. Answer c is invalid. For more information, see the section "Hubs," in this chapter.

13. **a.** A count to infinity occurs when two routers provide information on the same destination and so create a routing loop. All the other answers are invalid. For more information, see the section "Routers" in this chapter.

14. **a.** Each step in the path between a router and its destination is called a hop. The other terms are not used in networking. For more information, see the section "Routers," in this chapter.

15. **b.** A 16550 UART chip is capable of speeds up to 115,200bps. None of the other answers are valid. For more information, see the section "Modems," in this chapter.

APPLY YOUR KNOWLEDGE

16. **d.** The bridging method used on Ethernet networks is called *transparent* because the other network devices are unaware of the existence of the bridge. Source-route bridges are used on Token Ring networks, invisible is not a type of bridge, and cut-through is a switching method, not a type of bridge. For more information, see the section "Bridges," in this chapter.

17. **d.** RIP is a distance-vector routing protocol used on TCP/IP networks. ARP is a component of the TCP/IP protocol suite. NLSP is a link-state routing protocol used on IPX networks, and OSPF is a link-state routing protocol used on TCP/IP networks. For more information, see the section "Routers," in this chapter.

18. **c.** CSUs/DSUs are used to convert the digital signals used on a LAN to the digital signals used on a WAN. The process described in Answer a would be performed by a gateway, and the process described in Answer b would be performed by a modem. Answer d is not valid because WANs commonly use digital signals. For more information, see the section "CSU/DSU," in this chapter.

19. **a.** Routers make routing decisions based on the software-configured network address, which is protocol dependent. There is no such thing as an ARP address. Answers c and d are invalid. For more information, see the section "Routers," in this chapter.

20. **a, b, c.** You should verify bus compatibility, network compatibility, and hardware compatibility before you buy a new NIC. You do not typically need to concern yourself with cooling requirements of a component. For more information, see the section "Network Interface Cards (NICs)," in this chapter.

Suggested Readings and Resources

1. Sloan, Joseph D. *Network Troubleshooting Tools (O'Reilly System Administration)*. O'Reilly & Associates, 2001.

2. Habraken, Joe. *Absolute Beginner's Guide to Networking,* third edition. Que Publishing, 2001.

3. Haugdahl, J. Scott. *Network Analysis and Troubleshooting.* Addison-Wesley, 2000.

4. Cisco Systems, Inc. *Internetworking Troubleshooting Handbook,* second edition. Cisco Press, 2001.

5. Computer networking products and information, www.alliedtelesyn.com.

6. Computer networking device information, www.3com.com.

7. "Computer Networking Tutorials and Advice," compnetworking.about.com.

8. "TechEncyclopedia," www.techencyclopedia.com.

9. "Networking Technology Information from Cisco," www.cisco.com/public/products_tech.shtml.

10. "Network Cabling Help," www.datacottage.com.

This chapter covers the following CompTIA-specified objectives for the "Protocols and Standards" section of the Network+ exam:

Identify the seven layers of the OSI model and their functions.

▶ The OSI reference model provides a theoretical framework that is used to describe the processes and technologies associated with networking.

Identify the OSI layers at which various network components operate including:

- **Hubs**
- **Switches**
- **Bridges**
- **Routers**
- **Network interface cards (NICs)**

▶ Understanding how devices' functions relate to the OSI model can provide a greater understanding of networking principles.

CHAPTER 4

The OSI Model

OUTLINE

Introduction	**151**
Why Do We Need a Network Model?	**151**
OSI Reference Model 101	**151**
Layer 1: The Physical Layer	153
Layer 2: The Data-Link Layer	153
Layer 3: The Network Layer	154
Switching Methods	155
Network-Layer Addressing	156
Layer 4: The Transport Layer	157
Connection-Oriented Protocols	158
Connectionless Protocols	158
Flow Control	158
Layer 5: The Session Layer	159
Layer 6: The Presentation Layer	159
Layer 7: The Application Layer	160
OSI Model Summary	161
The Layers at Which Devices Operate	**162**
Hubs	162
Switches	162
Bridges	163
Routers	163
NICs	163
Summary of the Layers at Which Devices Operate	164
Chapter Summary	**164**
Apply Your Knowledge	**166**

STUDY STATEGIES

- ▶ Read the objectives at the beginning of the chapter.
- ▶ Study the information in the chapter, paying special attention to the tables, which summarize key information.
- ▶ Review the objectives again.
- ▶ Answer the exam questions at the end of the chapter and check your results.
- ▶ Use the ExamGear test on the CD-ROM that accompanies this book to answer additional exam questions concerning this material.
- ▶ Review the notes and exam tips in this chapter. Make sure you understand the information in the exam tips. If you don't understand the topic referenced in an exam tip, refer to the information in the chapter text and then read the exam tip again.

INTRODUCTION

One of the most important networking concepts to understand is the Open Systems Interconnect (OSI) reference model. This conceptual model, created by the International Organization for Standardization (ISO) in 1978 and revised in 1984, describes a network architecture that allows data to be passed between computer systems.

This chapter takes a detailed look at the OSI model and describes how it relates to real-world networking. It also examines how common network devices relate to the OSI model.

WHY DO WE NEED A NETWORK MODEL?

Because we are about to spend some of your valuable time discussing a theoretical model, it is only reasonable that we first discuss why we have such a model in the first place and how it can help us.

In simple terms, the OSI model provides a structure that helps us work with networks. By relating services and devices to a certain layer of the model, you can get a better idea of their function and purpose. For example, recall from Chapter 3, "Networking Components and Devices," that switches use the Media Access Control (MAC) address of the attached devices to make forwarding decisions. In the OSI model, MAC addresses are defined in the MAC sublayer of the data-link layer (Layer 2). If you knew that a bridge was also a data-link-layer device, you could quite reasonably draw the conclusion that it, too, works with MAC addresses—and you would be right. This example is perhaps one of the simplest that we could have used, but it serves the purpose well: It shows how the theoretical model can be translated into actual scenarios.

OSI REFERENCE MODEL 101

▶ Identify the seven layers of the OSI model and their functions.

| 7 - Application |
| 6 - Presentation |
| 5 - Session |
| 4 - Transport |
| 3 - Network |
| 2 - Data-link |
| 1 - Physical |

FIGURE 4.1
The OSI reference model.

FIGURE 4.2
How data travels between two devices.

The OSI model consists of seven layers, which is why it is sometimes called the OSI seven-layer model. In diagram form, as shown in Figure 4.1, the model is drawn from bottom to top in the following order: physical, data-link, network, transport, session, presentation, and application layers. The physical layer is classified as Layer 1, and the application layer is classified as Layer 7. In many cases, devices are referred to in relationship to the numbered layers at which they operate. For example, a router is said to be a Layer 3 (network layer) device.

The model is used to relate the transport of data from one host to another. If the data were being sent from an application, such as a Web browser, to a Web server, it would travel down through all the layers on the sending device, across the network media, and up through all the layers on the receiving device. Figure 4.2 shows a representation of how this works.

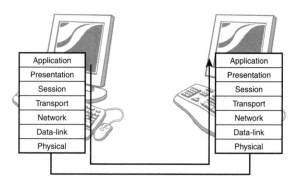

As data is passed up or down through the OSI model structure, headers are added (going down) or removed (going up) at each layer—a process called *encapsulation* (addition) or *decapsualtion* (removal). Figure 4.3 shows how this works.

The information added by each device at the sending end is removed by the corresponding layer at the receiving end. Each layer defines a certain aspect of the communication process, and as data travels up and down the model, the information is sorted into logical groups of bits. The exact term used to refer to the logical group of bits depends on the layer. Table 4.1 contains the terminology used at each layer of the OSI model.

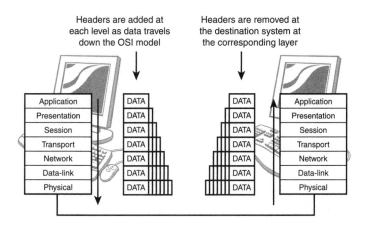

FIGURE 4.3
Encapsulation and decapsulation.

TABLE 4.1

TERMINOLOGY USED FOR LOGICAL GROUPS OF BITS AT THE LAYERS OF THE OSI MODEL

Layer	Terms Used
Application	Packets and messages
Presentation	Packets
Session	Packets
Transport	Packets, segments, and datagrams
Network	Packets and Datagrams
Data-link	Packets and frames
Physical	Packets and bits

As you can see, at every layer the term *packet* is used, and in some cases, other terms are used as well. Each layer of the OSI model defines specific functionality. The following sections look at each of the layers separately and discuss the function of each.

Layer 1: The Physical Layer

The physical layer (sometimes referred to incorrectly as the hardware layer) is the layer of the OSI model that defines the physical characteristics of the network. The physical characteristics can include the cable and connector type, the format for pinouts for cables, and so on. It also defines how the data actually travels across the network.

N O T E

OSI Numbering   Some discussions of the OSI model examine it from top to bottom, and others examine it in reverse. Both methods are valid, but remember that the numbering starts from the bottom and works up. Therefore, it seems most logical to us to explain the model starting at Layer 1 and working up.

The physical layer also defines the voltage that is used on the cable and the frequency at which the signals that carry the data are transitioned from one state to another. Such characteristics directly affect the speed (bandwidth) of a given media as well as the maximum distance over which a certain media type can be used.

Because the physical layer defines the physical connection to the network, it also defines the physical topology of the network. Recall that there are a number of common physical topologies, including star, ring, bus, mesh, and hybrid, with star being the most common.

Various standards are defined at the physical layer—for example, the Institute of Electrical and Electronics Engineers (IEEE) 802.3 Ethernet standard and the 802.5 Token Ring standard. If you think about it, this is very reasonable: An Ethernet network card has different physical characteristics than a Token Ring network card. However, you should know that some of these standards overlap more than one layer of the OSI model. For example, the Ethernet standard also defines the media access method, which is a function of the data-link layer.

Layer 2: The Data-Link Layer

The data-link layer is responsible for sending data to the physical layer so that it can be transmitted across the network. The data-link layer can perform *checksums* and *error detection* on the data to make sure that the data that was sent is the same as the data that is received.

The data-link layer is different from the other layers of the OSI model because it has two distinct sublayers—the Logical Link Control (LLC) sublayer and the Media Access Control (MAC) sublayer. Each has a very specific role:

◆ **LLC**—The LLC sublayer, which is defined by the IEEE 802.2 standard, controls the access of the media, allowing multiple high-level protocols to use a single network link.

◆ **MAC**—The MAC sublayer manages and controls access to the network media for the protocols that are trying to use it. The MAC address is defined at this layer.

As discussed in Chapter 1, "Introduction to Networking," there is a difference between the physical topology (how a network looks) and the logical topology (how the network works). Whereas the physical layer sees it from a physical topology perspective, the data-link layer sees the network from a logical topology perspective.

Layer 3: The Network Layer

The network layer of the OSI model is primarily concerned with providing a mechanism by which data can be moved between two networks or systems. The network layer does not define how the data is moved; rather, it is concerned with providing the mechanism that can be used for that purpose. The mechanisms that can be used include defining network addressing and conducting route discovery and maintenance.

When a system attempts to communicate with another device on the network, network-layer protocols attempt to identify that device on the network. When the target system has been identified, it is then necessary to identify the service that is to be accessed. This is achieved by using a *service identifier.* On Transmission Control Protocol/Internet Protocol (TCP/IP) networks, service identifiers are commonly referred to as *ports,* and on Internetwork Packet Exchange/Sequenced Packet Exchange (IPX/SPX) networks they are called *sockets,* although technically the terms can be used interchangeably.

Switching Methods

An important concept related to the network layer is switching methods. The switching method describes how the data sent from one node reaches another. Three types of switching are used on networks:

EXAM TIP

Know the Switching Methods   Be prepared to identify switching methods on the Network+ exam.

◆ **Circuit switching**—The best example of circuit switching is a telephone call. The link between caller and receiver is created, after which there is a dedicated communications link between the two points (hence the term *circuit*). The circuit cannot be broken, which is good because it means that no one else can use the line. In a data communications environment, however, this is a disadvantage because the data often originates from various sources.

◆ **Message switching**—In a message-switching environment, transmissions are broken down into messages that can traverse the network by the fastest means available. It might be that all messages travel over the same path or it might be that messages travel on different paths. At each point in the journey, the message is stored by a node before it is forwarded to the next hop on the journey. Such a mechanism gives rise to the phrase *store and forward.* The message-switching system works well in environments in which the amount of data being moved around varies at different times, but it also causes problems such as where to store the data before it is forwarded.

◆ **Packet switching**—Although both circuit switching and message switching can get the job done, both have some serious drawbacks that make them unsuitable for use in a modern network environment. Today, most networks use packet switching, which includes the good points of both circuit and message switching and does not include the bad points. In a packet-switched network, data is broken down into packets that can then be transported around the network. Most modern networks use packet switching as the switching method.

> **NOTE**
>
> **More on Switching** A more comprehensive discussion of switching methods, in particular how they relate to wide area networks, is included in Chapter 7, "WAN Technologies."

Network-Layer Addressing

From a network administrator's perspective, one of the most important aspects of the network layer is addressing. Network addresses allow a system to be identified on the network by a *logically assigned address.* This is in contrast to the physically assigned MAC addresses used on the data-link layer. The logical assignment of addresses means that schemes can be created that allow a more hierarchical approach to addressing than MAC addresses provide. By using a hierarchy, it is possible to assign a certain address to logical groups of systems as well as to the systems themselves. The result is that network addressing can be used to create portions of the network called *subnets.*

Hierarchical addressing systems are possible only with *routable* network protocols. The most common routable protocol in use today is TCP/IP, although IPX/SPX can still be found on many networks. Other routable protocols, such as AppleTalk, have all but been replaced with TCP/IP.

Of course, you don't have to use a routable protocol. Other non-routable protocols, such as NetBEUI, can be used, although they are of limited use in today's modern networking environments, where routable protocols are the order of the day. A more detailed discussion of networking protocols is included in Chapter 5, "Overview of Network Protocols."

Another function of the network layer is *route selection,* which refers to determining the best path for the data to take throughout the network. Recall from Chapter 3 that there are two ways in which routes can be configured: *statically* and *dynamically.* In a static routing environment, the network administrator must manually add routes to the routing tables. In a dynamic routing environment, routing protocols such as Routing Information Protocol (RIP) and Open Shortest Path First (OSPF) are used. These protocols work by automatically communicating routing information between devices on the network.

Layer 4: The Transport Layer

The basic function of the transport layer is, as its name suggests, to transport data from one host to another. The transport layer handles the actual processing of data between devices. This includes functions such as segmenting data so that it can be sent over the network and then reassembling the segmented data on the receiving end. The transport layer also deals with some of the errors that can occur in a stream of data, such as dropped and duplicated packets. In addition, the transport layer deals with some of the problems that can be produced by the fragmentation and reassembly process performed by the network layer.

The protocols that operate at the transport layer are those that are directly concerned with the transporting of data across the network. The following are some of the most commonly used transport-layer protocols:

◆ **TCP**—Part of the TCP/IP protocol suite, TCP provides a connection-oriented transport mechanism.

◆ **User Datagram Protocol (UDP)**—Part of the TCP/IP protocol suite, UDP provides a connectionless transport mechanism.

◆ **IPX**—Part of Novell's IPX/SPX protocol suite, IPX provides a connectionless transport mechanism

◆ **SPX**—Part of Novell's IPX/SPX protocol suite, SPX provides a connection-oriented transport mechanism.

Connection-Oriented Protocols

As you can see from the descriptions of the protocols in the preceding section, some are connection oriented and others are connectionless. In a connection-oriented session, the communication dialog between two systems is established, maintained, and then broken when the communication is complete. In technical jargon, this is often referred to as the *setting up* and *tearing down* of a session. While we are on the subject of sessions, we should make something clear: The session layer is also responsible for setting up, maintaining, and closing sessions with other hosts, but it does so at the application level rather than the network level. TCP and other transport-layer protocols maintain the sessions at the network level.

Connection-oriented protocols, such as TCP, enable the delivery of data to be guaranteed because the receipt of each packet that is sent must be acknowledged by the receiving system. Any packet that is not received is re-sent. This makes for a very reliable communication system, though the additional steps necessary to guarantee delivery mean that connection-oriented protocols have higher overhead than do connectionless protocols.

> **EXAM TIP**
>
> **Connection-Oriented Protocols** Connection-oriented protocols are able to accommodate lost or dropped packets by asking the sending device to retransmit. You should note this for the exam.

Connectionless Protocols

In contrast to connection-oriented communication, connectionless protocols offer only a *best-effort* delivery mechanism. A connectionless communication is a "fire and forget" mechanism in which data is sent but no acknowledgments of receipt are sent. This mechanism has a far lower overhead than the connection-oriented method, and it places the onus of ensuring complete delivery on a higher layer, such as the session layer.

> **EXAM TIP**
>
> **Know the Protocols** Be prepared to identify both connection-oriented and connectionless protocols on the Network+ exam.

Flow Control

Flow control also occurs at the transport layer. As the name suggests, flow control deals with the acceptance of data. It controls the data flow in such a way that the receiving system is able to accept the data at an adequate rate. Two methods of flow control are commonly used:

◆ **Buffering**—In a buffering system, data is stored in a holding area and waits for the destination device to become available. A system that uses this strategy encounters problems if the sending device is able to send data much faster than the receiving device is able to accept it.

◆ **Windowing**—Windowing is a more sophisticated approach to flow control than buffering. In a windowing environment, data is sent in groups of segments that require only one acknowledgment. The size of the window (that is, how many segments can be sent for one acknowledgment) is defined at the time the session between the two devices is established. As you can imagine, the need to have only one acknowledgment for every, say, five segments can greatly reduce overhead.

Layer 5: The Session Layer

The session layer is responsible for managing and controlling the synchronization of data between applications on two devices. It does this by establishing, maintaining, and breaking sessions. Whereas the transport layer is responsible for setting up and maintaining the connection between the two devices, the session layer performs much the same function on behalf of the application.

> **EXAM TIP**
>
> **About the OSI Layers** The Network+ exam touches very lightly on the upper layers of the OSI model; therefore, only a very basic explanation of them is provided here.

Layer 6: The Presentation Layer

The presentation layer's basic function is to convert the data intended for or received from the application layer into another format. Such conversion is necessary because the way in which data is formatted so it can be transported across the network is not necessarily readable by applications. Some common data formats handled by the presentation layer include the following:

◆ **Graphics files**—JPEG, TIFF, GIF, and so on are graphics file formats that require the data be formatted in a certain way.

◆ **Text and data**—The presentation layer is able to translate data into different formats such as American Standard Code for Information Interchange (ASCII) and Extended Binary Code Decimal Interchange Code (EBCDIC).

◆ **Sound/video**—MPEGs, QuickTime video, and MIDI files all have their own data formats to and from which data must be converted.

Another very important function of the presentation layer is encryption. *Encryption* is the scrambling of data so that it cannot be read by anything or anyone other than the intended destination. Data encryption is performed at the sending system, and *decryption* (that is, the unscrambling of data at the receiving end) is performed at the destination. Given the basic role of the presentation layer—that of data format translator—it is the obvious place for encryption and decryption to take place.

Layer 7: The Application Layer

The most common misconception about the application layer, the topmost layer of the OSI model, is that it represents applications that are used on a system such as a word processor or a spreadsheet. This is not correct. Instead, the application layer defines the processes that allow applications to use network services. For example, if an application needs to open a file from a network drive, the functionality is provided by components that reside at the application layer. However, some applications, such as email clients and Web browsers, do in fact reside at the application layer.

In simple terms, the function of the application layer is to take requests and data from the user and pass them to the lower layers of the OSI model. Incoming information is passed to the application layer, which then displays the information to the user. Some of the most basic application-layer services include file and print capabilities.

OSI Model Summary

Now that we have discussed the functions of each layer of the OSI model, it's time for a quick review. Table 4.2 lists the seven layers of the OSI model and describes some of the most significant points of each layer.

TABLE 4.2
OSI MODEL SUMMARY

REVIEW BREAK

EXAM TIP

Know Table 4.2 For the Network+ exam, as well as for your real-world experience, the information supplied in Table 4.2 should be sufficient.

OSI Layer	Major Functions
Application	Provides access to the network for applications and certain end user functions.
	Displays incoming information and prepares outgoing information for network access.
Presentation	Converts data from the application layer into a format that can be sent over the network.
	Converts data from the session layer into a format that can be understood by the application layer.
	Handles encryption and decryption of data. Provides compression and decompression functionality.
Session	Synchronizes the data exchange between applications on separate devices.
	Handles error detection and notification to the peer layer on the other device.
Transport	Establishes, maintains, and breaks connections between two devices.
	Determines the ordering and priorities of data.
	Performs error checking and verification and handles retransmissions if necessary.
Network	Provides mechanisms for the routing of data between devices across single or multiple network segments.
	Handles the discovery of destination systems and addressing.
Data-link	Has two distinct sublayers: LLC and MAC.
	Performs error detection and handling for the transmitted signals.
	Defines the method by which the media is accessed.
	Defines hardware addressing through the MAC sublayer.
Physical	Defines the physical structure of the network.
	Defines voltage/signal rates and the physical connection methods.
	Defines the physical topology.

THE LAYERS AT WHICH DEVICES OPERATE

▶ Identify the OSI layers at which various network components operate including:

- Hubs
- Switches
- Bridges
- Routers
- Network interface cards (NICs)

Now that we have examined the OSI network layer in some detail, we can look at how it relates to the network connectivity devices discussed in Chapter 3: hubs, switches, bridges, routers, and network interface cards (NICs). These devices are said to operate at certain layers of the OSI model based on their functions and roles in the network. Because these devices are covered in Chapter 3, this chapter does not describe them in detail. Instead, this chapter contains a brief description of each device, to jog your memory.

Hubs

Hubs act as the connectivity points of the network on systems that use twisted-pair cabling. There are two types of hubs: active and passive. Each performs the same basic function; they both provide a pathway along which the electrical signals that carry the data can travel. The difference between the two types of hubs is that an active hub has power and a passive hub does not. Even an active hub does nothing with a signal except regenerate it. Therefore, it is said to be a physical-layer device. Recall that the physical layer deals with placing signals on the media.

Switches

In Chapter 3 you learned that, like hubs, switches act as the connectivity points of the network on systems that use twisted-pair cable.

You also learned that a switch offers performance benefits over a hub because it forwards data only to the port on which the destination device is connected. This has the benefit of reducing network traffic because data isn't forwarded to all the ports on a switch. The switch does this by examining the MAC address of the devices connected to it. The use of the MAC address as an identifier places the switch at Layer 2 of the OSI model. Therefore, it is a data-link-layer device.

EXAM TIP

Layer 3 Switches and Layer 4 Switches For the Network+ exam you should consider switches as Layer 2 devices. In the real world, devices that are called Layer 3 switches and Layer 4 switches are available. These devices "switch" data but do so using other mechanisms.

Bridges

Bridges are used to divide a network into smaller areas through a process known as *segmentation*. Then, by learning which devices are located on which interface, a bridge is able to block or forward traffic between the interfaces. It does this by using the MAC address of the attached devices. The use of the MAC address makes a bridge a Layer 2 (that is, data-link-layer) device.

Routers

Routers are more complex and more functional than either bridges or switches because they are used to connect networks together and then manage the flow of data between the networks. Unlike switches and bridges, routers use software-configured logical network addresses. Because the routing function is implemented at the network layer of the OSI model, routers are referred to as Layer 3 devices.

NOTE

Brouters Chapter 2, "Cabling and Connectors," briefly discusses a device called a brouter. A brouter can route data that can be routed or bridge data that cannot be routed. Such a device is said to be both a Layer 2 device and a Layer 3 device.

NICs

A NIC provides the physical connectivity point to the network for a computer system. But although NICs are physical components, they are defined as data-link-layer devices because they are used in physical media access (which is handled at the MAC sublayer) and the logical access of the network media (which is handled at the LLC sublayer).

Know Where a Device Operates
In the Network+ exam you might be
asked to identify the layer at which
a given device operates.

Summary of the Layers at Which Devices Operate

Table 4.3 summarizes the devices discussed in the previous sections
and the corresponding layers at which they operate.

TABLE 4.3
THE OSI MODEL LAYERS AT WHICH VARIOUS DEVICES OPERATE

Device	OSI Layer at Which the Device Operates
Hub	Physical (Layer 1)
Switch	Data-link (Layer 2)
Bridge	Data-link (Layer 2)
Router	Network (Layer 3)
NIC	Data-link (Layer 2)

CHAPTER SUMMARY

KEY TERMS

- encapsulation
- OSI
- physical layer
- data-link layer
- network layer
- transport layer
- session layer

The OSI model is a conceptual model that defines seven layers.
Each of these layers performs a specific function that plays an
important part in the end-to-end communication between two
devices. The model allows us to relate the function of a certain protocol or service to a specific function of the model. For example, IP
is responsible for the discovery and establishment of routes through
the network. Therefore, it is reasonable to assume that IP is a
network-layer protocol because such functions are performed at the
network layer. The ability to draw parallels like this can be a useful
aid to understanding networking from both conceptual and practical
levels.

CHAPTER SUMMARY

Because the OSI model defines the functions that are performed at various layers, it can be said that network devices operate at certain layers of the OSI model. The layer at which a device operates is defined by the function of the device and the information the device uses to complete its task. Of the commonly used network devices, hubs operate at the physical layer; network cards, bridges, and switches operate at the data-link layer; and routers operate at the network layer.

Understanding the OSI model is important for networking. Even though it can sometimes be difficult to see how the OSI model is relevant in day-to-day tasks, it helps to reinforce networking theory and provides a framework in which to work.

KEY TERMS

- presentation layer
- application layer
- LLC
- MAC
- circuit switching
- packet switching
- message switching
- static routing
- dynamic routing
- TCP
- UDP
- SPX
- connectionless protocols
- connection-oriented protocols
- buffering
- windowing
- segmentation

APPLY YOUR KNOWLEDGE

Exercises

4.1   Identifying OSI Layers

Developing a real-world project in a chapter focusing on the OSI model is almost an impossible task. For the Network+ exam, you will need to be able to identify the various layers of the OSI model and the network devices that correspond to each level. With that in mind, in lieu of a hands-on project, this chapter provides a practical exercise to reinforce the concepts discussed in this chapter. Your ability to correctly complete this exercise will show sufficient knowledge of the OSI model to get you through any questions on it in the exam.

Estimated time: 10 minutes

1. Refer to the worksheet below and identify two functions for each layer of the OSI model.

2. Check your responses against the information in Table 4.2.

```
    ┌─────────────────────────────────────┐
    │ Layer Name _____ │
  7 │ Purpose/Function _____ │
    │ Purpose/Function _____ │
    └─────────────────────────────────────┘
    ┌─────────────────────────────────────┐
    │ Layer Name _____ │
  6 │ Purpose/Function _____ │
    │ Purpose/Function _____ │
    └─────────────────────────────────────┘
    ┌─────────────────────────────────────┐
    │ Layer Name _____ │
  5 │ Purpose/Function _____ │
    │ Purpose/Function _____ │
    └─────────────────────────────────────┘
    ┌─────────────────────────────────────┐
    │ Layer Name _____ │
  4 │ Purpose/Function _____ │
    │ Purpose/Function _____ │
    └─────────────────────────────────────┘
    ┌─────────────────────────────────────┐
    │ Layer Name _____ │
  3 │ Purpose/Function _____ │
    │ Purpose/Function _____ │
    └─────────────────────────────────────┘
    ┌─────────────────────────────────────┐
    │ Layer Name _____ │
  2 │ Purpose/Function _____ │
    │ Purpose/Function _____ │
    └─────────────────────────────────────┘
    ┌─────────────────────────────────────┐
    │ Layer Name _____ │
  1 │ Purpose/Function _____ │
    │ Purpose/Function _____ │
    └─────────────────────────────────────┘
```

FIGURE 4.4
A hands-on OSI model project.

Exam Questions

1. At which layer of the OSI model does a switch operate?

   a. Physical

   b. Data-link

   c. Network

   d. Session

2. Which of the following devices operate at Layer 2 of the OSI model? (Choose the three best answers.)

   a. Switch

   b. Network card

   c. Hub

   d. Bridge

APPLY YOUR KNOWLEDGE

3. Which layer of the OSI model is responsible for synchronizing the exchange of data between two devices at the application level?

   a. Transport

   b. Session

   c. Presentation

   d. Data-link

4. Which of the following transport-layer protocols offer guaranteed delivery? (Choose the two best answers.)

   a. SPX

   b. UDP

   c. IPX

   d. TCP

5. Which layer of the OSI model is responsible for route discovery?

   a. Session

   b. Data-link

   c. Network

   d. Transport

6. What are the two sublayers of the data-link layer?

   a. Logical link control

   b. Logical loop control

   c. Media access control

   d. Multiple access control

7. Which of the following are responsibilities of the transport layer? (Choose the two best answers.)

   a. Performs error detection and handling for the transmitted signals

   b. Synchronizes data exchange between two applications

   c. Performs error checking and verification

   d. Establishes, maintains, and breaks connections between devices

8. Which layer of the OSI model defines the method by which the network media are accessed on a logical level?

   a. Data-link

   b. Physical

   c. Session

   d. Presentation

9. At which layer of the OSI model does a hub operate?

   a. Application

   b. Network

   c. Physical

   d. Data-link

10. Which of the following terms is *not* used to describe a logical grouping of bits?

    a. Datagram

    b. Segment

    c. Package

    d. Packet

11. Which layer of the OSI model defines the signal rates and voltages that are used?

    a. Data-link

    b. Physical

    c. Session

    d. Presentation

APPLY YOUR KNOWLEDGE

12. At which layer of the OSI model does a bridge operate?

    a. Physical

    b. Data-link

    c. Network

    d. Transport

13. At which layer of the OSI model does an NIC operate?

    a. Physical

    b. Data-link

    c. Network

    d. Transport

14. At which layer of the OSI model do encryption and decryption take place?

    a. Physical

    b. Session

    c. Application

    d. Presentation

15. Which of the following are commonly used flow control strategies? (Choose the two best answers.)

    a. Buffering

    b. Segmentation

    c. Windowing

    d. Direct flow management

16. You have been called in to troubleshoot a 10Base2 network that is experiencing problems. After performing some tests, you determine that the problem lies with one of the terminators on the network. At which layer of the OSI model does the problem exist?

    a. Physical

    b. Data-link

    c. Network

    d. Session

17. Which of the following OSI layers is responsible for establishing connections between two devices?

    a. Session

    b. Network

    c. Transport

    d. Data-link

18. At which layer do the protocols that handle route discovery reside?

    a. Transport

    b. Network

    c. Session

    d. Application

19. At the transport layer, two types of protocols are used for sending data to a remote system. What terms are used to describe these protocols? (Choose the two best answers.)

    a. Connection oriented

    b. Connection reliant

    c. Connection dependent

    d. Connectionless

20. At which layer of the OSI model does a router operate?

    a. Application

    b. Session

APPLY YOUR KNOWLEDGE

c. Network

d. Transport

Answers to Exam Questions

1. **b.** A switch uses the MAC addresses of connected devices to make forwarding decisions and therefore operates at the data-link layer of the OSI model. None of the other answers apply. For more information, see the section "The Layers at Which Devices Operate," in this chapter.

2. **a, b, d.** Switches, bridges, and NICs operate at the data-link layer of the OSI model, which is also known as Layer 2. A hub is defined as a physical-layer (that is, Layer 1) device. For more information, see the section "The Layers at Which Devices Operate," in this chapter.

3. **b.** The synchronization of data between applications is performed at the session layer of the OSI model. None of the other answers apply. For more information, see the section "OSI Reference Model 101," in this chapter.

4. **a, d.** Both SPX and TCP are connection-oriented protocols that offer guaranteed delivery of data. UDP and IPX are both connectionless protocols. For more information, see the section "OSI Reference Model 101," in this chapter.

5. **c.** Route discovery is performed by protocols that operate at the network layer of the OSI model. None of the other answers are valid. For more information, see the section "OSI Reference Model 101," in this chapter.

6. **a, c.** The data-link layer of the OSI model is divided into two distinct sublayers: the LLC sublayer and the MAC sublayer. None of the other answers are valid. For more information, see the section "OSI Reference Model 101," in this chapter.

7. **c, d.** The network layer is responsible for, among other things, performing error checking and verification, and establishing, maintaining, and breaking connections between devices. None of the other answers are valid. For more information, see the section "OSI Reference Model 101," in this chapter.

8. **a.** Standards at the data-link layer define how the network is accessed on a logical level. You should not confuse the function of the data-link layer with that of the physical layer, which performs similar functions but at a physical rather than a logical level. For more information, see the section "OSI Reference Model 101," in this chapter.

9. **c.** A hub operates at the physical layer of the OSI model. None of the other answers are valid. For more information, see the section "The Layers at Which Devices Operate," in this chapter.

10. **c.** The term *package* is not valid when referring to a logical grouping of bits. All the other answers are valid terms. For more information, see the section "OSI Reference Model 101," in this chapter.

11. **b.** The physical layer of the OSI model defines the physical characteristics of the network, including voltages and signaling rates. None of the other answers are valid. For more information, see the section "OSI Reference Model 101," in this chapter.

12. **b.** Bridges use the MAC addresses of devices to make forwarding decisions. Therefore, they are classified as data-link-layer devices. None of the

APPLY YOUR KNOWLEDGE

other answers are valid. For more information, see the section "The Layers at Which Devices Operate," in this chapter.

13. **b.** NICs operate at the data-link layer of the OSI model. None of the other answers are valid. For more information, see the section "The Layers at Which Devices Operate," in this chapter.

14. **d.** Encryption is a function that takes place at the presentation layer of the OSI model. None of the other answers are valid. For more information, see the section "OSI Reference Model 101," in this chapter.

15. **a, c.** Windowing and buffering are commonly used flow control strategies. *Segmentation* is the term used to describe the division of packets to enable them to be transported across the network. Answer d is not valid. For more information, see the section "OSI Reference Model 101," in this chapter.

16. **a.** Cable and connectors are physical elements of the network, so they relate to the physical layer of the OSI model. None of the other answers are

valid. For more information, see the section "The Layers at Which Devices Operate," in this chapter.

17. **c.** The transport layer is responsible for establishing connections between two devices. None of the other answers are valid. For more information, see the section "OSI Reference Model 101," in this chapter.

18. **b.** Protocols at the network layer are responsible for route discovery. None of the other answers are valid. For more information, see the section "OSI Reference Model 101," in this chapter.

19. **a, d.** The two terms used to describe protocols at the transport layer are *connection oriented* and *connectionless*. The terms in Answers b and c are not valid. For more information, see the section "OSI Reference Model 101," in this chapter.

20. **c.** A router uses the logical network address to make decisions and is therefore a network-layer device. None of the other answers are valid. For more information, see the section "The Layers at Which Devices Operate," in this chapter.

Suggested Readings and Resources

1. Habraken, Joe. *Absolute Beginner's Guide to Networking,* third edition. Que Publishing, 2001.

2. Hallberg, Bruce A. *Networking: A Beginners Guide (Network Professional's Library).* Osborne McGraw-Hill, 2001.

3. "TechEncyclopedia," www.techencyclopedia.com.

4. "OSI Technical Information," www.cisco.com/univercd/cc/td/doc/cisintwk/ito_doc/osi_prot.htm.

5. "OSI Model Tutorial," www.itp-journals.com/search/t04124.htm.

6. Computer networking tutorials and advice, compnetworking.about.com.

This chapter covers the following CompTIA-specified objectives for the "Protocols and Standards" section of the Network+ exam:

Differentiate among the following protocols in terms of routing, addressing schemes, interoperability, and naming conventions:

- **TCP/IP**
- **IPX/SPX**
- **AppleTalk**
- **NetBEUI**

▶ For the Network+ exam, you will be expected to demonstrate an understanding of commonly used network protocols.

CHAPTER 5

Overview of Network Protocols

Introduction   **174**

Introduction to Protocols   **174**

The Function of Protocols   175
    Protocols from the Sending Device   176
    Protocols on the Receiving Device   176
Mapping Protocols to the OSI Model   177
    Application Protocols   177
    Transport Protocols   178
    Network Protocols   178

Transmission Control Protocol/Internet Protocol (TCP/IP)   **179**

A Brief History of TCP/IP   179
The TCP/IP Protocol Suite   180
TCP/IP Standards   180
TCP/IP Addressing   181
TCP/IP Interoperability   182
TCP/IP Naming   182
TCP/IP Routing Protocols   183
Mapping TCP/IP to the OSI Model   183

Internetwork Packet Exchange/ Sequenced Packet Exchange (IPX/SPX)   **183**

The IPX/SPX Protocol Suite   184
    Internetwork Packet Exchange (IPX)   184
    Sequenced Packet Exchange (SPX)   185

    Routing Information Protocol (RIP)   185
    NetWare Link State Protocol (NLSP)   185
    Service Advertising Protocol (SAP)   185
    NetWare Core Protocol (NCP)   185
IPX Addressing   186
Mapping IPX/SPX to the OSI Model   187
IPX/SPX Interoperability   187
IPX/SPX Naming   187

AppleTalk   **188**

AppleTalk Addressing   189
Mapping AppleTalk to the OSI Model   190
AppleTalk Interoperability   190
AppleTalk Routing   191
AppleTalk Naming   191

NetBEUI   **191**

Mapping NetBEUI to the OSI Model   191
NetBEUI Addressing   192

Protocol Overview and Comparison   **192**

Chapter Summary   **193**

Apply Your Knowledge   **195**

▶ Read the objectives at the beginning of the chapter.

▶ Study the information in this chapter, paying special attention to the tables, which summarize key information.

▶ Review the objectives again.

▶ Answer the exam questions at the end of the chapter and check your results.

▶ Use the ExamGear test on the CD-ROM that accompanies this book to answer additional exam questions concerning this material.

▶ Review the notes, tips, and exam tips in this chapter. Be sure you understand the information in the exam tips. If you don't understand the topic referenced in an exam tip, refer to the information in the chapter text and then read the exam tip again.

INTRODUCTION

In networks, as in every day life, rules and procedures govern communication. The rules and procedures that allow devices on a network to communicate with each other are referred to as *protocols*. Some protocols deal specifically with the process of transferring data from one system to another, and others are responsible for things like route discovery and providing client functionality.

This chapter identifies the protocols used on today's networks and the environments in which you are likely to see them. It also examines some of the characteristics of each protocol. Understanding these characteristics is very important for the Network+ exam.

NOTE

Protocols   The term *protocol* refers to any set of instructions that governs communication between two devices.

INTRODUCTION TO PROTOCOLS

▶ Differentiate among the following protocols in terms of routing, addressing schemes, interoperability, and naming conventions:

- TCP/IP
- IPX/SPX
- AppleTalk
- NetBEUI

When computers were restricted to standalone systems, there was little need for mechanisms to communicate between them. However, it wasn't long before the need to connect computers together for the purpose of sharing files and printers became a necessity. Establishing communication between network devices required more than a length of cabling; a method or a set of rules was needed to establish how systems would communicate. Protocols provide that method.

It would be nice if a single protocol facilitated communication between all devices, but this is not the case. A number of protocols can be used on a network, each of which has its own features, advantages, and disadvantages. What protocol you choose can have a significant impact on the functioning and performance of the network.

Protocols are grouped together into *protocol suites*. Each protocol suite defines a complete set of protocols that allow the devices to communicate. Within each protocol suite are a variety of different protocols, which can be broken down into three distinct categories:

◆ **Application protocols**—Application protocols deal with providing client functionality.

◆ **Transport protocols**—Transport protocols provide mechanisms for moving data around the network.

◆ **Network protocols**—Network protocols perform the underlying tasks that enable the movement of data.

Three main protocol suites are used today:

◆ **Transmission Control Protocol/Internet Protocol (TCP/IP)**—By far the most prevalent of all the protocols discussed in this chapter, the TCP/IP protocol suite is a comprehensive set of protocols, and versions of it are available for all common platforms.

◆ **Internetwork Packet Exchange/Sequenced Packet Exchange (IPX/SPX)**—Developed by Novell, IPX/SPX is a set of protocols originally designed for use on Novell networks. It is now less popular than it once was, due to the impact of TCP/IP.

◆ **AppleTalk**—Designed for use on networks that use Macintosh systems, AppleTalk is an advanced suite of protocols that provide high levels of functionality.

In addition to these protocol suites, certain other protocols, such as NetBIOS Extended User Interface (NetBEUI), are used on smaller networks. This chapter describes NetBEUI, but it mainly focuses on the three major suites.

The Function of Protocols

To get an idea of exactly how protocols facilitate communication between devices, let's look at the role protocols play at the sending and receiving computers. In the data communication process, the information that passes between computers on a network goes through certain steps at both the sending and receiving devices. The following sections discuss what takes place at each end of the communication process.

Protocols from the Sending Device

In order for a computer to send data, the following steps must be performed; keep in mind that these are general steps—the actual processes taken at the sending device are far more complex:

1. The protocol is responsible for breaking the data into smaller parts, called *packets*.

2. Addressing information is assigned to each of the individual packets. This addressing information is used to locate the destination computer on the network.

3. The data is prepared for transmission and sent through the network interface card (NIC) and on to the network.

You can match steps 1 through 3 to the OSI model, starting with the application layer and ending with the physical layer, where the data is passed through the NIC and onto the network media. This process is discussed in greater detail later in this chapter.

Protocols on the Receiving Device

The steps for the receiving device are pretty much the same as those for the sending device, but they occur in the opposite order:

1. When data reaches the destination computer, the data packets are taken off the network media and in through the system's NIC.

2. The addressing information added by the sending computer is stripped from the packets.

3. The data packets are reassembled.

4. The reassembled packets are passed to the specific application for use.

To accomplish these steps, the same protocol must be used on the sending and receiving devices. It is possible for two devices that use different protocols to communicate with each other, but a gateway—an intermediary device that has the ability to translate between two formats—is needed. For more information on gateways, refer to Chapter 3, "Networking Components and Devices."

Mapping Protocols to the OSI Model

As discussed previously in this chapter, three categories of protocols are used on networks: application protocols, transport protocols, and network protocols. These protocols can be matched to the OSI model, as shown in Figure 5.1.

Understanding how protocols map to OSI layers can be very useful as an aid in understanding how protocols within a suite work together. The following sections look more specifically at some of the protocols that reside at each level. First, let's look at application protocols.

Application Protocols

As shown in Figure 5.1, the application protocols work in the upper layers of the OSI seven-layer model: Application protocols map to the application, presentation, and session layers of the OSI model. The following are some of the specific application protocols from the various protocol suites:

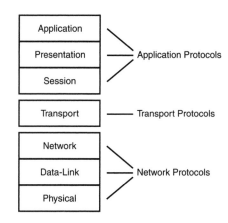

FIGURE 5.1
Matching protocol types to layers of the OSI model.

- ◆ **AppleTalk File Protocol (AFP)**—AFP is the protocol used by Macintosh systems for remote file management. It is part of the AppleTalk protocol suite.

- ◆ **File Transfer Protocol (FTP)**—FTP is one of the protocols that make up the TCP/IP protocol suite. It is used for transferring files.

- ◆ **NetWare Core Protocol (NCP)**—NCP is a protocol in the IPX/SPX suite that provides application-level functionality to client systems.

- ◆ **Simple Network Management Protocol (SNMP)**—SNMP is used to monitor network devices. Like FTP, SNMP is part of the TCP/IP protocol suite.

- ◆ **Simple Mail Transfer Protocol (SMTP)**—SMTP is the protocol used in the transporting of email. It is part of the TCP/IP protocol suite.

Although application protocols provide clients access to functionality, the transport protocols, which are described in the following section, actually move the data across the network.

Transport Protocols

Transport protocols map to the transport layer of the OSI model and are responsible for the transporting of data across the network. The following are some examples of transport protocols from the commonly used protocol suites:

◆ **AppleTalk Transaction Protocol (ATP)**—ATP is a connectionless protocol that is used with the AppleTalk protocol suite.

◆ **NetBEUI**—NetBEUI is a simple and fast network protocol that is used with NetBIOS.

◆ **SPX**—SPX is the NetWare communications protocol used to transport data across the network. It is a connection-oriented protocol.

◆ **TCP**—One of the protocols in the TCP/IP protocol stack, TCP is a connection-based protocol, and it is responsible for establishing connections between systems.

◆ **User Datagram Protocol (UDP)**—Part of the TCP/IP protocol suite, UDP is used instead of TCP when guaranteed data delivery is not required.

Although transport protocols are concerned with moving data around the network, they rely on network protocols, described in the following section, to provide the underlying services that enable the process.

Network Protocols

The network protocols provide the rules for communication between devices on the network. Network protocols are responsible for providing the addressing and routing information, error checking, and such things as retransmission requests for incomplete communications. The following are some examples of network protocols:

◆ **IP**—Part of the TCP/IP protocol suite, IP is used for addressing and route selection

◆ **IPX**—IPX is a communications protocol that is used for routing messages on networks that use the IPX/SPX protocol suite

◆ **Datagram Delivery Protocol (DDP)**—DDP provides connectionless service on AppleTalk networks

Now that you have seen how protocols are used on a network and some of the protocols used at the various layers, let's look at the specific protocols used in today's networks, starting with the most frequently used: TCP/IP.

TRANSMISSION CONTROL PROTOCOL/ INTERNET PROTOCOL (TCP/IP)

Not many technologies have survived the test of time, but TCP/IP can make this claim and then some. In the dynamic IT industry, technologies come and go; new and improved methods, procedures, and equipment replace the old at a staggering pace. TCP/IP is one of the few exceptions to the rule. Not only has it survived in a state that's very similar to its original, but as other networking protocols have fallen away, networks' dependency on TCP/IP has increased. There may have been pretenders to the protocol crown, but TCP/IP is truly the champion.

A Brief History of TCP/IP

In the late 1970s and early 1980s, the U.S. Department of Defense Advanced Research Projects Agency (ARPA) needed a system that would allow it to share the resources of its expensive mainframe computer systems. From this the ARPANET—the forerunner of today's Internet—was developed.

The original ARPANET network used a communication protocol known as NCP, but limitations were soon discovered, and a new protocol was needed to meet the new networking demands. That new protocol was TCP/IP. TCP/IP soon became the unquestioned leader in the protocol arena; increasingly, networks of all shapes and sizes were using it.

The history of the Internet and the development of TCP/IP have been closely linked and continue to be so today. ARPANET itself was retired in 1989, but its functions were steadily improved, and today we have the Internet. TCP/IP has always been at the root of the Internet; if you are working in network environments that require Internet access, you can expect to be using the TCP/IP protocol. All the major network operating systems include support for TCP/IP.

The TCP/IP Protocol Suite

Although TCP/IP is often referred to as a single protocol, the TCP/IP suite comprises a large number of protocols, many of which have been mentioned already in this chapter. Each of the protocols in the TCP/IP suite provides a different function, and together they provide the functionality we know as TCP/IP.

The TCP/IP protocol suite got its name from the two main protocols in the suite: TCP and the IP. TCP is responsible for providing reliable transmissions from one system to another, and IP is responsible for addressing and route selection. The following are some of the other protocols in the TCP/IP protocol suite:

◆ Address Resolution Protocol (ARP)

◆ FTP

◆ Internet Control Message Protocol (ICMP)

◆ IP

◆ Reverse Address Resolution Protocol (RARP)

◆ SMTP

◆ TCP

Chapter 6, "Working with TCP/IP," is dedicated to explaining the TCP/IP protocol suite. Therefore, the various protocols used in the suite are only listed here. For a complete discussion of the TCP/IP protocol suite and the specific protocols, refer to Chapter 6.

TCP/IP Standards

Unlike protocols such as AppleTalk and IPX, TCP/IP is not owned by any one party and is not licensed. As a result, anyone can develop TCP/IP compatibility for his or her products. This open approach has done much to advance TCP/IP as the protocol of choice across platforms and products.

Because of TCP/IP's open nature, development of TCP/IP is performed under a rather unique system. Standards pertaining to the TCP/IP protocol suite are published in documents known as Requests for Comments (RFCs). Any proposed idea for new standards or changes to old ones can be found in an RFC. The Internet Engineering Task Force (IETF) is responsible for maintaining and managing the list of RFCs, and any individual, company, or group can submit a new RFC or review and comment on an existing one. Information on the IETF can be found at www.ietf.org. This site also includes a complete list of the RFCs.

TCP/IP Addressing

Addressing in TCP/IP networks is a major topic, and it can take some getting used to. This section explores only the most basic principles of TCP/IP addressing. For a full discussion, refer to Chapter 6.

In TCP/IP networks, each node is identified by a unique address, as is each network segment. The IP address consists of four sets of 8 bits, referred to as *octets*, which are expressed in numbers and separated by periods. An example of an IP address is 192.168.1.1.

Because a single IP address represents both the IP address of the host and the IP address of the network to which the host is attached, a mechanism is needed to let the system know what part of the address refers to what. That mechanism is the *subnet mask*. The system uses the subnet mask to determine what part of the address refers to the network and what part refers to the node. If part of the address refers to the network, it is assigned a binary value of 1. If it is the node address, it's assigned a binary value of 0. So, if the subnet mask is 255.255.0.0, the first two parts of the address refer to the network and the last two refer to the node. Using our original address example (192.168.1.1) and a subnet mask of 255.255.0.0, the system is on a network called 192.168, and the node address is 1.1. Figure 5.2 shows how IP addressing works in a simple network.

IP addressing is a very complex subject that warrants more than just the basic discussion included here. Chapter 6 provides extensive coverage of the topic.

EXAM TIP

IANA The assignment of IP addresses is handled by suborganizations of a global organization called the Internet Assigned Numbers Authority (IANA). To find out more about IANA, go to www.iana.org.

FIGURE 5.2
TCP/IP addressing in a simple network.

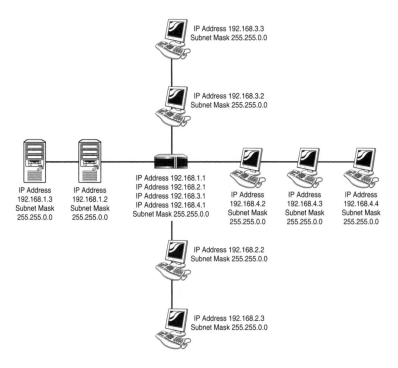

TCP/IP Interoperability

Of all the protocols discussed in this chapter, TCP/IP is by far the most interoperable—that is, TCP/IP is supported by all the popular operating systems. Over the years, TCP/IP has become the networking protocol of choice for almost all applications. The generic nature of TCP/IP means that systems using it can communicate with each other no matter what operating system is being used. This fact also allows TCP/IP-based services to be platform independent. For example, you might use a Windows 98 workstation on your desktop, but the server that resolves your Internet requests might be a Linux server, and the server that provides file and print services might be a NetWare server. TCP/IP even transcends platforms; it is available in versions for minicomputers and mainframes as well.

TCP/IP Naming

Hosts that run the TCP/IP protocol can be referred to either by their IP address, such as 192.168.4.3, or by a hostname, which can be a more human-readable name such as *server*. Other systems can then communicate by using the IP address or the hostname, although the latter must be resolved before it can be used. This resolution can be performed manually, through a text file, or dynamically, through a server running the Domain Name Server (DNS) service. Again, Chapter 6 provides more information.

TCP/IP Routing Protocols

TCP/IP is a fully routable protocol, making it very suitable for use on large networks. Routers on a TCP/IP network can communicate with each other using special protocols called *routing protocols*.

Two routing protocols are commonly used on TCP/IP-based networks: Routing Information Protocol (RIP) and Open Shortest Path First (OSPF). RIP is a distance-vector routing protocol, and OSPF is a link-state routing protocol. For more information on the differences between these two types of protocols, refer to Chapter 3.

Mapping TCP/IP to the OSI Model

Chapter 4, "The OSI Model," identifies the various levels of the OSI model. The OSI model provides a structure in which you can work; by placing services and devices in certain layers of the model, you can get a better idea of their function and purpose. The same is true of network protocols.

Figure 5.3 shows the core protocols of the TCP/IP suite and how they map to the layers of the OSI model.

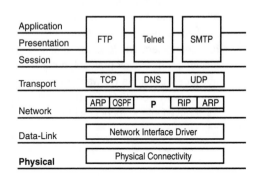

FIGURE 5.3
The OSI model and the TCP/IP protocol suite.

INTERNETWORK PACKET EXCHANGE/ SEQUENCED PACKET EXCHANGE (IPX/SPX)

IPX/SPX is the native protocol that was used, until recently, on Novell networks. Today even Novell, creator of IPX/SPX, has started using TCP/IP as the default protocol.

N O T E

NWLink   Many of today's networking environments are not restricted to a single server platform but instead use different servers on the same network. To accommodate this, Microsoft developed the NWLink protocol to allow interoperability between Novell NetWare networks and servers running Windows server platforms.

NWLink is a Windows implementation of the IPX/SPX protocol that lets Windows systems access applications running on a NetWare server. In turn, NetWare clients can use the NWLink protocol to access services running on Windows-based servers.

When IPX/SPX was a popular protocol for networks, such interoperability was mandatory. As the popularity of NetWare and the IPX/SPX protocol have diminished in recent years, the need for a means of interoperability has decreased. Windows 2000 still includes the NWLink protocol, but it is not widely used. As NetWare itself moves away from IPX/SPX, the need for the NWLink protocol is all but gone.

IPX/SPX was developed by Novell with a bit of help from Xerox. (IPX was based on an early protocol called Xerox Network System [XNS], and SPX was based on another Xerox protocol, Sequenced Packet Protocol [SPP].) During the reign of the Novell operating system, those working with networks would certainly have had to be very familiar with IPX/SPX. Today, however, you might never come in contact with it.

Despite its fading use, IPX offers certain distinct advantages: Addressing is almost completely automatic, IPX is a routable protocol, and, on small networks, IPX provides an excellent alternative to TCP/IP.

The IPX/SPX Protocol Suite

Like TCP/IP, IPX/SPX is a protocol suite that is made up of a variety of separate protocols, each of which has a different function and purpose. The individual protocols that form the IPX/SPX protocol suite include the following:

◆ Internetwork Packet Exchange (IPX)

◆ Sequenced Packet Exchange (SPX)

◆ Routing Information Protocol (RIP)

◆ NetWare Link State Protocol (NLSP)

◆ Service Advertising Protocol (SAP)

◆ NetWare Core Protocol (NCP)

Although a detailed discussion of each of these protocols is not required, the following sections briefly examine each of them and identify their purposes and functions.

Internetwork Packet Exchange (IPX)

IPX provides connectionless communication and is used to route messages from one node to another. Essentially, IPX is responsible for logical network addressing, route selections, and connection services. The route selections used are determined by tables created with another of the IPX/SPX protocols: RIP or OSPF. Because IPX is a connectionless protocol, it is unsuitable for some network applications. For this reason, it is used in conjunction with SPX.

Sequenced Packet Exchange (SPX)

SPX adds reliability to IPX. SPX is a connection-based protocol that is used when guaranteed message delivery is required on the network. Protocols that provide connection-oriented service are inherently slower than those that do not, because they are concerned with error control. Within the IPX/SPX protocol suite, SPX is responsible for fragmenting the packets into data, sequencing this data to ensure that the receiving device knows the correct order for the data, and reassembling the data.

Routing Information Protocol (RIP)

RIP is responsible for the routing of packets on an IPX/SPX network. RIP uses the distance-vector route-discovery method; it calculates routes based on the number of hops (that is, routers) that must be crossed to reach a particular device.

NetWare Link State Protocol (NLSP)

Both RIP and SAP are relatively old broadcast-based protocols that can function inefficiently in some network environments. To reduce broadcast traffic, you can use NLSP. NLSP uses a link-state route discovery method to build routing tables. Link-state protocols do not broadcast routing information periodically; rather, they broadcast routing information only when changes have been made to the routing information or at extended intervals. This process is more efficient than RIP.

Service Advertising Protocol (SAP)

NetWare uses SAP to allow systems providing services to the network, such as file and print services, to announce their services and addresses to the network. SAP lets NetWare clients know the location of the systems providing network resources. To let clients know if a service is available to them, SAP packet is broadcast every 60 seconds.

NetWare Core Protocol (NCP)

NCP is responsible for providing services to client applications. NCP is a connection-oriented protocol that provides the connection between clients and services.

IPX Addressing

Addressing for the IPX/SPX protocol suite is the responsibility of IPX. IPX addressing is somewhat simpler than TCP/IP addressing because rather than making up an addressing scheme and applying it to a network segment, IPX uses the Media Access Control (MAC) address that is assigned to each network interface. By combining this MAC address with an eight-character hexadecimal address, which is used to refer to the network segment, IPX creates a hierarchical addressing system that is routable.

An example of an IPX address is 0BAD33CE:0003FE7C06EC. The 0BAD33CE portion represents the IPX address for the network segment; 0003FE7C06EC is the MAC address of the node, which is used for the second part of the address. In addition to this format, IPX addresses can also be written with each group of four hexadecimal characters separated by colons (:)—for example, 0000:0007:003C:7F53:04CF. In some cases, any leading 0s on the network address portion are dropped. For example, 00000007 can be expressed simply as 7. The address would then be 7:003C:7F53:04CF.

Figure 5.4 shows how IPX addressing works in a sample network.

FIGURE 5.4
IPX addressing in a sample network.

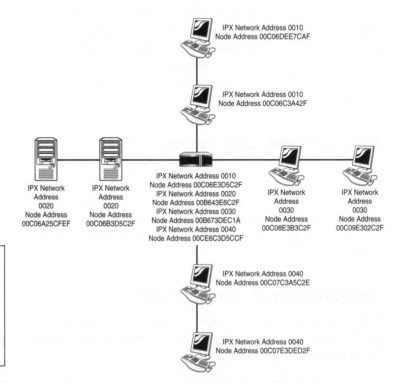

The IPX segment, or network, address is defined by the first server that comes up on a network. If another system that has a different number is subsequently brought onto the network, errors are generated. When a workstation system is brought onto the network, the IPX segment address is normally detected automatically. Alternatively, in some configurations it is possible to manually configure the address, although you don't need to do so under normal circumstances.

Mapping IPX/SPX to the OSI Model

Mapping the IPX/SPX protocol suite to the OSI model is not an easy task. As shown in Figure 5.5, the core protocols of the suite map to the network and transport layers of the OSI model.

IPX/SPX Interoperability

The IPX/SPX protocol suite is supported by Novell NetWare and by the Microsoft Windows platforms. Microsoft created its own implementation of the IPX/SPX protocol suite, called NWLink, which can be used with the Microsoft client software for NetWare to allow Windows systems to connect to a NetWare server. Even on a network with only Windows systems, some people prefer to use NWLink because it offers easier addressing of other protocols such as TCP/IP.

IPX/SPX Naming

As already mentioned, IPX addressing is essentially automatic. Naming also is not an issue with IPX/SPX because servers are normally the only parts of a network that are assigned addresses. These addresses are names of up to 47 characters (in current versions of NetWare). Workstations do not need such addresses and instead use IPX addressing.

For a time, IPX/SPX was the king of the network protocols, but over time it has given way to TCP/IP. Even Novell has, for many years, included TCP/IP with releases of its network operating systems; this is expected to be the beginning of the end for the once-proud IPX/SPX protocol suite.

EXAM TIP

NLSP and RIP Both NLSP and RIP function at more than one layer of the OSI model, but the details of how this works fall outside the scope of the Network+ exam.

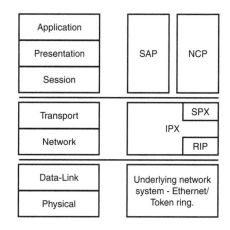

FIGURE 5.5
The OSI model and the IPX/SPX protocol suite.

APPLETALK

As you might have surmised, AppleTalk is the name given to the protocol used on Apple networks. The roots of the AppleTalk protocol can be traced back to the early 1980s. The first implementation of AppleTalk was limited and not suitable for internetworks. Late in the 1980s, however, significant improvements were made to the protocol; it then allowed for support of internetworking by supporting network addresses.

Like the IPX/SPX and TCP/IP protocol suites, the AppleTalk protocol suite is comprised of several protocols. The following are the AppleTalk protocols:

◆ **AppleShare**—AppleShare provides application-layer services. It comprises three different protocols: AppleShare File Server, AppleShare Print Server, and AppleShare PC.

◆ **AppleTalk Address Resolution Protocol (AARP)**—AARP maps the AppleTalk addresses to both Ethernet and Token Ring physical addresses.

◆ **AppleTalk Data Stream Protocol (ADSP)**—ADSP is a session-layer protocol that also performs transport-layer functions. At the session layer, ADSP establishes and releases connections. At the transport layer, it provides sequencing and handles flow control.

◆ **AppleTalk Filing Protocol (AFP)**—AFP manages file sharing on a network.

◆ **AppleTalk Session Protocol (ASP)**—Like ADSP, ASP works at the session layer and is used to establish and release connections between devices.

◆ **AppleTalk Transaction Protocol (ATP)**—ATP is a transport-layer connectionless protocol that is used to establish connections between computers.

◆ **Datagram Delivery Protocol (DDP)**—DDP provides connectionless service on an AppleTalk network.

◆ **EtherTalk Link Access Protocol (ELAP)**—ELAP is an implementation of the AppleTalk protocol that is compatible with the Ethernet protocol.

◆ **Name Binding Protocol (NBP)**—NBP maps computer host-names to network-layer addresses.

◆ **Printer Access Protocol (PAP)**—PAP is a session-layer protocol that is used to facilitate printing on an AppleTalk network. PAP also allows connections between file servers and workstations.

◆ **Routing Table Maintenance Protocol (RTMP)**—RTMP is a distance-vector routing protocol that is similar to the RIP, which is used by IPX/SPX and TCP/IP. RTMP maintains routing tables for a network.

◆ **TokenTalk Link Access Protocol (TLAP)**—TLAP is an implementation of the AppleTalk protocol that is compatible with the Token Ring protocol.

◆ **Zone Information Protocol (ZIP)**—ZIP divides network devices into logical groups called *zones*.

> **EXAM TIP**
>
> **Know the Functions of the Protocols** For the Network+ Exam, you should be sure you understand the functions of the protocols in the AppleTalk protocol suite.

AppleTalk Addressing

Like TCP/IP and IPX/SPX, AppleTalk requires two parts in the addressing system: the network part of the address and the node part. To get a node address, a system must simply be booted on an AppleTalk network. When the system is first brought up on the network, it generates a random node number that is then broadcast to the entire network. If by some unusual circumstance this number is already assigned to another system, a different node number is generated and broadcast to the network.

The node number must be used in conjunction with a network number, which is assigned by the administrator. When these numbers are used together, they form the network address of the computer.

AppleTalk addresses are 24 bits long; 16 of the bits are used for the network address, and 8 are used for the node address. Having only 8 bits available for node addresses means that there can be a maximum of 254 nodes on each network. However, you can use a strategy called *Extended AppleTalk Network* to get around this limitation. To use this technique, you assign a network a range of addresses rather than a single address.

> **NOTE**
>
> **LocalTalk** AppleTalk is a complete networking protocol that can be made compatible with both Token Ring and Ethernet; LocalTalk was developed for AppleTalk in Apple-only networks. LocalTalk uses carrier-sense multiple-access with collision avoidance (CSMA/CA) as an access method. A LocalTalk network uses shielded twisted pair (STP) media but can be configured to use regular unshielded twisted pair (UTP) or fiber-based media. LocalTalk uses a bus topology and can support up to 32 devices.

Another feature of AppleTalk networking that is worthy of note is the *zone*. Zones allow an administrator to divide an AppleTalk network into logical areas to simplify administration and make it easier for users to find network resources. Zones are generally used only in environments with large numbers of systems.

Mapping AppleTalk to the OSI Model

Like the other protocol suites, AppleTalk can be mapped to the OSI model. Table 5.1 shows the various AppleTalk protocols and the corresponding OSI levels.

TABLE 5.1

APPLETALK PROTOCOLS MAPPED TO THE OSI MODEL

OSI Layer	AppleTalk Protocols
Application	AppleTalk
Presentation	AFP
Session	ADSP, ZIP, PAP, AFP, ASP
Transport	ADSP, ATP, NBP, RTMP
Network	DDP, NBP, RTMP
Data-link	LocalTalk, AARP
Physical	LocalTalk, Ethertalk, TokenTalk

AppleTalk Interoperability

Of the three protocol suites discussed in this chapter, AppleTalk is the least interoperable; only Macintosh systems use it as the default protocol. AppleTalk support can be provided on certain other platforms, such as Microsoft Windows, but additional software is required to enable it.

AppleTalk Routing

AppleTalk is a routable protocol (although early versions were not). The routing functionality is enabled by RTMP. Like RIP, which is used on IP- and IPX-based networks, RTMP is a distance-vector routing protocol.

AppleTalk Naming

Systems on an AppleTalk network are assigned names so that users can locate resources more easily than by using network addresses. This functionality is provided by the NBP, which handles the resolution of computer names to network addresses.

NetBEUI

Despite the prominence of TCP/IP and the other protocols already discussed in this chapter, other protocols are used—and you can expect to encounter them at some point. One such protocol is NetBEUI. NetBEUI is a simple but fast protocol that was designed by Microsoft and IBM in the mid-1980s. The speed of NetBEUI can be attributed to the fact that it has very little overhead, but this fact in turn means that NetBEUI has limited functionality. Although it is not commonly used, NetBEUI has found a niche in small networks, such as those in home offices and small businesses.

The biggest limitation of the NetBEUI protocol is that it is not routable. Thus, an organization that requires more than a single segment cannot use NetBEUI. Bridges can be used to divide up a network that uses NetBEUI, but in reality few people bother to do this anymore and instead just use a protocol such as TCP/IP.

Mapping NetBEUI to the OSI Model

NetBEUI is a very simplistic network protocol and as such does not map to many layers of the OSI model. Specifically, the NetBEUI protocol operates only at the transport and network layers of the

OSI model. Because NetBEUI operates at only two layers, other protocols are needed to help in the network communication process. NetBEUI requires NetBIOS, which maps to the session layer of the OSI model, to establish a connection between two network devices; it needs a redirector to allow client systems to see network resources; and it needs the Server Message Block (SMB) protocol, which maps to the presentation layer of the OSI model, to provide communication between client redirectors and network servers.

NetBEUI Addressing

> **NOTE**
>
> **FQDN** As of Windows 2000, Microsoft has moved away from the NetBEUI addressing scheme described here. Instead of the 15-character naming, Windows 2000 uses the fully qualified domain name (FQDN) of the system.

Compared to the addressing schemes of IPX/SPX and TCP/IP, NetBEUI's is very simple. NetBEUI allows the computers on a network to be identified by *NetBIOS name*. The NetBIOS, or friendly, name must be no more than 15 characters in length, and it must be unique to the network. A NetBIOS name can be made up of any combination of characters, with the exclusion of certain special characters such as spaces (in Windows 2000).

You can create NetBEUI names such as *workstation1* and *fileserver*. As you can imagine, such a scheme works well in small environments that don't have many systems; in the few cases where you come across NetBEUI, they will be in exactly these kinds of environments.

NetBEUI was designed and is very well suited for small networks that have no need for routing. Its ease of configuration and maintenance also make it suitable for network environments in which administrative support is not always accessible. At the end of the day, however, its limitations exclude it from most networking environments, and therefore it is becoming extinct.

REVIEW BREAK

PROTOCOL OVERVIEW AND COMPARISON

As you've seen in this chapter, a number of protocols are used in modern networks, and TCP/IP is by far the most widely implemented of them. Each network protocol has unique characteristics some good and some not so good. Table 5.2 compares the characteristics of the major protocols.

TABLE 5.2
PROTOCOL COMPARISON

Protocol	Network OperatingSystem	Routable?	Configuration	Primary Use
TCP/IP	Used by default with Unix, Linux, NetWare, and Windows systems; supported by Macintosh and just about every other computing platform available	Yes	Comparatively difficult to configure; has a number of different configuration requirements.	Used on many networks of all shapes and sizes; is the protocol of the Internet
IPX/SPX	Used to be the default protocol for NetWare, but now TCP/IP is preferred; can also be used with Linux; Windows supports NWLink, a version of the IPX/SPX protocol suite that was created by Microsoft for cross-platform compatibility	Yes	Very easy to configure because most information is autoconfigured	Primarily used on legacy NetWare networks
AppleTalk	Used by Macintosh, with some support on other platforms	Yes	Minimal configuration difficulty; requires a node address (automatically assigned when systems boot) and a network address	Used on legacy Macintosh networks
NetBEUI	Used by Windows	No	Easy network configuration, requiring only the computer's NetBIOS name	Primarily used on smaller networks where routing is not required

CHAPTER SUMMARY

This chapter introduces the various protocols that are commonly found in modern network environments. A protocol is a set of rules that govern how communication and the exchange of data take place between devices on a network.

Several protocols are used today, including TCP/IP, IPX/SPX, AppleTalk, and NetBEUI. Each offers unique features, advantages, and disadvantages, so certain protocols are more suitable for some network implementations than others. Protocols such as TCP/IP, IPX/SPX, and AppleTalk are in fact protocol suites that consist of several other protocols. Each individual protocol provides a different function for the protocol suite.

KEY TERMS
- NetBEUI
- AppleTalk
- protocol suite
- application protocol
- transport protocol
- network protocol
- packet

CHAPTER SUMMARY

KEY TERMS

- ATP
- FTP
- SNMP
- SMTP
- TCP
- UDP
- SPX
- IPX
- IP
- TCP/IP addressing
- routing protocols
- NWLink
- RIP
- LocalTalk

TCP/IP is the protocol used for the Internet and is the most widely implemented protocol today. IPX/SPX has lost ground in recent years; even NetWare is putting more emphasis on TCP/IP in its network operating system, leaving IPX/SPX for older NetWare versions. AppleTalk is a protocol suite that is used for Macintosh networks. On smaller networks, the largely self-configuring NetBEUI can be used, but it has limitations that make it unsuitable for many of today's networked environments.

APPLY YOUR KNOWLEDGE

Exercises

5.1 Installing AppleTalk on a Windows 2000 Server

In this exercise, you learn how to install the AppleTalk protocol on a Windows 2000 server.

Estimated time: 10 minutes

1. Right-click the My Network Places icon on the desktop and select Properties from the menu that appears.

2. The Network and Dial-up Connections window appears, as shown in Figure 5.6. Right-click the icon that corresponds to your internal network card and select Properties from the menu. The Local Area Connection Properties dialog box appears.

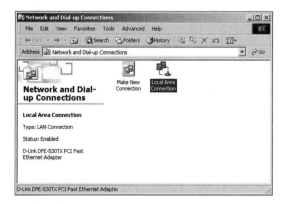

FIGURE 5.6
The Network and Dial-up Connections window.

3. Click the Install button to open the Select Network Component Type dialog box, which is shown in Figure 5.7.

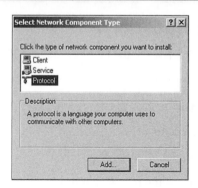

FIGURE 5.7
The Select Network Component Type dialog box.

4. In the Select Network Component Type dialog box, select the Protocol option and click the Add button.

5. The Select Network Protocol dialog box (shown in Figure 5.8) appears. Select AppleTalk protocol from the list and click OK.

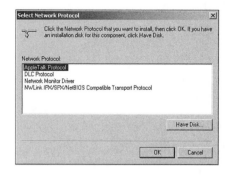

FIGURE 5.8
The Select Network Protocol dialog box.

6. The AppleTalk protocol is installed and is then listed in the Local Area Connection Properties dialog box. To configure the AppleTalk protocol, you can select it and then click the Properties button.

APPLY YOUR KNOWLEDGE

Exam Questions

1. At what layer of the OSI model does SPX operate?

   a. Physical

   b. Transport

   c. Network

   d. Session

2. Which of the following protocols is not routable?

   a. AppleTalk

   b. IPX/SPX

   c. NetBEUI

   d. TCP/IP

3. Which of the following are considered transport protocols? (Choose the two best answers.)

   a. TCP

   b. IP

   c. UDP

   d. NCP

4. Which of the following is an example of a NetBIOS name?

   a. 192.168.1.1

   b. workstation

   c. 00-23-F3-C8-5A-06

   d. 0C0E:0832:33EC:AE2C:11AC

5. Which of the following routing protocols has a version for both the TCP/IP and IPX/SPX protocol suites?

   a. RIP

   b. RTMP

   c. NLSP

   d. OSPF

6. Which of the following protocols is responsible for connectionless service on an AppleTalk network?

   a. DCP

   b. DLC

   c. DDP

   d. CCP

7. Which of the following are routing protocols that are used with the IPX/SPX protocol suite? (Choose the two best answers.)

   a. NLSP

   b. RIP

   c. NCP

   d. IPX

8. Which of the following protocol suites uses ZIP?

   a. AppleTalk

   b. NetBEUI

   c. TCP/IP

   d. IPX/SPX

9. Which of the following is an example of an IPX address?

   a. 0C0E:0832:33EC:AE2C:11AC

   b. 00-23-F3-C8-5A-06

   c. 192.168.1.1

   d. 0C0K:0832:33EC:AH2C:11AC

APPLY YOUR KNOWLEDGE

10. At which layer of the OSI model does the IPX protocol function?

    a. Network

    b. Session

    c. Application

    d. Data-link

11. You have been tasked with specifying a network for a customer. The network consists of three segments connected by two routers. When it is first installed, the network will have two Windows 2000 systems, one Linux server, and a NetWare server. In the near future, the client will be adding an IBM minicomputer running AS/400. Which of the following network protocols would you recommend for the installation?

    a. IPX/SPX

    b. AppleTalk

    c. NetBEUI

    d. TCP/IP

12. Which of the following protocols are distance-vector routing protocols? (Choose the two best answers.)

    a. RTMP

    b. ARP

    c. RIP

    d. RARP

13. Which of the following are considered application protocols? (Choose the two best answers.)

    a. TCP

    b. IP

    c. AFP

    d. FTP

14. Which of the following protocols is used by the IPX/SPX protocol suite to advertise the availability of resources on the network?

    a. RIP

    b. SAP

    c. NLSP

    d. NCP

15. NWLink is a version of what protocol suite?

    a. TCP/IP

    b. IPX/SPX

    c. NetBEUI

    d. AppleTalk

16. You are designing a new network installation for a client. The network consists of three segments separated by routers. The client wants to make sure that configuration of the workstation addresses is as simple as possible. Which of the following protocols are you most likely to recommend?

    a. TCP/IP

    b. AppleTalk

    c. NetBEUI

    d. IPX/SPX

17. In an AppleTalk network, what is the function of a zone?

    a. It defines physical boundaries on the network.

    b. It allows administrators to manage systems based on a system-generated zone ID.

c. It creates a password system that is common across a group of computers.

d. It allows the network to be broken up into logical administrative units.

18. Which of the following protocols is not part of the IPX/SPX protocol suite?

    a. NCP

    b. NLSP

    c. UDP

    d. RIP

19. TCP is an example of what kind of transport protocol?

    a. Connection-oriented

    b. Connection-reliant

    c. Connection-dependent

    d. Connectionless

20. In the IPX/SPX protocol suite, what is the function of NCP?

    a. It is used to advertise services on the network.

    b. It is a connectionless transport protocol.

    c. It provides application-level functionality to clients.

    d. It is a link-state routing protocol.

Answers to Exam Questions

1. **b.** SPX operates at the transport layer of the OSI model. None of the other answers are valid. For more information, see the section "Internetwork Packet Exchange/Sequenced Packet Exchange (IPX/SPX)," in this chapter.

2. **c.** NetBEUI is not a routable protocol. All the protocols listed are routable. For more information, see the section "NetBEUI," in this chapter.

3. **a, c.** Both UDP and TCP are transport protocols. IP is a network protocol, and NCP is an application protocol. For more information, see the section "Transport Protocols," in this chapter.

4. **b.** NetBIOS addresses are typically descriptive words such as *workstation*. Answer a is an IP address, Answer c is a MAC address, and Answer d is an example of an IPv6 address. For more information, see the section "NetBEUI," in this chapter.

5. **a.** Versions of RIP are available for both TCP/IP and IPX/SPX. RTMP is a routing protocol that is associated with AppleTalk, NLSP is a link-state routing protocol that is associated with the IPX/SPX protocol suite, and OSPF is a link-state routing protocol that is associated with TCP/IP. For more information, see the section "Transmission Control Protocol/Internet Protocol (TCP/IP)," in this chapter.

6. **c.** DDP provides connectionless communication on AppleTalk networks. None of the other answers are valid. For more information, see the section "AppleTalk," in this chapter.

7. **a, b.** NLSP and RIP are routing protocols that are used on IPX/SPX networks. NCP is an application protocol that is used on IPX/SPX networks, and IPX is a network protocol. For more information, see the section "Internetwork Packet Exchange/Sequenced Packet Exchange (IPX/SPX)," in this chapter.

8. **a.** AppleTalk uses ZIP. None of the other answers are valid. For more information, see the section "AppleTalk," in this chapter.

APPLY YOUR KNOWLEDGE

9. **a.** IPX addresses are expressed in hexadecimal format. Answer b is a MAC address, Answer c is an IP address, and Answer d is not a valid network address. For more information, see the section "Internetwork Packet Exchange/Sequenced Packet Exchange (IPX/SPX)," in this chapter.

10. **a.** IPX functions at the network layer of the OSI model. None of the other answers are valid. For more information, see the section "Internetwork Packet Exchange/Sequenced Packet Exchange (IPX/SPX)," in this chapter.

11. **d.** The only protocol suitable for this environment is TCP/IP. None of the other protocols accommodate all the computing platforms listed in the question. For more information, see the section "Transmission Control Protocol/Internet Protocol (TCP/IP)," in this chapter.

12. **a, c.** Both RTMP and RIP are distance-vector routing protocols. ARP is not a routing protocol; like RARP, it is an address resolution protocol. For more information, see the section "Transmission Control Protocol/Internet Protocol (TCP/IP)," in this chapter.

13. **c, d.** Both AFP and FTP are application protocols. TCP is a transport protocol, and IP is a network protocol. For more information, see the section "Transmission Control Protocol/Internet Protocol (TCP/IP)," in this chapter.

14. **b.** SAP is used by systems to advertise services on the network. RIP and NLSP are both routing protocols, and NCP is an application protocol. For more information, see the section "Transmission Control Protocol/Internet Protocol (TCP/IP)," in this chapter.

15. **b.** NWLink is a version of IPX/SPX that was created by Microsoft to allow for cross-platform compatibility. TCP/IP is supported natively on Windows platforms, as are NetBEUI and AppleTalk. For more information, see the section "Internetwork Packet Exchange/Sequenced Packet Exchange (IPX/SPX)," in this chapter.

16. **d.** Of the routable and widely supported protocols, IPX/SPX is the most suitable in this environment. TCP is a routable protocol, but the addressing of a TCP/IP network is more involved than IPX/SPX. NetBEUI is not routable and so could not be used in this configuration. For more information, see the sections "Transmission Control Protocol/Internet Protocol (TCP/IP)" and "Internetwork Packet Exchange/Sequenced Packet Exchange (IPX/SPX)," in this chapter.

17. **d.** A zone enables a network to be broken into logical administrative units. None of the other answers are valid. For more information, see the section "AppleTalk," in this chapter.

18. **c.** UDP is part of the TCP/IP protocol suite. All the other protocols are part of the IPX/SPX protocol suite. For more information, see the section "TCP/IP," in this chapter.

19. **a.** TCP is an example of connection-oriented communication. None of the other answers are valid. For more information, see the section "Transmission Control Protocol/Internet Protocol (TCP/IP)," in this chapter.

20. **c.** NCP provides application-level functionality to clients. None of the other answers are valid. For more information, see the section "Internetwork Packet Exchange/Sequenced Packet Exchange (IPX/SPX)," in this chapter.

APPLY YOUR KNOWLEDGE

Suggested Readings and Resources

1 Habraken, Joe. *Absolute Beginner's Guide to Networking,* third edition. Que Publishing, 2001.

2. Hallberg, Bruce A. *Networking: A Beginners Guide* (Network Professional's Library). Osborne McGraw-Hill, 2001.

3. "TechEncyclopedia," www.techencyclopedia.com.

4. Network protocol tutorial, www.wkmn.com/newsite/protocol.html.

5. Network+ network protocol tutorial, www.learnthat.com/courses/computer/networkplus/network11.shtml.

This chapter covers the following CompTIA-specified objectives for the "Protocols and Standards" section of the Network+ exam.

Define the purpose, function, and/or use of the following protocols within TCP/IP: IP, TCP, UDP, FTP, TFTP, SMTP, HTTP, HTTPS, POP/IMAP, Telnet, ICMP, ARP, and NTP.

▶ The TCP/IP protocol suite is composed of many different protocols. As a network administrator, you need to be able to identify the various protocols and their purposes.

Define the function of TCP/UDP ports and identify well-known ports.

▶ Understanding the function and role of ports in TCP/IP networking is a key skill for a network administrator.

Identify the purpose of the following network services: DHCP/BOOTP, DNS, NAT/ICS, WINS, SNMP.

▶ Many different TCP/IP-related services are used on networks. Understanding the services available and their functions is a key skill in network administration.

CHAPTER 6

Working with TCP/IP

Identify IP addresses (IPv4, IPv6) and their default subnet masks.

▶ IP addressing is perhaps one of the most complex principles in TCP/IP networking. This chapter introduces you to TCP/IP addressing as it relates to real-world networking scenarios.

Identify the purpose of subnetting and default gateways.

▶ Subnetting and default gateways are important elements of TCP/IP networking.

Identify the differences between public and private networks.

▶ Private network address ranges are now commonly used as a means to provide flexible TCP/IP addressing schemes within organizations. You are very likely to encounter private network addressing in the real world.

Introduction	**205**
TCP/IP Protocols	**205**
Internet Protocol (IP)	205
Transmission Control Protocol (TCP)	206
How TCP Works	206
User Datagram Protocol (UDP)	206
File Transfer Protocol (FTP)	207
Trivial File Transfer Protocol (TFTP)	209
Simple Mail Transfer Protocol (SMTP)	209
Hypertext Transfer Protocol (HTTP)	209
Hypertext Transfer Protocol Secure (HTTPS)	210
Post Office Protocol/Internet Message Access Protocol (POP/IMAP)	210
Telnet	211
Internet Control Message Protocol (ICMP)	211
Address Resolution Protocol (ARP)	212
Network Time Protocol (NTP)	213
TCP/IP Protocol Suite Summary	213
TCP/UDP Ports	**215**

TCP/IP-Based Network Services   **216**

Dynamic Host Configuration
  Protocol (DHCP)   217
    The DHCP Process   219
    Fault-Tolerant DHCP Configurations   219
    Should You Use DHCP?   220
BOOT Protocol (BOOTP)   220
Domain Name System (DNS)   220
    The DNS Namespace   222
    Types of DNS Entries   223
    DNS in a Practical Implementation   224
Network Address Translation (NAT)
  and Internet Connection Sharing (ICS)   224
    NAT   224
    How NAT Works   225
    ICS   226
Simple Network Management
  Protocol (SNMP)   226
    Components of SNMP   226
    SNMP Management Systems   227
    SNMP Agents   228
    Management Information
      Bases (MIBs)   228
SNMP Communities   230
Windows Internet Name Service (WINS)   230
    WINS in the Real World   232
TCP/IP Service Summary   232

IP Addressing   **233**

General IP Addressing Principles   233
IPv4   234
IP Address Classes   235
Subnet Mask Assignment   236
    Broadcast Addresses and "This
      Network"   236
    Classless Interdomain
      Routing (CIDR)   236
IPv6   237
    IPv6 Addressing   237
    Other Benefits of IPv6   238

Subnetting   **238**

Reasons to Subnet   **241**

Default Gateways   **241**

**Identifying the Differences Between
Public and Private Networks**   **242**

Private Address Ranges   244
Practical Uses of Public and Private IP
  Addressing   245

Chapter Summary   **246**

Apply Your Knowledge   **247**

STUDY STRATEGIES

▶ Read the objectives at the beginning of the chapter.

▶ Study the information in the chapter, paying special attention to the tables, which summarize key information.

▶ Review the objectives again.

▶ Answer the exam questions at the end of the chapter and check your results.

▶ Use the ExamGear test on the CD-ROM that accompanies this book to answer additional exam questions concerning this material.

▶ Review the notes, tips, and exam tips in this chapter. Make sure you understand the information in the exam tips. If you don't understand the topic referenced in an exam tip, refer to the information in the chapter text and then read the exam tip again.

INTRODUCTION

Transmission Control Protocol/Internet Protocol (TCP/IP) is so dominant that it warrants its own chapter. In fact, numerous chapters in this book in addition to this one also provide coverage of the many aspects of TCP/IP. This chapter deals with TCP/IP as a protocol suite, and Chapter 13, "Troubleshooting Connectivity," deals mainly with the troubleshooting aspects of TCP/IP. There is a great deal of ground to cover, so let's get started.

TCP/IP PROTOCOLS

▶ Define the purpose, function, and/or use of the following protocols within TCP/IP: IP, TCP, UDP, FTP, TFTP, SMTP, HTTP, HTTPS, POP3/IMAP4, Telnet, ICMP, ARP, and NTP.

As discussed in Chapter 5, "Overview of Network Protocols," the TCP/IP protocol suite is made up of many different protocols, each of which performs a specific task or function. The Network+ exam focuses on the following, which are some of the most commonly used and encountered protocols.

The following sections look at the functions of these protocols and their purposes.

Internet Protocol (IP)

IP, which is defined in RFC 791, is the protocol used to transport data from one node on a network to another. IP is connectionless, which means that it doesn't guarantee the delivery of data; it simply makes a best effort to do so. To ensure that transmissions sent via IP are completed, a higher-level protocol such as TCP is required.

> **NOTE**
>
> **IP and the OSI Model** IP operates at the network layer of the OSI model.

In addition to providing best-effort delivery, IP also performs fragmentation and reassembly tasks for network transmissions. Fragmentation is necessary because the maximum transmission unit (MTU) size is limited in IP. In other words, network transmissions that are too big to traverse the network in a single packet have to be broken up into smaller chunks and reassembled at the other end. Another function of IP is addressing. IP addressing is a complex subject, so there is a more detailed discussion of it later in this chapter, in the section "IP Addressing."

NOTE

TCP and the OSI Model   TCP operates at the transport layer of the OSI model.

NOTE

SYN Flooding   A problem with the TCP SYN/ACK system is that the TCP/IP protocol stack assumes that each of the SYN requests it receives is genuine. Although this is normally the case, crackers can also exploit this trust as a weakness by using an attack known as a *SYN flood*. In a SYN flood, large numbers of SYN requests are directed at a host, but the source address to which the system attempts to send an ACK is false, and therefore there is no acknowledgement of the ACK. The host, assuming that the lack of response is attributable to a network problem, keeps the SYN connections open for a period of time as a "just in case" precaution, and during this time, the connection cannot be used by another host. If enough false SYN requests are directed at a server, the result is that there aren't any connections left to service legitimate requests. To guard against this occurrence, some applications and operating systems have strategies that determine when a false connection is made, which helps prevent SYN flooding.

Transmission Control Protocol (TCP)

TCP, which is defined in RFC 793, is a connection-oriented protocol that uses IP as its transport protocol. Being connection oriented means that TCP requires a session to be established between two hosts before communication can take place. TCP provides reliability to IP communications. Specifically, TCP adds features such as flow control, sequencing, and error detection and correction. For this reason, higher-level applications that need guaranteed delivery use TCP rather than its lightweight and connectionless brother, UDP.

How TCP Works

When TCP wants to open a connection with another host, it follows this procedure:

1. It sends a message called a *SYN* to the target host.

2. The target host opens a connection for the request and sends back an acknowledgment message called an *ACK* (or SYN ACK).

3. The host that originated the request sends back another acknowledgment, saying that it has received the ACK message and that the session is ready to be used to transfer data.

When the data session has been completed, a similar process is used to close the session. This three-step session establishment and acknowledgment process is referred to as the *TCP three-way handshake*.

TCP is a reliable protocol because it has mechanisms that can accommodate and handle errors. These mechanisms include *timeouts*, which cause the sending host to automatically retransmit data if its receipt is not acknowledged within a given time period.

User Datagram Protocol (UDP)

UDP, which is defined in RFC 768, is the brother of TCP. Like TCP, UDP uses IP as its transport protocol, but the big difference is that UDP does not guarantee delivery like TCP does. In a sense, UDP is a "fire and forget" protocol; it assumes that the data sent will reach its destination intact. In fact, the checking of whether data is delivered is left to upper-layer protocols.

Unlike with TCP, with UDP there is no establishment of a session between the sending and receiving hosts, which is why UDP is referred to as a connectionless protocol. The upshot of this is that UDP has a much lower overhead than TCP. In fact, a TCP packet header has 14 fields. A UDP packet header has 4. Therefore, UDP is much more efficient than TCP. In applications that don't need the added features of TCP, UDP is much more economical in terms of bandwidth and processing effort.

NOTE   **UDP and the OSI Model**   UDP operates at the transport layer of the OSI model.

File Transfer Protocol (FTP)

As its name suggests, FTP provides for the uploading and downloading of files from a remote host that is running FTP server software. As well as uploading and downloading files, FTP allows you to view the contents of folders on an FTP server and rename and delete files and directories if you have the necessary permissions. FTP, which is defined in RFC 959, uses TCP as a transport protocol to guarantee delivery of packets.

FTP has security mechanisms that are used to authenticate users. However, rather than create a user account for every user, you can configure FTP server software to accept anonymous logons. When you do this, the username is anonymous, and the password is normally the user's email address. Most FTP servers that offer files to the general public operate in this way.

In addition to being very popular as a mechanism for distributing files to the general public over networks such as the Internet, FTP is also popular with organizations that need to frequently exchange large files with other people or organizations. For example, the chapters in this book were sent between the authors and Que Publishing using FTP. Such a system is necessary because the files we exchange are larger than can be accommodated using email.

All the common network operating systems offer FTP server capabilities, although whether you use them depends on whether you have a need for FTP services. All popular workstation operating systems offer FTP client functionality, although it is common to use third-party utilities such as CuteFTP and SmartFTP instead. Figure 6.1 shows an FTP session with the site ftp.redhat.com, from the FTP command-line client included with Windows 2000. Notice that this is an anonymous logon.

NOTE   **FTP and the OSI Model**   FTP is an application-layer protocol.

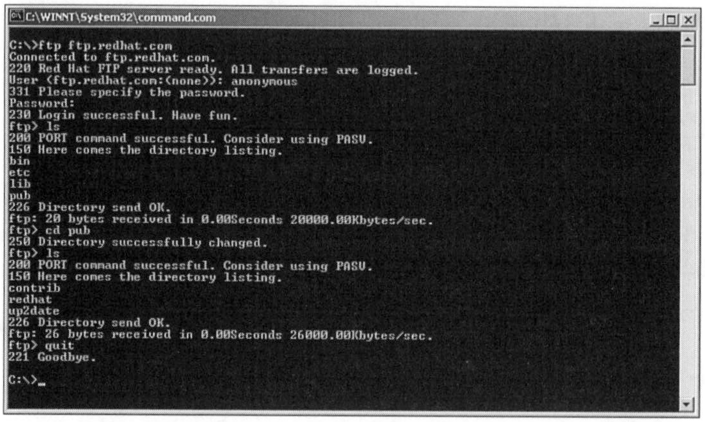

FIGURE 6.1
An FTP session, using the Windows 2000 FTP client.

```
C:\>ftp ftp.redhat.com
Connected to ftp.redhat.com.
220 Red Hat FTP server ready. All transfers are logged.
User (ftp.redhat.com:(none)): anonymous
331 Please specify the password.
Password:
230 Login successful. Have fun.
ftp> ls
200 PORT command successful. Consider using PASV.
150 Here comes the directory listing.
bin
etc
lib
pub
226 Directory send OK.
ftp: 20 bytes received in 0.00Seconds 20000.00Kbytes/sec.
ftp> cd pub
250 Directory successfully changed.
ftp> ls
200 PORT command successful. Consider using PASV.
150 Here comes the directory listing.
contrib
redhat
up2date
226 Directory send OK.
ftp: 26 bytes received in 0.00Seconds 26000.00Kbytes/sec.
ftp> quit
221 Goodbye.

C:\>_
```

FTP assumes that files being uploaded or downloaded are straight text (that is, ASCII) files. If the files are not text, which is quite likely, the transfer mode has to be changed to binary. With sophisticated FTP clients, such as CuteFTP, the transition between transfer modes is automatic. With more basic utilities, you have to perform the mode switch manually.

Unlike some of the other protocols discussed in this chapter that perform tasks transparently to the user, FTP is an application-layer service that is called upon frequently. Therefore, it can be useful to know some of the commands that are supported by FTP. If you are using a client such as CuteFTP, you might never need to use these commands, but they are useful to know in case you find yourself using a command-line FTP client. Table 6.1 lists some of the most commonly used FTP commands.

EXAM TIP

FTP Commands   On the Network+ exam, you might be asked to identify the appropriate FTP command to use in a given situation.

TABLE 6.1

COMMONLY USED FTP COMMANDS

Command	Purpose
ls	Lists the files in the current directory
cd	Changes working directory on the remote host
lcd	Changes working directory on the local host
put	Uploads a single file to the remote host
get	Downloads a single file from the remote host
mput	Uploads multiple files to the remote host

Command	*Purpose*
mget	Downloads multiple files from the remote host
binary	Switches transfers into binary mode
ascii	Switches transfers into ASCII mode (the default)

Trivial File Transfer Protocol (TFTP)

A variation on FTP is TFTP, which is also a file transfer mechanism. However, TFTP does not have either the security capability or the level of functionality that FTP has. TFTP, which is defined in RFC 1350, is most often associated with simple downloads, such as those associated with transferring firmware to a device such as a router and booting diskless workstations.

Another feature that TFTP does not offer is directory navigation. Whereas in FTP, commands can be executed to navigate around and manage the file system, TFTP offers no such capability. TFTP requires that you request not only exactly what you want, but also the particular location. Unlike FTP, which uses TCP as its transport protocol to guarantee delivery, TFTP uses UDP.

> **NOTE**
>
> **TFTP and the OSI Model** TFTP is an application-layer protocol that uses UDP, which is a connectionless transport-layer protocol. For this reason, TFTP is referred to as a connection-less file transfer method.

Simple Mail Transfer Protocol (SMTP)

SMTP, which is defined in RFC 821, is a protocol that defines how mail messages are sent between hosts. SMTP uses TCP connections to guarantee error-free delivery of messages. SMTP is not overly sophisticated, and it requires that the destination host always be available. For this reason, mail systems spool incoming mail so that users can read it at a later time. How the user then reads the mail depends on how the client accesses the SMTP server.

> **NOTE**
>
> **Sending and Receiving Mail** SMTP can be used for both sending and receiving mail. POP and IMAP can be used only for receiving mail.

Hypertext Transfer Protocol (HTTP)

HTTP, which is defined in RFC 2068, is the protocol that allows text, graphics, multimedia, and other material to be downloaded from an HTTP server. HTTP defines what actions can be requested by clients and how servers should answer those requests.

In a practical implementation, HTTP clients (that is, Web browsers) make requests in an HTTP format to servers running HTTP server applications (that is, Web servers). Files that are created in a special language such as Hypertext Markup Language (HTML) are returned to the client, and the connection is closed.

HTTP uses a uniform resource locator (URL) to determine what page should be downloaded from the remote server. The URL contains the type of request (for example, `http://`), the name of the server being contacted (for example, `www.novell.com`), and optionally the page being requested (for example, `/support`). The result is the syntax that Internet-savvy people are familiar with: `http://www.novell.com/support`.

Hypertext Transfer Protocol Secure (HTTPS)

One of the downsides of using HTTP is that HTTP requests are sent in clear text. For some applications, such as e-commerce, this method of exchanging information is not suitable—a more secure method is needed. The solution is HTTPS. HTTPS uses a system known as Secure Sockets Layer (SSL), which encrypts the information that is sent between the client and the host.

For HTTPS to be used, both the client and server must support it. All popular browsers now support HTTPS, as do Web server products, such as Microsoft Internet Information Server (IIS), Apache, and almost all other Web server applications that provide sensitive applications. When you are accessing an application that uses HTTPS, the URL starts with `https` rather than `http`—for example, `https://www.mybankonline.com`.

Post Office Protocol/Internet Message Access Protocol (POP/IMAP)

Both POP, which is defined in RFC 1939, and IMAP, the latest version of which is defined in RFC 1731, are mechanisms for downloading, or pulling, email from a server. They are necessary because, although the mail is transported around the network via SMTP, users cannot always read it immediately, so it must be stored in a central location. From this location, it needs to be downloaded, which is what POP and IMAP allow you to do.

POP and IMAP are very popular, and many people now access email through applications such as Microsoft Outlook, Netscape Communicator, and Eudora, which are POP and IMAP clients.

One of the problems with POP is that the password used to access a mailbox is transmitted acros the network in clear text. This means if someone wanted to, he or she could determine your POP password with relative ease. This is an area in which IMAP offers an advantage over POP. It uses a more sophisticated authentication system, which makes it harder for someone to determine a password.

Telnet

Telnet, which is defined in RFC 854, is a virtual terminal protocol. It allows sessions to be opened on a remote host, and then for commands to be executed on that remote host. For many years, Telnet was the method by which multiuser systems such as mainframes and minicomputers were accessed by clients. It was also the connection method of choice for Unix systems. Today, Telnet is still commonly used for accessing routers and other managed network devices.

One of the problems with Telnet is that it is not secure. As a result, remote session functionality is now almost always achieved by using alternatives such as Secure Shell (SSH).

Internet Control Message Protocol (ICMP)

ICMP, which is defined in RFC 792, is a protocol that works with the IP layer to provide error checking and reporting functionality. In effect, ICMP is a tool that IP uses in its quest to provide best-effort delivery.

ICMP can be used for a number of functions. Its most common function is probably the widely used and incredibly useful `ping` utility. `ping` sends a stream of ICMP echo requests to a remote host.

NOTE

Web-Based Mail—The Other, Other Email   Although there are many good points about accessing email by using POP and IMAP, such systems rely on servers to hold the mail until it is downloaded to the client system. In today's world, a more sophisticated solution to anytime/anywhere email access is needed. For many people, that solution is Web-based mail. Having an Internet-based email account allows you to access your mail from anywhere and from any device that supports a Web browser. Recognizing the obvious advantages of such a system, all the major email systems have, for some time, included Web access gateway products.

EXAM TIP

Telnet and Unix/Linux   Telnet is used to access Unix and Linux systems.

If the host is able to respond, it does so by sending echo reply messages back to the sending host. In that one simple process, ICMP enables the verification of the protocol suite configuration of both the sending and receiving nodes and any intermediate networking devices.

However, ICMP's functionality is not limited to just the use of the ping utility. ICMP is also able to return error messages such as Destination Unreachable and Time Exceeded messages. (The former message is reported when a destination cannot be contacted and the latter when the time to live (TTL) of a datagram has been exceeded.)

In addition to these and other functions, ICMP is able to perform *source quench*. In a source quench scenario, the receiving host is not able to handle the influx of data at the same rate as the data is being sent. To slow down the sending host, the receiving host sends ICMP source quench messages, telling the sender to slow down. This action prevents packets from being dropped and having to be re-sent.

ICMP is a very useful protocol. Although ICMP operates largely in the background, the ping utility alone makes it one of the most valuable of the protocols discussed in this chapter.

Address Resolution Protocol (ARP)

ARP, which is defined in RFC 826, is responsible for resolving IP addresses to Media Access Control (MAC) addresses. When a system attempts to contact another host, IP first determines whether the other host is on the same network it is on, by looking at the IP address. If IP determines that the destination is on the local network, it consults the ARP cache to see if it has a corresponding entry.

If there is not an entry for the host in the ARP cache, a broadcast on the local network asks the host with the target IP address to send back its MAC address. The communication is sent as a broadcast because without the target system's MAC address, the source system is unable to communicate directly with the target system.

Because the communication is a broadcast, every system on the network picks it up. However, only the target system replies because it is the only device whose IP address matches the request. The target system, recognizing that the ARP request is targeted at it, replies directly to the source system. It is able to do this because the ARP request contains the MAC address of the system that sent it. If the destination host is determined to be on a different subnet than the sending host, the ARP process is performed against the default gateway and then repeated for each step of the journey between the sending and receiving hosts.

> **EXAM TIP**
>
> **ARP Functions** The function of ARP is to resolve the IP address of a system to the MAC address of the interface on that system. Do not confuse ARP with DNS or WINS, which also perform resolution functions, but for different things.

Network Time Protocol (NTP)

NTP, which is defined in RFC 958, is the part of the TCP/IP protocol suite that facilitates the communication of time between systems. The idea is that one system configured as a time provider transmits time information to other systems that can be both the time receivers and the time providers to other systems.

Time synchronization is very important in today's IT environment because of the distributed nature of applications. Two very good examples of situations where time synchronization is important are email and directory services systems. In each of the these cases, having time synchronized between devices is important because without it there would be no way of keeping track of changes to data and applications.

In many environments, external time sources such as radio clocks, global positioning system (GPS) devices, and Internet-based time-servers are used as sources for NTP time. In others, the BIOS clock of the system is used. Regardless of what source is used, the time information is communicated between devices by using NTP.

> **NOTE**
>
> **NTP Rules** Specific guidelines dictate how NTP should be used. These "rules of engagement" can be found at www.eecis.udel.edu/~mills/ntp/servers.htm.

NTP server and client software is available for a wide variety of platforms and devices. If you are looking for a way to ensure time synchronization between devices, you should look to NTP as a solution.

REVIEW BREAK

TCP/IP Protocol Suite Summary

The details of each of protocols discussed in the preceding sections are summarized in Table 6.2. You can use this table for review before you take the Network+ exam.

TABLE 6.2
TCP/IP PROTOCOL SUITE SUMMARY

Protocol	Full Name	Description
IP	Internet Protocol	Connectionless protocol used for moving data around a network
TCP	Transmission Control Protocol	Connection-oriented protocol that offers flow control, sequencing, and retransmission of dropped packets
UDP	User Datagram Protocol	Connectionless alternative to TCP that is used for applications that do not require the functions offered by TCP
FTP	File Transfer Protocol	Protocol for uploading and downloading files to and from a remote host; also accommodates basic file management tasks
TFTP	Trivial File Transfer Protocol	File transfer protocol that does not have the security or error-checking capabilities of FTP; uses UDP as a transport protocol and is therefore connectionless
SMTP	Simple Mail Transfer Protocol	Mechanism for transporting email across networks
HTTP	Hypertext Transfer Protocol	Protocol for retrieving files from a Web server
HTTPS	Hypertext Transfer Protocol Secure	Secure protocol for retrieving files from a Web server
POP/IMAP	Post Office Protocol/Internet Message	Used for retrieving email from a server on which the mail is stored Access Protocol
Telnet	Telnet	Allows sessions to be opened on a remote host
ICMP	Internet Control Message Protocol	Used for error reporting, flow control, and route testing
ARP	Address Resolution Protocol	Resolves IP addresses to MAC addresses, to enable communication between devices
NTP	Network Time Protocol	Used to communicate time synchronization information between devices

TCP/UDP PORTS

▶ Define the function of TCP/UDP ports and identify well-known ports.

> **NOTE**
>
> **TCP and UDP Ports** CompTIA's objective for this section states "Describe the functions of TCP/UDP ports," which leaves you wondering if there is a difference between TCP and UDP ports. In reality there isn't. It's simply that some protocols use UDP and others use TCP.

The TCP/IP protocol suite offers so many services and applications that a mechanism is needed to identify to which protocol the incoming communications should be sent. That mechanism is a TCP/IP port.

Each TCP/IP protocol or application has a port associated with it. When a communication is received, the target port number is checked to see what protocol or service it is destined for. The request is then forwarded to that protocol or service. Take, for example, HTTP, whose assigned port number is 80. When a Web browser forms a request for a Web page, the request is sent to port 80 on the target system. When the target system receives the request, it examines the port number and when it sees that the port is 80, it forwards the request to the Web server application.

You can understand ports by thinking about the phone system of a large company. You can dial a central number (analogous to the IP address) to reach the switchboard, or you can append an extension number to get to a specific department directly (analogous to the port number). Another analogy is an apartment block. An apartment block has a single street address, but each apartment in the building has its own apartment number. And no, we are not going to suggest a poor comparison between an apartment suite and the TCP/IP protocol suite. Oops, too late!

TCP/IP has 65,535 ports available, but they are broken down into three designations:

- ◆ **Well-known ports**—The port numbers range from 0 to 1023. When CompTIA states "identify well-known ports," this is what it is referring to.

- ◆ **Registered ports**—The port numbers range from 1024 to 49151. Registered ports are used by applications or services that need to have consistent port assignments.

- ◆ **Dynamic or private ports**—The port numbers range from 49152 to 65535. These ports are not assigned to any protocol or service in particular and can be used for any service or application.

It is common for protocols to establish communication on one of the well-known ports and then move to a port in the dynamic range for the rest of the conversation. It's a bit like using a CB radio, in that you try to get a "breaker" on Channel 19, but then you go to another channel to have a conversation, leaving 19 open for others.

Understanding some of the most common TCP/IP port assignments is important because administrators are often required to specify port assignments when working with applications and configuring services. Table 6.3 shows some of the most well-known port assignments. For the Network+ exam, you should concentrate on the information provided in this table, and you should be able to answer any port-related questions you might receive.

NOTE: **IANA** You can obtain a list of port numbers from Internet Assigned Numbers Authority (IANA), at www.iana.org/assignments/port-numbers.

TABLE 6.3		

SOME OF THE MOST COMMON TCP/IP SUITE PROTOCOLS AND THEIR PORT ASSIGNMENTS

Protocol	Port Assignment	TCP/UDP Service
FTP	21	TCP
SSH	22	TCP
Telnet	23	TCP
SMTP	25	TCP
DNS	53	UDP
TFTP	69	UDP
HTTP	80	TCP/UDP
POP3	110	TCP
NNTP	119	TCP
NTP	123	TCP
IMAP4	143	TCP
SNMP	161	UDP
HTTPS	443	TCP

EXAM TIP

Port Numbers You should expect to know what port numbers are used for each protocol for the Network+ exam.

Although these are the standard ports for each of these protocols, in some cases it's possible to assign other port numbers to services. For example, you might choose to have one Web server application listen to the default port 80 while another listens to a different port. The result would be that if a user accesses the server but specifies a different port number, the user would be directed to the other Web server application running on the server.

TCP/IP-BASED NETWORK SERVICES

▶ Identify the purpose of the following network services: DHCP/BOOTP, DNS, NAT/ICS, WINS, and SNMP.

On its own, TCP/IP provides devices with a means to communicate, but combined with other services, such as the following, it can do even more:

◆ Dynamic Host Configuration Protocol (DHCP)

◆ BOOT Protocol (BOOTP)

◆ Domain Name System (DNS)

◆ Network Address Translation (NAT) and Internet Connection Sharing (ICS)

◆ Simple Network Management Protocol (SNMP)

◆ Windows Internet Name Service (WINS)

Services such as the ones discussed in the following sections provide functionality far beyond the basics of network communication. They provide a means to manage and administer a TCP/IP-based network. Today, it is quite likely that a network of any size will use one or all of the services discussed in the following sections. The first service we'll look at is one of the network administrator's best friends: DHCP.

Dynamic Host Configuration Protocol (DHCP)

Chapter 5 talks briefly about how IP addresses work. What it doesn't mention is that IP addresses can be assigned to devices statically or dynamically. Static IP addressing involves manually configuring the IP address of each system on the network; this is a potentially time-consuming process that provides plenty of opportunity for human error. For this reason, and because the reconfiguration of IP addressing is an equally arduous task, it's possible to have IP addresses assigned to systems automatically through a system called DHCP.

DHCP, which is defined in RFC 2131, allows ranges of IP addresses, known as *scopes*, to be defined on a system that is running a DHCP server application. When another system configured as a DHCP client is initialized, it asks the server for an address. If all things are as they should be, the server assigns an address to the client for a predetermined amount of time, which is known as the *lease* from the scope. Figure 6.2 shows a representation of DHCP.

FIGURE 6.2
An example of DHCP.

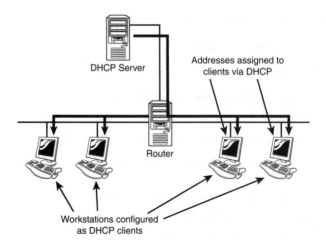

At various points during the lease (normally the 50% and 85% points), the client attempts to renew the lease from the server. If the server is unable to perform a renewal, the lease expires at 100%, and the client stops using the address.

In addition to an IP address and the subnet mask, many other pieces of information can be supplied by the DHCP server, although exactly what can be added depends on the DHCP server implementation. In addition to the address information, the default gateway is often supplied, along with Domain Name Service (DNS) information.

As well as having DHCP supply a random address from the scope, it's also possible to configure it to supply a specific address to a client. Such an arrangement is known as a *reservation*. Reservations are a means by which you can still use DHCP for a system but at the same time guarantee that it will always have the same IP address.

The advantages of using DHCP are numerous. First, administrators do not have to manually configure each system. Second, human error such as the assignment of duplicate IP addresses is eliminated. Third, DHCP removes the need to reconfigure systems if they move from one subnet to another or if you decide to make a wholesale change of the IP addressing structure. The downsides are that DHCP is a broadcast system that generates network traffic, albeit a very small amount, and that the DHCP server software must be installed and configured. After the initial configuration, though, DHCP is about as maintenance free as a service can get, with only occasional monitoring normally required.

> **NOTE**
>
> **Platform Independence**   DHCP is a protocol-dependent service, and it is not platform dependent. This means you can use, say, a Linux DHCP server for a network with Windows clients or a Novell DHCP server with Linux clients. Although the DHCP server offerings in the various network operating systems might differ slightly, the basic functionality is the same across the board.

The DHCP Process

When a system that is configured to use DHCP comes onto the network, it broadcasts a special packet that looks for a DHCP server. This packet is known as the DHCPDISCOVER packet. The DHCP server, which is always on the lookout for DHCPDISCOVER broadcasts, picks up the packet and compares the request with the scopes that it has defined. If it finds that it has a scope for the network from which the packet originated, it chooses an address from the scope, reserves it, and sends the address, along with any other information, such as the lease duration, to the client. This is known as the DHCPOFFER packet. Because the client still does not have an IP address, this communication is also achieved via broadcast.

When the client receives the offer, it looks at the offer to determine whether it is suitable. If more than one offer is received, which can happen if there is more than one DHCP server configured, the offers are compared to see which is best. *Best* in this context can involve a variety of criteria, but is normally the length of the lease. When the selection process is complete, the client notifies the server that the offer has been accepted, through a packet called a DHCPREQUEST packet, at which point the server finalizes the offer and sends the client an acknowledgment. This last message, which is sent as a broadcast, is known as a DHCPACK packet. When the client system has received the DHCPACK, it initializes the TCP/IP suite and is able to communicate on the network. You can see a representation of the DHCP process between a server and a client in Figure 6.3.

Fault-Tolerant DHCP Configurations

It is prudent to have more than one DHCP server to provide fault tolerance; however, you need to consider a number of factors when you use this approach. If multiple servers are used, the scopes defined on each server must not overlap, or else it is highly likely that systems will be assigned duplicate addresses from the different scopes. If you don't have enough addresses to create multiple, nonoverlapping scopes, you should consider configuring the DHCP server functionality on an additional server but not actually enabling the service. That way, if one of the DHCP servers goes down, the other system can be enabled quickly. Thanks to the lease renewal system, having the server down for a short amount of time is unlikely to cause too many problems. This, combined with a robust monitoring system, should ensure that the DHCP service is always available.

NOTE **What if the DHCP Server Is on a Different Subnet from the Client?** A common question about DHCP is "What happens if the DHCP server is on a different subnet from the client?" Normally, a router is configured not to forward a broadcast, but if the router is configured appropriately, it recognizes that the broadcast packet is a DHCP discovery packet and it therefore forwards the packet. When it does, however, it embeds in the packet information about which network the packet originated from. This allows the DHCP server to match the source network address with one of its ranges. This strategy allows a single DHCP server to serve the entire internetwork. If the router doesn't accommodate DHCP forwarding, a special service called a DHCP relay agent can be configured on a server. The DHCP relay agent forwards DHCP packets directly to the DHCP server rather than using broadcasts, allowing packets to traverse the routers.

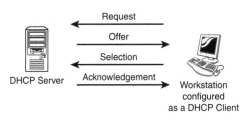

FIGURE 6.3
The DHCP process.

NOTE **Configuring Systems with DHCP Addresses** In some configurations, it might not be possible to configure a system with a DHCP address. In other cases, as with a server system, it might be possible but not recommended.

Should You Use DHCP?

Given the simplicity of DHCP's setup, the fact that all common network operating systems include a DHCP server free of charge, and the fact that running a DHCP server consumes very little server resources, it's hard to think of an environment in which a DHCP server is not a good idea. Unless you have a very small number of systems (fewer than, say, 10), a DHCP server is a very good idea indeed.

BOOT Protocol (BOOTP)

BOOTP was originally created so diskless workstations could obtain information—such as the TCP/IP address, subnet mask, and default gateway—needed to connect to the network. Such a system was necessary because diskless workstations had no way of storing the information.

When a system that is configured to use BOOTP is powered up, it broadcasts for a BOOTP server on the network. If there is such a server, it compares the MAC address of the system issuing the BOOTP request with a database of entries. From this database, it is able to supply the system with the appropriate information. It can also notify the workstation of a file that it must run on BOOTP.

In the unlikely event that you find yourself using BOOTP, you should be aware that, like DHCP, it is a broadcast-based system. Therefore, routers must be configured to forward BOOTP broadcasts.

Domain Name System (DNS)

DNS performs a very important function on TCP/IP-based networks. It resolves hostnames, such as www.quepublishing.com, to IP addresses, such as 24.67.164.63. Such a resolution system makes it possible for people to remember the names of, and refer to frequently used hosts, using the easy-to-remember hostnames rather than the hard-to-remember IP addresses.

In the days before the Internet, the network that was to become the Internet used a text file called HOSTS to perform name resolutions.

The file was regularly updated with changes and distributed to other servers. The following is a sample of some entries from a HOSTS file:

```
192.168.3.45     server1  s1            #The main
                                         file and
                                         print server
192.168.3.223    mail     mailserver    #The email server
```

As you can see, the IP address of the host is listed, along with the corresponding hostname. It is possible to add to a HOSTS file aliases of the server names, which in this example are s1 and mailserver. All the entries have to be added manually, and each system that is to perform resolutions has to have a copy of the file.

Even when the Internet was growing at a relatively slow pace, such a mechanism was both cumbersome and prone to error. It was obvious that as the network grew, a more automated and dynamic method of performing name resolution was needed. DNS became that method.

DNS solves the problem of name resolution by offering resolution through servers that are configured to act as name servers. The name servers run DNS server software, which allows them to receive, process, and reply to requests from systems that want to resolve hostnames to IP addresses. Systems that ask DNS servers for a hostname-to-IP address mapping are referred to as *resolvers*. Figure 6.4 shows an example of the DNS resolution process.

> **EXAM TIP**
>
> **The HOSTS File** On the Network+ exam, you might be asked to identify the purpose and function of a DNS HOSTS file.

> **EXAM TIP**
>
> **Comments in a HOSTS File** A comment in a HOSTS file is preceded by a hash symbol (#).

> **NOTE**
>
> **Resolution via the HOSTS File** HOSTS file resolution is still supported by practically every platform. If you need to resolve just a few hosts that will not change very often or at all, you can still use the HOSTS file for this.

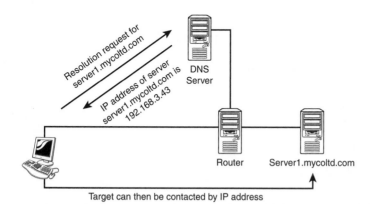

FIGURE 6.4
The DNS resolution process.

Because the DNS namespace, which is discussed in the following section, is very large, a single server is incapable of holding all the

N O T E

DDNS One of the problems with DNS is that despite all its automatic resolution capabilities, entries and changes to those entries must still be performed manually. A strategy to solve this problem is to use Dynamic DNS (DDNS), a newer system that allows hosts to automatically register themselves with the DNS server.

N O T E

FQDNs The domain name, along with any subdomains, is referred to as the fully qualified domain name (FQDN) because it includes all the components from the top of the DNS namespace to the host. For this reason, many people refer to DNS as *resolving FQDNs to IP addresses.*

records for the entire namespace. As a result, there is a good chance that a given DNS server might not be able to resolve the request for a certain entry. In this case, the DNS server asks another DNS server if it has an entry for the host.

The DNS Namespace

DNS operates in what is referred to as the *DNS namespace*. This space has logical divisions organized in a hierarchical structure. At the top level are domains such as .com and .edu, as well as domains for countries, such as .uk (United Kingdom) and .de (Germany). Below the top level are subdomains that are associated with organizations or commercial companies, such as Red Hat and Microsoft. Within these domains, hosts or other subdomains can be assigned. For example, the server ftp.redhat.com would be in the redhat.com domain, or another domain called, say, development, could be created, and hosts could be placed in that (that is, ftp.development.redhat.com). Figure 6.5 shows a graphical representation of a DNS hierarchical namespace.

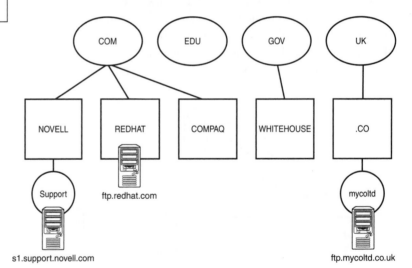

FIGURE 6.5
An example of a DNS hierarchical namespace.

The lower domains are largely open to use in whatever way the domain name holder sees fit. However, the top-level domains are relatively closely controlled. You can see a selection of the most widely used top-level DNS domain names in Table 6.4. Recently, a number of top-level domains were added, mainly to accommodate the increasing need for hostnames.

TABLE 6.4

SELECTED TOP-LEVEL DOMAINS IN THE DNS NAMESPACE

Top-Level Domain Name	Intended Purpose
com	Commercial organizations
edu	Educational organizations/establishments
gov	U.S. government organizations/establishments
net	Network providers/centers
org	Not-for-profit/other organizations
mil	Military
arpa	Reverse lookup
de	A country-specific domain, in this case Germany*

*In addition to country-specific domains, many countries have created subdomains that follow roughly the same principles as the original top-level domains (for example, co.uk, .gov.nz).

It should be noted that although the assignment of domain names is supposed to conform to the structure in Table 6.4, the assignment of names is not as closely controlled as you might think. It's not uncommon for some domain names to be used for other purposes. In particular, the .net and .org namespaces have been used for purposes other than what was intended.

Types of DNS Entries

Although the most common entry in a DNS database is an A (ADDRESS) record, which maps a hostname to an IP address, DNS can hold numerous other types of entries, as well. Some of particular note are the MX record, which is used to map entries that correspond to mail exchanger systems; and CNAME, or canonical record name, which can be used to create alias records for a system. A system can have an A record and then multiple CNAME entries for its aliases. A DNS table with all these types of entries might look like this:

```
fileserve.mycoltd.com   IN   A    192.168.33.2
email.mycoltd.com       IN   A    192.168.33.7
fileprint.mycoltd.com   IN CNAME fileserver.mycoltd.com
mailer.mycoltd.com      IN   MX   10    email.mycoltd.com
```

NOTE

Reverse Lookup Although the primary function of DNS is to resolves hostnames to IP addresses, it is also possible to have DNS perform an IP address-to-hostname resolution. This process is called *reverse lookup*.

As you can see, rather than map to an actual IP address, the CNAME and MX record entries map to another host, which DNS in turn can resolve to an IP address.

DNS in a Practical Implementation

In a real-world scenario, whether you use DNS is almost a nonissue. If you have Internet access, you will most certainly use DNS, but you are likely to use the DNS facilities of your Internet service provider (ISP) rather than have your own internal DNS server. However, if you operate a large, complex, multiplatform network, you might find that internal DNS servers are necessary. The major network operating system vendors are conscious of the fact that you might need DNS facilities in your organization, so they include DNS server applications with their offerings. It should also be noted that Microsoft Active Directory (see Chapter 9, "Network Operating Systems and Clients") requires DNS to operate.

It is common practice for workstations to be configured with the IP addresses of two DNS servers for fault-tolerance. You can see an example of this in Figure 6.6.

The importance of DNS, particularly in environments where the Internet is heavily used, cannot be overstated. If DNS facilities are not accessible, the Internet effectively becomes unusable, unless you can remember the IP addresses of all your favorite sites.

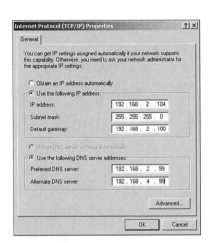

FIGURE 6.6
The DNS entries on a Windows 2000 Professional system.

Network Address Translation (NAT) and Internet Connection Sharing (ICS)

The need for almost every network, even small ones, to have Internet access has created the need for a mechanism to allow many computers to access the Internet through a single connection. Two mechanisms that make this possible are NAT and ICS.

NAT

The basic principle of NAT is that many computers can "hide" behind a single IP address. The main reason we need to do this (as you will see later in this chapter, in the section "IP Addressing") is because there simply aren't enough IP addresses to go around. Using NAT means that only one registered IP address is needed on the external interface of the system that is acting as the gateway between the internal and external networks.

NAT allows you to use whatever addressing scheme you like on your internal networks, although it is common practice to use the private address ranges, which are discussed later in the chapter, in the section "Identifying the Differences Between Public and Private Networks."

> **NOTE**
>
> **NAT and Proxy Servers** Don't confuse NAT with proxy servers, which are discussed in Chapter 12, "Securing the Network." The proxy service is very different from NAT, but many proxy server applications do include NAT functionality.

How NAT Works

When a system is performing NAT service, it funnels the requests that are given to it to the Internet. To the remote host, the request looks like it is originating from a single address. The system that is performing the NAT function keeps track of who asked for what and makes sure that when the data is returned, it is directed to the correct system. Servers that provide NAT functionality do so in different ways. For example, it is possible to statically map a specific internal IP address to a specific external one (known as the one-to-one NAT method), so that outgoing requests are always tagged with the same IP address. Alternatively, if you have a group of public IP addresses, you can have the NAT system assign addresses to devices on a first-come, first-served basis. Either way, the basic function of NAT is the same. Figure 6.7 shows a representation of NAT.

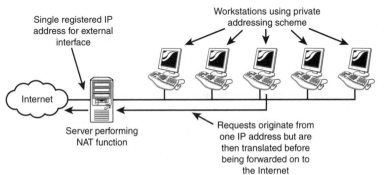

FIGURE 6.7
An example of NAT.

ICS

Although ICS is discussed separately from NAT, it is nothing more than an implementation of NAT on Windows platforms. More specifically, Windows Me, Windows XP, and Windows 2000 include the ICS feature, which makes it simple for users to create shared Internet connections.

Because ICS was intended as a simple mechanism for a small office network or a home network to share a single Internet connection, configuration is simple. However, simplicity is also the potential downfall of ICS. ICS provides no security, and the system providing the shared connection is not secure against outside attacks. For that reason, ICS should be used only when there are no other facilities available.

Simple Network Management Protocol (SNMP)

SNMP allows network devices to communicate information about their state to a central system. It also allows the central system to pass configuration parameters to the devices.

Components of SNMP

In an SNMP configuration, a central system known as a *manager* acts as the central communication point for all the SNMP-enabled devices on the network. On each device that is to be managed and monitored via SNMP, software called an SNMP agent is set up and configured with the IP address of the manager. Depending on the configuration, the SNMP manager is then able to communicate with and retrieve information from the devices running the SNMP agent software. In addition, the agent is able to communicate the occurrence of certain events to the SNMP manager as they happen. These messages are known as *traps*. Figure 6.8 shows how an SNMP system works.

NOTE

SNMP Is Not an NMS   SNMP is a protocol that facilitates network management functionality. It is not, in itself, a network management system (NMS).

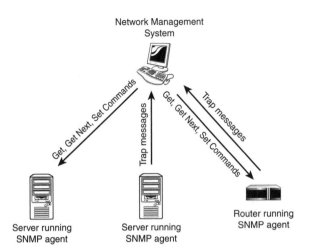

Network Management
System

Get, Get Next, Set Commands

Trap messages

Get, Get Next, Set Commands

Trap messages

Server running
SNMP agent

Server running
SNMP agent

Router running
SNMP agent

FIGURE 6.8
How SNMP works.

SNMP Management Systems

An SNMP management system is a computer running a special piece
of software called a Network Management System (NMS). These
software applications can be free, or they can cost thousands of dollars. The difference between the free applications and those that cost
a great deal of money normally boils down to functionality and support. All NMS systems, regardless of cost, offer the same basic functionality. Today, most NMS applications use graphical maps of the
network to locate a device and then query it. The queries are built in
to the application and are triggered by a point and click. You can
actually issue SNMP requests from a command-line utility, but with
so many tools available, it is simply not necessary.

Using SNMP and an NMS, it is possible to monitor all the devices
on a network, including switches, hubs, routers, servers, and printers, as well as any device that supports SNMP, from a single location. Using SNMP, you can see the amount of free disk space on a
server in Jakarta or reset the interface on a router in Helsinki—all
from the comfort of your desk in San Jose. Such power, though,
does bring with it some considerations. For example, because an
NMS gives you the ability to reconfigure network devices, or at least
get information from them, it is common practice to implement an
NMS on a secure workstation platform such as Linux or Windows
NT/2000 and to place the NMS PC in a secure location.

NOTE

Trap Managers   Some people refer
to SNMP managers or NMSs as "trap
managers." This reference is mislead-
ing because NMS is able to do more
than just accept trap messages from
agents.

SNMP Agents

Although the SNMP manager resides on a PC, each device that is part of the SNMP structure also needs to have SNMP functionality enabled. This is performed through a software component called an *agent*.

An SNMP agent can be any device that is capable of running a small software component that facilitates communication with an SNMP manager. SNMP agent functionality is supported by almost any device that is designed to be connected to a network.

As well as providing a mechanism for managers to communicate with them, agents are also able to tell SNMP managers when something happens. When a certain condition is met on a device that is running an SNMP agent, a trap is sent to the NMS, and the NMS then performs an action, depending on the configuration. Basic NMS systems may sound an alarm or flash a message on the screen. Other, more advanced, products may send a pager message, dial a cell phone, or send an email message.

Management Information Bases (MIBs)

Although the SNMP trap system may be the most commonly used aspect of SNMP, the manager-to-agent communication is not just a one-way street. In addition to being able to read information from a device using the SNMP commands Get and Get Next, SNMP managers can also issue the Set command. Having just three commands might make SNMP seem like a very limited mechanism, but this is not the case. The secret of SNMP's power is in how it uses those three commands.

To demonstrate how SNMP commands work, imagine that you and a friend each have a list on which the following four words are written: four, book, sky, and table. If you, as the manager, ask your friend for the first value, she, acting as the agent, will reply "four." This is analogous to an SNMP Get command. Now, if you ask for the next value, she would reply "book." This is analogous to an SNMP Get Next command. If you then say "set green," and your friend changes the word *book* to *green*, you will have performed the equivalent of an SNMP Set command. Sound simplistic? Well, if you can imagine expanding the list to include 100 values, you can see how you could navigate and set any parameter in the list, using

N O T E   **SNMP Versions**   The version of SNMP in widescale use now is Version 1. Other versions of SNMP are available, but they are not generally used due to a lack of standardization. Later versions of SNMP have more than just the three commands discussed here.

just those three commands. The key, though, is to make sure that you and your friend have exactly the same list, which is where Management Information Bases (MIBs) come in.

SNMP uses databases of information called MIBs to define what parameters are accessible, which of the parameters are read-only, and which are capable of being set. MIBs are available for thousands of devices and services, covering every imaginable need.

To ensure that SNMP systems offer cross-platform compatibility, MIB creation is controlled by the International Organization for Standardization (ISO). An organization that wants to create a MIB can apply to the ISO. The ISO then assigns the organization an ID under which it can create MIBs as it sees fit. The assignment of numbers is structured within a conceptual model called the *hierarchical name tree*. Figure 6.9 shows an example of the MIB hierarchical name tree.

EXAM TIP

Finding a MIB Do you want to find a MIB for a device on your network? MIB Central (`www.mibcentral.com`) provides a searchable database of nearly 2,400 MIBs for a wide range of equipment.

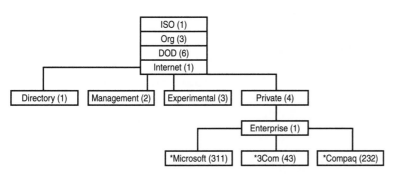

*Included for example purposes

FIGURE 6.9
An example of the MIB hierarchical name tree.

Table 6.5 extends the hierarchical tree further, to show the MIB entry on a Windows NT server, which corresponds to the number of DHCP offers that have been made by that server.

TABLE 6.5

EXTENDING MIB IDENTIFIERS TO THEIR CONCLUSION

Designator	Identifier
International Standards Organization	1
Organization	3

continues

TABLE 6.5   *continued*

EXTENDING MIB IDENTIFIERS TO THEIR CONCLUSION

Designator	*Identifier*
Department of Defense	6
Internet	1
Private	4
Enterprise	1
Microsoft	311
Software	1
DHCP	3
DHCPPar	1
ParDhcpTotalNoOfOffers	5.0

SNMP Communities

Another feature of SNMP that allows for manageability is communities. *SNMP communities* are logical groupings of systems. When a system is configured as part of a community, it communicates only with other devices that have the same community name. In addition, it accepts Get, Get Next, or Set commands only from an SNMP manager with a community name it recognizes. There are typically two communities defined by default: a public community that is intended for read-only use and a private community that is intended for read and write operations.

Whether you use SNMP depends on how many devices you have and how distributed your network infrastructure is. Even in environments that have just a few devices, SNMP can be very useful because it can act as your eyes and ears, notifying you in the event of a problem on the network.

Windows Internet Name Service (WINS)

On Windows networks, a system called WINS enables Network Basic Input/Output System (NetBIOS) names to be resolved to IP addresses.

NetBIOS name resolution is necessary on Windows networks so that systems can locate and access each other by using the NetBIOS computer name rather than the IP address. It's a lot easier for a person to remember that Mary's PC is called Mary than to remember its IP address, 192.168.2.34. However, even though the system can be accessed, from the user's perspective using the NetBIOS's computer name, this name still needs to be resolved to an IP address and subsequently to a MAC address (by ARP).

There are three ways a system can perform NetBIOS name resolution:

- ◆ **Statically**—A file called LMHOSTS can be manually updated with NetBIOS machine name-to-IP address mappings. It's also possible to make an entry in the file that points to a centrally located LMHOSTS file.

- ◆ **Via broadcast**—When a resolution is needed, the system can broadcast on the local network for the target host. The broadcast is picked up by all the devices on the local network, and each device looks at the target NetBIOS name to determine whether it is the target system. Only the intended target replies to the request.

- ◆ **By using dynamic name resolution**—When a WINS server is installed, WINS clients called *resolvers* are able to pass requests directly to the WINS server and have those requests answered from a database of records.

Of these three methods, the first requires that you manually configure at least one file with the entries. As you can imagine, this can be a time-consuming process, particularly if the systems on the network change frequently. You can forget using DHCP with static resolution. Unless you make reservations for each and every system on the network, the LMHOSTS file is likely to fall out of sync with the network fairly quickly.

The second method, broadcasts, works well in a small network environment, but if a large number of devices are on the network, the broadcast traffic can quickly become a problem. Add to that the fact that you can't browse across network segments (which is discussed shortly), and you'll see that the broadcast method is limited in its applications.

NOTE

NBNS   WINS is also referred to as the NetBIOS Name Service (NBNS).

EXAM TIP

Resolving NetBIOS Names   In a network that does not use WINS, there are two methods by which NetBIOS names can be resolved: via broadcasts or in the LMHOSTS file. Additionally, Windows 2000 can use DNS.

There are two basic reasons you might use a WINS server:

◆ **To reduce broadcasts**—In a network that does not have a WINS server, a system uses broadcasts to locate another system. On a large segment, these broadcasts can have a significant impact on network traffic.

◆ **To communicate across routers**—Because NetBIOS resolutions are broadcast based, they are not forwarded by routers. This makes it impossible for a NetBIOS name to be resolved from one segment to another. Although you can configure routers to forward these broadcasts, a more common practice is simply to use WINS. Because systems are configured with the address of the WINS server, it is possible for the client systems to query the server directly for name resolutions.

WINS in the Real World

WINS is a dynamic system. Each time a system is brought on to the network, it registers itself with a WINS server. When the system is taken off the network (that is, when it is powered down), it deregisters itself with the WINS server to make sure that the WINS database is kept up-to-date. For this and many other reasons, it is important that Windows systems are powered down in the correct manner.

It is possible to tune the NetBIOS name resolution by configuring the resolvers to use a specific order of resolution. For example, you can direct them to attempt a broadcast first and then contact a WINS server. Or you can direct them to only use a WINS server, and dispense with the broadcast resolution methods completely.

Although there are many environments in which you'll find WINS servers implemented, Microsoft is moving away from WINS as a resolution method and turning its focus to DNS. In particular, Windows 2000 offers DDNS, which basically eliminates the need for WINS.

R E V I E W   B R E A K

TCP/IP Service Summary

Table 6.6 helps you quickly identify the purpose and function of each of the TCP/IP services covered in the previous sections.

TABLE 6.6
SUMMARY OF TCP/IP SERVICES

Service	Purpose/Function
DHCP/BOOTP	Automatically assigns IP addressing information
DNS	Resolves hostnames to IP addresses
NAT/ICS	Translates private network addresses into public network addresses
SNMP	Provides network management facilities on TCP/IP-based networks
WINS	Resolves NetBIOS names to IP addresses

IP ADDRESSING

▶ Identify IP addresses (IPv4, IPv6) and their default subnet masks.

Addressing is perhaps the most challenging aspect of TCP/IP. It's certainly a topic that has many people scratching their heads for a while. The following sections look at how IP addressing works for both IPv4 and the newest version of the IP, IPv6. In today's IT environment, and certainly in the immediate future, IPv4 will remain the protocol of choice for networking. For that reason, this chapter dedicates considerably more time to it.

General IP Addressing Principles

To communicate on a network using the TCP/IP protocol, each system has to be assigned a unique address. The address defines both the number of the network to which the device is attached and the address of the node on that network. In other words, the IP address provides two pieces of information. It's a bit like a street name and a house number of a person's home address.

Each device on a logical network segment must have the same network address as all the other devices on the segment. All the devices must have different node addresses.

NOTE

IP Terminology   Two important phrases in IP addressing are network address and node address. The IP address defines both, but you must understand that the network address and the node address are different from one another. You need to be aware, also, that some people call the network address the network ID and the host address the host ID.

So how does the system know which part of the address is the network part and which is the node part? That is the function of a *subnet mask*. On its own, an IP address is no good to the system because it is simply a set of four numbers. The subnet mask is used in concert with the IP address to determine which portion of the IP address refers to the network address and which refers to the node address.

IPv4

An IPv4 address (which we just call an *IP address* from now on) is comprised of four sets of 8 bits, or octets. The result is that IP addresses are 32 bits in length. Each bit in the octet is assigned a decimal value. The leftmost bit has a value of 128, followed by 64, 32, 16, 8, 4, 2, and 1, left to right.

Each bit in the octet can be either a 1 or a 0. If the value is 1, it is counted as its decimal value, and if it is 0, it is ignored. If all the bits are 0, the value of the octet is 0. If all the bits in the octet are 1, the value is 255, which is 128+64+32+16+8+4+2+1. Figure 6.10 shows a chart representing the binary-to-decimal conversion. In Figure 6.10, the chart is used to derive the decimal of 195.

FIGURE 6.10
A binary-to-decimal conversion chart showing how 195 is derived.

128	64	32	16	8	4	2	1
1	1	0	0	0	0	1	1

By using the set of 8 bits and manipulating the 1s and 0s, any value between 0 and 255 can be obtained for each octet. Table 6.7 shows a few examples of this.

TABLE 6.7

EXAMPLES OF NUMBERS DERIVED THROUGH BINARY

Decimal Value	Binary Value	Decimal Calculation
10	00001010	8+2=10
192	11000000	128+64=192
205	11001101	128+64+8+4+1=205
223	11011111	128+64+16+8+4+2+1=223

As mentioned earlier, the IP address is composed of four sets of these bits, each of which is separated by a period. For this reason, an IP address is said to be expressed in dotted-decimal format.

IP Address Classes

IP addresses are grouped into logical divisions called *classes*. In the IPv4 address space, there are five address classes (A through E), although only three are used for assigning addresses to clients. Class D is reserved for multicast addressing, and Class E is reserved for future development.

Of the three classes available for address assignments, each uses a fixed-length subnet mask to define the separation between the network and the node address. A Class A address uses only the first octet to represent the network portion, a Class B address uses two octets, and a Class C address uses three octets. The upshot of this system is that Class A has a small number of network addresses but a very large number of possible host addresses. Class B has a larger number of networks but a smaller number of hosts, and Class C has an even larger number of networks, as well as an even smaller number of hosts. The exact figures are provided in Table 6.8.

TABLE 6.8

IPv4 ADDRESS CLASSES AND THE NUMBER OF AVAILABLE NETWORK/HOST ADDRESSES

Address Class	Range	Number of Networks	Number of Hosts per Network	Binary Value of First Octet
A	1–126	126	16,777,214	0xxxxxxx
B	128–191	16384	65,532	10xxxxxx
C	192–223	2,097,152	254	110xxxxx
D	224–247	NA	NA	1110xxxx
E	248–255	NA	NA	1111xxxx

Notice in Table 6.8 that the network number 127 is not included in any of the ranges. The 127 network ID is reserved for the local loopback. The local loopback is a function that is built in to the TCP/IP protocol suite and can be used for troubleshooting purposes.

EXAM TIP

Address Classes For the Network+ exam, you should be prepared to identify into which class a given address falls. You should also be prepared to identify the loopback address.

Subnet Mask Assignment

Like an IP address, a subnet mask is a 32-bit address expressed in dotted-decimal format. Unlike an IP address, though, a subnet mask performs just one function: It defines which parts of the IP address refer to the network address and which refer to the node address. Each of the classes of IP address that are used for address assignment has a standard subnet mask associated with it. The default subnet masks are listed in Table 6.9.

TABLE 6.9

DEFAULT SUBNET MASKS ASSOCIATED WITH IP ADDRESS CLASSES

Address Class	Default Subnet Mask
A	255.0.0.0
B	255.255.0.0
C	255.255.255.0

Broadcast Addresses and "This Network"

Two important concepts to keep in mind when working with TCP/IP are broadcast addresses and the addresses used to refer to "this network." When referring to "this network," the host ID portion of the address is expressed as 0s. So, for network number 192.168, the reference would be 192.168.0.0. For a Class A network number 12, it would be 12.0.0.0.

Broadcast addresses work much the same way as "this network" addresses, except that the host ID portion of the address is set to 255, to reflect that the message is going to be sent to all the hosts on that network. Using the preceding examples, the broadcast addresses would be 192.168.255.255 and 12.255.255.255.

Classless Interdomain Routing (CIDR)

Classless interdomain routing (CIDR) is a method of assigning addresses outside the standard Class A, B, and C structure. By specifying the number of bits in the subnet mask as a specific number, there is more flexibility than with the three standard class definitions.

Using CIDR, addresses are assigned using a value known as the
slash. The actual value of the slash is dependent on how many bits
of the subnet mask are used to express the network portion of the
address. For example, a subnet mask that uses all 8 bits from the
first octet and 4 from the second would be described as /12, or
"slash 12." A subnet mask that uses all the bits from the first three
octets would be called /24. Why the slash? In actual addressing
terms, the CIDR value is expressed after the address, using a slash.
So the address 192.168.2.1/24 means that the IP address of the
node is 192.168.2.1 and the subnet mask is 255.255.255.0.

IPv6

IPv4 has served faithfully for many years, and it seems that it is still
not yet ready to yield to the next version of IP, IPv6. However,
sooner or later we will be moved to IPv6, so an understanding of
what is involved in IPv6 and its addressing is both useful and
required for the Network+ exam.

IPv6 Addressing

By far the most significant aspect of IPv6 is its addressing capability.
The address range of IPv4 is nearly depleted, and it is widely
acknowledged that we are at just the beginning of the digital era.
Therefore, we need an addressing scheme that offers more
addresses than could possibly be used in the foreseeable future.
IPv6 delivers exactly that. Whereas IPv4 uses a 32-bit address,
IPv6 uses a 128-bit address that yields a staggering
340,282,366,920,938,463,463,374,607,431,768,211,456 possible
addresses. And no, the numeric pad on the PC didn't go nuts; that is
actually the number. Anyone for a subnetting exercise?

IPv6 addresses are expressed in a very different format from those
used in IPv4. An IPv6 address is composed of eight octet pairs in
hexadecimal, separated by colons. The following is an example of an
IPv6 address:

```
42DE:7E55:63F2:21AA:CBD4:D773:CC21:554F
```

Notice that the format of this address is similar to that used to
express a MAC address, although it is longer. Because the address is
expressed in hexadecimal format, only numbers and the letters A
though F are used in IPv6 addresses.

Other Benefits of IPv6

Although addressing is the biggest change in IPv6, the new version of the protocol will bring a number of other features, including the following:

◆ **Smaller header**—Some of the fields included in the IPv4 packet header format have been dropped or made optional. The upshot of this is that IPv6 has lower overhead than IPv4.

◆ **Packet labeling**—Packets can be labeled in such a way that they are recognized by a router as being special. This makes it possible for the router to prioritize data.

◆ **Improved authentication/security**—Realizing our increasing need for more security and authentication capabilities, the IPv6 specification includes extensions to support features such as IPSec (see Chapter 8, "Remote Access and Security Protocols," for more information).

Most manufacturers are building IPv6 support into their products now, to get ready for the time when we move to the new system. In the meantime, we will continue to use IPv4.

SUBNETTING

▶ Identify the purpose of subnetting and default gateways.

Now that we have looked at how IP addresses are used, we can discuss the process of subnetting. *Subnetting* is a process by which the node portions of an address are used to create more networks than you would have if you used the default subnet mask.

To illustrate subnetting, let's use an example. Suppose that you have been assigned the Class B address 150.150.0.0. Using this address and the default subnet mask, you could have a single network (150.150) and use the rest of the address as node addresses. This would give you a large number of possible node addresses, which in reality is probably not very useful. So, what you can do is "borrow" bits from the node portion of the address to use as network addresses. This would reduce the number of nodes per network, but chances are, you would still have more than enough.

EXAM TIP

IP Subnetting   IP subnetting is a very complex task, and it is hard to explain fully in the space available in this book. The information provided in this section is more than sufficient to answer any subnetting-related questions you might see on the Network+ exam. In fact, this material goes into more detail than is required. In the real world, subnetting is an important skill.

The simplest solution would be to use a subnet mask of 255.255.255.0 instead of the default Class B subnet mask of 255.255.0.0. This would give you 254 networks (150.150.1 through 254.0) and 254 nodes on each of those networks. The only problem arises if you need more than 254 nodes on each network. You then have to use a process sometimes referred to as *partial-octet* or *fractional subnetting.*

In partial-octet/fractional subnetting, only a portion of the octet is used to create more networks, and the rest of the octet is still available for assigning as node addresses. Here's how it works. Using the example of 150.150.0.0, let's say you want to create six networks. To do that, you need to take enough bits from the third octet to create six network addresses, and at the same time, you need to preserve as many node addresses as possible. If you take the first 3 bits, you can use combinations of the bits to create values as the network addresses. The values are shown in Table 6.10.

TABLE 6.10

VALUES OF SUBNETS WHEN USING 3 BITS FROM AN OCTET

Binary Value	Decimal Value
000	0
001	32
010	64
011	96
100	128
101	160
110	192
111	224

Because no portion of the address can be all 0s or all 1s, you can't use the 000 and 111 combination. Therefore, you lose the network assignments of 0 and 224. You are conveniently left with six possible networks.

NOTE

A Little Subnet Math   You can use a calculation to work out how many networks you'll get from a number of bits. For example, 2 to the power of the number of masked bits minus 2 equals the number of networks, and 2 to the power of the number of unmasked bits minus 2 will give you the number of nodes on the network. You have to subtract 2 from the total in each case because you can't have a portion of the address as all 1s or all 0s.

The bits you are taking are from the left side of the octet. To take this a step further, imagine that you use 5 bits of the octet instead of 3, as in the previous example. Using 5 bits, you would be taking the 128, 64, 32, 16, and 8 binary positions. The network numbers you could use would be 8, 16, 24, 32, 40, 48, 56, 64, and so on up to 248, in multiples of 8, which is the lowest number of the set that was used. In each instance, the available network IDs can be derived by taking the lowest number used, which in the first example is 32 and in this example is 8, and then multiplying up from there.

Let's look at another example. Imagine that you have been assigned the address 211.106.15.0. You need to have at least four networks. What would the subnet mask be, and what are the network IDs that you could use?

The subnet mask would be 255.255.255.224. To create four networks, you would need to use 3 bits (128, 64, and 32). This would give you six possible networks (32, 64, 96, 128, 160, and 192). It's simple! Remember that, as was discussed earlier, you can't use the values that correspond to all 0s or all 1s when working with subnets, which is why the network numbers 0 and 224 are not included.

The network addresses that can be derived from an address of 211.106.15.0 and a subnet mask of 255.255.255.224 are shown in Table 6.11, along with the usable address ranges for each network.

TABLE 6.11

SUBNETTED NETWORK ADDRESSES FROM THE ADDRESS 211.106.15.0

Network Address	Usable Address Range
211.106.15.32	211.106.15.33–211.106.15.63
211.106.15.64	211.106.15.65–211.106.15.95
211.106.15.96	211.106.15.97–211.106.15.127
211.106.15.128	211.106.15.129–211.106.15.159
211.106.15.160	211.106.15.161–211.106.15.191
211.106.15.192	211.106.15.193–211.106.15.223

The question that is normally on people's minds is "Okay, but how does this work in the real world?" Using the 211.105.15.0 example as a base, let's look at how the addressing would occur on the client systems. A system with the address 211.106.15.122 would be on the network 211.106.15.96, and the host ID would be 26 (96+26=122). The value of the third octet is the combination of the network address and the host ID.

As you can see, the use of subnetting makes addressing rather involved, but when you are used to it, it's really quite straightforward.

REASONS TO SUBNET

There are two main reasons for subnetting. First, it allows you to utilize IP address ranges more effectively. Second, it provides increased security and manageability to IP networking by providing a mechanism to create multiple networks rather than having just one.

DEFAULT GATEWAYS

▶ Identify the purpose of subnetting and default gateways.

Default gateways are the means by which a device is able to access hosts on other networks for which it does not have a route. Most workstation configurations actually default to just using default gateways rather than having any static routes configured.

When a system wants to communicate with another device, it first determines whether the host is on the local network or a remote network. If the host is on a remote network, the system looks in the routing table to determine whether it has an entry for the network that the remote host is on. If it does, it uses that route. If it does not, the data is sent to the default gateway.

In essence, the default gateway is simply the path out of the network for a given device. Figure 6.11 shows an example of how a default gateway fits into a network infrastructure.

EXAM TIP

Default Gateways For the Network+ exam, you will be expected to identify the purpose and function of a default gateway.

NOTE

Default Gateway Must Be Local Although it might seem obvious, it's worth mentioning that the default gateway must be on the same network as the nodes that use it.

FIGURE 6.11
The role of a default gateway.

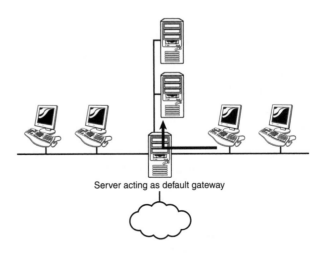

Server acting as default gateway

If a system is not configured with any static routes or a default gateway, it is limited to operating on its own network segment.

IDENTIFYING THE DIFFERENCES BETWEEN PUBLIC AND PRIVATE NETWORKS

▶ Identify the differences between public and private networks.

IP addressing involves many considerations, not least important of which is public and private networks. A *public network* is a network to which anyone can connect. The best, and perhaps only pure, example of such a network is the Internet. A *private network* is any network to which access is restricted. A corporate network or a school network would be considered a private network.

The main difference between public and private networks, apart from the fact that access to a private network is tightly controlled and access to a public network is not, is that the addressing of devices on a public network must be considered carefully, whereas addressing on a private network has a little more latitude.

As we have already discussed, in order for hosts on a network to communicate by using TCP/IP, they must have unique addresses.

The address defines the logical network each host belongs to and the host's address on that network. On a private internetwork with, say, three logical networks and 100 nodes on each network, addressing is not a particularly complex task. On a network on the scale of the Internet, however, addressing is very complex.

Each device on the Internet must be assigned a unique address, often referred to as a *registered address*, in light of the fact that it is assigned to a specific party. If two devices have the same address, chances are that neither will be able to communicate. Therefore, the assignment of addresses is carefully controlled by various organizations. Originally, the organization responsible for address assignments was the IANA, but it has since devolved some of the addressing responsibility to other organizations. Around the world, three organizations shoulder the responsibility for assigning IP addresses. In the Americas and parts of the Caribbean, address assignments are the responsibility of the American Registry for Internet Numbers (ARIN); in the Asia Pacific region, it is the Asia Pacific Network Information Centre (APNIC); and in Europe, the Middle East, and parts of Africa, it is Réseaux IP Européens Network Coordination Centre (RIPE NCC).

Between them, these organizations ensure that there are no IP address space conflicts and that the assignment of addresses is carefully managed.

If you are connecting a system to the Internet, you need to get a valid registered IP address from one of these organizations. Alternatively, you can obtain an address from an ISP. Because of the nature of their business, ISPs have large blocks of IP addresses that they can then use to assign to their clients. If you need a registered IP address, getting one from an ISP will almost certainly be a simpler process than going through a regional numbers authority. In fact, getting a number from an ISP is the way most people get addresses. Some ISPs' plans actually include blocks of registered IP addresses, working on the principle that businesses are going to want some kind of permanent presence on the Internet. Of course, if you discontinue your service with the ISP, you will no longer be able to use the IP address the ISP provided.

> **N O T E**
>
> **IPv4 Assignments**   You can view the IP address range assignments for IPv4 at www.iana.org/assignments/ ipv4-address-space.

Private Address Ranges

To provide flexibility in addressing and to prevent an incorrectly configured network from polluting the Internet, certain address ranges are set aside for private use. These address ranges are called *private ranges* because they are designated for use only on private networks. These addresses are special because Internet routers are configured to ignore any packets they see that use these addresses. This means that if a network "leaks" onto the Internet, it won't make it any further than the first router it encounters.

Three ranges are defined in RFC 1918, one each from Classes A, B, and C. You can use whichever range you want, although the Class A and Class B address ranges offer more addressing options than does Class C. The address ranges are defined in Table 6.12.

TABLE 6.12

PRIVATE ADDRESS RANGES

Class	Address Range	Default Subnet Mask
A	10.0.0.0–10.255.255.255	255.0.0.0
B	172.16.0.0–172.31.255.255	255.255.0.0
C	192.168.0.0–192.168.255.255	255.255.255.0

As you can see, the ranges offer a myriad of addressing possibilities. Even the Class C range offers 254 networks, with 254 nodes on each network, which is more than sufficient for the majority of network installations.

There is no requirement to use these addresses. In fact, many organizations choose not to use them and instead use an addressing scheme of another range. Such a strategy is fine if there is no chance the data from the network will find its way on to a public network. Given that the private ranges are created for this very reason and are flexible in terms of accommodating addresses, there is no reason not to use them.

Practical Uses of Public and Private IP Addressing

Having established the purpose of both public and private networks, and of public and private IP addressing, we can now look at how these fit into a practical scenario. It is common practice for a company to have only a handful of registered IP addresses and to configure the internal, private, network by using one of the private addressing schemes. Figure 6.12 shows the most basic example of this.

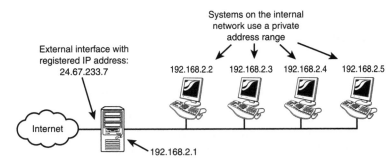

FIGURE 6.12
A basic example of public and private network address assignments.

The network in Figure 6.12 could provide Internet access to clients through the proxy server system. The external interface of the proxy server would have a registered IP address, and all the systems on the internal network would use one of the private ranges.

In this example, the external interface of the proxy server could use an ISP-assigned DHCP address. But what if the company wanted to have the same address all the time for a Web server or a Web access gateway for its email system? Then you would need to consider how you would assign IP addresses to the systems so that they could be accessed by an outside source.

CHAPTER SUMMARY

KEY TERMS

- IP
- TCP
- UDP
- FTP
- TFTP
- SMTP
- HTTP
- HTTPS
- POP
- IMAP
- Telnet
- ICMP
- ARP
- NTP
- DHCP
- BOOTP
- DNS
- HOSTS file
- NAT
- ICS
- SNMP
- WINS
- LMHOSTS file
- IP addressing
- subnet mask
- IPv4
- IPv6
- subnetting
- default gateways
- public network
- private network

This chapter discusses some of the aspects of the TCP/IP protocol suite. It looks at some of the most commonly used protocols in the suite, as well as the function of ports and the port assignments for some of the most common protocols. Understanding the functions of the protocols and their associated port assignments is very important when you're working with security products and reconfiguring services.

A network that uses TCP/IP has a number of services that offer needed functionality. Services such as DHCP and NAT offer a solution to the time-consuming and sometimes problematic task of IP addressing. DNS and WINS offer name resolution services that can allow users to access hosts by using easy-to-remember names rather than TCP/IP addressing. Another TCP/IP-based service, SNMP, allows a network to be managed from a central location.

IP addressing is a major topic, and it is very important for network administrators to understand it. Of particular importance are the structure of the addresses and the classes in which they fit. Understanding subnetting allows network administrators to use the allocated IP address space in the most efficient way possible.

An important component of configuring TCP/IP addressing on a system is the default gateway. Without a default gateway address, a system can communicate only with other systems on the same subnet.

This chapter also examines the purpose of private and public networks and their role in a TCP/IP network environment. As the IP address space continues to be depleted, such concepts will become increasingly important.

APPLY YOUR KNOWLEDGE

Exercises

6.1 Installing the DHCP Server Service and Configuring a DHCP Scope

In most networks, clients are able to obtain TCP/IP information from a DHCP server. Therefore, most network administrators are required to both install and manage a DHCP server.

In this exercise, you walk through the steps involved in installing a DHCP server on Windows 2000 Server, and you configure DHCP scopes.

NOTE

Authorizing DHCP Servers in Active Directory In an Active Directory environment, DHCP servers must be authorized in the directory before they can be used. This is beyond the scope of this exercise, but it must be understood in production environments.

Estimated time: 20 minutes

1. Select Start, Settings, Control Panel. The Windows 2000 Control Panel appears.

2. Locate and double-click the Add/Remove Programs icon in Control Panel. The Add/Remove Programs dialog box appears. Choose the Add/Remove Windows Components button on the left side of the screen.

3. The Windows Components Wizard dialog box, shown in Figure 6.13, appears.

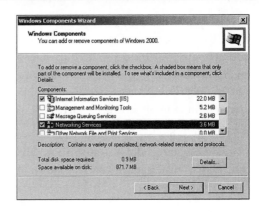

FIGURE 6.13
The Windows Components Wizard dialog box.

4. Select Network Services, and then click the Details button. The Networking Services dialog box, shown in Figure 6.14, appears.

FIGURE 6.14
The Networking Services dialog box.

5. From the Networking Services dialog box, it is possible to install a number of Windows 2000 network services. Select the DHCP option and click OK. The installation of the DHCP service begins.

6. If your system is already configured to use DHCP—for instance, if you use a DHCP address from your ISP—you need to enter a static IP address. For this exercise, you can use one of the private IP addresses discussed in this chapter. An example is 192.168.2.1.

7. After DHCP has been installed, you can access it by selecting Start, Administrative Tools, DHCP. The DHCP management console, shown in Figure 6.15, appears.

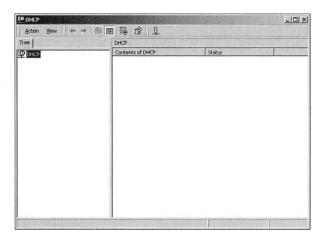

FIGURE 6.15
The DHCP management console.

8. Before you can install DHCP scopes, you have to add the DHCP server. To do this, select Action, Add Server. You are then prompted to add a server to the console. Enter the IP address of your server. In this case, you can use the private IP address 192.168.3.1. After you enter this address, click OK. The DHCP server becomes visible in the DHCP configuration screen.

9. Ensure that the IP address you entered as the DHCP server is the same as the IP address of

your internal network interface card. If it is not the same, the system will not recognize the DHCP server. Figure 6.16 shows the error message you get when the IP addresses of the internal NIC and the DHCP server do not match.

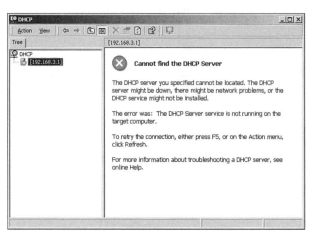

FIGURE 6.16
The Cannot Find the DHCP Server error message.

10. After you have ensured that the IP address of the internal NIC and the DHCP server are the same, you can configure a DHCP scope. To configure and set up a DHCP scope on the network, highlight the server in the left pane and then select the Action, New Scope.

11. The New Scope Wizard guides you through the process of establishing a scope for the network. Click Next to continue with the New Scope Wizard.

12. The second screen in the New Scope Wizard requires you to identify the name and description of the scope. This information is used for identification and to describe the purpose of the scope. Enter a name and a description, and then click Next.

APPLY YOUR KNOWLEDGE

13. The next screen in the wizard (see Figure 6.17) requires you to specify the range of addresses that the scope will use. These are the addresses that will be assigned to the client computers on the network. For this exercise, enter a range from the private address range; for instance, start at 192.168.2.3 and end at 192.168.2.50. This range allows 47 computer systems to automatically receive IP addresses from the DHCP server. Notice that when the start and end ranges are typed in, both the length and subnet mask are automatically filled in. Leave these settings as they are and click Next.

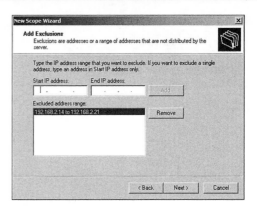

FIGURE 6.18
Excluded IP addresses in a DHCP scope.

15. The next screen in the wizard asks you to specify the lease duration. The lease duration is the length of time the client system can use the IP address from the DHCP scope. Select the desired duration and click Next.

16. You are prompted to configure the DHCP options. Select No, I Will Configure These Options Later, and click Next.

17. The final screen in the wizard indicates that you have successfully completed the New Scope Wizard.

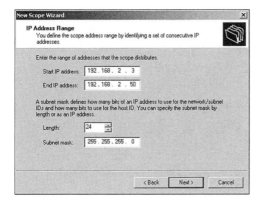

FIGURE 6.17
Inputting IP address ranges.

14. On this screen, identify any exclusions in the range of addresses. For this exercise, exclude the addresses from 192.168.2.14 to 192.168.2.21. Enter these addresses and click Add. The addresses are then excluded and will not be automatically assigned to client systems, but they can be manually assigned to other devices. Click Next to continue. Figure 6.18 shows the excluded IP address.

18. You are returned to the DHCP configuration screen, where the newly created scope appears. Notice in Figure 6.19 that beside the scope is a red arrow that points down. This lets you know that the scope is not yet active and cannot give IP addresses to clients. To activate the scope, right-click on the new scope and select Activate from the menu that appears.

APPLY YOUR KNOWLEDGE

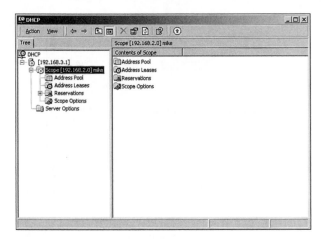

FIGURE 6.19
A deactivated DHCP scope.

19. When the scope has been activated, a green arrow appears by the scope. Figure 6.20 shows an activated DHCP scope.

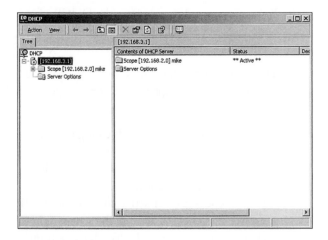

FIGURE 6.20
An activated DHCP scope.

Exam Questions

1. What is the function of HTTP?

   a. It allows files to be retrieved from Web servers.

   b. It provides a mechanism for time synchronization information to be communicated between hosts.

   c. It allows virtual terminal sessions to be opened on a remote host.

   d. It resolves NetBIOS names to IP addresses.

2. On a DHCP system, what term is given to the period of time for which a system is assigned an address?

   a. Rent

   b. Sublet

   c. Lease

   d. Assignment time

3. When using FTP, which command would you use to upload multiple files at once?

   a. mget

   b. put

   c. mput

   d. get

4. During a discussion with your ISP's technical support representative, he mentions that you might have been using the wrong FQDN. Which TCP/IP-based network service is he referring to?

   a. DHCP

   b. WINS

APPLY YOUR KNOWLEDGE

c. SNMP

d. DNS

5. What is the function of ARP?

   a. It resolves MAC addresses to IP addresses.

   b. It resolves NetBIOS names to IP addresses.

   c. It resolves IP addresses to MAC addresses.

   d. It resolves hostnames to IP addresses.

6. What is the function of NTP?

   a. It provides a mechanism for the sharing of authentication information.

   b. It is used to access shared folders on a Linux system.

   c. It is used to communicate utilization information to a central manager.

   d. It is used to communicate time synchronization information between systems.

7. Which port is assigned to the POP3 protocol?

   a. 21

   b. 123

   c. 443

   d. 110

8. You decide to move your network from NetBEUI to TCP/IP. For the external interfaces, you decide to obtain registered IP addresses from your ISP, but for the internal network, you choose to configure systems by using one of the private address ranges. Of the following address ranges, which one would you *not* consider?

   a. 192.168.0.0 to 192.168.255.255

   b. 131.16.0.0 to 131.16.255.255

   c. 10.0.0.0 to 10.255.255.255

   d. 172.16.0.0 to 172.31.255.255?

9. Which of the following addresses is a Class B address?

   a. 129.16.12.200

   b. 126.15.16.122

   c. 211.244.212.5

   d. 193.17.101.27

10. Consider the IP address 195.16.17.8. Assuming that the default subnet mask is being used, which part of the address would be considered the network address?

    a. 195.16

    b. 195.16.17

    c. 16.17.8

    d. 17.8

11. When you are configuring a new server application, the manual tells you to enable access through port 443. What kind of application are you configuring?

    a. A virtual terminal application

    b. A Web-based email application

    c. An FTP server

    d. A secure Web site

12. Which of the following is the correct broadcast address for the Class A network 14?

    a. 14.255.255.0

    b. 14.0.0.0

    c. 255.255.255.255

    d. 14.255.255.255

APPLY YOUR KNOWLEDGE

13. What is the purpose of a reverse lookup in DNS?

    a. It resolves IP addresses to hostnames.

    b. It resolves NetBIOS names to IP addresses.

    c. It resolves hostnames to IP addresses.

    d. It allows you to see who owns a particular domain name.

14. You ask your ISP to assign a public IP address for the external interface of your Windows 2000 server, which is running a proxy server application. In the email message you get that contains the information, the ISP tells you that you have been assigned the IP address 203.15.226.12/24. When you fill out the subnet mask field on the IP configuration dialog box on your system, what subnet mask should you use?

    a. 255.255.255.255

    b. 255.255.255.0

    c. 255.255.240.0

    d. 255.255.255.240

15. You are the administrator for a small network of 25 PCs. All the workstations are Windows 2000 Professional systems, and the server is a Windows 2000 Server system. Presently, the only Internet access is from a single PC that uses a modem, but your manager has asked you to get cable Internet access and share the connection with all the other workstations on the network. Which of the following services might you use to accomplish this?

    a. SNMP

    b. ICS

    c. DNS

    d. WINS

16. You are troubleshooting a problem with a system: A single workstation is unable to communicate with a server on another network; however, it is able to communicate with the other systems on its own segment. All the other workstations on the subnet are able to contact the server on the remote network. Which of the following is most likely the cause of the problem?

    a. The problem workstation has some faulty cabling.

    b. The IP address on the workstation is not configured correctly.

    c. There is an incorrectly configured or missing default gateway on the problem system.

    d. The remote server is unavailable.

17. Which of the following addresses is a valid IPv6 address?

    a. 211.16.233.17.12.148.201.226

    b. 42DE:7E55:63F2:21AA:CBD4:D773:CC21:554F

    c. 42DE:7E55:63G2:21AT:CBD4:D773:CC21:554F

    d. 42DE:7E55:63F2:21AA

18. While examining the data statistics for your network, you notice that there is a large amount of NetBIOS name resolution traffic being generated. What might you do to remedy this problem?

    a. Implement DHCP

    b. Implement WINS

    c. Implement NAT

    d. Implement SNMP

19. In SNMP, what message is sent by a system in the event of a threshold being triggered?

    a. Alert

    b. Trap

    c. Catch

    d. Signal

20. Which of the following port ranges is described as "well known"?

    a. 0 to 1023

    b. 1024 to 49151

    c. 49152 to 65535

    d. 65535 to 78446

Answers to Exam Questions

1. **a.** Web browsers use HTTP to retrieve text and graphic files from Web servers. Answer b describes NTP, Answer c describes SSH or Telnet, and Answer d describes the function of WINS. For more information, see the section "TCP/IP Protocols," in this chapter.

2. **c.** The term *lease* is used to describe the amount of time a DHCP client is assigned an address. All the other terms are invalid. For more information, see the section "TCP/IP-Based Network Services," in this chapter.

3. **c.** The mput command, which is an abbreviation for multiple put, allows more than one file to be uploaded at a time. mget is used to download multiple files in a single command, put is used to upload a single file, and get is used to download a single file. For more information, see the section "TCP/IP Protocols," in this chapter.

4. **d.** DNS is a system that resolves hostnames to IP addresses. The term *FQDN* is used to describe the entire hostname. None of the other services use FQDNs. For more information, see the section "TCP/IP-Based Network Services," in this chapter.

5. **c.** ARP resolves IP addresses to MAC addresses. Answer a describes the function of RARP, Answer b describes the process of WINS, and Answer d describes the process of DNS resolution. For more information, see the section "TCP/IP Protocols," in this chapter.

6. **d.** NTP is used to communicate time synchronization information between devices. All the other answers are invalid. For more information, see the section "TCP/IP Protocols," in this chapter.

7. **d.** POP3 uses port 110 for network communication. Port 21 is used for FTP, port 123 is used by NTP, and port 443 is used by HTTPS. For more information, see the section "TCP/UDP Ports," in this chapter.

8. **b.** The 131.16 range is not one of the recognized private IP address ranges. All the other address ranges are valid IP address ranges. For more information, see the section "IP Addressing," in this chapter.

9. **a.** Class B addresses fall into the range 128 to 191. Therefore, Answer a is the only one of the addresses listed that falls into that range. Answer b is a Class A address, and Answers c and d are both Class C IP addresses. For more information, see the section "IP Addressing," in this chapter.

10. **b.** The address given is a Class C address and therefore, if you are using the default subnet mask, the first three octets represent the network

APPLY YOUR KNOWLEDGE

address. None of the other answers are valid. For more information, see the section "IP Addressing," in this chapter.

11. **d.** Port 443 is used by HTTPS. Therefore, the application you are configuring is likely to be a secure Web site application. None of the other answers are valid. For more information, see the section "TCP/UDP Ports," in this chapter.

12. **d.** The broadcast address for a network uses the network ID, and all other octets in the address are set to all nodes, to indicate that every system should receive the message. Therefore, with a network address of 14, the broadcast address is 14.255.255.255. None of the other answers are valid. For more information, see the section "IP Addressing," in this chapter.

13. **a.** A reverse lookup resolves an IP address to a hostname rather than the hostname-to-IP address resolution normally performed by DNS. Answer b describes the functions of WINS, Answer c describes the process of a standard DNS resolution, and Answer d is not a valid answer. For more information, see the section "TCP/IP-Based Network Services," in this chapter.

14. **b.** In CIDR terminology, the number of bits to be included in the subnet mask is expressed as a slash value. If the slash value is 24, the first three entire octets form the subnet mask, so the value is 255.255.255.0. None of the other answers are correct. For more information, see the section "IP Addressing," in this chapter.

15. **b.** As its name implies, ICS allows a single Internet connection to be shared among multiple computers. None of the other services mentioned are used in shared Internet access. For more information, see the section "TCP/IP-Based Network Services," in this chapter.

16. **c.** The symptoms described indicate that the default gateway configuration on the system in question is likely incorrect. If Answer a or Answer b were correct, you would not be able to connect to other systems on the same subnet. If Answer d were correct, other systems would not be able to access the remote server, which, according to the question, you are able to do. For more information, see the section "Default Gateways," in this chapter.

17. **b.** IPv6 addresses are expressed in hexadecimal format and can therefore use only the letters A through F and numbers. They are also expressed in eight parts. None of the other answers fit these criteria. For more information, see the section "IP Addressing," in this chapter.

18. **b.** A WINS server allows client computers to perform NetBIOS name-to-IP address resolution without broadcasting. None of the services listed in the other answers can reduce the amount of NetBIOS resolution traffic. For more information, see the section "TCP/IP-Based Network Services," in this chapter.

19. **b.** The term used to refer to a message sent by an SNMP agent when a condition is met is *trap message*. None of the other terms are used to describe the message sent by SNMP. For more information, see the section "TCP/IP-Based Network Services," in this chapter.

20. **a.** Well-known ports are defined in the range 0 to 1023. Answer b describes the range known as registered ports 1024 to 49151. Answer c describes the dynamic, or private, ports, which range from 49152 to 65535. Answer d is not a valid answer. For more information, see the section "TCP/UDP Ports," in this chapter.

APPLY YOUR KNOWLEDGE

Suggested Readings and Resources

1. Habraken, Joe. *Absolute Beginner's Guide to Networking*, third edition. Que Publishing, 2001.

2. Shinder, Debra Littlejohn. *Computer Networking Essentials*. Cisco Press, 2001.

3. Comer, Douglas E. *Complete TCP/IP Training Course*, student edition. Prentice Hall PTR, 2001.

4. Hunt, Craig. *TCP/IP Network Administration*, third edition. O'Reilly & Associates, 2002.

5. Subnetting information, `www.howtosubnet.com`.

6. Computer networking tutorials and advice, `compnetworking.about.com`.

7. General TCP/IP and networking information, `www.cisco.com`.

8. "TechEncyclopedia," `www.techencyclopedia.com`.

9. Links to various TCP/IP resources, `www.private.org.il/tcpip_rl.html`.

This chapter covers the following CompTIA-specified objectives for the "Protocols and Standards" section of the Network+ exam.

Identify the basic characteristics (for example, speed, capacity, media) of the following WAN technologies:

- **Packet switching versus circuit switching**

- **ISDN**

- **FDDI**

- **ATM**

- **Frame Relay**

- **SONET/SDH**

- **T1/E1**

- **T3/E3**

- **OC-x**

▶ Wide area networking is one of the most interesting aspects of a network. Although for the Network+ exam, you will not be expected to understand detailed information about WANs, you will be expected to demonstrate a basic knowledge of the most commonly used WAN technologies.

CHAPTER 7

WAN Technologies

Introduction   260

Introduction to WAN Technologies   260

  Public Networks   261
    The Public Switched Telephone
     Network (PSTN)   261
    The Internet   262
    Public Networks: Advantages and
     Disadvantages   262

  Private Networks   263

  Switching Methods   264

  Packet Switching   265
    Virtual-Circuit Packet Switching   266
    Datagram Packet Switching   266

  Circuit Switching   267

  Message Switching   268

  Switching Methods Comparison   268

WAN Technologies   269

  Dial-up Modem Connections   270

  Integrated Services Digital
    Network (ISDN)   270
    Basic Rate Interface (BRI)   271
    Primary Rate Interface (PRI)   271
    BRI and PRI ISDN Comparison   272

  T-carrier Lines   272
    T1/E1 Lines   273
    T3/E3 Lines   273

  Fiber Distributed Data Interface (FDDI)   274
    FDDI Versus IEEE 802.5   274
    Implementing FDDI   275
    FDDI Fault Detection   275
    Advantages and Disadvantages
     of FDDI   275

  Asynchronous Transfer Mode (ATM)   277
    ATM Media   278

  X.25   278

  Frame Relay   278

  SONET/OCx   279

  WAN Technology Summary   280

Chapter Summary   281

Apply Your Knowledge   282

- ▶ Read the objectives at the beginning of the chapter.
- ▶ Study the information in the chapter, paying special attention to the tables, which summarize key information.
- ▶ Review the objectives again.
- ▶ Answer the exam questions at the end of the chapter and check your results.

- ▶ Use the ExamGear test on the CD-ROM that accompanies this book to answer additional exam questions concerning this material.
- ▶ Review the notes, tips, and exam tips in this chapter. Be sure you understand the information in the exam tips. If you don't understand the topic referenced in an exam tip, refer to the information in the chapter text and then read the exam tip again.

INTRODUCTION

In the beginning, there was a single computer. Soon it connected to other computers and became a local area network (LAN). LANs allowed files, printers, and applications to be shared freely and securely throughout an organization. For a short time, a LAN was sufficient in most organizations, but soon the need arose to interconnect LANs to provide enterprisewide data availability.

As you might imagine, connecting LANs together provided a challenge simply because of the distances separating them. Some were across town, and some were thousands of miles apart, which was a long way to run a segment of coaxial cable.

New technologies such as X.25 were introduced that could span these distances, and the wide area network (WAN) was born. Some technologies used by WANs are different from those used by LANs, and some WAN technologies are more complex than LAN technologies. Basically, though, a WAN does exactly what a LAN does: It provides connectivity between computers.

INTRODUCTION TO WAN TECHNOLOGIES

▶ Identify the basic characteristics (for example, speed, capacity, media) of the following WAN technologies:
  - Packet switching versus circuit switching
  - ISDN
  - FDDI
  - ATM
  - Frame Relay
  - SONET/SDH
  - T1/E1
  - T3/E3
  - OC-*x*

We'll start our examination of WANs by looking at perhaps the most significant consideration facing anyone who is implementing a

WAN: whether to use a public or a private network as a means of connectivity. Both the private and public WAN network services have good and bad points, and knowing the difference between them is a good place to start discussing the characteristics of WANs.

Public Networks

The bottom line for many of the decisions made in networking often has to do with money. This is often true when choosing a WAN networking method. To save money and a certain amount of administrative effort, you can choose to set up a WAN using an existing transmission infrastructure. Two key public networks can be used to establish a WAN: the public switched telephone network (PSTN) and the Internet. Each of these is discussed in the following sections.

The Public Switched Telephone Network (PSTN)

The *PSTN*, which is often called *plain old telephone system (POTS)*, is the entire collection of interconnected telephone wires throughout the world. Discussions of the PSTN include all the equipment that goes into connecting two points together, such as the cable, the networking equipment, and the telephone exchanges.

The modern PSTN is largely digital, with analog connections existing primarily between homes and the local phone exchanges. Modems are used to convert the computer system's digital signals to analog, so they can be sent out over the analog connection.

Using the PSTN to establish WAN connections is a popular choice, although the significant drawback is the limited transfer speeds. Transfer on the PSTN is limited to 56Kbps with a modem and 128Kbps with an Integrated Services Digital Network (ISDN) connection, and it's difficult to share large files or videoconferencing at such speeds. However, companies that need to send only small amounts of data remotely can use the PSTN as an inexpensive alternative for remote access, particularly when other resources such as the Internet are not available.

> **EXAM TIP**
>
> **Use PSTN to Save Money** If financial cost is a major concern, PSTN is the method of choice for creating a WAN.

Cable and DSL The increasing availability of cable and Digital Subscriber Line (DSL) services has meant that companies are increasingly looking toward these technologies as a means to establish VPN connections. Cable and DSL are particularly suited for such a purpose because they offer high speeds for comparatively low cost. They are also available 24/7 for an inclusive cost, which is a bonus over other methods such as ISDN, which is billed on a usage basis. Cable and DSL, in concert with VPNs, are making it possible for companies to establish low-cost, secure WAN links. Previously, many companies would not have been able to afford a solution that offers this kind of speed, availability, and security.

The Internet

The Internet has become very popular for establishing WAN connections. Using the Internet to provide remote access creates a cost-effective and reliable solution for interconnecting LANs. One of the most common methods of using the Internet for connecting LANs is through the use of *virtual private networks (VPNs)*. Essentially, a VPN uses a public network, such as the Internet, to connect private networks. Unlike private networks, VPNs can be used on an as-needed basis. A connection can be established to a remote location and then dropped when no transmissions are required. Many organizations use VPNs as dedicated links that permanently connect private LANs. Figure 7.1 shows a VPN connection over a public network.

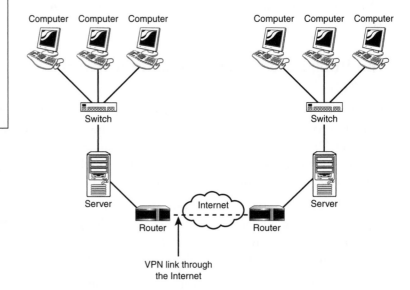

FIGURE 7.1
A VPN connecting two private LANs.

Public Networks: Advantages and Disadvantages

The biggest advantages of a public network such as the PSTN and the Internet are accessibility and availability. Public network access is everywhere, and perhaps more importantly, it is inexpensive. In addition, the technologies required to use public networks, such as VPNs, are moderately easy to configure and can be implemented in a short amount of time.

You are most likely to see public networks being utilized by small organizations, where the money for a private network is simply not available or needed. For many small organizations, the capabilities that the Internet provides are sufficient.

As you might have already surmised, there are some drawbacks in using a public network to interconnect LANs. First and foremost is security. When you establish a link over a public network, there is a risk that your data may be compromised by another user on that network. Technologies such as VPNs put a lot of emphasis on security measures such as encryption, which is aimed at reducing the security risk. However, if you are sending sensitive data over a public network, there is always a risk. Discussions about the degree of risk are best left to hackers, crackers, and security experts, and that debate is sure to go on for a long time.

In addition to the security risks, there are numerous other considerations concerning public lines, such as disconnections, logon troubles for modems, Internet failures, and a host of other likely and unlikely circumstances. Keep in mind that with a public network you are getting something for nothing—or at least very little—and you will have to make concessions. If you can't live with the drawbacks, you can always switch to a private network.

Private Networks

If we all had unlimited IT budgets, most of us would be using private networking to connect LANs together. Private networks provide a solid way to maintain connectivity between LANs, at least for those who can afford them.

A private network does not suffer from the same considerations of a public network. There are many technologies used to create private networks, and they vary in cost and implementation difficulty. The specific technologies used to create WANs over private networks are discussed in detail in this chapter; the most common private network technologies include Asynchronous Transfer Mode (ATM), Frame Relay, and X.25.

A private network can be designed and implemented from scratch based on an organization's specific needs. The network can be as complex or simple, expensive or inexpensive, secure or insecure as allowed by the budget, location, utilization, and data usage demands. The network can also be designed around the security needs of the data being carried over the network. For instance, fiber-based networks are more secure and more expensive than copper-based networks or wireless networks. A private network can employ various protocols based on security or performance needs. Basically, a private network gives the designer an opportunity to correct most of the problems presented by public networks.

Probably the biggest single disadvantage of a private network is the cost. Whereas the PSTN is yours for the asking at a nominal monthly fee, a private network requires that you purchase or lease every piece of cable, all the network cards, hubs, routers, switches, and so on, until you have enough equipment to go live.

Because of the required networking equipment, private networks often require more administrative effort than public networks, where the networking infrastructure is maintained by outside administrators. Often, a hidden cost associated with private networks is the need for qualified people to manage and maintain them. As the network grows—and it will—it becomes increasingly complex and requires more and more attention. Good administration is a must, or inefficiencies and lack of dependability will quickly consume the value of the private network. A company needs to carefully weigh administrative issues before getting into private networking.

Using a private WAN need not be a total do-it-yourself approach. In fact, most telephone companies provide managed WAN services, which include all the equipment you need to create a WAN. They also monitor and manage the connection for you, making sure that everything operates as it is supposed to. There is, of course, a price attached to such a service, but for many companies, a managed solution is money well spent.

Switching Methods

Before we go on to discuss the specific WAN technologies, we must first look at an important element of the WAN technologies—the switching methods. In order for systems to communicate on a network, there has to be a communication path between them on which the data can travel. To communicate with another entity, you need to establish a path that can be used to move the information from one location to another and back. This is the function of *switching*. It provides a path between two communication endpoints and switches the data, to make sure it follows the correct path. Three types of switching are used most often in networks today:

◆ Packet switching

◆ Circuit switching

Packet Switching

In packet switching, messages are broken down into smaller pieces called *packets*. Each packet is assigned source, destination, and intermediate node addresses. Packets are required to have this information because they do not always use the same path or route to get to their intended destination. Referred to as *independent routing*, this is one of the advantages of packet switching. Independent routing allows for a better use of available bandwidth by letting packets travel different routes, to avoid high-traffic areas. Independent routing also allows packets to take an alternate route if a particular route is unavailable for some reason. Figure 7.2 shows how packets can travel in a packet-switching environment.

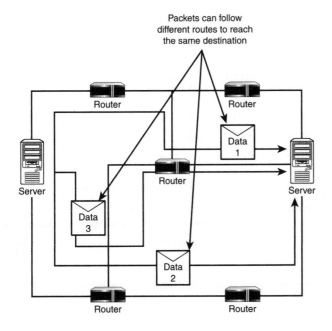

FIGURE 7.2
An example of packet switching.

NOTE **Packet Switching**   Packet switching is the most popular switching method for networks and is used on most LANs.

NOTE **Packet Size Restrictions**   The packet size is restricted in a packet-switching network, to ensure that the packets can be stored in RAM instead of on a hard disk. The benefit of this size restriction is faster access because retrieving data from RAM is faster than retrieving data from a hard disk.

NOTE **Datagram Packet Sizes**   The data packet size used with datagram packet switching is kept small in case of error, which would cause the packets to be resent.

In a packet-switching system, when packets are sent onto the network, the sending device is responsible for choosing the best path for the packet. This path might change in transit, and it is possible for the receiving device to receive the packets in a random or nonsequential order. When this happens, the receiving device waits until all the data packets are received, and then it reconstructs them according to their built-in sequence numbers.

Two types of packet-switching methods are used on networks: *virtual-circuit packet switching* and *datagram packet switching*. Each of these methods is described in the following sections.

Virtual-Circuit Packet Switching

When virtual-circuit switching is used, a logical connection is established between the source and the destination device. This logical connection is established when the sending device initiates a conversation with the receiving device. The logical communication path between the two devices can remain active for as long as the two devices are available or can be used to send packets once. After the sending process has completed, the line can be closed.

All the packets in virtual-circuit packet switching must follow the same path. That is, they travel through the logical communication path that is established. Virtual-circuit packet switching is commonly used for connection-oriented services such as real-time video.

Datagram Packet Switching

Unlike virtual-circuit packet switching, datagram packet switching does not establish a logical connection between the sending and transmitting devices. The packets in datagram packet switching are independently sent, meaning that they can take different paths through the network to reach their intended destination. To do this, each packet must be individually addressed, to determine where its source and destination are. This method ensures that packets take the easiest possible routes to their destination and avoid high-traffic areas.

Because in datagram packet switching the packets can take multiple paths to reach their destination, they can be received in a nonsequential order. The information contained within each packet header is used to reconstruct all the packets, and so the original message is received intact.

Circuit Switching

In contrast to the packet-switching method, *circuit switching* requires a dedicated physical connection between the sending and receiving devices. The most commonly used analogy to represent circuit switching is a telephone conversation, in which the parties involved have a dedicated link between them for the duration of the conversation. When either party disconnects, the circuit is broken and the data path is lost. This is an accurate representation of how circuit switching works with network and data transmissions. The sending system establishes a physical connection, the data is transmitted between the two, and when the transmission is complete, the channel is closed.

Some clear advantages to the circuit-switching technology make it well suited for certain applications. The primary advantage is that after a connection is established, there is a consistent and reliable connection between the sending and receiving device. This allows for transmissions at a guaranteed rate of transfer.

Like all technologies, circuit switching has downsides. As you might imagine, a dedicated communication line can be very inefficient. After the physical connection is established, it is unavailable to any other sessions until the transmission is complete. Again using the phone call analogy, this would be like a caller trying to reach another caller and getting a busy signal. Circuit switching can therefore be fraught with long connection delays. Figure 7.3 shows an example of circuit switching.

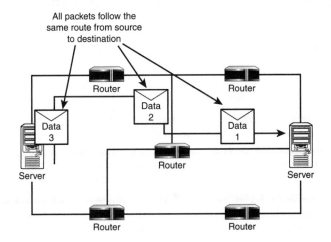

FIGURE 7.3
An example of circuit switching.

Message Switching

In some respects, *message switching* is similar to packet switching, but instead of using and sending packets, message switching divides data transmissions into messages. Like packets, each of these messages contains the destination address. Devices on the network that forward the message use this destination address. Each intermediate device in the message's path stores the message momentarily and then forwards it to the next device in the network, until it finally reaches its destination. Message switching is therefore often referred to as the *store-and-forward* method.

Message switching offers many advantages over circuit switching. Because message switching doesn't require a dedicated connection as does circuit switching, a larger number of devices can share the bandwidth of the network. A message-switching system also has the capability of storing messages, which allows the traffic on the network to clear. This strategy can significantly reduce the traffic congestion on the network.

The main drawbacks of the message-switching method are that the store-and-forward method makes it a poor choice for real-time applications, such as videoconferencing, in which the temporary storing of data would be disruptive to the message. A second drawback is that the intermediate devices, often PC systems, must be capable of temporarily storing messages by using their hard disk space.

REVIEW BREAK

Switching Methods Comparison

Table 7.1 summarizes the characteristics of the various switching methods.

TABLE 7.1
COMPARISON OF SWITCHING METHODS

Switching Method	Pros	Cons	Key Features
Packet switching	Packets can be routed around network congestion.	Packets can become lost while taking alternate routes to the destination.	Packets can travel the network independently, looking for the best route to the destination system.
	Packet switching makes efficient use of network bandwidth.	Messages are divided into packets that contain source and destination information.	There are two types of packet switching: datagram and virtual-circuit packet switching.

Switching Method	Pros	Cons	Key Features
Circuit switching	Offers a dedicated transmission channel that is reserved until disconnected.	Dedicated channels can cause delays because a channel is unavailable until one side disconnects.	Offers the capability of storing messages temporarily to reduce network congestion.
		Uses a dedicated physical link between the sending and receiving devices.	
Message switching	Multiple devices have the capability to share bandwidth.	The store-and forward system makes message switching impractical for many real-time applications.	Entire messages are sent during transmissions.
			Intermediate devices temporarily store and then forward messages.

WAN TECHNOLOGIES

Having looked at the differences between the various switching methods, we can now take a better look at the technologies used to create WANs. Several technologies, including the following, can be used to implement WANs:

◆ Dial-up modem connections

◆ ISDN

◆ T-carrier lines

◆ Fiber Distributed Data Interface (FDDI)

◆ ATM

◆ X.25

◆ Frame Relay

◆ Synchronous Optical Network (SONET)/OC-*x*

These technologies vary in terms of cost, complexity, and switching methods. We'll start our discussion by looking at perhaps the simplest of WAN technologies—the modem.

Dial-up Modem Connections

Today, people are more likely to associate a modem with a dial-up Internet service provider (ISP) account than with a WAN technology. But the reality is that for many years, and still today, modems have been used to provide WAN capabilities.

The biggest drawback of a modem connection is the speed, which is limited to 56Kbps. There are, however, a few advantages to modem connections. The cost of a modem link depends on the distance covered. In parts of the world such as North America, where local calls are free, modem links can provide an inexpensive WAN solution where there would otherwise be no WAN connectivity at all. All that is needed to create the modem WAN link is a phone line and a modem at each end of the link. You also need software to enable, support, and configure the link, but all modern network operating systems include this functionality, so this is not a problem.

Integrated Services Digital Network (ISDN)

ISDN is a dial-up technology capable of transmitting voice and data simultaneously over the same physical connection. Using ISDN, users are able to access digital communication channels via both packet- and circuit-switching connections. ISDN is much faster than a regular modem connection. To access ISDN, a special phone line is required, and this line is usually paid for through a monthly subscription. You can expect these monthly costs to be significantly higher than those for a dial-up modem account.

To establish an ISDN connection, you dial the number for the end of the connection, much as you would with a conventional phone call or modem dial-up connection. A conversation between the sending and receiving devices is then established. The connection is dropped when one end disconnects or hangs up. The line pickup of ISDN is very fast, allowing a connection to be established, or brought up, very quickly—much more quickly than a conventional phone line.

ISDN has two defined interface standards—Basic Rate Interface (BRI) and Primary Rate Interface (PRI)—which are discussed in the following sections.

Basic Rate Interface (BRI)

BRI defines a communication line that utilizes three separate channels. There are two B (that is, bearer) channels of 64Kbps each and one D (that is, delta) channel of 16Kbps. The two B channels are used to carry digital information, which can be either voice or data. The B channels can be used independently to provide 64Kbps access or combined together to utilize the entire 128Kbps. The D channel is used for out-of-band signaling.

> **EXAM TIP**
>
> **2B+D** BRI ISDN is sometimes referred to as 2B+D. This abbreviation simply refers to the available channels.

To use BRI ISDN, the connection point must be within 5,486 meters (18,000 feet) of the ISDN provider's BRI service center. In addition, to use BRI ISDN, special equipment is needed, such as ISDN routers and ISDN terminal adapters. Figure 7.4 shows a standard ISDN router.

FIGURE 7.4
An ISDN router.

Primary Rate Interface (PRI)

PRI is a form of ISDN that is generally carried over a T1 line (called E1 in Europe) and can handle transmission rates of up to 1.544Mbps. PRI is composed of 23 B channels (30 in Europe), each providing 64Kbps for data/voice, and one 64Kbps D channel.

> **NOTE**
>
> **Leased Lines** ISDN is considered a *leased line* because access to ISDN is leased from a service provider.

BRI and PRI ISDN Comparison

Table 7.2 compares BRI and PRI ISDN.

TABLE 7.2
BRI AND PRI ISDN COMPARISON

Characteristic	*PRI*	*BRI*
Speed	1.544Mbps	128Kbps
Channels	23B+D	2B+D
Transmission carrier	T1	PSTN

T-carrier Lines

T-carrier lines are high-speed lines that can be leased from telephone companies. T-carrier lines can support both voice and data transmissions and are often used to create point-to-point private networks. Four distinct types of T-carrier lines are available:

- ◆ **T1**—T1 lines offer transmission speeds of 1.544Mbps, and they can be used to create point-to-point dedicated digital communication paths. T1 lines have commonly been used for connecting LANs.

- ◆ **T2**—T2 leased lines offer transmission speeds of 6.312Mbps. It accomplishes this by using 96 64Kbps B channels.

- ◆ **T3**—T3 lines offer transmission speeds of up to 44.736Mbps, using 672 64Kbps B channels.

- ◆ **T4**—T4 lines offer impressive transmission speeds of up to 274.176Mbps by using 4,032 64Kbps B channels

Of these T-carrier lines, the ones commonly associated with networks are T1 and T3 lines, which are discussed further in the following sections.

T1/E1 Lines

T1 (also known as a leased line) is actually a dedicated digital circuit that is leased from the telephone company. This creates an always-open, always-available line between you and whomever you choose to connect to when you establish the service. T1 lines also eliminate the "one call per wire" limitation by using a method called *multiplexing,* or *muxing.* Using a device called a *multiplexer,* the signal is broken into smaller pieces and assigned identifiers. Multiple transmissions are divided by the multiplexer and transmitted across the wire simultaneously. When the signals reach their destination, they are put back in the proper order and converted back into the proper form.

Having T1 service used to be the way to show someone you were serious about your particular communication needs. T1 lines were expensive; however, their prices have fallen in the past few years, as other technologies have begun to rival their transmission rates. T1 offers speeds up to 1.544Mbps. The obvious advantages of a T1 line are its constant connection—no dial-up or other connection is required because it is always on—and it can easily be budgeted because it has a fixed monthly cost. In addition, the transfer rate is guaranteed because it, like a telephone call, is a private circuit. Many companies use T1 lines as their pipelines to the Internet.

NOTE — **E1 Lines** In Europe, the service provided by telephone companies that is similar to the T1 service is called *E1.* E1 supports speeds of 2.048Mbps

T3/E3 Lines

For a time, the speeds offered by T1 lines were sufficient for all but a few organizations. As networks and the data they support expanded, T1 lines did not provide enough speed for many organizations. T3 service answered the call by providing transmission speeds of 44.736Mbps.

T3 lines are dedicated circuits that provide very high capacity and are generally used by large companies, ISPs, or long-distance companies. T3 service offers all the strengths of a T1 service (just a whole lot more), but the costs associated with T3 limits its use to the few organizations that have the money to pay for it.

NOTE — **E3 Lines** In Europe, the service provided by telephone companies that is similar to the T3 service is called *E3.* E3 supports speeds of 34.368Mbps.

NOTE — **Fractional T** Due to the cost of a T-carrier solution, it is now possible to lease portions of a T-carrier service. Known as *fractional T,* you can subscribe and pay for service based on 64Kbps channels.

Fiber Distributed Data Interface (FDDI)

FDDI was introduced in the mid-1980s. FDDI is an American National Standards Institute (ANSI) topology standard that uses fiber-optic cable and token-passing media access. Recall from Chapter 1, "Introduction to Networking" that the token-passing method requires systems that are sending data on the network to have access to a token. The data is attached to the token and transported throughout the network.

FDDI can be used over both multimode and single-mode fiber cable and can reach transmissions speeds of up to 100Mbps. FDDI combines the strengths of Token Ring, the speed of Fast Ethernet, and the security of fiber-optic cable. Although not widely deployed, FDDI is used for creating network backbones and connecting private LANs to create WANs.

FDDI Versus IEEE 802.5

FDDI and the IEEE 802.5 standard share some common features. For instance, both standards use a token-passing access method, and both can use fiber-optic media. However, despite their surface similarities, if you dig a little deeper, there are some significant differences.

As mentioned previously, the FDDI standard uses a token-passing access method similar to that of the IEEE 802.5 standard, with one very notable difference. The original 802.5 standard specifies that only a single data frame can be attached to a token. However, a computer in an FDDI network can transmit as much data on the token as possible within a specified period. When the specified time has expired, the computer releases the token to the ring, and then it must wait until the token returns before it can send more data.

Another key difference between standards 802.5 and FDDI is that FDDI uses a dual-ring configuration. The first, or primary, ring is used to transfer the data around the network, and the secondary ring is used for redundancy and fault tolerance; the secondary ring waits to take over if the primary ring fails. If the primary ring fails, the secondary ring kicks in automatically, with no disruption to network users. Figure 7.5 shows an FDDI dual-ring configuration.

> **N O T E**
>
> **CDDI**   The Copper Distributed Data Interface (CDDI) standard defines FDDI over copper cable rather than fiber-optic cable. CDDI has an even lower level of popularity than FDDI.

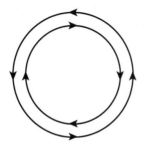

FIGURE 7.5
An example of an FDDI configuration.

Even though the second ring sits dormant, you can connect network devices to both rings. Network devices that attach to both rings are referred to as *Class A stations*, or *dual attached stations (DASs)*. Network devices that connect to a single ring are called *Class B stations*, or *single attached stations (SASs)*. Class A stations are the more reliable of the two because they continue to function in the event that one of the rings fails—a technique known as *wrapping*. SASs, on the other hand, are not fault tolerant; if the ring attached to the device fails, the device becomes isolated from the network. Figure 7.6 shows an example of DASs and SASs on an FDDI network.

NOTE

Wrapping In the FDDI topology, *wrapping* refers to the capability of a network device to continue to operate if one of the rings fails.

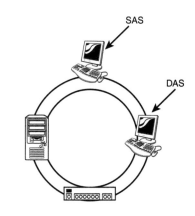

FIGURE 7.6
An FDDI ring with both a SAS and a DAS.

Implementing FDDI

If you are implementing or troubleshooting an FDDI network, you need to keep in mind a few factors. The practical limitations of an FDDI network are 500 workstations and a maximum of 100 kilometers of cable. The FDDI specification calls for multimode fiber-optic cable with a 62.5-micrometer core. Two kilometers (6,561 feet) is the maximum cable segment length; to cover a longer distance with FDDI, a repeating device is needed every two kilometers (6,561 feet).

FDDI Fault Detection

The FDDI standard uses a technique called *beaconing* to detect faults on a network. When a computer on an FDDI network detects an error, it sends a continual signal called a *beacon* to its immediately upstream neighbor until it hears a beacon response from the upstream neighbor. This process continues until the only computer system still beaconing is the one immediately downstream from the one with the fault. Of course, the upstream system cannot respond to the beacon because there is a fault between it and the sending computer, disabling the connection between the two devices. To identify the location of the cable break, the network administrator looks for the computer sending the beacons and then looks upstream for the problem.

Advantages and Disadvantages of FDDI

FDDI has a few significant advantages, some of which stem directly from the fact that it uses fiber-optic cable as its transmission media.

The following list contains some of the advantages associated with FDDI:

- **Immune to electromagnetic interference (EMI)**—Fiber is not susceptible to the influences of EMI.

- **Secure**—Fiber is more secure than copper-based media. Eavesdropping and tapping into the line are far more difficult with fiber-optic cable than with copper-based cable.

- **Long cable distances**—Fiber-optic cable has a transmission range of more than two kilometers (6,561 feet).

In addition to the advantages provided by the fiber-optic cable, FDDI itself has a few strong points:

- **Fault-tolerant design**—By using a dual-ring configuration, FDDI is able to provide some fault tolerance. If one cable fails, the other can be used to transmit the data throughout the network.

- **Speed due to the use of multiple tokens**—Unlike the IEEE 802.5 standard, FDDI uses multiple tokens, which increases the overall network speed.

- **Beaconing**—FDDI uses beaconing as a built-in error-detection method, making finding faults such as cable breaks a lot easier.

FDDI also has a few key drawbacks, including the following:

- **High cost**—The costs associated with FDDI and the devices and cable needed to implement an FDDI solution are very costly—too costly for many small organizations.

- **Implementation difficulty**—FDDI setup and management can be very complex, requiring trained professionals with significant experience to manage and maintain the cable and infrastructure.

Because of the cost, FDDI is implemented in only a limited number of environments. As a result, your chances of encountering FDDI in the real world are relatively low.

Asynchronous Transfer Mode (ATM)

Most of us got our first look at ATM in the early 1990s, when it was introduced. ATM was heralded as a breakthrough technology for networking because it was an end-to-end solution, ranging in use from a desktop to a remote system. Though promoted as both a LAN and WAN solution, ATM did not live up to its hype due to associated implementation costs and a lack of standards. The introduction of Gigabit Ethernet, which offered great transmissions speeds and compatibility with existing network infrastructure, further dampened the momentum of the ATM bandwagon. ATM has, however, found a niche with some ISPs and is also commonly used as a network backbone.

ATM is a packet-switching technology that provides transfer speeds ranging from 1.544Mbps to 622Mbps. It is well suited for a variety of data types, such as voice, data, and video. Using fixed-length packets, or cells, that are 53 bytes long, ATM can operate much more efficiently than variable-length-packet packet-switching technologies such as Frame Relay. Having a fixed-length packet allows ATM to be concerned only with the header information of each packet. It does not need to read every bit of a packet to determine the beginning and end of the packet. ATM's fixed cell length also makes it easily adaptable to other technologies as they develop. Each cell has 48 bytes available for data, with 5 bytes reserved for the ATM header.

ATM is a circuit-based network technology because it uses a virtual circuit to connect two networked devices. Two types of circuits are used in an ATM network:

- **Switched virtual circuits (SVCs)**—SVCs are set up only for the duration of a conversation or data transmission. An SVC is a temporary connection that is dropped when the transmission is complete.

- **Permanent virtual circuits (PVCs)**—PVCs are permanently established virtual circuits between two devices.

In the following sections we look at some of the characteristics of ATM.

ATM Media

ATM is compatible with the most widely used and implemented networking media types available today, including single-mode and multimode fiber, coaxial cable, unshielded twisted-pair, and shielded twisted-pair. Although it can be used over various media, the limitations of some of the media types make them impractical choices. ATM can also operate over other media, including FDDI, T1, T3, SONET, OC-3, and Fiber Channel.

X.25

X.25 was one of the original packet-switching technologies, but today it has been replaced in many applications by Frame Relay. Various telephone companies, along with network providers, developed X.25 in the mid-1970s to transmit digital data over analog signals on copper lines. Because so many different entities had their hands in the development and implementation of X.25, it works well on many different kinds of networks with different types of traffic. X.25 is one of the oldest standards, and therein lie both its greatest advantage and its greatest disadvantage. On the upside, X.25 is a global standard that can be found all over the world. On the downside, its maximum transfer speed is 56Kbps—which is quite reasonable when compared to other technologies in the mid-1970s but quite slow and cumbersome today.

Because X.25 is a packet-switching technology, it uses different routes to get the best possible connection between the sending and receiving device at a given time. As conditions on the network change, such as increased network traffic, so do the routes that the packets take. Consequently, each packet is likely to take a different route to reach its destination during a single communication session. The devices that make it possible to use X.25 service are called *packet assemblers/disassemblers* (PADs). A PAD is required at each end of the X.25 connection.

Frame Relay

Frame Relay was designed to provide standards for transmitting data packets in high-speed bursts over digital networks, using a public data network service. Frame Relay is a packet-switching technology that uses variable-length packets. Essentially, Frame Relay is a streamlined version of X.25. It uses smaller packet sizes and fewer error-checking mechanisms than X.25, and consequently it has less overhead than X.25.

A Frame Relay connection is built by using PVCs that establish end-to-end circuits. This means that Frame Relay is not dependent on the best-route method of X.25. Frame Relay can be implemented on 56Kbps, T1, T3, and ISDN lines.

SONET/OCx

In 1984 the U.S. Department of Justice and AT&T reached an agreement stating that AT&T was a monopoly that needed be divided into smaller, directly competitive companies. This created a challenge for local telephone companies, which were then faced with the task of connecting to an ever-growing number of independent long-distance carriers, each of which had a different interfacing mechanism. Bell Communications Research answered the challenge by developing SONET, a fiber-optic WAN technology that delivers voice, data, and video at speeds in multiples of 51.84Mbps. Bell's main goals in creating SONET were to create a standardized access method for all carriers within the newly competitive U.S. market and to unify different standards around the world. SONET is capable of transmission speeds between 51.84Mbps and 2.488Gbps

One of Bell's biggest accomplishments with SONET was that it created a new system that defined data rates in terms of Optical Carrier (OC) levels. Table 7.3 contains the OC levels you should be familiar with.

TABLE 7.3

OC LEVELS AND TRANSMISSION RATES

OC Level	Transmission Rate
OC-1	51.84Mbps
OC-3	155.52Mbps
OC-12	622.08Mbps
OC-24	1.244Gbps
OC-48	2.488Gbps

NOTE

SDH Synchronous Digital Hierarchy (SDH) is the European counterpart to SONET.

WAN Technology Summary

Table 7.4 summarizes the main characteristics of the various WAN technologies discussed in this chapter. You can use this table as an aid in reviewing before you take the Network+ exam.

TABLE 7.4
WAN TECHNOLOGY OVERVIEW

WAN Technology	Supported Speed	Switching Media	Key Method Used	Characteristics
ISDN	BRI: 64Kbps to 128Kbps PRI: 64Kbps to 1.5Mbps	Copper/fiber-optic	Can be used for circuit-switching or packet-switching connections	ISDN can be used to transmit all types of traffic, including voice, video, and data.
				BRI uses 2B+D channels, PRI uses 23B+D channels. B channels are 64Kbps. ISDN uses the public network and requires dial-in access.
T-carrier (T1, T3)	T1: 1.544Mbps T3: 44.736Mbps	Copper/fiber-optic	Circuit switching	T-carrier is used to create point-to-point network connections for private networks.
FDDI	100Mbps	Fiber-optic	N/A	Uses a dual-ring configuration for fault tolerance.
				Uses a token-passing media-access method.
				Uses beaconing for error detection.
ATM	1.544Mbps to 622Mbps	Copper/fiber-optic	Cell switching	ATM uses fixed cells that are 53 bytes long.
X.25	56Kbps	Copper/fiber-optic	Packet switching	X.25 is limited to 56Kbps.
				X.25 provides a packet-switching network over standard phone lines.
Frame Relay	56Kbps to 1.544Mbps	Copper/fiber-optic	PVCs and SVCs	Frame Relay is a packet-oriented protocol, and it uses variable-length packets.
SONET	51.8Mbps to 2.4Gbps	Fiber-optic	N/A	SONET defines synchronous data transfer over optical cable. The European equivalent of SONET is SDH.

CHAPTER SUMMARY

This chapter outlines the technologies used to create WANs. Each of these technologies has advantages and disadvantages, making some of them well suited for certain environments and completely impractical in others. Each of the technologies varies in terms of media, speed, availability, and cost.

Public networks such as the PSTN and the Internet are the most widely used methods of establishing WANs due in part to their availability, accessibility, and perhaps most importantly, their cost. The downsides of using these networks are security and speed issues.

Private networks allow secure communications between devices; however, the costs of dedicated private networks make them unattainable for many small companies. In addition, the implementation and management of private networks can often be more complex than that of public networks.

Several switching methods are used to establish communication between devices. With packet switching, messages are broken down into smaller pieces, with each packet assigned source, destination, and intermediate node addresses. These packets are independently routed toward the destination address. Circuit switching, on the other hand, requires a dedicated physical connection between the sending and receiving devices. Data transmissions follow the dedicated path to the receiving device. Message switching sends the entire message via intermediate devices, such as computers, temporarily storing and then forwarding the messages.

KEY TERMS

- public network
- PSTN
- private network
- message switching
- packet switching
- circuit switching
- independent routing
- virtual circuit packet
- datagram packet switching
- modem
- ISDN
- BRI
- PRI
- T-carrier
- T1/E1
- T3/E3
- FDDI
- Beaconing
- ATM
- SVC
- PVC
- X.25
- Frame Relay
- SONET/OC-x

APPLY YOUR KNOWLEDGE

Exercises

7.1 Investigating WAN Options

Estimated time: 30 minutes

Because you are unlikely to have the equipment or facilities to create your own WAN, this exercise requires that you investigate the WAN options that would be available to you if you were to create a WAN from your location to another.

Your research should include visiting the Web site of a local telecommunications provider and ascertaining the options open to you. Given that financial considerations are generally a major factor in a decision such as this, you should look at the lower-cost options such as cable, DSL, or ISDN in preference to leased-line circuits, such as T1 lines. From your research you should be able to answer the following questions:

◆ Which services are available in your location?

◆ Which services offer the best value for the money, based on available bandwidth, cost of installation, ongoing costs (line/equipment rental), maintenance, and call charges, if applicable?

◆ Which of the available services would you choose, and what would the estimated annual cost be for that service?

Although you should not sign up for any of the services during the course of this exercise, through this exercise you will gain valuable information because this is exactly the kind of project you are likely to be assigned when working in a real-world situation as an administrator. Evaluation and recommendation of products is an important element of a network administrator's role.

Exam Questions

1. Your company currently use a standard PSTN communication link to transfer files between LANs. Until now, the transfer speeds have been sufficient for the amount of data that needs to be transferred. Recently, a new application has been purchased that requires a minimum transmission speed of 1.5Mbps. You have been given the task of finding the most cost-effective solution to accommodate the new application. Which of the following technologies would you use?

   a. T3

   b. X.25

   c. T1

   d. BRI ISDN

2. Which of the following terms is used to describe a station on an FDDI network that is attached to both rings?

   a. DUS

   b. SAS

   c. DAS

   d. DRS

3. Which of the following statements are true of ISDN? (Choose the two best answers.)

   a. BRI ISDN uses 2B+1D channels.

   b. BRI ISDN uses 23B+1D channels.

   c. PRI ISDN uses 2B+1 D channels.

   d. PRI ISDN uses 23B+1D channels.

APPLY YOUR KNOWLEDGE

4. You have been hired to establish a WAN connection between two offices—one in Vancouver and one in Seattle. The transmission speed can be no less than 2Mbps. Which of the following technologies could you choose?

   a. T1

   b. PSTN

   c. T3

   d. ISDN

5. A customer calls you and wants information on FDDI. Which of the following are true of FDDI? (Choose the two best answers.)

   a. DASs are linked to both rings on FDDI.

   b. SASs are linked to both rings on FDDI.

   c. FDDI uses fiber-based media.

   d. FDDI uses copper-based media.

6. Which if the following technologies use exclusively fiber-based media? (Choose the two best answers.)

   a. FDDI

   b. T1

   c. SONET

   d. ISDN

7. Due to recent cutbacks, your boss approaches you, demanding an alternative to the company's costly dedicated T1 line. Only very small amounts of data will require transfer over the line. Which of the following are you likely to recommend?

   a. ISDN

   b. FDDI

   c. The PSTN

   d. X.25

8. Which of the following technologies requires a logical connection between the sending and receiving devices?

   a. Circuit switching

   b. Virtual-circuit packet switching

   c. Message switching

   d. High-density circuit switching

9. Which of the following technologies requires dial-up access? (Choose the two best answers.)

   a. FDDI

   b. ISDN

   c. Packet switching

   d. The PSTN

10. Which of the following is an advantage of ISDN over the PSTN?

    a. ISDN is more reliable.

    b. ISDN is cheaper.

    c. ISDN is faster.

    d. ISDN uses 53Kbps fixed-length packets.

11. Which of the following best describes the process of creating a dedicated circuit between two communication endpoints and directing traffic between those two points?

    a. Multiplexing

    b. Directional addressing

    c. Addressing

    d. Circuit switching

APPLY YOUR KNOWLEDGE

12. Which of the following technologies uses fixed-length packets, or cells, that are 53 bytes in length?

    a. ATM

    b. ISDN

    c. VPN

    d. FDDI

13. You need to implement a low-cost WAN implementation. Which of the following are considered public networks? (Choose the two best answers.)

    a. ATM

    b. The Internet

    c. FDDI

    d. The PSTN

14. Which of the following switching methods is associated with the store-and-forward technique?

    a. Packet switching

    b. Message switching

    c. Circuit switching

    d. Virtual-circuit packet switching

15. Which of the following are packet-switching technologies? (Choose the two best answers.)

    a. ATM

    b. X.25

    c. FDDI

    d. Frame Relay

16. Which of the following are disadvantages of a public network?

    a. Security

    b. Accessibility

    c. Availability

    d. Cost

17. Which of the following circuit-switching strategies are used by ATM? (Choose the two best answers.)

    a. SVC

    b. VCD

    c. PVC

    d. PCV

18. On an ISDN connection, what is the purpose of the D channel?

    a. It carries the data signals.

    b. It carries signaling information.

    c. It allows multiple channels to be combined, to provide greater bandwidth.

    d. It provides a temporary overflow capacity for the other channels.

19. Which of the following technologies uses a PAD?

    a. ISDN

    b. ATM

    c. X.25

    d. OC-3

APPLY YOUR KNOWLEDGE

20. Of the following technologies, which are limited to 56Kbps? (Choose the two best answers.)

    a. Modem

    b. ISDN

    c. X.25

    d. Frame Relay

Answers to Exam Questions

1. **c.** A T1 line has a transmission capability of 1.544Mbps and is considerably cheaper than a T3 line. X.25 and BRI ISDN cannot provide the required transmission speed. For more information, see the "WAN Technologies" section in this chapter.

2. **c.** *DAS* describes a device that occupies both rings on an FDDI network. None of the other answers are valid. For more information, see the "WAN Technologies" section in this chapter.

3. **a, d.** BRI ISDN uses 2B+1D channels, which are two 64Kbps data channels, and PRI-ISDN uses 23B+1D channels. The other answers are not valid. For more information, see the "WAN Technologies" section in this chapter.

4. **c.** The only technology in this question that is capable of transfer speeds above 2Mbps is a T3 line. None of the other technologies listed can provide the transmission speed required. For more information, see the "WAN Technologies" section in this chapter.

5. **a, c.** DASs in an FDDI network connect to both rings, creating a fault-tolerant measure for the Class A device. FDDI is implemented over a fiber-based media. Answer b is incorrect because an SAS is connected to only one ring. Answer d is incorrect because FDDI can be implemented only over fiber-optic cable. For more information, see the "WAN Technologies" section in this chapter.

6. **a, c.** FDDI is implemented as two counter-rotating rings using fiber-based media. SONET is a fiber-based standard that was developed by Bell Communications Research, following the AT&T breakup in 1984. T1 and ISDN can both be implemented over copper-based cable. For more information, see the "WAN Technologies" section in this chapter.

7. **c.** When very little traffic will be sent over a line, the PSTN is the most cost-effective solution, although it is limited to 56Kbps. All the other WAN connectivity methods accommodate large amounts of data and are expensive in comparison to the PSTN. For more information, see the "WAN Technologies" section in this chapter.

8. **b.** When virtual circuit switching is used, a logical connection is established between the source and the destination device. None of the other answers are valid. For more information, see the "Introduction to WAN Technologies" section in this chapter.

9. **b, d.** Both the PSTN and ISDN require dial-up connections to establish communication sessions. The other answers are not valid. For more information, see the "WAN Technologies" section in this chapter.

10. **c.** One clear advantage that ISDN has over the PSTN is its speed. ISDN can combine 64Kbps channels for faster transmission speeds than the PSTN can provide. ISDN is no more or less

APPLY YOUR KNOWLEDGE

reliable than the PSTN. ISDN is more expensive than the PSTN. Answer d describes ATM. For more information, see the "WAN Technologies" section in this chapter.

11. **d.** Circuit switching is the process of creating a dedicated circuit between two communication endpoints and directing traffic between those two points. None of the other answers are valid types of switching. For more information, see the "Introduction to WAN Technologies" section in this chapter.

12. **a.** ATM uses fixed packets, or cells, with lengths of 53 bytes—48 bytes for data information and 5 bytes for the header. None of the other technologies listed use this cell format. For more information, see the "WAN Technologies" section in this chapter.

13. **b, d.** The Internet and the PSTN are considered public networks and are therefore the most cost-effective data transmission solutions. ATM and FDDI are examples of private networking technologies. For more information, see the "Introduction to WAN Technologies" section in this chapter.

14. **b.** Message switching uses a store-and-forward switching method. This method is impractical for real-time data transmissions but well suited for other applications, such as email. None of the other switching methods are associated with store-and-forward. For more information, see the "Introduction to WAN Technologies" section in this chapter.

15. **b, d.** X.25 and Frame Relay are both packet-switching technologies. ATM and FDDI are not considered packet-switching technologies. For more information, see the "WAN Technologies" section in this chapter.

16. **a.** There are many advantages of a public network, but security is a concern because data transmissions can be intercepted. All the other answers are advantages of using a public network. For more information, see the "Introduction to WAN Technologies" section in this chapter.

17. **a, c.** ATM uses two types of circuit switching—PVC and SVC. VCD and PCV are not the names of switching methods. For more information, see the "WAN Technologies" section in this chapter.

18. **b.** The D channel on an ISDN link carries signaling information, whereas the B, or bearer, channels carry the data. The other answers are not valid. For more information, see the "WAN Technologies" section in this chapter.

19. **c.** A PAD is associated with X.25 networks. None of the other technologies listed use PADs. For more information, see the "WAN Technologies" section in this chapter.

20. **a, c.** Both modem links and X.25 are limited to 56Kbps. ISDN and Frame Relay are both capable of greater speeds than either X.25 or modems. For more information, see the "WAN Technologies" section in this chapter.

APPLY YOUR KNOWLEDGE

Suggested Readings and Resources

1. Habraken, Joe. *Absolute Beginner's Guide to Networking,* third edition. Que Publishing, 2001.

2. Shinder, Debra Littlejohn. *Computer Networking Essentials.* Cisco Press, 2001.

3. McCarty, Ronald W. *Cisco WAN Quick Start.* Cisco Press, 2000.

4. Cisco Systems Inc. *Internetworking Troubleshooting Handbook,* second edition. Cisco Press, 2001.

5. Marcus, Scott J. *Designing Wide Area Networks and Internetworks: A Practical Guide.* Addison-Wesley, 1999.

6. Frame Relay and associated WAN information, `www.mywanonline.com/fr_online_learning.htm`.

7. WAN technology information from Cisco, `www.cisco.com/univercd/cc/td/doc/cisintwk/ito_doc/introwan.htm`.

8. General WAN info and links, `www.techfest.com/networking/wan.htm`.

9. Computer Networking Tutorials and Advice, `compnetworking.about.com`.

10. "TechEncyclopedia," `www.techencyclopedia.com`.

11. Networking technology information from Cisco, `www.cisco.com/public/products_tech.shtml`.

This chapter covers the following CompTIA-specified objectives for the "Protocols and Standards" section of the Network+ exam:

Define the function of the following remote access protocols and services:

- **Remote Access Service (RAS)**

- **Point-to-Point Protocol (PPP)**

- **Point-to-Point Tunneling Protocol (PPTP)**

- **Independent Computing Architecture (ICA)**

▶ Remote access is a common feature of today's networks. An understanding of the common remote access protocols and services is a must for any network administrator.

Identify the following security protocols and describe their purpose and function:

- **Internet Protocol Security (IPSec)**

- **Layer 2 Tunneling Protocol (L2TP)**

- **Secure Sockets Layer (SSL)**

- **Kerberos**

▶ Providing remote access facilities for a network brings with it a multitude of security concerns. To address these concerns, security protocols are available to ensure that only the intended users can access the network and the data transmitted to it.

CHAPTER 8

Remote Access and Security Protocols

OUTLINE

Introduction   **291**

Remote Access Protocols and Services   **292**

Remote Access Service (RAS)   292
     RAS Client Support   293
Serial Line Internet Protocol (SLIP)   294
Point-to-Point Protocol (PPP)   295
     PPP Authentication Protocols   295
     The PPP Dial-up Sequence   296
PPTP   297
Independent Computing Architecture (ICA)   298

Security Protocols   **299**

IPSec   300
L2F   301
Layer Two Tunneling Protocol (L2TP)   301
Secure Sockets Layer (SSL)   302
Kerberos   303
SSH   303
Remote Authentication Dial-In User
   Service (RADIUS)   304

Types of Remote Access   **304**

Dial-up Remote Access   305
Virtual Private Networks   305

Chapter Summary   **306**

Apply Your Knowledge   **307**

STUDY STRATEGIES

▶ Read the objectives at the beginning of the chapter.

▶ Study the information in the chapter, paying special attention to the tables, which summarize key information.

▶ Review the objectives again.

▶ Answer the exam questions at the end of the chapter and check your results.

▶ Use the ExamGear test on the CD-ROM that accompanies this book to answer additional exam questions concerning this material.

▶ Review the notes, tips, and exam tips in this chapter. Make sure you understand the information in the exam tips. If you don't understand the topic referenced in an exam tip, refer to the information in the chapter text and then read the exam tip again.

INTRODUCTION

Networks are no longer restricted to the confines of a single location or even a small group of locations. Users can, and do, connect to remote networks from virtually anywhere. The ability to remotely access networks has changed the way we work and do business. Today, anywhere/anytime access to computer networks is an expectation rather than a bonus. Whether a user is working from home, his or her car, or a branch office, the ability to access the corporate network has become a critical requirement.

Modern network and workstation operating systems facilitate remote access by providing the means and methods to do it. By using remote access capabilities, it's possible to create a secure, transparent connection that lets remote corporate users feel as if they were operating from the local network.

Traditionally, remote access has been achieved by using a modem and a dial-up connection. Although this method is still widely used and is by far the most popular method of remote connectivity, new technologies continue to emerge, increasing the variety of ways that networks can be accessed remotely. Technologies such as fixed wireless, Internet access using cable, and Digital Subscriber Line (DSL) have opened up new possibilities for remote access through their increased speed and reduced costs. These high-speed remote access methods mean that instead of just using the connection to transfer a file or two, remote workers can use a variety of technologies such as videoconferencing.

Regardless of the technique used for remote access or the speed at which access is achieved, certain technologies need to be in place in order for the magic to happen. These technologies include the protocols both to allow the access to the server and to secure the data transfer after the connection is established. Also necessary are methods of access control that make sure only authorized users are using the remote access features.

All the major operating systems include built-in support for remote access. They provide both the access methods and security protocols necessary to secure the connection and data transfers.

This chapter focuses on the protocols and services used to establish and secure remote network access. It begins by looking at the remote access protocols and the protocols used for security. Finally, the chapter examines two remote access methods—dial-in access and virtual private networks (VPNs)—and the protocols they use to establish and secure remote connections.

REMOTE ACCESS PROTOCOLS AND SERVICES

▶ Define the function of the following remote access protocols and services:

• Remote Access Service (RAS)

• Point-to-Point Protocol (PPP)

• Point-to-Point Tunneling Protocol (PPTP)

• Independent Computing Architecture (ICA)

Protocols and services are needed for establishing remote connections. The following sections discuss these protocols and services:

◆ Remote Access Service (RAS)

◆ Serial Line Internet Protocol (SLIP)

◆ Point-to-Point Protocol (PPP)

◆ Point-to-Point Tunneling Protocol (PPTP)

◆ Independent Computing Architecture (ICA)

Each of these protocols and services has advantages, disadvantages, and limitations, but each has a place in establishing remote connectivity.

This chapter begins its discussion of remote access technologies by looking at the remote access mechanism used on Windows Server platforms: the RAS, which is the most popular form of remote connectivity.

Remote Access Service (RAS)

RAS is a full-featured remote access solution that is included with Windows Server products. The popularity of RAS has a lot to do with the popularity of Windows, but RAS is also feature rich, easy to configure, and easy to use. As a result of this ease of use, many companies that previously had not used remote access now embrace it. (The fact that RAS is included with Windows has probably also had something to do with its popularity.)

Any system that supports the appropriate dial-in protocols can connect to a RAS server. Most commonly, the clients are Windows systems that use the dial-up networking feature; but any operating system that supports dial-up client software will work. Connection to a RAS server can be made over a standard phone line, using a modem, over a network, or via an Integrated Services Digital Network (ISDN) connection.

When a connection is made to the RAS server, the client is authenticated and the system that is dialing in becomes a part of the network, although it is connected over a slow link. Depending on the configuration of the RAS server, the client is then able to access just the RAS server or the entire network. The number of RAS connections is normally limited by the number of dial-in connections the system can physically accommodate, but there are also some limits built in to the software. Windows NT 4 Server, for example, supports up to 256 remote connections, whereas workstation products such as Windows NT Workstation and Windows 2000 Professional support only a single RAS connection. Figure 8.1 shows an example of remote access through a RAS server.

NOTE **RRAS** In Windows 2000 Microsoft renamed the RAS service to Routing and Remote Access Service (RRAS). The basic RAS functionality, however, is the same as in previous versions of Windows.

NOTE **RAS Server Callbacks** RAS includes a feature called *callback* that allows for an extra degree of security. When a call is placed to a RAS server, the server hangs up and calls back either a predetermined number or a number that can be input by the remote user. When a predetermined number is used, only calls that originate from that number will be serviced, which is more secure than allowing calls from any number.

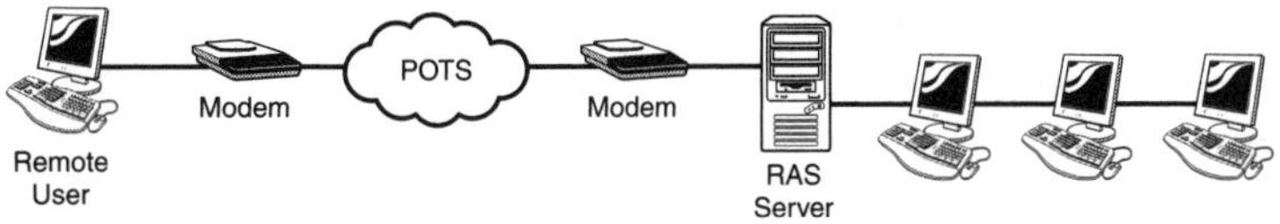

FIGURE 8.1
Remote access through a RAS server.

RAS Client Support

RAS supports remote connectivity from all the major client operating systems available today, including the following:

◆ Windows for Workgroups–based clients

◆ LAN Manager–based clients

◆ Windows 95–based clients

◆ Windows NT Workstation–based clients

◆ Windows NT Server–based clients

◆ Windows 2000 Professional–based clients

◆ Unix-based/Linux clients

◆ Macintosh-based clients

◆ OS/2-based clients

Although the system is called RAS, the underlying technologies that enable the RAS process are dial-up protocols such as PPP and SLIP.

Serial Line Internet Protocol (SLIP)

EXAM TIP

SLIP   SLIP is not actually included in the CompTIA objectives, but it is included here because it is still used in real-world applications, though on a decreasing basis.

In the 1970s, students at the University of California, Berkley, developed SLIP. SLIP was designed to allow data to be transmitted via Transmission Control Protocol/Internet Protocol (TCP/IP) over serial connections in a Unix environment. SLIP did an excellent job, but time proved to be its enemy. SLIP was developed in an atmosphere in which security was not an overriding concern; consequently, SLIP does not support encryption or authentication. It transmits all the data used to establish a connection (username and password) in clear text, which is, of course, dangerous in today's insecure world.

SLIP also does not provide error checking or packet addressing, so it can be used only in serial communications. It supports only TCP/IP, and login is accomplished through a terminal window. You can avoid the terminal window logon by utilizing scripts, but doing so can be difficult as well.

Is SLIP a bad protocol? No, in its day, it performed its intended duties perfectly; it is just not a match for today's computing environment or the new dial-up protocols that are available.

Many operating systems still provide at least minimal SLIP support for backward capability to older environments, but SLIP has been replaced by a newer and more secure alternative: PPP. SLIP is still used by some government agencies and large corporations in Unix remote access applications, so you might come across it from time to time.

Point-to-Point Protocol (PPP)

PPP, which is described in RFC 1661, is the standard remote access protocol in use today. PPP is actually a family of protocols that work together to provide connection services. PPP provides solutions to most of SLIP's shortcomings.

Because PPP is an industry standard, it offers interoperability between different software vendors in various remote access implementations. PPP provides a number of security enhancements compared to SLIP, the most important being the encryption of usernames and passwords during the authentication process. PPP allows remote clients and servers to negotiate data encryption methods and authentication methods and support new technologies. PPP even gives administrators the ability to choose which particular local area network (LAN) protocol to use over a remote link. A Windows 2000 administrator can choose among NetBIOS Extended User Interface (NetBEUI), NWLink (Internetwork Packet Exchange/ Sequenced Packet Exchange [IPX/SPX]), AppleTalk, or TCP/IP.

PPP Authentication Protocols

During the establishment of a PPP connection between the remote system and the server, the remote server needs to authenticate the remote user and does so by using the PPP authentication protocols. PPP accommodates a number of authentication protocols; the protocol used in the authentication process depends on the security configurations established between the remote user and the server. The following are some of the common authentication protocols used by PPP:

◆ **Challenge Handshake Authentication Protocol (CHAP)**— CHAP is an authentication system that uses the MD5 encryption scheme to secure authentication responses. CHAP is a commonly used protocol, and as the name suggests, anyone trying to connect is challenged for authentication information. When the correct information is supplied, the systems "shake hands," and the connection is established.

◆ **Microsoft Challenge Handshake Authentication Protocol (MS-CHAP)**—MS-CHAP was developed to authenticate remote Windows-based workstations. There are two versions of MS-CHAP; the main difference between the two is that

Z
O
T
E   **ATCP**   Macintosh users can dial in to a Windows 2000 server by using PPP over AppleTalk Control Protocol (ATCP). ATCP is installed when the AppleTalk protocol is installed, or it can be installed separately.

MS-CHAP version 2 offers mutual authentication. This means that both the client and the server must prove their identities in the authentication process. Doing so ensures that the client is connecting to the expected server.

◆ **Password Authentication Protocol (PAP)**—PAP is the least secure of the authentication methods that use unencrypted passwords. PAP is often not the first choice of protocols used; rather, it is used when more sophisticated types of authentication fail between a server and a workstation.

◆ **Extensible Authentication Protocol (EAP)**—EAP is an extension made to standard PPP. EAP has additional support for a variety of authentication schemes. It is often used with VPNs to add security against brute-force or dictionary attacks.

◆ **Shiva Password Authentication Protocol (SPAP)**—SPAP is an encrypting authentication protocol used by Shiva remote access servers. SPAP offers a higher level of security than other authentication protocols such as PAP, but it is not as secure as CHAP.

The PPP Dial-up Sequence

The following specific steps are performed when a remote connection is established:

1. To allow communication between devices to occur, framing rules are established between the client and the server.

2. The remote client system is authenticated by the authentication server, using one of the PPP authentication protocols: CHAP, MS-CHAP, EAP, or PAP.

3. Network control protocols (NCPs) configure the remote client for the correct LAN protocols, TCP/IP, and so on.

After these steps are successfully completed, the server and the client can begin to exchange data.

E
X
A
M   TIP

SLIP and PPP   If you are working on a network that uses SLIP, you should try to move to PPP as soon as possible because it is more flexible and secure than PPP.

PPTP

PPTP, which is documented in RFC 2637, is often mentioned together with PPP. Although it's used in dial-up connections as PPP is, PPTP provides very different functionality: It creates a secure *tunnel* between two points on a network, over which other connectivity protocols, such as PPP, can be used. This tunneling functionality is the basis for VPNs, which are discussed later in this chapter.

VPNs are created and managed by using the PPTP protocol, which builds on the functionality of PPP, making it possible to create dedicated point-to-point tunnels through a public network such as the Internet. Figure 8.2 shows an example of a PPTP connection through a public network.

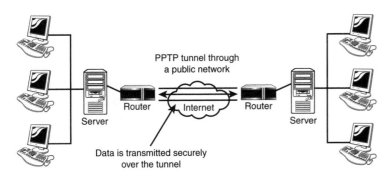

FIGURE 8.2
A PPTP connection.

To establish a PPTP session between a client and server, a TCP connection known as a *PPTP control connection* is required to create and maintain the communication tunnel. The PPTP control connection exists between the IP address of the PPTP client and the IP address of the PPTP server, using TCP port 1723. It is the function of the PPTP control connection to pass the PPTP control and management messages used to maintain the PPTP communication tunnel between the remote system and the server. Examples of these control and management messages are included in Table 8.1.

TABLE 8.1

PPTP CALL CONTROL AND MANAGEMENT MESSAGES

PPTP Control Message	Function
Start Control Connection Request	The initial message sent by the client to create the PPTP control connection. To establish a PPTP tunnel, this control connection must be initiated before any other PPTP messages can be sent.
Start Control Connection Reply	The response sent by the server, acknowledging the client's request.
Outgoing Call Request	The request sent by the client to establish the PPTP tunnel.
Outgoing Call Reply	The server's reply to the Outgoing Call Request message.
Call Clear Request	The request sent by the PPTP client, indicating the termination of the tunnel.
Call Disconnect Notify	The message sent by the server in response to the Call Clear Request message.
Stop Control Connection Request	The request sent by either the PPTP client or the PPTP server to indicate that the control connection is being terminated.

PPTP uses the same authentication methods as PPP, including MS-CHAP, CHAP, PAP, and EAP.

Independent Computing Architecture (ICA)

The Citrix ICA protocol allows client systems to access and run applications on a server, using the resources of the server, with only the user interface, keystrokes, and mouse movement being transferred between the client and server computers. In effect, although you are working at a remote computer, the system functions as if you were physically sitting at the server itself. Such technology is often referred to as *thin client* because only a very small piece of software is need on the client system.

NOTE

The X Window System   ICA is similar to the X Window System, which is used in Unix/Linux environments.

Because ICA requires only minimal traffic back and forth between the client and the server, the connection is not bandwidth intensive, allowing clients to simultaneously use ICA. In addition, processing is performed on the server rather than on the client workstation. This enables client systems to use applications they would not normally be able to run. For example, using ICA, it would be possible for a user on a 486 computer with only 16MB of RAM to run the latest Office suite or a complex graphics system. Doing so would be impossible using only the resources of the client system.

ICA is platform independent. It provides client software for all the major operating systems, including Windows, Macintosh, and Linux, and it even supports handheld devices.

NOTE

ICA Support ICA works over all standard network protocols, such as TCP/IP, NetBEUI, IPX/SPX, and PPP. It also supports the commonly used transport mechanisms, such as ISDN, Frame Relay, and Asynchronous Transfer Mode (ATM).

SECURITY PROTOCOLS

▶ Identify the following security protocols and describe their purpose and function:
  - Internet Protocol Security (IPSec)
  - Layer 2 Tunneling Protocol (L2TP)
  - Secure Sockets Layer (SSL)
  - Kerberos

Any discussion of remote access is sure to include security, and for a good reason: As its name implies, remote access literally opens your network to remote users. Although you'd like to think that only authorized users would try to connect from remote locations, the reality is that an equal number of illegitimate users will probably attempt to connect. Because many of the methods used to establish remote access are over public networks, securing the data you send and the points at which you connect is an important consideration. A significant element of this security is encryption.

Encryption is the process of encoding the data sent over remote connections, and it involves scrambling the usernames and passwords used to gain access to the remote network. *Encryption* is simply the process of encoding data using a mathematical algorithm that makes it difficult for unauthorized users to read the data if they are able to intercept it. The algorithm is actually a mathematical value known as a *key*. The key is required in order to read the encrypted data.

Encryption techniques use public and private keys; public keys can be shared and private keys cannot.

A key is a binary number that has a large number of bits. As you might imagine, the bigger the number or key, the harder it is to guess. Today, simple encryption strategies use 40 to 56 bits. On a 40-bit encryption, there are 2^{40} possible keys; 56-bit encryption has 2^{56} possible keys—that's more than 65 trillion possible keys. Remember that without the correct key, the data cannot be accessed. Although the number of keys associated with lower-grade encryption may seem amazing, they have been cracked by some very high-end, specialized systems. That makes necessary higher-grade encryption: Many online transactions require 128-bit encryption, and other applications support encryption as high as 1,024 bits. (If you have time, try to calculate the key combinations for these higher-grade encryption strategies.)

Using and managing remote access connections requires knowledge of security protocols and what they are designed to do. The following sections examine several different security protocols:

- ◆ IP Security (IPSec)
- ◆ Layer Two Forwarding (L2F)
- ◆ Layer 2 Tunneling Protocol (L2TP)
- ◆ Secure Sockets Layer (SSL)
- ◆ Kerberos
- ◆ Secure Shell (SSH)
- ◆ Remote Authentication Dial-In User Service (RADIUS)

IPSec

IPSec is designed to encrypt data during communication between two computers. The function of IPSec is to ensure that data on a network cannot be viewed, accessed, or modified by those who should not have access to it. IPSec provides security for both internal and external networks. It might seem that protection on an internal network is less necessary than on an external network; however, much of the data you send across networks has little or no protection, allowing unwanted eyes to access it.

IPSec provides three key security services:

◆ **Data verification**—It verifies that the data received is from the intended source.

◆ **Protection from data tampering**—It ensures that the data has not been tampered with and changed between the sending and receiving devices.

◆ **Private transactions**—It ensures that the data sent between the sending and receiving devices is unreadable by any other devices.

IPSec operates at the network layer of the Open Systems Interconnect (OSI) model and provides security for protocols that operate at higher layers of the OSI model. Thus, by using IPSec, you can secure practically all TCP/IP-related communications.

> **NOTE**
>
> **Using IPSec** IPSec was created by the Internet Engineering Task Force (IETF) and can be used on both IPv4 and IPv6 networks.

> **EXAM TIP**
>
> **IPSec and TCP/IP** IPSec can only be used on TCP/IP networks. If you are using another network protocol, you need to use a security protocol such as L2TP.

L2F

L2F is a proprietary protocol and technology that was developed by Cisco Systems. It allows tunneling to be utilized as a connection method over insecure networks. L2F is still around today; it has been folded into new implementations of tunneling protocols, and it is included in the new and improved L2TP.

Layer Two Tunneling Protocol (L2TP)

L2TP is a combination of PPTP and Cisco's L2F technology. L2TP, as the name suggests, utilizes tunneling to deliver data. It authenticates the client in a two-phase process: It first authenticates the computer and then the user. By authenticating the computer, it prevents the data from being intercepted, changed, and returned to the user in what is known as a *man-in-the-middle attack*. L2TP assures both parties that the data they are receiving is exactly the data sent by the originator.

L2TP and PPTP are both tunneling protocols, so you might be wondering which you should use. Here is a quick list of the some of the advantages of each, starting with PPTP:

◆ PPTP has been around the longest; it offers more interoperability than L2TP.

> **NOTE**
>
> **L2TP Tunneling Without Encryption** It is possible to create an L2TP tunnel without using encryption, but this is not a true VPN and, obviously, lacks a certain amount of security.

> **EXAM TIP**
>
> **L2TP and the Data-Link Layer** Unlike IPSec, which operates at the network layer of the OSI model, L2TP operates at the data-link layer, making it protocol independent. This means that an L2TP connection can support protocols such as IPX and AppleTalk.

◆ PPTP is an industry standard.

◆ PPTP is easier to configure than L2TP because L2TP requires
digital certificates.

◆ PPTP has less overhead than L2TP.

The following are some of the advantages of L2TP:

◆ L2TP offers greater security than PPTP.

◆ L2TP supports common public key infrastructure technology.

◆ L2TP provides support for header compression.

Secure Sockets Layer (SSL)

SSL is a security protocol that is used on the Internet. Originally
developed by Netscape for use with its Navigator browser, SSL uses
public key encryption to establish secure connections over the
Internet. SSL provides three key services:

◆ **Server authentication**—SSL allows a user to confirm a server's
identity. For example, you can use this ability when you are
purchasing something online with a credit card but first want
to verify the server's identity.

◆ **Client authentication**—SSL allows a server to confirm a
user's identity. This functionality is often used when a server is
sending sensitive information—such as banking information
or sensitive documents—to a client system and wants to verify
the client's identity.

◆ **Encrypted connections**—It is possible to configure SSL to
require all information sent between a client and a server to be
encrypted by the sending software and decrypted by the
receiving software. Doing this establishes private and secure
communication between two devices. In addition, SSL has a
mechanism to determine whether the data sent has been tampered with or altered in transit.

You can see SSL security on the Web when you access a secure universal resource locator (URL). Secure Web sites begin with `https://`
instead of `http://`. Hypertext Transfer Protocol over SSL (HTTPS)
connections require a browser to establish a secure connection.

Kerberos

Seasoned administrators can tell you about the risks of sending clear-text, unencrypted passwords across any network. The Kerberos network authentication protocol is designed to ensure that the data sent across networks is encrypted and safe from attack. Its purpose is to provide authentication for client/server applications.

Kerberos was created at Massachusetts Institute of Technology to provide a solution to network security issues. With Kerberos, the client must prove its identity to the server, and the server must also prove its identity to the client. Kerberos provides a method to verify the identity of a computer system over an insecure network connection.

Kerberos is distributed freely, as is its source code, allowing anyone interested to view the source code directly. Kerberos is also available from many different vendors that provide additional support for its use.

EXAM TIP

Tickets For the exam, you should know that the security tokens used in Kerberos are known as *tickets*.

SSH

Because Unix- and Linux-based systems are prominent in modern network environments, network administrators face huge security interoperability concerns. Windows-based clients often use Telnet to remotely access Unix/Linux servers. Unfortunately, Telnet is a very insecure remote access method; it sends the entire session—including passwords and login information—in clear text. (*Clear text* simply means that the information is sent unencrypted, and anyone can intercept with a packet capture program, and read the data with his or her favorite word processor.)

SSH provides a secure multiplatform replacement for Telnet. SSH allows users to connect to a remote server, and it encrypts the entire session. SSH has become an IETF standard, and development for SSH now includes a number of operating systems besides Linux and Unix. Using SSH, Windows 9x/NT/2000 as well as Macintosh systems can securely access remote servers.

To download and try SSH, go to www.freessh.org and download the client software.

Remote Authentication Dial-In User Service (RADIUS)

Among the potential issues network administrators face when implementing remote access are utilization and the load on the remote access server. As a network's remote access implementation grows, reliance on a single remote access server might be impossible, and additional servers might be required. RADIUS can help in this scenario.

RADIUS is a protocol that allows a single server to become responsible for all remote access authentication, authorization, and auditing (or accounting) services. The RADIUS protocol can be implemented as a vendor-specific product such as Microsoft's Internet Authentication Server (IAS).

RADIUS functions as a client/server system. The remote user dials in to the remote access server, which acts as a RADIUS client, or network access server (NAS), and connects to a RADIUS server. The RADIUS server performs authentication, authorization, and auditing (or accounting) functions and returns the information to the RADIUS client (which is a remote access server running RADIUS client software); the connection is either established or rejected based on the information received.

RADIUS can also be configured in a fault-tolerant architecture that provides backup servers that process requests when other RADIUS servers fail. Because RADIUS is actually a set of protocols based on RFCs, it works with many remote access servers—it is not a Microsoft-only implementation.

TYPES OF REMOTE ACCESS

Having looked at the protocols required to establish remote access, let's now look at two types of remote access—dial-up remote access and virtual private networking—and how they use remote access protocols. All the major operating systems offer these types of remote access.

Dial-up Remote Access

Perhaps the simplest and most common of all remote access connections is dial-up access. A dial-up connection is established when the modem of one system contacts a modem on another system and communication begins between the two systems. All the major network operating systems support dial-up remote access. To connect to a server via modem, the server needs to be capable of answering and authenticating a remote access client (for example, a RAS server). The server performing this function is known as the *remote access server*.

> **NOTE**
>
> **Dial-up Remote Access** Dial-up remote access is best suited for a small, remote user population that requires minimal data transfers that can be supported with analog or ISDN performance.

Virtual Private Networks

In the mid-1990s, Microsoft, IBM, and Cisco began working on a technology called *tunneling*. By 1996 more companies had become interested and involved in the work, and the project soon produced two new virtual private networking solutions: PPTP and L2TP. Ascend, 3Com, Microsoft, and U.S. Robotics had developed PPTP, and Cisco Systems had introduced L2F.

From these developments, VPNs became one of the most popular methods of remote access. Essentially, a VPN is an extension of a LAN that establishes a remote connection, using a public network such as the Internet. A *VPN* is a point-to-point dedicated link over a public IP network.

A VPN encapsulates encrypted data inside another datagram that contains routing information. The connection between two computers establishes a switched connection that is dedicated to the two computers. The encrypted data is encapsulated inside PPP, and that connection is used to deliver the data.

A VPN allows anyone with an Internet connection to use the infrastructure of the public network to dial in to the main network and access resources as if he or she were logged on to the network locally. It also allows two networks to be connected to each other securely.

Many elements are involved in establishing a VPN connection, including the following:

◆ **A VPN client**—The VPN client is the computer that initiates the connection to the VPN server.

◆ **A VPN server**—The VPN server authenticates connections from VPN clients.

◆ **An access method**—As mentioned, a VPN is most often established over a public network such as the Internet; however, some VPN implementations use a private intranet. The network that is used must be IP based.

◆ **VPN protocols**—Protocols are required to establish, manage, and secure the data over the VPN connection. PPTP and L2TP are commonly associated with VPN connections.

VPNs have become very popular because they allow the public Internet to be safely utilized as a wide area network (WAN) connectivity solution. (A complete discussion of VPNs would easily fill another book and goes beyond the scope of the Network+ objectives.)

CHAPTER SUMMARY

KEY TERMS

- RAS
- SLIP
- PPP
- CHAP
- MS-CHAP
- PAP
- EAP
- SPAP
- PPTP
- ICA
- security protocol
- encryption
- IPSec
- L2F
- L2TP
- SSL
- Kerberos
- SSH
- RADIUS
- VPN

Remote access has become an important part of modern business, and companies have come to depend on the ability to access network applications and services from a remote location. To facilitate remote access, all the major operating systems offer the protocols necessary to connect a remote client to a server system. Some of the most common remote access protocols are SLIP, PPP, PPTP, RAS, L2TP, and ICA.

Implementing remote access for an organization introduces another issue for the network administrator: security. You must understand and use security protocols to ensure that data is not compromised. The common security protocols include IPSec, SSL, and Kerberos.

APPLY YOUR KNOWLEDGE

Exercises

8.1   Enabling the Remote Access Service on a Computer Running Windows 2000 Server

Whether through a RAS, a VPN, or some other method, the ability to configure remote access methods has become an important consideration for network administrators. In this exercise, you'll configure a server to allow incoming remote access.

Estimated time: 15 minutes

1. Select Start, Programs, Administrative Tools, Routing and Remote Access. The Routing and Remote Access window shown in Figure 8.3 appears.

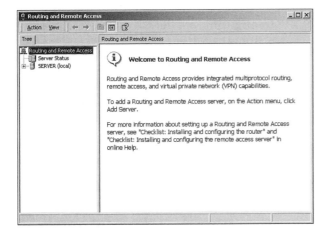

FIGURE 8.3
The Routing and Remote Access window.

2. To make the system a RAS server, select the Add Server option from the Action menu. The Add Server dialog box appears. Select the This Computer radio button, as shown in Figure 8.4.

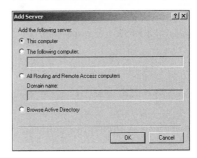

FIGURE 8.4
The Add Server dialog box.

3. In the left pane of the Routing and Remote Access window, right-click on your server and choose Configure and Enable Routing and Remote Access. The Routing and Remote Access Server Setup Wizard opens. Click Next to start the wizard.

4. Select the appropriate Remote Access Server radio button, as shown in Figure 8.5, and then click Next.

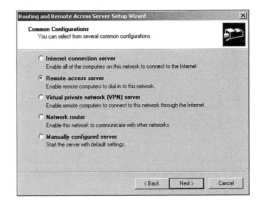

FIGURE 8.5
The Routing and Remote Access Server Setup Wizard.

APPLY YOUR KNOWLEDGE

5. The next screen in the wizard requires you to choose which protocols your clients will be able to use to connect to the remote access server. Accept the default, TCP/IP, and click Next.

6. You need to decide how to handle client IP addressing. For now, accept the default setting of Automatically, as shown in Figure 8.6, and then click Next.

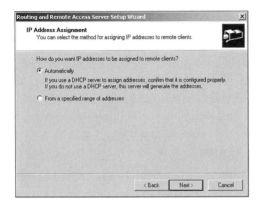

FIGURE 8.6
Configuring automatic IP addressing for remote clients.

7. In the next wizard screen, you have the option to set up a RADIUS server. Opt not to do so at this time and click Next.

8. The final wizard screen acknowledges the successful configuration of a Windows RAS server. Click Next, and the RAS service attempts to start automatically. Figure 8.7 shows the Routing and Remote Access window, with a successfully installed RAS server.

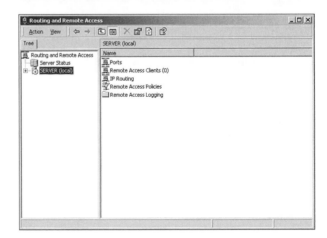

FIGURE 8.7
The Routing and Remote Access window with an installed RAS server.

8.2 Configuring a Client System to Access a Remote Server

After you have the server side of a remote access connection configured, you can configure the client side. To create a dial-up connection that allows a user to connect to a resource as a dial-up client, follow the steps in this exercise.

Estimated time: 15 minutes

1. Select Start, Settings, Network and Dial Up Connections. The Network and Dial-up Connections window shown in Figure 8.8 appears.

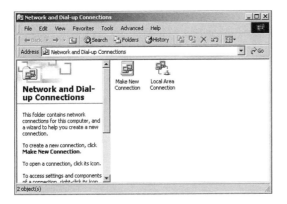

FIGURE 8.8
The Network and Dial-up Connections window.

2. Double-click the Make New Connection icon to start the Network Connection Wizard. Click Next to configure the connection.

3. The first screen of the Network Connection Wizard allows you to choose the type of network connection you want to create. Select the Dial-up to Private Network option, as shown in Figure 8.9, and then click Next. The Phone Number to Dial dialog box appears.

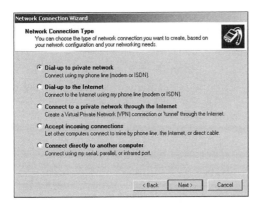

FIGURE 8.9
The Network Connection Type dialog box.

4. Enter the telephone number of the remote access server (a line that the remote access server will use to accept incoming calls). For this exercise, enter your personal telephone number. Click Next, and the Connection Availability screen appears. It allows you to limit the use of this dial-up connection to your personal logon or to anyone who logs on to this computer.

5. Make sure For All Users is selected, as shown in Figure 8.10, and then click Next.

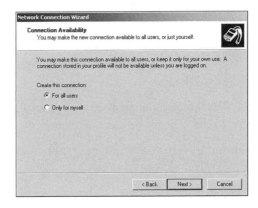

FIGURE 8.10
The Connection Availability dialog box.

6. The next screen lets you choose whether you will let other users access resources through this connection. For this exercise, leave the Internet Connection Sharing box unchecked. Click Next.

7. The Completing the Network Connection Wizard dialog box appears. You need to enter a descriptive name for the connection you are creating, so for this connection, enter **Real World Project Test**. Select Add a Shortcut to My Desktop, and then click Finish. A shortcut icon appears on your desktop.

APPLY YOUR KNOWLEDGE

8. In a real-world scenario, you can now establish a connection to a remote access server by double-clicking the shortcut icon.

Exam Questions

1. Which of the following statements best describes a VPN?

    a. It is any protocol that allows remote clients to log in to a server over a network such as the Internet.

    b. It provides a system whereby only screen display and keyboard and mouse input travel across the link.

    c. It is a secure communication channel across a public network such as the Internet.

    d. It is a protocol used for encryption of user IDs and passwords.

2. Which of the following is a disadvantage of SLIP?

    a. It transmits passwords and usernames in clear text.

    b. It can be used only on Linux systems.

    c. It can be used only on Microsoft Windows systems.

    d. It is not a Network Driver Interface Specification (NDIS)-compliant protocol.

3. What is the function of SSL?

    a. It provides a mechanism for data downloaded from and information uploaded to a Web site to be secured against unauthorized viewing.

    b. It allows a secure remote connection to be established to a remote host for the purposes of opening a session on the remote host.

    c. It allows an insecure remote connection to be established to a remote host for the purposes of opening a session on the remote host.

    d. It allows a remote system to dial in to a server and uses the resources of that server as a gateway to the network.

4. What is the function of RAS?

    a. It allows an insecure remote connection to be established to a remote host for the purposes of opening a session on the remote host.

    b. It provides a mechanism for data downloaded from and information uploaded to a Web site to be secured against unauthorized viewing.

    c. It allows a secure remote connection to be established to a remote host for the purposes of opening a session on the remote host.

    d. It allows a remote system to dial in to a server and uses the resources of that server as a gateway to the network.

5. In a remote access scenario, what function does PPP serve?

    a. It is a secure technology that allows information to be securely downloaded from a Web site.

    b. It is a dial-up protocol used over serial links.

    c. It is a technology that allows a secure tunnel to be created through a public network.

    d. It provides a public key/private key exchange mechanism.

APPLY YOUR KNOWLEDGE

6. At what layer of the OSI model does IPSec operate?

   a. Physical

   b. Data-link

   c. Network

   d. Transport

7. Which of the following are PPP authentication methods? (Choose the two best answers.)

   a. SLAP

   b. CHAP

   c. MS-CHAP

   d. POP

8. Which of the following protocols is used in thin-client computing?

   a. ICA

   b. PPP

   c. PPTP

   d. RAS

9. SSH is a secure alternative to which of the following?

   a. Telnet

   b. DHCP

   c. PPTP

   d. Kerberos

10. Kerberos is an authentication system that can be used on what operating systems?

    a. Windows 2000

    b. Linux

    c. Unix

    d. All of the above

11. What encryption method does CHAP use when replying to an authentication request?

    a. Kerberos

    b. MDA

    c. MD5

    d. PPTP

12. How does the callback feature work in RAS?

    a. It allows the RAS server to call a preset number any time it receives a connection.

    b. It allows the RAS server to call a user-defined number any time it receives a connection.

    c. It allows the RAS server to call a preset or user-defined number any time it receives a connection.

    d. It allows the RAS server to generate a random number to call each time it receives a connection.

13. Which of the following URLs is using SSL?

    a. `http:ssl//www.comptia.org`

    b. `http://www.comptia.org`

    c. `httpssl://www.comptia.org`

    d. `https://www.comptia.org`

14. Which of the following is not an authentication protocol?

    a. IPSec

    b. CHAP

    c. PAP

    d. EAP

APPLY YOUR KNOWLEDGE

15. In a thin-client scenario, what information is propagated across the communications link between the client and the server?

    a. Any data retrieved by the client from Web sites

    b. Screen updates and keyboard and mouse input

    c. Any file that is opened by the client during the session

    d. Only the graphics files used to create the user's desktop, screen updates, and keyboard and mouse input

16. Which of the following is a reason to use L2TP rather than IPSec to create a VPN connection?

    a. You need to have a secure connection.

    b. You are a using a protocol other than TCP/IP.

    c. You are using Microsoft Windows systems.

    d. You are using public key/private key encryption.

17. You are on-site as a consultant. The client's many remote access users are experiencing connection problems. Basically, when users try to connect, the system is unable to service their authentication requests. What kind of server might you recommend to alleviate this problem?

    a. RADIUS server

    b. IPSec server

    c. Proxy server

    d. Kerberos server

18. Your company wants to create a secure link between two networks over the Internet. Which of the following protocols would you use to do this?

    a. PPP

    b. VPN

    c. PPTP

    d. SLIP

19. Which of the following protocols does PPTP use to establish connections?

    a. DHCP

    b. FTP

    c. SSH

    d. TCP

20. You are working for a client on a remote access connectivity solution. The client wants to use the RAS service for up to 10 clients at the lowest possible cost. Which of the following operating systems would you recommend to the client?

    a. Windows Me

    b. Novell NetWare 5.x

    c. Windows 2000 Professional

    d. Windows 2000 Server

Answers to Exam Questions

1. **c.** A VPN provides a secure communication path between devices over a public network such as the Internet. None of the other answers describes a VPN. For more information, see the section "Types of Remote Access," in this chapter.

APPLY YOUR KNOWLEDGE

2. **a.** SLIP transmits passwords and usernames in clear text and is therefore insecure. SLIP is usable across all platforms that support it, including Linux and Windows. Answer d is not valid. For more information, see the section "Remote Access Protocols and Services," in this chapter.

3. **a.** SSL provides a mechanism for securing data across a network. Answer b describes SSH, and Answer d describes RAS. Answer c is not valid. For more information, see the section "Security Protocols," in this chapter.

4. **d.** RAS allows a remote system to dial in to a network and use the resources of the network. All the other answers are not valid. For more information, see the section "Remote Access Protocols and Services" in this chapter.

5. **b.** PPP is a protocol that allows for dial-up connections over serial links. Answer a describes SSL, Answer c describes a VPN, and Answer d describes PKI. For more information, see the section "Remote Access Protocols and Services," in this chapter.

6. **c.** IPSec operates at the network layer of the OSI model. All the other answers are incorrect. For more information, see the section "Security Protocols," in this chapter.

7. **b, c.** Both CHAP and MS-CHAP are PPP authentication methods. The other answers are not valid authentication protocols. For more information, see the section "Remote Access Protocols and Services," in this chapter.

8. **a.** The ICA protocol is used in thin-client networking, where only screen, keyboard, and mouse inputs are sent across the line. PPP is a dial-up protocol used over serial links, PPTP is a technology used in VPNs, and RAS is a remote

access service. For more information, see the section "Remote Access Protocols and Services," in this chapter.

9. **a.** SSH is a secure alternative to Telnet. None of the other answers are valid. For more information, see the section "Security Protocols" in this chapter.

10. **d.** Kerberos is available for all the major operating systems. For more information, see the section "Security Protocols," in this chapter.

11. **c.** CHAP uses the MD5 encryption method. None of the other answers are correct. For more information, see the section "Remote Access Protocols and Services," in this chapter.

12. **c.** The callback feature in RAS allows it to call a preset or user-defined number when it receives a connection. None of the other answers are valid. For more information, see the section "Remote Access Protocols and Services," in this chapter.

13. **d.** You can identify when SSL is used by the s in the URL (in this case `https://www.comptia.org`). Answer b is a valid HTTP URL, but it is not secure. None of the other answers are valid URLs. For more information, see the section "Security Protocols," in this chapter.

14. **a.** IPSec is not an authentication protocol. All the other protocols listed are classed as authentication protocols. For more information, see the section "Security Protocols," in this chapter.

15. **b.** Only screen, keyboard, and mouse inputs are sent across the communications link in a thin-client scenario. This allows the processing to be handled by the server. None of the other answers are valid. For more information, see the section "Remote Access Protocols and Services," in this chapter.

APPLY YOUR KNOWLEDGE

16. **b.** You need to use L2TP instead of IPSec when you are using a protocol other than TCP/IP. IPSec can be used only with TCP/IP. None of the other answers are valid. For more information, see the section "Security Protocols," in this chapter.

17. **a.** By installing a RADIUS server, it is possible to move the workload associated with authentication to a dedicated server. A proxy server would not improve the dial-up connection's performance. There is no such thing as a Kerberos server or an IPSec server. For more information, see the section "Security Protocols," in this chapter.

18. **c.** To establish the VPN connection between the two networks, you should use PPTP. PPP is a protocol used on dial-up links. A VPN is a type of network, not a protocol. SLIP is a nonsecure dial-up protocol. For more information, see the section "Types of Remote Access," in this chapter.

19. **d.** PPTP uses TCP. None of the other answers are valid. For more information, see the section "Remote Access Protocols and Services," in this chapter.

20. **d.** Windows 2000 Server supports more than 10 remote clients. Windows Me is not capable of being a RAS server. Novell NetWare does not include RAS server capability because RAS is a Microsoft product. Windows 2000 Professional supports only a single dial-in RAS connection. For more information, see the section "Remote Access Protocols and Services," in this chapter.

Suggested Readings and Resources

1. Habraken, Joe. *Absolute Beginner's Guide to Networking*, third edition. Que Publishing, 2001.

2. Shinder, Debra Littlejohn. *Computer Networking Essentials*. Cisco Press, 2001.

3. Fortenberry, Thaddeus. *Windows 2000 Virtual Private Networking*. New Riders Publishing, 2000.

4. Yuan, Ruixi, W. Timothy Strayer. *Virtual Private Networks: Technologies and Solutions*. Addison-Wesley, 2001.

5. Computer networking tutorials and advice, compnetworking.about.com.

6. "TechEncyclopedia," www.techencyclopedia.com.

7. Information on L2TP from Cisco, www.cisco.com/warp/public/cc/pd/iosw/tech/l2pro_tc.htm.

8. Microsoft RAS information, www.microsoft.com/technet/treeview/default.asp?url=/technet/itsolutions/network/default.asp.

9. Thin client (ICA) information from Citrix, www.citrix.com.

10. Independent thin client information, www.mcc.ac.uk/Thin/gothin.htm.

11. Information on VPNs, including security protocols, www.vpnc.org.

This chapter covers the following CompTIA-specified objectives for the "Network Implementation" section of the Network+ exam:

Identify the basic capabilities (i.e., client support, interoperability, authentication, file and print services, application support, and security) of the following server operating systems:

- **Unix/Linux**
- **NetWare**
- **Windows**
- **Macintosh**

▶ Operating systems are the means by which functionality is provided on a network. Each of the common operating systems has its own features and characteristics, and a capable network administrator must be familiar with them.

Identify the basic capabilities of client workstations (i.e., client connectivity, local security mechanisms, and authentication).

▶ Knowing how workstation operating systems connect to the network and accommodate users is an important part of the network administrator's skill set.

CHAPTER 9

Network Operating Systems and Clients

Introduction   **319**

**Introduction to Network Operating
Systems**   **319**

Choosing a Network Operating System   320
Which Network Operating System
  Is Best?   321

Windows NT 4   **324**

Domains and Workgroups   325
Windows NT 4 System Requirements   327
Windows NT 4 File Systems   327
Windows NT 4 Monitoring and
  Performance Tools   328
    Performance Monitor   328
    Network Monitor   330
    Task Manager   330
    Event Viewer   330
Windows NT 4 User Management Basics   331
Verifying Network Settings in
  Windows NT 4   332
Windows NT 4 Authentication   333
Windows NT 4 File and Print Services   333
Windows NT 4 Application Support   334
Windows NT 4 Security   334

Windows 2000   **335**

Windows 2000 Active Directory and
  Domains   335
Windows 2000 System Requirements   336
Windows 2000 File Systems   337

Windows 2000 Monitoring and
  Performance Tools   337
    Event Viewer   338
    The Performance Console   338
    The System Information Console   340
    Task Manager   340
    The Recovery Console   340
Managing Windows 2000 Disk Drives   341
Windows 2000 User Management Basics   342
Windows 2000 Authentication   342
Windows 2000 File and Print Services   343
Windows 2000 Application Support   344
Windows 2000 Security   344

Novell NetWare   **344**

NetWare System Requirements   345
NetWare File Systems   345
NetWare Performance-Monitoring Tools   346
NetWare User Administration   347
NetWare Server Configuration   348
Viewing and Changing a NetWare
  Network Configuration   349
NetWare Authentication   350
NetWare File and Print Services   351
NetWare Application Support   351
NetWare Security   352

Linux   **353**

Linux System Requirements   355
Linux File Systems   355
Linux Monitoring and Performance Tools   356
    The Top Utility   356
    Process File System   357
    Graphical Utilities   357

OUTLINE

Managing Linux Disk Drives 358
Linux User Management Basics 358
Verifying Linux Network Settings 360
Linux Authentication 360
Linux File and Print Services 360
Linux Application Support 361
Linux Security 362

Operating System Interoperability **363**

Using Windows with NetWare 364
Using Windows and Linux Servers 364
Using NetWare and Linux Servers 365

Operating System Client Support **365**

Windows Server Client Support 365
NetWare Server Client Support 366
Linux Server Client Support 366

Client Operating Systems **367**

Windows 95, Windows 98, and
  Windows Me 367
    Application Support for Windows 95,
      Windows 98, and Windows Me 368
    Local Security Mechanisms for
      Windows 95, Windows 98, and
      Windows Me 368
    Authentication for Windows 95,
      Windows 98, and Windows Me 368

Windows NT Workstation, Windows 2000
Professional, and Windows XP
Professional 369
    Application Support for Windows NT
      Workstation, Windows 2000
      Professional, and Windows XP
      Professional 369
    Client Connectivity for Windows NT
      Workstation, Windows 2000
      Professional, and Windows XP
      Professional 370
    Local Security Mechanisms for
      Windows NT Workstation,
      Windows 2000 Professional, and
      Windows XP Professional 370
    Authentication for Windows NT
      Workstation, Windows 2000
      Professional, and Windows XP
      Professional 370
Linux 370
    Applications for Linux 371
    Client Connectivity for Linux 371
    Local Security Mechanisms for Linux 372
    Authentication for Linux 372
Macintosh 372
    Application Support for Macintosh 373
    Client Connectivity for Macintosh 373

Chapter Summary **374**

Apply Your Knowledge **375**

- ▶ Read the objectives at the beginning of the chapter.
- ▶ Study the information in the chapter, paying special attention to the tables, which summarize key information.
- ▶ Review the objectives again.
- ▶ Answer the exam questions at the end of the chapter and check your results.

- ▶ Use the ExamGear test on the CD-ROM that accompanies this book to answer additional exam questions concerning this material.
- ▶ Review the notes, tips, and exam tips in this chapter. Make sure you understand the information in the exam tips. If you don't understand the topic referenced in an exam tip, refer to the information in the chapter text and then read the exam tip again.

INTRODUCTION

Network operating systems are some of the most powerful and complex software available today. This chapter looks at a number of operating systems that are widely used in today's network environments. Each network operating system has unique strengths and weaknesses, and each has its share of the competitive network operating system market. As a network administrator, it is your responsibility to maintain and manage these operating systems and ensure that they provide the network services they were designed to provide. Even though the Network+ exam does not require that you be an expert in the operating systems discussed in this chapter, a basic knowledge is required. For those who find themselves working with operating systems, further study is almost certainly warranted.

A network requires both a network operating system and client operating systems. This chapter outlines the characteristics of the client operating systems that are most commonly used today.

The information described in this chapter is not intended to provide a complete tutorial on any of the operating systems discussed. Rather, this chapter provides an overview of each operating system, along with information on commands used for setting up, installing, and configuring each operating system.

> **EXAM TIP**
>
> **Operating Systems** The information included in this chapter is intended to provide the information necessary to answer any related question on the Network+ exam. Apart from studying the information provided, you should research and learn more about each of these operating systems for your own interest.

INTRODUCTION TO NETWORK OPERATING SYSTEMS

▶ Identify the basic capabilities (i.e., client support, interoperability, authentication, file and print services, application support, and security) of the following server operating systems:

- Unix/Linux
- NetWare
- Windows
- Macintosh

Early network operating systems provided very few network services, such as file and printer sharing. Today's network operating systems offer a far broader range of network services; some of these services are used in almost every network environment and others are used in only a few.

Despite the complexity of operating systems, the basic function and purpose of a network operating system is straightforward: to provide services to the network. Network operating systems provide several services for the client systems on the network. The following are some of the most common of these services:

◆ Authentication

◆ File and print services

◆ Web server services

◆ Firewall and proxy services

◆ Dynamic Host Configuration Protocol (DHCP) and Domain Name System (DNS) services

These are just a few of a large number of services that a network operating system can provide. When you take the time to list all the different aspects of network operating systems, you gain an appreciation for their complexity and the many functions they are designed to perform.

Choosing a Network Operating System

When it comes to choosing a network operating system, you have a few choices. A network administrator needs to carefully choose a network operating system according to the needs of the organization. The following network operating systems are used in today's network environments:

◆ **Windows NT/2000/XP/.Net**—Windows is the most popular network operating system in use today. With the introduction of Windows XP/.Net, which is both a server platform and a desktop solution, Windows will continue its push to become the network operating system of choice in organizations of all sizes. Many people like the Windows-based network operating systems because of their familiar and easy-to-navigate graphical interfaces, even though these same graphical utilities and menus place increased demands on a server's hardware resources.

◆ **Novell NetWare**—Novell NetWare has long been one of the most widely used network operating systems. In the past, NetWare was viewed primarily as a file and print platform, but in reality, it can do much more. NetWare can be implemented in small networks, but it truly shines in a large corporate environment. Novell has lost a great deal of ground to the Windows and Linux platforms, although it still has a solid base of users.

◆ **Unix and Linux**—Some people might think that Linux is the new kid on the block, but in fact, Linux has been around for quite some time, and the operating system it is based on, Unix, has been around for decades. Linux is a free, open-source operating system and has found considerable popularity as a server operating system. In addition, although Unix is not free, it has been the network operating system of choice for many large organizations. Be prepared, however; although they are powerful, these network operating systems are not as pretty and graphically intensive as what you might be used to. Working with them requires some command-line input and a better understanding of the underlying technologies than you need when you use some of the other network operating systems.

◆ **Macintosh**—Although not nearly as prevalent as the other network operating systems discussed in this list, Macintosh systems can be used in a server role.

Which Network Operating System Is Best?

The debate over which is the *best* network operating system is an ongoing one, and one that will not be resolved in the pages of this book. All network operating systems have good and bad points, and each provides a solid choice for most modern network environments. Over time, functionality has been added to each of the operating systems, and today, in terms of functionality, there is little difference between these offerings. Similarity in service offerings aside, several points will influence an organization's choice of network operating system. The following are some of the factors you should consider when choosing a network operating system:

◆ **Hardware compatibility**—Maintaining a network involves maintaining the hardware on the server. If you intend to use existing hardware in a server, you should verify that the network operating system supports that hardware. Some network operating systems support a wider range of hardware than others, although the best hardware from the mainstream manufacturers is supported by all the major network operating systems. Network operating system manufacturers have a vested interest in supporting the broadest range of hardware possible, and unless you are using some weird and wonderful hardware device, you should not encounter any problems. If you have a selection of unusual hardware, you should ensure that your chosen operating system will support it. Manufacturers publish lists of hardware devices that have been verified as compatible, so be sure to check these lists if you intend to use unusual hardware. These *hardware compatibility lists* are available on the network operating system vendors' Web sites.

◆ **Technical capabilities**—Small organizations often have server administrators who double as teachers, secretaries, or data entry clerks. In environments where a dedicated server administrator is nonexistent and available technical skills are few, choosing the most user-friendly network operating system might be an important consideration. It might be easier for the administrator/data entry clerk to add a new user to a Windows 2000 server from a graphical screen than to enter a cryptic command at a command prompt. The inability of existing personnel to support a product would almost certainly cause more problems than it would cure. There are of course alternatives: Training can bridge the knowledge gap where necessary.

◆ **Application support**—Most software manufacturers go to great lengths to ensure that the software they are designing is available to all network operating system platforms. Sometimes, however, a manufacturer cannot or does not ensure that its software will work on every network operating system, so it is important that you check. For example, if your company is using an application database that is not supported by Linux, this would make the installation of a Linux server out of the question.

◆ **Budget**—Many choices in IT boil down to the money that is available, and choosing a network operating system is often one such choice. If a Linux server provides all the functionality and services your organization needs and does it for free, why pay for Windows? For those used to paying the price for a desktop operating system, the cost of a network operating system can be quite surprising because it is considerably higher.

◆ **Technical support**—An important factor in choosing a network operating system is technical support. Each of network operating system manufacturer offers support for its product(s); however, the cost and the usefulness of this support might not be in line with what you need. One thing is for sure: Support and network management go hand in hand. Of the network operating systems we have discussed, Novell, Microsoft, and Unix have very defined support structures. Linux has a less-well-defined support structure, although some Linux distributors offer very comprehensive technical support programs. Other Linux distributors take a more hands-off approach, leaving you to rely on Internet newsgroups and your own savvy.

Now that we have looked at some of the considerations when selecting a network operating system, we'll take a more detailed look at common NOSs and some of the utilities and procedures associated with them. We will also look at each of the CompTIA-prescribed criteria related to network operating systems:

◆ **Authentication**—Authentication is a fundamental security-related consideration for networks. Authentication is essentially the process of verifying the identity of the person trying to access a resource on the system. The most common use of authentication is the logon process, in which a user's identity is validated. A detailed discussion of authentication methods used by the various network operating systems is not required for the Network+ exam; however, a basic knowledge of how each of the network operating systems handles authentication is an asset in real-world network administration.

◆ **File and print services**—One of the fundamental and most commonly used network services is file and print services. Each of the network operating systems is fully capable of providing these services to network users, but each provides these services in its own way and with a unique set of features.

NOTE

Third-Party Vendors The term *third-party* is used to refer to an entity besides the original manufacturer or your own organization that creates a product. In this context, a third-party application is one that is not created by the network operating system manufacturer or you.

NOTE

Resource Security Models   Two ways are commonly used to secure files that are shared over a network: user-level security and share-level security. Networks that use user-level security apply rights to user accounts for specific resources such as files, directories, or printers. Networks that use share-level security require that passwords be assigned to individual files or network resources; users who need access to a specific printer, for instance, would require a password to access it.

◆ **Application support**—What applications are supported by a network operating system plays a major part in how the network operating system is used and in its popularity.

◆ **Security**—A discussion of network operating system security is difficult to capture in a single chapter. In fact, you will find that there are volumes of books dedicated to discussions on how to establish security and how to work around it. This chapter provides only a brief introduction to the security measures taken in network operating systems. Security is a major consideration on networks, and the skills and strategies needed to properly secure a network against inside and outside threats is one of the most valuable skills for network administrators to have.

WINDOWS NT 4

Windows NT 4 is a network operating system that was introduced after the Windows NT 3.51 operating system. Because Windows NT 3.51 is not found in many organizations today and is not on the Network+ exam, this chapter does not discuss it. You will, however, know if you are working on a Windows NT 3.51 server because the graphics might look unfamiliar. Windows NT 3.51 uses the graphical interface of Windows 3.x, whereas Windows NT 4 and later versions have the look of the Windows 95/98/Me type of desktop.

Two types of Windows NT 4 are available: Windows NT Workstation and Windows NT Server. The former is designed for desktop use, and the latter is for servers. Windows NT Workstation is a scaled-down version of Windows NT Server. It is based on the same structure as Windows NT Server, and the two versions share a similar look and similar features. Unlike Windows 95 client systems, which accommodate games and older DOS-based programs, Windows NT Workstation was built for reliability and security.

Although Windows NT 4 has been superseded by Windows 2000 and Windows XP, many servers are still operating with Windows NT 4 today. Microsoft is providing less and less support for Windows NT now because it hopes that organizations will make the switch to the new generation of Windows products. Still, Windows

NT continues to function adequately for many organizations, making the likelihood that you will encounter Windows NT very great.

Domains and Workgroups

One of the key considerations for anyone installing or working with Windows NT 4 is whether to use a workgroup or domain model. Domains and workgroups are logical groups of computers that are created for the purposes of administration and resource access. A Windows NT 4 system can be configured as either a member of a workgroup or a member of a domain. Workgroups are used in small networks of usually no more than 10 computers. In a workgroup scenario, a dedicated, or centralized, network server is nonexistent, and each system in the workgroup is able to offer services to and use services from other systems in the workgroup. Security in a workgroup model is handled by each system; that is, each computer has its own list of users who can access the system. There is no centralized database of user accounts, which results in a situation that can lead to a variety of administrative headaches. For example, changing user passwords and making sure that they are changed on each system in the workgroup can be an administrative nightmare. Also, when a new user joins the company, an account must be created on every system to which the user needs access.

Domains are very different from workgroups. In a Windows environment, a *domain model* is a network model that uses a centralized approach to resource management, meaning that computers within the domain can access data and network services from a central location. A Windows NT server that is configured in the domain model can be set up to perform three different roles on the network:

◆ **Primary domain controller (PDC)**—The PDC is the main server and is responsible for the majority of server-related tasks on the network, including authentication and managing the network user account information. A Windows NT domain can have only a single PDC, and every effort should be made to ensure that it is running at all times. Without a PDC, certain administrative tasks, such as adding users, cannot be completed. If the PDC is the only Windows NT server system on the network, its role is even more important because without it, users are unable to log on.

◆ **Backup domain controller (BDC)**—As a company grows, its reliance on a single server can create a problem because a single server represents a single point of failure, and in many cases, a single server cannot handle the workload for an entire network. That is where a BDC comes in. The BDC holds a second copy of the information that is stored on the PDC, including the database of user accounts and other important network information. Having duplicate information provides a level of fault tolerance for the network and a second server to help with the network load. If the PDC goes offline for any reason, the BDC holds the information necessary to authenticate users and keeps the network functioning. Depending on the size of the network, there might be several BDCs on a single network. If the PDC on a network fails, a BDC can be promoted to a PDC through a simple process. After the problem with the PDC has been corrected and the PDC has been brought back online, the BDC's role can be reversed again. Whereas a domain can have only a single PDC, many BDCs can be used.

◆ **Member server**—The member server does not take part in domain authentication and does not hold a copy of the user account database. Member servers provide file, print, and application services.

Figure 9.1 shows a typical Windows NT network layout, which includes a PDC, a BDC, a member server, and client computers.

FIGURE 9.1
A Windows NT network with a PDC, a BDC, a member server, and clients.

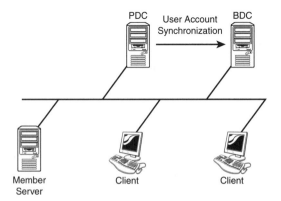

Windows NT 4 System Requirements

Windows NT has perhaps the lowest hardware requirements of all the network operating systems discussed in this chapter except for Linux. The hardware requirements for operating systems are listed on the respective manufacturers' Web sites. Many of these hardware requirements represent the bare minimum hardware requirements and are only enough to get the network operating system up and running. When additional applications are added and network services are needed, the minimum requirements will not meet the demands of the network. Table 9.1 shows the vendor-suggested hardware requirements for Windows NT 4.

TABLE 9.1

MINIMUM SERVER REQUIREMENTS FOR WINDOWS NT 4

Hardware	Minimum Requirement
Processor	486/33 CPU
RAM	16MB
Hard disk space	125MB

Windows NT 4 File Systems

Windows NT can use two different file systems: file allocation table (FAT) and New Technology File System (NTFS). FAT is a file system that is used with Windows 95 and 98, and although it can be used on a Windows NT system, it is not recommended because it does not provide any security. In contrast, NTFS provides file-level security, which is generally an important issue for all Windows server platforms. In addition to the security benefits, NTFS has performance advantages over FAT32 on large disk partitions and offers compression capabilities.

NOTE **Windows NT and FAT32**   Although later Windows server platforms such as Windows 2000 now support the FAT32 file systems, FAT32 was not supported by Windows NT 4.

When using NTFS partitions, it is important to know that FAT can be converted to NTFS, but after a partition has been set as NTFS, it cannot be changed back to FAT. On a local system, NTFS partitions

NOTE

Managing NTFS Partitions
Managing NTFS partitions, including NTFS security features, is an important part of a network administrator's role when working with Windows network operating systems.

cannot be read locally by non–NTFS-capable Windows desktop operating systems such as Windows 95/98 and Me. This can cause problems when a system is configured as a dual-boot system (that is, when a system is loaded with more than one operating system). In such a configuration, any area of the disk that is formatted with NTFS would be unavailable when the system is booted with a non-NTFS-capable operating system.

Windows NT 4 Monitoring and Performance Tools

One of the features that has contributed to the success of Windows server software is the easy-to-navigate graphical administration utilities and performance-monitoring tools. A network administrator who is managing a Windows NT server can expect to become very familiar with these utilities. Four of the most popular utilities are Performance Monitor, Network Monitor, Task Manager, and Event Viewer. Together, these tools can provide a comprehensive view of a Windows NT system. If you know what you are looking for, these tools can provide you with information on every aspect of a Windows NT system and network performance. When you are establishing system performance baselines, these are the tools to use.

NOTE

Baselines Baselining is the process of taking measurements of system performance for the purposes of future comparison. Taking baselines under normal, medium, and high network usage conditions allows you to determine whether the system is behaving abnormally at a later date.

Performance Monitor

Performance Monitor is a tool that is used to view the current performance statistics of a Windows NT system. Using Performance Monitor, you can analyze the performance of a single piece of hardware, such as memory, as well as view the impact a particular application is having on the system in general. Performance Monitor is also used to determine whether a system is having any problems or bottlenecks due to insufficient or malfunctioning hardware. Figure 9.2 shows a sample Performance Monitor screen for Windows NT 4.

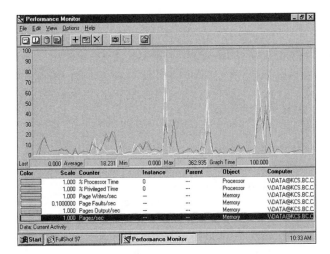

FIGURE 9.2
A Windows NT 4 Performance Monitor screen.

Performance monitoring is part of proactive administration. Using Performance Monitor allows an administrator to find and locate a problem before it has a noticeable impact on the network. Of the many different performance areas that can be viewed with Performance Monitor, some of the most common are the following:

◆ **Memory Available Bytes**—This counter identifies the amount of physical memory that is free. If this counter is low, there might be a RAM shortage.

◆ **Memory Pages/Sec**—This counter shows the number of pages requested from virtual memory. For this counter, a number above 10 indicates a potential problem and means that more memory might be required.

◆ **% Processor Time**—This counter shows the amount of processor usage. If this counter indicates that the processor usage is consistently at 100%, the processor might not be able to handle the load. Keep in mind, however, that a processor might surge to a high count and then drop again. To be a true indicator of a processor bottleneck, the processor count would have to remain high for an extended period of time.

◆ **% Disk Time**—If this counter is consistently over 65% to 70%, the server probably has a performance problem. This counter indicates the number of hard disk read and write requests. Installing more memory might solve a problem indicated by this counter.

N O T E **Hard Disk Counters**   For the hard disk counters to appear in Windows NT 4.0 Performance Monitor, you need to run the command `diskperf.exe -y` from the command prompt.

◆ **Disk Queue Length**—If the disk queue length is consistently over 2, there is definitely disk performance degradation, and you will have to upgrade to improve performance.

Network Monitor

One of the tasks that network administrators are most frequently responsible for is monitoring what the network is doing. In Windows NT 4, Network Monitor is used to capture and analyze a range of network-related statistics, and it is one of the key utilities to use for network troubleshooting and capacity planning. Network Monitor can help you identify whether and where there are bottlenecks in a network. In Windows NT 4, the standard Network Monitor tool allows you to view the network information only for the system on which it is running. An enhanced version that is available separately allows you to view information from other nodes on the network as well.

Task Manager

As in other Windows desktop operating systems, pressing Ctrl+Alt+Del in Windows NT displays a Windows dialog box. However, the menu screen that appears in Windows NT is unique: It displays a Windows Security dialog box. From this dialog box, you have the option of starting the Windows Task Manager utility. Task Manager has three tabs, each showing different information: The Applications tab shows which applications are running, the Processes tab shows which processes are running and their approximate memory and CPU usage, and the Performance tab shows overall system resource usage. Figure 9.3 shows the Performance tab in Task Manager.

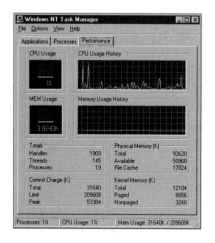

FIGURE 9.3
The Performance tab in Task Manager.

Event Viewer

Events in all server systems are logged somewhere. In Windows NT 4, many of the system logs are kept in the Event Viewer. The Event Viewer can record an error in the system or in a specific application. The information is recorded in three log files:

◆ **Security log**—This log contains such information as successful and unsuccessful logon attempts and failed resource access.

Unless the auditing feature is turned on, the security log is
likely to show little or no information.

◆ **Application log**—This log contains information logged by
applications, such as a problem with a database application or
a problem with a DHCP server application. Vendors of third-
party applications can use the Application log as a destination
for error messages generated by their applications.

◆ **System log**—This log records information about components
or drivers in the server. This is the place to look when you're
troubleshooting a problem with a hardware device on your
system or a problem with network connectivity. For example,
messages related to the client element of DHCP appear in
this log.

Windows NT 4 User Management Basics

The management of user accounts in Windows NT 4, including
adding and removing accounts, is done by using a utility called User
Manager for Domains. This utility can be used from either a PDC
or a BDC, although the accounts you make are created on the PDC,
and the newly created account is replicated to the BDC for fault-
tolerant purposes. After a user account is created on the PDC, the
user can use that account to access the network. Figure 9.4 shows
the User Manager for Domains window.

EXAM TIP

Locking the Server   The Windows
Security dialog box has an option
that allows you to lock the server,
thus disabling the screen and preventing unauthorized user access.
It is a good idea to lock the server
whenever a Windows NT 4 server is
left unattended. To access the
Security dialog box, press
Ctrl+Alt+Del.

NOTE

**User Accounts and Account
Management**   When supporting
clients using any network operating
system, an understanding of user
accounts and account management
is required. Each of the network operating systems handles account
management a little differently, but the
underlying principles are the same
throughout all platforms. A detailed
knowledge of account management for
networks is not required for the
Network+ exam, but you need to know
the fundamentals.

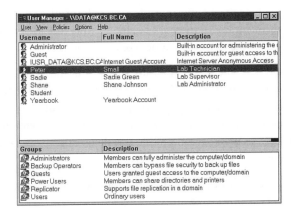

FIGURE 9.4
The Windows NT 4 User Manager for Domains
window.

> **WARNING**
>
> **Using the Administrator Account**
> To perform your role as a network administrator in a Windows environment, it is necessary to have access to an Administrator account. For security reasons, network users should never be given access to the Administrator account. Even if they have access to the Administrator account, server administrators should log on as regular users most of the time, using the Administrator account only when making administrative changes.

During the creation of accounts, security measures are applied to each account, such as password regulations, permitted logon times, and other logon restrictions. Each account can also be afforded permissions according to the groups to which it belongs. In Windows NT, a special account called Administrator is created, and when a user is logged on using this account, he or she has rights to perform administrative actions on the entire system. In addition, there is a group called Administrators, the members of which are assigned the same rights as the Administrator account. Because of its omnipotence, the Administrator account should be used only when absolutely necessary.

Verifying Network Settings in Windows NT 4

The management of network-related tasks on a Windows NT server is done from the Network Settings dialog box. Most network-related tasks can be performed from this dialog box, including installing and configuring protocols, managing network interface cards (NICs), and installing additional services. You can access the Network Settings dialog box by right-clicking on the Network Neighborhood Desktop icon and selecting Properties or by double-clicking the Network applet in the Control Panel.

To test a network's connectivity, you can use several utilities. The following are some of the utilities used on Windows NT 4 server platforms:

◆ `ping`—Perhaps the mostly widely used Transmission Control Protocol/Internet Protocol (TCP/IP) utility, the `ping` utility tests connectivity between networked devices.

◆ `ipconfig`—The `ipconfig` utility displays all the TCP/IP configurations for a server. The most common command syntax used with this utility is `ipconfig /all`, which displays information on all NICs in the system, including the gateway and the subnet mask. `ipconfig` can also be used to release and renew addresses obtained via DHCP.

◆ `tracert`—This utility verifies the route to a remote system. `tracert` is often used after a failed `ping` request, to see where packets were dropped.

The utilities used to troubleshoot connectivity in a TCP/IP network are covered in greater detail in Chapter 13, "Troubleshooting Connectivity."

Windows NT 4 Authentication

Windows NT is a secure operating system in that users have to provide a user ID and password in order to gain access to the system. When a user logs on, the information provided is compared with a database of user information that is maintained on the server. If the user ID and password are valid, restrictions such as logon times and workstation restrictions are compared. If there are no restrictions in force, a token is generated by the system and passed back to the authentication system, which then allows the user access.

The token created for the user contains information such as the user's ID (which is expressed as a number called a *security identifier* [SID] rather than the user's name) and any group memberships that the user holds. Each time a user attempts to access a protected resource, the token is compared against the access control list for that resource. If you add a user to a group after the user has logged on, the user must log off and log back on again in order for the change to take effect.

Windows NT 4 File and Print Services

As with other operating systems, file and print services are at the core of the services offered by Windows NT 4. Any folder on any drive on the server can be made available to clients through a process called *sharing*. Sharing involves nominating a certain folder to be available to clients and then setting up the parameters that govern how it is shared. These parameters can include a share name (which can be different from the folder name), the number of users that are able to connect to the share, and the security of the folder.

The security capabilities of the folder depend on which file system the disk that holds the folder is using. Folders on a FAT partition can be secured at the share point, and the rights assigned at that point are in effect from that point in the directory structure down. For folders on NTFS partitions, it is possible to combine the share-level permissions with the NTFS permissions, which can then be assigned to each file or directory.

Print services are provided in much the same way. Any printer that is defined on the server system can be shared with users.

Windows NT 4 Application Support

Windows NT 4 has been around for a number of years, and it is largely responsible for putting a dent in the vast market share that other operating systems, such as Novell NetWare, have enjoyed. Its proliferation has led to the development of a huge number of third-party applications, covering every need from the most basic to the most complex. If you have a Windows NT 4 server and are looking for an application, you are likely to have a great deal of choice.

Nearly every application that an organization could want is provided with Windows NT 4,including DHCP and DNS server programs, a Web server application, a backup utility, performance-monitoring and system-management utilities, and even (perhaps inappropriately for a server system) a selection of games. Windows NT 4 also includes various products for integration with other operating systems, so it is one of the most comprehensive single-package network operating system offerings available.

Windows NT 4 Security

The Windows server platforms, like the other network operating systems, provide a range of security options for securing the resources on a network. The following are some of the security areas commonly used on Windows-based servers:

◆ **Object-based security**—Object-based security refers to the ability to establish access control over specific devices and resources on the server. To be able to access a resource such as a printer, users must have permissions to access it. Permissions to devices, resources, or files on the network can be granted to an individual user, or they can be assigned to entire groups of users.

◆ **User authentication**—To access a Windows-based network and the resources on the network, a user needs a logon username and password. Windows uses a feature known as *single sign-on*, which allows a user to log on to the network domain once and authenticate to any computer in the domain.

◆ **File and directory security**—Windows server systems can use NTFS. NTFS has many advantages over the FAT file system found in Windows desktop systems. NTFS allows file-level security, meaning that individual files, such as spreadsheets or documents, can require access permissions.

Although Windows NT 4 was a major product in the IT landscape for a number of years, Microsoft has built on the success of Windows NT by introducing a new and updated version, Windows 2000, which is discussed in the following section.

> **EXAM TIP**
>
> **Watch the Cap Locks**   To log on to a Windows NT 4 system, a valid username and password are required. The password is case sensitive, but the username is not.

WINDOWS 2000

Windows 2000 was the follow-up to the popular Windows NT 4 network operating system, and it quickly established itself as a reliable and robust operating system. Windows 2000 built on the success of its predecessor and offered many improvements and advancements. In many ways, Windows 2000 functions in the same way as Windows NT 4. In others, it functions very differently.

The biggest difference between the two operating systems is the addition of Active Directory—a directory services system that provides improved user account management capabilities—in Windows 2000. Many tasks have been streamlined in Windows 2000, and additional wizards are available to assist with administrative tasks.

Three different versions of Windows 2000 are available for server platforms: Windows 2000 Server, Advanced Server, and Datacenter Server. There are some subtle and not-so-subtle differences between these respective offerings, such as processor support and cost. Windows 2000 is also available as a workstation operating system: Windows 2000 Professional. As Windows NT Workstation is to Windows NT Server, Windows 2000 Professional has the majority of features, capabilities, and strengths of Windows 2000 Server products but omits the server-type network services and capabilities.

Windows 2000 Active Directory and Domains

Many administrators have found user management in Windows NT awkward, especially in large organizations. In the past, NetWare had the preferred method of account management for large numbers of user accounts. For this reason, Microsoft introduced its new approach to user and account management in Windows 2000 platforms—Active Directory. Active Directory is a cornerstone concept for Windows 2000 because it significantly affects the layout and makeup of a Windows 2000–based network.

Active Directory is a directory services system that allows network objects such as users and groups to be placed into logical areas of a database. This database can then be distributed among various servers, all of which participate in the Active Directory structure. Because all the network object information is placed in a single database, albeit a distributed database, it can be used by any network application or subsystem, eliminating the need for duplicate information.

Active Directory put an end to the old Windows NT PDC and BDC network layout. Instead, servers on a Windows 2000 network can either be domain controllers or member servers. Domain controllers are servers that have Active Directory installed and configured on them. Domain controllers store user account information and provide network authentication. Unlike a Windows NT domain, which can have only a single PDC, a Windows 2000 domain can have several domain controllers, with each one having a read/write copy of the Active Directory database. For fault-tolerant reasons, this is a good strategy to employ.

Member servers are not involved in the authentication of network users and do not take part in the Active Directory replication process. Member servers are commonly employed as file and print servers, or with additional software, as database servers, firewalls, or servers for other important network services.

Windows 2000 System Requirements

One of the initial concerns for the Windows 2000 platform has to do with the high level of hardware required to support the network operating system. Table 9.2 lists the minimum recommended hardware requirements for Windows 2000 Server, but these are just barely enough to install Windows 2000. To actually take advantage of Windows 2000 features, the hardware requirements should be significantly higher.

EXAM TIP

Active Directory Active Directory is a complex subject, and much of the information in this section is not needed for the Network+ exam. For further information on Active Directory, refer to Microsoft's Web site (www.microsoft.com).

TABLE 9.2

MINIMUM SERVER REQUIREMENTS FOR WINDOWS 2000 SERVER

Hardware	*Minimum Requirement*
Processor	Pentium at 133MHz
RAM	128MB
Hard disk space	1GB (2GB during installation)

> **NOTE**
>
> **Windows OS Requirements** The figures identified in Table 9.2 show the requirements for Windows 2000 Server. The hardware requirements for other Windows server products such as Windows 2000 Advanced Server and Windows Datacenter are higher.

Windows 2000 File Systems

Another difference between Windows NT and Windows 2000 has to do with the file systems they support. Windows 2000 supports the FAT, FAT32, and NTFS file systems, whereas Windows NT 4 offers only FAT and NTFS.

In addition to its support for FAT32, Windows 2000 introduces a newer version of NTFS, which provides more options and capabilities, including support for Active Directory and increased security options. Remember that Active Directory and other security-related features are available only on NTFS partitions. To convert from FAT or FAT32 to NTFS in Windows 2000, you use the same command, convert.exe, at a command prompt as you would in Windows NT 4. This command has the same considerations in both operating systems in that it cannot be converted back again.

> **NOTE**
>
> **FAT32** Windows client systems often use the FAT32 file system, which supports the larger hard disks that are now available.

> **EXAM TIP**
>
> **NTFS** It is recommended that, whenever possible, you format a drive as NTFS when you are creating partitions rather than convert from FAT to NTFS at a later date. Drives originally formatted with NTFS have less fragmentation and better performance than those converted from FAT.

Windows 2000 Monitoring and Performance Tools

Like Windows NT, Windows 2000 offers a variety of graphical monitoring and performance utilities. Many of the utilities are the same as those found in Windows NT, and others are enhanced versions of some of the utilities. Despite a few differences, network administrators who are used to the way these utilities function in Windows NT will be able to make the switch and use the Windows 2000 utilities.

Access to the performance and monitoring tools in Windows 2000 is different than that in previous Windows server platforms. Windows 2000 uses the Microsoft Management Console (MMC) to centralize the location of Windows 2000 performance and administrative tools. These management tools, referred to as *snap-ins*, are added to the MMC to manage the hardware, software, and networking components of the server. Some of the most common tools used as snap-ins are Event Viewer, Device Manager, Computer Management, Performance Logs and Alerts, and System Information and Services.

Event Viewer

Like Windows NT, Windows 2000 includes the familiar Event Viewer. Windows 2000 adds some new logs to the Event Viewer, including those for recording DNS events and file replication events. For the most part, you will want to keep a close eye on the System log and perhaps the Security log. The System log tracks events related to server hardware components. Figure 9.5 shows the Windows 2000 Event Viewer.

> N O T E   **Log Files**   Application logs and System logs can be viewed by any user. Security logs can be viewed only by users who are using accounts with administrative privileges.

FIGURE 9.5
The Windows 2000 Event Viewer.

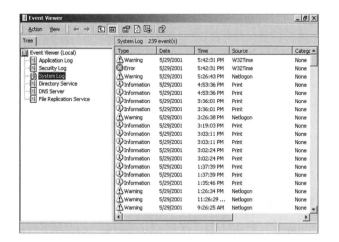

The Performance Console

The Performance console, shown in Figure 9.6, provides two snap-ins: System Monitor and Performance Logs and Alerts. These tools are responsible for providing very different but equally critical system performance–related information:

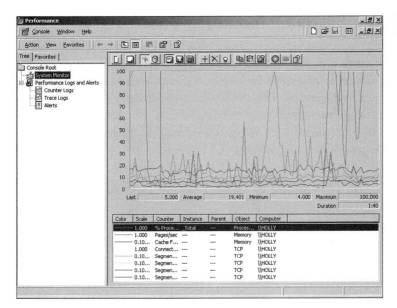

FIGURE 9.6
The Windows 2000 Performance console.

◆ **System Monitor**—System Monitor allows you to monitor the components within the server and determine whether they are causing bottlenecks. The counters that can be viewed in System Monitor are similar to those for Windows NT, but Windows 2000 adds a few more counters to the mix. System Monitor enables you to obtain real-time performance statistics for the server.

◆ **Performance Logs and Alerts**—This monitoring tool allows you to capture performance-related statistics from the local computer or even a remote computer. The information gathered can then be viewed with System Monitor. Perhaps the key feature in Performance Logs and Alerts is the ability to set alerts. By right-clicking on the Alerts icon and choosing New Alert Settings, you can set thresholds; when these thresholds are exceeded, an alert message can be sent. For instance, if a hard disk is reaching its capacity, an alert message can be sent to the administrator, warning him or her of the situation before it becomes a problem on the network.

The System Information Console

The System Information console is used to view and manage hardware on a Windows 2000 server. The System Information console provides a comprehensive look at the hardware and configurations used in the system. This utility allows you to determine whether there are any resource conflicts on the system. It is a valuable tool for troubleshooting hardware-related problems. Figure 9.7 shows the System Information console.

FIGURE 9.7
The System Information console.

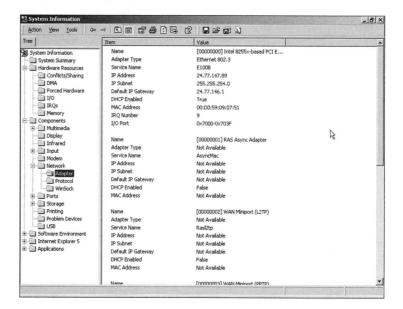

Task Manager

For those who enjoyed using Task Manager in Windows NT, there is good news. Task Manager is included in Windows 2000, and it provides similar features to the Windows NT version. It, too, can be used to view resources in use, end processes, and lock the console for security purposes.

The Recovery Console

New to Windows 2000 is the Recovery console. Unlike many other utilities, it is a command-line utility. The Recovery console is used primarily to recover from failed servers.

If a server refuses to boot, you can start the Recovery console from the Windows 2000 setup disks, from the Windows 2000 Server CD, or from the system itself, if the utility is installed. (If the Recovery console is installed, it appears as a boot option on the startup menu screen.) Because this utility consumes only 7MB of space, it's worthwhile to have it installed.

Managing Windows 2000 Disk Drives

Many network administrators do not like the look and design of the Windows NT Disk Administrator tool, so it was replaced in Windows 2000 by the Disk Management utility, which can be found in the Computer Management console. The look of the Disk Management utility might be different from the look of the Disk Administrator, but the basic functioning is the same. Disk Management is used to create and delete volumes, format disks, and create fault-tolerant configurations.

A new concept in Windows 2000 disk administration is *dynamic disks*, which allow a range of capabilities, including setting up and configuring Redundant Arrays of Inexpensive Disks (RAID). Another new addition to Disk Management is the Network Disk Management tool, which allows an administrator to manage the disks on other Windows 2000 systems on the network. Figure 9.8 shows the Disk Management pane in the Computer Management console.

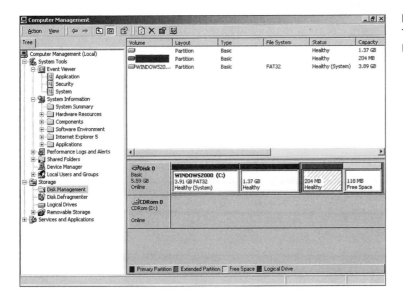

FIGURE 9.8

The Disk Management pane in the Computer Management console.

Windows 2000 User Management Basics

Local User Administration If a server is installed without Active Directory, local user administration is performed through the Computer Management applet, which is found in the Administrative Tools applet of the Control Panel.

Windows NT 4 administrators who are looking for the User Manager for Domains tool to manage user accounts in Active Directory are out of luck. Although User Manager for Domains is still available for managing Windows NT 4 domains, it has been replaced in Windows 2000. Account management in Windows 2000 is accomplished in the Active Directory Users and Computers MMC snap-in, which is accessed through the Administrative Tools menu.

Although the look of the Active Directory Users and Computers screen is somewhat different from that of User Manager for Domains, the basic functions of creating, adding, and deleting user accounts remain the same as in Windows NT. There are a few more bells and whistles and some additional template groups in Windows 2000, but if you are comfortable in Windows NT, it won't take you long to understand basic procedures in Active Directory Users and Computers.

As with Windows NT, in Windows 2000, the Administrator account is king. Care must be taken when using this account, and it should not be given to anyone except people who need to perform administrative tasks on the server.

Windows 2000 Authentication

The Windows authentication process allows users logging on to the network to access all network resources to which they have permissions. This means it is necessary to log on only once to access all the resources on the network. In Windows 2000, two processes are required for a successful logon:

◆ **Interactive logon**—This logon is used to confirm the identity of the person logging on to the domain or local system.

◆ **Network authentication**—This logon is used to verify the user's identification for access to network resources.

A few industry-supported types of authentication are used in Windows 2000. The type of authentication used depends on what is being accessed. Table 9.3 shows the various types of authentication used by Windows 2000.

TABLE 9.3	

WINDOWS 2000 AUTHENTICATION METHODS

Authentication Method	*Description*
Kerberos version 5	Kerberos is an authentication mode that is used for interactive logon and the default method of network authentication for services.
NT LAN Manager (NTLM)	NTLM is used for authentication in a mixed-mode network configuration. *Mixed-mode network* is a Microsoft term that describes a network that uses a combination of Windows NT and Windows 2000 systems. If a network exclusively uses one or the other, NTLM authentication is not required. An example of NTLM authentication is a Windows NT workstation authenticating to a Windows 2000 Server system.
Secure Sockets Layer/Transport Layer Security (SSL/TLS)	SSL/TLS is an authentication method that is used when a user is attempting to access a secure Web server.

Windows 2000 File and Print Services

Like Windows NT, Windows 2000 provides file and print services. Similarly to Windows NT, Windows 2000 uses shares to make areas of the disk available to clients. And as in Windows NT, in Windows 2000 these shares can be secured by file permissions if they are resident on NTFS partitions. In addition to these features, which are common in Windows NT, Windows 2000 also includes some new features, such as the following:

- ◆ **Disk quotas**—The amount of disk space available to a user can be restricted and managed through disk quotas. This is a useful element of control over disk usage.

- ◆ **Encrypting File System (EFS)**—EFS allows files to be encrypted while on the disk, preventing unauthorized access.

- ◆ **Distributed File System (DFS)**—DFS allows multiple directories on distributed servers to be represented through a single share point, simplifying access for users and administration.

All these features combine to make Windows 2000 a very solid choice as a file and print server.

Windows 2000 Application Support

Of all the network operating systems discussed in this chapter, Windows 2000 has perhaps the best overall level of support by third-party applications. Why is Windows so well supported? If you were a software developer, wouldn't you rather develop a program for the most popular operating system than for one of the others? The answer is probably yes, and this is perhaps the largest factor that influences application development for Windows. Another lesser factor is that the programming tools for Windows are easy-to-use, graphical tools created by Microsoft. Therefore, Windows is an easy platform for which to develop applications.

In addition to having superb third-party application support, Windows 2000 Server comes with a complete set of tools and services that satisfy almost every need a company could have from a network operating system. These applications include DNS and DHCP server services, performance-monitoring tools, and Web server applications.

Windows 2000 Security

Windows 2000 brings with it a full range of security features that make for a very strong operating system. Authentication security is provided through Kerberos version 5, files system security and encryption are provided through NTFS permissions and EFS, and network communication can be protected by IPSec (which is discussed in Chapter 8, "Remote Access and Security Protocols"). These features are combined with the underlying features introduced in Windows NT 4.

NOTE

NetWare Versions   The information this chapter provides on Novell NetWare is intended to apply to NetWare 5 and 6. If you find yourself working on an older version of NetWare, you might find that some of the commands and utilities are different from those discussed here.

NOVELL NETWARE

Once the network operating system of choice for all but a few networks, NetWare's popularity has declined somewhat. However, NetWare is still widely used in many large organizations. The latest version of NetWare, version 6, has garnered a number of awards and continues to prove that Novell can produce a world-leading network operating system.

One of the features that really put NetWare on the networking map was Novell Directory Services (NDS). Like Microsoft's Active Directory, NDS (which has been around since 1994) is a directory services system that allows network objects to be stored in a database. This database can then be divided up and distributed among different servers on the network. These processes are known as *partitioning* (the dividing up) and *replication* (the distribution among servers on the network). Although introduced as NDS with NetWare 4.x, Novell has now renamed the product eDirectory and has made it platform independent.

Like the other network operating systems, NetWare is a full-featured operating system that offers all the functions required by an organization, including file and print services, DNS and DHCP servers, and FTP and Web servers. NetWare also supports a wide range of third-party hardware and software.

> **EXAM TIP**
>
> **NDS** Although a detailed understanding of NDS is not required for the Network+ exam, working with a NetWare server will most certainly require a thorough knowledge of NDS.

> **NOTE**
>
> **NDS Versions** NDS was originally created for NetWare, but versions are now available for other platforms, including Linux, Windows NT/2000, and various versions of Unix.

NetWare System Requirements

In terms of hardware, NetWare system requirements are quite modest, and even moderately powered servers can provide adequate levels of performance to a relatively large numbers of users. Table 9.4 shows the basic NetWare 6 Server requirements.

TABLE 9.4

MINIMUM SERVER REQUIREMENTS FOR NETWARE 6

Hardware	Minimum Requirement
Processor	Pentium II or better
RAM	256MB
Hard disk space	Approximately 2GB

NetWare File Systems

Unlike Windows NT/2000, which uses share points to make disk resources available to users, NetWare has a more versatile approach, in which all areas of the disk are available to all users who have permissions. There is no concept of share points, although it is possible for a user to connect to a specific folder on the server if necessary.

NOTE

NSS   In some versions of NetWare, Novell has offered a service called Novell Storage Services (NSS). NSS allows for larger volume sizes and improves the performance of file serving.

Instead, users can map a drive to an area of a disk called a *volume*. Only the areas of the volume to which the user has been assigned permissions are available to that user.

Novell offers compatibility with client operating systems by using special software drivers known as *name spaces* to make drives available to clients. Different name space drivers are available, depending on which clients are being used. Most commonly, the driver that mimics the file properties of Windows clients, which is called "long," is used.

Part of NetWare's reputation as a very high-performance file server is related to the way it handles file caching. When a volume is initialized, the file allocation table is copied into memory, as are parts of another table, called the *directory entry table*. When a file is requested, the tables are searched for the location of the file, and the file is read from the disk. The holding of tables in memory makes this process very fast, and the caching of files in memory helps to increase the speed of the process. In fact, any memory that is available on a NetWare server after the server modules and workspace are loaded is assigned to the caching of files.

NetWare Performance-Monitoring Tools

Similar to the Windows server platforms, NetWare includes utilities that enable you to gauge the performance of the server system. The main tool is NetWare Monitor (see Figure 9.9), which provides an exhaustive range of information. The following are some of the most commonly used performance indicators in NetWare Monitor:

◆ **Processor Utilization**—This indicates how busy the processor is at any given time. If the counter is consistently high, the processor is unable to keep up with the load.

◆ **Total Cache Buffers**—This is the amount of memory available for file caching. You should ensure that this counter does not run too low (below 40%). Insufficient RAM for caching degrades server performance considerably.

◆ **Dirty Cache Buffers**—A dirty cache buffer is an area of memory that holds data waiting to be written to disk. Excessively high numbers of cache buffers can indicate that the disk channel is unable to keep up with disk demands.

◆ **Long Term Cache Hits**—A cache hit is recorded when a piece of data is found in memory rather than on the disk. If the amount of RAM in the server is sufficient, the Long Term Cache Hits setting should be high (97% to 99%). If the figures start to consistently drop below 95%, memory usage on the server should be examined.

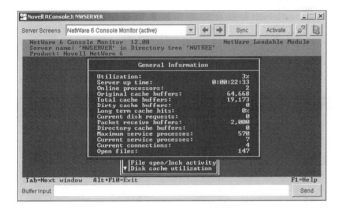

FIGURE 9.9
The Monitor screen from a NetWare 6 server.

NetWare User Administration

One of the differences between working with Windows servers and working with NetWare servers is that with NetWare much of the configuration of the server is actually performed from a workstation, not from the server itself, although Novell is moving toward a more server-centric model in this respect. Performing administrative tasks from the workstation is a good practice because fewer server resources are used for administration and more are available for carrying out user requests.

Two basic tools are used for administering NetWare: NetWare Administrator and ConsoleOne. Both utilities are Windows based, but ConsoleOne is a Java-based application, whereas NetWare Administrator is a standard 32-bit Windows application. NetWare Administrator and ConsoleOne can be used to manage practically all network objects, including users, groups, printing, and the server file system. Another Windows tool, NDS Manager, can be used to manage the structure of the NDS. Also, a range of browser-based management tools can be used on the NetWare server console and on a version of ConsoleOne. Figure 9.10 shows an example of a screen from the NetWare Administrator utility, and Figure 9.11 shows an example of the workstation version of ConsoleOne.

FIGURE 9.10
The NetWare Administrator utility.

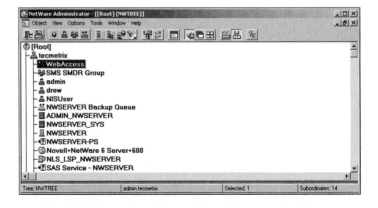

FIGURE 9.11
The NetWare ConsoleOne utility.

NetWare Server Configuration

On a NetWare server, network and user administration is typically performed from a workstation; however, disk management and other hardware configurations are normally performed directly on the server. NetWare uses several different utilities for hardware configurations, but the most common is the nwconfig utility, which is used for administering disk partitions, volumes, and RAID configurations. Utilities are also available for networking configuration (inetcfg) and for working with the NDS structure (dsrepair).

> **NOTE**
>
> **NetWare Administration** In NetWare 6, some of the disk-management tasks have been moved from the nwconfig utility to ConsoleOne.

Although they are not configuration tools per se, there are a number of other useful NetWare server console commands. Some of the most useful of these are listed in Table 9.5.

TABLE 9.5

USEFUL NETWARE SERVER COMMANDS

Command	Function
config	Displays network configuration information, including network addresses and protocol information
version	Displays the NetWare version currently installed on the server
display servers	Lists the servers that are visible to this server; useful for troubleshooting connectivity problems
reset router	Clears the server's routing table

Viewing and Changing a NetWare Network Configuration

From a NetWare server, the primary tool for configuring network settings is the Internetworking Configuration utility (inetcfg). Figure 9.12 shows a sample screen from the inetcfg utility, which is similar to many of the NetWare server utilities that use a menu-based format.

FIGURE 9.12
A sample screen from the inetcfg utility.

Table 9.6 summarizes the NetWare tools used for network configuration.

TABLE 9.6

NETWARE NETWORK CONFIGURATION COMMANDS

Command	Function
inetcfg	Configures network settings
config	Displays network configuration and other information, such as the NDS context of the server
ping	Simultaneously tests connectivity to multiple TCP/IP hosts
tping	Tests connectivity to a single TCP/IP host
ipxping	Tests connectivity between two hosts running Internetwork Packet Exchange (IPX)
tcpcon	Displays TCP/IP statistics and configuration in the familiar menu-based format
iptrace	Verifies the route to a remote system.

NetWare Authentication

NOTE

NetWare Passwords Passwords in NetWare are not case-sensitive.

As with all the other network operating systems discussed in this chapter, NetWare authentication is performed by using a username and password combination. As well as supplying this information, users also need to tell client software which NDS tree to authenticate to and the location of the user object in the NDS tree.

After a user has been validated, an assortment of restrictions is verified, including allowed logon times and station restrictions, which prevent users from logging on from certain workstations. Information about the user account and what the user can and can't access is stored in the NDS. For this reason, a copy of the NDS must be available in order for the user to be able to log on. Also, each time a user attempts to access a resource, her authentication status is checked in the NDS to make sure she is who she says she is and that she is allowed to access the resource.

NetWare File and Print Services

As mentioned earlier in this chapter, NetWare has long been regarded as the king of file and print services, and indeed, for many years, it was *the* operating system of choice for this purpose. Although that might no longer be the case, many people in the IT industry still see NetWare as primarily a file and print server platform.

Of all the network operating systems discussed in this chapter, NetWare has by far the most comprehensive (and complex) file system security structure. In addition to allowing an administrator to assign a comprehensive set of rights to users and groups, NetWare provides file permission inheritance systems, as well as the ability to block the inherited rights if needed. All this adds up to a sophisticated file system security method that can take some getting used to.

In addition to file permission rights, files can also be assigned a range of attributes. These attributes work the same as file attributes in DOS and Windows, except that the Windows file permissions are limited to attributes such as read-only and hidden, whereas the NetWare file attributes include such possibilities as rename inhibit and copy inhibit.

Printing with NetWare can be implemented in a variety of ways. Traditionally, printers were defined on the server, and print queues were associated with those printers. In NetWare 6, a feature called Novell Distributed Print Services allows a more dynamic printing environment to be created, with increased functionality. NetWare 6 also includes a new feature called iPrint, which allows users to see graphical maps of the network and point and click to access network devices.

To access a printer on NetWare, clients capture the output that would normally be directed to a local printer port and send it to the network printer. In early versions of NetWare, this was a process performed by using a command-line utility, called capture. Today, the process has been hidden behind the graphical interface of the client software and is largely unnoticed.

> **NOTE**
>
> **NDS—It Wasn't Always Like That**
> Any discussion of Novell NetWare now invariably involves NDS, or eDirectory. The functionality provided by the directory services system is so ingrained in NetWare that without it the system is little more than a collection of software programs. It wasn't always like this, though. In versions of NetWare up to and including 3.x, NetWare used a system called the *Bindery* to store user, group, and printing information. The Bindery was actually a group of three files that were stored on each server and were not shared between servers in the same way as directory services databases are shared. If a user needed access to more than one server, the user's account needed to be created on each server. Although numerous strategies and products eased the administrative burden that this created, Novell realized that a more dynamic approach was needed, hence the introduction of NDS.

NetWare Application Support

Although application support will always be a topic of much debate, the reality is that third-party application support for NetWare is not nearly at the same level as it is for the Windows server platforms. In terms of third-party application support, NetWare would even have a hard time competing against Linux. However, many applications are available for NetWare, and you are likely to have a choice of applications for any given purpose.

Even though third-party support might be lacking, the applications included with the NetWare package leave little to be desired. Included in NetWare are a DHCP server, a DNS server, a Web server application (and two of them in NetWare 6), and a range of other services. Pretty much any application that is needed in a modern networking environment is available in the network operating system.

NetWare Security

Like the other network operating systems, NetWare has many security features to help secure the server and the network. The key areas of NetWare security include the following:

◆ **Resource access**—Resource access in NetWare is controlled, as is everything else related to security, through directory services. For a user to gain access to a network resource—whether it be a file, directory, printer, server, or gateway—the appropriate permissions must be applied through the directory. Permissions can be granted to the user, to a group to which the user belongs, or to an NDS container object in which the user resides. Rights to objects can be inherited or gained from other user IDs through a process called *security equivalence.*

◆ **User authentication**—As with the other network operating systems, accessing a NetWare server and network resources requires a username and password combination. To log on to a NetWare server, the context of the user must also be specified and, in some instances, the name of the NDS tree must also be provided. *Context* is a term used to refer to the user IDs location in the NDS tree. Without the correct context, the security subsystem is unable to identify the correct user ID and does not grant access to the server. Because the context can be quite complex and because the tree name is generally not used except at the point of login, it's common practice to configure users' workstations to default to a certain tree and context, so that users do not need for them to supply that information. This way, a user needs to provide only a username and password.

◆ **File and directory security**—NetWare provides a very comprehensive file and directory permissions system, which allows rights to be assigned to users, groups, and other NDS objects. Rights are inheritable, which means that rights assigned at one directory level flow down through the directory structure until they reach the end of the directory tree, unless they are countered by an inherited rights mask or by an explicit trustee assignment. Much the same process is used to manage and assign rights within the NDS directory tree, although the actual set of rights that can be assigned is different.

Like the Windows console, the NetWare console can and should be locked for security purposes. You can lock the NetWare console by using a utility called scrsaver, which you run from the server command line.

With the proliferation of Microsoft Windows server platforms, you might not actually get to work with a NetWare server. But if you do, you'll find that there is good reason why NetWare was king of the network operating system hill for so long.

LINUX

Providing a summary of Linux in a few paragraphs is a difficult task. Unlike other operating systems, each of which has only a single variation, Linux has many different distributions, each offering a slightly different approach. Some of the most common Linux distributions include Red Hat, SuSE, Debian, and Caldera. In light of the many versions of Linux, if a command or an approach is listed in this section and is not available in the version of Linux you are using, you can look for an equivalent command or approach in your version, and you will very likely find one.

The history of Linux can be traced back to 1991, when Linus Torvalds, then a student at the University of Helsinki, set out to make a Unix-like operating system. After developing the original

---

EXAM TIP

Accessing a NetWare Server To gain access to a NetWare server, four pieces of information are normally required: a username, a password, a directory context, and the name of the tree to which the user wants to log in. In addition, you can specify a server name, although this is not required.

EXAM TIP

Headless Operation As an extra security precaution, NetWare supports *headless* operation, which means that the NetWare server can run without a keyboard, mouse, and monitor. It is safe to plug these devices back in while the system is running if you want to gain access.

Linux kernel, the core of the operating system, he distributed it on the Internet and asked anyone who was interested to develop it. Many eager developers jumped on the programming bandwagon, and in a few short years, Linux had progressed into a viable alternative to the commercially available network operating systems.

Today, the development of Linux continues in much the same way as it always has: Anyone who wants to can develop Linux to further enhance its capabilities. To ensure that this is always the case, the Linux kernel is protected under a licensing agreement which implies that the source code will always be available to anyone who wants access. More information on Linux licensing and development can be found at www.gnu.org.

The following are some of the key features of the Linux operating system:

◆ **Multitasking**—Linux supports multitasking, which is the ability for several programs to run simultaneously.

◆ **Multiplatform**—Linux is able to operate on a number of different platforms, not just on Intel machines.

◆ **Multiprocessor support**—Linux supports multiple processors, meaning that it recognizes multiple processors in a system.

◆ **Development**—In all the noncommercial programs available for Linux, the source code is available. This allows you to customize and further develop Linux.

◆ **Virtual consoles**—Linux supports virtual consoles, which are essentially independent logon sessions.

◆ **File system support**—In addition to the Linux native file systems, such as EXT2, Linux supports a wide range of file systems, including FAT (for DOS), HFS (for Macintosh), VFAT (for Windows 95, Windows 98, and Windows Me), and CDFS (for CD-ROMs).

◆ **Network support**—Linux has the ability to connect to a variety of network environments. Linux includes TCP/IP networking such as FTP, Telnet, and NFS; support for AppleTalk server; and Internetwork Packet Exchange/Sequenced Packet Exchange (IPX/SPX) and NetWare connectivity software.

Linux System Requirements

Linux is a very dynamic and diverse network operating system, and therefore, it is almost impossible to make a blanket statement about the hardware needed to get a Linux server up and running. You can be reasonably sure, however, that the minimum hardware requirements for a Linux system are lower than those for any other operating system. Linux users are quick to point out the limited hardware that is required for a Linux system, and it really is quite amazing. One of the many reasons that Linux has the ability to run on limited hardware is because it offers graphical utilities but is a command-line operating system. Windows, on the other hand, is a graphical operating system that offers some command-line utilities. It is the graphical nature of the operating systems that increases the need for faster and more extensive hardware.

You can find the minimum hardware requirements for each of the different Linux distributions at the distributors' respective Web sites, but they are all fairly similar. To give you an idea of the hardware requirements for a Linux system, Table 9.7 lists the system requirements for Red Hat Linux 7.

TABLE 9.7

MINIMUM SERVER REQUIREMENTS FOR RED HAT LINUX 7

Hardware	Minimum Requirement
Processor	486 CPU
RAM	32MB
Hard disk space	650MB

Linux File Systems

The number of file systems supported by Linux is really remarkable. The default Linux file system is called EXT2, but to coexist on the same partition as a Windows operating system, Linux also supports the FAT file system. The EXT2 file system is the most widely used on Linux systems and provides support for large hard disks.

IN THE FIELD

HARDWARE VERIFICATION

Verifying the hardware that goes into a Linux server is very important—perhaps more important than with any of the other network operating systems. Linux has had compatibility issues with certain hardware configurations, and verifying hardware support before purchasing hardware for a Linux system is a good idea. Each of the various distributors of Linux offers hardware compatibility lists on its Web site (although these lists can be hard to find). In addition to a hardware compatibility list, many server administrators turn to newsgroups to post questions about hardware compatibility. The Linux hardware compatibility lists are not as comprehensive as Novell's or Microsoft's, and they sometimes require some additional digging.

Linux Monitoring and Performance Tools

Network administrators who are used to the slick graphical performance tools of the Windows server environments might be taken aback by the visual presentation of some of the Linux utilities used to monitor performance. Many Linux distributions do provide graphical tools, but many Linux servers are command-line driven and do not provide a graphical interfaces.

When you get past the appearance of the utilities, you will find that the actual performance and monitoring that these tools provide is second to none. Performance tools vary somewhat among Linux distributions, but they all offer a variety of performance-monitoring tools. The following sections discuss a few ways to view system resources and usage.

The Top Utility

Top is a command-line utility that displays the processes that are currently being run on the system and how much of the system's resources these processes are using. Similar information is provided in Windows 2000 on the Processes tab in the Task Manager utility.

Also included in the display are various counters that show how physical memory is being used, the amount of swap space in use, and the total number of processes in use. One of the best features about the Top utility is that it is dynamic, and every few seconds, the information is updated, to give you the most current picture of your system.

Process File System

A Linux system has a /proc directory, which is a virtual directory that is used to view just about any aspect of a Linux system. All the mainstream Linux distributions include /proc directories, and as a network administrator, you can expect to be spending some time looking in this directory when working on Linux machines.

The components that can be viewed with the proc command are listed in the /proc directory. The most useful switches for the proc command include the following:

◆ /proc/dma—Provides information on the Direct Memory Access (DMA) channels in use

◆ /proc/cpuinfo—Lists complete information about the CPU

◆ /proc/apm—Includes information on power management, if it is supported

◆ /proc/meminfo—Includes information on physical memory and the swap file

◆ /proc/net—Provides networking information

◆ /proc/pci—Provides information on the Peripheral Component Interconnect (PCI) devices within the system

Graphical Utilities

The two most common Linux graphical interfaces, GNOME and the K Desktop Environment (KDE), provide a number of easy-to-use performance-monitoring utilities. Figure 9.13 shows a system-monitoring tool from a Linux system that uses the KDE graphical interface.

FIGURE 9.13

A system-monitoring tool in the KDE.

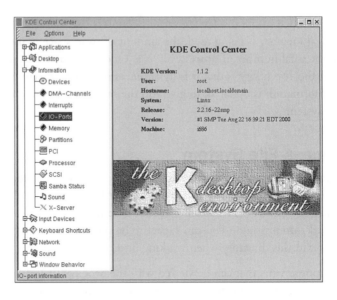

Managing Linux Disk Drives

Linux partitions are usually managed through the Fdisk utility. Administrators who are used to the cleaner Microsoft Disk Management utility might have to take some time to get used to Linux Fdisk. In inexperienced hands, Fdisk can be a dangerous utility; it should be used only by server administrators who are comfortable with it.

In addition to Fdisk, many of the major Linux distributions also have their own disk-management utilities. Red Hat uses Disk Druid, Mandrake Linux uses Disk Drake, and Caldera Linux uses LIZARD. Each of these utilities does essentially the same thing: partition and manage the hard disks. Figure 9.14 shows an example of the Disk Druid disk-management utility that is used in Red Hat Linux.

Linux User Management Basics

At first, the management of users' accounts in Linux might seem awkward, and compared to user management in other network operating systems, it is. You typically add users on a Linux system by using the useradd command from the command line, with the following syntax:

```
useradd <USERNAME>
```

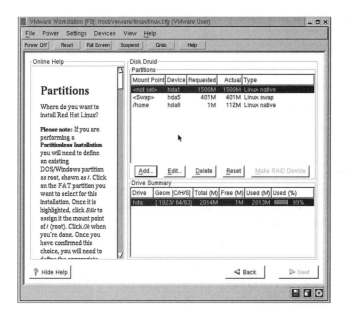

FIGURE 9.14
The Disk Druid utility on Red Hat Linux.

The next step is to set a password for the user account that was created; to do this, you use the passwd command. After you type the command, Linux prompts you to enter the password and then to enter it again for confirmation. Various graphical utilities are available that can also be used for adding user accounts. If you prefer, you can use one of them instead of the command-line utilities.

User account information is stored in a file called passwd in the /etc directory. This file is a text file, and in a standard configuration, passwords are also stored in this file, in plain text. Because this represents a security issue, it is common to use a process called *password shadowing* in which the password is stored and encrypted in a separate file, called /etc/shadow. Group accounts are created in much the same way as user accounts, except the command used is groupadd.

Linux has a more distributed method of security than either NetWare or Windows, in that it relies more heavily on the security capabilities of applications than on the core user accounts. This is one of the features that makes Linux the most customizable of the operating systems described in this chapter.

NOTE

Linux Graphical Utilities   Although many Linux administrators prefer to use command-line utilities for tasks such as adding users, there are a number of graphical utilities available.

Verifying Linux Network Settings

Network settings, much like anything else in Linux, are stored in text files that normally are located in the /etc/ directory or subdirectories of this directory. Network settings can be configured through a variety of command-line and graphical utilities.

The following are the commands that are most commonly used to verify and test network connectivity in a Linux environment:

◆ ifconfig—ifconfig shows detailed information—including TCP/IP address, default gateway, and subnet mask—about all network interfaces. It also provides very basic usage statistics for each interface.

◆ ping—ping works the same way as with the other network operating system server platforms: It tests network connectivity between two devices. The ping command in Linux uses a simple syntax: ping <IP address>.

◆ traceroute—traceroute displays the network path between two nodes. At each hop, information about the hop, including the response time and IP address, is shown. The syntax for the traceroute command is traceroute <IP address>.

Linux Authentication

People who are used to working on a Windows-based system will no doubt discover that administration on a Linux system is very different from what they are used to. For instance, authentication information such as a list of users is kept in a text file. This file, /etc/ passwd, controls who can and who cannot log on to the system.

For a user to log on to the system, a valid username and password combination must be supplied. Both of these pieces of information are case-sensitive.

Linux File and Print Services

Although it is not the most obvious choice for a file and print server platform, Linux can perform the role of a file and print server admirably. In a base configuration, the volumes on a Linux server are not available to network clients. To make them available, one of two file sharing services is commonly used:

◆ **NFS**—NFS is the original file-sharing system used with Linux. NFS makes it possible for areas of the hard disk on a Linux system to be shared with other clients on the network. Once the share has been established from the client side, the fact that the drive is on another system is transparent to the user.

◆ **Samba**—Samba provides Server Message Block functionality so that areas of the Linux server disks can be made available to Windows clients. In much the same way as on Windows servers, Samba facilitates the sharing of folders that can then be accessed by Windows client computers. Samba also makes it possible for Linux printer resources to be shared with Windows clients.

As with Windows NT/2000 and NetWare, Linux has a file system permission structure that makes it possible to restrict access to files or directories. In Linux, each file or directory can be assigned a very basic set of file rights that dictate the actions that can be performed on the file. The basic rights are Read, Write, and Execute. The rights can be expressed in an alphabetic format (that is, RWX) or a numeric format (777). The rights to a file can be derived from the file ownership, from a group object, or from an "everyone" designator, which covers all users who are authenticated on the server. The Linux file permission structure might not be as sophisticated as those found in other network operating systems, but it is still more than sufficient in many environments.

Printing on a Linux system occurs through a service called the Line Printer daemon. The Line Printer functionality can be accessed by any user on the network who is properly authorized and connected. Some distributions of Linux have started to provide a more enhanced printing system called the Common Unix Printing System (CUPS). Many people, however, still prefer to use the traditional Line Printer system because of its simplicity and efficiency.

Linux Application Support

If you can think of an application that you might need, chances are that it is available for Linux in some form. As well as highly sophisticated commercial applications produced by large software companies, you can find software for the Linux platform that is written by an equally enthusiastic army of small software development companies and individuals. This means that application support for Linux is on par with if not greater than that in other network operating systems, such as NetWare, even if it has not yet reached the levels achieved by Windows server platforms.

In a sense, all applications created for Linux are third-party applications in that Linux itself is only an operating system kernel. The applications that run on this kernel are what provide Linux with functionality.

On the assumption that a network server will have a number of requirements, it is common practice for the Linux kernel to be bundled with various applications and provided to customers as a package, which, as we discussed earlier, are called *distributions*.

One respect in which Linux certainly has the edge over the other operating systems discussed is that many Linux applications are free of charge. Developed in the same spirit as Linux itself, and in many cases governed by the same licensing types, these free applications can seriously reduce the cost of maintaining a network server. Although it can be said that there are also free server-type applications for Windows and NetWare, there are certainly not as many of them as there are for Linux. (Note that we are referring to server applications, not applications targeted at workstation or end-user applications.)

Linux Security

Considerable effort has been put into making Linux a very secure network operating system, and those efforts are evident. When it is configured correctly, Linux is a very secure operating system, and therefore it is often chosen to be used as a company's firewall server. The following are a few highlights of Linux security:

◆ **Resource access**—As in the other network operating systems, access to resources on a Linux network is controlled through permissions. Access control lists identifying which systems and who can access what resources are held in text files such as hosts.deny and hosts.allow. Permissions for network resources and services can be assigned to an individual user or to a group of users.

◆ **User authentication**—To access the local system resources or any network resources, user authentication, in the form of a username and a password, is required. The user account information is kept in a text file known as the `/etc/passwd` file in the Linux system.

◆ **File and directory security**—The default file system used by Linux is the EXT2 file system. Like NTFS, which is used with Windows servers, EXT2 allows administrators to assign permissions to individual files and folders. These permissions are used to control who is allowed access to specific data on the server. A secure server should have permissions set on the important data in the system.

As Linux continues to grow in popularity, it will become an increasingly common sight in server rooms of organizations of all sizes. As a network administrator, you should prepare yourself for *when* you encounter a Linux system—not *if*.

EXAM TIP

Logging on to Linux Servers   To log on to a Linux server, the user must supply a valid username and password. Both of these values are case sensitive. You should know this for the exam.

OPERATING SYSTEM INTEROPERABILITY

Rather than use the same network operating system on all servers, modern networks often work in multivendor environments, meaning that you might encounter more than one of the major network operating systems functioning on the same network. In such a scenario, you might, for example, have a NetWare server that handles authentication as well as file and print services, a Windows 2000 server that hosts the corporate email system, and two Linux systems—one acting as a server and the other providing firewall services. It is possible to use a single operating system for all these tasks, but in some situations a more flexible approach is required.

To facilitate such environments, network operating system manufacturers build in features and services that allow their operating systems to coexist on networks with other vendors' operating systems. In some cases, the manufacturers appear to do so grudgingly, but in the IT environment of the 21st century, it would be a bold move indeed not to provide such services.

The following sections take a brief look at how well some of the major network operating systems "play" with each other.

Using Windows with NetWare

A typical combination in many environments is the use of Windows and NetWare servers. Unfortunately for NetWare, some of these situations are part of a migration to a completely Windows-based system. In other environments, organizations leverage the power of NDS (or eDirectory) and NetWare for file and print services and use a Windows server product for application hosting. Because it realizes that there will be such environments, Microsoft supplies a range of tools, including the following, to help in the communication between Windows server products and NetWare:

♦ **Client Services for NetWare (CSNW)**—CSNW is designed to allow Windows client systems to access file and print services on a NetWare server. CSNW is installed on a client system and allows only that client to connect to the NetWare server.

♦ **Gateway Services for NetWare (GSNW)**—GSNW is used to allow systems in a Windows domain to access resources on a NetWare server. GSNW is installed on the server and allows all permitted Windows clients to connect to the NetWare server through it.

♦ **File and Print Services for NetWare (FPNW)**—FPNW is used for NetWare clients to access file and print services from a Windows server system. Basically, it makes a Windows Server system look like a NetWare server or a reasonable facsimile thereof.

EXAM TIP

CSNW and FSNW   You should understand the functions of CSNW and GSNW for the Network+ exam. You should also understand where they are installed.

Using Windows and Linux Servers

In today's environments, Linux and Windows servers are commonly used together, and therefore, clients and the servers themselves must be able to communicate. One of the programs used to increase interoperability between Linux and Windows is Samba. Samba is a software package for Linux that allows Linux workstations to share resources with Windows workstations in a Windows-based network. Samba is available free of charge and is commonly installed by default during a Linux installation. Connection to a Samba server requires the use of the Microsoft network client, which is installed by default with most Windows client operating systems.

Using NetWare and Linux Servers

NetWare and Linux servers are fully interoperable and are often found together in network environments. For instance, a NetWare file and print server might coexist with a Linux firewall and proxy server. In addition, it is possible, by using eDirectory, to integrate the management of Linux servers into the directory services system in order to streamline administration.

To make these scenarios possible, Linux supports both IPX/SPX, which is required for NetWare 3.x and 4.x, and TCP/IP, which is used in the later NetWare versions. However, many of the Linux distributions do not natively support IPX/SPX. If you use one of those distributions, you need to download extra software and perform additional configuration.

EXAM TIP

Samba You might be asked to identify the function and purpose of Samba for the Network+ exam.

OPERATING SYSTEM CLIENT SUPPORT

Because many different client systems—including Linux, Windows, and Macintosh systems—are used in today's networks, network operating systems need to support each of these client systems. Of the three client systems mentioned, Microsoft Windows is by far the most popular. However, in recent years, other platforms have experienced a surge in popularity.

Windows Server Client Support

Windows-based servers support all the client software that is used on networks today. Many types of client software, including Windows 95, Windows 98, and Windows Me, Windows NT Workstation, Windows XP Professional, Windows 2000 Professional, Windows 3.x, and editions of Windows NT Server, are natively supported by Windows servers and can be integrated with relative ease. To connect to a Windows server, Client for Microsoft Networks needs to be installed on the client systems.

Unix systems are fully configurable with Windows servers, via a special add-on pack called Windows Services for Unix. This add-on pack provides compatibility with the Unix NFS and a variety of Unix utilities. Macintosh, on the other hand, requires the Services for Macintosh product, which allows Macintosh clients to use TCP/IP and access shared files, directories, and printers on a Windows 2000 server.

NetWare Server Client Support

As a major player in the network operating system world, NetWare provides support for a variety of clients. When connecting Windows systems in a NetWare environment, you need to consider the following:

◆ To connect a Windows NT/2000 workstation to a NetWare 3.x or 4.x network, you need the NWLink protocol and you need CSNW installed. NetWare 5.x does not specifically require the NWLink protocol, but it does requires client software to access the NetWare server. Alternatively, you can use the Novell-supplied client software, which, in fact, offers more functionality than the CSNW product.

◆ Connecting a Windows server system to a NetWare server to act as a gateway requires NWLink and GSNW.

◆ To connect Windows desktop systems to a NetWare 3.x or 4.x network, IPX/SPX (or Microsoft's own version of it, NWLink) is required on the workstation, as is CSNW or the Novell client software. NetWare 5.x does not specifically require IPX/SPX, and NetWare 6 does not necessarily require client-side software.

NOTE

NetWare 6 Client Access NetWare 6 allows for Windows access to NetWare networks without client software installed on the system.

Linux Server Client Support

Because a Linux workstation uses the same operating system that is running on the server, client support is both integrated and seamless. Linux client systems can access all the resources offered by a Linux server with ease. The most common resources are file sharing, which is normally facilitated through NFS, and printing, which is made available through the Line Printer daemon.

As discussed earlier in this chapter, Windows clients are able to access resources on a Linux server through the Samba product. Macintosh clients can also use the Samba functionality.

CLIENT OPERATING SYSTEMS

◆ Identify the basic capabilities of client workstations (i.e., client connectivity, local security mechanisms, and authentication).

Whereas a network operating system works behind the scenes, providing the services that make the network function, the workstation operating systems act as the window to the network. For that reason, network administrators must be aware of the operating systems that grace the front end of the network.

As stated previously, Microsoft's Windows products dominate the desktop operating systems market. The other operating systems discussed in this chapter hold single-figure percentages of the market share. However, these other systems are readily available, and their numbers are growing.

Windows 95, Windows 98, and Windows Me

Perhaps the most widely used client operating systems are the Windows-based clients, Windows 95, Windows 98, and Windows Me. These clients are used in network environments of all sizes, ranging from small office and home office environments to large corporations. Their popularity can be attributed to the familiar, easy-to-navigate graphical interfaces, compatibility with most of the current popular applications, and their low cost, at least in comparison to other Windows products, such as Windows NT Workstation and Windows 2000 Professional.

Application Support for Windows 95, Windows 98, and Windows Me

Windows 95, Windows 98, and Windows Me systems support all but a few of the major applications used today. They were designed to be used with office productivity tools such as spreadsheets and word processors. In addition, they support a range of entertainment applications. Of all the operating systems in use today, they have the greatest commercial software support.

Local Security Mechanisms for Windows 95, Windows 98, and Windows Me

If there is one failing in Windows 95, Windows 98, and Windows Me–based clients, it is their local security. Windows clients have no file system security, which means that the files you save on your system can be accessed by anyone who uses your computer. There are third-party products designed to either hide folders and files or password-protect them.

Windows 95, Windows 98, and Windows Me clients also do not provide a mechanism to prevent tampering with systems and application settings. Perhaps even more significantly, anyone can use a Windows 95, Windows 98, and Windows Me system without providing a username and password.

The lack of a local security mechanism makes Windows 95, Windows 98, and Windows Me clients an unsuitable operating system for many network environments and for particular categories of users on a network. If local security is required, an operating system such as Windows NT or 2000 should be used.

Authentication for Windows 95, Windows 98, and Windows Me

Windows 95, Windows 98, and Windows Me clients require a username-and-password combination in order for users to log on to the network and access network resources. The system is then authenticated by the server that is being used. Authentication is a function of the server operating system rather than the local workstation.

Windows NT Workstation, Windows 2000 Professional, and Windows XP Professional

Windows NT Workstation, Windows 2000, and Windows XP Professional were introduced to provide robust, secure, high-performance alternatives to Microsoft's other workstation operating systems, such as Windows 95, Windows 98, and Windows Me. Since the introduction of Windows NT Workstation as a business-oriented operating system, Microsoft has succeeded it with two other versions: Windows 2000 Professional and its latest offering, Windows XP Professional. Built on the same basic building blocks as Windows NT Server, these products are popular in corporate environments where local workstation security is as important as the security of the server. Windows NT Workstation, Windows 2000, and Windows XP Professional use the same authentication mechanisms as their corresponding server products, and they support NTFS for file system security.

Application Support for Windows NT Workstation, Windows 2000 Professional, and Windows XP Professional

Application support for Windows NT Workstation, Windows 2000, and Windows XP Professional Workstation is very high, although certain applications are simply not supported. All the operating systems discussed in this chapter have the ability to support DOS applications and 16-bit and 32-bit Windows applications, as well as some other platforms. In general, this compatibility works flawlessly, although certain applications can cause problems. One such problem is that any application that interfaces directly with hardware won't work. This is because Windows NT Workstation, Windows 2000, and Windows XP Professional have a special set of drivers that intercept calls made to the hardware. Only applications that understand the function of these drivers and know how to interface with them can be used on these systems.

Client Connectivity for Windows NT Workstation, Windows 2000 Professional, and Windows XP Professional

Windows NT Workstation, Windows 2000, and Windows XP Professional are intended to be suitable clients for any of the common network operating systems. To connect to NetWare servers, Microsoft provides CSNW, although Novell offers client software that has more functionality. To connect to a Linux server running Samba, no additional software is required.

Local Security Mechanisms for Windows NT Workstation, Windows 2000 Professional, and Windows XP Professional

Windows NT Workstation, Windows 2000, and Windows XP Professional share the same security subsystem as their server counterparts and use the same security mechanisms. User accounts can be defined locally on the workstation, or the system can be made a member of a domain, in which case user accounts from the central user account database can be used to log on to the workstation and therefore the domain as well.

Authentication for Windows NT Workstation, Windows 2000 Professional, and Windows XP Professional

Two pieces of information are required to log on to a Windows NT or Windows 2000 system: a username and a password. Of the two, the username is not case-sensitive, but the password is. If the workstation has also been made a member of the domain, an additional dialog box allows you to specify whether you want to log on as an account from the local workstation or as a user account from the domain.

Linux

Although Linux has not experienced the same success as a workstation operating system as it has at the server level, it is increasingly being looked to as an alternative to the other offerings. Many Linux distributions actually include a "workstation" option that can be selected during the installation process. Instead of installing server-type applications (proxy server, Web server, and so on), the installation focuses on workstation-type applications and utilities.

Applications for Linux

One of the myths that has traditionally surrounded Linux is the lack of applications that have been written for it. In the early stages of Linux, this might have been true, but it is certainly no longer the case. The range and quality of applications and utilities available for Linux is truly impressive.

As the popularity of Linux has increased, so has the number of software companies developing Linux-friendly applications. One of the most high profile of these companies is Corel, which has developed a WordPerfect Office suite for Linux. Commercially available software for Linux is licensed in the same way as the software for other operating systems: You need a license to install the product, and you do not receive the source code for the program.

In addition to commercially available software, there is also a larger amount of "free" Linux software. For every commercially available Linux software package, there is an equivalent that is available free of charge. A good example of free software is StarOffice, which is an office suite from Sun Microsystems that includes a spreadsheet, word processor, and all the productivity tools required by desktop users. Free Linux software does not end there. You can get firewall software, proxy software, and backup software—just about any software you need to use Linux as a server or desktop solution.

Client Connectivity for Linux

In either a server or client configuration, Linux supports many networking protocols, giving it the capability to operate as a client in many network environments. The latest versions of Linux include support for TCP/IP, IPX/SPX, and other protocols. This allows Linux clients to interoperate with common network operating systems, although you might need to install client software on either the client or the server to facilitate connectivity.

In NetWare 6, native file access makes it possible for Linux clients to access NetWare server resources without additional software.

Local Security Mechanisms for Linux

Linux is an inherently secure operating system, although the system administrator might need to have a detailed understanding of the operating system to make it completely bulletproof. For local security measures, a username and password combination is required to log on to the system, providing the basis of user verification. In the past, username and password information was stored in a plain-text format, which constitutes a security risk. Today, it is far more common to use the password shadowing technique discussed earlier in this chapter, in the section "Linux User Management Basics."

For file system security, the EXT2 file system, and others, can be used to secure the files that are held on a system.

Note that unlike Windows systems, where there are differences in the security measures and mechanisms from version to version, a Linux system used as a workstation and a Linux system used as a server utilizes the same underlying operating system. Therefore, the information provided earlier about security on Linux servers is equally applicable to Linux clients.

Authentication for Linux

Linux authentication is based on a username and password combination. Without a valid user ID, it is very difficult to access a local system. Of important note is that on a Linux system, there is a root account that can be authenticated on any system. The root account is comparable to the Administrator account on Windows networks. On a Linux system, both the username and password are case sensitive.

Macintosh

Since its introduction, Macintosh has supplied network connectivity features including hardware as well as protocols to facilitate communications. Early systems included a networking interface called a

LocalTalk adapter. Networking functionality was also built in to the operating system, using AppleTalk (discussed in Chapter 5, "Overview of Network Protocols") as the protocol suite.

Although today's Macintosh computers might look very different from those early systems, their networking legacy remains intact. A Macintosh makes a great client for all the common network operating systems. However, depending on the type and version of network operating system and MAC OS being used, additional software might be required at either the server end or the client end.

> **N O T E**
>
> **MAC OS X** MAC OS X includes functionality that allows connectivity to Windows and Linux/Samba server platforms without additional software.

Application Support for Macintosh

There is no shortage of software for Macintosh computers. In fact, many of the programs Windows users have come to know and love were first written for the Macintosh and, according to Macintosh users, worked better on Macintosh than they do on Windows. Some areas of particular software strength for Macintosh computers include graphical and desktop publishing applications and educational programs.

In addition, Macintosh systems can use Windows applications by using a process called *emulation*. This allows Windows-based programs to run on Macintosh, but there are performance losses, and in some cases, the programs won't run at all.

Client Connectivity for Macintosh

Macintosh computers make suitable clients for most network operating systems, but in some cases, there is a need for additional software. For example, to connect to a NetWare server, special client software is required. NetWare now includes native file access that can allow Macintosh clients to access a NetWare file system without additional software. For Windows NT/2000 servers, a product called Services for Macintosh can be installed; this product makes selected shares and printers available to Macintosh clients.

CHAPTER SUMMARY

KEY TERMS

- authentication
- file and print services
- Web server services
- firewall and proxy services
- Novell NetWare
- Unix
- Linux
- Macintosh
- workgroup
- domain
- PDC
- BDC
- tracert
- ipconfig
- ping
- Active Directory
- FAT
- FAT32
- NTFS
- NDS
- config
- inetcfg
- ipxping
- NLM
- multitasking
- ifconfig
- traceroute
- NFS
- Samba
- CSNW
- GSNW
- FPNW

Network operating systems are specialized and complex software packages that are used to provide network services such as authentication and file and print services to client computers.

A few key network operating systems are used in modern network environments, each with a unique share of the market. These operating systems include NetWare, Linux, and the various Windows server platforms. As a network administrator, you will be required to know how each of these operating systems functions in order to adequately manage a network. Each of these network operating systems has certain characteristics and deals with network functionality in its own way.

Workstation operating systems provide the interface that allows clients to access network resources and facilities. Therefore, an awareness of the common client operating systems and their characteristics is necessary for any network administrator.

APPLY YOUR KNOWLEDGE

Exercises

9.1   Installing Windows 2000 Advanced Server

Perhaps the best way to understand how a network operating system works and how it is configured is to install it. In this project, you go through the steps involved in installing a network operating system. In this exercise, you install Windows 2000 Advanced Server. Before you begin, make sure you have the following:

◆ A system that includes a 2GB partition with at least 1GB of free space.

◆ A copy of Microsoft Windows 2000 Advanced Server. You can obtain a 120-day evaluation copy at www.microsoft.com/windows2000 or at www.microsoft.com/servers/evaluation/trial. You can either download a copy or order it on CD-ROM.

◆ A system that meets the minimum required hardware configuration.

> **NOTE**
>
> **Dual-Boot Configuration** This project can be performed on a computer that currently has Microsoft Windows 95, Windows 98, or Windows NT installed. The installation you perform in this project will automatically configure the machine to operate in dual-boot mode, although you must be very careful not to install the new version of Windows over the old. When the computer starts, the user is presented with a choice of booting with either the original operating system or the newly installed Windows 2000 Advanced Server.

The installation of Windows 2000 Advanced Server begins in a text-based mode. After the preliminary steps are completed, the computer reboots and is then in a graphical user interface–based mode for the duration of the installation. This exercise utilizes default configuration settings for everything except the computer name and the TCP/IP settings. Using these steps, you will install Windows 2000 Advanced Server as a member of a workgroup named EXAMPREP.

As you go through the installation, be aware that some screens perform extended configuration routines and can take a few minutes.

Estimated time: 60 minutes

1. Place the Windows 2000 CD in the CD-ROM drive. The CD should run automatically. (If you downloaded the software from the Web, go to the download folder and double-click the Setup icon.)

2. When the Setup notification screen appears, press Enter.

3. When the Welcome to Setup screen appears, press Enter.

4. When the Windows 2000 Licensing Agreement appears, read the agreement, and then press F8 to accept the licensing terms. (If you do not accept the licensing terms, you will exit Setup.)

5. A list of existing partitions appears. Choose the one on which you want to install Windows 2000 Advanced Server, and press Enter. (Alternatively, you can create a partition on the disk or format an existing partition and install Windows 2000 onto the *new partition*.)

6. Next, you receive a list of formatting options for the partition you have chosen. Choose Format the Partition Using the NTFS File System.

APPLY YOUR KNOWLEDGE

7. The partition is formatted and examined. Files are then copied from the Windows 2000 source (either the CD or the download location) into the Windows 2000 installation folders.

8. When the file transfer is complete, the computer automatically reboots. Make sure that any floppies are removed and that the CD remains in the CD-ROM drive. (This ends the text-based section of the installation.)

9. When the computer restarts, you see the Welcome to the Windows 2000 Server Setup Wizard. Click Next or wait for the installation to proceed after a few seconds. Windows 2000 detects and installs devices. You will be pleasantly surprised by its abilities.

10. The Regional Settings page eventually appears. Accept the defaults by clicking Next.

11. On the Personalize Your Software page, type your name and organization name in the appropriate boxes.

12. The Your Product Key page appears. Input the key provided with the download or use the one printed on the CD-ROM.

13. The Licensing Mode page appears. This is where you tell the software whether you will run in per-server mode, which allows only as many connections to the server as you have purchased licenses for, or the per-seat mode, which allows unlimited connections based on the number of per-seat licenses you have purchased. Choose Per Server, if it is not chosen for you. In the Number of Concurrent Connections box, type the number **10** for this exercise. Click Next.

14. The all-important Computer Name and Administrator Password page appears. Enter a name for your computer and a password for the

Administrator account. (If you leave the Administrator password blank, you will not have to use a password to log on with this account. This is *never* a good idea. Give this account a secure password. Click Next.

15. The Windows 2000 Components page appears. This is where you choose which components you want to add to the installation. Accept the default choices, and after you familiarize yourself with this information, click Next.

16. The Date and Time Settings page appears. Make the necessary adjustments, and then click Next.

17. The Network Settings page appears, telling you that Windows 2000 is in the process of installing networking components. You are eventually asked to choose Typical or Custom network settings. Choose Custom, and then click Next.

18. When the Networking Components page appears, click Internet Protocol (TCP/IP), and then click Properties.

19. In the Internet Protocol (TCP/IP) Properties dialog box, choose Use the Following IP Address, and then type **192.168.1.200**. You are assigning a static IP address for this server, using 192.168.1.200 because it is part of the reserved private IP address scope. Note that when you type in the IP address, Windows 2000 automatically inputs a subnet mask for you. For now do not set any other information such as DNS server addresses. Click Next.

20. The Workgroup or Computer Domain screen appears. Recall that the two network types are peer-to-peer and client/server. On this screen, you tell Windows 2000 what type of network it will be in. Let's set it up as a peer-to-peer network for now to keep this exercise simple.

APPLY YOUR KNOWLEDGE

Verify and choose either No, This Computer Is Not on a Network or choose Is on a Network Without a Domain. Notice that you can give the workgroup a name. For this exercise, name it REALWORLD. Any other computers that have their workgroup names set to REALWORLD will be able to be members of this new workgroup. Click Next.

21. The Installing Components dialog box appears and informs you that Setup is installing Windows 2000 components. Eventually, the Performing Final Tasks page appears and tells you that Setup is performing a final set of installation tasks. Sometimes, this can take a few minutes.

22. When the Completing the Windows 2000 Setup Wizard page appears, click Finish.

23. Remove the CD from the drive and restart the computer. You will either boot to Windows 2000, or, if you are dual-booting, you will eventually see a text-based menu with Windows 2000 selected as the default operating system choice. You have 30 seconds to make a different selection before the computer boots into Windows 2000.

    Windows 2000 starts up and presents you I with a logon informational screen. Press Ctrl+Alt+Delete, and you will be presented with the logon screen. In the username box, type **Administrator**. In the password box, type the password you used in step 14. Remember that the password is case sensitive: Make sure you type it *exactly* as you did in step 14. You then see the Windows 2000 desktop.

    At this point, you can click Start in the lower-left corner of the screen, and then select Shutdown,

Restart, or any of the other choices that are available in the drop-down list.

Exam Questions

1. Which of the following Windows NT 4 commands is used on the command line to display detailed network configuration information?

   a. ipconfig

   b. ipconfig /all

   c. ifconfig

   d. config

2. Which of the following commands would you use to display the network configuration on a NetWare server?

   a. ifconfig

   b. config

   c. ipconfig

   d. ping

3. Which of the following should you consider when selecting a network operating system? (Choose the three best answers.)

   a. Application support

   b. Technical capabilities

   c. Distribution media

   d. Existing infrastructure

4. You have been instructed to install a Novell NetWare server onto your network. All the other servers are Windows NT 4 systems. You want Windows 98 clients to be able to access both the Windows NT systems and the NetWare server.

APPLY YOUR KNOWLEDGE

Which of the following strategies could you adopt? (Choose the two best answers.)

a. Install the Novell NetWare client for Windows 98 on each workstation.

b. Install Gateway Services for NetWare on the server.

c. Install Gateway Services for NetWare on the clients.

d. Install the Microsoft Network Client, and select NetWare during the installation.

5. What is the name of the Java-based utility that can be used on a NetWare server or on a workstation to manage NDS objects?

a. NetWare Administrator

b. NetWare Console

c. nwadmin

d. ConsoleOne

6. You are troubleshooting a hardware problem on a server, and you use the top command to get detailed hardware information. Which operating system are you running on your server?

a. Novell NetWare

b. Linux

c. Windows 2000

d. Windows Me

7. Which of the following security systems are associated with Windows 2000? (Choose the two best answers.)

a. NTLM

b. Shadow passwords

c. The Bindery

d. Kerberos

8. Which of the following services can be installed on a Windows NT 4 server to enable Windows clients to access the resources on a NetWare server?

a. IPSec

b. NDS

c. CSNW

d. GSNW

9. On a Linux system, which file holds user account information?

a. /etc/users

b. /etc/shadow

c. /etc/passwd

d. /etc/userinfo

10. What is the maximum number of PDCs allowed in a Windows NT domain?

a. 1

b. 10

c. 256

d. Unlimited

11. Which of the following is a common disk-management tool used in a Linux environment?

a. nwconfig

b. partmgr

c. Fdisk

d. Disk Administrator

APPLY YOUR KNOWLEDGE

12. Which of the following file systems are supported by Windows 2000? (Choose the three best answers.)

    a. FAT

    b. FAT32

    c. NTFS

    d. NSS

    e. EXT2

13. Which of the following is a reason not to use Windows 98 in a business environment?

    a. It requires powerful hardware.

    b. It has limited application support.

    c. It does not offer any local security.

    d. It does not have full network connectivity features.

14. You are given the task of installing a DHCP server system on your network. You currently run Windows NT, Windows 2000, Novell NetWare 5, and Linux servers. On which of the server platforms could you implement DHCP server functionality?

    a. Novell NetWare

    b. Linux

    c. Windows NT/2000

    d. Any of the above

15. Which of the following utilities would you use to configure the network settings on a NetWare 5.x server?

    a. `ipconfig`

    b. `config`

    c. `inetcfg`

    d. `ifconfig`

16. Which of the following services would you install on a Windows 2000 system to enable Macintosh clients to use the resources on the server?

    a. Services for Macintosh

    b. MacGW

    c. GSNW

    d. MacGate

17. You are given the task of specifying an operating system for use as a file and print server platform. Security is a priority, as are hardware and application support. Which of the following operating systems are you most likely to consider? (Choose the three best answers.)

    a. Linux

    b. Macintosh

    c. Windows 2000

    d. Windows Me

    e. Novell NetWare

18. Which of the following services is required to make the file and print resources of a Linux server available to Windows clients?

    a. Squid

    b. GSFL

    c. FP4Linux

    d. Samba

APPLY YOUR KNOWLEDGE

19. Which of the following commands can be used to test TCP/IP network connectivity in Windows 2000 Server?

    a. `ping`

    b. `tping`

    c. `ifconfig`

    d. `inetcfg`

20. On a Linux server, which of the following is the preferred file system?

    a. FAT

    b. HPFS

    c. EXT2

    d. NTFS

Answers to Exam Questions

1. **b.** The command `ipconfig /all` is used to show detailed network configuration information. The `ipconfig` command can be used alone, but it shows much less information when it is not used with the `/all` option. `ifconfig` is a utility used on Linux, Unix, and Macintosh systems to view configuration information for network interfaces. The `config` command does the same on a NetWare server. For more information, see the section "Windows 2000," in this chapter.

2. **b.** The `config` command is used to display network configuration information on a NetWare server. `ifconfig` is a utility that is used on Linux, Unix, and Macintosh systems to view configuration information for network interfaces. The `ipconfig` command is used to view network configuration on Windows systems. The `ping` utility

is used to verify network connectivity between two devices. For more information, see the section "NetWare," in this chapter.

3. **a, b, d.** Application support, technical capabilities, and existing infrastructure are all important considerations in choosing a network operating system. The distribution media would not be a concern because all modern network operating systems are available on a variety of media. For more information, see the section "Introduction to Network Operating Systems," in this chapter.

4. **a, b.** To facilitate connection to a NetWare server from Windows clients, you can install the Novell client on each workstation or install Gateway Services for NetWare on the server. In addition, Microsoft supplies a client for NetWare that can be used. GSNW is a server-based service and would not be installed on the client. Answer d is not valid. For more information, see the section "NetWare," in this chapter.

5. **d.** ConsoleOne is the Java-based utility used to manage the NDS. NetWare Administrator is not a Java-based utility, and NetWare Console is a server utility. `nwadmin` is the abbreviated term used to refer to NetWare Administrator. For more information, see the section "NetWare," in this chapter.

6. **b.** The Top utility is used on Linux systems to provide system information. The other operating systems do not provide or accommodate the Top utility. For more information, see the section "Linux," in this chapter.

7. **a, d.** NTLM and Kerberos are security systems that are available on Windows 2000 systems. Shadow passwords are associated with Linux. The Bindery is associated with NetWare versions up

APPLY YOUR KNOWLEDGE

to 4. For more information, see the section "Windows 2000," in this chapter.

8. **d.** GSNW can be installed on the server to allow Windows clients to access a NetWare server. IPSec is a security protocol and does not provide access to a NetWare server. NDS is the directory services system that is provided on NetWare. CSNW is installed on the client to allow it to connect to a NetWare server. For more information, see the section "Operating System Interoperability," in this chapter.

9. **c.** The /etc/passwd file is where user account information is stored on a Linux-based system. The etc/shadow file is used for storing encrypted passwords. The other files are not valid. For more information, see the section "Linux," in this chapter.

10. **a.** Only one PDC can be used on a Windows NT 4 network. Numerous BDCs can be used to provide functionality in case of a PDC failure. The other answers are invalid. For more information, see the section "Windows NT 4," in this chapter.

11. **c.** Fdisk is a commonly used Linux disk-management utility. None of the other utilities are available for Linux. For more information, see the section "Linux," in this chapter.

12. **a, b, c.** Windows 2000 supports the FAT, FAT32, and NTFS file systems. NSS is a file system that is associated with NetWare. EXT2 is a Linux/Unix file system. For more information, see the section "Windows 2000," in this chapter.

13. **c.** Windows 98 does not offer any local security mechanisms and therefore is not suited for many business environments. All the other answers *are* valid reasons to use Windows 98. For more

information, see the section "Client Operating Systems," in this chapter.

14. **d.** All these operating systems support the use of DHCP. For more information, see the sections "Windows 2000," "Linux," and "NetWare" in this chapter.

15. **c.** The inetcfg utility is used on NetWare servers to configure a network. The config utility can be used to view, but not set, the network configuration on a NetWare server. The other answers are not valid NetWare utilities or commands. For more information, see the section "NetWare," in this chapter.

16. **a.** Services for Macintosh needs to be loaded on a Windows server to allow Macintosh clients to access file and print services in a Windows environment. None of the other answers are valid. For more information, see the section "Client Operating Systems," in this chapter.

17. **a, c, e.** When you need security, application, and hardware support, you can use Linux, Windows 2000, and NetWare. Macintosh does provide these services, but there are possible hardware compatibility issues. Windows Me is a workstation operating system, so it is not used as a server operating system. For more information, see the sections " Windows 2000," "Linux," and "NetWare," in this chapter.

18. **d.** Samba is used to provide Windows clients with file and print services from a Linux server. None of the other options are valid. For more information, see the section "Operating System Interoperability," in this chapter.

19. **a.** The ping command is used to test connectivity on a Windows 2000 system. tping is a NetWare-specific utility, as is inetcfg. ifconfig is used on

APPLY YOUR KNOWLEDGE

Unix, Linux, and Macintosh systems to view and configure network interfaces. For more information, see the section "Windows 2000," in this chapter.

20. **c.** The native and most-used file system on Linux is the EXT2 file system. Linux supports FAT, but it is not the file system of choice, and neither is HPFS. Linux does not support NTFS. For more information, see the section "Linux," in this chapter.

Suggested Readings and Resources

1 Habraken, Joe. *Absolute Beginner's Guide to Networking,* third edition. Que Publishing, 2001.

2. Nemeth, Evi, Garth Snyder, Trent Hein. *Linux Administration Handbook.* Prentice Hall, 2002.

3. Williams, G Robert, Mark Walla. *The Ultimate Windows 2000 Systems Administrators Guide.* Addison-Wesley, 2000.

4. Peek, Jerry D, Grace Todino, John Strange. *Learning Unix Operating System.* O'Reilly & Associates, 2002.

5. Ray, John, William C. Ray. *MAC OS X Unleashed.* Sams Publishing, 2001.

6. Windows 2000 information, www.microsoft.com/windows2000/default.asp.

7. Novell NetWare information, www.novell.com/products/netware.

8. Unix information and links, www.unixtools.com.

9. Linux information and links, www.linux.org.

10. Macintosh information, www.mac.com.

11. Computer networking tutorials and advice, compnetworking.about.com.

12. "TechEncyclopedia," www.techencyclopedia.com.

This chapter covers the following CompTIA-specified objectives for the "Network Implementation" section of the Network+ exam:

Identify the purpose and characteristics of fault tolerance.

▶ For a network to be effective as a business tool, it must be available. In the quest for network availability, many technologies are employed so that failure of a specific piece of equipment will not necessarily mean that the network becomes unavailable.

Identify the purpose and characteristics of disaster recovery.

▶ The old saying goes "…when things go wrong, as they usually will…." The need for businesses to ensure the availability of the network and the data on it, no matter what the circumstance, is a key consideration in network planning. A network administrator plays a key role in this strategy.

Identify the main characteristics of VLANs.

▶ VLANs are used in modern networks to create divisions within the networks. Although they are not as widely implemented as some other network technologies, VLANs are deployed in many organizations.

Identify the main characteristics of network attached storage (NAS).

▶ In recent years, the placement of storage on the network has become a driving force in network planning and implementation. One of the most significant technologies associated with this area of the industry is NAS.

CHAPTER 10

Fault Tolerance, Disaster Recovery, VLANs, and NAS

Introduction   386

Understanding Fault Tolerance   386

RAID   388
    RAID 0   389
    RAID 1   390
    RAID 2   392
    RAID 3   393
    RAID 4   393
    RAID 5   393
    RAID 10   395
    Choosing a RAID Level   396
    Hardware and Software RAID   398
Other Fault-Tolerance Measures   398
    Preparing for Faulty Power Supplies   399
    Having Spare Memory   399
    Preventing Processor Failures   399
    Providing Fault Tolerance for NICs   400
    Using Standby Servers   400
    Server Clustering   401
    Using Uninterruptable Power
      Supplies   401

Disaster Recovery   403

Backup Methods   403
    Full Backups   403
    Incremental Backups   404
    Differential Backups   405
A Comparison of Backup Methods   405
Backup Rotation Schedules   406
Backup Best Practices   407

VLANs   408

VLAN Membership   409
    Protocol-Based VLANs   409
    Port-Based VLANs   410
    MAC Address–Based VLANs   410

Network Storage   411

Traditional File Server Storage   411
Network Attached Storage (NAS)   412
SANs   413

Chapter Summary   414

Apply Your Knowledge   416

▶ Read the objectives at the beginning of the chapter.

▶ Study the information in the chapter, paying special attention to the tables, which summarize key information.

▶ Review the objectives again.

▶ Answer the exam questions at the end of the chapter and check your results.

▶ Use the ExamGear test on the CD-ROM that accompanies this book to answer additional exam questions concerning this material.

▶ Review the notes, tips, and exam tips in this chapter. Make sure you understand the information in the exam tips. If you don't understand the topic referenced in an exam tip, refer to the information in the chapter text and then read the exam tip again.

INTRODUCTION

When you come right down to it, the most important responsibility of network administrators is to ensure data availability. When users, customers, or clients need access to network data, it should be ready to go. Many organizations depend on data availability; without it, they could not function.

Two key strategies help ensure data availability: fault tolerance and disaster recovery. In order to fulfill the role of network administrator, is it essential that you have a clear understanding of how to use these strategies.

In addition to fault tolerance and disaster recovery, two additional objectives covered in this chapter have to do with network attached storage (NAS) and virtual local area networks (VLANs). NAS is becoming increasingly popular in modern network environments. It provides a means to offload data storage from server systems and onto dedicated storage devices that are connected directly to the network. VLANs, on the other hand, are used to segment a network for the purposes of organization and security.

It might seem unusual to include VLANs and network storage in a chapter about fault tolerance and disaster recovery because the topics do not appear to be related. However, we need to stick to the CompTIA objectives as closely as possible to make it as easy as possible for you to find exam information. The downside of this approach is that the objectives do not always follow a logical order.

UNDERSTANDING FAULT TOLERANCE

▶ Identify the purpose and characteristics of fault tolerance.

In networking, *fault tolerance* refers to the ability for a device or system to continue operating in the event of a failure. Fault tolerance should not be confused with disaster recovery, which is the ability to respond to and recover from catastrophic events with no loss of data and no loss of data availability.

In practical terms, fault tolerance involves ensuring that when network hardware or software fails, users on the network can still access the data and continue working with little or no disruption of service. Developing a strong fault-tolerant system that ensures continual access to data is not an easy task, and it involves attention to many details. The following sections explore fault tolerance, establishing a fault-tolerant network design, and the impact failure can have on the network.

Today's business world relies heavily on networks and network servers. If these networks and servers were to fail, many businesses would be unable to function. Thus every minute a network is not available costs money. The exact amount of money it costs depends on the size of the organization and can range from a mild economic inconvenience to a crippling financial blow. The potential impact of a network failure often dictates the fault tolerance measures an organization implements.

Unfortunately, no fault-tolerance measures can guarantee 100% availability to network data or services, and fault-tolerance solutions that strive to meet this goal can be very expensive. But the costs associated with any fault-tolerance solution must be compared to the costs of losing access to network services and the reconstruction of network data.

Some hardware components are more likely than others to fail. Implementing a strong fault-tolerance strategy involves identifying the weakest links and employing strategies that can compensate when those weak links fail. Figure 10.1 provides a quick look at the failure rates of server hardware components.

As shown in Figure 10.1, 50% of all server failures can be attributed to hard disks. The hard disk is 50 times more likely to fail than the motherboard and 12 times more likely to fail than memory. It should come as no surprise that when configuring a fault-tolerant system, hard drives receive special attention; after all, they do hold all the data. (Of course, it would be unwise not to consider fault-tolerance measures for other hardware devices as well.) The following sections identify common fault tolerance measures, beginning with the best known: Redundant Array of Inexpensive Disks (RAID).

FIGURE 10.1
Server hardware failure rates.

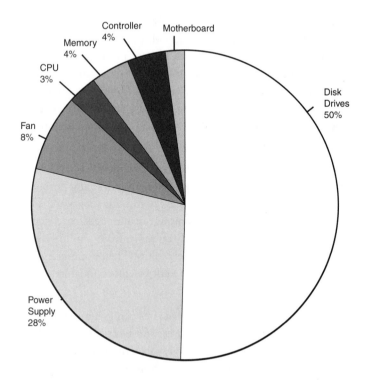

RAID

RAID is a strategy for implementing fault-tolerance solutions that prevent hard disk failure. RAID combines multiple hard disks together in such a way that more than one disk is responsible for holding data. Instead of using a single large disk, information is written to several smaller disks.

Such a design offers two key advantages. First, the failure of one disk does not, in fault-tolerant RAID configurations, compromise the availability of data. Second, reading (and sometimes writing) to multiple smaller disks is simply faster with multiple hard disks than when using one large disk, thus offering a performance boost.

The goals of a RAID solution are clear: Decrease the costs associated with downtime, secure network data, minimize network disruption, and (selfishly) reduce the stress on the network administrator(s). Because a well-designed RAID system can accomplish all these goals, RAID is widely implemented and found in organizations of all sizes.

Several RAID strategies are available, and each has advantages and disadvantages. It is important to know what you are protecting and why before you implement any RAID solution; the particular RAID strategy used will depend on many factors, including associated costs, the server's role, and the level of fault tolerance required. The following sections discuss the characteristics of the various RAID strategies.

RAID 0

Although it is classified as a RAID level, RAID 0 is in fact not fault tolerant. As such, RAID 0 is not recommended for servers that maintain mission-critical data. RAID 0 works by writing to multiple hard drives simultaneously, allowing for faster data throughput. RAID 0 offers a significant performance increase over a single disk—but, as with a single disk, all data is lost if any disk in the RAID set fails. With RAID 0 you actually increase your chances of losing data compared to using a single disk because RAID 0 uses multiple hard disks, creating multiple failure points. Essentially, the more disks you use in the RAID 0 array, the more at risk the data is. A minimum of two disks is required to implement a RAID 0 solution.

RAID 0 writes data to the disks in the array by using a system called *striping*. Striping works by partitioning the hard disks into stripes and writing the data across the stripes, as shown in Figure 10.2. This strategy is also used by RAID 2, RAID 3, RAID 4, and RAID 5.

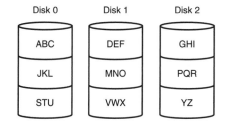

FIGURE 10.2
RAID 0 with disk striping.

Advantages of RAID 0

Despite the fact that it is not fault tolerant, RAID 0 is well suited for some environments. The following are some of the advantages of RAID 0:

◆ **Ease of implementation**—RAID 0 offers easy setup and configuration.

◆ **Good input/output (I/O) performance**—RAID 0 offers a significant increase in performance over a single disk and other RAID solutions by spreading data across multiple disks.

◆ **Minimal hardware requirements**—RAID 0 can be implemented with as few as two hard drives, making it a cost-effective solution for some network environments.

Disadvantages of RAID 0

You cannot have the good without the bad. For a number of reasons, a RAID 0 solution may not be appropriate:

◆ **No fault tolerance**—Employing a RAID solution that does not offer data protection is a major drawback. This factor alone limits a RAID 0 solution to only a few network environments.

◆ **Increased failure points**—A RAID 0 solution has as many failure points as there are hard drives. For instance, if your RAID 0 configuration has five disks and any one of those drives fails, the data on all drives will be lost.

◆ **Limited application**—Because of the lack of fault tolerance, a RAID 0 solution is practical for few applications. Quite simply, it's limited to environments where the performance of I/O outweighs the importance of data availability.

Despite its drawbacks, you might encounter RAID 0.

Recovering from a Failed RAID 0 Array

Anyone relying on a RAID 0 configuration to hold sensitive data is bold. The bottom line is, there is no way to recover from a failed RAID 0 array, short of restoring the data from backups. Both the server and the services it provides to the network are unavailable while you rebuild the drives and the data.

RAID 1

RAID 1 is a fault-tolerant configuration known as *disk mirroring*. A RAID 1 solution uses two physical disk drives. Whenever a file is saved to the hard disk, a copy of the file is automatically written to the second disk. The second disk is always an exact mirrored copy of the first one. Figure 10.3 illustrates a RAID 1 array.

RAID 1 writes the same data to the hard drives simultaneously. The benefits of having a duplicate copy of all saved data are clear, and on the surface, RAID 1 may seem like a very fault-tolerant solution. However, it has a couple drawbacks. First, RAID 1 has very high overhead because an entire disk must be used to provide the mirrored copy. Second, a RAID 1 solution is limited to two hard drives, which limits the available storage capacity.

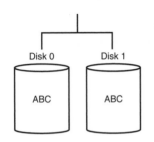

FIGURE 10.3
A RAID 1 array.

Another RAID strategy that falls under the category of RAID 1 is disk duplexing. *Disk duplexing* is a mirrored solution that incorporates a second level of fault tolerance by using a separate hard disk controller for each hard drive. Putting the hard disks on separate controllers eliminates the controller as a single point of failure. The likelihood of a failed disk controller is not nearly as high as the likelihood of a failed hard disk, but the more failure points covered, the better. Figure 10.4 shows a disk duplexing configuration.

Advantages of RAID 1

Although it is far from perfect, RAID 1 is widely implemented in many different network environments. The following are a few of the advantages of RAID 1:

◆ **Fault tolerance**—RAID 1 is a fault-tolerance solution that maintains a mirrored image of data on a second hard drive in case of failure. Disk duplexing adds extra fault tolerance by using dual hard drive controllers.

◆ **Reduced cost**—RAID 1 provides fault tolerance by using only two hard disks, thereby providing a cost-effective method of implementing a fault-tolerance solution.

◆ **Ease of implementation**—Implementing a RAID 1 solution is not difficult; it can be set up quite easily. The procedures and methods for implementing the hardware and software are well documented.

Disadvantages of RAID 1

Several factors exclude RAID 1 from being used in many network environments. The following are some of the disadvantages associated with RAID 1:

◆ **Limited disk capacity**—Because RAID 1 uses only two hard disks, limited disk space is available for use. Even if you purchased two 80GB drives, your network would have only 80GB of storage space. The applications and data storage needs of many of today's businesses would exceed this limitation quickly.

◆ **High disk space overhead**—RAID 1 has 50% overhead— that is, half of the hard disk space needs to be used for RAID. So for every megabyte used for other purposes, another is needed for RAID.

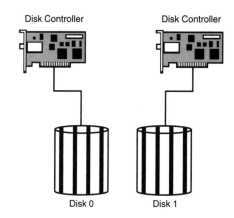

FIGURE 10.4
A disk duplexing configuration.

NOTE

Sizing the Mirror   Because mirroring involves making a duplicate copy of the data, the volumes used on each disk are the same size. If you set up the mirrored environment with a 500MB volume and a 700MB volume, the result will be only a 500MB volume. The system will use the lowest common amount of free space to construct the mirrored volume.

◆ **Limited hot-swap support**—Because RAID 1 is often implemented through software rather than hardware, RAID 1 configurations often don't support the ability to hot swap drives, meaning that you might have to shut down the server to replace a damaged hard disk. In some environments, powering down a server is a major consideration that is avoided at all costs. In such environments, a software RAID 1 solution is not practical.

Although disk mirroring is a reliable fault-tolerance method, it provides for only a single disk failure.

Recovering from a Failed RAID 1 Array

RAID 1 can handle the failure of a single drive; if one fails, a complete copy of the data exists on an alternate hard drive. Recovering from a failed RAID 1 array typically involves breaking the mirror set, replacing the failed drive with a working one, and reestablishing the mirror. The data will be automatically rebuilt on the new drive.

The recovery process may cause network disruption while a new hard drive is installed. The server can continue to function with a single drive, but there is no fault tolerance until the RAID 1 array is rebuilt.

It is possible—however unlikely—for multiple drives to fail, and RAID 1 cannot handle such a situation.

RAID 2

A few RAID levels have fallen into obscurity, and it is unlikely that you will see them in modern network environments. RAID 2 falls into this category. RAID 2 is described here to provide a complete look at the RAID picture.

RAID 2 is a fault-tolerant RAID level that writes error-correction data across several disks and uses this code to re-create data in case of failure. RAID 2 offered an error-detection method that used *hamming code*. Hamming code was designed to be used with drives with no built-in error detection. SCSI hard disks today all have built-in error-detection, making this feature useless. RAID 2 no longer has any real-world practical applications.

RAID 3

RAID 3 is another obsolete RAID level. RAID 3 stripes data across several hard disks, like RAID 0 does, but it also uses an additional disk for parity information. If a hard drive fails, the separate parity disk can be used to re-create the missing data, and business can continue without disruption to network service. Using a dedicated disk as a parity disk puts undue stress on a single disk because the parity information is constantly being written to the disk. The increased workload placed on a single disk can slow performance and cause the disk to fail more quickly than the other disks in the array.

RAID 4

RAID 4, like RAID 3, stripes information across all hard drives and uses a single dedicated disk for parity information. The main difference between the two is that RAID 4 uses *block-level striping*. However, due to the use of a single parity disk, RAID 4 suffers from the same shortcomings as RAID 3, and you are unlikely to encounter it today.

RAID 5

RAID 5 is the preferred hard disk fault-tolerance strategy for most environments; it is trusted to protect the most sensitive data. RAID 5 stripes the data across all the hard drives in the array.

Instead of reserving a single disk for parity information as RAID 3 and 4 do, RAID 5 spreads parity information across all the disks in the array. Known as *distributed parity*, this approach allows the server to continue to function in the event of disk failure. The system can calculate the information that is missing from the failed drive by using the parity information on the disks. A minimum of three hard drives is required to implement RAID 5, but more drives are recommended, up to 32. When calculating how many drives you will be using in a RAID 5 array, remember that the parity distributed across the drives is equivalent to one disk. Thus if you have four 10GB hard disks, you will have 30GB of storage space.

You can expect to work with and maintain a RAID 5 array in your network travels. Figure 10.5 shows a RAID 5 array.

> **NOTE**
>
> **Long Shots**   The chances of encountering RAID levels 2, 3, and 4 in a modern network environment are similar to the odds of being struck by lightning and winning the lottery on the same day.

> **NOTE**
>
> **Drive Failures**   The key advantage of RAID 5 is that a single drive can fail and the server can continue operation.

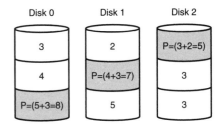

FIGURE 10.5
A RAID 5 array.

Advantages of RAID 5

There are several reasons RAID 5 has become a widely implemented fault-tolerance strategy. The following are some of the key advantages of RAID 5:

◆ **Minimal network disruption**—When a hard disk crashes in a RAID 5 array, the rest of the drives will continue to function with no disruption in data availability. Network users can keep working, and costs associated with network downtime are minimized. Although there is no disruption to data access, the performance of the system decreases until the drive has been replaced.

◆ **Performance**—Because RAID 5 can access several drives simultaneously, the read performance over that of a single disk is greatly improved. Increased performance is not necessarily a reason to use a fault-tolerant solution, but it is an added bonus.

◆ **Distributed parity**—By writing parity over several disks, RAID 5 avoids the bottleneck of writing parity to a single disk, which occurs with RAID 3 and 4.

Disadvantages of RAID 5

The disadvantages of RAID 5 are few, and the benefits certainly outweigh the costs. The following are the disadvantages of RAID 5:

◆ **Poor write performance**—Because parity is distributed across several disks, multiple writes must be performed for every write operation The severity of this performance lag will depend on the application being used, but its impact is minimal enough to make it a factor in only a few environments.

◆ **Regeneration time**—When a hard disk is replaced in a RAID 5 array, the data must be regenerated on it. This process is typically performed automatically and demands extensive system resources. However, this factor is unlikely to become a concern.

◆ **Data limitations**—RAID 5 that is implemented using software (such as Windows NT) is unable to include the system or boot partitions in the stripe set, so you must use an alternative method to secure the system and boot partitions. For example, some organizations use RAID 5 for data and a mirrored set to provide fault tolerance for the system and boot partitions. This limitation does not include hardware RAID 5 solutions, which can stripe the system and boot partitions.

Recovering from a RAID 5 Array Failure

RAID 5 ensures data availability even in the event of failed hard disks. A RAID 5 system will still be able to service requests from clients in the event of a failure, by using the parity information from the other disks to identify the data that is now missing because it was on the failed drive.

At some point, you must replace the failed hard disks to rebuild the array. Some systems let you remove the failed hard drive (that is, they are hot swappable) and insert the new one without powering down the server. The new hard disk is configured automatically as part of the existing RAID 5 array, and the rebuilding of data on the new drive occurs automatically. Other systems may require you to power down the server to replace the drive. You must then manually perform the rebuild. Because RAID 5 continues to run after a disk failure, you can schedule a time to replace the damaged drive and minimize the impact on network users.

IN THE FIELD

HOT SWAP VERSUS HOT SPARE

Two strategies are commonly associated with minimizing data disruption with RAID: hot swappable drives and hot spare drives. A hot spare drive sits unused in a RAID array, waiting to be called into action. For instance, if a hard disk fails in a RAID 5 array, the hot spare is already installed and ready to take over.

Hot swapping, on the other hand, refers to the ability to replace a device such as a hard disk without having to power down the system. Hot swapping is not reserved for hard disks; many other types of server and workstation hardware support hot swapping.

RAID 10

In some server environments, it makes sense to combine RAID levels. One such strategy is RAID 10, which combines RAID 1 and RAID 0. RAID 10 requires four hard disks—two for the data striping and two to provide a mirrored copy of the striped pair.

NOTE

Implementing RAID 10 There are various ways of implementing RAID 10, depending on how many drives you have available and what the system configuration is.

What's in a Name?   RAID 10 has many names. It's sometimes referred to as RAID 1/0, RAID 0/1, or RAID 1+0.

RAID 10 combines the performance benefits of RAID 0 with the fault-tolerant capability of RAID 1, without requiring the parity calculations. However, RAID 10 also combines the limitations of RAID 0 and RAID 1. Mirroring the drives somewhat reduces the performance capabilities of RAID 0, and the 50% overhead of a RAID 1 solution is still in effect. Even with these limitations, RAID 10 is well suited for many environments, and you might find yourself working with or implementing such a solution. Figure 10.6 shows a possible configuration for a RAID 10 solution.

FIGURE 10.6
A RAID 10 solution.

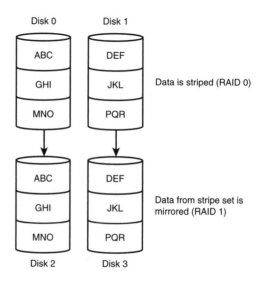

Choosing a RAID Level

Deciding whether to use a fault-tolerant solution on a network is the first and most obvious step for you to take when you design a network. The next, less simple, decision is which RAID level to implement. Your first inclination might be to choose the best possible RAID solution, but your budget might dictate otherwise. You should consider the following when choosing a specific RAID level:

◆ **Data protection and availability**—First and foremost, you must consider the effect of downtime on the organization. If minutes will cost the organization millions, you need a very strong fault-tolerant solution. On the other hand, if you are able to go offline for an hour or more and suffer nothing more than an inconvenience, a costly RAID solution might be overkill. Before choosing a RAID solution, be sure what impact data unavailability will have on you and your network.

◆ **Cost**—We would all like the best RAID solution, but high-end RAID solutions are out of the price range of many organizations. You are left to choose the best solution for the price.

◆ **Capacity**—Some organizations' data needs are measured in megabytes, and others organizations' needs are measured in gigabytes. Before choosing a RAID solution, you need to know the volume of data. RAID 1, for instance, provides far less space than RAID 5.

◆ **Performance**—Speed is an important consideration. With some of the RAID solutions the network suffers a performance hit, whereas with others performance can be increased over the performance using a single disk. Choosing the correct RAID solution might involve understanding the performance capabilities of each of the different RAID levels.

Table 10.1 summarizes the main characteristics of the various RAID levels.

TABLE 10.1
RAID CHARACTERISTICS

RAID Level	Description	Key Features Required	Minimum Disks
RAID 0	Disk striping	No fault tolerance; improved I/O performance	2
RAID 1	Disk mirroring	Provides fault tolerance but at 50% disk overhead; can also be used with separate disk controllers, a strategy known as disk duplexing	2 (2 is also the maximum number of disks used for RAID 1.)
RAID 2	Disk striping with hamming code	Limited use	3
RAID 3	Disk striping with single-parity disk	Limited use	3
RAID 4	Disk striping with single-parity disk	Limited use	3
RAID 5	Disk striping with distributed parity	Widely used RAID solution; uses distributed parity	3
RAID 10	Striping with mirrored volumes	Increased performance withperformance with striping and offers mirrored fault tolerance	4

Hardware and Software RAID

After you've decided to implement a RAID solution, you must also decide whether to use a software or hardware RAID solution. The decision is not easy, and your budget might again be the deciding factor.

Software RAID is managed by the network operating system or third-party software and as such requires server resources to operate. As a result, the overhead associated with software RAID can affect the performance of the server by taking resource time away from other applications. Some variations of RAID require more from the server than others; for example, RAID 1 is commonly implemented using software RAID because it requires less overhead than RAID 5.

Software RAID has one definite advantage: It's inexpensive. For instance, Linux and Windows NT/2000 have RAID capability built in, allowing RAID to be implemented at no extra cost, apart from the costs associated with buying multiple disks. These operating systems typically offer support for RAID levels 0, 1, and 5.

Hardware RAID is the way to go if your budget allows. Hardware RAID uses its own specialized controller, which takes the RAID processing requirements away from the server. The server's resources can thus focus on other applications. Hardware RAID also provides the ability to use cache memory on the RAID controller, further adding to its performance capabilities over software RAID.

> **NOTE**
>
> **Arrays and Volumes**   When discussing RAID, you'll often encounter the terms *array* and *volume*. An *array* is a group of disks that are part of a single RAID configuration. For instance, you would say, "There are two disks in a RAID 1 array." A *volume* is a logical disk space within an array. Typically, a volume only refers to data storage and capacity.

Other Fault-Tolerance Measures

Although hard drives represent the single largest failure point in a network, they are not the only failure points. Even the most costly RAID solution cannot save you from a faulty power supply or memory module. To fully address data availability, you must consider all hardware. This section provides a brief overview of some of the other common fault-tolerance measures you can take to further ensure data availability:

◆ Preparing for faulty power supplies

◆ Having spare memory

◆ Preventing processor failures

◆ Providing fault tolerance for network interface cards (NICs)

◆ Using standby servers

◆ Server clustering

◆ Using uninterruptable power supplies (UPSs)

Preparing for Faulty Power Supplies

If you work with servers or workstations, you know that from time to time a power supply will fail. When it fails in a workstation, you simply power down the system and replace the power supply. On a server, where downtime is often measured in dollars and cents, powering down to replace a faulty power supply can be a major issue.

You can prepare for a faulty power supply by using redundant, hot-swappable power supplies. As you might expect, such a strategy has associated costs that must be weighed against the importance of continual access to data.

Having Spare Memory

After memory is installed and confirmed to be working, it generally works for a long time. Sometimes, however, memory is at the root of server problems. Unfortunately, no fault-tolerance strategies will cope with failed memory; there is no hot swapping of memory, so you have to power down the server during the repair. The best you can do is minimize the impact of the failure.

Some environments have spare memory available at all times in case of failure. When memory does fail, a spare is ready to go. Such planning requires considerable forethought, but when you need such a solution, the preparation pays off.

Preventing Processor Failures

Processors are hardy, and processor failure is extremely uncommon. In fact, processor failure is so unusual that few organizations include processors in their fault-tolerance designs. Environments that consider processors may have a spare or, more likely, a standby server (discussed later in this chapter).

Some multiprocessor machines have a built-in safeguard against a single processor failure. In such a machine, the working processor maintains the server while a replacement for the nonfunctioning processor is found.

Providing Fault Tolerance for NICs

A faulty NIC can disable access to data quickly because a failed NIC effectively isolates the server. Several strategies are used to provide fault tolerance for NICs. Many systems employ a hot spare in the system that can be put to work as soon as the primary NIC fails.

Another strategy, called *adapter teaming*, uses multiple NICs configured to act as a single unit. Adapter teaming is a relatively new technology and as such is not widely implemented, but it's expected to become increasingly popular. In addition to providing fault tolerance, adapter teaming can increase bandwidth capability and let you manage network traffic more effectively.

Using Standby Servers

In addition to instituting fault-tolerance measures for individual components, many larger organizations use server fault-tolerance measures. In this scenario, if one server fails, a second is fully configured and waiting to take over. The second server is sometimes located in a separate building, in case of fire or flood damage to the location where the first server is kept.

A second strategy used for complete server fault tolerance is *server failover*. A server failover configuration has two servers wired together, with one acting as the primary server and the other acting as the secondary server. The systems synchronize data between them, ensuring that they are always current with each other. If the secondary server detects that the primary is offline, it switches to failover mode and becomes the primary server for the network. The whole procedure is transparent to the network user, and very little downtime, if any, is experienced.

As you might imagine, the costs associated with having a redundant server are very high. For this reason, few organizations use the failover and hot-spare server measures.

NOTE

Warm Swaps Some systems support *warm swaps*. Warm swapping involves powering down an individual bus slot to change a NIC. Doing so prevents you from having to power down the entire system to replace an NIC.

Server Clustering

Continuing our journey into incredibly expensive fault-tolerance strategies, we come to server clustering. For companies that cannot afford even a second of downtime, the costs of server clustering are easily justified.

Server clustering involves grouping several computers into one logical unit. This strategy can, depending on the configuration, provide fault tolerance as well as increased performance and load balancing. Because the servers within the cluster are in constant contact with each other, they are able to detect and compensate for a failing server system. A well-configured server cluster will provide failover without any disruption to network users.

The advantages of clustering are obvious. Clustering affords the highest possible availability of data and network services. Clusters are the foundational configuration for the "five nines" level of service—that's 99.999% uptime, which translates to less than 10 minutes of downtime in a year.

The fundamental downside to server clustering is its cost. Clustering requires a separate network to be constructed between the servers, installation and configuration of additional software, additional hardware, and additional administrative support.

Using Uninterruptable Power Supplies

No discussion of fault tolerance can be complete without a look at power-related issues and the mechanisms used to combat them. When you're designing a fault-tolerant system, your planning should definitely include UPSs. A UPS serves many different functions and is a major part of server consideration and implementation.

On a basic level, a UPS is a box that holds a battery and a built-in charging circuit. During times of good power, the battery is recharged; when the UPS is needed, it's ready to provide power to the server. Most often, the UPS is required to provide enough power to give the administrator time to shut down the server in an orderly fashion, preventing any potential data loss from a dirty shutdown.

NOTE

Overloading UPSs One mistake often made by administrators is the overloading of UPSs. UPSs are designed for server systems, and connecting monitors, printers, or other peripheral devices to them reduces their effectiveness.

Why Use a UPS?

Organizations of all shapes and sizes need UPSs as part of their fault-tolerance strategies. A UPS is as important as any other fault-tolerance measure. Three key reasons make a UPS necessary:

◆ **Data availability**—The goal of any fault-tolerance measure is data availability. A UPS ensures access to the server in the event of a power failure—or at least as long as it takes to save your file.

◆ **Data loss**—Fluctuations in power or a sudden power down can damage the data on the server system. In addition, many servers take full advantage of caching, and a sudden loss of power could cause the loss of all information held in cache.

◆ **Hardware damage**—Constant power fluctuations or sudden power downs can damage hardware components within a computer. Damaged hardware can lead to reduced data availability while the hardware is being repaired.

Power Threats

In addition to keeping a server functioning long enough to safely shut it down, a UPS also safeguards a server from inconsistent power. This inconsistent power can take many forms. A UPS protects a system from the following power-related threats:

◆ **Blackout**—A totalfailure of the power supplied to the server.

◆ **Spike**—A spike is a very short (usually less than a second) but very intense increase in voltage. Spikes can do irreparable damage to any kind of equipment, especially computers.

◆ **Surge**—Compared to a spike, a surge is a considerably longer (sometimes many seconds) but usually less intense increase in power. Surges can also damage your computer equipment.

◆ **Sag**—A sag is a short-term voltage drop (the opposite of a spike). This type of voltage drop can cause a server to reboot.

◆ **Brownout**—A brownout is a drop in power supply that usually lasts more than a few minutes.

Many of these power-related threats can occur without your knowledge; if you don't have a UPS, you cannot prepare for them. For a few hundred dollars, it is worth buying a UPS, if for no other reason than to sleep better at night.

DISASTER RECOVERY

▶ Identify the purpose and characteristics of disaster recovery.

Besides implementing fault-tolerance measures in a network you need to consider disaster recovery—the things to do when your carefully implemented fault-tolerance measures fail. Disaster recovery and fault tolerance are two separate entities, and both are equally important. *Disaster recovery* is defined as measures that allow a network to return to a working state.

Backups and backup strategies are key components of disaster recovery. The following sections identify the various backup strategies that are commonly used and why these strategies are such an important part of a network administrator's role.

Backup Methods

You can choose from several backup methods. You shouldn't select one at random; you should choose carefully, to match the needs of your organization.

The backup method you choose will most likely be affected by the amount of time you have available. Many organizations have a time window in which backup procedures must be conducted. Outside that window, the backup procedure can impede the functioning of the network by slowing down the server and the network. Organizations with large amounts of data require more time for a backup than those with small amounts of data. Although both small and large organizations require full backups, the strategy each uses will be different. With that in mind, let's look at the various backup methods, which include full backups, incremental backups, and differential backups.

EXAM TIP

Tape Cleaning Tips   When backing up to tape, you must periodically clean the tape drive with a cleaning cartridge. If your system is unable to access a tape, you should first try another tape. If that doesn't work, you should use a cleaning tape. Remember these tips for the exam!

Full Backups

If you have time, a full backup is usually the best type of backup. A full backup copies all the files on the hard disk. In case of disaster, the files from a single backup set can be used to restore the entire system.

Despite the advantages of full backups, they are not always a practical solution. Depending on the amount of data that needs to be backed up, the procedure can take a long time. Many administrators try to run full backups in the off hours, to reduce the impact on the network. Today, many networks do not have off hours, making it difficult to find time to squeeze in full backups.

Full backups are often used as the sole backup method in smaller organizations that have only a few gigabytes of data. Larger organizations that utilize hundreds of gigabytes of data storage are unlikely to rely on full backups as their sole backup strategy.

IN THE FIELD

BACKUPS AND SECURITY

Having your entire hard drive stored on a single tape has obvious advantages but also some not-so-obvious disadvantages, including security concerns. A tape holding all your sensitive data can be restored by you or by anyone who has access to the tape. There are well-documented cases of stolen tapes and the resulting stolen data. When you make any backups, you're responsible for storing the tapes in a secure location.

Incremental Backups

An incremental backup is much faster than a full backup because only the files that have changed since the last full or incremental backup are included in it. For example, if you do a full backup on Tuesday and an incremental on Thursday, only the files that have changed since Tuesday will be backed up. Because an incremental backup copies less data than a full backup, backup times are significantly reduced.

On the other hand, incremental backups take longer to restore than full backups. When you are restoring from an incremental backup, you need the last full backup tape and each incremental tape done since the last full backup. In addition, these tapes must be restored in order. Suppose you do a full backup on Friday and incremental backups on Monday, Tuesday, and Wednesday. If the server fails on Thursday, you will need four tapes: Friday's full backup and the three incremental backups.

Differential Backups

Many people confuse differential backups and incremental backups, but they are very different from one another. Whereas an incremental backup backs up everything from the last full or incremental backup, a differential backup backs up only the files that have been created or changed since the last full backup.

When restoring from a differential backup, you need only two tapes: the latest full backup and the latest differential. Depending on how dynamic the data is, the differential backup could still take some time. Essentially, differential backups provide the middle ground between incremental and full backups.

EXAM TIP

What to Use in a Backup Cycle In a backup cycle, incremental backups and a differential backup must be combined with a full backup to get a complete copy of the data on a drive.

EXAM TIP

Understand the Backup Types For the Network+ exam, be sure you understand what is involved in backing up and restoring data for all the backup types (for example, how many tapes are used and in what order they must be restored).

REVIEW BREAK

A Comparison of Backup Methods

The backup software determines what data has changed since the last full backup, by checking a setting known as the *archive bit*. When a file is created, moved, or changed, the archive bit is set to indicate that the changed file must be backed up.

Full backups do not concern themselves with the archive bit because all data is backed up. However, a full backup resets the archive bit after the files have been copied to the tape. Differential backups use the archive bit but do not clear it because the information is needed for the next differential backup. Incremental backups clear the archive bit so that unnecessary files aren't backed up. Table 10.2 summarizes the characteristics of the different backup methods.

EXAM TIP

Clearing the Archive Bit On the Network+ exam it is likely that you will be asked to identify what backup methods clear the archive bit from a changed or created file.

TABLE 10.2
COMPARISON OF BACKUP METHODS

Method	What Is Backed Up	Restore Procedure	Archive Bit
Full	All data	All data is restored from a single tape.	Does not use the archive bit but clears it after files have been copied to tape

continues

TABLE 10.2   *continued*
COMPARISON OF BACKUP METHODS

Method	What Is Backed Up	Restore Procedure	Archive Bit
Incremental	All data changed since the last full or incremental backup	The restore procedure requires several tapes: the latest full backup and all incremental tapes since the last full backup.	Uses the archive bit and clears it after a file is saved to disk
Differential	All data changed since the last full backup	The restore procedure requires the latest full backup tape and the latest differential backup tape.	Uses the archive bit but does not clear it

Backup Rotation Schedules

You can use a backup rotation schedule in conjunction with a backup method. Organizations use many different rotations, but most are variations on a single popular rotation strategy: the Grandfather-Father-Son (GFS) rotation.

GFS is the most widely used rotation method. It uses separate tapes for monthly, weekly, and daily backups. A common GFS strategy requires 12 tapes. Four tapes are used for daily backups, Monday through Thursday; these are the son tapes. Five tapes are used for weekly backups, perhaps each Friday; these are the father tapes. Finally, three tapes are used for a monthly rotation; these are the grandfather tapes.

Using the GFS rotation, you can retrieve lost information from the previous day, previous week, and several previous months. Adding tapes to the monthly rotation lets you go back even further to retrieve data. Of course, the further back you go, the less current (and perhaps less usable) the information is. More tapes also make the rotation more complex.

Many organizations don't follow the GFS strategy by the book; instead, they create their own backup regimes. Regardless of the backup strategy used, a well-designed backup rotation is an integral part of system administration and should follow guidelines that allow for several retrieval points.

Backup Best Practices

When you're designing a backup strategy, you should consider some general best practices. These best practices ensure that when you need it, the backup you are depending on will be available:

◆ **Test your backups**—After a backup is completed, you have no idea whether the backup was successful and whether you will be able to retrieve needed data from it. Learning this information when your system has crashed is too late. To make sure the backups work, it is important to periodically restore them.

◆ **Confirm the backup logs**—Most backup software generates log files after a backup procedure. After a backup is completed, you should read the backup logs to look for any documented errors that may have occurred during the backup procedure. Keep in mind that reading the backup-generated logs is no substitute for occasionally testing a restore. A completely unsuccessful backup might generate no documented errors.

◆ **Label the backup cartridges**—When you use many tapes in a rotation, you should label the cartridges to prevent reusing a tape and recording over something you need. The label should include the date of the backup and whether it was a full, incremental, or differential backup.

◆ **Rotate backups offsite**—Keeping all the tape backups in the server room or elsewhere in the same location as the server can be a problem. If the server location is damaged (by fire or flood, for example), you could lose all the data on the server as well as all your backups. You should use an off-site tape rotation scheme to store current copies of backups in a secure off-site location.

◆ **Use new tapes**—Over time, tape cartridges can wear out and become unreliable. To combat this problem, you should periodically introduce new tapes into the tape rotation and destroy the old tapes.

◆ **Password-protect the backups**—As an added measure of security, it is a good idea to password-protect your backups. That way, if they fall into the wrong hands, they are protected by a password.

EXAM TIP

Write Protection   Tape cartridges often use a write protection tab similar to the ones found on 3.5-inch floppy disks. It is a good idea to write-protect a tape cartridge after a backup so it will not be overwritten accidentally.

Designing an effective backup strategy is one of the most important considerations for a network administrator, and therefore, it is an important topic area for the Network+ exam. Remember that the preservation of data is a foremost consideration when approaching network management.

VLANs

▶ Identify the main characteristics of VLANs.

The word *virtual* is used a lot in the computing world—perhaps too often. In the case of VLANs, the word *virtual* does little to help explain the technology. Perhaps a more descriptive name for the VLAN concept might have been "segmented LAN."

VLANs involve network segmentation, a strategy that significantly increases the performance capability of the network and removes potential performance bottlenecks. A VLAN is a group of computers that are connected together and act as if they are on their own network segments, even though they might not be. For instance, suppose you work in a three-story building in which the advertising employees are spread over all three floors. A VLAN can let all the advertising personnel use the network resources as if they were connected on the same segment. This virtual segment can be isolated from other network segments. In effect, it would appear to the advertising group that they were on a network by themselves.

VLANs offer some clear advantages. Being able to create logical segmentation of a network gives administrators flexibility beyond the restrictions of the physical network design and cable infrastructure. VLANs allow for easier administration because the network can be divided into well-organized sections. Further, you can increase security by isolating certain network segments from others. For instance, you can segment the marketing personnel from finance or the administrators from the students. VLANs can ease the burden on overworked routers and reduce broadcast storms. Table 10.3 summarizes the benefits of VLANs.

EXAM TIP

802.1q   802.1q is the Institute of Electrical and Electronics Engineers (IEEE) specification developed to ensure interoperability of VLAN technologies from the various vendors.

EXAM TIP

VLANs   VLANs allow you to create multiple broadcast domains on a single switch. In essence, this is the same as creating separate networks for each VLAN.

TABLE 10.3

BENEFITS OF VLANS

Advantage	Description
Increased security	By creating logical (virtual) boundaries, network segments can be isolated.
Increased performance	By reducing broadcast traffic throughout the network, VLANs free up bandwidth.
Organization	Network users and resources that are linked and communicate frequently can be grouped together in a VLAN.
Simplified administration	With a VLAN the network administrator's job is easier when moving users between LAN segments, recabling, addressing new stations, and reconfiguring hubs and routers.

VLAN Membership

You can use several methods to determine VLAN membership or how devices are assigned to a specific VLAN. The following sections describe the common methods of determining how VLAN membership is assigned.

Protocol-Based VLANs

With protocol-based VLAN membership, computers are assigned to VLANs by using the protocol that is in use and the Layer 3 address. For example, this method allows an Internetwork Packet Exchange (IPX) network or a particular Internet Protocol (IP) subnet to have its own VLAN.

It is important to note that although VLAN membership may be based on Layer 3 information, this has nothing to do with routing or routing functions. The IP numbers are used only to determine the membership in a particular VLAN—not to determine routing.

Port-Based VLANs

Port-based VLANs require that specific ports on a network switch be assigned to a VLAN. For example, ports 1 through 8 may be assigned to marketing, ports 9 through 18 may be assigned to sales, and so on. Using this method, a switch determines VLAN membership by taking note of the port used by a particular packet. Figure 10.7 shows how the ports on a server could be used for port-based VLAN membership.

FIGURE 10.7
Port-based VLAN membership.

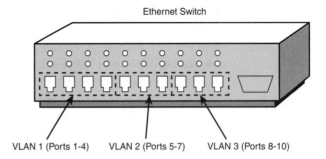

Ethernet Switch

VLAN 1 (Ports 1-4)   VLAN 2 (Ports 5-7)   VLAN 3 (Ports 8-10)

MAC Address–Based VLANs

As you may have guessed, the Media Access Control (MAC) address type of VLAN assigns membership according to the MAC address of the workstation. To do this, the switch must keep track of the MAC addresses that belong to each VLAN. The advantage of this method is that a workstation computer can be moved anywhere in an office without needing to be reconfigured; because the MAC address does not change, the workstation remains a member of a particular VLAN. Table 10.4 provides an example of the membership of a MAC address–based VLAN.

TABLE 10.4

MAC ADDRESS–BASED VLANS

MAC Address	VLAN	Description
44-45-53-54-00-00	1	Sales
44-45-53-54-13-12	2	Marketing
44-45-53-54-D3-01	3	Administration
44-45-53-54-F5-17	1	Sales

Although the acceptance and implementation of VLANs has been slow, the ability to logically segment a LAN provides a new level of administrative flexibility, organization, and security.

NETWORK STORAGE

▶ Identify the main characteristics of network attached storage (NAS).

Data storage and retrieval are fundamental services that networks are required to provide. A network can provide this functionality many different ways; the one you choose will depend on many factors, including the organization's budget and data storage needs. This section explores some of the different data storage choices, including traditional file server storage, NAS, and storage area networks (SANs).

EXAM TIP

File Servers and SANs Although only NAS devices are included in the CompTIA objectives, this chapter includes information on file servers and SANs, to give you a better idea of where NASs fit into the storage picture.

Traditional File Server Storage

Perhaps the most widely used type of network data storage involves using an existing server to store data. This approach is commonly used by small organizations that can't afford a more costly solution or that don't have a volume of data large enough to warrant a more advanced and costly solution.

A traditional file server typically uses a full-featured network operating system and may or may not be dedicated as a file server. In many network environments, the server provides numerous network services, including print services, authentication, and even proxy or firewall service.

You will probably be working with traditional file servers, as these are prevalent in almost every company. Figure 10.8 shows a traditional file server solution.

FIGURE 10.8
A traditional network file server.

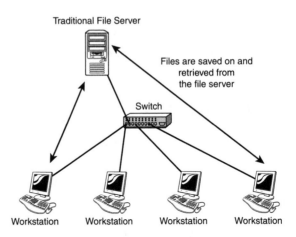

Traditional File Server

Files are saved on and
retrieved from
the file server

Switch

Workstation   Workstation   Workstation   Workstation

Network Attached Storage (NAS)

As the storage needs of organizations of all sizes increase, new technologies must be developed to accommodate those needs. One strategy for increased storage needs is NAS. Essentially, NAS is a specialized file server that is designed specifically and used exclusively as a file server.

NAS is a box that typically has no mouse, keyboard, or monitor, and that has a very streamlined operating system. Several hard disks and perhaps a tape drive hold the network files. Additional hard drives can be added to the NAS to increase storage capacity. Clients typically access a NAS over an Ethernet connection; each NAS box is seen as a node on the network and requires an IP address.

Because NAS systems are not attached to a server, they must be able to communicate on the network by using an application protocol designed for file access. Most commonly, the Network File System (NFS) protocol or Server Message Block (SMB) protocol is supported by NAS devices for this purpose.

Because NAS is dedicated to data storage, it's a more costly solution than providing data storage from an existing server. However, the advantages of NAS over the traditional file server are compelling. First, NAS can provide higher data availability; as a dedicated device, the NAS is less likely than a traditional file server to be brought down or to crash, disabling file access. Second, a NAS system is more secure and less susceptible to security attacks than a traditional file server. Third, and somewhat subjectively, a NAS system offers easy administration. Figure 10.9 shows an example of a NAS.

> **EXAM TIP**
>
> **File System Access Protocols**   For the Network+ exam, you should be prepared to identify the file system access protocols (sometimes referred to as *application protocols*) that are commonly supported by NAS devices.

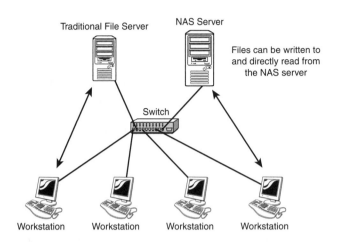

FIGURE 10.9
A NAS system.

SANs

A SAN is a redundant network that utilizes servers and various storage devices, allowing all data to be stored and accessed very quickly. However, whenever the word *redundant* is used with networks, you know you are facing a costly solution.

Users typically access a SAN by using a fast interconnection technology called fiber channel. Thanks to fiber channel, a SAN can support transfer rates of up to 1Gbps. A SAN consists of servers that share and store data on RAID arrays or tape drives. All the devices are connected via fiber channel and offer very high-speed data transfer.

Creating a SAN can be as simple as adding a few new servers and storage devices to an existing network, using fiber channel adapters. As the SAN grows, you can add fiber channel hubs and switches for more efficient utilization. Because all the servers and storage devices have alternate paths to each other, a server failure does not make data unavailable. The data is distributed across all the servers and is not server-centric.

SANs are relatively new; as of this writing, many aspects of the technology do not have standards. SANs are an excellent way to handle large amounts of data, but buyers should beware. It is generally accepted that the best way to implement a SAN is to hire a SAN vendor and purchase a turnkey solution. Interoperability problems exist between SANs, and each has unique peculiarities.

Currently, the single biggest disadvantage of SANs is currently their cost. Successful SAN implementation tends to be expensive and involves many people as well.

As the amount and utilization of stored data increases, other technologies must assuredly surface to allow us to continue to maintain and protect data. SANs are likely to be an influence in major storage situations, especially as standards begin to be developed for this technology.

CHAPTER SUMMARY

KEY TERMS

- fault tolerance
- RAID
- RAID 0
- disk mirroring
- disk striping with parity
- RAID 10
- power supply
- memory
- processor
- NIC
- standby server
- server clustering
- UPS
- blackout
- spike
- surge

This chapter explores two important networking concepts: fault tolerance and disaster recovery. Although many people think fault tolerance and disaster recovery are one and the same, they are in fact very different, but equally important, concepts.

Fault tolerance usually refers to the measures network administrators use to ensure that data and network services are always available to network users. A strong fault-tolerance strategy does not happen by accident; rather, you must consider many factors when choosing the best fault-tolerance strategies for a specific organization.

Because availability is such a huge issue and server downtime is so costly, most of the hardware components within a server need to be considered as part of a fault-tolerance solution. Hard drives typically receive the most attention because they're 50% more likely to fail than any other component. The mechanism used to protect against such failures is RAID.

Several RAID levels are available today. The most common are RAID levels 0, 1, and 5. Although RAID 0 is a RAID level, it does not offer any fault tolerance, but it does offer performance improvements over using a single disk. RAID 1 uses disk mirroring to establish fault tolerance but suffers from 50% overhead and limited storage capacity. The RAID level of choice for organizations that can afford it is RAID 5. RAID 5 stripes data and parity information over several disks. The parity information can be used to re-create data in the event that a hard drive in the array fails.

CHAPTER SUMMARY

Other fault-tolerance measures include using UPSs, redundant components, and sometimes redundant servers.

Disaster recovery involves having in place measures that can be used when the system goes down. To protect data from disaster, you need backups. Three key types of backups are available: full, incremental, and differential. A full backup makes a copy of all data, an incremental backup makes a copy of the data that has changed since the last full backup or the latest incremental backup, and a differential backup saves everything that has changed since the last full backup.

In addition to backup methods, a backup rotation strategy ensures that data is sufficiently recoverable. The most common backup rotation strategy is the GFS rotation. This type of rotation requires numerous tapes for daily, weekly, and monthly backups.

In some networks, VLANs are used to segment a LAN into logical segments. This segmentation allows for increased organization and security for the logical LANs. Although VLANs have been slow to catch on, many people feel they will soon be common in large organizations.

As the volume of data used in modern networks continues to increase, better data storage technologies have been developed. Two of these strategies are NAS and SANs. A SAN solution is very costly and therefore limited to large organizations that have the money and resources to support such a strategy.

KEY TERMS

- sag
- brownout
- disaster recovery
- full backup
- incremental backup
- differential backup
- archive bit
- backup rotation
- GFS
- VLAN
- protocol-based VLAN
- port-based VLAN
- MAC address–based VLAN
- network storage
- traditional file server
- NAS
- SAN
- fiber channel

APPLY YOUR KNOWLEDGE

Exercise

10.1   Performing a Full Backup

You have recently been employed as the network administrator for a large pharmaceutical company. On your first day of work, you notice that no backup has been performed for more than six months. You immediately decide to perform a full backup and schedule backups to occur at regular intervals.

You use Windows 2000 Server's Backup Wizard utility to back up a few data files and automate the process to reoccur automatically based on a schedule you construct.

Estimated time: 20 minutes

1. Select Start, Programs, Accessories, System Tools, Backup. The Backup [Untitled] screen appears.

2. Select the Schedule Jobs tab and click the Add Job button. The Backup Wizard screen appears.

3. Click Next on the Backup Wizard screen.

4. Choose Back Up Selected Files, Drives, or Network Data and click Next.

5. Select the data you would like to back up. The window contains a directory of files similar to Windows Explorer, with one added twist: A check box appears next to each directory item. Click the box to select an item to be backed up. Note that if you click on a folder, you will back up everything from that point in the directory down.

6. Choose one or two folders that contain a few files. Click Next.

7. Choose the media type to which you want to save your data. In this project, you'll save your

backup to disk, so choose the File in the Backup Media Type drop-down box.

8. If the directory you want to use doesn't exist, you can create it by clicking the Browse button and navigating to where you want to put the backup file you are about to create. (Click the New Folder icon in the browse window.)

9. Specify the type of backup you want to perform. Choose Normal and click Next.

10. Select Verify Data After Backup if you want the operating system to check to make sure the backup has been made. Click Next.

> **Test Recoveries**   You should continue to perform test recoveries to be sure you can restore your data.
>
> *— NOTE*

11. Choose whether you want to add this backup to the end of any previous backups or if you want to replace an old backup with this new one. For this project, choose Replace the Data on the Media with This Backup. Click Next.

12. The next window lets you assign Backup Label and Media Label names. Leave the defaults in place and click Next. A Set Account Information dialog box might appear. Windows 2000 allows you to run the job under another account name/password if you would like. If you get this choice, enter your administrator account username and password. (The password will be whatever you established when you installed Windows 2000 Server or whatever you changed it to.)

13. The When to Backup screen appears. Give the backup job you are creating the name BackupTest and click Set Schedule.

APPLY YOUR KNOWLEDGE

14. The Schedule Job screen appears, and you can schedule when you want the backup job to occur. Set whatever schedule you would like and click OK. You return to the When to Backup Screen; click Next.

15. On the Completing the Backup Wizard screen, click Finish to create the job. The backup utility creates the job, and the folders/files you selected will be backed up according to the schedule you selected.

16. You can view the status of the backup job or make changes to it by using the Task Scheduler. To use the Task Scheduler, choose Start, Settings, Control Panel. When the Control Panel opens, double-click the Scheduled Tasks icon. You should see the backup job you just created. You can double-click it to edit the job.

Exam Questions

1. What is the minimum number of disks required for a RAID 5 array?

    a. 2

    b. 5

    c. 1 physical and 1 logical

    d. 3

2. What RAID level uses disk mirroring to provide fault tolerance?

    a. RAID 1

    b. RAID 0

    c. RAID 5

    d. RAID 2

3. Which of the following backup methods require the archive bit to be cleared? (Choose the two best answers.)

    a. Full

    b. Incremental

    c. Differential

    d. Mirror image

4. As network administrator, you have been asked to implement a backup and restore method that requires only a total of two tape sets. Which of the following backup pairs would you use?

    a. Full, incremental

    b. Differential, incremental

    c. Full, differential

    d. This cannot be done.

5. Which of the following are valid ways to assign computers to a VLAN? (Choose the three best answers.)

    a. Protocol assignment

    b. Port-based assignment

    c. NetBIOS computer name

    d. MAC address

6. How many hard disks are required to establish a RAID 1 solution?

    a. 8

    b. 4

    c. 6

    d. 2

APPLY YOUR KNOWLEDGE

7. You are the network administrator for a company that operates from 7 a.m. to 9 p.m. Monday through Friday. Your boss requires that a backup be performed nightly but does not want the backup to interfere with network operations. Full backups have been started at 9:30 p.m. and have taken until 8 a.m. to complete. What strategy would you suggest to correct the backup issue?

   a. Weekly full backups, incremental backups on Mondays, and differential backups every other weekday

   b. Full backup performed on the weekend and incremental backups performed on weekdays

   c. Differential backups performed on weekends and a full backup every other weekday evening

   d. Weekly full backups combined with weekend differential backups

8. Which of the following power-related problems is associated with a short-term voltage drop?

   a. Surge

   b. Brownout

   c. Sag

   d. Spike

9. Which of the following fault-tolerant RAID levels offers the best read and write performance?

   a. RAID 0

   b. RAID 1

   c. RAID 5

   d. RAID 10

10. Which of the following are fault-tolerance measures associated with network adapters? (Choose the two best answers.)

    a. Warm swapping

    b. Adapter teaming

    c. Packet fragment recovery

    d. Secondary I/O recovery

11. Which of the following devices cannot be implemented in a fault-tolerant configuration?

    a. Power supply

    b. Processor

    c. NIC

    d. Memory

12. What is the storage capacity of a RAID 1 array that uses two 40GB hard disks?

    a. 80GB

    b. 40GB minus the parity calculation

    c. 40GB

    d. 80GB minus the parity calculation

13. Which of the following are valid reasons to use a UPS? (Choose the three best answers.)

    a. Data availability

    b. To prevent damage to hardware

    c. Increased network speeds

    d. To prevent damage to data

14. How many tapes are typically used in a GFS tape rotation?

    a. 14

    b. 13

APPLY YOUR KNOWLEDGE

c. 12

d. 11

15. As a network administrator, you have been asked to implement a RAID solution that offers high performance. Fault tolerance is not a concern. Which RAID level are you likely to use?

  a. RAID 0

  b. RAID 1

  c. RAID 2

  d. RAID 5

  e. RAID 10

16. What is the best way to verify that your backup procedures are working?

  a. Check the system logs

  b. Perform periodic test restores

  c. Introduce new cartridges into the tape rotation

  d. Use the verify option when backing up data

17. What file system access protocols are commonly supported by a NAS device?

  a. FAT

  b. NFS

  c. SMB

  d. NTFS

18. Which of the following uses redundant hard disk controllers?

  a. Disk duplexing

  b. RAID 0

  c. Disk duplication

  d. RAID 5

19. You have installed five 15GB hard disks for your server in a RAID 5 array. How much storage space will be available for data?

  a. 75GB

  b. 60GB

  c. 30GB

  d. 45GB

20. While digging through an old storage closet, you find two 10GB hard disks. What RAID levels could you implement with them? (Choose the two best answers.)

  a. RAID 5

  b. RAID 0

  c. RAID 10

  d. RAID 1

Answers to Exam Questions

1. **d.** At least three hard disks are required in a RAID 5 array. None of the other answers are valid. For more information, see the section "Understanding Fault Tolerance," in this chapter.

2. **a.** Disk mirroring is defined by RAID 1. Raid 0 is disk striping, which offers no fault tolerance. RAID 5 is disk striping with parity. RAID 2 is not a commonly implemented RAID level. For more information, see the section "Understanding Fault Tolerance," in this chapter.

3. **a, b.** The archive bit is reset in both a full backup and an incremental backup. Differential backups do not change the status of the archive bit. Mirror image is not an accepted backup type.

APPLY YOUR KNOWLEDGE

For more information, see the section "Disaster Recovery," in this chapter.

4. **c.** A full backup combined with a differential backup will require only two tapes to do a complete restore, assuming that each backup set fits on a single tape. Full and incremental backups might need more than two tapes. Differential and incremental backups must be combined with a full backup to be effective. Answer d is not valid. For more information, see the section "Disaster Recovery," in this chapter.

5. **a, b, d.** VLANs can be created by using protocol assignments, by defining the ports on a device as belonging to a VLAN, or by using MAC addresses. VLANs cannot be created by using the NetBIOS computer name. For more information, see the section "VLANs," in this chapter.

6. **d.** Two disks are required to create a RAID 1 array. All the other answers are invalid. For more information, see the section "Understanding Fault Tolerance," in this chapter.

7. **b.** By making a full backup on the weekend and incremental backups during the week, you should be able to complete the backups without interfering with the normal working hours of the company. All the other answers are invalid. For more information, see the section "Disaster Recovery," in this chapter.

8. **c.** A sag is a short-term voltage drop. A brownout is also a voltage drop, but it lasts longer than a sag. A surge is an increase in power that lasts a few seconds. A spike is a power increase that lasts a few milliseconds. For more information, see the section "Understanding Fault Tolerance," in this chapter.

9. **d.** RAID 10 offers the performance advantages of RAID 0 and the fault-tolerance capabilities of RAID 1. RAID 0 is not a fault-tolerant solution. RAID 1 and RAID 5 offer fault tolerance but do not increase performance. For more information, see the section "Understanding Fault Tolerance," in this chapter.

10. **a, b.** In server systems, warm swapping allows network adapters to be swapped out without the server being powered off. Adapter teaming allows multiple NICs to be logically grouped together. If one of the NICs fails, then the other NICs in the group can continue to provide network connectivity. Adapters in a team can also be grouped together to increase the available bandwidth. Answers c and d are not valid answers. For more information, see the section "Understanding Fault Tolerance," in this chapter.

11. **d.** There is no accepted fault-tolerance strategy for coping with a failed memory module. All the other hardware components listed can be implemented in a fault-tolerant configuration. For more information, see the section "Understanding Fault Tolerance," in this chapter.

12. **c.** A RAID 1 array requires an amount of disk space equivalent to that of the mirrored drive. Therefore, in a RAID 1 array of 80GB, only 40GB will be available for data storage. None of the other answers are valid. For more information, see the section "Understanding Fault Tolerance," in this chapter.

13. **a, b, d.** UPSs can prevent damage to hardware and damage to data caused by fluctuations in the power supply. They can also promote the availability of data by keeping a server running in the event of a power outage. A UPS does not increase

APPLY YOUR KNOWLEDGE

the speed of the network. For more information, see the section "Understanding Fault Tolerance," in this chapter.

14. **c.** The standard GFS rotation uses 12 tapes. None of the other answers are valid. For more information, see the section "Disaster Recovery," in this chapter.

15. **a.** RAID 0 offers the highest level of performance but does not offer any fault tolerance. If the performance of RAID 0 is required along with fault tolerance, RAID 10 is a better choice. RAID 1 offers fault tolerance but no increase in performance. For more information, see the section "Understanding Fault Tolerance," in this chapter.

16. **b.** Performing periodic test restores is the only way to be absolutely sure that your backup and restore procedures and systems are working correctly. All the other options are best practices, but doing a test restore is the only way to be sure that the backups are working. For more information, see the section "Disaster Recovery," in this chapter.

17. **b, c.** NAS devices typically support NFS and SMB file system access protocols. NTFS and FAT are file systems, not file system access protocols.

For more information, see the section "NAS," in this chapter.

18. **a.** Disk duplexing is an implementation of RAID 1 (disk mirroring) that places each of the drives on a separate controller. None of the other answers are valid. For more information, see the section "Understanding Fault Tolerance," in this chapter.

19. **b.** In a RAID 5 configuration, a space equivalent to one whole drive is used for the storage of parity information. In this question, this requirement equates to 15GB. Therefore, in a 75GB RAID 5 array, 60GB is available for data storage. None of the other answers are valid. For more information, see the section "Understanding Fault Tolerance," in this chapter.

20. **b, d.** Both RAID 0 and RAID 1 use two disks. The difference between the two implementations is that RAID 1 offers fault tolerance through disk mirroring, whereas RAID 0 stripes the data across the drives but does not offer any fault tolerance. RAID 5 requires at least three disks, and RAID 10 requires at least four disks if the entire hard disk is to be used. For more information, see the section "Understanding Fault Tolerance," in this chapter.

Suggested Readings and Resources

1. Toigo, Jon William. *Disaster Recovery Planning: Preparing for the Unthinkable,* third edition. Prentice Hall, 2002.

2. Overview of disaster recovery procedures, www.labmice.net/disaster.htm.

3. Disaster recovery information for Windows 2000, www.microsoft.com/windows2000/library/operations/fileandprint/recovery.asp.

4. General disaster recovery information, www.tekcentral.com/teknetwork/disaster_recovery.

This chapter covers the following CompTIA-specified objectives for the "Network Implementation" and "Network Support" sections of the Network+ exam.

Given a remote connectivity scenario (IP, IPX, dial-up, PPPoE, authentication, physical connectivity, etc.) configure the connection.

▶ Configuring remote connectivity is a common task for a network administrator. Although many of the technologies used for configuring remote connectivity are the same as those used to configure connectivity on a LAN, some technologies are specific to remote connectivity.

Given a network configuration, select the appropriate NIC and network configuration settings (DHCP, DNS, WINS, protocols, NetBIOS/hostname, etc.)

▶ The ability to install and configure network connectivity is one of the most fundamental skills a network administrator must master. To do this effectively requires an understanding of the software and hardware configurations involved.

CHAPTER 11

Configuring Network Connectivity

Given specific parameters, configure a client to connect to the following servers:

- **Unix/Linux**
- **NetWare**
- **Windows**
- **Macintosh**

▶ Each network operating system requires client systems to be configured differently. Many environments now use multiple network operating systems, which brings an extra level of complexity to client configuration.

Given a scenario, predict the impact of modifying, adding, or removing network services (e.g., DHCP, DNS, WINS, etc.) on network resources and users.

▶ Understanding the effect that adding or removing a service will have on the network and its users is an important skill for a network administrator.

Introduction   **426**

Configuring Remote Connectivity   **426**

    Physical Connections   427
    Protocols   428
    Software   429
    Dial-up Access   430
       Dial-up Connection Troubleshooting   431
    Security   432

Selecting an NIC and Network Configuration Settings   **432**

    Choosing an NIC   433
    Installing an NIC   433
    Connecting the PC to the Network   435
    Testing and Troubleshooting the NIC   436
    Configuring the NIC Settings   437
       Configuring Client Systems for
         TCP/IP   439
       Configuring DNS Server Information   441
       Configuring WINS Server Information   441
    Using DHCP   442

Outline

Configuring Clients to Access Servers   **443**

  Configuring Microsoft Windows Clients   443
    Client for Microsoft Networks on
      Windows 95/98/Me   444
    Client for Microsoft Networks on a
      Windows NT/2000 System   444
    Novell Client Software   444
  Unix/Linux Client Software   446

**Adding, Modifying, or Removing
Network Services**   **446**

  Adding, Modifying, or Removing DHCP   447
    DHCP Traffic   447
  Adding, Modifying, or Removing WINS   448
  Adding, Modifying, or Removing DNS   449

Chapter Summary   **450**

Apply Your Knowledge   **451**

Study Strategies

▶ Read the objectives at the beginning of the chapter.

▶ Review the objectives again.

▶ Answer the exam questions at the end of the chapter and check your results.

▶ Use the ExamGear test on the CD-ROM that accompanies this book to answer additional exam questions concerning this material.

▶ Review the notes, tips, and exam tips in this chapter. Make sure you understand the information in the exam tips. If you don't understand the topic referenced in an exam tip, refer to the information in the chapter text and then read the exam tip again.

INTRODUCTION

Configuring network connectivity—whether on a remote network connection or with systems on a local area network (LAN)—is one of the daily responsibilities of a network administrator. Configuring network connectivity encompasses many different skills, including working with protocols, system hardware, and a variety of network services.

All the major client operating systems, including Linux, Macintosh, and Windows, handle the configuration of network connectivity very differently. Those who are proficient in establishing network connectivity from a Windows platform, for instance, are in for a surprise if they try to do the same from a Linux command line. Although the means to configure connectivity information might be different from one platform to another, the information required is often the same. This means that although the configuration of Dynamic Host Configuration Protocol (DHCP) client connectivity in Linux is done with a text file and Windows might use a graphical interface dialog box, the information that must be provided is much the same in each instance.

This chapter focuses on the network settings required for network connectivity across all platforms. It starts with a look at the protocols and procedures required to configure remote network connectivity.

CONFIGURING REMOTE CONNECTIVITY

▶ Given a remote connectivity scenario (IP, IPX, dial-up, PPPoE, authentication, physical connectivity, etc.) configure the connection.

The capability to remotely access networks has become an important part of the modern IT infrastructure. All organizations, from the smallest business to the largest corporation, are taking advantage of the potential that remote network access provides. Therefore, today's network administrators are as likely to be responsible for managing remote network access as they are for LAN access. Configuring and managing remote access requires knowledge of the protocols and procedures involved in establishing a remote connection.

The following sections explore some of the common considerations in configuring a remote connection, including a discussion of physical connections, protocols (which facilitate the connection), software (which establishes the connection), the dial-up connection method, and security.

For information on remote access protocols, refer to Chapter 8, "Remote Access and Security Protocols." For more information on troubleshooting remote access, refer to Chapter 13, "Troubleshooting Connectivity."

> **NOTE**
>
> **Remote Access** The focus of this section is remote access—that is, the use of a remote system to dial in to a private network. This is important because in certain cases, even though the Internet might be used as a means to access a private network, it is not required.

Physical Connections

There are many ways to connect to a remote network. Some, such as the plain old telephone system (POTS), offer a direct connection between you and the remote host. Others, such as cable and Digital Subscriber Lines (DSL), allow you to connect, but the connection occurs over a public network (the Internet), which can bring additional considerations such as authentication and security problems. The methods that can be used to establish a remote connection are discussed in detail in Chapter 8. For that reason, only a brief recap is included in this section:

◆ **Public switched telephone network (PSTN)**—The PSTN offers by far the most popular method of remote connectivity. A modem and a POTS line allow for inexpensive and reliable, if not fast, remote access.

◆ **Integrated Services Digital Network (ISDN)**—ISDN is a dial-up technology that works much like the PSTN, but instead of using analog signals to carry the data, ISDN uses digital signals. This makes it faster than the PSTN.

◆ **Cable**—In an effort to take advantage of the increasing demand for high-speed Internet access, cable TV providers now offer broadband Internet access over the same connection that is used to carry cable TV signals.

◆ **DSL**—DSL services are the telecom companies' broadband offering. *x*DSL (that is, the family of DSL services) comes in many different varieties, and as with cable, you need a special modem in order to use it.

◆ **Satellite**—Perhaps the least popular of the connection methods discussed here, satellite provides wireless Internet access, although in some scenarios a PSTN connection is also required for upstream access. Of the technologies discussed in this section, satellite is the least suitable for remote access.

Protocols

When you have decided on the physical aspect of the connection, the next consideration is the protocols that allow you to make a connection to the remote server.

To facilitate a connection between a remote system and a remote access server, common protocols must be used between the systems. Two types of protocols are required to establish a remote connection. You first need to have the protocols that communicate at the data-link layer, including the following:

◆ **Point-to-Point Protocol (PPP)**—PPP is actually a family of protocols that work together to provide connection services. PPP allows remote clients and servers to negotiate authentication between devices. PPP can employ a variety of encryption methods to secure transmissions.

◆ **Serial Line Internet Protocol (SLIP)**—SLIP is an older connection protocol than PPP, and it was originally designed to allow data to be transmitted via Transmission Control Protocol/Internet Protocol (TCP/IP) over serial connections in a Unix environment. Unfortunately, SLIP does not support encryption or authentication and therefore has largely fallen out of favor. If you have users that use SLIP to connect from remote systems, you should move them to PPP connections as soon as possible.

◆ **Point-to-Point Protocol over Ethernet (PPPoE)**—PPPoE is a method of using PPP connections over Ethernet. Using PPPoE and a broadband connection such as xDSL or cable Internet access, it is possible for individual users to have authenticated access to high-speed data networks, which provides an efficient way to create a separate connection to a remote server for each user. This strategy allows Internet access and billing on a per-user basis rather than a per-site basis.

Users accessing PPPoE connections require the same information as required with standard dial-up phone accounts, including a username and password combination. As with a dial-up PPP service, an Internet service provider (ISP) will most likely automatically assign configuration information such as the IP address, subnet mask, default gateway, and DNS server information.

After a data link has been established the as connection between the devices, other network-layer and transport-layer protocols are required to facilitate signal transmission. Examples of these protocols include the following:

◆ **TCP/IP**—TCP/IP is the most widely used protocol today, and it is the protocol that is most commonly used to configure remote connectivity. As with access for systems on a LAN, remote access requires unique TCP/IP addressing. The most common way for remote clients to get IP information from the remote server is through automatic assignment from a DHCP server. However, it is possible to manually assign IP addresses from a static pool of addresses that have been assigned to the remote access server by the network administrator.

◆ **Internetwork Packet Exchange/Sequenced Packet Exchange (IPX/SPX)**—Like TCP/IP, IPX/SPX is a fully routable protocol, and it can therefore be used for connecting to a remote system. However, just as TCP/IP is replacing IPX/SPX on LANs, it is also replacing IPX/SPX on remote access links.

Generally speaking, TCP/IP is the protocol suite to use for remote access. However, popular remote access solutions such as Microsoft Remote Access Service (RAS) can accommodate connections established using IPX/SPX, so you should be aware of the fact that IPX/SPX can be used.

> **NOTE**
> **Using PPPoE** How do you know if your ISP is using PPPoE? If you have xDSL or cable, you can just open your browser and be online. With PPPoE, authentication is required before you can access the Internet.

Software

With the physical connection and the protocols in place, you are almost ready to establish a connection. You just need some software to make the magic happen.

FIGURE 11.1
The Connect To screen on a Windows client system.

FIGURE 11.2
Routing and Remote Access configuration screen.

To establish a remote connection, the remote system typically requires software that initiates contact with the remote server. This software can take many forms: In some Windows client systems, for example, a remote connection can be configured by using Dial-Up Networking. Figure 11.1 shows the Connect To screen on a Windows Me system.

In addition to the client-side software that initiates the remote connection, server-side software that is responsible for answering the request is required. The server responding to the remote access requests is referred to as the *remote access server*. On Windows server platforms, the network service responsible for handling remote client connections is RAS. Figure 11.2 shows the Routing and Remote Access Service dialog box on a Windows 2000 system. (The steps required to install RAS are described in Chapter 8.)

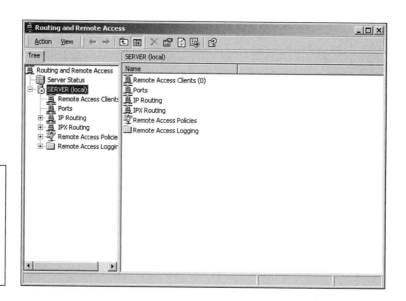

Dial-up Access

As noted previously, dial-up is one of the most popular methods of gaining remote access to a LAN. There was a time when dial-up referred to using a modem on a POTS line, but today the term is applied generally to any connection that must be manually established to a remote system. For example, the establishment of a virtual private network (VPN) connection to a remote system over a cable Internet connection would be considered a dial-up connection.

The specifics of configuring dial-up access to a remote server depend on the client system being used. Linux, Macintosh, and the various Windows client systems all have different methods and means of connecting to a remote server via a dial-up connection. Instead of individually documenting the procedures for configuring each of the respective client systems, the following list identifies the configuration information and hardware required by all client systems to access a remote server using a dial-up connection:

◆ **Hardware**—In order to access the remote server, the client system has to have the correct hardware installed to make the connection. Most dial-up remote connections require a modem on the client and a modem on the server system.

◆ **Phone number, hostname, or IP address**—To connect to a remote access server over a dial-up connection, you need to have the phone number of the remote server, the IP address, or the hostname.

◆ **Transmission protocols**—You need to choose the compatible protocol used by the remote server—NetBIOS Extended User Interface (NetBEUI), TCP/IP, or IPX/SPX. If the server is using TCP/IP, you might need to configure the IP configuration information manually, or this information might be assigned through a remote DHCP server.

◆ **Security**—On the client system, you might need to establish security information so it can be authenticated by the server. The security information includes a username-and-password combination that will be verified by the remote server, as well as data encryption options.

◆ **Client connection options**—On the client side, you can configure connection options such as redialing or disconnecting after a certain amount of time.

Dial-up Connection Troubleshooting

It would be nice if every time you dialed in to a remote server, it answered, and you were authenticated to the network. Although this usually happens most of the time, there are times when you just can't connect. If you are unable to establish the remote connection through dial-up, consider the following:

◆ **Verify that the remote access server is operational**—You might be trying to log on to a remote server that is down. This might require a call to the remote network administrator to confirm.

◆ **Verify that you have correct authentication information**—To access the remote access server, you need a valid user account for the remote network and permissions to access the server.

◆ **Confirm that you are calling the correct number or trying to connect to the correct server**—Frequently, the cause of a problem can be traced to something simple. In the case of remote connectivity, this can often be using the wrong phone number or IP address for the remote server.

◆ **Verify local settings**—In order to connect to the remote server, the client system needs to be correctly configured to access the server. These configuration settings include protocol information and compatible security settings.

Security

In today's world, it is necessary to establish security measures for remote network connections. In the same way users on local network systems must be authenticated to use network services and resources, remote clients must also be authenticated. The intention of remote authentication is to ensure that only users who have permission to access the remote network can access it. Most remote authentication requires at least a username and password combination, similar to that required for local network connections. More sophisticated systems use token generators or special authentication devices.

SELECTING AN NIC AND NETWORK CONFIGURATION SETTINGS

▶ Given a network configuration, select the appropriate NIC and network configuration settings (DHCP, DNS, WINS, protocols, NetBIOS/hostname, etc.).

Part of the role of the network administrator is to install and configure network interface cards (NICs) in client and server systems. Today, this is a fairly simple process, although you need to consider many factors. We'll start with perhaps the most basic of considerations—how to choose an NIC.

Choosing an NIC

The choice of what NIC to use depends on certain criteria, including the following:

◆ **Bus compatibility**—Some older systems have only Industry Standard Architecture (ISA) slots, but most modern systems have either Peripheral Component Interconnect (PCI) slots or both PCI and ISA slots. Either way, you should verify that there is an expansion slot of the correct type available.

◆ **Type of network**—As mentioned in the discussion on NICs in Chapter 3, "Networking Components and Devices," unless you are using a networking system other than Ethernet, you should not need to specify another type of NIC.

◆ **Media compatibility**—As mentioned in Chapter 3, NICs can come with one, two, or even three types of network connectors.

Besides these criteria, which dictate to a certain extent which cards you can use, the choice then depends on manufacturer, cost, and requirements. The NIC might come preinstalled in the system or, as in an increasing number of cases, the network interface might be built on to the system board. In either of these situations, you do not have to install an NIC.

Installing an NIC

The physical installation of an NIC is similar to the installation of any other system expansion card. To install an NIC, you must insert it into an available expansion slot on the system board. The NIC must be pressed firmly into the expansion slot and then screwed into place. Figure 11.3 shows the physical installation of an NIC.

FIGURE 11.3
The physical installation of an NIC.

After the NIC has been physically installed into the computer system, it has to be configured to use the appropriate system resources. Specifically, an NIC requires a unique input/output (I/O) address and a unique interrupt request (IRQ) address. If either the I/O address or the IRQ address is the same as that of another device in the system, one or both of the devices will probably fail to work.

Windows client systems and the latest Windows server systems support plug and play, which automatically assigns system resources to expansion cards such as NICs. In non–plug-and-play Windows platforms and other operating systems, that do not support plug-and-play, the system resources are configured manually.

Regardless of the kind of NIC being used, you need driver software to make the NIC work properly with the chosen operating system. Installing driver software normally involves downloading the latest software from the manufacturer's Web site. Although the NIC might be supplied with a driver disk or the operating system might have a driver for the NIC, neither are likely to contain the latest driver, so downloading from the Web is almost certainly the best method of obtaining the driver.

Connecting the PC to the Network

With the NIC installed and functioning, the next step is to connect the PC to the network. This can be a simple process or a complicated process, depending on the type of network you are using. The following are some of the factors you should consider when connecting a new system to an existing network:

◆ **Connecting to a coaxial network**—The biggest consideration when connecting to a coaxial network is that it might be necessary to break the coaxial segment to insert a British Naval Connector (BNC) T-connector to physically connect the PC. Recall from Chapter 1, "Introduction to Networking," that breaking a coaxial cable segment prevents any device connected to it from working. So if you are adding a computer to a coaxial segment and you need to add a length of cable and a connector, you need to either arrange with network users for a few minutes when the network will be unavailable or add the cable and connector before or after working hours. The good news is that you can leave spare BNC T-connectors in the coaxial cable segment as a just-in-case precaution. Doing so can mean that you can add a system to the coaxial segment without affecting users other than the one whose system you are connecting.

◆ **Connecting to a twisted-pair network**—Twisted-pair is the easiest of all the network types to connect to. All you need to connect is a cable (referred to as a *patch cable*) that connects the system to a hub or switch. In environments that use a structured cable system, the cable can be connected to a wall jack or a jack in a floor box. In a less structured environment, the cable can be run directly between the system and the hub or switch. One item worthy of note is that if you are using a Token Ring network, you must configure the NIC to work at the correct speed. Twisted-pair Ethernet networks can accommodate different speeds, if the networking hardware supports a speed higher than the base 10Mbps. Token Ring networks do not offer this function; all devices on the ring must operate at the same speed (4Mbps or 16Mbps). Connecting a system to the network with an NIC configured for the wrong speed prevents the system from communicating on the network, and it might even cause problems with other devices on the segment.

After the physical connection to the network has been established, you need to consider which other parameters need to be set. In the case of twisted-pair Ethernet networks, these parameters can include the following:

◆ **Speed of the network**—Unlike coaxial networks that operate at 10Mbps, twisted-pair networks can run at speeds of 10Mbps, 100Mbps, or even 1Gbps. Most NICs are able to automatically sense the speed of the network to which they are connected, although it is normally possible to configure the speed manually.

◆ **Duplex settings**—Recall from Chapter 3 that one of the advantages of Ethernet switches is that they allow you to use full-duplex links between the switch and the client computer. Full-duplex links allow the system and the switch to "talk" in both directions at the same time. Most modern NICs are able to automatically detect whether a full-duplex link is available and then use it. If you are using a switched network and have NICs that are able to support full-duplex links, you should make sure that this feature is being utilized.

Testing and Troubleshooting the NIC

With the NIC installed and the PC connected to the network, the next step is to test whether the NIC is functioning correctly and whether the link to the network is established.

With today's plug-and-play environment and software configurable NICs that have a range of autodetection features, testing whether the NIC is operating should be a matter of routine. You might not even have to test the NIC specifically, but just configure the NIC through the operating system and connect to the network. If all is working correctly, you should be able to connect, and by doing so prove that everything is working as it should be.

However, there is always a possibility that the installation of the NIC might have some problems. Understanding how to fix such problems is an important network administration skill.

Before considering troubleshooting the NIC at a protocol level, you should ensure that the NIC is installed and operating correctly.

There are a couple ways to do this:

◆ **Use the tools in the operating system**—Most operating systems include utilities that report the status of hardware devices installed in the system. For example, on a Windows system, the Device Manager reports the status of an installed NIC. Figure 11.4 shows an example of the General tab of the Properties dialog box for a network adapter on a Windows 2000 system.

◆ **Use a diagnostic tool**—Many NIC manufacturers provide utilities that help you test to make sure the NIC is operating correctly. The same utilities are often used to configure the NIC, as well. Figure 11.5 shows the Diagnostics tab in one such utility—the Intel PROSet utility.

Depending on the results of the tests, you might need to further troubleshoot the installation of the NIC. If you are using a manufacturer-supplied testing utility, and it reports that it can't find the NIC, you might have the wrong utility for the NIC, or the NIC might not be working at all. Manufacturer-supplied testing utilities do not need separate driver software, so if the testing utility can't find the NIC, you can eliminate the drivers as the cause of the problem.

Configuring the NIC Settings

When you have confirmed that the NIC is operating correctly, you can configure the software settings for the NIC. The settings and configuration information you need depend on the protocol you are using.

Choosing the correct protocol is an important consideration when configuring a network or adding systems to an existing network. The client and the server must use the same protocol in order for communication to take place. This section provides a brief summary of the commonly used protocols. For a complete description of the various protocols, refer to Chapter 5, "Overview of Network Protocols."

◆ **TCP/IP**—By far the most prevalent of network protocol suites, TCP/IP is available for almost every computing

FIGURE 11.4
Information for an NIC in the Windows 2000 Device Manager utility.

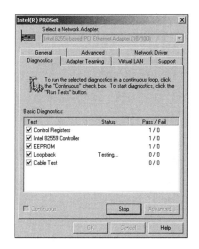

FIGURE 11.5
The Diagnostics tab in the Intel PROSet utility.

platform and has widespread industry support. The majority of LANs now use TCP/IP as the default protocol. Configuring TCP/IP connectivity requires the use of an IP address, a subnet mask, a default gateway, and possibly Domain Name Service (DNS) server information and Windows Internet Naming System (WINS) information.

◆ **IPX/SPX**—Novell invented and implemented IPX/SPX when it introduced NetWare in the 1980s. At that time, TCP/IP was for the most part an academic/military/government protocol, and Novell realized the need for a robust, routable protocol. IPX/SPX is one of the main reasons that Novell owned the networking market through the 1980s and most of the 1990s. IPX/SPX was also easy to install and configure. Today, TCP/IP has largely displaced IPX. One of the advantages of IPX is that workstation configuration is very simple. Generally speaking, the only item that might need to be configured is the frame type, which determines the format in which data is grouped into the frames that are placed on the network. Older versions of NetWare use a frame type called 802.3, whereas newer versions use a frame type called 802.2. Fortunately, most client software is able to detect the frame type automatically.

IN THE FIELD

A NEW LEASE ON LIFE FOR IPX?

With the advent of the Internet, IPX/SPX has found a new home as a security tool. To ensure that internal network resources are not exposed to unauthorized people from external networks, such as the Internet, some administrators are using IPX/SPX on the internal network. IPX/SPX provides a routable protocol, allowing the construction of large, efficient internal networks that are automatically isolated from the outside world. Administrators can use hardware and software implementations that translate information to and from the Internet. Many administrators like this extra level of security for their internal networks. You can consider using IPX/SPX in NWLink and NetBEUI network environments.

◆ **NWLink**—When Microsoft began working on adding support for interoperability with NetWare, it opted to develop its own fully compatible version of Novell's proprietary IPX/SPX.

This development was necessary because earlier versions of NetWare did not support authentication over TCP/IP.

◆ **NetBEUI**—Microsoft chose IBM's NetBEUI as the protocol for its first networking implementation in the mid-1980s. One of the reasons Microsoft chose to base its early networking efforts on NetBEUI was the protocol's simplicity and speed. Microsoft wanted to offer a very simple, easy workgroup configuration. Name services and addressing are both handled automatically with NetBEUI. There are no configuration issues, other than setting up the NIC and installing NetBEUI as the protocol. Because of NetBEUI's simplicity, administrators sometimes use it to troubleshoot hard-to-find communication problems between two machines. The simplicity of NetBEUI also created problems for Microsoft as the 1980s progressed. NetBEUI is a nonroutable protocol, and as networks began to interconnect, Microsoft found its clients stranded within the confines of small LANs.

EXAM TIP

NWLink Versus IPX/SPX   On the Network+ exam, be careful when determining whether connectivity to a NetWare server is required from a Microsoft client. NWLink is the required protocol because Microsoft does not directly support IPX/SPX. Watch for this same situation in reverse as well: NetWare uses IPX/SPX to communicate with a Windows NT Server running NWLink.

As mentioned earlier, TCP/IP is by far the most common of the networking protocols in use today. For that reason, we will take a more in-depth look at configuring client systems to use TCP/IP.

Configuring Client Systems for TCP/IP

Configuring a client system for TCP/IP can be a relatively complex task, or it can be simple. Any complexity involved is related to the possible need to configure TCP/IP manually. The simplicity is related to the fact that TCP/IP configuration can occur automatically via DHCP. We'll discuss DHCP later in this chapter; this section looks at some of the basic information required to make a system function on a network, using TCP/IP. At the very least, a system needs an IP address and a subnet mask. The default gateway, DNS server, and WINS server are all optional, but network functionality is limited without them. The following list briefly explains the IP-related settings used to connect to a TCP/IP network:

◆ **IP address**—Each system must be assigned a unique IP address so it can communicate on the network.

◆ **Subnet mask**—The subnet mask allows the system to determine what portion of the IP address represents the network address and what portion represents the node address.

TCP/IP Connection Requirements
At the very minimum, an IP address and a subnet mask are required to connect to a TCP/IP network. With just this minimum configuration, connectivity is limited to the local segment, and DNS and WINS resolution are not possible.

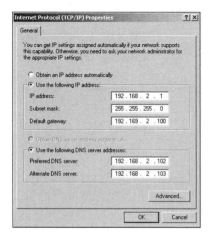

FIGURE 11.6
The Internet Protocol (TCP/IP) Properties dialog box on a Windows 2000 system.

FIGURE 11.7
The TCP/IP Properties dialog box on a Windows Me system.

◆ **Default gateway**—The default gateway allows the system to communicate with systems on a remote network, without the need for explicit routes to be defined.

◆ **DNS server addresses**—DNS servers allow dynamic host-name resolution to be performed. It is common practice to have two DNS server addresses defined so that if one server becomes unavailable, the other can be used.

◆ **WINS server addresses**—A WINS server enables Network Basic Input/Output System (NetBIOS) names to be resolved to IP addresses. As with DNS servers, it is common practice to enter two WINS server addresses, to provide a degree of fault tolerance.

Exactly how this information is entered on the client depends on the operating system being configured. For example, Figure 11.6 shows the Internet Protocol (TCP/IP) Properties dialog box on a Windows 2000 system. As you can see, the system represented in Figure 11.6 is fully configured for operation on a private network.

The configuration screens for other systems are slightly different. Figure 11.7 shows the IP Address tab of the TCP/IP Properties dialog box on a Windows Me system.

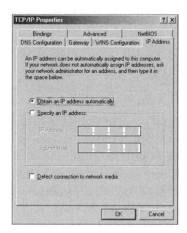

In any case, the parameters required need to be entered into the respective dialog boxes carefully. In the case of Windows Me, the DNS Configuration and WINS Configuration tabs must be used to input the DNS and WINS information. In Windows 2000, the DNS server fields are on the same screen as the main IP address.

Other systems use different utilities to allow TCP/IP configuration information to be entered. Figure 11.8 shows the TCP/IP configuration screen on a Macintosh OS9 system, and Figure 11.9 shows the TCP/IP configuration screen in the netconfig utility on a Red Hat Linux system.

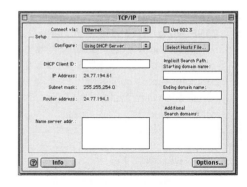

FIGURE 11.8
The TCP/IP configuration screen on a Macintosh system.

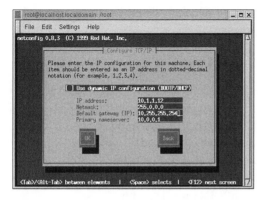

FIGURE 11.9
The TCP/IP configuration screen in the netconfig utility on a Red Hat Linux system.

Configuring DNS Server Information

DNS is used on TCP/IP networks for name resolution. It resolves fully qualified domain names (FQDNs) to IP addresses. For example, DNS would resolve the address www.comptia.org to its IP address, 216.119.103.72.

Regardless of the operating systems used, at least one DNS server must be accessible by a client system in order for dynamic name resolution to take place. Clients on the TCP/IP network must be configured with the IP address of the DNS server. Figure 11.10 shows the DNS configuration tab of the Advanced TCP/IP Settings dialog box on a Windows 2000 system. (You can find more information on DNS in Chapter 6.)

Configuring WINS Server Information

WINS is used to convert NetBIOS names to IP addresses. NetBIOS names are the friendly names by which we refer to the computers on the network (for example, sales1, Maryscomp, secretary).

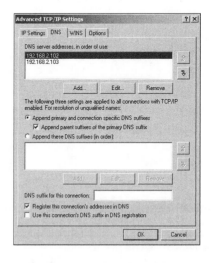

FIGURE 11.10
The DNS configuration screen on a Windows 2000 system.

NOTE **WINS Proxy**   Even clients that are not WINS enabled can use WINS—by using WINS proxies. A *WINS proxy* is a computer that is configured to act on behalf of a client system that is not WINS enabled.

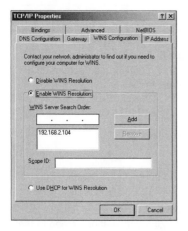

FIGURE 11.11
The WINS configuration screen on a Windows Me system.

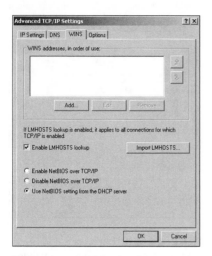

FIGURE 11.12
The WINS configuration screen on a Windows 2000 server system.

Many client operating systems are WINS enabled, which means they can be configured to use WINS servers. WINS-enabled clients use the WINS server to resolve NetBIOS names to IP addresses, allowing communication across subnets and reducing broadcast traffic. The following is a partial list of the client systems that can use WINS:

◆ Windows 2000 Server/Professional

◆ Windows NT Workstation/Server

◆ Windows 95/98/Me

◆ Windows for Workgroups

◆ OS/2

◆ Unix/Linux (requires Samba)

Each of the WINS-enabled client systems needs to be configured to use WINS. To do so, the IP address of the WINS server is required. Figure 11.11 shows the WINS Configuration tab of the TCP/IP Properties dialog box on a Windows Me system, and Figure 11.12 shows the WINS Configuration tab of the Advanced TCP/IP Settings dialog box on a Windows 2000 system. (You can find more information on WINS in Chapter 6.)

Using DHCP

Now that we have discussed how TCP/IP configuration information is entered manually, it's time to kick back a little and look at how you can handle this configuration with a single click—thanks to DHCP. As mentioned previously, DHCP is a protocol that is used to simplify the assignment of IP configuration information on a TCP/IP network. DHCP allows you to dynamically assign IP addressing information to client systems on the network, reducing possible human error and administrative overhead. DHCP is not restricted to a single platform; it is a generic technology that is supported by all the major operating systems.

When DHCP is used on a network, the client systems must be configured to use DHCP. Each of the client operating systems has some method of configuring the system to receive IP information from the DHCP server. Configuring a client to use DHCP is often as simple as clicking a check box or selecting a radio button.

When client systems are configured to use DHCP, they can receive more than just the IP address. They can also be assigned any of the other TCP/IP information, such as the default gateway, subnet mask, and any DNS or WINS servers. In addition, some DHCP server platforms support a range of other information as well. (You can find more information on DHCP in Chapter 6.)

When the networking configuration is complete, the system should be able to function on the network. However, to connect to a server system and use its resources, the system needs client software, which is discussed in the following section.

CONFIGURING CLIENTS TO ACCESS SERVERS

▶ Given specific parameters, configure a client to connect to the following servers:

  • Unix/Linux

  • NetWare

  • Windows

  • Macintosh

Many clients can be used on modern networks, and a network administrator must be prepared to manage and support client connectivity in a multiplatform network environment. Learning how to connect the various clients to the major network operating systems used today is a hands-on task. To prepare you for the inevitable, the following sections provide an overview of the various client operating systems and what is required to connect them to common network operating systems.

Configuring Microsoft Windows Clients

The most widely used of all client platforms is Microsoft Windows. Configuring Microsoft Windows clients for server connectivity depends on which version of Windows you are using and to what server you want to connect. Versions of Windows, such as 98 and Me, require that client software be installed in order to connect to a Windows Server platform. Products such as Windows 2000

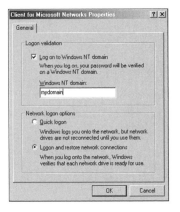

FIGURE 11.13
The Client for Microsoft Networks Properties
dialog box on a Windows Me system.

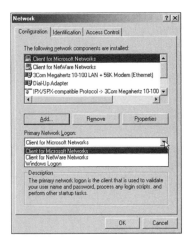

FIGURE 11.14
Setting the Primary Network Logon in Windows Me.

Professional assume that a connection to a server will be forthcom-
ing and therefore install the client software automatically. The following sections look at these various options.

Client for Microsoft Networks on
Windows 95/98/Me

The Client for Microsoft Networks can be installed on a Windows
95/98/Me system to facilitate connection to a Windows Server platform such as Windows NT 4 Server or Windows 2000 Server. The
client is included on the workstation operating system distribution
CD and is installed through the Network dialog box, which can be
accessed through the Network Control Panel or a variety of other
methods.

No information is needed to install the client software, but to con-
figure the software, you must open the Client for Microsoft
Networks Properties (see Figure 11.13), check the Log on to
Windows NT Domain box, and specify the domain name.

After you change these settings, you need to set the primary network
logon to the type of client you are using—in this case the Client for
Microsoft Networks. An example of the dialog box where you do
this is shown in Figure 11.14.

Client for Microsoft Networks on a
Windows NT/2000 System

Because networking functionality is built in to Windows NT/2000,
you do not need to add extra client software. However, you must
still configure the domain to which the system is supposed to
authenticate. Before you can "join" a domain, you must first create
an account for the system, or the computer must be joined to the
domain with a user account that is able to create a computer
account automatically.

Novell Client Software

Novell produces a full range of client software for Windows platforms. The client software is supplied when you buy a copy of
NetWare, or it can be downloaded free of charge from the Novell

download Web site, at `http://download.novell.com`. There are different versions of the client for Windows 95/98/Me, NT/2000, and XP. The client downloads vary in size but are generally quite large (around 13MB). On a high-speed Internet connection, this is not a problem, but you might want to avoid downloading these clients over a modem connection.

Installing the Novell client software is much like installing any other application. After the client software is installed, the system normally needs to be rebooted. When the system boots back up again, the Novell client appears automatically. On systems that require local login, such as Windows NT Workstation and Windows 2000 Professional, the Novell client replaces the Microsoft authentication dialog box but still offers the capability to log on to the local system.

To connect to a Novell network, certain criteria need to be supplied to the client software, including the following:

◆ **Username**—This is the name of the user ID that is being used to authenticate.

◆ **Password**—The password is not case-sensitive.

◆ **Tree**—This is the name of the Novell Directory Services (NDS) tree to which you want to connect.

◆ **Context**—This is the name of the NDS container in which the user object you are trying to log in as resides. This parameter is optional, but if it is not supplied, the username must be typed in, along with the full path to the user's container.

◆ **Server**—This field is optional. Specifying a server causes the client to connect to a specific server. If none is specified, the nearest server that is able to authenticate the user into NDS is used.

For the Tree, Context, and Server fields, navigation boxes to the right of each field allow you to browse the network for suitable resources. Figure 11.15 shows an example of the Novell Login dialog box with the fields completed.

When the Novell Login dialog box first opens on a system, it is displayed in a simplified format, with just the Username and Password fields. You must click the Advanced button to display the screen shown in Figure 11.15.

N O T E

Logging on to NDS   To log on to NDS, you must specify at least a username, a context, and a tree name. It is possible to combine the username and context into a single entry, although it is not common to do so.

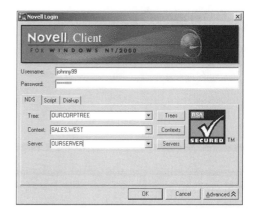

FIGURE 11.15
The Novell Login dialog box.

NOTE

NetWare Versions   The information in this section assumes that you are trying to connect to a NetWare 4.x, 5.x, or 6 system, rather than to an earlier version of NetWare.

If you prefer not to use the Novell software, you can use the client Microsoft supplies that can be used with NetWare networks. Like any other network service, this client is added through the Network applet in the Control Panel or through the properties of a network connection in Windows 2000. The basic functionality of the Novell-supplied client and the Microsoft-supplied client is the same, but in terms of advanced features, the Novell Client exceeds the Microsoft offering, by providing support for features such as ZENWorks, Novell's client system management software, and Novell Distributed Printing Services (NDPS).

Unix/Linux Client Software

NOTE

Daemons   You cannot talk about Linux configuration without talking about Linux daemons. *Daemons* are the applications that run in the background of Linux systems and provide services to the system or network. Daemon services start automatically, or they can be started manually. Some of the most common daemon services for networks include the dhcpd daemon for DHCP services and the named daemon for DNS services. When you configure DHCP or DNS in one of the Linux graphical utilities, these daemon files are being modified.

Unix/Linux systems are actually hybrid systems in that such a system can act as either a client or a server or both. In the Unix/Linux world, every machine is called a *host*, and a host can perform as either a client or a server or both.

Unix and Linux utilize the Network File System (NFS) protocol to provide file-sharing capabilities between computers. NFS, like TCP/IP, is actually a suite of protocols, and many people refer to NFS as an *application*. The most widely used version of NFS is version 2, which is based on RFC 1094. Version 3, which is documented in RFC 1813, exists but has not been widely implemented at the present time. You can find more information on NFS at the Sun Microsystems Web site, www.sun.com.

NFS is a popular system for sharing files between Linux and Unix systems; however, it does little to allow Windows-based clients to access the same shares (although NFS software is available for Windows). To get around this limitation, Windows clients use the Samba (SMB) service. Samba allows Windows-based clients to access resources such as files and printers on a Linux server. The smbd daemon provides the Samba service to the network.

ADDING, MODIFYING, OR REMOVING NETWORK SERVICES

▶ Given a scenario, predict the impact of modifying, adding, or removing network services (e.g., DHCP, DNS, WINS, etc.) on network resources and users.

All network services require a certain amount of network resources in order to function. The amount of resources required depends on the exact service being used. Before implementing or removing any service on a network, it is very important to understand the impact that these services can have on the entire network. To provide some idea of the demands various services place on the network, this section outlines some of the most common network services and the impact their addition, modification, or removal might have on the network and clients.

Adding, Modifying, or Removing DHCP

DHCP automatically assigns TCP/IP addressing to computers when they join the network and automatically renews the addresses before they expire. The advantage of using DHCP is the reduced number of addressing errors, which makes network maintenance much easier. Remember from earlier in this chapter that each computer on a TCP/IP network requires a unique IP address.

One of the biggest benefits of using DHCP is that the reconfiguration of IP addressing can be performed from a central location, with little or no effect on the clients. In fact, you can reconfigure an entire IP addressing system without the user noticing. There is, as always, a cost associated with everything good, and with DHCP, the cost is increased network traffic.

DHCP Traffic

You know what the function of DHCP is and the service it provides to the network, but what impact does the DHCP service have on the network itself? Some network services can consume huge amounts of network bandwidth, but DHCP is not one of them. The traffic generated between the DHCP server and the DHCP client is minimal during normal usage periods.

The bulk of the network traffic generated by DHCP occurs during two phases of the DHCP communication process: when the lease of the IP address is initially granted to the client system and when that lease is renewed. The entire DHCP communication process takes less than a second, but if there is a large number of client systems, the communication process can slow down the network.

For most network environments, the traffic generated by the DHCP service is negligible. For environments where DHCP traffic is a concern, you can reduce this traffic by increasing the lease duration for the client systems, thereby reducing communication between the DHCP client and the server.

IN THE FIELD

DHCP LEASES

Some network administrators choose to allow infinite DHCP leases, but this strategy is not always practical. In any network, there can be changes; for example, computers can be added or taken away, remote laptops can be used to connect to the main LAN, and NICs might need to be replaced. If a system is removed from a network that uses infinite DHCP leases, the IP address used by the removed system will be unavailable for reuse. A better option is to choose long duration periods ranging from one to two weeks. This ensures that the IP address will be able to be reused in the future.

If DHCP functionality is removed from the network (which is unusual), each system needs to be manually configured with IP addressing information.

DHCP is covered in greater detail in Chapter 6.

Adding, Modifying, or Removing WINS

WINS is used on Microsoft networks to facilitate communications between computers by resolving NetBIOS names to IP addresses. Each time a computer starts up, it registers itself with a WINS server by contacting that server over the network. If the system then needs to contact another system, it can contact the WINS server to get the NetBIOS name resolved to an IP address. If you are thinking about not using WINS, you should know that the alternative is for computers to identify themselves and resolve NetBIOS names to IP addresses via broadcasts. Broadcasts are inefficient because all data is transmitted to every device on the network segment. Broadcasts can be a significant problem for large network segments. Also, if a network has more than one segment, you will be unable to browse to remote segments because broadcasts are not typically forwarded by routers, which should eliminate this method of resolution.

Because WINS actually replaces the broadcast communication on a network, it has a positive impact on network resources and bandwidth usage. This does not mean that WINS does not generate any network traffic—just that the traffic is more organized and efficient. The amount of network traffic generated by WINS clients to the WINS server is minimal and should not have a negative impact in most network environments.

WINS server information can be entered manually into the TCP/IP configuration on a system, or it can be supplied via DHCP. If the WINS server addresses change and the client configuration is being performed manually, each system needs to be reconfigured with the new WINS server addresses. If you are using DHCP, you need to update only the DHCP scope with the new information.

Removing WINS from a network increases the amount of broadcast traffic and can potentially limit browsing to a single segment.

NOTE **WINS Traffic** When you are estimating the amount of traffic WINS will generate, it is important to consider the network topology and the design or configuration of the routers in the network.

Adding, Modifying, or Removing DNS

As previously mentioned, the function of DNS is to resolve hostnames to IP addresses. Without such a service, network users would have to identify a remote system by its IP address rather than by its easy-to-remember hostname.

Name resolution can be provided dynamically by a DNS server, or it can be accomplished statically, using the HOSTS file on the client system. If you are using a DNS server, the IP address of the DNS server is required. DNS server addresses can be entered manually, or they can be supplied through a DHCP server.

A more detailed discussion of DNS is presented in Chapter 6.

CHAPTER SUMMARY

KEY TERMS

- remote connectivity
- PSTN
- ISDN
- cable Internet
- xDSL
- satellite Internet
- PPP
- SLIP
- PPPoE
- dial-up
- coaxial network
- twisted-pair
- duplex settings
- IP address
- subnet mask
- default gateway
- DNS server address
- WINS server address
- FQDN
- NetBIOS
- DHCP
- context
- tree
- NFS

This chapter focuses on the protocols and procedures involved in establishing and configuring network connectivity. Each of the major operating systems has to be correctly configured before remote users can log on to a network. Although the information needed to access these networks is the same, the methods for configuring the information is different across operating system platforms.

Configuring remote access involves a number of different software configurations. To access a remote network, a user must have a valid protocol, a means of accessing the remote network (such as a dial-up account), and a valid user account. Accessing a remote network requires considerable configuration on both the client and server computer systems.

To log on to a network, a number of settings have to be configured on the client system. These settings include DNS, DHCP, WINS, NetBIOS names, and protocols. If you do not correctly configure these settings, the client system might be unable to access the network. Although the need to configure these, or similar, settings is the same for all operating systems, the method of configuring these settings in each of the operating systems varies. Network administration requires a knowledge of how each of the different client-based operating systems is configured.

APPLY YOUR KNOWLEDGE

Exercises

11.1   Installing WINS

In this exercise, you walk through the steps involved in installing WINS.

Estimated time: 10 minutes

1. Select Start, Settings, Control Panel.

2. Double-click the Add/Remove Programs icon. The Add/Remove Programs dialog box appears.

3. Click the Add/Remove Windows Components button on the left side of the screen. The Windows Components Wizard dialog box (see Figure 11.16) appears.

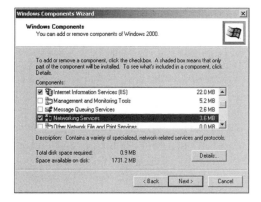

FIGURE 11.16
The Windows Components Wizard dialog box.

4. Select Networking Services from the menu, and then click the Details button at the bottom of the screen. The Networking Services dialog box appears (see Figure 11.17).

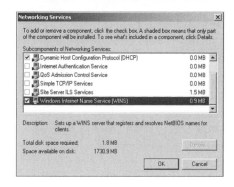

FIGURE 11.17
The Networking Services dialog box.

5. Place a checkmark in the Windows Internet Name Service (WINS) box, and then click OK. You are taken back to the Windows Components Wizard.

6. Click Next to continue the installation. WINS is installed. It might be necessary to insert the Windows 2000 CD to complete the installation.

11.2   Setting a Client System to Obtain IP Information from a DHCP Server

Many organizations today use DHCP to configure TCP/IP information on client systems for both convenience and reducing errors made by manually inputting TCP/IP information. This exercise shows you how to set up a client system to obtain IP information from a DHCP server.

Estimated time: 10 minutes

1. On the Desktop, right-click the My Network Places icon. Choose Properties from the menu. The Network and Dial-Up Connections window appears.

2. Right-click the Local Area Connection icon, and then choose Properties from the menu that appears. The Local Area Connection Properties dialog box appears (see Figure 11.18).

FIGURE 11.18
The Local Area Connection Properties dialog box.

3. Select Internet Protocol (TCP/IP), and then click the Properties button. The Internet Protocol (TCP/IP) Properties dialog box appears (see Figure 11.19).

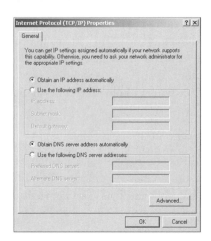

FIGURE 11.19
The TCP/IP Properties dialog box.

4. Select Obtain an IP Address Automatically, and then click OK.

5. Click OK to close the Local Area Connection Properties dialog box. Your computer is now configured to obtain IP addressing information from a DHCP server automatically upon startup.

Exam Questions

1. You are configuring new Windows 98 systems for connection to a NetWare server. After installing the client software and rebooting the system, which of the following information do you need to supply to log in to NDS? (Choose the three best answers.)

    a. Tree name

    b. Username

    c. Domain name

    d. Password

2. Which service must be installed on a Linux system in order to make the file and print capabilities of the server available to clients?

    a. Squid

    b. Samba

    c. DNS

    d. WINS

3. Which of the following data-link-layer protocols are used to establish a remote access connection? (Choose the two best answers.)

    a. PPP

    b. TCP

c. SLIP

d. IPX

4. Which of the following pieces of information are required to configure a system for TCP/IP connectivity? (Choose the two best answers.)

   a. DNS server addresses

   b. Default gateway

   c. IP address

   d. Subnet mask

5. You are configuring DHCP functionality on a network that has 100 Windows NT Workstation systems. Which of the following network operating system platforms can you use to supply DHCP server functionality?

   a. Windows 2000

   b. NetWare

   c. Linux

   d. All of the above

6. While troubleshooting a Windows 2000 server, you disable the DNS service. What effect will this have on the network users?

   a. Users cannot receive IP addresses dynamically.

   b. Users cannot contact servers using hostnames.

   c. Broadcast traffic increases.

   d. Systems cannot use VPNs.

7. As the network administrator for a very large network, you have been asked to reduce the traffic generated by the DHCP service. Which of the following would be the best course of action?

   a. Reinstall DHCP.

   b. Increase the DHCP lease time.

c. Decrease the DHCP lease time.

d. Manually assign DHCP addresses.

8. You have just added 15 new workstations on a network. Which of the following is the easiest way to assign these systems WINS and DNS configuration information?

   a. Use the LMHOST and HOSTS files.

   b. Provide users with the configuration information.

   c. Use Windows 2000 WINS/DNS Proxy Service (WDPS).

   d. Use DHCP.

9. When configuring a client to log on to a Windows 2000 domain, which two of the following actions must be completed?

   a. Choose to log on to the Windows NT domain.

   b. Install the Internetwork Protocol Client (IPC).

   c. Select the appropriate tree and context.

   d. Supply the domain name.

10. You are installing an NIC in a client system. Which of the following sources is preferred for obtaining the NIC drivers?

   a. Software that shipped with the NIC

   b. Another system with a similar NIC

   c. The NIC manufacturer's Web site

   d. Standard NE2000 drivers

APPLY YOUR KNOWLEDGE

11. Which of the following are required when choosing an NIC for your network? (Choose the two best answers.)

    a. DNS compatibility

    b. Bus compatibility

    c. Correct authentication method

    d. Correct type of network

12. You are installing a new system on a 10BaseT network. What would you tell the users on the network to which the system will be connected?

    a. The network will be unavailable while the new system is added.

    b. The network will slow down while the new system is added.

    c. The network will be unaffected by the addition of the new system.

    d. The network server will need to be rebooted before users can access network resources.

13. Which of the following applications are used by Linux clients to access disk resources on a Unix system?

    a. NFS

    b. Client software for Unix

    c. Client software for Linux

    d. PHS

14. You have been given the task of troubleshooting a failed remote connection. Which of the following are valid troubleshooting steps in determining the cause of a remote connection failure? (Choose the two best answers.)

    a. Verify the phone number called.

    b. Verify the authentication information.

    c. Verify the modem bus compatibility.

    d. Verify that CHAP is installed.

15. You are required to connect a new Windows 98 system to an existing Windows 2000 server. What client software is required?

    a. TCP/IP

    b. Microsoft Client for Windows 98

    c. Client for Microsoft Networks

    d. No additional client software is required

16. You are connecting a new workstation to a 10Base2 segment and discover that no connector is currently available. You must add a new connection. The user, a department manager, needs the system right away. What should you tell the other users on the segment?

    a. The network will be unaffected by the addition of the new system.

    b. Their manager is impatient.

    c. The network server will need to be rebooted before they can access network resources.

    d. The network will temporarily be unavailable while the new connector is being added to the network.

17. Which of the following are required when installing a new NIC into a system? (Choose the two best answers.)

    a. A unique IRQ address

    b. A network-assigned IRQ address

    c. A DHCP-assigned I/O address

    d. A unique I/O address

APPLY YOUR KNOWLEDGE

18. While troubleshooting your Windows 2000 server, you disable WINS. What effect will this have on the network users?

    a. Users cannot be assigned IP addresses dynamically.

    b. Users cannot resolve hostnames to IP addresses.

    c. Users cannot browse across subnets.

    d. Authentication for new users fails.

19. Which of the following are required to establish a remote connection? (Choose the three best answers.)

    a. Windows Dial-Up Networking

    b. A physical means of connection

    c. A protocol to establish the connection

    d. A protocol to establish the communication

20. Which of the following remote connectivity methods is least likely to be used in a network?

    a. Satellite

    b. PSTN

    c. ISDN

    d. xDSL

Answers to Exam Questions

1. **a, b, d.** To connect to a NetWare server, you need to supply a valid username and password, as well as the name of the NDS tree to which you want to connect. A domain name is not required because domains, in this context, are associated with Windows NT/2000 based networks. For more information, see the section "Configuring Clients to Access Servers," in this chapter.

2. **b.** The Samba service can be loaded on a Linux system to provide file and print functionality to Windows clients. None of the other services listed provide this service. For more information, see the section "Configuring Clients to Access Servers," in this chapter.

3. **a, c.** PPP and SLIP are data-link-layer protocols that can be used to establish remote connectivity between two devices. TCP and IPX are both transport-layer protocols. For more information, see the section "Configuring Remote Connectivity," in this chapter.

4. **c, d.** To configure TCP/IP, you only need an IP address and the subnet mask. However, without a default gateway, network functionality is limited to the local network segment, and DNS or WINS resolutions are not available. For more information, see the section "Configuring Clients to Access Servers," in this chapter.

5. **d.** DHCP is part of the TCP/IP protocol suite and is therefore platform independent. DHCP server functionality is provided by all common network operating systems, so any of the platforms listed would make suitable DHCP servers. For more information, see the section "Configuring Clients to Access Servers," in this chapter.

6. **b.** If you disable the DNS service, users will not be able to contact servers on the network by using the hostnames and will instead have to use IP addresses. Answer a describes the DHCP service, so disabling DNS will not affect IP address assignment. DNS resolutions cannot be achieved via broadcasts, so these will not increase as a

APPLY YOUR KNOWLEDGE

result. Answer d is not valid. For more information, see the section "Adding, Modifying, or Removing Network Services," in this chapter.

7. **b.** If you increase the DHCP lease duration, there will be fewer lease renewal requests on the system. However, this brings with it many other considerations that might make it impractical. None of the other strategies would reduce DHCP-related traffic. For more information, see the section "Adding, Modifying, or Removing Network Services," in this chapter.

8. **d.** If you are configuring network settings, by far the easiest way to supply the information to client system is to use DHCP. Answers a and b are valid, but they are both time-consuming. Answer c is invalid. For more information, see the section "Configuring Clients to Access Servers," in this chapter.

9. **a, d.** When authenticating to a Windows 2000 server, the domain name must be supplied and the desire to log on to the domain must be selected. Answer b is not a valid answer. Answer c is related to logging on to a NetWare server. For more information, see the section "Configuring Clients to Access Servers," in this chapter.

10. **c.** The latest drivers for an NIC can be found on the NIC manufacturer's Web site. Answers a and b are possible, but they are not guaranteed to provide the latest driver. Answer d is not valid. For more information, see the section "Selecting an NIC and Network Configuration Settings," in this chapter.

11. **b, d.** When choosing an NIC, you should consider bus compatibility and the type of network to which you are going to connect. Answers a and c are not valid considerations for selecting a network card. For more information, see the section "Selecting an NIC and Network Configuration Settings," in this chapter.

12. **c.** When connecting a system to a network that uses twisted-pair cabling (as 10BaseT does), other users on the segment will be unaffected by the addition of a new system. None of the other answers are valid. For more information, see the section "Selecting an NIC and Network Configuration Settings," in this chapter.

13. **a.** The Network File System (NFS) application is used to access areas of a disk on other systems that have made them available to clients. None of the other answers are valid. For more information, see the section "Configuring Remote Connectivity," in this chapter.

14. **a, b.** Verifying that the correct number is being called and that the authentication information is correct are both valid troubleshooting steps. Answers c and d are both invalid. For more information, see the section "Configuring Remote Connectivity," in this chapter.

15. **c.** Client for Microsoft Networks is required to connect a Windows 98 system to a Windows server. TCP/IP might be required, but the Microsoft client software can be used over a number of protocols. Answers b and d are invalid. For more information, see the section "Configuring Clients to Access Servers," in this chapter.

16. **d.** On a coaxial network segment, it is necessary to break the cable to add another connector for a new system. For the duration of the break, users on the segment are unable to access the network. None of the other answers are correct. For more information, see the section "Selecting an NIC and Network Configuration Settings," in this chapter.

APPLY YOUR KNOWLEDGE

17. **a, d.** When installing an NIC, you must ensure that there are a unique I/O address and a unique IRQ address available for the NIC. Answers b and c are invalid. For more information, see the section "Selecting an NIC and Network Configuration Settings," in this chapter.

18. **c.** If you disable WINS, users will be unable to browse across subnets. Answer a describes what would happen if you disabled DHCP, and Answer b describes what would happen if you disabled DNS. Answer d is invalid. For more information, see the section "Adding, Modifying, or Removing Network Services," in this chapter.

19. **b, c, d.** To establish a remote connection, you need the physical connection method, a protocol to establish the connections, and a protocol to communicate with the remote system. Windows Dial-Up Networking is not necessarily required. For more information, see the section "Configuring Remote Connectivity," in this chapter.

20. **a.** Of those listed, satellite is the least suitable method for remote access because it has limited upload speeds and requires both a satellite and a dial-up connection. All the other options are valid and widely used methods of Internet access. For more information, see the section "Configuring Remote Connectivity," in this chapter.

Suggested Readings and Resources

1. Habraken, Joe. *Absolute Beginner's Guide to Networking,* third edition. Que Publishing, 2001.

2. Nemeth, Evi, Garth Snyder, Trent Hein. *Linux Administration Handbook.* Prentice Hall, 2002.

3. Williams, G Robert, Mark Walla. *The Ultimate Windows 2000 Systems Administrators Guide.* Addison-Wesley, 2000.

4. Peek, Jerry D, Grace Todino, John Strange. *Learning Unix Operating System.* O'Reilly & Associates, 2002.

5. Ray, John, William C. Ray. *MAC OS X Unleashed.* Sams Publishing, 2001.

6. Windows 2000 information, www.microsoft.com/windows2000/default.asp.

7. Novell NetWare information, www.novell.com/products/netware.

8. Unix information and links, www.unixtools.com.

9. Linux information and links, www.linux.org.

10. Macintosh information, www.mac.com.

11. Computer networking tutorials and advice, compnetworking.about.com.

12. "TechEncyclopedia," www.techencyclopedia.com.

This chapter covers the following CompTIA-specified objectives for the "Network Implementation" section of the Network+ exam:

Identify the purpose, benefits, and characteristics of using a firewall.

▶ Firewalls are a means by which to secure a network from outside intruders. With the proliferation of the Internet and WAN connectivity, the use of firewalls is becoming commonplace.

Identify the purpose, benefits, and characteristics of using a proxy server.

▶ The Internet provides many benefits to a modern business. One of the challenges associated with being connected to the Internet, though, is providing access to all users within an organization in a controlled manner. Proxy servers are the tools that allow us to do this.

Given a scenario, predict the impact of a particular security implementation on network functionality (e.g., blocking port numbers, encryption, etc.).

▶ The measures used to protect networks also add a layer of complexity to these networks. Understanding how these measures operate and the consequences of changing or removing services are key skills for a network administrator.

CHAPTER 12

Securing the Network

Introduction	**462**
Threats to Security	**462**
Security Responsibilities of a Network Administrator	464
Physical and Logical Security	**465**
Physical Security	465
Logical Security	466
Authentication, Passwords, and Password Policies	466
File System Security	471
Firewalls	**475**
The Purpose and Function of a Firewall	476
Packet-Filtering Firewalls	476
Circuit-Level Firewalls	477
Application Gateway Firewalls	477
Demilitarized Zones	478

Proxy Servers	**479**
Caching Proxy Servers	480
Using a Proxy Server	482
Understanding How Security Affects a Network	**482**
Blocking Port Numbers	483
Port Blocking and Network Users	484
Encryption	484
Internet Protocol Security (IPSec)	485
Data Encryption Standard (DES)	485
3DES	486
Pretty Good Privacy (PGP)	486
Auditing	487
Chapter Summary	**488**
Apply Your Knowledge	**489**

▶ Read the objectives at the beginning of the chapter.

▶ Study the information in the chapter, paying special attention to the tables, which summarize key information.

▶ Review the objectives again.

▶ Answer the exam questions at the end of the chapter and check your results.

▶ Use the ExamGear test on the CD-ROM that accompanies this book to answer additional exam questions concerning this material.

▶ Review the notes, tips, and exam tips in this chapter. Make sure you understand the information in the exam tips. If you don't understand the topic referenced in an exam tip, refer to the information in the chapter text and then read the exam tip again.

INTRODUCTION

Today, more than ever, the security of networks is a major consideration for network administrators. Notwithstanding the risks associated with the fact that most networks are now connected by some means to the Internet, security from a more local perspective is a big issue.

For a network administrator to fully understand the security risks associated with the network, he or she must take a holistic view and consider every aspect, threat, and possible weakness. The network administrator must assume that someone will attempt to gain unauthorized access to the network or the systems attached to it at some point. This might sound a little dramatic, but there are plenty of network administrators who can attest to the fact that it is a reality.

There are, of course, certain environments in which security is more of a concern than in others. If you work for, say, a bank or a branch of the government, security is likely to be a high priority. For a chain of florists in Fresno, security is likely to be less of an issue, but it must still be considered.

Security today is not just about stopping corporate espionage or preventing theft of equipment. It's about protecting the physical assets and, perhaps more importantly, the data of the organization. The cracker coming in through your firewall and entering 50 bogus orders for gift hampers might think it's funny. Your boss is likely to find it less amusing.

In essence, security is about ensuring the privacy, integrity, and quality of a network's data and the systems that hold it, with the purpose of ensuring business continuity. Determining what measures are required to ensure this security is the concern of the network administrator.

THREATS TO SECURITY

Before we look at the measures you can take to secure your network, let's first look at what you are trying to protect against. The following are some possible threats to a network's security:

◆ **Internal threats**—It is a sad fact that the most common source of security problems in an organization is from the employees of that organization. For example, a user might decide to "borrow" the apparently unused hub from the equipment cupboard on the third floor, or he might really want to know just how much money the president of the company actually earns. In more extreme cases, a user might attempt to pass valuable corporate information to an outside party. Sound far-fetched? It's not; it happens every day.

◆ **Deliberate data damage**—To most people, the idea of deliberately damaging someone else's property is, to say the least, distasteful. Unfortunately, not everyone operates with the same values. Whether "just for fun" or with more shady intent, some people might delight in corrupting data or deleting it completely. Either way, business continuity will almost certainly be affected.

◆ **Industrial espionage**—This rather James Bond–sounding security threat involves the process of a person retrieving data from a server for a purpose. The intruder might want to get her hands on the latest blueprints of your new widget, or she might want financial information for a buyout bid. Either way, the integrity (and in some cases, the future viability) of the business can be affected by such events.

◆ **Physical equipment theft**—Although it is less of an issue than theft of data, theft of physical equipment can affect business continuity as well. If an important piece of equipment is stolen (for example, the server or a backup tape), the intruder will have access to your data. Insurance normally takes care of replacing the actual equipment, but data is generally not insured, unless specified, so the cost of restructuring the data is not provided for.

You might be fortunate enough not to suffer from any of these threats. Certainly, in a small organization that performs a seemingly uninteresting (to outsiders) business, there might not be any occurrences of security threats. But as an organization grows, so too do the amount of information, the number of methods that can be used to access it, and the number of people who are interested in finding out about the business. As the number of employees grows, the chance that a "bad apple" will find its way into the cart increases as well. Sadly, it is a fact of life.

Security Responsibilities of a Network Administrator

To combat possible security threats, what is expected of you, as a network administrator? The exact network security responsibilities you have depend on the kind of environment in which you are working. In large companies, there might be an individual or a group that is specifically responsible for security issues. You might be part of that group or be under its direction. In small companies, the entire onus of network security might lie on you—the network administrator's shoulders. This chapter assumes that as a network administrator, you are primarily responsible for network security. Assume that you need to do the following, to ensure network security in your organization:

◆ **Ensure that a security policy is in place**—A security policy defines the security measures, how they function, what is involved in their operation, and how problems are dealt with. The security policy should be created with the support of management.

◆ **Ensure that the security policy is enforced**—There is no point in having a policy if it is not enforced. As the network administrator, you need to make sure that the security policy works and is implemented as described.

◆ **Ensure that any infractions of the security policy are dealt with**—Perhaps the most undesirable part of a network administrator's security responsibilities involves dealing with infractions of the security policy. Because the majority of security-related incidents occur with people inside the company, this can often be an unpleasant task.

◆ **Ensure that the security situation is continually evaluated, revised, and updated**—Networks change, as does the company structure. The security needs of an organization should be evaluated constantly. Any changes deemed necessary should be incorporated into the security policy, again with the cooperation of management.

This is just a brief look at the responsibilities a network administrator has in implementing security on a network. Depending on the environment you work in, you might have to consider more or fewer security-related responsibilities. Now that you have an idea of some of the basic security responsibilities, let's look at the two types of network security: physical and logical.

PHYSICAL AND LOGICAL SECURITY

Security can be broken down into two distinct areas: physical security and logical security. *Physical security* refers to the issues related to the physical security of the equipment that comprises or is connected to the network. Physical security includes controlling access to equipment, supervising visitors, and enforcing the security measures that are in place, to control physical access to areas that contain networking equipment.

Logical security is concerned with security of data while it is on the systems that are connected to the network. Logical security involves controlling passwords and password policies, controlling access to data on servers through file system security, controlling access to backup tapes, and perhaps most importantly, preventing sources outside the network from gaining access to the network through a connection from another network, such as the Internet. Because logical security is a large and complex topic, this chapter covers only topics related to the Network+ exam and some supporting information.

Physical Security

Physical security is concerned with the prevention of unauthorized access to the physical equipment that makes up the network or the systems attached to it.

Perhaps the biggest consideration related to physical security is restricting access to networking equipment and servers. Most commonly, the people you are trying to protect against in this respect are the employees of the company rather than malicious outsiders.

Specific physical security considerations include the following:

> ◆ **Controlling access to equipment**—Networking equipment should be kept in a secure location. For example, you might have a dedicated, environmentally controlled room in which all the network servers and networking equipment are kept.

> **EXAM TIP**
>
> **Physical Security** The Network+ exam focuses much more on logical security than on physical security. For this reason, the discussion of physical security is confined to just the basics.

Alternatively, as in many small organizations, networking equipment might be stored in a cupboard or even a rack. Wherever your equipment is located, access control systems (including locks and keys) should be in place to prevent unauthorized access.

◆ **Creating and enforcing visitor policies**—Even if you have a dedicated server room, it's highly likely that there will be other equipment in the room, such as telephone systems, air-conditioning units, and fire-protection systems. Each of these systems will have a scheduled maintenance program, which means that you will periodically have visitors in the server room. Procedures should be in place so that the identities of visitors are verified, and that when these visitors are in the equipment room, they are supervised.

◆ **Securing the area**—The physical security of the network environment should be examined from a big-picture perspective. If a dedicated room is used for the server, determine the security of the room. Are there windows in the room that might represent a security risk? Are there windows that could facilitate someone outside the building seeing in? All these aspects and more must be factored in when considering physical security.

Logical Security

Logical security is a much more involved subject than physical security. Not only are there more ways in which data can be threatened logically than physically, but the measures available to secure data are equally diverse. This section focuses on two of the most significant aspects of logical security: authentication and file system security.

Authentication, Passwords, and Password Policies

Although there are many different methods of authentication, none have attained the level of popularity of username and password combinations. The reason is that, apart from the fact that usernames and passwords do not require any additional equipment, which practically every other method of authentication does, the username and password process is familiar to users, easy to implement, and

Hacker or Cracker? The terms *hacker* and *cracker* are tossed about quite freely when it comes to network security, but the two terms describe very different individuals. A *hacker* is someone who attempts to disassemble or delve into a computer program with the intention of understanding how it works, normally in order to make it better. A *cracker*, on the other hand, is someone who attempts to gain access to a computer system or application without authorization, with the intention of using the application illegally or viewing the data. Crackers, not hackers, are the people network administrators need to be concerned with.

relatively secure. In the future, other authentication methods, such as biometrics (for example, fingerprint recognition, retinal scans), might overtake usernames and passwords in popularity, but if they ever do, that day is some time away.

Before we talk about some of the specific considerations for working with usernames and passwords, we should perhaps answer a simple question. Why do we need usernames and passwords in the first place? The obvious answer, of course, is that they provide a mechanism for users to prove that they are entitled to access the network or a specific resource. But there is another reason: accountability. If users must prove their identity, they are made accountable for their actions. This is particularly relevant in environments in which the auditing of system events is performed because it allows events to be attributed to certain users, based on their usernames. Without some form of authentication—be it usernames and passwords or something else—users cannot be held accountable for their actions.

Passwords are a relatively simple form of authentication in that only a string of characters can be used. However, how the string of characters is used and what policies you can put in place to govern them make usernames and passwords such an excellent form of authentication.

> **NOTE**
>
> **Passphrases** In some environments, passwords are called *passphrases*.

Password Policies

All popular network operating systems include password policy systems that allow the network administrator to control how passwords are used on the system. The exact capabilities vary between network operating systems. However, generally they allow the following:

◆ **Minimum length of password**—Shorter passwords are easier to guess than longer ones. Setting a minimum password length does not prevent a user from creating a longer password than the minimum, although each network operating system has a limit on how long a password can be.

◆ **Password expiration**—Also known as the *maximum password age*, password expiration defines how long the user can use the same password before having to change it. A general practice is that a password is changed every month or every 30 days. In high-security environments, you might want to make this value shorter, but you should generally not make it any longer.

Having passwords expire periodically is an important feature because it means that if a password is compromised, the unauthorized user will not have access indefinitely.

◆ **Prevention of password reuse**—Although a system might be able to cause a password to expire and prompt the user to change it, many users are tempted to simply use the same password again. A process by which the system remembers the last, say, 10 passwords is most secure because it forces the user to create completely new passwords.

◆ **Prevention of easy-to-guess passwords**—Some systems have the capability to evaluate the password provided by a user to see if it meets a required level of complexity. This prevents users from having passwords such as *password* or *12345678*.

The process of setting password policies differs between network operating systems. As an example, Figure 12.1 shows the Password Policy configuration screen on a Windows 2000 Server system.

FIGURE 12.1
The Password Policy configuration screen in Windows 2000.

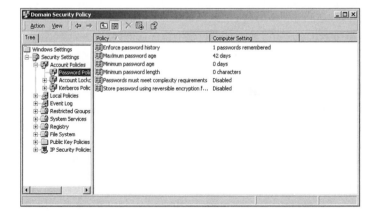

Each network operating system uses slightly different terms to describe the parameters that can be set in the password policy, although the options are similar across all network operating systems. For more information, consult the documentation for your network operating system. (Exercise 12.2 at the end of this chapter describes how to set the password policy on a Windows 2000 Active Directory system.)

Understanding Password Strength

No matter how good a company's password policy, it is only as effective as the passwords that are created within it. A password that is hard to guess, or *strong*, is more likely to protect the data on a system than one that is easy to guess, or *weak*.

To understand the difference between a strong password and a weak one, consider this: A password of six characters that uses only numbers and letters and is not case-sensitive has 10,314,424,798,490,535,546,171,949,056 possible combinations. That might seem like a lot, but to a password-cracking program, it's really not much security. A password that uses eight case-sensitive characters, with letters, numbers, and special characters has so many possible combinations that a standard calculator is not able display the actual number.

There has always been debate over how long a password should be. It should be sufficiently long that it is hard to break but sufficiently short that the user is able to easily remember it (and type it). In a normal working environment, passwords of 8 characters are seen as sufficient. Certainly, they should be no fewer than 6 characters. In environments where security is a concern, passwords should be 10 characters or more.

Users, You Are the Weakest Link

For all your efforts to create and implement a strong password policy and system, there is normally one weak link in the chain—the user. You can specify that passwords be a minimum of 10 characters and that the user is not allowed to reuse an old password. However, that still doesn't stop the user from using a password like *peterdecember* for December and *peterjanuary* in January. As discussed earlier in this chapter, some authentication systems do have mechanisms that try to detect easy-to-guess passwords and prevent users from setting them, but its effectiveness is limited to only basic character sequences/dictionary words. For example, they would not dispute a Social Security number combined with the user's name. This might constitute a strong password in terms of characters used to create it and length, but it would still be potentially easy to guess for a password cracker.

NOTE

The Administrator's Password The password used to log on to the Administrator account are, without question, the most valuable of all the passwords on the system. For that reason, you should treat them with an even greater level of respect than the passwords for normal user IDs. Administrator account passwords should, ideally, be changed more often than standard user account passwords, and they should also be as hard to guess or crack as possible.

NOTE

Weak Passwords The Computer Emergency Response Team (CERT) Coordination Center estimates that four out of five network security incidents are caused by weak passwords.

The best way to deal with these situations is education. You must educate users so they understand why passwords are used, their purpose, and what the rules are to create them. You should also tell users what are and are not considered acceptable passwords. In the 21st century, you might think that users would automatically understand the need for strong and hard-to-guess passwords, but the reality is different. Users are notorious for choosing easy-to-guess passwords, such as their surname, a spouse's name, a pet's name, a home address, or a vehicle license plate number. This is the kind of information that a password cracker will try first when attempting to crack a password.

Users should be encouraged to use a password that is considered strong. A strong password has at least eight characters; has a combination of letters, numbers, and special characters; uses mixed case; and does not form a proper word. Examples might include *3Ecc5T0h* and *e1oXPn3r*. Such passwords might be secure, but users are likely to have problems remembering them. For that reason, a strategy that is popular is to use a combination of letters and numbers to deform phrases or long words. Examples include *d1eTc0La* and *tAb1eT0p*. These passwords might not be quite as secure as the preceding examples, but they are still very strong and a whole lot better than the name of the user's household pet.

Passwords: The Last Word

One last password-related topic is worth mentioning. A password is effective only if just the intended users have it. As soon as a password is passed to someone else, its effectiveness as an authentication mechanism is diminished, and as a tool for accountability, the password is almost useless. Passwords are a means of accessing a system and the data on it. Passwords that are known by anyone other than the intended user(s) might as well not be set at all.

IN THE FIELD

SECURITY OF BACKUP TAPES

One of the most overlooked aspects of security is ensuring that backup tapes are made, transported, and stored securely. Backup tapes make an attractive target for anyone who wants to get hold of your data. It's much easier to steal a backup tape than a hard disk. To make sure data is available in the event of a disaster, backup tapes are often taken offsite, away from the secure environment created just to secure the data.

To provide an extra measure of security for your backups, consider password-protecting backup media, using a registered courier service to transport the media between locations, and ensuring that the tapes are secure at the remote location. As an extra measure, if your budget allows, you could also consider using an encryption system that would scramble the data on the tape, making it very difficult to read should it fall into the wrong hands.

File System Security

Because they are the heart of the system, network operating systems are chock full of security-related features and subsystems. All popular network operating systems have robust authentication systems that control access to the network and file system security measures which ensure that users can view and use only the data they are supposed to. Chapter 9, "Network Operating Systems and Clients," discusses the authentication methods used by the various network operating systems, so this chapter does not cover that again. Instead, the following sections take a more in-depth look at the file system security measures on the popular network operating systems.

After logon security, file system security is perhaps the most important aspect of system security. If you have a solid file system security structure in place, even if someone does manage to gain unauthorized access to the system, the amount of damage he or she is able to do can be limited.

Novell NetWare File System Security

File system security on NetWare is the most sophisticated of any of the popular network operating systems. In addition to a full set of file permissions, NetWare also accommodates file permission inheritance, as well as filters to cancel out that inheritance. For those who are unfamiliar with the various features of NetWare file system security, it can seem a bit bewildering. When you are used to it, though, you realize that it allows an extremely high level of control over files and directories.

At the core of NetWare file system security are the basic permissions. These permissions can be assigned to individual files or, where appropriate, directories (that is, folders). The file system rights available on a NetWare server are listed in Table 12.1.

NOTE

Inheritance The term *inheritance* is used to describe the process of rights flowing down the directory tree. For example, rights are assigned at the top of the directory structure, and unless they are blocked at a lower level, they flow to the bottom of the structure. All common network operating systems employ file inheritance in one way or another.

TABLE 12.1

FILE PERMISSIONS ON A NETWARE SERVER

Right	Description
Supervisor	Supervisory—implies all rights
Read	Allows the file to be read
Write	Allows the file to be written to
Create	Allows new files to be created
Erase	Allows files to be deleted
Modify	Allows the attributes of the file to be changed
Filescan	Allows the file to be viewed
Access Control	Allows the file permissions to be manipulated

Figure 12.2 shows a file permission assignment on a NetWare 6 server.

FIGURE 12.2

File permission assignment on a NetWare 6 server.

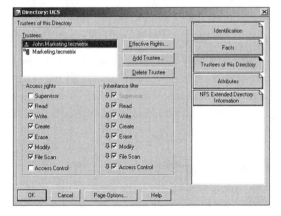

Unix/Linux File System Security

Of the platforms discussed in this chapter, Unix and Linux have the most simplistic approach to file system security, although for most environments, this approach is more than sufficient. File permissions can be assigned to either the creator of a file or directory, a group, or the entity "everyone," which includes any authenticated user.

Unix and Linux have only three rights that can be assigned. These rights are listed in Table 12.2.

TABLE 12.2

FILE PERMISSIONS ON UNIX/LINUX

Right	Description
Read	Allows files to be listed, opened, and read
Write	Allows files to be created, written to, or modified
Execute	Allows the file to be executed (that is, run)

Figure 12.3 shows a directory listing from a Linux server with the assigned permissions for each file or directory. The file permissions are listed to the right of the file. The first value specifies whether the file is a file (-) or a directory . The next three values specify the file rights for the user, the next three for the group, and the next three for the "everyone" assignment.

FIGURE 12.3
A directory listing from a Linux server, showing file and directory permissions.

Windows NT 4 and Windows 2000 File System Security

Both Windows NT 4 and Windows 2000 use the New Technology File System (NTFS) to provide file system security. Rights can be assigned to users, groups, and some special entities, which include the "everyone" assignment. Table 12.3 describes the basic file permissions that can be used with NTFS on Windows NT 4 and Windows 2000.

FIGURE 12.4
The Disk Properties screen, through which file permissions are assigned.

> **EXAM TIP**
>
> **Know the File Permissions** On the Network+ exam, you might be asked to identify valid and invalid file permissions for certain platforms.

TABLE 12.3

FILE PERMISSIONS WITH NTFS ON WINDOWS NT 4 AND WINDOWS 2000

Right	Description
Full Control	Provides all rights
Modify	Allows files to be modified
Read & Execute	Allows files to be read and executed (that is, run)
List Folder Contents	Allows the files in a folder to be listed
Read	Allows a file to be read
Write	Allows a file to be written to

Figure 12.4 shows the Disk Properties screen, through which file permissions are assigned.

An added complexity to file system security on Windows platforms is that the shares created to allow users to access folders across the network can also be assigned a set of permissions. Although these permissions are quite basic (Full Control, Change, and Read), they must be considered because they can be combined with NTFS permissions. The rule when this situation occurs is that the most restrictive permissions assignment applies. For example, if a user connects through a share with Read permission and then tries to access a file to which he has the NTFS Full Control right, the actual permissions would be Read. The most restrictive right (in this case, Read) overrides the other permissions assignment.

File Permissions Best Practices

In an ideal world, each and every file and directory would be assigned exactly the needed set of permissions that allows each and every user only the required level of access. If you have just a few dozen files, such an approach might be possible. But in the real world, where servers might have 200,000 files or more, it's simply not feasible.

The commonly adopted solution is to assign rights to directories (that is, folders) rather than files and then try to group files that have a similar level of access together in one location. If such a system is implemented carefully, it can work very well. However, it requires certain considerations, such as whether there are groups of files that require the same access, and it can be implemented only in environments where file system security is not a great concern.

FIREWALLS

▶ Identify the purpose, benefits, and characteristics of using a firewall.

Even though a firewall is considered a logical security measure, it deserves its own section because it is a specific objective for the Network+ exam.

A firewall is a system or group of systems that controls the flow of traffic between two networks. The most common use of a firewall is to protect a private network from a public network such as the Internet. However, firewalls are also increasingly being used as a means to separate a sensitive area of a private network from other, less-sensitive, areas of the private network.

At its most basic, a *firewall* is a device (it could be a computer system or a dedicated hardware device) that has more than one network interface and manages the flow of network traffic between those interfaces. How it manages the flow and what it does with certain types of traffic depend on its configuration. Figure 12.5 shows the most basic firewall configuration.

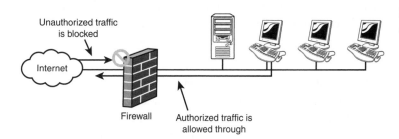

FIGURE 12.5
A basic firewall implementation.

Strictly speaking, a firewall performs no action on the packets it receives besides the basic functions just described. However, in a real-world implementation, a firewall is likely to offer other functionality, such as Network Address Translation (NAT) and proxy server services. Without NAT, any host on the internal network that needs to send or receive data through the firewall needs a registered IP address.

Although there are such environments, most people have to settle for using a private address range on the internal network and therefore rely on the firewall system to translate the outgoing request into an acceptable public network address.

The Purpose and Function of a Firewall

Although the fundamental purpose of a firewall is to protect one network from another, you need to configure the firewall to allow some traffic through. If you don't need to allow traffic to pass through a firewall, you can dispense with it entirely and completely separate your network from other networks.

A firewall can employ a variety of different methods to ensure security. A firewall can use just one of these methods, or it can combine different methods to produce the most appropriate and robust configuration. The following sections discuss the various firewall methods that are commonly used: packet filtering firewalls, circuit-level firewalls, and application gateway firewalls.

Packet-Filtering Firewalls

Of the firewall methods discussed in this chapter, *packet filtering* is the most commonly implemented. Packet filtering allows the firewall to examine each and every packet that passes through it and determine what to do with the packet, based on the configuration. A packet-filtering firewall deals with packets at the data-link and network layers of the Open Systems Interconnect (OSI) model. The following are some of the criteria by which packet filtering can be implemented:

◆ **IP address**—By using the IP address as a parameter, the firewall is able to allow or deny traffic, based on the source or destination IP address. For example, you can configure the firewall so that only certain hosts on the internal network are able to access hosts on the Internet. Alternatively, you can configure it so that only certain hosts on the Internet are able to gain access to a system on the internal network.

◆ **Port number**—As discussed in Chapter 6, "Working with TCP/IP," the Transmission Control Protocol/Internet Protocol (TCP/IP) protocol suite uses port numbers to identify what service a certain packet is destined for. By configuring the firewall to allow certain types of traffic, you can control the flow. You might, for example, open port 80 on the firewall to allow Hypertext Transfer Protocol (HTTP) requests from users on the Internet to reach the corporate Web server. You might also, depending on the application, open the HTTP Secure (HTTPS) port, port 443, to allow access to a secure Web server application.

◆ **Protocol ID**—Because each packet transmitted with IP has a protocol identifier in it, a firewall is able to read this value and then determine what kind of packet it is. If you are filtering based on protocol ID, you specify which protocols you will and will not allow to pass through the firewall.

◆ **MAC address**—This is perhaps the least used of the packet-filtering methods discussed, but it is possible to configure a firewall to use the hardware-configured MAC address as the determining factor in whether access to the network is granted. This is not a particularly flexible method, and it is therefore suitable only in environments where you can closely control who uses which MAC address. The Internet is not such an environment.

Circuit-Level Firewalls

Circuit-level firewalls are similar in operation to packet-filtering firewalls, but they operate at the transport layer of the OSI model. The biggest difference between a packet-filtering firewall and a circuit-level firewall is that a circuit-level firewall forwards all requests to the other network, using its own IP address rather than the IP address of the internal system that sent the request. This serves to "hide" the identity of the inside system, which is good from a security standpoint because outside users cannot see the internal network.

Application Gateway Firewalls

The application gateway firewall is the most functional of all the firewall types. As its name suggests, the application gateway firewall functionality is implemented through an application. Application gateway firewall systems can implement sophisticated rules and closely control traffic that passes through. Features of application

EXAM TIP

The Three Firewall Methods The three firewall methods described in this chapter are often combined into a single firewall application. Packet filtering is the basic firewall function. Circuit-level functionality provides NAT, and an application gateway firewall provides proxy functionality. This is a good thing to remember for the Network+ exam.

N O T E

Personal Firewalls   For exactly the same reasons that a firewall is implemented on a corporate network, you should consider protecting your personal computer at home with a firewall as well. The increasing use of always-on Internet access methods such as cable means that you are just as likely to become the target of an intruder at home as you are at work. Remember that most intruders are not looking for anything in particular; they are just looking for anything. If you connect to the Internet from a computer system, you are exposing yourself to millions of other users, some of whom would love to have a look at your hard drive to see if there is anything of interest. The solution is to implement a personal firewall, of which there are now quite a few. For a relatively small amount of money, you can protect your system against all but the most determined of intruders. Even if you have nothing to hide, you should still be aware of problems such as Distributed Denial of Service attacks (DDoS), which can use your system as a host to launch an attack on another host on the Internet.

gateway firewalls can include user authentication systems and the ability to control which systems an outside user can access on the Internal network.

Demilitarized Zones

An important firewall-related concept is demilitarized zones (DMZs). A DMZ is part of a network on which you place servers that must be accessible by sources both outside and inside your network. However, the DMZ is not connected directly to either network, and it must always be accessed through the firewall. The military term DMZ is used because it describes an area in which there is little or no enforcement or policing.

Using DMZs provides an extra level of flexibility, protection, and complexity to your firewall configuration. Figure 12.6 shows an example of a DMZ configuration.

By using a DMZ, you can create an additional step that makes it more difficult for an intruder to gain access to the internal network. In Figure 12.6, for example, an intruder who tried to come in through Interface 1 would have to spoof a request from either the Web server or proxy server into Interface 2 before it could be forwarded to the internal network. Although it is not impossible for an intruder to gain access through a DMZ, it is very difficult.

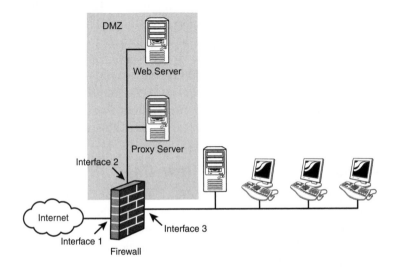

FIGURE 12.6
A DMZ configuration.

Firewalls have become common in businesses of all sizes. As the Internet becomes an ever more hostile place, firewalls and the individuals who understand them are likely to become an essential part of the IT landscape.

PROXY SERVERS

▶ Identify the purpose, benefits, and characteristics of using a proxy server.

Proxy servers provide what is now an essential feature of any modern network—Internet access. A *proxy server* acts as an intermediary between a user on the internal network and a service on the external network (normally the Internet). The proxy server takes requests from a user and then performs those requests on behalf of the user. To the external system, the request looks as if it originated from the proxy server, not from the user on the internal network. Figure 12.7 shows how a proxy server fits into a network configuration.

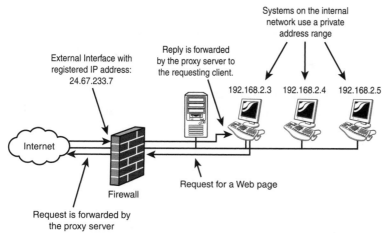

FIGURE 12.7
A proxy server in a typical network configuration.

There are a couple reasons to implement a proxy server:

◆ **To perform NAT functions**—A proxy server is able to process and execute commands on behalf of clients that have "private" IP addresses. This enables an organization with only one registered IP address to provide Internet access to a large number of computers.

N O T E

Single IP Address Representation A proxy server enables a network to appear to external networks as a single IP address—that of the external network interface of the proxy server.

N O T E **Proxy Servers Versus Firewalls** The function of a proxy server should not be confused with the function of a firewall, even though some applications integrate the functionality of both. In basic terms, a proxy server is a centralized point of access to the Internet. It also, generally, provides caching capabilities.

◆ **To allow Internet access to be controlled**—Having a centralized point of access allows for a great deal of control over the use of the Internet. By using the functionality of a proxy server application or by using an add-on feature, proxy servers can filter requests made by clients and either allow or disallow them. You could, for example, implement uniform resource locator (URL) filtering, which allows or denies users access to certain sites. More sophisticated products can also perform tests on retrieved material, to see if it fits acceptable criteria. Such measures are intended to prevent users from accessing inappropriate Internet Web pages. As an "after the event" feature, proxy server applications also normally provide logging capabilities so that Internet usage can be monitored.

Although the most common function of a proxy server is to provide access to the World Wide Web for internal clients, that is not its only function. A proxy server, by definition, can be used as an intermediary for anything, not just HTTP requests. Other services can be supported by a proxy server, depending on the proxy server application being used and the configuration. For example, you might configure a proxy server to service HTTP requests (TCP port 80), Post Office Protocol 3 (POP3) email retrieval (TCP port 110), Simple Mail Transfer Protocol (SMTP) mail sending (TCP port 25), and HTTPS requests (TCP port 443).

With an understanding of what a proxy server is designed to do, you can look at one additional feature built into proxy server functionality: caching.

Caching Proxy Servers

N O T E **Proxy Servers and Protocols** Proxy servers are sometimes referred to as *HTTP proxies* or *HTTP proxy servers*. In reality, most proxy servers provide proxy services for multiple protocols, not just HTTP.

An additional feature offered by many proxy server applications is caching; such a system is known as a *caching proxy server*. Caching allows the proxy server to store pages that it retrieves as files on disk. Consequently, if the same pages are requested again, they can be provided more quickly than if the proxy server had to go back to the Web server from which the pages were originally retrieved. This approach has two benefits:

◆ **Significantly improves performance**—Performance is improved particularly in environments such as a school, where there is a great likelihood that more than one user might retrieve the same page.

◆ **Reduces demands on Internet connections**—Because there are fewer requests to the Internet when a caching proxy server is in use, there is reduced demand on the Internet connection. In some cases, this results in a general speed improvement. In extreme cases, it might even be possible to adopt a less expensive Internet connectivity method because of the lower level of demand.

As with any technology, with caching proxy servers there are issues to be considered. Sometimes a sizable amount of hard disk space is required to store the cached pages. With the declining cost of hard disk space in recent years, this is not likely to be much of a problem, but it still needs to be considered.

Another factor is that it's possible for pages held in the cache to become stale. As a result, a user might retrieve a page and believe it is the latest version when in fact it has since changed but the new page has not been updated in the proxy server cache. To prevent this problem, caching proxy servers can implement measures such as aging of cached information so that it is removed from the cache after a certain amount of time. Some proxy applications are also able to check to make sure that the page stored in the cache is the same as the page currently available on the Internet. If the page in the cache is the same as the one on the Internet, it is served to the client from the cache. If the page is not the same, the newer page is retrieved, cached, and supplied to the client.

More advanced features of caching proxy servers are Internet Cache Protocol (ICP) and Caching Array Routing Protocol (CARP). Using these protocols, a proxy server can ask another proxy server if it has a user-requested page in its cache. If it does, the page is retrieved from the other proxy server, stored in cache, and then supplied to the client. Such an arrangement can be used only in environments where there are multiple proxy servers. The increasing availability of broadband and high-speed Internet access is making such environments increasingly rare.

FIGURE 12.8
The Proxy Settings configuration screen in
Internet Explorer.

Using a Proxy Server

Before clients can use a proxy server, it is necessary to configure the client applications to use it, and in some cases, additional client software is needed. In the case of Web browsers, it is necessary to manually tell the application that it needs to use a proxy server. Figure 12.8 shows the configuration screen in Microsoft Internet Explorer that allows the configuration of proxy parameters.

Other applications besides Web browsers might need to use the proxy server functionality. In some cases, you might need to actually load client software. In essence, this client software modifies elements of the TCP/IP software on the system, to either make it aware of or allow it to cope with the existence of a proxy server.

By now, you might have realized that both firewalls and proxy servers play an important part in the network infrastructure. For that reason, many applications are now available that combine the functionality of both roles. These "firewalling proxy servers" provide a convenient means for an organization to control and secure the access of its network, and at the same time provide the benefits of Internet access to users.

UNDERSTANDING HOW SECURITY AFFECTS A NETWORK

▶ Given a scenario, predict the impact of a particular security implementation on network functionality (e.g., blocking port numbers, encryption, etc.).

Implementing security measures has an effect on the network. How much of an effect it has depends on which security measures are implemented and the habits of the network users. CompTIA specifies two examples of network security measures (blocking ports and encryption) and asks that you determine what effect the implementation of those measures will have on the network. The following sections help you prepare for this part of the exam.

Blocking Port Numbers

Port blocking is one of the most widely used security methods on networks. Port blocking is associated with firewalls and proxy servers, although in fact it can be implemented on any system that provides a means to manage network data flow, according to data type.

Essentially, when you block a port, you disable the ability for traffic to pass through that port. Port blocking is typically implemented to prevent users on a public network from accessing systems on a private network, although it is equally possible to block internal users from external services by using the same procedure.

Depending on the type of firewall system in use on a network, you might find that all the ports are disabled (blocked) and that the ones you need traffic to flow through must be opened. The benefit of this strategy is that it forces the administrator to choose the ports that should be unblocked rather than specify those that need to be blocked. This ensures that you allow only those services that are absolutely necessary into the network.

What ports remain open largely depends on the needs of the organization. For example, the ports associated with the services listed in Table 12.4 are commonly left open.

TABLE 12.4

COMMONLY OPENED PORT NUMBERS AND THEIR ASSOCIATED USES

Port Number	Protocol	Purpose
80	HTTP	Web browsing
443	HTTPS	Secure Web transactions
21	FTP	File transfers
25	SMTP	Email sending
110	POP3	Email retrieval
53	DNS	Hostname resolution

These are, of course, only a few of the services you might need on a network, and allowing other services on a network is as easy as opening the port. Keep in mind that the more ports that are open, the more vulnerable you become to outside attacks. You should never open a port on a firewall unless you are absolutely sure that you need to open it.

Port Blocking and Network Users

Before you implement port blocking, you should have a very good idea of what the port is used for. Although it is true that blocking unused ports does not have any impact on internal network users, if the wrong port is blocked, you can suffer many headaches.

For instance, a network administrator was given the task of reducing the amount a spam emails received by his company. He decided to block port 25. He succeeded in blocking the spam email, but in the process, he also prevented users from sending and receiving email.

Encryption

Encryption is the process of encoding data so that, without the appropriate unlocking code, the encrypted data can't be read. Encryption is increasingly being used as a means of protecting data from unauthorized users. If you have ever used a secure Web site, you have used encryption.

On private networks, encryption is generally not a very big issue. Modern network operating systems often implement encryption so that passwords are not transmitted openly throughout the network. On the other hand, normal network transmissions are not usually encrypted, although they can be if the need arises. A far more common use for encryption is for data that is sent across a public network such as the Internet. In this case, the administrator has little or no control over the path the data takes to get to its destination. During data transmission, there is plenty of opportunity for someone to take the data from the network and then read the contents of the packets. This process is often referred to as *packet sniffing*.

By sniffing packets from the network and reading their contents, unauthorized users can gain access to private information. But packet sniffing is not possible with encrypted data. Without the necessary code to decrypt the data, the sniffer is able to see only jumbled code. There is a chance that the sniffer might be able to work out what the code is, but the stronger the form of encryption used, the harder it is for the sniffer to work out the code. Therefore, the stronger the encryption method that is used, the better protected the data is.

A number of encryption methods are commonly used. The following sections explain some of the most popular ones:

◆ IP Security (IPSec)

◆ Data Encryption Standard (DES)

◆ Triple DES (3DES)

◆ Pretty Good Privacy (PGP)

Internet Protocol Security (IPSec)

IPSec is a set of protocols developed by the Internet Engineering Task Force to establish secure transmission of data packets between computer systems. IPSec is commonly used for transmitting data across public networks, where privacy and security are an ever-present concern. Therefore, IPSec is often used to, among other things, create virtual private networks (VPNs).

IPSec works at the network layer of the OSI model. Therefore, all applications and services that use IP for the transport of data can use IPSec security. In comparison, security mechanisms such as Secure Sockets Layer (SSL), which operate above the network layer, provide security only for applications that can use SSL, such as Web browsers.

Data Encryption Standard (DES)

DES was originally developed by IBM in the mid-1970s, and it became a standard in 1977. DES encrypts and decrypts data in 64-bit chunks, using a 64-bit key. Although the key is 64 bits, the actual encryption key used by DES is a 56-bit key. This is because 1 bit in every byte is reserved for parity, which leaves 56 bits.

For a time, DES was a proven and trusted encryption method. However, over time, attacks against DES encryption methods were successful, and data security was compromised. Quite simply, as faster and less expensive computer systems became available, 56-bit key encryption became inadequate.

Interestingly, DES cracking contests in the late 1990s highlighted DES weaknesses. One system, which was developed for $250,000 and code-named the DES Cracker, shattered DES encryption in less than three days. Today's systems reduce both the cost and time necessary to crack DES encryption.

However, some companies still use the DES encryption method. But for organizations whose data is more sensitive, something stronger is needed.

3DES

Often referred to as "triple DES," 3DES is an improvement on the DES encryption standard and is much more widely used due to the increased difficulty involved in cracking 3DES encryption. Although 3DES is based on the DES standard, it is a much stronger version, and it is able to provide significantly more security for data than traditional DES.

3DES gets its name from the fact that it performs encryption the same way as regular DES, but it does it three times. Regular DES uses a 64-bit key encryption method, whereas 3DES uses three 64-bit keys, for an overall key length of 192 bits. Like DES, 1 of the bits in each byte is reserved for parity; therefore, the actual key is 168 bits.

Pretty Good Privacy (PGP)

Intended mainly as a mechanism to encrypt email transmission, PGP is a public-key encryption method created by Phil Zimmerman. PGP can be downloaded and used by anyone who wants to add a degree of security to email messages. A detailed discussion of PGP falls outside the scope of the Network+ objectives. For more information and PGP downloads, go to www.pgpi.org.

Auditing

Auditing is an important part of system security. It provides a means to track events that occur on a system. Auditing increases accountability on a network by making it possible to isolate events to certain users. For instance, it is possible to log failed logon attempts that might indicate that someone is trying to gain access to the network by guessing a username or password.

A network administrator might need to audit many different events on a system. Some of these events include failed/successful logons, audit printer access, file and directory access, and remote access. Reviewing the log files generated by auditing allows an administrator to better gauge the potential threats to the network. (Exercise 12.1 at the end of this chapter describes the procedures involved in enabling auditing on a Windows 2000 server.)

IN THE FIELD

ESCALATION PROCEDURES

One of the most important aspects of network security is knowing what to do when a security problem occurs. The exact actions you take depend on the circumstances surrounding the breach and what the breach actually is.

For example, your reaction to the discovery that two users are sharing the same user account would be very different from your reaction if you found that a cracker had gained access to your e-commerce Web server during the night. In either case, *after* an event has happened is not the time to think, "What do I do now?"

If there is one blanket rule to security breaches, it is that as soon as is practically possible, management should be informed of the problem. As discussed at the beginning of the chapter, the implications of a security issue can affect the viability and continuation of the business. For such incidents to be dealt with and to ensure that the business is not affected, management participation is necessary.

CHAPTER SUMMARY

KEY TERMS

- physical security
- logical security
- file system security
- authentication
- password policy
- inheritance
- firewalls
- packet filtering
- port number
- MAC address
- circuit-level firewall
- application gateway firewall
- DMZ
- personal firewalls
- proxy server
- NAT
- caching proxy server
- encryption
- IPSec
- DES
- 3DES

Network security is a complex subject, and it should be a primary focus for any network administrator.

Being able to effectively secure a network involves understanding the risks that can be a threat to the network as well as what the result of a breach in security might entail.

There is a distinction between physical security and logical security. Physical security involves physically protecting data by controlling access to the network equipment or servers that hold that data. Logical security involves protecting the data on a network from being accessed by unauthorized personnel.

Network operating systems include features that allow you to protect the data on a network by providing authentication capabilities, logon restrictions, file system rights, and in some cases, auditing. Depending on the environment, you might not use all these features, but you are sure to use some of them.

Two important elements of a network security picture are the use of proxy servers and firewall systems. A firewall system acts as a protective layer to network access by controlling the traffic that passes between the interfaces on the system. Proxy servers allow you to centralize access to the Internet and therefore provide a way to control and monitor network access.

Understanding how implementing security features such as port blocking and encryption will affect the network and the users on it is another important aspect of network security.

As well as implementing measures that serve to protect the network, you must also be able to detect intrusions to the network and provide procedures that define what steps should be taken when a breach does occur. All these elements must be combined in order to have an effective network security policy.

APPLY YOUR KNOWLEDGE

Exercises

12.1 Activating Logon Auditing on a Windows 2000 Server

Many different elements go into developing an effective security strategy. Two of these elements are configuring and setting up a password policy and configuring system auditing. In this exercise, you learn the procedures involved in activating the auditing feature on a Windows 2000 Server system. (Remember that to enable auditing, you need to have administrative privileges.)

Estimated time: 15 minutes

1. Select Start, Programs, Administrative Tools, and then select Local Security Policy. The Local Security Settings dialog box, shown in Figure 12.9, appears.

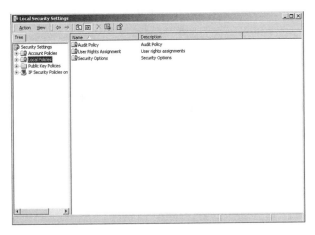

FIGURE 12.9
The Local Security Settings dialog box in Windows 2000 Server.

2. On the left side of the dialog box, click on the Local Policies folder, and then double-click the Audit Policy file folder on the right side of the dialog box. The auditable policies are displayed. Figure 12.10 shows the auditable policies.

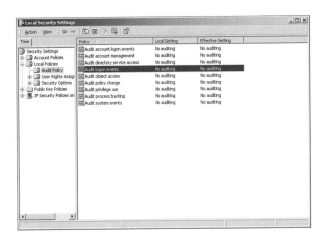

FIGURE 12.10
The auditable policies on a Windows 2000 Server system.

3. Double-click the Audit Logon Events icon. This opens the Local Security Policy Setting dialog box, which is shown in Figure 12.11.

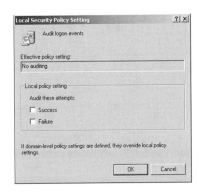

FIGURE 12.11
The Local Security Policy Setting dialog box in Windows 2000 Server.

APPLY YOUR KNOWLEDGE

4. Select the Success and Failure check boxes to audit both successful and failed logon attempts, and then click OK.

5. View the Local and Effective Setting columns to view the new auditing configuration. (Note that if the domain-level security policy is defined for these values, they will override the local security policy settings.)

12.2   Setting Password Policies

As a network administrator, you might be required to establish a password policy for the organization. In this exercise, you identify where password policies are set in Windows 2000 and how to set them. Specifically, you set a specific maximum password age.

Estimated time: 10 minutes

1. Select Start, Programs, Administrative Tools, and then select Domain Security Policy from the menu. The Domain Security Policy dialog box, shown in Figure 12.12, appears.

FIGURE 12.12
The Domain Security Policy dialog box in Windows 2000.

2. On the left side of the dialog box, click the Account Policies icon, and then double-click the Password Policy option on the right side of the dialog box. The password policy options are displayed.

3. Double-click the Maximum Password Age option. The Security Policy Setting dialog box, which is shown in Figure 12.13, appears.

FIGURE 12.13
The Security Policy Setting dialog box in Windows 2000.

4. In the Passwords Expire In field, enter the number of days before the password expires. Click OK. The new password policy is now active for the system.

12.3   Testing Password Strength

Network administrators are required to set strong passwords and ensure that users also set strong passwords. In this exercise, you test password strength.

Estimated time: 10 minutes

1. Log on to the Internet, and type **https://www.securitystats.com** in the address box of your browser. You arrive at the Secure Stats Web site.

2. On the left side of the screen, under the Awareness Tools menu, click the Password Strength option.

APPLY YOUR KNOWLEDGE

3. You are redirected to the Password Security Web site. In the Test the Strength of a Sample Password field, type the password you would like to test.

4. The password strength is displayed in a bar graph, ranging from Weak Passwords to Strong Passwords. After getting the results on the password strength, try to increase the password's strength by using different characters or by using uppercase and lowercase letters.

Exam Questions

1. Which of the following are benefits of using a proxy server? (Choose the three best answers.)

   a. It allows costs associated with Internet access to be reduced.

   b. It provides a central point of Internet access.

   c. It allows Internet access to be controlled.

   d. It allows hostnames to be resolved to IP addresses.

2. On a packet-filtering firewall, which of the following is not used as a criterion for making forwarding decisions?

   a. IP address

   b. MAC address

   c. TCP/IP port

   d. NetBIOS service name

3. What is the basic reason for implementing a firewall?

   a. It reduces the costs associated with Internet access.

b. It provides NAT functionality.

c. It provides a mechanism to protect one network from another.

d. It allows Internet access to be centralized.

4. Which of the following is the strongest password?

   a. *password*

   b. *WE300GO*

   c. *l00Ka1ivE*

   d. *lovethemusic*

5. Which of the following best describes 3DES?

   a. It uses 56-bit key encryption.

   b. It is Windows platform specific.

   c. It uses 192-bit encryption.

   d. It uses triple 168-bit encryption.

6. When defining a password policy for an organization, which of the following would you consider setting? (Choose the three best answers.)

   a. Minimum password length

   b. Password expiration period

   c. Prevention of password reuse

   d. Maximum password length

7. What is the name for an area that is connected to a firewall but is neither in the private network area nor the public network area?

   a. Area of no return

   b. Demilitarized zone

   c. No man's land

   d. Forbidden zone

APPLY YOUR KNOWLEDGE

8. At which two layers of the OSI model does a packet-filtering firewall operate? (Choose the two best answers.)

   a. Network

   b. Data-link

   c. Transport

   d. Application

9. You have installed a proxy server on a network and configured it to allow all the hosts on the internal network to access the Internet through it. None of the users on the internal network are able to access the Internet, although they could before you implemented the proxy server. What is the most likely cause of the problem?

   a. The proxy server is not configured correctly.

   b. The Internet connection is not working.

   c. The Web browser on the client system needs to be reconfigured to use a proxy server.

   d. The HTTP proxy service is not enabled on the system.

10. What is the purpose of auditing?

    a. It allows you to be notified when a security breach is detected.

    b. It allows you to determine whether there has been a security breach.

    c. It allows you to prevent security breaches.

    d. It allows you to control Internet access from a single point.

11. After noticing that there have been several attempts to access your network from the Internet, you decide to block port 53. Which of the following services is associated with port 53?

    a. WINS

    b. DNS

    c. SMTP

    d. POP3

12. At which level of the OSI model does a circuit-level firewall operate?

    a. Transport

    b. Data-link

    c. Network

    d. Physical

13. Which of the following is not a valid file permission on a Unix/Linux system?

    a. Read

    b. Write

    c. Execute

    d. Erase

14. You suspect that an employee in the company has been logging on to the system from a remote connection and attempting to look through files that he should not have access to. Which mechanism could you use to discover the identity of the person trying to dial in?

    a. Auditing

    b. File permissions

    c. Password policy

    d. Intruder detection

APPLY YOUR KNOWLEDGE

15. Which of the following network operating system platforms uses inheritance filters to prevent file permissions from flowing through the directory structure?

    a. NetWare

    b. Linux

    c. Windows 2000

    d. Windows 98

16. Which of the following is not a valid file permission on a NetWare server?

    a. Read

    b. Write

    c. Full Control

    d. Modify

17. Your company is moving from a client-based email system to a Web-based solution. After all the users have been successfully moved to the new system, what are you likely to do on the corporate firewall? (Choose the two best answers.)

    a. Block port 53

    b. Block port 110

    c. Block port 80

    d. Block port 25

18. Which of the following is considered a physical security measure?

    a. Password policy

    b. Locks on equipment cabinets

    c. Auditing policy

    d. Firewall

19. Which of the following is not a valid file permission on a Windows 2000 NTFS partition?

    a. Full Control

    b. Read

    c. Modify

    d. Change

20. You are a network administrator for a small company in Alaska that makes knitted hats. It is expected that your company will experience huge growth, and a competitive company is seeking the design for your company's latest toque, which is code-named "Frost Killer." Your manager is concerned that a rogue employee might be preparing to sell the design to the competition, so you have been given the task of securing the company's data on your Windows 2000 server. Which of the following would you do?

    a. Block ports.

    b. Use a proxy server.

    c. Implement file system security.

    d. Install a firewall.

Answers to Exam Questions

1. **a, b, c.** A proxy server allows the costs associated with Internet access to be reduced, provides a central point of Internet access, and allows Internet access to be controlled. Answer d describes the function of a DNS server. For more information, see the section "Proxy Server," in this chapter.

APPLY YOUR KNOWLEDGE

2. **d.** Firewalls do not make forwarding decisions based on the NetBIOS service name, which is fictitious. All the other answers are valid means by which a firewall can make filtering decisions. For more information, see the section "Firewalls," in this chapter.

3. **c.** Implementing a firewall allows you to have protection between networks, typically from the Internet to a private network. All the other answers describe functions offered by a proxy server. Note that some firewall systems do offer NAT functionality, but NAT is not a firewall feature; it is an added benefit of these systems. For more information, see the section "Firewalls," in this chapter.

4. **c.** Strong passwords include a combination of letters and numbers and upper- and lowercase letters. In this question Answer c is by far the strongest password. Answer a is not a strong password because it is a standard word, contains no numbers, and is all in lowercase. Answer b mixes letters and numbers, and it is not a recognized word, so it is a strong password, although it is not as strong as Answer c. Answer d is too easy to guess and contains no numbers. For more information, see the section "Physical and Logical Security," in this chapter.

5. **c.** 3DES uses a 192-bit encryption key. None of the other answers are valid. For more information, see the section "Understanding How Security Affects a Network," in this chapter.

6. **a, b, c.** When creating a password policy, you should set a minimum password length, parameters limiting reusing the old password, and a password expiration period. You may even want to set a maximum password length. For more

information, see the section "Physical and Logical Security," in this chapter.

7. **b.** A DMZ is an area of a network where you would place systems that must be accessed by users outside the network. All the other answers are invalid. For more information, see the section "Firewalls," in this chapter.

8. **a, b.** Packet-filtering firewalls work at the data-link and network layers of the OSI model. None of the other answers are valid. For more information, see the section "Firewalls," in this chapter.

9. **c.** In order for Web browsers to access the Internet through a proxy server, they must be correctly configured. Given the scenario, Answer c is the most likely answer. For more information, see the section "Proxy Servers," in this chapter.

10. **b.** Auditing is a process of reviewing security logs so that breaches can be detected. Answer a describes the function of alerting. The other answers are not valid. For more information, see the section "Understanding How Security Affects a Network," in this chapter.

11. **b.** DNS uses port 53. None of the other services use port 53. For more information, see the section "Understanding How Security Affects a Network," in this chapter.

12. **a.** A circuit-level firewall works at the transport layer of the OSI model. None of the other answers are valid. For more information, see the section "Firewalls," in this chapter.

13. **d.** Erase is not a valid file permission on Linux or Unix systems. Read, Write, and Execute are all valid Linux file permissions. For more information, see the section "Physical and Logical Security," in this chapter.

APPLY YOUR KNOWLEDGE

14. **a.** To determine the user ID of a person trying to log on, you would implement auditing. File permissions, password policies, and intruder detection would not help you to do this. For more information, see the section "Understanding How Security Affects a Network," in this chapter.

15. **a.** Novell NetWare uses filters to prevent file permissions from flowing through the directory tree. None of the other network operating systems use inheritance filters as part of their file system security structure. For more information, see the section "Physical and Logical Security," in this chapter.

16. **c.** Full Control is not a valid right. The equivalent on a NetWare server is Supervisor. All the other answers are valid NetWare file permissions. For more information, see the section "Physical and Logical Security," in this chapter.

17. **b, d.** Because users will access their email via a Web browser, the firewall will not need to accommodate POP3 (port 110) and SMTP (port 25).

Blocking port 53 would disable DNS lookups, and blocking port 80 would disable Web browsing (HTTP). For more information, see the section "Understanding How Security Affects a Network," in this chapter.

18. **b.** Locks on a cabinet would be considered a physical security measure. All the other answers are considered logical security measures. For more information, see the section "Physical and Logical Security," in this chapter.

19. **d.** Change is not a valid NTFS file permission. All the other permissions are valid on an NTFS partition. For more information, see the section "Physical and Logical Security," in this chapter.

20. **c.** Implementing file system permissions can help secure data on the internal network. Blocking ports would prevent external users but would likely have no effect on internal users. The same is true of implementing a proxy server. Answer d is not a valid option. For more information, see the section "Physical and Logical Security," in this chapter.

APPLY YOUR KNOWLEDGE

Suggested Readings and Resources

1. Habraken, Joe. *Absolute Beginner's Guide to Networking,* third edition. Que Publishing, 2001.

2. Shinder, Debra Littlejohn. *Computer Networking Essentials.* Cisco Press, 2001.

3. Northcutt, Steven, David Mclachlan, Judy Novak. *Network Intrusion Detection: An Analysis Handbook,* second edition. New Riders Publishing, 2000.

4. Zwicky, Elizabeth D., Simon Cooper, Brent Chapman, Deborah Russell. *Building Internet Firewalls,* second edition. O'Reilly & Associates, 2000.

5. Norberg, Stephan, Deborah Russell. *Securing Windows NT/2000 Servers for the Internet.* O'Reilly & Associates, 2000.

6. Linux security information, www.linuxsecurity.com.

7. Windows NT/2000 security information, www.ntsecurity.net.

8. Computer Security Institute, www.gocsi.com.

9. Computer networking tutorials and advice, compnetworking.about.com.

10. "TechEncyclopedia," www.techencyclopedia.com.

This chapter covers the following CompTIA-specified objectives for the "Network Support" section of the Network+ exam.

Given a troubleshooting scenario, select the appropriate TCP/IP utility from among the following:

- `tracert`
- `ping`
- `arp`
- `netstat`
- `nbtstat`
- `ipconfig/ifconfig`
- `winipcfg`
- `nslookup`

▶ Many TCP/IP troubleshooting utilities are available. Knowing which one to use in a given scenario is an essential skill for the real world and the Network+ exam.

Given a troubleshooting scenario involving a small office/home office network failure (e.g., xDSL, cable, home satellite, wireless, POTS), identify the cause of the problem.

▶ The proliferation of small office and home office networks has given rise to a new type of specialized troubleshooting—one that has some very different considerations than those involved in working on a corporate network.

CHAPTER 13

Troubleshooting Connectivity

Given a troubleshooting scenario involving a remote connectivity problem (e.g., authentication failure, protocol configuration, physical connectivity) identify the cause of the problem.

▶ Today remote connectivity is the norm rather than the exception. As a network administrator, you will be expected to be able to troubleshoot remote connectivity issues.

Introduction	**500**
Troubleshooting Tools	**500**
The ping Utility	501
Troubleshooting with ping	502
Switches for ping	503
The Trace Route Utility	504
The arp Utility	506
The ARP Cache	506
Switches for arp	507
The netstat Utility	507
Switches for netstat	508
The nbtstat Utility	509
The ipconfig and ifconfig Utilities	511
The ipconfig Utility	511
The ifconfig Utility	512
The winipcfg Utility	512
The nslookup Utility	513
The route Utility	515
Troubleshooting in a Small Office/ Home Office Environment	**516**
DSL Internet Access	520
DSL Troubleshooting Procedures	522
Cable Internet Access	523
Cable Troubleshooting Procedures	524

Home Satellite Internet Access	525
Home Satellite Troubleshooting Procedures	526
Wireless Internet Access	526
Wireless Troubleshooting Procedures	527
POTS Internet Access	528
POTS Troubleshooting Procedures	529
Troubleshooting Poor Connection Speeds	531
Modem-Specific Troubleshooting	532
Calling Technical Support	533

Troubleshooting Remote Connectivity Errors **534**

Troubleshooting Authentication Failure	534
Troubleshooting Physical Connectivity Problems	535
Troubleshooting Protocol Configuration Problems	536

Chapter Summary **537**

Apply Your Knowledge **539**

Study Strategies

▶ Read the objectives at the beginning of the chapter.

▶ Study the information in the chapter, paying special attention to the tables, which summarize key information.

▶ Review the objectives again.

▶ Pay close attention to the example scenarios. They focus on specific areas of knowledge for the Network+ exam.

▶ Answer the exam questions at the end of the chapter and check your results.

▶ Use the ExamGear test on the CD-ROM that accompanies this book to answer additional exam questions concerning this material.

▶ Review the notes, tips, and exam tips in this chapter. Make sure you understand the information in the exam tips. If you don't understand the topic referenced in an exam tip, refer to the information in the chapter text and then read the exam tip again.

EXAM TIP

Windows   Although the Network+ exam is touted as being vendor independent, CompTIA appears to have written the objectives and the exam with the Windows platform firmly in mind. Where necessary for the Network+ exam, this chapter provides information for the utilities on other platforms.

INTRODUCTION

There are two certainties in the networking world. The first is that you will be working on networks that use Transmission Control Protocol/Internet Protocol (TCP/IP). The second is that at some point, you will be troubleshooting those networks. This chapter focuses on identifying the TCP/IP utilities that are commonly used when working with TCP/IP networks and explains how to use those utilities in the troubleshooting process.

TROUBLESHOOTING TOOLS

▶ Given a troubleshooting scenario, select the appropriate TCP/IP utility from among the following:

- `tracert`
- `ping`
- `arp`
- `netstat`
- `nbtstat`
- `ipconfig/ifconfig`
- `winipcfg`
- `nslookup`

The best way to work through this chapter is to try each of the utilities discussed, to get a better idea of how they are used and what they were designed to do. These tools are the core utilities used in the troubleshooting of TCP/IP networks and are used extensively real-world environments. The following sections describe these utilities:

- ◆ `ping`
- ◆ Trace route
- ◆ `arp`
- ◆ `netstat`
- ◆ `nbtstat`
- ◆ `ipconfig` and `ifconfig`

◆ winipcfg

◆ nslookup

◆ route

Note that not all the tools discussed here are available on every operating system. However, the discussion begins by looking at one that is not only available on all platforms but is arguably the most used—and most useful—of all troubleshooting utilities: ping.

The ping Utility

ping is a command-line utility designed to test connectivity between systems on a TCP/IP-based network. Its basic function is to answer one simple question: "Can I see another host?" ping can be a network administrator's right hand; most TCP/IP troubleshooting procedures begin with the ping utility and, if necessary, work from there. We say "if necessary" because the information provided by the ping command can often isolate the cause of a problem so that further action is not needed.

ping works by using Internet Control Message Protocol (ICMP) packets to ascertain whether another system is connected to the network and able to respond. A successful ping request requires that a packet, called an *ICMP echo request*, be sent to a remote host. If the remote host receives the packet, it sends an *ICMP echo reply* in return, and the ping is a success. Figure 13.1 shows the output from a successful ping request.

EXAM TIP

Command Output For each of the commands discussed in this chapter, be sure that you are able to identify the output. On the Network+ exam, you will likely be asked to identify the output from these commands.

```
C:\WINNT\System32\command.com

C:\>ping 24.67.184.1

Pinging 24.67.184.1 with 32 bytes of data:

Reply from 24.67.184.1: bytes=32 time=40ms TTL=64
Reply from 24.67.184.1: bytes=32 time=40ms TTL=64
Reply from 24.67.184.1: bytes=32 time=40ms TTL=64
Reply from 24.67.184.1: bytes=32 time=30ms TTL=64

Ping statistics for 24.67.184.1:
    Packets: Sent = 4, Received = 4, Lost = 0 (0% loss),
Approximate round trip times in milli-seconds:
    Minimum = 30ms, Maximum = 40ms, Average = 37ms

C:\>
```

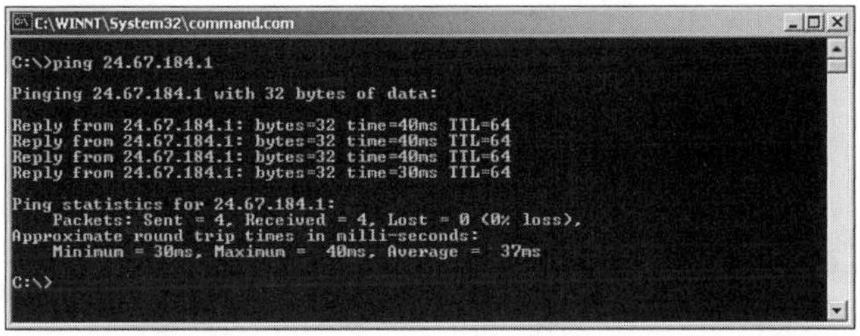

FIGURE 13.1
A successful ping request.

Notice in Figure 13.1 that four packets are sent to the remote host. These packets are 32 bytes in size and took 40ms, 40ms, 40ms, and 30ms to reach their destination. The time= section of the ping command output is often important, because a high number could indicate congestion on the network or a routing problem. The version of the ping utility shown in Figure 13.1 is from a Windows 2000 system. Other versions might send more packets or larger packets.

Sometimes ping requests fail. When a ping fails, you know that you are unable to connect to a remote host. Figure 13.2 shows the output from a failed ping command.

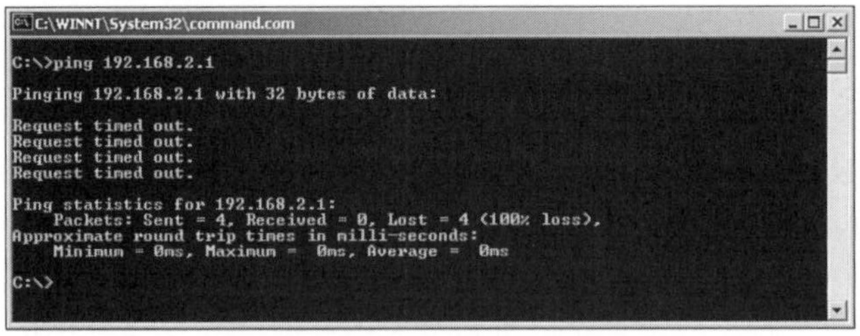

FIGURE 13.2
A failed ping command.

```
C:\WINNT\System32\command.com                                    _|□|×|

C:\>ping 192.168.2.1

Pinging 192.168.2.1 with 32 bytes of data:

Request timed out.
Request timed out.
Request timed out.
Request timed out.

Ping statistics for 192.168.2.1:
    Packets: Sent = 4, Received = 0, Lost = 4 (100% loss),
Approximate round trip times in milli-seconds:
    Minimum = 0ms, Maximum = 0ms, Average = 0ms

C:\>
```

> **NOTE**
>
> **The Loopback Adapter** The *loopback adapter* is a special function within the protocol stack that is supplied for troubleshooting purposes. The Class A IP address 127.X.X.X is reserved for the loopback; although convention dictates that you use 127.0.0.1, you can use any address in the 127.X.X.X range, except for the network number itself (127.0.0.0) and the broadcast address (127.255.255.255). You can also ping by using the default hostname for the local system, which is called localhost (for example, ping localhost).

Troubleshooting with ping

Although ping does not completely isolate problems, you can use it to help identify where a problem lies. When troubleshooting with ping, you take the following steps:

1. ping the IP address of your local loopback adapter, using the command ping 127.0.0.1. If this command is successful, you know that the TCP/IP protocol suite is installed correctly on your system and functioning. If you are unable to ping the local loopback adapter, TCP/IP might need to be reloaded or reconfigured on the machine you are using.

2. ping the IP address of your local network interface card (NIC). If the ping is successful, you know that your interface is functioning on the network and has TCP/IP correctly installed. If you are unable to ping the local interface, TCP/IP might not be bound correctly to the card or the network card drivers might be improperly installed.

3. ping the IP address of another node on your local network. By doing so you can determine whether the computer you are using is able to see other computers on the network. If you can ping other devices on your local network, you have network connectivity.

If you cannot `ping` other devices on your local network and you were able to `ping` your local network card, you might not be connected to the network correctly, or there might be a cable problem on the computer. After you've confirmed that you have network connectivity for the local network, you can verify connectivity to a remote network by sending a `ping` to the IP address of the default gateway.

4. If you are able to `ping` the default gateway, you can verify remote connectivity by sending a `ping` to the IP address of a system on a remote network.

Using just the `ping` command in these steps, you can confirm network connectivity on not only the local network but also on a remote network. The whole process requires as much time as it takes to type in the command—and you can do it all from a single location.

If you are an optimistic person, you can perform step 5 first. If that works, all the other steps will also work, saving you the need to test them. If your step 4 trial fails, you can go back to step 1 and start the troubleshooting process from the beginning.

Switches for `ping`

If you've spent any time working with command-line utilities, you no doubt already know that every command is accompanied by a number of switches, or options. The switches let you customize the behavior of the command. Although some switches (we'll call them that from now on) are rarely used, others come in handy under a The `ping` command offers several switches, the most widely used of which, `-t`, sends continuous packets rather than just a few. This switch sets the `ping` command to continue to `ping` the remote host until it is stopped by keyboard input. This switch is particularly helpful when you're troubleshooting connectivity issues such as a suspect cable. Table 13.1 shows the available switches for the `ping` command on a Windows 2000 system.

EXAM TIP

Connectivity Problems   On the Network+ exam, you might be asked to relate the correct procedure for using `ping` for a connectivity problem.

EXAM TIP

Testing TCP/IP Installations   To test a system to see if TCP/IP is installed, working, and configured correctly, you can `ping` the loopback address and then `ping` the IP address of the local system (`localhost`).

EXAM TIP

`ping` Using DNS   The `ping` examples used in this section show the `ping` command using the IP address of the remote host. It is also possible to `ping` the Domain Name Service (DNS) name of the remote host (for example, `ping www.comptia.org`, `ping server1`); this, of course, can be done only if your network uses a DNS server. On a Windows-based network, you can also `ping` by using the Network Basic Input/Output System (NetBIOS) computer name.

EXAM TIP

Switches   Even the most obscure switches for the commands discussed in this chapter might appear on the Network+ exam.

More Options   Newer versions of Windows such as Windows XP have more switches for the `ping` command. These extra switches are not included on the Network+ exam.

More Switches   Of the switches listed in Table 13.1, the ones most likely to appear on the Network+ exam are the `-t`, `-a`, and `-n` switches.

`ping` Example Scenario   Suppose you have been asked to troubleshoot a computer system that is unable to print to a network printer. You have verified that the computer is logged on to the network with the correct username and password and that the printer is online and functioning. However, you are still unable to print.

`ping` Example Solution   In this scenario, it would be a good idea to use the `ping` command to determine whether the computer can see the printer. To do this, you can `ping` the IP address of the printer. If you successfully `ping` the printer, then you know that the printer is working, as least as far as network connectivity is concerned. If you are unable to `ping` the network printer, then there is a network problem. Try to `ping` a different device on the network; if you're successful, the network problem is likely with the printer.

TABLE 13.1

`ping` SWITCHES ON A WINDOWS 2000 SYSTEM

Switch	Description
`-t`	`ping`s a device on the network until stopped. To stop it, press Ctrl+C.
`-a`	Tells the `ping` utility to resolve the IP address to a hostname as well as perform the `ping`.
`-n count`	Specifies the number of `ping` requests to send to the remote host. Example: `ping -n 15 <IP address>`.
`-l size`	Specifies the size of the `ping` request to send.
`-f`	Specifies that the "Don't Fragment" flag is set in the packet.
`-i TTL`	Specifies the time to live for the packet.
`-v TOS`	Specifies the type of service for the packet to be sent.
`-r count`	Records the route hops that the packet takes on its journey.
`-w timeout`	Specifies the timeout, in milliseconds, during which the `ping` utility should wait for each reply.

The Trace Route Utility

Sometimes `ping` just isn't enough. In such cases, you need to reach for something a little stronger. Trace route is a TCP/IP utility that is used to track the path a packet takes to reach a remote host. Each of the network operating systems, with the exclusion of NetWare, provides a trace route utility, but the name of the command and the output vary slightly in each. Table 13.2 shows the trace route command syntax used in various operating systems.

TABLE 13.2

TRACE ROUTE UTILITY COMMANDS

Operating System	Trace Route Command Syntax
Windows 2000/NT	`tracert <IP address>`
Novell NetWare	`iptrace.nlm`
Linux/Unix	`traceroute <IP address>`
OS/2	`tracerte <IP address>`

What exactly does the trace route command trace? The simple answer, of course, is routes. Local area networks (LANs) and wide area networks (WANs) can have several routes that packets can follow to reach their destinations. These routes are kept in routing tables that hold the information used to tell the packets how they will travel through the network. The trace route utility lets you track the path a packet takes through the network. Figure 13.3 shows the results of a successful trace route command in Windows 2000.

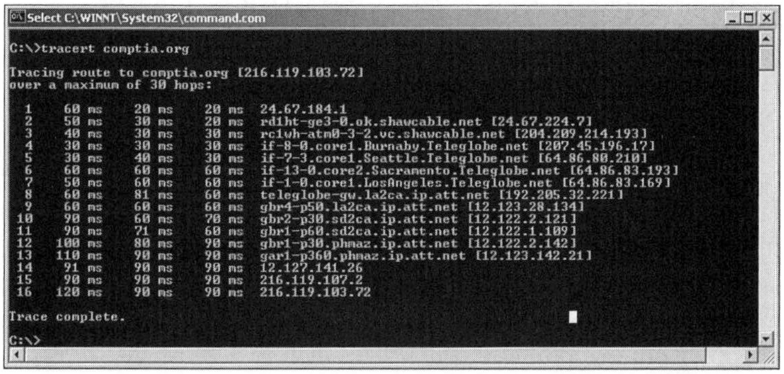

FIGURE 13.3
A trace route command in Windows 2000.

Not all trace route commands are as successful as the one in Figure 13.3. A trace route command that has an asterisk (*) in the entries shows that the particular hop was timed out. Several consecutive asterisks indicate a problem with the routing information or congestion on the network. Figure 13.4 shows an example of a failed trace route command.

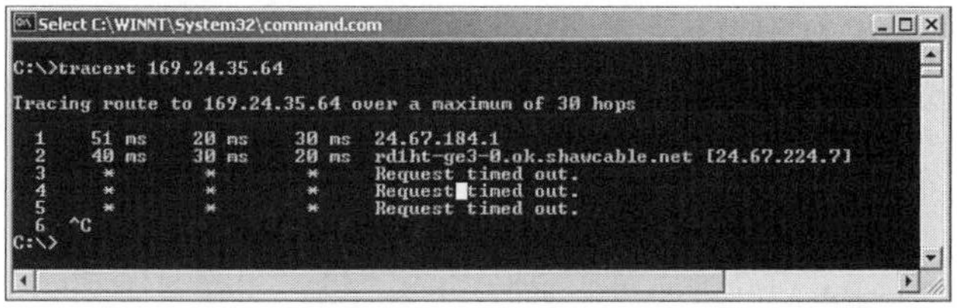

FIGURE 13.4
A failed trace route command from a Windows 2000 system.

In the example shown in Figure 13.4, the route is traced over a number of hops before it times out on the next hop of the route. In this example, pressing Ctrl+C terminates the trace; but if the trace route command were left to its own devices, it would run to 30 steps, like the successful trace.

EXAM TIP

Isolating Bottlenecks Because trace route reports the amount of time it takes to reach each host in the path, it is useful tool for isolating bottlenecks in a network. You need to know this for the exam.

NOTE

Trace Route Example Scenario
Suppose a user on your network complains that she is unable to access files located in an offsite location. However, she can access all files within the local network.

Trace Route Example Solution   In this case, you could use the trace route command to determine how far the packet travels before it fails. You would probably perform the trace route command with the IP address of the computer holding the files in the offsite location. The results from the command would determine how far the packet reaches before it's dropped.

In a network troubleshooting situation, trace route is often used in concert with ping. First, you use trace route to determine where on a route the connectivity problem lies. Then, from the point of the problem, you can determine the possible cause of the problem by using ping.

The arp Utility

As discussed in Chapter 6, "Working with TCP/IP," Address Resolution Protocol (ARP) is the part of the TCP/IP suite that resolves IP addresses to Media Access Control (MAC) addresses. Such a translation is necessary because even though systems use IP addresses to find each other, the low-level communication between devices occurs using the MAC address.

When two systems on an IP network want to communicate, they first establish each other's location by using the IP address. Then, ARP requests are sent to ascertain the MAC address of the devices so that they can communicate with each other. In a sense, the IP address is the name by which a system can be found in a phone book, and the MAC address is the actual phone number used to establish communication.

The ARP Cache

ARP translations are typically stored locally on systems in the ARP cache. But how does the MAC address from another computer system end up in your system's ARP cache? Each time you access another host, your system broadcasts to the ARP component of every host on the network. Because the IP address is embedded in the request, all systems other than the chosen one ignore the request, but the target system receives the request and replies accordingly. At this point both hosts record each other's MAC address in their local ARP cache, and these entries remain in the cache until they are timed out, which depends on how often they are accessed. If the ARP entry is reused, the time period is extended further.

The ARP table can hold two different types of entries: static and dynamic. Static entries do not expire and can be added to the ARP cache manually via the -s switch. Dynamic entries are added as the system accesses other hosts on the network.

EXAM TIP

ARP and OSI   ARP operates at the network layer of the Open Systems Interconnect (OSI) model.

To view the ARP cache on a Windows 2000 computer, you use the arp -a command. Figure 13.5 shows an example of an ARP cache, the result of using arp -a.

FIGURE 13.5
An ARP cache.

Switches for arp

As with the other command-line utilities discussed in this chapter, arp has a few associated switches. Table 13.3 lists some of the switches commonly used with the arp command.

TABLE 13.3

COMMONLY USED arp COMMAND SWITCHES

Switch	Description
-a	Displays the current ARP entries. If there is more than one interface, ARP resolution for each interface is displayed.
inet_addr	Resolves the MAC address of a remote system identified in the inet_addr field.
-N if_addr	Displays the ARP entries for a specific network interface.
-d inet_addr	Deletes the entry for the specified host.
-s inet_addr eth_addr	Allows you to add a static entry to the ARP cache. Must be used with both the IP address (inet_addr) and the MAC address (eth_addr).

> **NOTE**
>
> **arp Example Scenario** Suppose you receive a message on a client machine, stating that a duplicate IP address is being used on the network. What do you do?
>
> **arp Example Solution** The ARP command is well suited for troubleshooting duplicate IP addresses on a network. The ARP cache holds information, which includes the MAC address and its associated IP address. From this information, it is possible to determine where the IP conflict lies.

The netstat Utility

The netstat command displays packet statistics such as how many packets have been sent and received as well as other related protocol information. It is also used to view both inbound and outbound TCP/IP network connections. This utility is popular with seasoned network administrators whose information needs go far beyond what utilities such as ping can provide.

On a Windows system, there are essentially four columns to view when using the netstat command without switches. The first is Proto, which identifies the protocol being used. The second is the Local Address column, which specifies the local address and the local port being used. Next is the Foreign Address column, which identifies the destination address and port used. Finally, the State column lists whether the connection has been established; this column is used to determine the current status of your TCP connections.

As with the other command-line utilities, you can use a number of available switches with the netstat command. Without using any of these switches, the output from a netstat command would resemble the output shown in Figure 13.6.

FIGURE 13.6
Output from a netstat command in Windows 2000.

Switches for netstat

A handful of switches are used with the netstat command. Table 13.4 shows the various switches on a Windows system.

TABLE 13.4

netstat SWITCHES IN WINDOWS

Switch	Description
-a	Displays a list of the current connections and listening ports on the system.

Switch	Description
-e	Displays statistical information for the network interfaces.
-n	Specifies IP addresses and port numbers in numeric form rather than as hostnames if resolution is available and has been performed.
-p *proto*	Shows a list of the connections, on a per-protocol basis, where *proto* is the protocol.
-r	Displays the routing table for the system.
-s	Displays a complete list of protocol statistics, on a protocol-by-protocol basis, including TCP, UDP, and IP.
interval	Redisplays selected statistics, pausing the number of seconds specified by the interval second between each display. You can stop the updates by pressing Ctrl+C. If the interval switch is omitted, netstat prints the current configuration information once.

Of these switches, you're likely to use one far more than any other: -r. The netstat -r command provides an easy way to see the routes configured on the system. The information provided in Table 13.6 can seem cryptic at first glance; but study it a bit longer, and it will start to make sense. Routing tables can become incredibly complicated, but they all work fundamentally the same way, no matter how many routes are included.

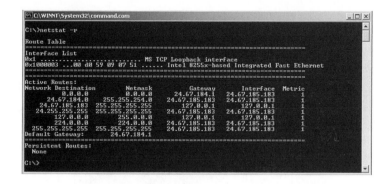

The nbtstat Utility

The NetBIOS statistic command, nbtstat, can be used to display protocol and statistical information for NetBIOS over TCP/IP (sometimes called NetBT) connections. Among other things, the nbtstat utility displays the NetBIOS names of systems that have been resolved.

EXAM TIP

In time, you will be able to read a routing table and determine whether there is a routing problem on the network. Figure 13.7 shows the output from the netstat -r command.

EXAM TIP

netstat -r command The netstat -r command is commonly used to view routing information. You are likely to be asked about it on the Network+ exam.

NOTE

netstat Example Scenario
Suppose you are unable to access a system on a remote network, but you know that the system is up and running. What should you try?

netstat Example Solution It might be necessary to view the current routing table by using the netstat -r command to determine whether the route to the remote host is correct.

FIGURE 13.7
Output from the netstat -r command.

Strange But True   Although it sounds backward, it is true: Windows NT boots from the system partition and then loads the system from the boot partition.

Because nbtstat is used for the resolution of NetBIOS names, it's available only on Windows systems. Neither NetWare nor Linux supports NetBIOS.

Table 13.5 shows some of the most frequently used switches for nbtstat.

TABLE 13.5

nbtstat SWITCHES

Switch	Description
-a	(Adapter status) Lists the NetBIOS resolution table of a remote system identified by its hostname.
-A	(Adapter status) Lists the NetBIOS resolution table for a remote system identified by its IP address.
-c	(Cache) Lists the NetBIOS name cache along with the IP address of each name in the cache.
-n	(Names) Displays the NetBIOS local name table.
-r	(Resolved) Provides statistical information about resolutions.
-R	(Reload) Reloads the NetBIOS names from the LMHOSTS file.
-S	(Sessions) Shows the NetBIOS sessions table, with the state of connection on a hostname basis.

nbstat Example Scenario   Suppose a Windows system is having problems communicating with another system on the network. You can connect to the system by using an IP address but not by using the NetBIOS name. What should you do?

nbstat Example Solution   To solve the problem, check to see if NetBIOS name resolution is operating correctly by looking at the list of resolved names in the NetBIOS name cache. You get to the NetBIOS name cache by using the nbtstat command.

Figure 13.8 shows the output from using nbtstat -r in Windows 2000.

FIGURE 13.8
The output from the nbtstat -r command.

When you look at the output from certain nbtstat commands, you may see reference to a scope ID. Do not confuse this with Dynamic

Host Configuration Protocol (DHCP) scopes. In NetBIOS, you can create scopes to logically group systems together. It is this grouping that the scope ID information refers to.

The `ipconfig` and `ifconfig` Utilities

When it comes to troubleshooting connectivity on a network, the ipconfig and `ifconfig` commands provide much of the configuration information you will require. The `ipconfig` utility shows the IP configuration of Windows systems, whereas `ifconfig` is a Linux, Unix, and OS/2 utility that you can use to obtain configuration information and to configure network interfaces. We'll look at the two separately, beginning with the Windows utility `ipconfig`.

The `ipconfig` Utility

The `ipconfig` command shows the IP configuration information for all network cards installed within a system. Information provided includes the IP address, the subnet mask, and the current default gateway. To find additional information, the ipconfig command is often used with the /all switch, which includes additional information on Windows Internet Name Service (WINS) servers, DNS configuration, the MAC address of the interface, and whether DHCP is enabled. If DHCP is enabled, information about the lease is provided, including how much time is left on the lease.

Because it provides such a wealth of information, `ipconfig` is the utility of choice for network administrators; therefore, you can expect it to be on the Network+ exam. Figure 13.9 shows the output from the ipconfig /all command.

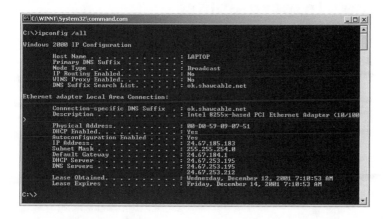

FIGURE 13.9
Output from the `ipconfig /all` command.

> **NOTE**
>
> **New `ipconfig` Switches** The Windows 2000 version of `ipconfig` has some new switches that allow you to perform tasks, among other things, such as re-registering with a Dynamic DNS server.

Multiple NICs   Using the `ipconfig` command with the flags listed in Table 13.6 will affect all the interfaces on the system. This is fine if you have only one network interface, but on systems with more than one network interface it's possible to specify which interface rather than have the command applied to all interfaces.

`config` and `inetcfg`   On a NetWare server, you can use the `config` command to obtain information about network interface configuration. You can use the `inetcfg` command to reconfigure network interface settings.

The `ipconfig` Command Line   You can use `ipconfig` from the command line on Windows 95, Windows 98, and Windows Me systems.

Running the `winipcfg` Utility   You can run the `winipcfg` utility from within Windows clients by selecting Start, Run, and then typing **`winipcfg`** in the dialog box.

Only a limited number of switches are available for the ipconfig command, but they are important. Table 13.6 lists some of the commonly used switches and what they do.

TABLE 13.6

COMMONLY USED `ipconfig` SWITCHES

Switch	Description
/?	Provides a list of the switches available for the `ipconfig` command. Exact switches vary between Windows platforms.
/all	Displays all TCP/IP configuration information.
/renew	Releases all TCP/IP information and then queries a DHCP server for new information. After the command is issued, you can use `ipconfig /all` to confirm that the `ipconfig /renew` command was successful.
/release	Releases the DHCP lease. The result is that the system will not have any IP configuration information.

The `ifconfig` Utility

As mentioned previously, ipconfig is a Windows-based utility. The equivalent on a Linux, Unix, or OS/2 platform is `ifconfig`. Because Linux relies more heavily on command-line utilities than Windows, much more functionality is incorporated into `ifconfig` than into `ipconfig`. You can get information about the usage of the `ifconfig` command by using `ifconfig --help`.

The `winipcfg` Utility

winipcfg is the Windows 95, Windows 98, and Windows Me equivalent of the ipconfig command. Although it provides similar information to `ipconfig`, it is a graphical utility rather than a command-line utility. The `winipcfg` dialog box, which is shown in Figure 13.10, has two parts. The top part of the dialog box displays information such as the hostname and the address of the DNS server; the bottom part of the dialog box displays the local IP configuration information. The information shown includes the MAC address, IP address, subnet mask, gateway, and DHCP address and lease information.

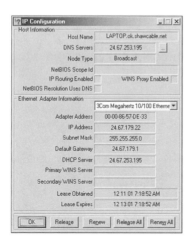

NOTE

`winipcfg` Example Scenario
Suppose you are working from home
and although you are able to use your
system normally, you are unable to
log on to the Internet. What should
you do?

`winipcfg` Example Solution   You can
use the `winipcfg` utility on your computer to determine whether you are
getting a valid IP address from the
Internet service provider's (ISP's)
DHCP server. If an IP address is listed, it might not be valid. Use the
Renew All button to refresh and reload
the TCP/IP configuration.

The `nslookup` Utility

The nslookup command is a TCP/IP diagnostic tool that is used to
troubleshoot DNS problems. It lets you interact with a DNS server
and locate records by performing manual DNS lookups. The basic
syntax is that you add the IP address of the DNS server after the
nslookup command. Figure 13.11 shows an example of `nslookup`
usage and its output.

FIGURE 13.11
nslookup output.

If you provide a server name with nslookup, the command performs
a DNS lookup and returns the IP address for the server name you
entered. If you provide an IP address with `nslookup`, the command
performs a reverse DNS lookup and provides you with the server
name.

Entering `nslookup` by itself at the command prompt and pressing
Enter starts the `nslookup` utility in interactive mode. Instead of
being returned to the command prompt, you stay in the utility and
receive a > prompt. At the > prompt, you can issue more commands
or switches. A list of some of the `nslookup` switches for the interactive mode is provided in Table 13.7. You can get a full list of the
switches by typing **?** at the > command prompt.

TABLE 13.7

nslookup SWITCHES IN INTERACTIVE MODE

Switch	*Description*
option	Sets a switch.
all	Displays a list of the currently set switches, including the current server and domain.
[no]debug	Turns display of debug information on/off.
[no]d2	Turns display of exhaustive debugging information on/off.
[no]defname	Causes the domain specified in defname to be appended to each query.
[no]recurse	Specifies that the query should be recursive.
[no]search	Specifies that nslookup should use the domain search list.
[no]vc	Specifies that nslookup should use a virtual circuit.
domain=*NAME*	Sets the default domain name to the name specified in *NAME*.
srchlist=*N1*[/*N2*/.../*N6*]	Sets the domain to *N1* and the search order to the values specified inside [ ].
root=*NAME*	Sets the root server to the root server specified in *NAME*.
retry=*X*	Specifies the number of retries, where *X* is the number.
timeout=*X*	Sets the initial timeout value, in seconds, to the value specified in *X*.
type=*X*	Specifies the type of query that nslookup should perform, such as A, ANY, CNAME, MX, NS, PTR, SOA, or SRV.
querytype=*X*	The same switches as for type.
class=*X*	Specifies the query class.
[no]msxfr	Tells nslookup to use the Microsoft fast zone transfer system.
server *NAME*	Sets the default server to the value specified in *NAME*.
exit	Exits the nslookup program and returns you to the command prompt.

> **NOTE**
>
> **nslookup Example Scenario**
> Suppose you are experiencing problems using the Internet but you have verified that the IP configuration of your workstation is valid and you are able to ping a remote server by using its IP address. What should you do?
>
> **nslookup Example Solution**   To solve your problem, use nslookup to validate the configuration and function of your DNS servers.

The route Utility

A rather odd omission from the CompTIA Network+ objectives is the route command. We're not sure why they elected not to include it; but because it is an often-used and very handy tool, we cover it here. Based on the fact that route is not included in the objectives, we can say with some confidence that you will not be asked about it on the exam. However, you never know when CompTIA might decide that it fits into another objective.

The route command lets you display and modify the routing table on your Windows and Linux systems. Figure 13.12 shows the output from a route print command on a Windows 2000 system.

> NOTE
>
> **Linux and the route Command** The discussion here focuses on the Windows 2000 route command, but other operating systems have equivalent commands. On a Linux system, for example, the command is also route, but the usage and switches are different.

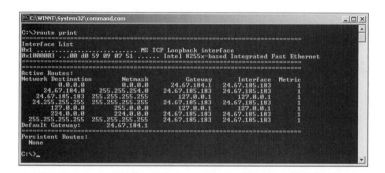

FIGURE 13.12
The output from a route print command on a Windows 2000 system.

As well as displaying the routing table, the Windows 2000 version of the route command has a number of other switches, detailed in Table 13.8. For complete information about all the switches available with the route command in Windows 2000, use the command route at the command line. To see a list of the route command switches on a Linux system, use the command route --help.

TABLE 13.8

SWITCHES FOR THE route COMMAND IN WINDOWS 2000

Switch	Description
add	Allows you to add a route to the routing table.
delete	Allows you to remove a route from the routing table.
change	Allows you to modify an existing route.

continues

| TABLE 13.8 | *continued* |

SWITCHES FOR THE route COMMAND IN WINDOWS 2000

Switch	Description
-p	When used with the add command, makes the route permanent. If the -p switch is not used when a route is added, the route is lost upon reboot.
print	Allows you to view the routing table of the system.
-f	Removes all gateway entries from the routing table.

TROUBLESHOOTING IN A SMALL OFFICE/HOME OFFICE ENVIRONMENT

▶ Given a troubleshooting scenario involving a small office/home office network failure (e.g., xDSL, cable, home satellite, wireless, POTS), identify the cause of the problem.

Today, networks aren't limited to businesses in office buildings. An increasing number of households have more than one computer, and in the same way that businesses have realized the advantages of networking computers together, so, too, have homes. In addition to the growing proliferation of home networks, more people are now working from home, further increasing the need for home-based networks. For these reasons, as a network troubleshooter, you are just as likely today to be spending time in people's homes troubleshooting networks as in a corporate office.

Small office and home office networks are generally quite simple. Whereas an office-based network might have multiple WAN links, complex routing structures, and expensive equipment, a small office/home office environment is likely to consist of a few PCs and perhaps a printer, connected to a hub or switch. One common denominator, though, is that almost every home or small office network has some form of Internet connection, be it a modem, cable, Digital Subscriber Line (DSL), or satellite link.

Troubleshooting in a small office/home office environment brings with it some unique technical challenges. Here are just a few of them:

◆ **Each situation is different**—Unlike a tech who works for a company at a single location, those troubleshooting home or small office networks often face unfamiliar setups. Therefore, it's very important to understand the problem fully before you begin working.

◆ **You should assume that the client has no tools**—It's a good idea to take your own tools and equipment when you go to a small office/home office network. In a corporate IT environment, when you need to make a boot disk, you can probably mosey over to another PC and make one. In a home office with a single PC, you simply don't have that luxury. Many techs like to carry a laptop system for exactly that reason. Another factor to consider is that in a home environment, you might not have the opportunity to troubleshoot through substitution. Most small office/home office network owners do not have a spare network card, nor are they likely to warm up to the idea of you removing one from another system (if they have one). You should take spare parts such as network cards, cables, and hubs.

◆ **You should be prepared for an audience**—Many people, particularly when you are working on their PCs, want to watch. It can make for an uncomfortable experience, particularly if the troubleshooting process is not going as well as you expected. Be patient and think calm thoughts.

◆ **No other techs are likely to be onsite**—In a corporate environment, the chances are great that someone else who is responsible for the network and who understands the problem is available. In a small office/home office environment, you might not have such a luxury.

◆ **You need to examine the obvious**—As discussed shortly, problems that simply wouldn't occur in a corporate environment may have had a hand in the failure of a small office/home office network. Before trying to debug an IP packet trace, you should check the connections and power source.

◆ **You should assume that the user has tried to fix it**—In a corporate environment, employees attempting to fix a problem is a big no-no. In a small office/home office environment, you can almost guarantee that some kind of fix has been attempted. Be sure to discuss what has been tried already, and then assume that none of the steps were performed correctly. Ascertaining what has already been attempted should give you warning signs for potential problems.

Perhaps the biggest difference you'll find between small office/home office networks and corporate networks is the lack of control over systems and networking equipment in a small office/home office network. By day, the front office might serve as the workplace of an architect or lawyer. By night, it might become the secret place of little Johnny when he's playing hide-and-go-seek. During those dull times when he's waiting for his friend to find him, who's to say that Johnny doesn't unplug cables from the plastic box under the desk? So, what was plugged in before is now unplugged, and in the morning Mom can't log on to the Internet. This is a simple example, but you would be surprised just how often this kind of thing happens.

Basic problems you'll face when working on a small office/home office network are the same as those that you'd face in any networked environment. Therefore, we'll leave them to Chapter 15, "Network Troubleshooting," which covers troubleshooting procedures and best practices in detail.

IN THE FIELD

WORKING IN PEOPLE'S HOMES AND SMALL OFFICES

Just as working in people's homes and small offices brings with it certain technical challenges, you should also consider professional factors. Here are a few tips you might want to bear in mind:

· **Keep your appointments**—If you are 30 minutes late to an office, someone can probably still let you in to work on the network. People who keep home offices might not be around all day; if you are late, you might find yourself waiting on the doorstep.

· **Have some kind of identification**—Just as a worker from the local utility might be asked for identification, you can fully expect to be challenged for ID when you turn up at someone's house. In reality, you are just as likely to be asked when you are visiting an office, so it's always a good idea to have some kind of ID on you.

- **Respect the house**—When you're working in an office, people will probably be less sensitive to your moving around while working on a problem or tracing a cable. In someone's house, it's inappropriate to go wandering off while searching for a cable junction box or tracking a network cable.

- **Don't be nosy**—Many computers in small offices or homes serve both as the business computer and the household PC. Limit your use of the computer strictly to the problem at hand and resist wandering through the PC's hard drive.

One of the most common needs for a small office or home business is the Internet, and nothing is likely to be more urgent for a user than not being able to log on and get email or download the latest batch of work. Whereas office-based businesses tend to connect to the Internet using either leased lines or Integrated Services Digital Network (ISDN) connections, small office or home-based businesses tend to use a variety of other methods, depending on their needs and their budgets.

We might be entering the broadband era, but the most popular method of connecting to the Internet is still via modem and phone line. This method is the least expensive available, and although the maximum speed is limited (in comparison to other methods), it is sufficient for most email messages and even moderate-sized uploads and downloads.

Sometimes, however, a dial-up connection simply is not fast enough. There are a variety of other methods to choose from. When it comes to high-speed Internet access, many small businesses and homes use cable or one of the DSL family members (that is, xDSL). Although neither of these technologies can provide Ethernet-like speeds, they let you surf the Web, download files, and view online movies relatively easily.

DSL and cable might be the most widely used connection methods, but they are not the only kids on the block. Many small companies and home users employ other technologies such as home satellite, plain old telephone system (POTS), and wireless communication. The following sections identify the main characteristics of each of these technologies and what you can expect when troubleshooting them.

DSL Internet Access

DSL is an Internet access method that uses a standard phone line to provide high-speed Internet access. DSL is available only in certain areas, although as the telephone companies try to cash in on the broadband Internet access market, the areas of coverage are likely to increase.

DSL offers phone and data transmissions over a standard phone connection. DSL is most commonly associated with high-speed Internet access; because it is less expensive than technologies such as ISDN, it is often used in homes and small businesses. With DSL, a different frequency can be used for digital and analog signals, which means you can talk to a friend on the phone while you're uploading data.

DSL arrived on the scene in the late 1990s, and it brought with it a staggering number of flavors. Together, all these variations are known as xDSL. The following are some of the most common types of DSL:

◆ **Asymmetric DSL (ADSL)**—Probably the most common of the DSL varieties is ADSL. The word *asymmetric* describes different channels on the line: one channel is used for POTS and is responsible for analog traffic, the second channel is used to provide upload access, and the third channel is used for downloads. With ADSL, downloads are faster than uploads.

◆ **Symmetric DSL (SDSL)**—SDSL offers the same speeds for uploads and for downloads, making it most suitable for business applications such as Web hosting, intranets, and e-commerce. It is not widely implemented in the home/small business environment and cannot share a phone line.

◆ **ISDN DSL (IDSL)**—ISDN DSL is a symmetric type of DSL that is commonly used in environments where SDSL and ADSL are unavailable. IDSL does not support analog phones.

◆ **Rate Adaptive DSL (RADSL)**—RADSL is a variation on ADSL that can modify its transmission speeds based on the signal quality. RADSL supports line sharing.

◆ **Very High Bit Rate DSL (VHDSL)**—VDSL is an asymmetric version of DSL and, as such, can share a telephone line.

◆ **High Bit Rate DSL (HDSL)**—HDSL is a symmetric technology that offers identical transmission rates in both directions. HDSL does not allow line sharing with analog phones.

Why are there are so many DSL variations? The answer is quite simply that each flavor of DSL is aimed at a different user, business, or application. Businesses with high bandwidth needs are more likely to choose a symmetric form of DSL, whereas budget-conscious environments such as home offices are likely to opt for an option that allows phone line sharing at the expense of bandwidth. When you're working in a home/small office environment, you should expect to work with an ADSL system.

Users commonly complain that other Internet access methods are slow or provide inconsistent access. Supporters of DSL claim that it does not suffer from either of these problems. But how much speed does DSL provide? Table 13.9 summarizes the expected speeds of the various DSL options.

TABLE 13.9

EXPECTED DSL SPEEDS

DSL Variation	Upload Speed	Download Speed
ADSL	1Mbps	8Mbps
SDSL	1.5Mbps	1.5Mbps
IDSL	144Kbps	144Kbps
RADSL	1Mbps	7Mbps
VHDSL	1.6Mbps	13Mbps
HDSL	768Kbps	768Kbps

Although DSL services are affordable, several factors affect the quality of the connection, including location (how close you are to the DSL provider) and security (how much the service opens your computer to crackers).

DSL Troubleshooting Procedures

Troubleshooting DSL is similar to troubleshooting any other Internet connection. The following are a few things to check when users are experiencing problems with a DSL connection:

◆ **Physical connections**—The first place to look when troubleshooting a DSL problem is the network cable connections. From time to time, these cables can come loose or inadvertently be detached, and they are often overlooked as the cause of a problem.

◆ **The NIC**—While you're checking the cable at the back of the system, take a quick look to see if the network card light-emitting diode (LED) is lit. If it is not, something could be wrong with the card. It might be necessary to swap out the network card and replace it with one that is known to be working.

◆ **Drivers**—Confirm that the network card is installed and has the correct drivers. Many times, simply using the most up-to-date driver can resolve connectivity issues.

◆ **Protocol configuration**—The device you are troubleshooting might not have a valid IP address. Confirm the IP address by using the appropriate tool for the operating system being used—for example, winipcfg, `ipconfig`, or `ifconfig`. If the system requires the automatic assignment of an IP address, confirm that the system is set to obtain an IP address automatically. It might be necessary to use the `ipconfig /release` and `ipconfig /renew` commands to get a new IP address.

◆ **DSL LEDs**—Each DSL box has an LED on it. The light sequences are often used to identify connectivity problems or problems with the box itself. Refer to the manufacturer's Web site for information about error codes and LEDs.

Ultimately, if none of these steps cure or indicate the cause of the problem, you might have to call the DSL provider for assistance. You can find more information about using technical support services later in this chapter, in the section "Calling Technical Support."

NOTE

DSL Example Scenario   Suppose you have been asked to specify an Internet access method that provides for high speeds and dedicated access. What would you choose?

DSL Example Solution   In such a case, you should contact your local phone company and determine whether DSL is available in the area.

Cable Internet Access

Cable Internet access is an always-on Internet access method that is available in areas that have digital cable television. Not all cable TV providers offer Internet access, but an increasing number are taking advantage of the relatively simple jump from being cable providers to being ISPs.

Cable Internet access is attractive to many small businesses and home office users because it is both inexpensive and reliable. Most cable providers do not restrict how much use is made of the access. Connectivity is achieved by using a device called a cable modem; it has a coaxial connection for connecting to the provider's outlet and an unshielded twisted-pair (UTP) connection for connection directly to a system or to a hub or switch. Figure 13.13 shows a cable modem.

FIGURE 13.13
A cable modem.

Cable providers often supply a cable modem free of charge, although of course you are paying for the rental of the modem in a monthly service fee. Many cable providers offer free or low-cost installation of cable Internet service, which includes installing a network card in a PC. Some providers also do not charge for the network card.

NOTE

MDI-X Ports   A cable modem is generally equipped with a medium-dependent interface crossed (MDI-X) port, so a straight-through UTP cable can be used to connect the modem to a system.

One of the biggest disadvantages of cable access is cited (by DSL providers at least) as the fact that you share the available bandwidth with everyone else in your cable area. As a result, during peak times, performance of a cable link might be poorer than in low-use periods. In residential areas, busy times are evenings and weekends, and particularly right after school. In general, though, performance with cable systems is good, and in low-usage periods it can be very fast.

Cable Troubleshooting Procedures

In general, cable Internet access is a low-maintenance system with very few problems. When problems do occur, you can try various troubleshooting measures:

◆ **Check the user's end**—Before looking at the cable modem, make sure that the system is configured correctly and that all cables are plugged in. If a hub or switch is used to share the cable Internet access among a group of computers, ensure that the hub or switch is on and functioning correctly. If the device acts as a basic firewall/DHCP server, be sure none of the settings have changed.

◆ **Check the physical connections**—Cable modems have three connections: one for the cable signal, one for the local network, and one for the power. Make sure they are all plugged in appropriately.

◆ **Ensure that the protocol configuration on the system is valid**—If an IP address is assigned via DHCP, the absence of an address is a sure indicator that connectivity is at fault. Try obtaining a new IP address by using the appropriate command for the platform. If the IP addresses are statically configured, make sure they are set correctly. Trying to use any address other than that specified by the ISP might prevent a user from connecting to the network.

◆ **Check the indicator lights on the modem**—Most cable modems have indicator lights that show the status of the modem. Under normal conditions, a single light labeled Ready or Online should be lit. Most cable providers provide a manual with the modem that details the functions of the lights and what they indicate in certain states. Generally speaking, any red light is bad.

◆ **Cycle the power on the modem**—Cycling the power on the modem is a sure-fire way of resetting it. Cable providers prefer that you don't disconnect the signal cable, although exactly why is unclear.

◆ **Call the technical support line**—If you are sure the connectors are all in place and the configuration of the system is correct, the next step is to call the technical support line of the cable provider. If the provider is experiencing problems that affect a great number of users, you might get a message while you're on hold, informing you of the fact. If not, you will eventually get to speak to someone who can help you troubleshoot the problem. One of the good things about cable access is that the cable company can remotely monitor and reset the modem. It should be able to tell you if the modem is functioning correctly.

Unless the modem is faulty, which is not that common, by this point the user should be back on the Internet or at least you should fully understand why the user cannot connect. If the problem is with the cable provider's networking equipment, you and the user simply have to wait for the system to come back on.

NOTE

Cable Example Scenario Suppose you are troubleshooting a user's cable Internet connection and are unable to get an IP address. What should you do?

Cable Example Solution You should verify that the protocol configuration is correct and that all cables are connected correctly. During your investigation, you notice that the Online light of the cable modem is red. After you cycle the power to the modem, the light remains red; you are still unable to obtain a valid IP address. The next step is to contact the cable service provider's technical support line.

Home Satellite Internet Access

A few years ago, the only family with home-based satellite access was the Jetsons. Today, however, it is becoming increasingly evident that the use of satellites for providing broadband Internet access to the home and small business user is going to become very popular.

Two different types of broadband Internet satellite services are deployed: one-way and two-way systems. A *one-way satellite system* requires a satellite card and a satellite dish installed at the end user's site; this system works by sending outgoing requests on one link using a phone line, with inbound traffic returning on the satellite link. A *two-way satellite system,* on the other hand, provides data paths for both upstream and downstream data. Like a one-way system, a two-way system also uses a satellite card and a satellite dish installed at the end user's site; bidirectional communication occurs directly between the end user's node and the satellite.

Home satellite systems are asymmetric; that is, download speeds are faster than upload speeds. In fact, a home satellite system is likely to use a modem for the upline traffic, with downloads coming over the satellite link. The exact speeds you can expect with satellite Internet depend on many factors. As with other wireless technologies, atmospheric conditions can significantly affect the performance of satellite Internet access. One additional consideration for satellite Internet is increased *propagation time*—the time it takes for the signal to travel back and forth from the satellite. In networking terms, this time is very high; depending on atmospheric conditions, it can range from .5 seconds to 5 seconds.

Home Satellite Troubleshooting Procedures

Your ability to troubleshoot satellite Internet connections might be very limited. Home satellite Internet is a line-of-sight wireless technology, and the installation configuration must be very precise. Because of this requirement, many satellite companies insist that the satellite be set up and configured by trained staff members. In fact, if you install a satellite system in a way that does not accord with the manufacturer's recommendations, you might void any warranties.

Given this limitation, troubleshooting satellite connections often requires you to concentrate less on connectivity issues and more on physical troubleshooting techniques. Perhaps more than for any other Internet technology, calls to technical support occur very early in the troubleshooting process.

Wireless Internet Access

For some time, office buildings have been built with networks in mind. Until recently, most houses and small offices have not. For this reason, wireless networks in homes and small offices are particularly popular. Using a wireless network provides the flexibility to work from anywhere in the range of the access point, and it negates the need to drill holes in walls and run cables through ventilation and heating ducts (which is not recommended).

Generally, wireless Internet access is provided only in areas such as metropolitan centers, where the number of possible users is sufficiently high to warrant the expensive installations.

In reality, wireless Internet access is a much more popular mechanism for truly mobile users than for users looking for Internet access from a small office or home setup. However, some people prefer the flexibility of a completely wireless solution, and more and more users will sign up as additional providers offer wireless service.

Wireless Troubleshooting Procedures

Wireless Internet access requires a wireless network adapter and a wireless access service. Troubleshooting wireless access is normally confined to ensuring that the adapter is functioning correctly and configured properly.

The main factors that can affect wireless access are environmental conditions and outside interference. Many people who live in areas that often have fog or other damp conditions experience poor performance (or none at all) from wireless Internet service. In other areas, the conditions are perfect for wireless communication. Electrical interference can also be a factor.

Here are some specific things you should check when troubleshooting a wireless connection:

- ◆ **Check the configuration of the wireless interface**—This step includes checking to make sure the system is recognizing the device, that the drivers are enabled and configured, and that all protocols and bindings are correct.

- ◆ **Move the computer around to find out if it's in a dead spot**—Some construction materials or electrical equipment can block or weaken the signal. Moving around will help you discover this kind of problem.

- ◆ **Check with other people**—If possible, and if you know other people who have the same Internet access method, check to see if they are also experiencing problems. It might be that there is a problem with the service rather than just the user's system.

If you are sure that everything is configured correctly, you might have to contact the wireless provider to see if anything is amiss.

Given the availability, speed, and relatively low cost of other Internet access methods, wireless Internet access seems like it might take some time to get a foothold in the Internet access market. But for people who simply have to have 100% mobility, it's the way to go.

POTS Internet Access

The most popular means of connecting to the Internet or a remote network is still the good old telephone line and modem. Because the same line used for a household phone is used for dial-up access, it is referred to as the POTS method of access. Although many parts of the world are served by broadband providers offering services such as those discussed so far in this chapter, more people still connect with a modem.

Internet access through a phone system requires two things: a modem and a dial-up access account through an ISP. As you might recall from Chapter 2, "Cabling and Connectors," modems are devices that convert the digital signals generated by a computer system into analog signals that can travel across a phone line. A computer can have either an internal or external modem. External modems tend to be less problematic to install and troubleshoot because they don't require reconfiguration of the host system. Internal modems use one of the serial port assignments (that is, a COM port) and must therefore be configured not to conflict with other devices.

The second piece of the puzzle, the dial-up ISP account, can easily be obtained by contacting one of the many local, regional, or national ISPs. Most ISPs offer a range of plans that are normally priced based on the amount of time the user is allowed to spend online. Almost without exception, ISPs offer 56Kbps access, the maximum possible under current standards. Most ISPs also provide email accounts, access to newsgroup servers, and often small amounts of Web space.

It is a good idea to research an ISP choice carefully. Free services exist, but they generally restrict users to a certain number of online hours per month or use extensive banner advertising to pay for the services. Normally, you pay a monthly service fee for an ISP; doing so provides a degree of reassurance because the ISP can be held accountable. Paid-for service also tends to provide a higher level of support.

Another big consideration for dial-up Internet access is how many lines the ISP has. ISPs never have the same number of lines as subscribers; instead, they work on a first-come, first-served basis for dial-up clients. This means that on occasion, users get busy signals when they try to connect. Before signing up for a dial-up Internet access account, you should ask the company what its ratio of lines to subscribers is and use that figure as part of your comparison criteria.

With a modem and an ISP account, you are ready to get connected. But what happens if things do not run as planned? Welcome to the interesting and sometimes challenging world of troubleshooting dial-up connections.

POTS Troubleshooting Procedures

Troubleshooting a dial-up connection problem can be tricky and time-consuming because you must consider many variables. The following are some places to start your troubleshooting under various conditions.

If the user is unable to dial out, try the following:

◆ **Check physical connections**—The most common problem with modem connections is that something has become unplugged; modems rarely fail after they initially work. For an external modem, you also need to verify that the modem has power.

◆ **Check that there is a dial tone on the line**—You can do this by plugging a normal phone into the socket and seeing if you can dial out. A modem generally has a speaker, and you can set up the modem to use the speaker so you can hear what is going on.

If the user can dial out but can't get a connection, try the following:

◆ **Make sure the user is dialing the correct number**—This suggestion sounds obvious, but sometimes numbers change or are entered incorrectly.

◆ **Call the ISP**—You can call the ISP to determine whether it is having problems.

◆ **Check the modem speaker**—Find out if you are getting busy signals from the ISP by turning on the modem speaker.

NOTE

Technical Support In some cases, users may not use an ISP at all and instead dial another system directly. In that case, all the troubleshooting steps in this section apply, except that you have to rely on the technical support capabilities of the person responsible for the remote system rather than the ISP if you have a problem.

If the user can dial out and can get a connection but is then disconnected, try the following:

◆ **Ensure that the modem connection is configured correctly**—The most common modem configuration is 8 data bits, 1 stop bit, and no parity.

◆ **Check the username and password**—Make sure the correct username and password combination is configured for the dial-up connection.

◆ **Verify that the connection settings are correct**—Pay particular attention to things such as the IP address. Most ISPs assign IP addresses through DHCP, and trying to connect with a statically configured IP address is not permitted.

◆ **Make sure the user has not exceeded a preset connection time limit**—Some ISPs restrict the number of monthly access hours. If the user has such a plan, check to make sure some time credit is left.

◆ **Try specifying a lower speed for the connection**—Modems are designed to negotiate a connection speed with which both devices are comfortable. Sometimes, during the negotiation process, the line can be dropped. Initially setting a lower speed might get a connection. You can then increase the modem speed to accommodate a better connection.

IN THE FIELD

CALL WAITING

If you are troubleshooting a dial-up connection that randomly slows down or disconnects completely, check to see if the line has a call-waiting function on it. As you might know, when call waiting is used, a tone informs you during the call that someone is trying to get through. This tone interferes with the modem connection and can cause it to either slow down for a period of time or drop the connection altogether.

Call-waiting problems are hard to troubleshoot because they occur only when a call is coming in and when you are on that line. Moving the system to another line might make the connection work properly and leave all concerned scratching their heads. The good news is

that the solution to the call-waiting problem is simple. The telephone company can give you a code to can add to the beginning of
the modem dial string to temporarily disable call waiting for the
duration of the call. In most cases, the telephone company or ISP
can help you configure the disabling of call waiting if you need such
help.

Troubleshooting Poor Connection Speeds

Even if you are not having a problem connecting, you might find
that the speed of modem connections is problematic. Such problems
are not uncommon. The modem might say it can handle 56Kbps,
and the ISP might advertise the same, but quite often you simply
cannot get 56Kbps speed on a dial-up connection. There are many
possible reasons; some of them you can do something about, and
some of them you can't. Here are some of the reasons speeds might
not be as fast as expected:

◆ **Poor line quality**—In some areas, the quality of the telephone
  lines and exchange equipment can reduce the maximum possible connection speed.

◆ **Incorrectly configured modem**—The modem configuration
  is very important in ensuring the highest possible connection
  speed. In particular, for external modems, the configuration of
  the serial port the modem is connected to should be checked.
  Defaults sometimes restrict the speed of the port.

◆ **Poor-quality modems**—Perhaps less of an issue now than in
  the past, poor-quality modems can contribute to poor connection speeds and connectivity problems. Paying the extra
  money for a good-quality modem is worth the savings in frustration alone.

After saying all this, it is worth mentioning that after you establish a
connection, whatever the speed, you are still at the mercy of the ISP.
Even a 56Kbps link might be too slow if the ISP's networking
equipment or Internet connection can't keep up with demand.
Unfortunately, there is no way to know if the bottleneck is with the
ISP or the modem.

Modem-Specific Troubleshooting

Typically, modems are reliable devices. They have no moving parts, and chances are that after you have installed, configured, and tested a modem, you won't have to play around with it again. However, there can be exceptions, and you should be aware of the following modem-specific troubleshooting measures:

◆ **Ensure that you have the latest drivers**—For any type of modem, you should make sure the latest drivers are installed. The drivers supplied with modems typically are not up-to-date, and a visit to the modem manufacturer's Web site (from another computer) might yield more up-to-date drivers. Try to avoid using generic drivers where possible. Even if they work, which they often don't, they probably won't offer all the features of the proper drivers.

◆ **Check for resource conflicts**—For internal modems, you need to make sure there are no conflicts with other system resources. For external devices, you need to make sure serial ports are enabled and configured correctly.

◆ **Check for firmware updates**—Both internal and external modems have updatable firmware chips. Check the modem manufacturer's Web site to ensure that you have the latest version of the firmware. (Note that firmware updates should be completed before installation, and then only if they fix a specific problem you are having.)

If you are confident that a modem is installed and configured correctly, but it's still not working properly, you can test and configure it by using special commands called the *AT command set*. These commands are mentioned briefly in Chapter 2, but they are worthy of a more detailed discussion here; they are often useful for troubleshooting modems and related connectivity problems.

You can use AT commands through a communications application to talk directly to the modem. On Windows platforms, you can use the HyperTerminal utility. On most common Linux distributions, you can use the `minicom` utility. After you have established a session with the modem, you can issue AT commands directly to the modem, which will respond different ways, depending on the command. Table 13.10 lists some of the most commonly used AT commands.

TABLE 13.10	
COMMONLY USED AT COMMANDS	
AT Command	*Result*
ATA	Sets the modem to auto-answer.
ATH	Hangs up an active connection.
ATD	Dials a number.
ATZ	Resets the modem.
ATI3	Displays the name and model of the modem.

In general, getting the modem to respond to an ATZ command is a good enough indicator that the modem is functioning.

Calling Technical Support

When troubleshooting any kind of Internet access, there is a chance that your efforts will not be successful and that you will need to call technical support. If you find yourself in such a situation, you can take the following steps to ensure that you get the answers you need:

◆ **Be prepared**—Have on hand all the information you might be asked for. This includes account numbers, user IDs for the connection, and other information. Do not give technical support representatives the administrator or equivalent account information for your system.

◆ **Be prepared to wait**—Many service providers seem to think that a 20-minute (or more) wait is a reasonable level of customer service. Even if you don't agree, there is little you can do about it, so call from a hands-free phone or headset if possible so you can do other things while you wait.

◆ **Try fixes during the call**—If possible, avoid ending a technical support call to try things and then calling back if they don't work. Make the call while you're in front of the system with the problem. You are far more likely to get a speedy resolution if you can try fixes with the tech support representative on the phone.

EXAM TIP

AT Commands   You should be prepared to identify the function of basic AT commands for the Network+ exam.

NOTE

POTS Example Scenario   A customer calls and complains that she is often disconnected during a dial-up session. Other times, the connection is fine. What should you do?

POTS Example Solution   You check all the modem configurations, and they appear to be correct. You should find out if call waiting is enabled on the line; if it is, you should modify the modem dial string to disable call waiting before dialing an Internet connection.

With the help of a technical support staff person, you should be able to correct the problem. But what if you are on the other end of the phone? What if you are the one trying to solve remote connectivity problems for a customer? The next section offers some guidance.

TROUBLESHOOTING REMOTE CONNECTIVITY ERRORS

▶ Given a troubleshooting scenario involving a remote connectivity problem (e.g., authentication failure, protocol configuration, physical connectivity) identify the cause of the problem.

As networks have moved away from single locations and telecommuting has increased in popularity, a new world of troubleshooting has opened up: that of remote connectivity errors. Remote connectivity errors are bugs that prevent you from dialing in to the office, remotely dialing in to your home computer, or logging on to your ISP. People have come to rely on the ability to remotely access the office, and the Internet has become so closely integrated with modern business that many organizations come to a standstill without it.

Although many means and methods are available for establishing remote connectivity, network administrators can focus their attention on three hot spots when troubleshooting errors: authentication failure, protocol configuration problems, and physical connectivity problems.

Troubleshooting Authentication Failure

Authentication problems are typically the first place to look when a user is experiencing remote connectivity errors. All forms of remote connectivity should require some form of authentication to confirm that those trying to access the remote resources have permission to do so. Most of us are aware of authentication in the form of usernames and passwords.

As a network administrator, you can expect to become very familiar with authentication troubleshooting. Quite often, authentication errors result from users incorrectly entering usernames and/or passwords. As you might expect and hope, when this happens, users are unable to access the network. Many systems use case-sensitive passwords; when you are troubleshooting authentication failure, be sure you know whether case-sensitive passwords are required.

Authentication issues can also arise as a result of permissions changes in users' accounts. In all kinds of networks, network administrators need to sometimes make changes to accounts. Whether due to security reasons, network maintenance, or an accident, at some point accounts change. When incorrect changes to accounts are made, it is the responsibility of the network administrator to correct them before the user tries to log on, or at least to notify the user of a potential problem. If you're troubleshooting remote connectivity and you have confirmed that the correct username and password are used, you should confirm that everything is as it should be with the user's account.

The third and perhaps least likely cause for authentication failure is a downed authentication server. If the server providing the authentication for the remote access goes down, then no one who is authenticated through that server will be able to log on. In such a circumstance, you are likely to receive numerous calls regarding authentication difficulty—not just one or two.

Troubleshooting Physical Connectivity Problems

When you're troubleshooting remote connectivity errors, it is often easy to forget the most basic troubleshooting practices. By this we mean ensuring that all the physical connections are in place. When you suspect a physical connectivity problem, here are a few key places to look:

◆ **Faulty cable**—Either through accident or by wear and tear, sometimes cables break. If you suspect a faulty cable as the cause of a connectivity error, replace the cable with one that is known to be working to confirm your suspicion.

◆ **Improperly connected cable**—Troubleshooting a connectivity issue might be as simple as plugging in a cable. You should ensure that all cables are securely attached to the correct ports.

EXAM TIP

Caps Lock If you're troubleshooting authentication failure, you should ensure that Caps Lock is turned off on the keyboard.

NOTE

Authentication Example Scenario Suppose you are employed to provide telephone support for a large ISP. A customer calls, complaining that she is unable to dial in to your ISP service and access the Internet.

Authentication Example Solution When isolating remote connectivity errors, you should first determine whether customers are using the correct authentication information. In this case, it would be necessary to confirm that the correct username and password are being used. If you are using an authentication system that is case sensitive, you should ensure that the correct case is being used.

NOTE

Physical Connectivity Example Scenario   One of your company's remote users calls you and is angry that he is unable to dial in and access the local network from his remote location. He insists he is using the correct username and password.

Physical Connectivity Example Solution   When you receive calls for remote connectivity errors, try to think of problems that are associated with physical connectivity. If the user is accessing a remote location using a modem, confirm that the modem is correctly cabled both in the computer and into the phone jack. If the user requires a network card to access remote services, ensure that the network cable is installed correctly. You can also try a different jack and phone cable.

◆ **Incorrect cable**—If you are troubleshooting a new connection, you should make sure the correct cable is being used.

◆ **Faulty interface**—A faulty network card can stop data flow in a hurry.

◆ **Faulty networking devices**—Hubs, switches, and routers may be the sources of your problem; just because the lights are on, don't assume that a device is working correctly. If possible, substitute the device for one that is known to be working so that you can eliminate it from your inquiries.

You should also try these troubleshooting measures:

◆ **Use observation techniques and connectivity tools**—You should approach physical connectivity problems in a methodical manner and use tools such as ping to locate problems. Most networking devices have indicator LEDs that you can use to determine the status of the device.

◆ **Be aware of EMI and crosstalk**—As discussed in Chapter 2, you must be aware of the effects of electromagnetic interference (EMI) and crosstalk on network media. If you have an intermittent or hard-to-trace problem, you should certainly consider this factor.

Troubleshooting Protocol Configuration Problems

Many, but not all, of the problems you encounter with remote connectivity can be addressed with the measures listed previously. You might encounter a time when you have confirmed that the network user is using the correct username and password combination, that no changes have been made to the user's account information, that all physical connections are in place, and that the user still cannot establish a remote connection.

The next most likely client connectivity problem is protocol configuration. Protocol configuration issues are usually on the client side of the network. Each client computer must have a unique address in order to participate on the network. Failure to obtain addressing information could indicate a problem with a DHCP server.

You should check the DHCP server to make sure it is functioning and that addresses are available for assignment.

One of the most frustrating troubles to deal with as an administrator is duplicate IP addresses. This problem is usually is the result of manually assigning IP addresses or improperly configuring subnet assignments on multiple DHCP servers. As mentioned earlier in this chapter, you can use the arp command along with the ping utility to find MAC addresses that have the same IP address.

Administrators should also be aware of whether the network operating system will automatically assign private IP addresses when the DHCP server cannot be located. On a Windows 2000 network, if the client runs ipconfig and reports an IP address beginning with 169, then you know the client has been provided with a private IP address, and this means the DHCP server is either down, unreachable, or has run out of available IP addresses for assignment.

> **NOTE**
>
> **Unauthorized Configurations** Some operating systems are better at protecting against unauthorized configuration changes than others. Windows 2000 and Linux, for example, require special rights to change network configurations. Windows 95 and Windows 98, on the other hand, do not. If you are working on an operating system that does not control reconfigurations, be sure to check carefully for changes.

CHAPTER SUMMARY

Knowing how to troubleshoot network connectivity is an important part of a network administrator's role. Fortunately, many utilities are designed to make the process of determining and correcting connectivity issues easier. The most common utilities for this type of troubleshooting include ping, ipconfig, trace route, nbstat, and netstat. Variations of these commands are available on each of the major operating systems.

Today, small offices and home networks alike rely on Internet access for business and/or recreation. There are many different ways to get Internet access, including using xDSL, cable, home satellite, wireless, and POTS.

The DSL family of products is referred to as xDSL and includes ADSL, RADSL, IDSL, SDSL, HDSL, and VHDSL. Each DSL method is used for different applications. Only asymmetric DSL flavors such as ADSL and RADSL can share lines with a regular phone line. DSL is an always-on type of Internet access, which means a computer that uses it could be subjected to security risks from the outside.

KEY TERMS

- ping
- ICMP
- localhost
- trace route
- arp
- ARP cache
- netstat
- nbtstat
- ipconfig
- ifconfig
- winipcfg
- nslookup

CHAPTER SUMMARY

KEY TERMS

- route
- DSL
- cable Internet
- xDSL
- home satellite
- wireless Internet access
- POTS

Cable Internet is becoming increasingly popular because it offers fast and reliable transfer speeds. Cable Internet is widely available from most cable TV companies. Both wireless and home satellite Internet access target a very specific market. Wireless is used when mobility is required, and home satellite is used where other forms of Internet access are not available. POTS is regular modem Internet access; the maximum Internet speed available on POTS is 56Kbps.

How you troubleshoot each type of Internet connectivity depends on the exact type being used. General troubleshooting guidelines include using observation techniques, confirming physical connectivity, and verifying the protocol configuration.

As an administrator in today's networks, you will probably find yourself troubleshooting remote connectivity errors. Three common troubleshooting areas for remote access include authentication failure, protocol configuration problems, and physical connectivity problems. Before calling for technical support, network administrators should verify functionality in each of these areas.

APPLY YOUR KNOWLEDGE

Exercises

13.1   Using the `ipconfig` Command

By using the troubleshooting commands, you can reinforce the knowledge you need for the Network+ exam. Because the emphasis of the material in the Network+ curriculum is on the Windows platform, in this exercise you will use a Windows 2000 system. In this exercise, you learn how to use the ipconfig command.

Estimated time: 10 minutes

1. Open a command prompt by selecting Start, Run and then typing **cmd** in the Run dialog box.

2. At the command prompt, type **ipconfig**. Note what information is displayed.

3. At the command prompt, type **ipconfig /all**. Note what additional information is displayed.

4. Determine whether you are using DHCP by looking for the entry for the DHCP server. If you are using DHCP, when was your address assigned? How much time is left on the lease?

5. If you are using DHCP, attempt to renew the address lease by using the command ipconfig /renew. Note whether you are able to renew the lease.

6. To see the updated lease information, type **ipconfig /all**. The date and time for the DHCP lease information should now be updated.

13.2   Using the `ping` Utility

In this exercise, you follow the ping troubleshooting sequence. How far you are able to go will depend on your network connectivity. If you are able to connect to the Internet, you should be able to complete all the steps in this exercise.

Estimated time: 10 minutes

1. `ping` the local loopback of your system by using the command `ping 127.0.0.1`.

2. Determine your IP address by using the ipconfig command.

3. `ping` the IP address of your system by using the `ping <IP ADDRESS>` command.

4. Use the ipconfig command to determine the address of your default gateway and then `ping` it.

5. `ping` a remote host. If you are able to determine (from the address) that your DNS server is on a remote network, then `ping` that. Otherwise, you can try `ping 216.119.103.72`.

6. If you have DNS capability (which is very likely, if you are connected to the Internet), you can also try to `ping` a remote host by its hostname (for example, ping comptia.org).

13.3   Using the `arp` Command

In this exercise, you use the arp command to look at the local ARP cache and observe the process of the ARP cache being updated. As in the previous exercise, being connected to a network will make a big difference in the amount and variety of information displayed in this exercise.

Estimated time: 10 minutes

1. View the ARP cache on your local system by using the **arp -a** command. Note how many devices are listed in the ARP cache.

2. Determine the IP address of your default gateway by using the ipconfig command. `ping` the IP address of your default gateway system. Does the first `ping` take longer than the subsequent `ping`s?

APPLY YOUR KNOWLEDGE

If it does, why do you think it does? Immediately run the ping utility again. Is the first ping quicker than the first ping of the first attempt?

3. Using the arp -a command again, view the ARP cache. Note whether any entries have been added. Write down the IP address and MAC address of the default gateway; you'll use them later in the exercise.

4. By using the ipconfig command, determine the IP address of your default gateway, and then ping the address.

5. Immediately view the ARP cache again. Note whether any new entries have been added.

6. Wait about three minutes and then view the ARP cache again. Is the entry for the default gateway still there?

7. Using the information you wrote down in step 3, add a static entry for your default gateway by using the following command:

```
arp -s <IP ADDRESS OF DEFAULT GATEWAY>
  <MAC ADDRESS OF DEFAULT GATEWAY>
```

For help with the syntax, type **arp** at the command line to display the help screen.

8. After you have successfully added the new entry, view the ARP cache. The static entry should now be listed.

9. Delete the static entry you just created by using the following command:

```
arp -d <IP ADDRESS OF DEFAULT GATEWAY>
```

10. View the ARP cache one last time, to ensure that the static entry has been removed.

13.4 Using the Trace Route Utility

In this exercise, you use the tracert command in Windows 2000 to look at how a trace route works.

Estimated time: 10 minutes

1. Ascertain the IP address of your DNS server by using the ipconfig /all command.

2. Trace the route to your DNS server by using the command tracert <ADDRESS OF DNS SERVER>. Note how many hops you are from your DNS server and how long the round trip took.

3. Trace the route to the CompTIA Web server by using the command tracert www.comptia.org. Note how many hops you are away from the Web server and how long the round trip took.

4. Use the same command as in step 3, but add the -d switch to the command line, as follows: tracert www.comptia.org.com -d. Note what changes in the output from the command.

Exam Questions

1. Which of the following TCP/IP utilities can be used to view routing tables on a Windows 2000 system? (Choose the two best answers.)

   a. netstat

   b. nbtstat

   c. route

   d. ping

   e. tracert

APPLY YOUR KNOWLEDGE

2. Which of the following commands can be used to purge and reload the remote cache name table?

   a. nbtstat -R

   b. nbtstat -n

   c. nbtstat -r

   d. nbtstat -S

3. Which of the following commands can be used to display the protocol statistics on a per-protocol basis?

   a. netstat -S

   b. netstat -r

   c. netstat -R

   d. netstat -s

   e. netstat -a

4. The following is output from which of the following commands?

   ```
   Active Connections
   Proto Local Address Foreign Address State
   TCP     laptop:1026    127.0.0.1:50000
   ➥ESTABLISHED
   TCP     laptop:50000   127.0.0.1:1026
   ➥ESTABLISHED
   ```

   a. nbtstat

   b. netstat

   c. arp

   d. ipconfig

5. Which of the following best describes the function of the ARP command?

   a. It resolves IP addresses to MAC addresses.

   b. It resolves NetBIOS names to IP addresses.

   c. It resolves fully qualified domain names to IP addresses.

   d. It resolves hostnames to IP addresses.

6. From your Windows 2000 system you try unsuccessfully to ping a remote host on another network. What utility might you use to determine where the packet was dropped?

   a. arp

   b. netstat

   c. tracert

   d. nbtstat

7. You are troubleshooting a client connectivity problem in which a system is unable to log on to the network. The client system uses the Linux operating system. Which of the following commands would you use to view the current IP configuration?

   a. ipconfig

   b. ipconfig /all

   c. ifconfig

   d. config

8. Which of the following switches is used to perform a continuous ping?

   a. -c

   b. -d

   c. -t

   d. -ct

APPLY YOUR KNOWLEDGE

9. Which utility is used to view NetBIOS over TCP/IP statistics?

   a. `ping -t`

   b. `netstat`

   c. `nbtstat`

   d. `arp`

   e. `tracert`

10. Which of the following commands allows you to view the ARP cache?

    a. `arp -a`

    b. `arp -C`

    c. `arp -c`

    d. `arp -A`

11. Which utility would produce the following output?

```
6  55 ms  27 ms  42 ms  so-1-0-0.XL1.VAN1.NET
[152.63.137.130]
7  55 ms  41 ms  28 ms  0.so-7-0-0.TL1.VAN1.NET
[152.63.138.74]
8  55 ms  55 ms  55 ms  0.so-2-0-0.TL1.SAC1.NET
[152.63.8.1]
9  83 ms  55 ms  55 ms  0.so-7-0-0.XL1.SAC1.NET
[152.63.53.249]
10 82 ms  41 ms  55 ms  POS6-0.BR5.SAC1.NET
[152.63.52.225]
11 55 ms  68 ms  55 ms  uu-gw.ip.att.net
[192.205.32.125]
12 55 ms  68 ms  69 ms  tbr2-p013802.ip.att.net
[12.122.11.229]
13 96 ms  69 ms  82 ms  tbr1-p012801.ip.att.net
[12.122.11.225]
14 82 ms  82 ms  69 ms  tbr2-p012402.ip.att.net
[12.122.11.221]
15 82 ms  83 ms  68 ms  gbr2-p20.ip.att.net
[12.122.11.254]
16 55 ms  69 ms  69 ms  gbr1-p60.ip.att.net
[12.122.1.109]
17 123 ms 96 ms  96 ms  gbr1-p30.ip.att.net
[12.122.2.142]
```

```
18 83 ms  96 ms  97 ms  gar1-p360.ip.att.net
[12.123.142.21]
19 96 ms  82 ms  96 ms  12.127.141.26
20 124 ms 96 ms  96 ms  216.119.107.2
21 124 ms 82 ms  110 ms 216.119.103.72
```

   a. `nbtstat -R`

   b. `netstat -R`

   c. `arp -s`

   d. `tracert`

12. Which of the following commands would you use to check whether a modem is working through a communications program?

    a. ARP

    b. ATZ

    c. ATG

    d. AMP

13. Which of the following is *not* likely to be the cause of slow connections over a dial-up link?

    a. No dial tone

    b. Incorrect modem configuration

    c. Poor line quality

    d. Incorrect serial port configuration.

14. When using cable Internet access, which of the following is not a valid troubleshooting step?

    a. Plugging the cable connection into a TV

    b. Ensuring that all physical connections are in place

    c. Calling the support line of the cable service provider

    d. Checking to make sure you have a valid IP address

APPLY YOUR KNOWLEDGE

15. When troubleshooting a network connectivity problem, you are able to `ping` your local loop-back, the IP address of your system, and the IP address of another system on your network. However, you cannot `ping` the default gateway. Which of the following is *not* a valid reason for this problem?

    a. The default gateway is not operational.

    b. The IP address of the default gateway is not configured correctly.

    c. Routing is disabled on your workstation.

    d. There is no default gateway present.

16. When using trace route to determine the cause of a network connectivity problem, you notice that asterisks (*) are being displayed. What does this mean?

    a. The hop after this router is invalid.

    b. The host is unable to forward the request any further along the route.

    c. The router is not authorized to provide a hostname to requestors.

    d. The request was not returned in time and was therefore timed out.

17. When contacting technical support personnel, which of the following information should you be prepared to give? (Choose the three best answers.)

    a. Administrator passwords for your server systems

    b. Account information for the dial-up account

    c. Details of what fixes you have already tried

    d. A detailed description of the problem

18. You attempt to `ping` the Web server `web.comptia.org` but receive a Host Not Found error. When you try to `ping` the server, using its IP address, you are successful. What is the most probable cause of the problem?

    a. The `web.comptia.org` system is not up and running.

    b. Name resolution is not configured correctly.

    c. Your default gateway is not configured correctly.

    d. The server has an invalid IP address.

19. Which of the following commands would you use to add a static entry to the ARP table of a Windows 2000 system?

    a. `arp -a <IP ADDRESS> <MAC ADDRESS>`

    b. `arp -s <MAC ADDRESS> <IP ADDRESS>`

    c. `arp -s <IP ADDRESS> <MAC ADDRESS>`

    d. `arp -i <IP ADDRESS> <MAC ADDRESS>`

20. Which of the following is not a valid troubleshooting step when you are having connectivity problems with a cable modem?

    a. Use the AT command set to initialize the modem.

    b. Cycle the power on the modem.

    c. Check all the physical connections to the modem and the network.

    d. Verify the network settings.

APPLY YOUR KNOWLEDGE

Answers to Exam Questions

1. **a, c.** Both route and netstat can be used to view the routing table on a Windows 2000 system. nbtstat is used to view NetBIOS over TCP/IP statistics, and ping is used to test connectivity between two devices. tracert is used to trace the route between two devices on a network. For more information, see the section "Troubleshooting Tools," in this chapter.

2. **a.** The nbtstat -R command purges and reloads the remote cache name table. The -n switch displays the local name table, -r provides resolution information, and -S shows the NetBIOS session table. For more information, see the section "Troubleshooting Tools," in this chapter.

3. **d.** The netstat -s command displays statistics on a per-protocol basis. The -S and -R switches are not valid with netstat. Answer b (-r) causes netstat to display the routing table, and Answer e (-a) checks connections. For more information, see the section "Troubleshooting Tools," in this chapter.

4. **b.** The output is from a netstat command. All the other utilities listed provide different output. For more information, see the section "Troubleshooting Tools" in this chapter.

5. **a.** The ARP command resolves IP addresses to MAC addresses. Answer b describes the function of WINS, and Answers c and d describe the function of DNS. For more information, see the section "Troubleshooting Tools," in this chapter.

6. **c.** On a Windows system, the tracert command can be used to track the path a packet takes between hosts on the network. Of the commands listed, only tracert can perform this function.

For more information, see the section "Troubleshooting Tools," in this chapter.

7. **c.** The ifconfig command displays the configuration of the network interfaces on a Linux system. Answers a and b are Windows-based utilities, and Answer d is a NetWare command. For more information, see the section "Troubleshooting Tools," in this chapter.

8. **c.** The ping -t command issues a continuous stream of ping requests until it is interrupted. None of the other answers are valid switches for the ping command. For more information, see the section "Troubleshooting Tools," in this chapter.

9. **c.** The nbtstat command can be used to view NetBIOS over TCP/IP statistics. The ping command is used to test connectivity between devices, netstat is used to view TCP/IP protocol statistics, the arp command is used to view a list of IP address to MAC address resolutions, and tracert is used to track the path between two devices on the network. For more information, see the section "Troubleshooting Tools," in this chapter.

10. **a.** On a Windows 2000 system, the arp -a command displays the contents of the ARP cache. None of the other answers are valid switches for the ARP command. For more information, see the section "Troubleshooting Tools," in this chapter.

11. **d.** The output is from the Windows 2000 tracert command. All the other utilities listed provide different output. For more information, see the section "Troubleshooting Tools," in this chapter.

APPLY YOUR KNOWLEDGE

12. **b.** The ATZ command resets the modem. If the command can be executed successfully, the modem is working correctly. None of the other commands are valid AT command set commands. For more information, see the section "Troubleshooting in a Small Office/Home Office Environment," in this chapter.

13. **a.** The lack of a dial tone would mean that no link could be established—not even a slow one. All the other answers are valid reasons for a slow dial-up link. For more information, see the section "Troubleshooting in a Small Office/Home Office Environment," in this chapter.

14. **a.** Although the physical connections for cable TV and a cable modem are the same, the data signal on a coaxial cable would be ignored by a TV, making this an invalid troubleshooting step. All the other steps are valid troubleshooting steps. For more information, see the section "Troubleshooting in a Small Office/Home Office Environment," in this chapter.

15. **c.** The routing functionality of the workstation is irrelevant in this scenario. All the other answers are valid reasons for the problem. For more information, see the section "Troubleshooting Tools," in this chapter.

16. **d.** The asterisk symbol is returned when a reply is not received from a host within a specified time limit. The other answers may be the cause of the problem, but it is not possible to determine

which of them is the error, given just this result. For more information, see the section "Troubleshooting Tools," in this chapter.

17. **b, c, d.** When contacting technical support, you should be prepared to give the username and password for the account, information about what fixes you have attempted, and a detailed description of the problem. You should not, however, give a technical support person passwords for the user accounts—especially the Administrator account—on the internal network. For more information, see the section "Troubleshooting in a Small Office/Home Office Environment," in this chapter.

18. **b.** The scenario indicates that there is a problem with name resolution. None of the other answers would produce this symptom. For more information, see the section "Troubleshooting Tools," in this chapter.

19. **c.** This command would correctly add a static entry to the ARP table. None of the other answers are valid ARP switches. For more information, see the section "Troubleshooting Tools," in this chapter.

20. **a.** The AT command set is for use with conventional modems, not with cable or DSL modems. All the other steps are valid for troubleshooting cable modems. For more information, see the section "Troubleshooting in a Small Office/Home Office Environment," in this chapter.

APPLY YOUR KNOWLEDGE

Suggested Readings and Resources

1. Sloan, Joseph D. *Network Troubleshooting Tools (O'Reilly System Administration).* O'Reilly & Associates, 2001.

2. Habraken, Joe. *Absolute Beginner's Guide to Networking,* third edition. Que Publishing, 2001.

3. Haugdahl, J. Scott. *Network Analysis and Troubleshooting.* Addison-Wesley, 2000.

4. Cisco Systems, Inc. *Internetworking Troubleshooting Handbook,* second edition. Cisco Press, 2001.

5. Computer networking products and testing tools, `www.trendware.com`.

6. Network cable information, `www.techfest.com/networking/cabling.htm`.

7. Computer networking tutorials and advice, `compnetworking.about.com`.

8. "TechEncyclopedia," `www.techencyclopedia.com`.

9. Networking Technology Information from Cisco, `www.cisco.com/public/products_tech.shtml`.

10. "Network Cabling Help," `www.datacottage.com`.

This chapter covers the following CompTIA-specified objectives for the "Network Support" section of the Network+ exam.

Given a wiring task, select the appropriate tool (e.g., wire crimper, media tester, punch-down tool, tone generator, optical tester).

▶ Working with wiring, or cable as it is often called, is a common task for network administrators. To do so effectively, you must understand the tools and concepts associated with making and testing cables.

Given a network scenario, interpret visual indicators (e.g., link lights, collision lights) to determine the nature of the problem.

▶ Sometimes finding the source of a problem is as simple as looking at indicator lights. Many network devices have visual indicators that help you troubleshoot.

Given output from a diagnostic utility (e.g., tracert, ping, ipconfig), identify the utility and interpret the output.

▶ Software utilities provide the network troubleshooter with information about the configuration of a system and a means to test connectivity with other systems on the network. Understanding how to interpret the information supplied by software utilities is a key skill for a network administrator.

CHAPTER 14

Troubleshooting Tools and Utilities

OUTLINE

Introduction	**549**
Selecting the Appropriate Tool for Wiring	**549**
Wire Crimpers	550
Punchdown Tools	550
Tone Generators	551
Media Testers	552
Hardware Loopback Connectors	553
Interpreting Visual Indicators	**553**
LEDs on Networking Devices	554
LEDs on NICs and Other Devices	555
Using LEDs in Troubleshooting	556
Using Diagnostic Utilities	**557**
ping	557
The Destination Host Unreachable Message	557
The Request Timed Out Message	558
The Unknown Host Message	559
The Expired TTL Message	560
The tracert Command	560
The netstat Command	563
netstat -e	564
netstat -a	565
netstat -r	566
netstat -s	567
The ipconfig Command	568
The winipcfg Command	570
Chapter Summary	**571**
Apply Your Knowledge	**572**

STUDY STRATEGIES

▶ Read the objectives at the beginning of the chapter.

▶ Study the information in this chapter, paying special attention to the tables, which summarize key information.

▶ Review the objectives again.

▶ Study the output from the various commands demonstrated in this chapter.

▶ Answer the exam questions at the end of the chapter and check your results.

▶ Use the ExamGear test on the CD-ROM that accompanies this book to answer additional exam questions concerning this material.

▶ Review the notes, tips, and exam tips in this chapter. Make sure you understand the information in the exam tips. If you don't understand the topic referenced in an exam tip, refer to the information in the chapter text and then read the exam tip again.

INTRODUCTION

A large part of network administration involves having the right tools for the job and knowing when and how to use them. Selecting the correct tool for a networking job sounds like an easy task, but network administrators can choose from a mind-boggling number of tools and utilities.

Given the diverse range of tools and utilities available, it is unlikely that you will encounter all the ones that are available—or even all those that are discussed in this chapter. For the Network+ exam, however, you are required to have a general knowledge of the tools available and what they are designed to do.

SELECTING THE APPROPRIATE TOOL FOR WIRING

▶ Given a wiring task, select the appropriate tool (e.g., wire crimper, media tester, punchdown tool, tone generator, optical tester).

Until networks become 100% wireless, network administrators can expect to spend some of their time using a variety of media-related troubleshooting and installation tools. Some of these tools (such as the tone generator and locator) may be used for troubleshooting media connections, and others (such as wire crimpers and punchdown tools) are used to create network cables and connections.

IN THE FIELD

THE BASIC TOOLS

Although many costly, specialized networking tools and devices are available to network administrators, the most widely used tools cost only a few dollars: the standard screwdrivers we use on almost a daily basis. As a network administrator, you can expect to take the case off a system to replace a network interface card (NIC) or perhaps remove the cover from a hub to replace a fan with amazing regularity. Advanced cable testers and specialized tools will not help you when you need a screwdriver.

Cable Caveat   When making cables, always order more connectors than you need; there will probably be a few mishaps along the way.

FIGURE 14.1
A wire crimper for RJ-45 and RJ-11 cables. (Photo courtesy of TRENDware International, www.trendware.com.)

Make or Buy?   There is some debate about whether it is better to buy network cables from a cable manufacturer or make your own. The advantage of buying cables is simply that they are guaranteed to work because they are tested before being sent out. Homemade cables are often made incorrectly and can create hard-to-troubleshoot errors. For example, loose connectors that work when the cable is in one position may not work it's in another. Those who make cables claim that the cost savings over buying cables is a clear benefit. However, if the associated labor costs were introduced into the equation, it is a more difficult argument to make. Many network administrators take the best from both worlds, buying network cable when standard cable lengths are needed and making their own when specific cable lengths are required.

Wire Crimpers

Wire crimpers are tools you might find yourself using on a regular basis. Like many things, making your own cables can be fun at first, but the novelty soon wears thin. Basically, a wire crimper is a tool that you use to attach media connectors to the ends of cables. For instance, you use one type of wire crimper to attach RJ-45 connectors on unshielded twisted-pair (UTP) cable, and you use a different type of wire crimper to attach British Naval connectors (BNCs) to coaxial cabling. Figure 14.1 shows an example of a wire crimper for crimping both RJ-11 and RJ-45 connectors.

In a sense, you can think of a wire crimper as a pair of special pliers. You insert the cable and connector separately into the crimper, making sure the wires in the cable align with the appropriate connectors. Then, by squeezing the crimper's handles, you force metal connectors through the wires of the cable, making the connection between the wire and the connector.

When you crimp your own cables, you need to be sure to test them before putting them on the network. It only takes a momentary lapse to make a mistake when creating a cable, and you can waste time later trying to isolate a problem in a faulty cable. The section "Media Testers," later in this chapter, includes a discussion of how you can test whether a cable is working correctly.

Punchdown Tools

If you have ever looked in a network closet, you have probably seen a distribution block, more commonly called a patch panel. A *patch panel* is a freestanding or wall-mounted unit with a number of port connections on the front. In a way, it looks like a wall-mounted hub without the light-emitting diodes (LEDs). The patch panel provides a connection point between network equipment such as hubs and switches and the ports to which PCs are connected, which are normally distributed throughout a building. Figure 14.2 shows three patch panels.

Behind each of the individual RJ-45 jacks on the patch panel are connectors to which are attached the eight wires from a piece of twisted-pair cable. These wires are commonly attached to the patch panel by using a tool called a *punchdown tool*. To use the punchdown tool, you place a wire in the tip of the tool and push it into the connector at the back of the patch panel. The insulation is stripped, and the wire is firmly embedded into the connector. Because the connector strips the insulation on the wire, it is known rather grandiosely as an insulation displacement connector (IDC). (Most networks administrators choose to refer to it as a *thingy*, if they call it anything at all.) Figure 14.3 shows an example of a typical punchdown tool.

Using a punchdown tool is much faster than using wire strippers to prepare each individual wire and then twisting the wire around a connection pole or tightening a screw to hold the wire in place. In many environments, cable tasks are left to a specialized cable contractor. In others, the administrator is the one with the task of connecting wires to a punchdown block.

Tone Generators

A tone generator is a device that can save a network installer many hours of frustration. Strangely, the tone generator has a partner that goes wherever it goes but is seldom mentioned: the tone locator. You might hear the tone generator and the tone locator referred to as the *fox and hound*.

As you might expect, the purpose of the tone generator is to generate a signal that is transmitted on the wire you are attempting to locate. At the other end, you press the tone locator against individual wires. When it makes contact with the wire that has the signal on it, the locator emits an audible signal or tone.

The tone locator is a useful device, but it does have some drawbacks. First, it often takes two people to operate—one at each end of the cable. Of course, one person could just keep running back and forth; but if the cable is run over great distances, this can be a problem. Second, using the tone generator is a time-consuming process because it must be attached to each cable independently.

NOTE

Direct Cable Connections Not all environments use patch panels. In some environments, cables are run directly between systems and a hub or switch. This is an acceptable method of connectivity, but it is not as easy to make tidy as a structured cabling system that uses a patch panel system and wall or floor sockets.

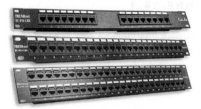

FIGURE 14.2
A selection of patch panels. (Photo courtesy of TRENDware International, `www.trendware.com`.)

FIGURE 14.3
A punchdown tool. (Photo courtesy of TRENDware International, `www.trendware.com`.)

NOTE

Labeling Cables Many problems that can be discovered with a tone generator are easy to prevent by simply taking the time to properly label cables. If the cables are labeled at both ends, you will not need to use such a tool to locate them.

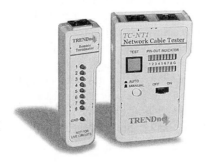

FIGURE 14.4

An example of a media tester. (Photo courtesy of TRENDware International, www.trendware.com.)

Media Testers

A media tester, also called a cable tester, is used to test whether a cable is working properly. Any tool that facilitates the testing of a cable can be deemed a cable tester. One of the simplest cable-testing devices is a multimeter. By using the continuity setting, you can test for shorts in a length of coaxial cable; or, if you know the correct cable pinouts and have needlepoint probes, you can test twisted-pair cable. Various other single-purpose and multipurpose devices allow you to test cables. Some of these devices tell you if the cable is working correctly and, if it's not, give you some idea why it's not. Figure 14.4 shows an example of a media tester. Note that there are two parts to the media tester: one for each end of the cable.

Because the majority of network cabling is copper based, most of the tools designed to test cabling are designed for copper-based cabling. However, when you test fiber-optic cable, you need an optical tester.

An optical cable tester performs the same basic function as a wire media tester, but on optical media. The most common problem with an optical cable is a break in the cable that prevents the signal from reaching the other end. Due to the extended distances that can be covered with fiber-optic cables, degradation is rarely an issue in a fiber-optic LAN environment.

Ascertaining whether a signal reaches the other end of a fiber-optic cable is a relatively easy task, but when you determine that there is a break, the problem becomes locating the break. That's when you need a tool called an optical time-domain reflectometer (OTDR). By using an OTDR, you can locate how far along in the cable the break occurs. The connection on the other end of the cable might be the source of the problem, or perhaps there is a break halfway along the cable. Either way, an OTDR can pinpoint the problem.

Unless you work extensively with fiber-optic cable, you're unlikely to have an OTDR or even a fiber-optic cable tester in your toolbox. Specialized cabling contractors will have them, though, so knowing they exist is important.

Hardware Loopback Connectors

Hardware loopback connectors are simple devices that redirect outgoing transmissions from a system directly back into it. Hardware loopback connectors are used in conjunction with diagnostic software for diagnosing transmission problems. Loopback connectors are available for a number of ports, including RJ-45, serial, and parallel ports.

Specifically, a hardware loopback connector loops the outgoing data signal wires back into the system on the incoming data signal line. It in effect tricks the system into thinking that the PC is sending and receiving data on the network, when in fact the data being sent is just being rerouted back in. Note that in some cases, a hardware loopback connector is referred to as an adapter or a plug.

For the purposes of this discussion, we're interested in the hardware loopback connector used with twisted-pair network ports (10BaseT, 100BaseT, and so on). You can buy hardware loopback plugs or make your own. The wiring of a hardware loopback connector is fairly simple: Pin 1 is wired to Pin 3, and Pin 2 is wired to Pin 6. A picture is worth a thousand words in this case; Figure 14.5 shows a graphical representation of the wiring of a hardware loopback connector. The wiring pinouts for a hardware loopback connector are the same as those for a UTP crossover cable.

INTERPRETING VISUAL INDICATORS

▶ Given a network scenario, interpret visual indicators (e.g., link lights, collision lights) to determine the nature of the problem.

One of the first and easiest methods to spot signs of trouble on a network or with a network component is to look at the LEDs that appear on most network components. Many of the devices used in modern networks—such as hubs, routers, switches, and even NICs—have LEDs that let you know what, if anything, is going wrong. The following sections examine some of the common networking devices and what you can learn from their LEDs.

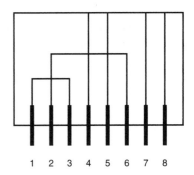

FIGURE 14.5
The wiring for a hardware loopback connector.

> **NOTE**
>
> **Software Versus Hardware Loopback** Chapter 13, "Troubleshooting Connectivity," discusses the use of the local loopback address (127.0.0.1) as a means of testing the Transmission Control Protocol/Internet Protocol (TCP/IP) connectivity of a system. Although this test is an effective way of ensuring that the TCP/IP protocol suite is operating correctly, it does not ensure that the network is functional at a physical level because the software loopback functionality is built in to the protocol suite. In other words, a software loopback never makes it as far as the physical NIC or connection. A hardware loopback takes the test one step further by providing a mechanism to test the physical connectivity. The software loopback test is still a useful tool, however, because without a functioning network card, operating systems generally won't allow the protocol suite to be tested.

LEDs on Networking Devices

If you have seen a hub or a switch, you have no doubt noticed the LEDs on the front of the device. Each individual RJ-45 connector has one or two dedicated LEDs. These LEDs are designed to provide the network administrator with a quick idea of the status of a connection or to a potential problem. Table 14.1 provides some examples of link-light indicators functioning on a hub.

Note that the LEDs' sequencing and meanings vary among the different hub manufacturers and therefore may be different from those listed in Table 14.1.

TABLE 14.1

LINK-LIGHT INDICATOR LEDS FOR A NETWORK HUB

LED State	Meaning
Solid green	A device is connected to the port, but there is no activity on the device.
Blinking green	There is activity on the port. The connected system is sending or receiving data.
No LED lit	There is no detectable link. Either there's a problem with the connection between the device and the hub (such as an unplugged cable) or the remote system is powered down.
Fast continuous blinking for extended periods	This often indicates a fault with the connection, which can commonly be attributed to a faulty network card.
Blinking amber	There are collisions on the network. A few orange LEDs flashing intermittently are okay, but continuously blinking amber LEDs indicate a problem.

In addition to link-light indicators, some hubs and switches have port-speed LEDs that, when lit, indicate the speed at which the connected device is functioning. Some also have LEDs that indicate whether the link is operating in full-duplex mode. These LEDs are often labeled FDX, FX, FD, or Full. Figure 14.6 shows an example of LEDs on an Ethernet switch.

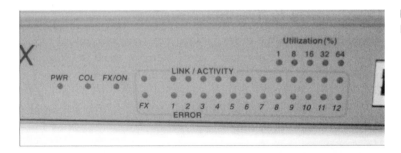

FIGURE 14.6
LEDs on a hub.

By understanding the function of the lights on networking devices, you can tell at a glance the status of a device and the systems connected to it. You should take the time to familiarize yourself with the specific indicator lights on the network devices you work with and their various states.

LEDs on NICs and Other Devices

In addition to hubs and switches, most other networking devices have LEDs that provide a variety of information. Most NIC have at least one LED that indicates whether there is a link between the system and the network into which it is plugged. The link light operates at a physical level; in other words, it should be lit when the PC is on, regardless of whether the networking software is loaded, the network configuration is correct, or the user is logged on to the network. In addition to the link LED, many NICs have additional lights to indicate the speed at which the network connection is established and/or when there is network activity on the link. Figure 14.7 shows a NIC that has a link light (right), an activity LED (middle), and an LED that indicates whether the link is at 100Mbps (left).

LEDs are also included on cable modems and DSL modems, which are increasingly common as people want faster methods to connect to the Internet.

The number of LEDs on a device and their functionality depends on the device. For example, the cable modem we use has four LEDs: one that indicates that the modem is online, a Send indicator, a Receive indicator, and one labeled Message.

FIGURE 14.7
A NIC with indicator LEDs.

> **NOTE**
>
> **Reading the Lights** The trick to using indictor lights on networking equipment is knowing how they function in normal operation. Then, when a deviation occurs, you can recognize that something is wrong.

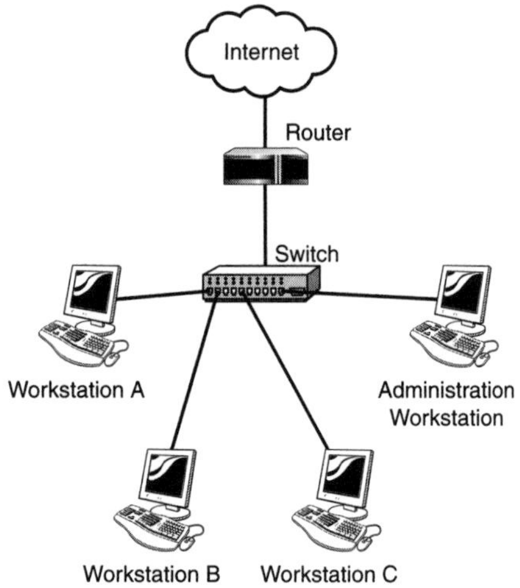

FIGURE 14.8
A sample network.

> **EXAM TIP**
>
> **Identify the Link Lights** Expect to be asked to identify the purposes of link lights on the Network+ exam. You might be presented with diagrams and asked how you would use LEDs in the troubleshooting process.

Using LEDs in Troubleshooting

The usefulness of LEDs in troubleshooting scenarios cannot be overstated. LEDs provide an instant, visual indicator about the state of a network link. In some cases, as with collision lights, they can even alert you to problems on the network. Understanding how to interpret information provided by LEDs is important for the real world and for the Network+ exam.

To demonstrate how LEDs can be used for troubleshooting, consider the sample network layout in Figure 14.8.

Imagine a scenario in which a user who is working at Workstation A calls and tells you she is unable to access the Internet. The Internet connection could be down, but by connecting to the Internet yourself, you determine that it is working correctly; therefore, it is safe to assume that the problem is on the user's end rather than with the Internet connectivity. Next, you decide to visit the user's workstation to see if you can ping the Internet router. Before you begin the ping test, you look at the back of the system and see that the link LED on the NIC is not lit. You can be fairly sure at this point that the ping test will not work because without the link light, there is no connectivity between the NIC and the switch.

Now you have narrowed the problem to one of a few things. Either the NIC or the cable is faulty, the switch to which the user is connected is not functioning, or the port on the switch to which the user is connected is faulty.

The easiest way to test whether the cable is the problem is to borrow a known working cable from Workstation B or C and plug it into Workstation A. When you try this, if the link light does not come on, you can deduce that the NIC is faulty. If the light does come on, you can deduce that either the port on the switch or a cable is faulty. The next step is to swap the cable out or try the original cable in another port switch.

Whatever the actual problem, link lights play an important role in the troubleshooting process. They give you an easy method of seeing what steps do and don't work.

USING DIAGNOSTIC UTILITIES

▶ Given output from a diagnostic utility (e.g., tracert, ping, ipconfig), identify the utility and interpret the output.

You can use many different tools to monitor and troubleshoot TCP/IP networks. Chapter 13 discusses how to use these tools; this chapter looks at the output from the various utilities and what you can learn in each case.

ping

ping is perhaps the most widely used of all network tools; it is primarily used to verify connectivity between two network devices. On a good day, the results from the ping command will be successful, and the sending device will receive a reply from the remote device. Not all ping results are that successful, and to be able to effectively use ping, you must be able to interpret the results of a failed ping command.

When you're troubleshooting with the ping command, four key error messages can be returned: two of the error messages are quite common, and two are a little less common. The following sections describe these results of a ping command.

The Destination Host Unreachable Message

The Destination Host Unreachable error message means that a route to the destination computer system cannot be found. To remedy this problem, you might need to examine the routing information on the local host to confirm that the local host is correctly configured, or you might need to make sure the default gateway information is correct. Listing 14.1 shows an example of a ping failure that gives the Destination Host Unreachable message.

LISTING 14.1

A ping FAILURE WITH THE DESTINATION HOST UNREACHABLE

```
Pinging 24.67.54.233 with 32 bytes of data:
Destination host unreachable.
Destination host unreachable.
Destination host unreachable.
Destination host unreachable.
Ping statistics for 24.67.54.233:
    Packets: Sent = 4, Received = 0, Lost = 4 (100% loss),
Approximate round trip times in milli-seconds:
    Minimum = 0ms, Maximum =  0ms, Average =  0ms
```

The Request Timed Out Message

The Request Timed Out error message is very common when you use the ping command. Essentially, this error message indicates that your host did not receive the ping message within the designated time period. This is typically an indicator that the destination device is not connected to the network, is powered off, or is not configured correctly. It could also mean that some intermediate device is not operating correctly. In some rare cases, it can also indicate that there is so much congestion on the network that timely delivery of the ping message could not be completed. It might also mean that the ping is being sent to an invalid IP address or that the system is not on the same network as the remote host, and an intermediary device is not configured correctly. In any of these cases, the failed ping should initiate a troubleshooting process that may involve other tools, manual inspection, and possibly reconfiguration. Listing 14.2 shows the output from a ping to an invalid IP address.

LISTING 14.2

THE OUTPUT FOR A ping TO AN INVALID IP ADDRESS

```
C:\>ping 169.76.54.3
Pinging 169.76.54.3 with 32 bytes of data:

Request timed out.
Request timed out.
Request timed out.
Request timed out.
```

```
Ping statistics for 169.76.54.3:
    Packets: Sent = 4, Received = 0, Lost = 4 (100%
Approximate round trip times in milli-seconds:
    Minimum = 0ms, Maximum =  0ms, Average =  0ms
```

Refer to Chapter 13 for information on troubleshooting procedures using ping.

During the ping request, you might receive some replies from the remote host that are intermixed with Request Timed Out errors. This is often a result of a congested network. An example follows; notice that the example in Listing 14.3, which was run on a Windows Me system, uses the -t switch to generate continuous pings.

LISTING 14.3

THE -t SWITCH GENERATING CONTINUOUS pings

```
C:\>ping -t 24.67.184.65
Pinging 24.67.184.65 with 32 bytes of data:

Reply from 24.67.184.65: bytes=32 time=55ms TTL=127
Reply from 24.67.184.65: bytes=32 time=54ms TTL=127
Reply from 24.67.184.65: bytes=32 time=27ms TTL=127
Request timed out.
Request timed out.
Request timed out.
Reply from 24.67.184.65: bytes=32 time=69ms TTL=127
Reply from 24.67.184.65: bytes=32 time=28ms TTL=127
Reply from 24.67.184.65: bytes=32 time=28ms TTL=127
Reply from 24.67.184.65: bytes=32 time=68ms TTL=127
Reply from 24.67.184.65: bytes=32 time=41ms TTL=127

Ping statistics for 24.67.184.65:
    Packets: Sent = 11, Received = 8, Lost = 3 (27% loss),
Approximate round trip times in milli-seconds:
    Minimum = 27ms, Maximum =  69ms, Average =  33ms
```

In this example, three packets were lost. If this continued on your network, you would need to troubleshoot to find out why packets were being dropped.

The Unknown Host Message

The Unknown Host error message is generated when the hostname of the destination computer cannot be resolved. This error usually occurs when you `ping` an incorrect hostname, as shown in the following example, or try to use `ping` with a hostname when hostname resolution (via DNS or a `HOSTS` text file) is not configured:

```
C:\>ping www.comptia.ca
Unknown host www.comptia.ca
```

If the `ping` fails, you need to verify that the `ping` is being sent to the correct remote host. If it is, and if name resolution is configured, you have to dig a little more to find the problem. This error might indicate a problem with the name resolution process, and you might need to verify that the DNS or WINS server is available. Other commands, such as `nslookup`, can help in this process.

The Expired TTL Message

The Time to Live (TTL) is an important consideration in understanding the `ping` command. The function of the TTL is to prevent circular routing, which occurs when a `ping` request keeps looping through a series of hosts. The TTL counts each hop along the way toward its destination device. Each time it counts one hop, the hop is subtracted from the TTL. If the TTL reaches 0, the TTL has expired, and you get a message like the following:

```
Reply from 24.67.180.1: TTL expired in transit
```

If the TTL is exceeded with `ping`, you might have a routing problem on the network. You can modify the TTL for `ping` on a Windows system by using the `ping -i` command.

The tracert Command

The `tracert` command, which is short for *trace route,* does exactly what its name implies—it traces the route between two hosts by using Internet Control Message Protocol (ICMP) echo packets to report back at every step in the journey. The `tracert` command provides a lot of useful information, including the IP address of every router connection it passes through, and in many cases the name of the router (although this depends on the router's configuration). `tracert` also reports the length, in milliseconds, of the round trip the packet made from the source location to the router and back. This information can tell you a lot about where network bottlenecks or breakdowns may be. Listing 14.4 shows an example of a successful `tracert` command on a Windows 2000 system.

LISTING 14.4

A tracert **COMMAND**

```
C:\>tracert 24.7.70.37
Tracing route to c1-p4.sttlwa1.home.net [24.7.70.37] over a
maximum of 30 hops:
  1    30 ms    20 ms    20 ms   24.67.184.1
  2    20 ms    20 ms    30 ms   rd1ht-ge3-0.ok.shawcable.net
➥[24.67.224.7]
  3    50 ms    30 ms    30 ms   rc1wh-atm0-2-1.vc.shawcable.net
➥[204.209.214.193]
  4    50 ms    30 ms    30 ms   rc2wh-pos15-0.vc.shawcable.net
➥[204.209.214.90]
  5    30 ms    40 ms    30 ms   rc2wt-pos2-0.wa.shawcable.net
➥[66.163.76.37]
  6    30 ms    40 ms    30 ms   c1-pos6-3.sttlwa1.home.net
➥[24.7.70.37]
Trace complete.
```

The tracert display on a Windows-based system includes several
columns of information. The first column represents the hop
number. The next three columns indicate the round-trip time, in
milliseconds, that a packet takes in its attempts to reach the destination. The last column is the hostname and the IP address of the
responding device.

Of course, not all tracert commands are successful. Listing 14.5
shows the output from a tracert command that doesn't manage to
get to the remote host.

LISTING 14.5

A tracert **COMMAND THAT DOESN'T GET TO THE
REMOTE HOST**

```
C:\>tracert comptia.org

Tracing route to comptia.org [216.119.103.72]
over a maximum of 30 hops:
  1    27 ms    28 ms    14 ms   24.67.179.1
  2    55 ms    13 ms    14 ms   rd1ht-ge3-0.ok.shawcable.net
➥[24.67.224.7]
  3    27 ms    27 ms    28 ms   rc1wh-atm0-2-1.shawcable.net
➥[204.209.214.19]
  4    28 ms    41 ms    27 ms   rc1wt-pos2-0.wa.shawcable.net
➥[66.163.76.65]
  5    28 ms    41 ms    27 ms   rc2wt-pos1-0.wa.shawcable.net
➥[66.163.68.2]
```

continues

LISTING 14.5   *continued*

A tracert COMMAND THAT DOESN'T GET TO THE REMOTE HOST

```
6    41 ms    55 ms    41 ms    c1-pos6-3.sttlwa1.home.net
➥[24.7.70.37]
7    54 ms    42 ms    27 ms    home-gw.st6wa.ip.att.net
➥[192.205.32.249]
8    *        *        *        Request timed out.
9    *        *        *        Request timed out.
10   *        *        *        Request timed out.
11   *        *        *        Request timed out.
12   *        *        *        Request timed out.
13   *        *        *        Request timed out.
14   *        *        *        Request timed out.
15   *        *        *        Request timed out.
```

EXAM TIP

Trace Route Names   The CompTIA objectives refer to the tracert utility by name. However, the trace route functionality has different names on other platforms. The output is much the same across all platforms.

In this example, the tracert only gets to the seventh hop, at which point it fails; this failure indicates that the problem lies on the far side of the device in step 7 or on the near side of the device in step 8. In other words, the device at step 7 is functioning but might not be able to make the next hop. The cause of the problem could be a range of things, such as an error in the routing table or a faulty connection. Alternatively, the seventh device might be operating 100%, but Device 8 might not be functioning at all. In any case, you can isolate the problem to just one or two devices.

The tracert command can also help you isolate a heavily congested network. In the following example, the trace route packets fail in the midst of the tracert but subsequently are able to continue. This behavior can be an indicator of network congestion, as shown in Listing 14.6.

LISTING 14.6

A TRACE ROUTE PACKET FAILURE DURING THE tracert

```
C:\>tracert comptia.org

Tracing route to comptia.org [216.119.103.72]over a maximum of
30 hops:
1    96 ms    96 ms    55 ms    24.67.179.1
2    14 ms    13 ms    28 ms    rd1ht-ge3-0.ok.shawcable.net
➥[24.67.224.7]
3    28 ms    27 ms    41 ms    rc1wh-atm0-2-1.shawcable.net
➥[204.209.214.19]
```

```
4     28 ms    41 ms    27 ms   rc1wt-pos2-0.wa.shawcable.net
➥[66.163.76.65]
5     41 ms    27 ms    27 ms   rc2wt-pos1-0.wa.shawcable.net
➥[66.163.68.2]
6     55 ms    41 ms    27 ms   c1-pos6-3.sttlwa1.home.net
➥[24.7.70.37]
7     54 ms    42 ms    27 ms   home-gw.st6wa.ip.att.net
➥[192.205.32.249]
8     55 ms    41 ms    28 ms   gbr3-p40.st6wa.ip.att.net
➥[12.123.44.130]
9      *         *        *      Request timed out.
10     *         *        *      Request timed out.
11     *         *        *      Request timed out.
12     *         *        *      Request timed out.
13    69 ms    68 ms    69 ms   gbr2-p20.sd2ca.ip.att.net
➥[12.122.11.254]
14    55 ms    68 ms    69 ms   gbr1-p60.sd2ca.ip.att.net
➥[12.122.1.109]
15    82 ms    69 ms    82 ms   gbr1-p30.phmaz.ip.att.net
➥[12.122.2.142]
16    68 ms    69 ms    82 ms   gar2-p360.phmaz.ip.att.net
➥[12.123.142.45]
17   110 ms    96 ms    96 ms   12.125.99.70
18   124 ms    96 ms    96 ms   light.crystaltech.com
➥[216.119.107.1]
19    82 ms    96 ms    96 ms   216.119.103.72
Trace complete.
```

> **NOTE**
>
> **route Interpretation** This section explores the results from the Windows `tracert` command, but interpreting `route` command results is similar throughout the various other operating system platforms.

Generally speaking, `tracert` allows you to identify the location of a problem in the connectivity between two devices. After you have determined this location, you might need to use a utility such as `ping` to continue troubleshooting. In many cases, as in the examples provided in this chapter, the routers might be on a network such as the Internet and so not be within your control. In that case, there is little you can do except inform your ISP of the problem.

The `netstat` Command

As discussed in Chapter 13, the `netstat` command displays the protocol statistics and current TCP/IP connections. Used without any switches, the `netstat` command shows the active connections for all outbound TCP/IP connections. In addition, several switches are available that change the type of information `netstat` displays.

The following sections show the output from several `netstat` switches and identify and interpret the output from each command.

netstat -e

The netstat -e command shows the activity for the NIC and displays the number of packets that have been both sent and received. An example of the netstat -e command is shown in Listing 14.7.

LISTING 14.7

AN EXAMPLE OF THE nestat -e COMMAND

```
C:\WINDOWS\Desktop>netstat -e
Interface Statistics

                             Received              Sent

Bytes                        17412385          40237510
Unicast packets                 79129             85055
Non-unicast packets               693               254
Discards                            0                 0
Errors                              0                 0
Unknown protocols                 306
```

As you can see, the netstat -e command shows more than just the packets that have been sent and received. The following list briefly explains the information provided in the netstat -e command:

◆ **Bytes**—The number of bytes that have been sent or received by the NIC since the computer was turned on.

◆ **Unicast packets**—Packets sent and received directly to this interface.

◆ **Non-unicast packets**—Broadcast or multicast packets that were picked up by the NIC.

◆ **Discards**—The number of packets rejected by the NIC, perhaps because they were damaged.

◆ **Errors**—The errors that occurred during either the sending or receiving process. As you would expect, this column should be a low number. If it is not, it could indicate a problem with the NIC.

◆ **Unknown protocols**—The number of packets that were not recognizable by the system.

netstat -a

The netstat -a command displays statistics for both the TCP and User Datagram Protocol (UDP). Listing 14.8 shows an example of the netstat -a command.

LISTING 14.8

AN EXAMPLE OF THE netstat -a COMMAND

```
C:\WINDOWS\Desktop>netstat -a

Active Connections

  Proto  Local Address        Foreign Address       State
  TCP    laptop:1027          LAPTOP:0              LISTENING
  TCP    laptop:1030          LAPTOP:0              LISTENING
  TCP    laptop:1035          LAPTOP:0              LISTENING
  TCP    laptop:50000         LAPTOP:0              LISTENING
  TCP    laptop:5000          LAPTOP:0              LISTENING
  TCP    laptop:1035          msgr-ns41.msgr.       ESTABLISHED
                              hotmail.com:1863
  TCP    laptop:nbsession     LAPTOP:0              LISTENING
  TCP    laptop:1027          localhost:50000       ESTABLISHED
  TCP    laptop:50000         localhost:1027        ESTABLISHED
  UDP    laptop:1900          *:*
  UDP    laptop:nbname        *:*
  UDP    laptop:nbdatagram    *:*
  UDP    laptop:1547          *:*
  UDP    laptop:1038          *:*
  UDP    laptop:1828          *:*
  UDP    laptop:3366          *:*
```

As you can see, the output includes four columns, which show the protocol, the local address, the foreign address, and the state of the port. The TCP connections show the local and foreign destination address and the current state of the connection. UDP, however, is a little different; it does not list a state status because as mentioned throughout this book, UDP is a connectionless protocol and does not establish connections. The following list briefly explains the information provided by the `netstat -a` command:

◆ **Proto**—The protocol used by the connection.

◆ **Local Address**—The IP address of the local computer system and the port number it is using. If the entry in the local address field is an asterisk (*), it indicates that the port has not yet been established.

◆ **Foreign Address**—The IP address of a remote computer system and the associated port. When a port has not been established, as with the UDP connections, `*:*` appears in the column.

◆ **State**—The current state of the TCP connection. Possible states include established, listening, closed, and waiting.

netstat -r

The `netstat -r` command is often used to view the routing table for a system. A system uses a routing table to determine routing information for TCP/IP traffic. Listing 14.9 shows an example of the `netstat -r` command from a Windows Me system.

NOTE

Getting Routing Information The routing information provided by the `netstat -r` command on a Windows system is the same as that produced by the `route print` command.

LISTING 14.9

AN EXAMPLE OF THE `netstat -r` COMMAND

```
C:\WINDOWS\Desktop>netstat -r
Route table

============================================================
============
============================================================
============
Active Routes:
Network Destination        Netmask          Gateway
Interface  Metric
         0.0.0.0          0.0.0.0       24.67.179.1
         ➥24.67.179.22       1
      24.67.179.0    255.255.255.0     24.67.179.22
      ➥24.67.179.22       1
      24.67.179.22  255.255.255.255        127.0.0.1
      ➥127.0.0.1        1
   24.255.255.255  255.255.255.255     24.67.179.22
   ➥24.67.179.22       1
         127.0.0.0        255.0.0.0        127.0.0.1
         ➥127.0.0.1        1
```

```
          224.0.0.0       224.0.0.0    24.67.179.22
        ➥24.67.179.22        1
   255.255.255.255  255.255.255.255   24.67.179.22
   ➥2           1
Default Gateway:        24.67.179.1
================================================================
=============
Persistent Routes:
  None

Active Connections

   Proto Local Address   Foreign Address          State
   TCP     laptop:1030   n239.audiogalaxy.com:ftp
➥ESTABLISHED
   TCP     laptop:1035   msgr-ns41.msgr.hotmail.com:1863
➥ESTABLISHED
   TCP     laptop:1027   localhost:50000          ESTABLISHED
   TCP     laptop:50000  localhost:1027           ESTABLISHED
```

> **N O T E**　**TCP Information in Windows**　In some versions of Windows, the TCP connection information section at the bottom of the screen is not shown.

netstat -s

The netstat -s command displays a number of different statistics related to the TCP/IP protocol suite. Understanding the purpose of every field in the output is beyond the scope of the Network+ exam, but for your reference, sample output from the netstat -s command is shown in Listing 14.10.

LISTING 14.10

AN EXAMPLE OF THE netstat -s COMMAND

```
C:\>netstat -s

IP Statistics

  Packets Received             = 389938
  Received Header Errors       = 0
  Received Address Errors      = 1876
  Datagrams Forwarded          = 498
  Unknown Protocols Received   = 0
  Received Packets Discarded   = 0
  Received Packets Delivered   = 387566
  Output Requests              = 397334
  Routing Discards             = 0
  Discarded Output Packets     = 0
  Output Packet No Route       = 916
  Reassembly Required          = 0
  Reassembly Successful        = 0
```

continues

LISTING 14.10 | *continued*

AN EXAMPLE OF THE netstat -s COMMAND

```
Reassembly Failures               = 0
Datagrams Successfully Fragmented = 0
Datagrams Failing Fragmentation   = 0
Fragments Created                 = 0

ICMP Statistics

                              Received    Sent
Messages                      40641       41111
Errors                        0           0
Destination Unreachable       223         680
Time Exceeded                 24          0
Parameter Problems            0           0
Source Quenches               0           0
Redirects                     0           38
Echos                         20245       20148
Echo Replies                  20149       20245
Timestamps                    0           0
Timestamp Replies             0           0
Address Masks                 0           0
Address Mask Replies          0           0

TCP Statistics

Active Opens                  = 13538
Passive Opens                 = 23132
Failed Connection Attempts    = 9259
Reset Connections             = 254
Current Connections           = 15
Segments Received             = 330242
Segments Sent                 = 326935
Segments Retransmitted        = 18851

UDP Statistics

Datagrams Received  = 20402
No Ports            = 20594
Receive Errors      = 0
Datagrams Sent      = 10217
```

The ipconfig Command

The ipconfig command is a technician's best friend when it comes to viewing the TCP/IP configuration of a Windows system—at least most Windows-based systems. The ipconfig command cannot be used on Windows 95 and Windows 98 systems. Used on its own, the `ipconfig` command shows basic information such as the name of the network interface, the IP address, the subnet mask, and the default gateway. Combined with the `/all` switch, it shows a detailed set of information, as you can see in Listing 14.11.

LISTING 14.11

AN EXAMPLE OF THE `ipconfig /all` COMMAND

```
C:\>ipconfig /all
Windows 2000 IP Configuration
    Host Name . . . . . . . . . . . . : server
    Primary DNS Suffix  . . . . . . . : write
    Node Type . . . . . . . . . . . . : Broadcast
    IP Routing Enabled. . . . . . . . : Yes
    WINS Proxy Enabled. . . . . . . . : No
    DNS Suffix Search List. . . . . . : write
                                        ok.anyotherhost.net
Ethernet adapter Local Area Connection:

    Connection-specific DNS Suffix  . : ok.anyotherhost.net
    Description . . . . . . . . . . . : D-Link DFE-530TX PCI Fast
    Ethernet
    Physical Address. . . . . . . . . : 00-80-C8-E3-4C-BD
    DHCP Enabled. . . . . . . . . . . : Yes
    Autoconfiguration Enabled . . . . : Yes
    IP Address. . . . . . . . . . . . : 24.67.184.65
    Subnet Mask . . . . . . . . . . . : 255.255.254.0
    Default Gateway . . . . . . . . . : 24.67.184.1
    DHCP Server . . . . . . . . . . . : 24.67.253.195
    DNS Servers . . . . . . . . . . . : 24.67.253.195
                                        24.67.253.212
    Lease Obtained.. . . . . : Thursday, February 07, 2002 3:42:00 AM
    Lease Expires .. . . . . : Saturday, February 09, 2002 3:42:00 AM
```

As you can imagine, you can use the output from an `ipconfig /all` command in a massive range of troubleshooting scenarios. Table 14.2 lists some of the most common troubleshooting symptoms, along with where to look for clues about solving them in the `ipconfig /all` output.

EXAM TIP

Check the `ipconfig` Information
When looking at `ipconfig` information, you should be sure that all information is present and correct. For example, a missing or incorrect default gateway parameter would limit communication to the local segment. Be sure to know this for the exam.

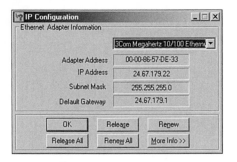

FIGURE 14.9
The basic `winipcfg` screen.

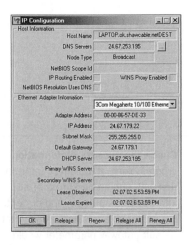

FIGURE 14.10
A detailed `winipcfg` screen.

TABLE 14.2

COMMON TROUBLESHOOTING SYMPTOMS THAT ipconfig CAN HELP SOLVE

Symptom	Field to Check in ipconfig Output
User is unable to connect to any other system	Make sure the TCP/IP address and subnet mask are correct. If the network uses DHCP, make sure DHCP is enabled.
User is able to connect to another system on the same subnet but is not able to connect to a remote system	Make sure the default gateway is correctly configured.
User is unable to browse the Internet	Make sure the DNS server parameters are configured correctly.
User is unable to browse across remote subnets	Make sure the WINS server parameters are configured correctly, if applicable.

The `winipcfg` Command

On a Windows 95, Windows 98, or Windows Me system, the `winipcfg` command is used instead of the `ipconfig` command. The difference between the two utilities is that `winipcfg` is a graphical utility. Figure 14.9 shows the `winipcfg` graphical screen.

As you can see, in basic mode, `winipcfg` shows information including the Media Access Control (MAC) address and IP address of the interface, the subnet mask, and the default gateway. For detailed information, similar to that produced with `ipconfig /all`, a More Info button allows you to switch into a much more detailed screen (see Figure 14.10).

The same troubleshooting scenarios, with the same solutions, apply to `winipcfg` as to `ipconfig`. Refer to Table 14.2 to see some explanations of common problems and solutions.

CHAPTER SUMMARY

This chapter focuses on the tools and utilities network administrators use to manage and troubleshoot networks, including tools for wiring tasks, visual indicators, and software-based utilities.

You'll use many different types of tools when working with network media. Wire crimpers are used for attaching connectors to cables, and punch down tools are used for wiring patch panels. These two tools are used to create the physical network connections, and others tools, such as optical testers, media testers, and tone generators, are used after the network is established for network maintenance and troubleshooting.

Many network devices, such as switches and hubs, have indicator lights that provide information about the status of the device and systems connected to it. Indicator lights provide an easy way to determine whether devices are functioning properly.

Working with networks requires knowledge of the software utilities used to manage and troubleshoot them. Being able to interpret the output from these utilities is a key skill identified in the CompTIA objectives.

KEY TERMS

- wire crimper
- media tester
- punch down tool
- tone generator
- optical tester
- link lights
- collision lights
- tracert
- ipconfig
- ping
- hardware loopback connector
- LEDs
- netstat
- winipcfg

┌─────────────────────────────────┐
APPLY YOUR KNOWLEDGE
└─────────────────────────────────┘

Exercises

14.1 Examining the Output from a Successful ping

When you're troubleshooting and managing networks, using and interpreting the results from diagnostic utilities is an important skill to learn. In this exercise, you take a look at the output for a successful ping.

This exercise assumes that you are using Windows 2000.

Estimated time: 10 minutes

1. Open a command prompt on your system by selecting Start, Run. In the Open field of the Run dialog box, type **command** and click OK.

2. At the command prompt, type the command **ping comptia.org**. You should receive four Reply From messages indicating a successful ping.

3. Determine what the minimum, maximum, and average times taken to complete the round trip were.

14.2 Simulating a Bad Connection or a Communication Problem

This exercise shows you how to simulate a bad connection or communication problem by disconnecting the network cable during a continuous ping of a remote host.

This exercise assumes that you are using Windows 2000 and have an Internet connection.

Estimated time: 10 minutes

1. At the command prompt, type the command **ping -t comptia.org**.

2. After the pinging process has started, unplug the UTP cable from the NIC in your system. Look at the screen. What message do you receive?

3. Plug the cable back into the NIC. The output from the command should return to the normal Reply From messages.

4. Press Ctrl+C to stop the ping process. Leave the command screen open, but minimize it.

14.3 Simulating What Happens When the Default Gateway Parameter on a System Is Missing or Incorrectly Configured

This exercise shows how to simulate a missing or incorrectly configured default gateway parameter. This exercise assumes that you are using Windows 2000.

Estimated time: 5 Minutes

1. Right-click My Network Places and select Properties. The Network and Dial-up Connections dialog box appears.

2. Right-click the Local Area Connection icon and select Properties from the menu. The Local Area Connection Properties dialog box appears.

3. Select Internet Protocol (TCP/IP) and click the Properties button. The Internet Protocol (TCP/IP) Properties dialog box appears.

┌───┐
│ **W A R N I N G** **Record Your Settings** Before you │
│ complete step 4, make a note of all │
│ the current settings for your TCP/IP │
│ configuration. If you are using DHCP, │
│ this might be as simple as noting │
│ that addresses will be assigned via │
│ DHCP. If you are using static │
│ addresses, double-check the infor- │
│ mation you have noted before │
│ proceeding to step 4. │
└───┘

APPLY YOUR KNOWLEDGE

4. Select the Use the Following IP Address radio button. Enter the private address 192.168.2.1 and the subnet mask 255.255.255.0. Leave the Default Gateway field blank. The screen should look like the dialog box shown in Figure 14.11.

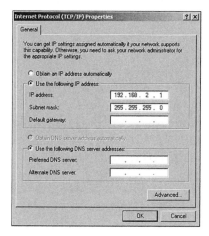

FIGURE 14.11
The Internet Protocol (TCP/IP) Properties dialog box.

5. Click OK to return to the Local Area Connection Properties dialog box. Click OK, and the system initializes the new TCP/IP settings.

6. Restore the command prompt that was mini-mized in step 4 of Exercise 14.2.

7. Type the command **ping 216.119.103.72**. What is the result?

8. Repeat steps 1 through 3 and use the information you originally collected before step 4 to restore your original configuration.

Exam Questions

1. As a network administrator, you find yourself working in a wiring closet where none of the cables have been labeled. Which of the following tools are you most likely to use to locate the physical ends of the cable?

   a. Tone generator

   b. Wire crimper

   c. Punch down tool

   d. ping

2. You are trying to use the tracert command to determine the route a packet takes. You receive five successful hops, followed by several asterisks (*). What is the likely cause of the problem?

   a. The destination host is not online.

   b. The router at step 4 or 5 has a problem.

   c. The router at step 5 or 6 has a problem.

   d. The router at step 5 is not powered on.

3. During a visual inspection, you notice that one of the indicator lights on your hub is continuously and rapidly flashing. How might you interpret the LED?

   a. The system connected to the port is not powered on.

   b. You are using a crossover cable.

   c. This is normal activity.

   d. You might have a faulty NIC.

4. You are trying to ping a remote host with the command ping desertforme.co.uk. The ping

APPLY YOUR KNOWLEDGE

returns an Unknown Host error message. What is the cause of the problem?

  a. The remote host is not responding.

  b. The name of the destination computer cannot be resolved.

  c. The route to the destination computer is incorrect.

  d. WINS is not configured.

5. You are installing a new system into an existing star network and need a cable that is 45 feet long. Your local vendor does not stock cables of this length, so you are forced to make your own. Which of the following tools will you need to complete the task?

  a. Optical tester

  b. Punch down tool

  c. Crimper

  d. UTP splicer

6. You are working with a standard hub. Each hub has a single LED to indicate link and activity. You notice a solid green light on several of the hub ports. What does this most likely indicate?

  a. Collisions on the port

  b. A connected device with no activity on the device

  c. A connected device sending information to the network

  d. A crossover cable connecting the device to the hub

7. You are attempting to troubleshoot an IP configuration problem on a Windows 98 system.

Which of the following commands could you use to view the TCP/IP configuration information? (Choose the two best answers.)

  a. `winipcfg`

  b. `ifconfig`

  c. `config`

  d. `ipconfig`

8. You are troubleshooting a connectivity problem in which the user is unable to connect to any remote systems. The connectivity to local systems appears to work correctly. Based on the following output from an `ipconfig /all` command, what is the most likely cause of the problem?

```
C:\>ipconfig /all
Windows 2000 IP Configuration
    Host Name . . . . . . . . . . . . : server
    Primary DNS Suffix  . . . . . . . : write
    Node Type . . . . . . . . . . . . : Broad
➥cast
    IP Routing Enabled. . . . . . . . : Yes
    WINS Proxy Enabled. . . . . . . . : No
    DNS Suffix Search List. . . . . . : write

➥ok.anyotherhost.net
Ethernet adapter Local Area Connection:

    Connection-specific DNS Suffix  . :
➥ok.anyotherhost.net
    Description . . . . . . . . . . . : D-Link
➥DFE-530TX PCI Fast Ethernet
    Physical Address. . . . . . . . . : 00-80-C8-
➥E3-4C-BD
    DHCP Enabled. . . . . . . . . . . : Yes
    Autoconfiguration Enabled . . . . : Yes
    IP Address. . . . . . . . . . . . :
➥24.67.184.65
    Subnet Mask . . . . . . . . . . . :
➥255.255.254.0
    Default Gateway . . . . . . . . . :
    DHCP Server . . . . . . . . . . . :
➥24.67.253.195
    DNS Servers . . . . . . . . . . . :
➥24.67.253.195
```

APPLY YOUR KNOWLEDGE

```
24.67.253.212
Lease Obtained.. . . . . : Thursday, February
➡07, 2002 3:42:00 AM
Lease Expires .. . . . . : Saturday, February
➡09, 2002 3:42:00 AM
```

    a. The DNS server information is missing.

    b. The node type is set to broadcast.

    c. The default gateway parameter is missing.

    d. DHCP is enabled.

9. You are troubleshooting a network printer in a busy accounting office. When you try to `ping` the printer, some of the `ping` requests are returned but others are not. What is the most likely explanation of this problem?

    a. The printer keeps going online and off line.

    b. The network is congested or the NIC in the printer is unable to keep up with the printing demands.

    c. The network cable connecting the printer is faulty.

    d. The NIC in the printer is faulty.

10. Consider the following output from the `netstat -e` command. What might you determine from this information?

	Received	Sent
Bytes	17412385	40237510
Unicast packets	79129	85055
Non-unicast packets	693	254
Discards	0	
Errors	2233654	0
Unknown protocols	306	

    a. The NIC in this system is faulty.

    b. This is normal.

    c. Errors are being generated on the network, but not by this system.

    d. This system is generating errors.

11. You are troubleshooting a problem with a workstation and have managed to narrow it down to a single patch cable. What tool might you use to troubleshoot the problem further?

    a. Tone generator/locator

    b. OTDR

    c. `ping`

    d. Media tester

12. What tool can be used to find a break in a length of fiber-optic cable?

    a. Tone generator

    b. TDR

    c. OTDR

    d. Fox and hare

13. Examine the following output from the `tracert` command. What, if anything, is wrong with this trace route?

```
C:\>tracert 24.7.70.37
Tracing route to c1-pos6-3.sttlwa1.home.net
➡[24.7.70.37] over a maximum of 30 hops:
  1    30 ms    20 ms    20 ms  24.67.184.1
  2    20 ms    20 ms    30 ms  rd1ht-ge3-
➡0.ok.shawcable.net [24.67.224.7]
  3    50 ms    30 ms    30 ms  rc1wh-atm0-2-
➡1.vc.shawcable.net [204.209.214.193]
  4    50 ms    30 ms    30 ms  rc2wh-pos15-
➡0.vc.shawcable.net [204.209.214.90]
  5    30 ms    40 ms    30 ms  rc2wt-pos2-
➡0.wa.shawcable.net [66.163.76.37]
  6    30 ms    40 ms    30 ms  c1-pos6-
➡3.sttlwa1.home.net [24.7.70.37]
Trace complete.
```

APPLY YOUR KNOWLEDGE

a. The IP address is invalid.

b. There is nothing wrong with this output.

c. The trace was not completed.

d. The maximum hop count has restricted the number of hops reported.

14. Examine the following output from the ping command. Based on this information, what are you likely to check first in your troubleshooting process? (Choose the two best answers.)

```
Pinging 24.67.54.233 with 32 bytes of data:
Destination host unreachable.
Destination host unreachable.
Destination host unreachable.
Destination host unreachable.
Ping statistics for 24.67.54.233:
    Packets: Sent = 4, Received = 0, Lost = 4
➥(100% loss),
Approximate round trip times in milli-
➥seconds:
    Minimum = 0ms, Maximum =  0ms, Average =
➥0ms
```

a. That the remote host is online

b. The default gateway setting of the system

c. The routing table on the system

d. The patch cable for the system

15. A tone generator and locator are commonly referred to as what?

a. Fox and rabbit

b. Fox and hare

c. Fox and hound

d. Fox and dog

16. During a support call with a remote user, you need to know the default gateway parameter on the user's Windows 2000 system. Which of the following commands could you use to view this information? (Choose the two best answers.)

a. `ipconfig /all`

b. `ipconfig`

c. `winipcfg`

d. `ping`

17. Which of the following commands would generate a Request Timed Out error message?

a. `ping`

b. `netstat`

c. `ipconfig`

d. `nbtstat`

18. A user calls to report a problem with his workstation when trying to connect to the server. You are able to connect to the server without a problem. When you visit the user's desk, you notice that the link light on the network card is not lit. Which of the following is not a possible cause of the problem?

a. The NIC in the workstation

b. The NIC in the server

c. The patch cable between the user's system and the switch

d. The network switch port to which the user is connected

19. What tool would you use when working with an IDC?

a. Wire crimper

b. Media tester

APPLY YOUR KNOWLEDGE

   c. OTDR

   d. Punch down tool

20. Which of the following commands would you use to discover what connections have been established by TCP on a system?

   a. `nbtstat`

   b. `ipconfig`

   c. `tracert`

   d. `netstat`

Answers to Exam Questions

1. **a.** The tone generator tool, along with the tone locator, can be used to trace cables. Crimpers and punch down tools are not used for locating a cable. The `ping` utility would be of no help in this situation. For more information, see the section "Selecting the Appropriate Tool for Wiring," in this chapter.

2. **c.** The router at step 5 or 6 is the likely source of the problem. Because all steps up to and including step 5 have been successful, the problem lies either on the far side of Router 5 or the near side of the router in step 6. Answer a is incorrect because if the destination host were not online, you would receive no successful replies. Answer b is incorrect because if the router at step 4 were having a problem, you would receive only four successful replies and not five. Answer d is incorrect because if the router were powered off, you would receive no successful replies. For more information, see the section "Using Diagnostic Utilities," in this chapter.

3. **d.** When an LED is continually and rapidly flashing, you might have a faulty NIC in the system. None of the other answers are valid explanations for this scenario. For more information, see the section "Interpreting Visual Indicators," in this chapter.

4. **b.** In this case, the problem is caused because the hostname of the destination computer cannot be resolved. In Answer a, the hostname would have to first be resolved before you could draw this conclusion. Answer c is incorrect; if the route to the destination could not be determined, you would receive a Destination Unreachable message. Answer d is incorrect because WINS is not used for name resolution on the Internet. For more information, see the section "Using Diagnostic Utilities," in this chapter.

5. **c.** When attaching RJ-45 connectors to UTP cables, the wire crimper is the tool you use. None of the other tools are used in the construction of UTP cable. For more information, see the section "Selecting the Appropriate Tool for Wiring," in this chapter.

6. **b.** A solid green indicator light normally indicates that the device is connected but not sending any data. Collisions are normally indicated by a rapidly flashing LED, and a device sending data will normally cause the LED to flash sporadically. The use of a crossover cable to connect the device to the hub will cause a connectivity failure, and in that case the LED would most likely not be lit at all. For more information, see the section "Interpreting Visual Indicators," in this chapter.

7. **a, d.** The `winipcfg` and `ipconfig` commands can be used to verify IP information on a Windows 98 client system. The `ipconfig` command is run

APPLY YOUR KNOWLEDGE

from the Windows command prompt. The `ifconfig` utility is used on Linux and OS/2 systems to view and set interface configurations. The `config` utility is used on NetWare to view configuration information. For more information, see the section "Using Diagnostic Utilities," in this chapter.

8. **c.** The default gateway parameter is missing from the `ipconfig /all` output. For more information, see the section "Using Diagnostic Utilities," in this chapter.

9. **b.** If you're trying to `ping` a remote system and you receive intermittent Request Timed Out errors, these errors might indicate a congested network or trouble with the NIC in the remote system. All the other answers are valid, although they are much less likely than Answer b. For more information, see the section "Using Diagnostic utilities," in this chapter.

10. **c.** A high number of errors in the Received column in the `netstat -e` output indicates that errors are being generated on the network. However, the 0 value in the Sent column suggests that this system is not generating the errors. The other answers for this question are not valid. For more information, see the section "Using Diagnostic Utilities," in this chapter.

11. **d.** If you suspect a problem with a patch cable, you can use a media tester to test it. An OTDR is used to test optical cables, and so it would not be used on UTP, which is copper-based cable. The other tools discussed in this question would not be used. For more information, see the section "Selecting the Appropriate Tool for Wiring," in this chapter.

12. **c.** An OTDR can be used to find a break in a length of fiber-optic cable. The other tools listed cannot be used to troubleshoot a break in a fiber-optic cable. For more information, see the section "Selecting the Appropriate Tool for Wiring," in this chapter.

13. **b.** This is normal output from a `tracert` command. For more information, see the section "Using Diagnostic Utilities," in this chapter.

14. **b, c.** A Destination Host Unreachable message in response to a `ping` suggests either a problem with the default gateway or an error in the routing table. Answer a is incorrect; if the remote host were online, the `tracert` should be successful. Answer d would result in a series of failed `tracert` requests. For more information, see the section "Using Diagnostic Utilities," in this chapter.

15. **c.** A tone generator and locator are commonly referred to the fox and hound. None of the other answers are valid. For more information, see the section "Selecting the Appropriate Tool for Wiring," in this chapter.

16. **a, b.** Both the `ipconfig` and `ipconfig /all` commands show the default gateway information on a Windows 2000 system. `winipcfg` cannot be used on a Windows 2000 system. `ping` does not show IP configuration for a system. For more information, see the section "Using Diagnostic Utilities," in this chapter.

17. **a.** The `ping` command generates a Request Timed Out error when it is unable to receive a reply from the destination system. None of the other commands produce this output. For more information, see the section "Using Diagnostic Utilities," in this chapter.

APPLY YOUR KNOWLEDGE

18. **b.** The NIC in the server would not cause the problem in this scenario because you are still able to access the server. All the other answers could be the potential cause of the problem. For more information, see the section "Using Diagnostic Utilities," in this chapter.

19. **d.** You use a punch down tool when working with an IDC. All the other tools are associated with making and troubleshooting cables, but they are not associated with IDCs. For more information, see the section "Selecting the Appropriate Tool for Wiring," in this chapter.

20. **d.** The `netstat` command can be used to see what connections have been established by TCP. `nbtstat` is used to view Network Basic Input/Output System (NetBIOS) over TCP/IP connection information, `ipconfig` is used to view TCP/IP configuration information, and `tracert` is used to troubleshoot connectivity between two devices on a network. For more information, see the section "Using Diagnostic Utilities," in this chapter.

Suggested Readings and Resources

1. Sloan, Joseph D. *Network Troubleshooting Tools (O'Reilly System Administration).* O'Reilly & Associates, 2001.

2. Habraken, Joe. *Absolute Beginner's Guide to Networking,* third edition. Que Publishing, 2001.

3. Haugdahl, J. Scott. *Network Analysis and Troubleshooting.* Addison-Wesley, 2000.

4. Cisco Systems, Inc. *Internetworking Troubleshooting Handbook,* second edition. Cisco Press, 2001.

5. Computer networking products and testing tools, `www.trendware.com`.

6. Network Cabling Information, `www.techfest.com/networking/cabling.htm`.

7. "Computer Networking Tutorials and Advice," `compnetworking.about.com`.

8. "TechEncyclopedia," `www.techencyclopedia.com`.

9. Networking technology information, `www.cisco.com/public/products_tech.shtml`.

10. "Network Cabling Help," `www.datacottage.com`.

This chapter covers the following CompTIA-specified objectives for the "Network Support" section of the Network+ exam:

Given a network problem scenario, select an appropriate course of action based on a general troubleshooting strategy. This strategy includes the following steps.

- **Establish the symptoms**

- **Identify the affected areas**

- **Establish what has changed**

- **Select the most probable cause**

- **Implement a solution**

- **Test the results**

- **Recognize the potential effects of the solution**

- **Document the solution**

▶ In order for troubleshooting to be successful, it must be approached in a structured manner. These steps describe a troubleshooting methodology that has been proven in the field.

Given a troubleshooting scenario involving a network with a particular physical topology (i.e. bus, star/hierarchical, mesh, ring, and wireless) and including a network diagram, identify the network area affected and the cause of the problem.

▶ Physical topology problems are infrequent, but they do occur. You will need to be able to identify the symptoms of a topology error and the steps necessary to correct them.

CHAPTER 15

Troubleshooting Procedures and Best Practices

Given a network troubleshooting scenario involving a client connectivity problem (e.g. incorrect protocol/client, software/ authentication configuration, or insufficient rights/permissions), identify the cause of the problem.

▶ Client connectivity problems are common. The fact that users are involved in the troubleshooting process adds an interesting twist. Communication skills are often as important as technical skills in the solution of a problem.

Given a network troubleshooting scenario involving a wiring/infrastructure problem, identify the cause of the problem (e.g. bad media, interference, network hardware).

▶ Although wiring is resilient to failure, it can and does become faulty. It can also be affected by outside sources, which can create some challenges for troubleshooters. In addition, the devices used to create networks can fail, which often renders entire sections of a network, or the whole network, unusable.

Introduction	**584**
Troubleshooting Basics	**584**
Troubleshooting Servers and Workstations	585
General Troubleshooting Considerations	586
The Art of Troubleshooting	**588**
Establishing What the Symptoms Are	589
Information from the Computer	589
Information from the User	590
Observation Techniques	591
Effective Questioning Techniques	591
Identifying the Affected Area	592
Establishing What Has Changed	592
Changes to the Network	592
Changes to the Server	593
Changes to the Workstation	594
Selecting the Most Probable Cause of the Problem	594
Implementing a Solution	595
Testing the Results	596
Recognizing the Potential Effects of the Solution	596
Documenting the Solution	597
Troubleshooting Topology Errors	**598**
Bus Network Errors	598
Star Network Errors	599
Ring Network Errors	601

Mesh Network Errors	601
Wireless Network Errors	602

Troubleshooting Client Connectivity Errors **602**

Protocol Errors	603
Protocol-Specific Issues	603
Authentication	604
Permissions Errors	605
Physical Connectivity Errors	606

Troubleshooting Wiring- and Infrastructure-Related Problems **607**

Troubleshooting Wiring	608
Determining Your Wiring	608
Where the Cable Is Used	608
Troubleshooting the Infrastructure	609
Baselines and Performance Monitoring	610

Troubleshooting Checklists **611**

Troubleshooting Cable Problems	611
Troubleshooting Network Connectivity	612
Troubleshooting Network Printing	613
Troubleshooting Data Access	613
Troubleshooting NICs	614

Chapter Summary **615**

Apply Your Knowledge **617**

OUTLINE

STUDY STRATEFIES

► Read the objectives at the beginning of the chapter.

► Study the information in the chapter, paying special attention to the tables that summarize key information.

► Review the objectives again.

► Pay close attention to the "Troubleshooting Scenario and Solution" sidebars. They focus on specific areas of knowledge for the Network+ exam.

► Answer the exam questions at the end of the chapter and check your results.

► Use the ExamGear test on the CD-ROM that accompanies this book to answer additional exam questions concerning this material.

► Review the notes, tips, and exam tips in this chapter. Make sure you understand the information in the exam tips. If you don't understand the topic referenced in an exam tip, refer to the information in the chapter text and then read the exam tip again.

INTRODUCTION

Even the most well-designed and maintained networks will fail at some point. Such a failure might be as dramatic as a failed server taking down the entire network or as specific and undramatic as a single computer system being unable to print. Regardless of the problem you face, as a network administrator, you will spend a sizable portion of your time troubleshooting problems with the network, the devices connected to it, and the people who use it. In each case, the approach to the problem is as important as the troubleshooting process itself. Although some steps are common to the troubleshooting process, very few problems you face will be alike because so many variables will be involved.

As you will see in this chapter, troubleshooting is about more than just fixing a problem: It includes isolating the problem and taking the appropriate actions to prevent it from happening again. The ability to effectively troubleshoot network-related problems goes beyond technical knowledge and includes the ability to think creatively to get to the root of a problem. In addition, strong communication skills can turn a difficult and seemingly impossible troubleshooting task into an easy one. Although the role of the network administrator can be a cellular one, you will be surprised at just how much interaction there is with users and at how important this element of your role will be.

This chapter provides a comprehensive look into the many facets that make up an effective troubleshooting strategy. In addition, it examines specific skills and techniques you can use to quickly isolate a network-related problem. It also examines scenarios in which these troubleshooting skills come into play.

NOTE

Who Says? Ask 10 network administrators about troubleshooting best practices, and you will no doubt get 15 different answers. There really is no universally accepted definition or procedural acceptance of troubleshooting best practices. With this in mind, the information provided in this chapter specifies troubleshooting best practices identified by CompTIA. Whether these are the best practices in real-world application is a matter of debate. However, there is no debate that these are the best practices that will be on the exam.

TROUBLESHOOTING BASICS

There is really no magic or innate ability that makes a good network troubleshooter. You will hear tales of people who have a gift for troubleshooting, but there is nothing necessarily gifted about those who can troubleshoot well. Instead, good troubleshooters have a special combination of skills. The ability to competently and confidently troubleshoot networks comes from experience, a defined methodology, and sometimes just plain luck.

One of the factors that makes troubleshooting such a difficult task is the large number of variables that can come into play. Although it is difficult to preemptively list all the factors you have to consider while troubleshooting networks, this chapter lists a few to make you start thinking in the right direction. When you are troubleshooting, thinking in the right direction is half the battle. Considering that most network administrators spend the majority of their troubleshooting time working on the devices connected to the network rather than on the network infrastructure itself, it is worth looking at some of the factors that can affect troubleshooting of devices connected to the network. First, let's look at the difference between troubleshooting a server and troubleshooting a workstation system.

Troubleshooting Servers and Workstations

One often overlooked but very important distinction in troubleshooting networks is the difference between troubleshooting a server computer and troubleshooting a workstation system. Although the fundamental troubleshooting principles of isolation and problem determination are often the same in different networks, the steps taken for problem resolution are often very different from one network to another. Make no mistake: When you find yourself troubleshooting a server system, the stakes are much higher than with workstation troubleshooting, and therefore it's considerably more stressful. Let's take a look at a few of the most important distinctions between workstation and server troubleshooting:

◆ **Pressure**—It is difficult to capture in words the pressure you feel when troubleshooting a downed server. Troubleshooting a single workstation with one anxious user is stressful enough, and when tens, hundreds, or even thousands of users are waiting for you to solve the problem, the pressure can be enough to unhinge even the most seasoned administrator.

◆ **Planning**—Troubleshooting a single workstation often requires very little planning. If work needs to be done on a workstation, it can often be done during a lunch break, after work, or even during the day. If work needs to be done on a server, particularly one that is heavily accessed, you might need to wait days, weeks, or even months before you have a good time to take down the server so you can work on it and fix the problem.

◆ **Time**—For many organizations, every minute a server is unavailable is measured as much in dollars as it is in time. Servers are often relied on to provide 24-hour network service—and anything less is often considered unacceptable. Although it might be necessary to take a server down at some point for troubleshooting, you will be expected to account for every minute that it is down.

◆ **Problem determination**—Many people who have had to troubleshoot workstation systems know that oftentimes finding the problem involves a little trial and error. (Swap out the RAM; if that doesn't work, replace the power supply, and so on.) Effective server troubleshooting involves very little trial and error—if any at all. Before the server is powered down, the administrator is expected to have a very good idea of the problem.

◆ **Expertise**—Today, many people feel comfortable taking the case off their personal computers to add memory, replace a fan, or just have a quick peek. Although it is based on the same technologies as PC hardware, server hardware is often more complex, and those who manage and maintain servers are expected to have an advanced level of hardware and software knowledge, often reinforced by training and certifications.

These are just a few of the differences in the troubleshooting practices and considerations between servers and workstations. As this chapter discusses troubleshooting, attention is focused mainly on the server side of troubleshooting. This helps explain why some of the troubleshooting procedures might seem rigid and unnecessary on a workstation level.

General Troubleshooting Considerations

Knowing the differences between procedures and approaches for troubleshooting servers and for troubleshooting workstations is valuable, but there are a seemingly endless number of other considerations. Each of these other factors can significantly affect the way you approach a problem on the network. The following list contains some of the obvious and perhaps not so obvious factors that come into play when troubleshooting a network:

◆ **Time**—The time of day can play a huge role in the troubleshooting process. For instance, you are likely to respond differently to a network problem at 10 a.m., during high network use, than at 8 p.m., when the network is not being utilized as much. The response to network troubleshooting during high-use periods is often geared toward a Band-Aid solution, just getting things up and running as soon as possible. Finding the exact cause of the problem and developing a permanent fix generally occurs when there is more time.

◆ **Network size**—The strategies and processes used to troubleshoot small networks of 10 to 100 computer systems can be very different from those used to troubleshoot networks consisting of thousands of computers.

◆ **Support**—Some network administrators find themselves working alone, as a single IT professional working for a company. In such cases, the only available sources might include telephone, Internet, or manufacturer support. Other network administrators are part a large IT department. In that type of environment, the troubleshooting process generally includes a hierarchical consultation process.

◆ **Knowledge of the network**—It would be advantageous if there was uniformity in the installation of all networks, but there isn't. You could be working on a network with ring, bus, or star topology. Before you start troubleshooting a network, you need to familiarize yourself with its layout and design. The troubleshooting strategies you employ will be affected by your knowledge of the network.

◆ **Technologies used**—Imagine being called in to troubleshoot a wide area network (WAN) that includes multiple Linux servers, a handful of NetWare servers, an old Windows NT 3.51 server, and multiple Macintosh workstations. Your knowledge of these technologies will dictate how, if at all, you are going to troubleshoot the network. There is no shame in walking away from a problem you are unfamiliar with. Good network administrators always recognize their knowledge boundaries.

> **Workstations and Servers** The Network+ exam does not require you to identify any specific differences between workstation and server troubleshooting but does require background knowledge of general troubleshooting procedures and the factors that influence how a network problem is approached.

These are just a few of the factors that will affect your ability to troubleshoot a network. There are countless others—far too many to list.

THE ART OF TROUBLESHOOTING

▶ Given a network problem scenario, select an appropriate course of action based on a general troubleshooting strategy. This strategy includes the following steps.

- Establish the symptoms
- Identify the affected areas
- Establish what has changed
- Select the most probable cause
- Implement a solution
- Test the results
- Recognize the potential effects of the solution
- Document the solution

There is little question that at some point in your networking career, you will be called on to troubleshoot network-related problems. Correctly and swiftly identifying these problems is not done by accident; rather, effective troubleshooting requires attention to some specific steps and procedures. Although some organizations have documented troubleshooting procedures for their IT staff members, many do not. Whether you find yourself using these exact steps in your job is debatable, but the general principles will remain the same. The CompTIA objectives list the troubleshooting steps as follows:

1. Establish what the symptoms are.

2. Identify the affected areas.

3. Establish what has changed.

4. Select the most probable cause.

5. Implement a solution.

6. Test the results.

7. Recognize the potential effects of the solution.

8. Document the solution.

The following sections examine each of these areas, as well as an additional step that you might want to include in the troubleshooting process.

Establishing What the Symptoms Are

Troubleshooting a problem can be difficult, but trying to do it with limited information is often a fool's quest. Lacking information can cause you to troubleshoot the wrong problem. You might find yourself replacing a toner cartridge when someone actually just used the wrong password.

Therefore, the first step in the troubleshooting process is to establish exactly what the symptoms of the problem are. This stage of the troubleshooting process is about information gathering—a process that requires experience with the operating system being used, communication skills, and, perhaps most importantly, patience. It is very important to get as much information as possible about the problem before you charge out the door with that toner cartridge under your arm. You can glean information from three key sources: the computer (in the form of logs and error messages), the computer user, and your own observation. These sources are examined in the following sections.

Information from the Computer

If you know where to look and what to look for, a computer can help reveal where a problem lies. Many operating systems provide error messages when a problem is encountered. A Linux system, for instance, might present a Segmentation Fault error message, which indicates a memory-related error. Windows, on the other hand, might display an Illegal Operation error message to indicate a possible memory or application failure. Both of these system error messages can be cross-referenced with the operating systems' Web site information to identify the root of the problem. The information provided in these error messages can at times be cryptic, so finding the solution might be tricky.

In addition to the system-generated error messages, network operating systems can be configured to generate log files after a hardware or software failure. An administrator can then view these log files to

EXAM TIP

Error Message Storage   For the Network+ exam, you do not need to know where error messages are stored on the respective operating systems; you only need to know that the troubleshooting process requires you to read system-generated log errors.

NOTE

Installation Policies   Many organizations have strict policies about what can and cannot be installed on computer systems. These policies are not in place to exercise the administrator's control but rather to prevent as many crashes and failures as possible.

NOTE

Gathering Information   Your communication skills will be most needed when you are gathering information from end users.

see when the failure occurred and what was being done when the crash occurred. Window NT/2000 displays error messages in the Event Viewer, Linux stores many of its system log files in the /var/log directory, and NetWare creates a file called abend.log, which contains detailed information about the state of the system at the time of the crash. When you start the troubleshooting process, make sure you are familiar enough with the operating system that is being used to be able to determine whether it is trying to give you a message.

Information from the User

Getting accurate information from a computer user or anyone with limited technical knowledge can be a tricky task. Having a limited understanding of computers and technical terminology can make it difficult for a non-technical person to relay the true symptoms of a problem. However, users can convey what they are trying to do and what is not working. When you interview an end user, you will likely want the following information:

◆ **Error frequency**—If it is a repeating problem, ask for the frequency of the problem. Does the problem occur at regular intervals or sporadically? Does it happen daily, weekly, or monthly?

◆ **Applications in use**—You will definitely want to know what applications were in use at the time of the failure. Only the end user will know this information.

◆ **Past problems**—Ask whether this error has been a problem in the past. If it has and it was addressed, you might already have your fix.

◆ **User modifications**—A new screensaver, a game, or other such programs have ways of ending up on users' systems. Although many of these applications can be installed successfully, sometimes they create problems. When you are trying to isolate the problem, ask the user whether any new software additions have been made to the system.

◆ **Error messages**—Network administrators cannot be at all the computers on a network all the time. Therefore, they are likely to miss an error message when it is displayed onscreen. The end user might be able to tell you what error message appeared.

Observation Techniques

Finding a problem often involves nothing more than using your eyes, ears, and nose to locate the problem. For instance, if you are troubleshooting a workstation system and you see a smoke cloud wafting from the back of the system, looking for error messages might not be necessary. If you walk into a server room and hear the CPU fan screaming, you are unlikely to need to review the server logs to find the problem.

Observation techniques often come into play when you're troubleshooting connectivity errors. For instance, looking for an unplugged cable and confirming that the light-emitting diode (LED) on the network interface card (NIC) is lit requires observation on your part. Keeping an eye as well as a nose out for potential problems is part of the network administrator's role and can help in identifying a situation before it becomes a problem.

Effective Questioning Techniques

Regardless of the method you are using to gather information about a problem, there are some important questions you will need to have answered. When approaching a problem, consider the following questions:

◆ Is only one computer affected, or has the entire network gone down?

◆ Is the problem happening all the time, or is it intermittent?

◆ Does the problem happen during specific times, or does it happen all the time?

◆ Has this problem occurred in the past?

◆ Has any network equipment been moved recently?

◆ Have any new applications been installed on the network?

◆ Has anyone else tried to correct the problem; if so, what has that person tried?

◆ Is there any documentation that relates to the problem or to the applications or devices associated with the problem?

By answering these questions, as well as others, you will gain a better idea of exactly what the problem is.

EXAM TIP

Observation Techniques For the Network+ exam, remember that observation techniques play a large role in the preemptive troubleshooting process, which can result in finding a small problem before it becomes a large one.

NOTE

Troubleshooting Scenario A user calls you to complain that he is unable to access the network. You confirm that he is using the correct username and password and that his account is active. He was able to access the network the previous day.

Troubleshooting Solution This situation might suggest a physical connectivity problem. Confirm that the link LED is lit on the back of the NIC and that the cable is physically attached.

Be Thorough   On the Network+ exam, you might be provided with either a description of a scenario or a description augmented by a network diagram. In either case, you should read the description of the problem carefully, step by step. In most cases, the correct answer is fairly logical and the wrong answers can be identified easily.

Troubleshooting Scenario   You are a network administrator managing a network that has four separate network segments: sales, administration, payroll, and advertising. Late on Tuesday evening, you get a call from several members of the sales staff, complaining that they are unable to access a network printer.

Troubleshooting Solution   Because the reported problem has a common thread, the sales department, it is likely that there is a connectivity issue with the network segment the sales group is on. The problem could be a downed router, switch hub, or authentication server. Whatever the cause, you can more easily isolate the problem if you know the location. Consider how this troubleshooting scenario would be handled differently if the error reports came simultaneously from the sales, payroll, and advertising groups.

Identifying the Affected Area

Some computer problems are isolated to a single user in a single location; others affect several thousand users spanning multiple locations. Establishing the affected area is an important part of the troubleshooting process, and it will often dictate the strategies you use in resolving the problem.

Problems that affect many users are often connectivity issues that disable access for many users. Such problems can often be isolated to wiring closets, network devices, and server rooms. The troubleshooting process for problems that are isolated to a single user will often begin and end at that user's workstation. The trail might indeed lead you to the wiring closet or server, but that is not likely where the troubleshooting process would begin. Understanding who is affected by a problem can provide you with the first clues about where the problem exists.

Establishing What Has Changed

Whether there is a problem with a workstation's access to a database or an entire network, keep in mind that they were working at some point. Although many claim that the "computer just stopped working," it is unlikely. Far more likely is that there have been changes to the system or the network that caused the problem. As much as users try to convince you that computers do otherwise, computer systems do not reconfigure themselves. Therefore, establishing what was done to a system will lead you in the right direction to isolate and troubleshoot a problem.

Changes can occur on the network, on a server, or on a workstation. Each of these is discussed in the following sections.

Changes to the Network

Most of today's networks are dynamic and continually growing to accommodate new users and new applications. Unfortunately, these network changes, although intended to increase network functionality, may inadvertently cause additional problems. For instance, a new computer system added to a network might be installed with a duplicate computer name or IP address, which would prevent another computer that has the same name or address from accessing the network. Other changes that can create problems on the network include adding or removing a hub or switch, changing the network's routing information, or adding or removing a server. In fact, almost every change that the network administrator makes to the network can potentially have an undesirable impact elsewhere on the network. For this reason, all changes made to the network should be fully documented and fully thought out.

Changes to the Server

Part of a network administrator's job involves some tinkering with the server. Although this might be unavoidable, it can sometimes lead to several unintentional problems. Even the most mundane of all server tasks can have a negative impact on the network. The following are some common server-related tasks that can cause problems:

◆ **Changes to user accounts**—For the most part, changes to accounts do not cause any problems, but sometimes they do. If after making changes to user accounts a user or several users are unable to log on to the network or access a database, the problem is likely related to the changes made to the accounts.

◆ **Changes to permissions**—Data is protected by permissions that dictate who can and cannot access the data on the drives. Permissions are an important part of system security, but changes to permissions can inadvertently prevent users from being able to access specific files.

◆ **Patches and updates**—Part of the work involved in administering networks is to monitor new patches and updates for the network operating system and install them as needed. It is not uncommon for an upgrade or a fix to an operating system to cause problems on the network.

◆ **New applications**—From time to time, new applications and programs—such as productivity software, firewall software, or even virus software—have to be installed on the server. When any kind of new software is added to the server, it might cause problems on the network. Knowing what has recently been installed can help you isolate a problem.

◆ **Hardware changes**—Either because of failure or expansion, hardware on the server might have to be changed. Changes to the hardware configuration on the server can cause connectivity problems.

EXAM TIP

The Obvious Solutions In the Network+ exam, avoid discounting a possible answer because it seems too easy. Many of the troubleshooting questions are based on possible real-world scenarios, many of which do have very easy or obvious solutions.

NOTE

Faulty Hardware Although recent changes to systems or networks account for many network problems, some problems do happen out of the blue. Faulty hardware is a good example.

> **Troubleshooting Scenario**   A system that could previously log on to the network now receives an error message, saying that it cannot log on due to a duplicate IP address.
>
> **Troubleshooting Solution**   A duplicate IP address means that there are two systems on the network that are attempting to connect to the network using the same IP address. As you know, there can be only one. This often happens when a new system has been added to a network where Dynamic Host Configuration Protocol (DHCP) is not being used.

Changes to the Workstation

The changes made to the systems on the network are not always under the control of the network administrator. Often, configuration changes and some software installations are performed by the end user. Such changes can be particularly frustrating to troubleshoot, and many users are unaware that the changes they make can cause problems. When looking for changes to a workstation system, consider the following:

◆ **Network settings**—One of the configuration hotspots for workstation computer systems is the network settings. If a workstation is unable to access the network, it is a good idea to confirm that the network settings have not been changed.

◆ **Printer settings**—Many printing problems can be isolated to changes in the printer configuration. Some client systems, such as Linux, are more adept at controlling administrative configuration screens than others; for example, Windows leaves such screens open to anyone who wants to change the configuration. When printing problems are isolated to a single system, changes in the configuration could be the cause.

◆ **New software**—Many users love to download and install nifty screensavers or perhaps the latest 3D adventure games on their work computers. Although it may be more interesting being Zaxon the Level 43 Wizard than John the data entry clerk, the addition of extra software can cause the system to fail. Confirm with the end user that new software has not been added to the system recently.

Selecting the Most Probable Cause of the Problem

There can be many different causes for a single problem on a network, but with appropriate information gathering, it is possible to eliminate many of them. When looking for a probable cause, it is often best to look at the easiest solution first and then work from there. Even in the most complex of network designs, the easiest solution is often the right one. For instance, if a single user cannot log on to a network, it is best to confirm network settings before replacing the NIC. Remember, though, that at this point you are only trying to determine the most probable cause, and your first guess might in fact be incorrect. It might take a few tries to determine the correct cause of the problem.

IN THE FIELD

DEVELOPING A PLAN FOR THE SOLUTION

Although developing a plan for solving a network problem is not specifically listed in the CompTIA objectives, after identifying a cause, but before implementing a solution, you should develop a plan for the solution. This is particularly a concern for server systems in which taking the server or network offline is a difficult and undesirable prospect. After identifying the cause of a problem on the server, it is absolutely necessary to plan for the solution. For instance, the plan must include when the server or network should be taken offline and for how long, what support services are in place, and who will be involved in correcting the problem.

Planning is a very important part of the whole troubleshooting process and can involve formal or informal written procedures. Those who do not have experience troubleshooting servers may be wondering about all the formality, but this formality ensures the least amount of network or server downtime and the maximum data availability.

As far as workstation troubleshooting is concerned, very rarely is a formal planning procedure required, and this makes the process easier. Planning for workstation troubleshooting typically involves arranging a convenient time with end users in order to implement a solution.

Implementing a Solution

At this point, you should be ready to implement a solution—that is, apply the patch, replace the hardware, plug in a cable, or implement some other solution. In an ideal world, your first solution would fix the problem, although unfortunately this is not always the case. If your first solution does not fix the problem, you will need to retrace your steps and start again.

It is important that you attempt only one solution at a time. Trying several solutions at once can make it very unclear which one actually corrected the problem.

NOTE

Troubleshooting Scenario   A user calls you to inform you that she is unable to access email. After asking a few questions, you determine that the user has only recently started with the company and has been unable to get email since her start date.

Troubleshooting Solution   In this scenario, there can be several causes of the problem: perhaps network connectivity, perhaps a bad NIC, or perhaps (most likely) email has never been configured on her workstation. Check to see if email has been configured. If it has not, configure it. If it has and it is working correctly, consider the next most likely cause of the problem.

NOTE

Escalation Procedures   One of the important but often neglected parts of the planning process is the development of escalation procedures. Although many technicians have difficulty admitting that they might need help with a problem, sometimes they need to do it. Unless there are formal escalation procedures defined by an organization, the rule of thumb is simply to determine the closest available suitable source of help and start from there.

EXAM TIP

Rollback Plans   A common and mandatory step that you must take when working on servers and some mission-critical workstations is to develop a rollback plan. The purpose of a rollback plan is to provide a method to get back to where you were before attempting the fix. Troubleshooting should not make the problem worse!

NOTE

Avoiding False Starts   When you have completed a fix, you should test it as thoroughly as you can before informing users of the fix. Users would generally rather wait for a real fix than have two or three false starts.

NOTE

Virus Activity   Keep in mind when troubleshooting a network or systems on a network that the problem might be virus related. Viruses can cause a variety of problems that can often disguise themselves as other problems. Part of your troubleshooting toolkit should include a bootable virus disk with the latest virus definitions. Indicators that you might have a virus include increased error messages and missing and corrupt files.

Testing the Results

After the corrective change has been made to the server, network, or workstation, it is necessary to test the results. This is where you find out if you were right and the remedy you applied actually worked. Don't forget that first impressions can be deceiving, and a fix that *seems* to work on first inspection may not actually have corrected the problem.

The testing process is not always as easy as it sounds. If you are testing a connectivity problem, it is not difficult to ascertain whether your solution was successful. However, changes made to an application or to databases are typically much more difficult to test. It might be necessary to have people who are familiar with the database or application run the tests with you in attendance.

In an ideal world, you would want be able to fully test a solution to see if it indeed corrected the problem. However, you might not know if you were successful until all users have logged back on, the application has been used, or the database has been queried. As a network administrator, you will be expected to take the testing process as far as you realistically can, even though you might not be able to simulate certain system conditions or loads. The true test will be in a real-world application.

Recognizing the Potential Effects of the Solution

Sometimes, you will apply a fix that corrects one problem but creates another problem. Many such circumstances are hard to predict—but not always. For instance, you might add a new network application, but the application requires more bandwidth than your current network infrastructure can support. The result would be that overall network performance would be compromised.

Everything done to a network can have a ripple effect and negatively affect another area of the network. Actions such as adding clients, replacing hubs, and adding applications can all have unforeseen results. It is very difficult to always know how the changes you make to a network are going to affect the network's functioning. The safest thing to do is assume that the changes you make are going to affect the network in some way and realize that you just have to figure out how. This is where you might need to think outside the box and try to predict possible outcomes.

Documenting the Solution

Although it is often neglected in the troubleshooting process, documentation is as important as any of the other troubleshooting procedures. Documenting a solution involves keeping a record of all the steps taken during the fix—not necessarily just the solution.

For the documentation to be of use to other network administrators in the future, it must include several key pieces of information. When documenting a procedure, you should include the following information:

- **Date**—When was the solution implemented? It is important to know the date because if problems occur after your changes, knowing the date of your fix makes it easier to determine whether your changes caused the problems.

- **Why**—Although it is obvious when a problem is being fixed why it is being done, a few weeks later, it might become less clear why that solution was needed. Documenting why the fix was made is important because if the same problem appears on another system, you can use this information to reduce time finding the solution.

- **What**—The successful fix should be detailed, along with information about any changes to the configuration of the system or network that were made to achieve the fix. Additional information should include version numbers for software patches or firmware, as appropriate.

- **Results**—Many administrators choose to include information on both successes and failures. The documentation of failures may prevent you from going down the same road twice, and the documentation of successful solutions can reduce the time it takes to get a system or network up and running.

- **Who**—It might be that there is information left out of the documentation or someone simply wants to ask a few questions about a solution. In both cases, if the name of the person who made a fix is in the documentation, he or she can easily be tracked down. Of course, this is more of a concern in environments where there are a number of IT staff or if system repairs are performed by contractors instead of actual company employees.

EXAM TIP

Log Books   Many organizations require that a log book be kept in the server room. This log book should maintain a record of everything that has been done on the network. In addition, many organizations require that administrators keep a log book of all repairs and upgrades made to networks and workstations.

NOTE

Troubleshooting Scenario   You have been away on a sunny vacation for three weeks, and when you return, there are several error messages on your company's server.

Troubleshooting Solution   Part of the role of a network administrator is to review the network documentation. To troubleshoot this scenario, you should look for any documented changes that were made to the system in your absence. Specifically, you should look for network configuration changes and added software applications or operating system patches. It is likely that one of these modifications will be at the root of the problem.

TROUBLESHOOTING TOPOLOGY ERRORS

▶ Given a troubleshooting scenario involving a network with a particular physical topology (i.e. bus, star/hierarchical, mesh, ring, and wireless) and including a network diagram, identify the network area affected and the cause of the problem.

As discussed in Chapter 1, "Introduction to Networking," several different topologies are used for networks. Each of these different types of network designs has failure points that are specific to the topology being used. To get a better idea of what is involved in troubleshooting these topology errors, the following sections provide specific troubleshooting scenarios and identify the potential causes of the problems.

Bus Network Errors

Recall from Chapter 1 that a bus topology connects all computer stations in a linear fashion. In the early days of Ethernet, the bus topology was the most widely used topology, and network administrators during that time were very experienced with the techniques involved in troubleshooting a bus network.

Before looking at specific bus troubleshooting scenarios, let's review the following characteristics of the bus topology:

◆ The cable used on a bus network has two distinct physical endpoints. Each of these cable ends requires a terminator. Terminators are used to absorb electronic signals so that they are not reflected back on the media, compromising data integrity. A failed or missing terminator will render the entire network segment unusable.

Troubleshooting Scenario   You have been called in to troubleshoot a network. The network has six computers and one printer connected in a bus topology. You question the network users and discover that although all devices on the network are able to access each other's system, data failures are occurring intermittently and some print jobs are failing.

Troubleshooting Solution
Intermittent data failures on a bus network can be the result of improper termination or grounding. Improper termination can also prevent the network from functioning altogether. A bus network requires a 50-ohm terminator on each of the physical ends of the bus. One of the ends of the bus also needs to be grounded.

◆ The addition, removal, or failure of a device on the network might prevent the entire network from functioning. Also, the coaxial cable used in a bus network can be damaged very easily. Moving cables in order to add or remove devices can cause cable problems.

◆ A bus topology must be continuous. A break in the cable at any point will render the entire segment unusable. If the location of the break in the cable is not apparent, you can check each length of cable systematically from one end to the other to identify the location of the break, or you can use a tool such as a time domain reflectometer.

◆ One end of the bus network should be grounded. Intermittent problems or a high occurrence of errors may indicate poor or insufficient grounding.

Now that we have looked at some of the considerations for bus topologies, we can examine some possible troubleshooting scenarios and solutions.

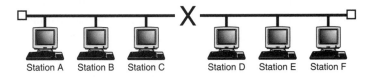

Star Network Errors

A star network is the most commonly used network topology today. With a star topology, each computer connects to a centralized device, and each system requires its own cable. Troubleshooting a star network has different considerations from troubleshooting a bus topology. As a network administrator today, you can expect to troubleshoot star networks.

NOTE

Troubleshooting Scenario You have been asked to come in on the weekend and install two new computer systems for the new employees who are starting Monday. On Monday morning, all employees are able to use their local computer resources but are unable to print or access the Internet through the proxy server. What is the likely cause of the problem?

Troubleshooting Solution Network failure after the installation of new systems on a bus topology can often be traced to improper cabling during the installation. If devices are unable to access network resources, you should ensure that the network is properly cabled, with all the network devices connected to each other.

FIGURE 15.1
A bus network failure.

NOTE

Troubleshooting Scenario You are called to troubleshoot a bus topology. When you arrive, you find that none of the devices on the network can communicate with each other. Using the information provided in Figure 15.1, identify the cause of the problem.

Troubleshooting Solution The cable in a bus network segment must be a contiguous length. In Figure 15.1, you can see a break in the cable that would stop Workstations A, B, and C from accessing Workstations D, E, and F. However, because the terminators are at each end of the broken segment, neither part of the network sections would be able to function.

N O T E

Troubleshooting Scenario   After an unhealthy lunch, you receive several calls from star network users, complaining that they are unable to access the network. Upon further investigation, you are able to confirm that all the users are members of the sales department. Using Figure 15.2 as a reference, what is the likely cause of the problem?

Troubleshooting Solution   On a star network, the hub or switch provides a single point of failure. In this example, all the members of the sales department are connected to Hub 1. Therefore, it might be that a faulty hub is the cause of the problem.

Troubleshooting Scenario   A single user calls you, complaining that he is unable to access the star network. Upon investigation, you discover that neither the NIC LED nor the LED associated with that user's computer on the hub is lit. What steps can you take to identify the problem?

Troubleshooting Solution   In this scenario, you can take troubleshooting steps from both the workstation and the wiring closet. The first step is to check the physical connections between the two devices. If they are okay, consider trying another network cable or another port on the hub or switch. If it is convenient, you could try the network cable in an alternative system to see if the problem lies with the workstation's NIC.

FIGURE 15.2
A star topology failure.

The following list contains a few of the main characteristics of the star topology and some pointers to potential steps you can take when troubleshooting a star network:

◆ Each device on the network requires its own cable, which is connected to a centralized device such as a hub. A cable failure should affect only the device connected to that cable length.

◆ Devices can be added or removed from a star network without affecting the existing users on the network. If other stations are affected by the addition or removal of devices, there might be a problem with a hub or switch.

◆ A centralized device provides a single point of failure in a star network. If a hub were to fail, for instance, all devices connected to it would be unable to access the network. When you know this and the fact that a cable problem should affect only a single system, you can significantly reduce the amount of time needed to isolate a problem in a star network.

◆ Hubs and switches have indicator lights, or LEDs, that show the states of connected devices as well as representations of network utilization and collision statistics. You can use the lights as a resource when troubleshooting a problem. No lights means no power. Most modern hubs and switches cannot operate without power.

◆ Hubs and switches can be connected to each other to provide more capacity on the network. If all the devices connected to one hub can see each other but not the rest of the network, you should suspect a problem with the hub-to-hub or switch-to-switch connection.

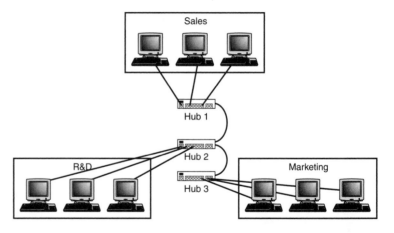

Ring Network Errors

A ring topology is not commonly used in today's network environments, but just in case you are working with a ring network, it is worthwhile knowing what to look for when troubleshooting one. The following is a review of the characteristics of a ring topology:

◆ The failure of a single computer or section of cable can cause complete network disruption.

◆ Only one computer can send data onto the network at a time, and the sending computer must have access to the *token* to send the data.

◆ Ring topologies are seen in Token Ring and Fiber Distributed Data Interface (FDDI) networks. Each of these systems uses fault-tolerant strategies.

> **NOTE**
>
> **Troubleshooting Scenario**   All users of a ring network are unable to log on to the network. After checking the connectivity between the workstation and the multistation access unit (MSAU), you are satisfied that all the workstation connections are secure and correct. What is the problem?
>
> **Troubleshooting Solution**   Ensure that the ring is complete. On an MSAU, the ring completion is achieved by connecting the first MSAU in the ring to the last one. If the ring connection is not complete, devices on the network will not be able to communicate with each other.

Mesh Network Errors

A mesh topology offers high redundancy by providing several paths for data to reach its destination. In a true mesh network, each device on the network is connected to every other device, and if one cable fails, there is another to provide an alternative data path. Given the number of cables involved, a mesh network can be somewhat tricky to troubleshoot.

Let's review the characteristics of a mesh topology and look at some of the factors that can affect troubleshooting in mesh systems:

◆ A mesh topology interconnects all devices on the network, offering the highest level of redundancy of all the topologies. In a pure mesh environment, all devices are directly connected to all other devices. In a hybrid mesh environment, some devices are connected only to certain others in the topology.

◆ Although a mesh topology can accommodate failed links, mechanisms should still be in place so that failed links are detected and reported.

◆ Design and implementation of a true mesh network can be complex and often requires specialized hardware devices.

NOTE

> **Troubleshooting Scenario** After numerous problems with connectivity between remote sites, your manager asks to you to design and specify a new topology that has the maximum amount of fault tolerance.
>
> **Troubleshooting Solution** You can implement a mesh topology between all your WAN devices and configure the topology to accommodate a network link failure.

> **Troubleshooting Scenario** Users connecting to a wireless access point are experiencing random problems such as lost connections, poor speed, and network errors.
>
> **Troubleshooting Solution** Check to see if the wireless devices are operating within the accepted range of the wireless access point. Also find out if there are any environmental considerations that have not been fully taken into account, such as construction materials and heavy machinery that can interfere with the quality of the signal.

Mesh networks are so rare that it's unlikely that you will be faced with troubleshooting one but there will likely be questions on the Network+ exam that focus on mesh networks.

Wireless Network Errors

Wireless networks do not require physical cable to connect computers; rather, they use wireless media. The benefits of such a configuration are clear—users have remote access to files and resources without the need for physical connections. Wireless networking eliminates cable faults and cable breaks. It does, however, introduce its own considerations: signal interference and security.

The following list summarizes the characteristics of a wireless network:

◆ A wireless network allows for a remote connection without requiring cumbersome cabling.

◆ Users can be added to an existing network without disruption to current users.

◆ Common media types for wireless networks include infrared, radio waves, and satellite communication. The most common method used for wireless local area network (LAN) implementations is radio waves.

◆ It is possible to eavesdrop on wireless signals. Therefore, security must be carefully considered.

◆ Wireless communication has limited speed compared to cabled Ethernet networks.

◆ Some types of wireless communications require a point-to-point direct line-of-sight connection.

TROUBLESHOOTING CLIENT CONNECTIVITY ERRORS

▶ Given a network troubleshooting scenario involving a client connectivity problem (e.g. incorrect protocol/client, software/authentication configuration, or insufficient rights/permissions), identify the cause of the problem.

Any network administrator is likely to tell you that client connectivity errors are one of the most common sources of network-related problems. Client connectivity errors range from plain old user error to more complex protocol and cabling issues as well as administrative mistakes. With so many possibilities, it is no wonder that client connectivity persists as one of the biggest network troubleshooting hotspots. The following sections explore the common sources of client connectivity problems and provide scenarios that network administrators might encounter.

Protocol Errors

The client system has to have a protocol assigned or bound to its NIC in order to access resources. You can use specialized tools to verify that a protocol is being used by the system; for example, on Windows NT/2000/XP systems you use the ipconfig command, on older Windows client systems you use the winipcfg command, and on Linux systems you use the ifconfig command.

Protocol-Specific Issues

You need to consider a number of factors related to network protocols when you troubleshoot a network. The following list describes some of the protocol-specific issues you should be aware of when dealing with client protocol configurations:

♦ **Transmission Control Protocol/Internet Protocol (TCP/IP)**—For a system to operate on a TCP/IP-based network, it must have at the very least a unique IP address, the correct subnet mask for the network to which it is connected, and (for cross-network connectivity) a default gateway entry. In addition, Domain Name Service (DNS) server addresses may be required.

♦ **Internetwork Packet Exchange/Sequenced Packet Exchange (IPX/SPX)**—Each system on an IPX/SPX network must have a unique address, although the addresses are generated and assigned automatically. Care must be taken to ensure that the correct frame type is being used, although systems are usually able to autodetect the frame type that is in use.

◆ **Network BIOS Extended User Interface (NetBEUI)**—Each system on a network that uses NetBEUI must have a unique name to identify the computer on the network. For name resolution between network segments, a network needs either a Windows Internet Naming System (WINS) server or manual name resolution through an LMHOSTS file.

◆ **AppleTalk**—Each system on an AppleTalk network must have a unique address.

On networks that use TCP/IP, DHCP is often used to automatically assign protocol information to clients. When DHCP is not used, protocol information has to be entered manually, and many errors can arise—most commonly duplicate IP addresses.

When protocol settings are correctly configured, protocol problems are infrequent. Unless settings are manually changed, very little can go wrong.

Authentication

Before users can log on to the system, their identities must be verified. By far the most common type of authentication used is the standard username and password combination. When a user account is created, it is good practice for the administrator to set a password. The user should change that password immediately so that the administrator no longer knows it.

Users should be forced to change their logon passwords periodically, although that often creates the problem of users forgetting their passwords. Mechanisms should therefore be in place that allow users to get new passwords quickly.

Most user password problems can be traced to users entering an incorrect password or entering the correct password incorrectly. All common operating systems offer the capability for the administrator to change a user's password, but none offer the capability to determine the user's existing password. Therefore, if a user does forget his or her password, a new one has to be created and issued.

Little can be done about users incorrectly typing passwords, except that you can encourage users to be careful. Note that Linux and Windows NT/2000 and some NetWare platforms used case-sensitive passwords. Therefore, if a user is having trouble logging on, he or she should ensure that the Caps Lock key is on or off as appropriate.

Permissions Errors

Access to programs and data across the network is controlled by permissions. Permissions are responsible for protecting the data on the network and ensuring that only those who should have access to it do.

The first rule of permissions troubleshooting is to remember that permissions do not change themselves. If a user cannot access a file, the first question to the user should always be, "Could you ever access the file?" If the user says "Yes, but now I can't access the file," you should check server change logs or documentation to see if any changes have been made in the permissions structure.

If no changes have been made, you should verify that the user is in fact allowed access to that file or directory. In large environments, trying to keep track of who should have access to what can be a tricky business—one that is best left to defined policies and documentation.

The following are some other items you should consider when troubleshooting permissions problems:

◆ On some operating systems, rights and permissions can be inherited from parent directories or other directories that are higher in the directory structure. A change in the permissions assignments at one level may have an effect on a lower level in the directory tree.

◆ File permissions can be gained from objects other than the user's account. Depending on the operating system being used, rights can also be gained from group membership, other network objects, or security equivalence. When you are troubleshooting a permissions problem, be sure that you understand where rights are supposed to originate.

◆ File attributes can override file permissions, and they can prevent actions from being performed on certain files. To the uninitiated, this might seem like a file permissions problem, but in fact it is correct operation. For example, on a NetWare file system, the Rename Inhibit permission prevents changes to the name of a file, even if the user has the Supervisory File System permission.

NOTE

Cooling Fans   Most networking devices have only one moving part: the cooling fan. You should not underestimate the importance of the fan, and you should always make sure that hubs, switches, and routers have adequate cooling and that the fan is working.

NOTE

Troubleshooting Scenario   A user calls and says that he is unable to log on to the network. After checking that he is using the correct username and password combination, you decide that there may be a connectivity issue, so you visit the user at his desk.

Troubleshooting Solution   Upon reaching the user's desk, you determine that the cable is indeed plugged in to the NIC, but you also notice that the link light on the NIC is not on. As a precaution, you attempt to log on anyway, but you are unsuccessful. You receive a message saying that no logon server could be found. Noting the connection number for the wall socket to which the problem system is connected, you proceed to the server room to check the switch to which the system is connected. You check the physical connection into the switch, and everything appears to be in order. You grab a spare network cable and head back to the user's desk. You swap out the existing cable with the new one, and the link light comes on. The user attempts to log on again and is successful.

◆ You need to determine that there is actually a problem. Users sometimes decide to clean up by deleting files they think are no longer used. Permissions may have been set that prevent users from doing this, and rightly so, but the user might identify this as a permissions problem and report it as such. To a lesser extent, the same situation can occur if a user tries to manipulate a file while it is in use by another application or user.

IN THE FIELD

APPLICATION PROBLEMS AND FILE PERMISSIONS

A malfunctioning application can sometimes be traced back to a file permissions problem. Many types of applications write temporary files, which they then need to delete when a certain operation is completed or the application is closed. File permissions and attributes can prevent this process, and in some cases, the result is that the application misbehaves or stops working completely. If you have an application problem you can't nail down, make sure that it is not related to file permissions or attribute problems.

Troubleshooting permissions problems can be both challenging and enjoyable. As with many other IT troubleshooting scenarios, you can solve most permissions problems effectively if you fully understand what you are troubleshooting and the factors that affect the situation.

Physical Connectivity Errors

Although many of the problems associated with client connectivity can be traced to software-based problems such as configuration, authentication, and permissions issues, physical connectivity is often the root of the problem.

When you are troubleshooting physical connectivity errors, the first place to look is at the network cables. Although it is rare, cables can become loose or disconnected from NICs or from the ports on a hub or switch. Oftentimes, this is the result of other cables being plugged in or unplugged, or of activity on the connections around the one that is having the problem. Other cable considerations include exceeded maximum lengths, cable breaks, and improperly terminated or made cables, although these are only a consideration in exceptional cases.

Physical connectivity errors also involve the devices used to establish the physical client/server connectivity. This can include hubs, switches, MSAUs, NICs, routers, and connectivity hardware. As discussed earlier in this chapter, these devices normally have LEDs that indicate the state of the network and the respective links with devices. Although it is possible to have a problem with a single port on one of the aforementioned devices, it is more likely that the entire unit will malfunction. Thankfully, networking devices are very resilient devices that normally provide many years of reliable service, with few or no problems.

Troubleshooting physical connectivity errors often requires some trial and error. For example, you might switch a cable to a different port in a hub to test whether the port is at fault or replace a cable or NIC with one that is known to be working to see if it fixes the problem. If you are fortunate enough to have them, you can use instruments and devices that are aimed at reducing the hit-or-miss approach to the troubleshooting process, but they are costly devices and they actually often come a distant second to the trial-and-error method.

TROUBLESHOOTING WIRING- AND INFRASTRUCTURE-RELATED PROBLEMS

▶ Given a network troubleshooting scenario involving a wiring/infrastructure problem, identify the cause of the problem (e.g. bad media, interference, network hardware).

You will no doubt find yourself troubleshooting wiring and infrastructure problems considerably more infrequently than you'll troubleshoot client connectivity problems—and thankfully so. Wiring- and infrastructure-related problems can be very difficult to trace, and sometimes a very costly solution is needed to remedy the situation. When troubleshooting these problems, a methodical approach is likely to pay off.

NOTE

Troubleshooting Scenario You receive several calls from users on the second floor, reporting that they have become disconnected from the network. You know that on the second floor there is a printer with a network connection, so you attempt to ping the IP address of the printer but are unsuccessful. What could be the problem?

Troubleshooting Solution Because numerous people are reporting problems, you can be sure that the problem is not with a specific workstation or network connection. The problem is more likely with one of the switches that is used for second-floor connections. Upon reaching the server room, you notice that one of the switches in the rack is powered off and that none of the LEDs on it are lit. All the other switches in the rack are on and operating correctly. After you attempt to cycle the power on the failed switch, nothing happens. You deduce that the switch must have failed and proceed to replace a hub as a temporary measure.

Wiring problems are related to the actual cable used in a network. For the purposes of the Network+ exam, infrastructure problems are classified as those related to network devices such as hubs, switches, and routers.

Troubleshooting Wiring

Troubleshooting wiring involves knowing what wiring your network uses and where it is being used.

Determining Your Wiring

As mentioned in Chapter 2, "Cabling and Connectors," the cable used has certain limitations, in terms of both speed and distance. It might be that the network problems are the result of trying to use a cable in an environment or a way for which it was not designed. For example, you might find that a network is connecting two workstations that are 130 meters apart with Category 5 UTP cabling. Category 5 UTP is specified for distances up to 100 meters, so exceeding the maximum cable length could be a potential cause of the problem.

Determining the type of cable used by a network is often as easy as reading the cable. The cable should be stamped with its type—whether it is, for example, UTP Category 5, RG-58, or something else. As you work with the various cable types used to create networks, you'll get to the point where you can easily identify them. However, you should be careful when identifying cable types because some cable types are almost indistinguishable. After you have determined the cable being used, you can compare the characteristics and limitations of that cable against how it is being used on the network.

Where the Cable Is Used

Imagine that you have been called in to track down a problem with a network. After some time, you discover that clients are connected to the network via standard UTP cable run down an elevator shaft. Recall from Chapter 2 that UTP has very poor resistance to electromagnetic interference (EMI) and therefore UTP and the electrical equipment associated with elevators react to each other like oil and water. The same can be said of cables that are run close to fluorescent light fittings. Such problems might seem farfetched, but you would be surprised at just how many environments you will work in that have random or erratic problems that users have lived with for a long time and not done anything about.

Part of troubleshooting wiring problems is to identify where the cable is run, to isolate whether the problem is a result of crosstalk or EMI. You need to be aware of problems associated with interference and the distance limitations of the cable being used.

If you find a problem with a network's cable, there are various things you can do to correct the problem. For cables that exceed the maximum distance, you can use a repeater to regenerate the signal, try to reroute the cable over a more economical route, or even replace the type of cable with one that has greater resistance to attenuation. The method you choose will often depend on the network's design and your budget.

For cable that is affected by EMI or other interference, you should consider replacing the cable with cable that is more resistant to such interference or rerouting the cable away from the source of the interference. If you do reroute cable, pay attention to the maximum distance, and make sure that as you're curing one problem you don't create another.

> **NOTE**
>
> **Risers** In many buildings, risers are used for running cables between floors. A *riser* is a column that runs from the bottom of the building to the top. Risers are used for running all kinds of cables, including electrical and network cables.

> **NOTE**
>
> **Test Cable** Never assume that the cable you are using is good until you test it and confirm that it is good. Sometimes cables break, and bad media can cause network problems.

Troubleshooting the Infrastructure

If you are looking for a challenge, troubleshooting infrastructure problems is for you. It is often not an easy task, and it usually involves many processes, including baselining and performance monitoring. Only by using a variety of tools and methods can you identify the infrastructure as the cause of your troubles.

You can experience three types of basic problems when troubleshooting infrastructure problems:

◆ **Specific failures**—A device such as a hub or switch can cease to function and cause an entire section of the network to fail. Such problems tend to be quite easy to troubleshoot. If you are armed with the network documentation, it should be fairly simple to pinpoint the source of the problem.

◆ **Nonspecific failures**—Sometimes users experience random problems with the network, but there doesn't seem to be any common thread to the problems. Such problems can be hard to isolate because it is often difficult to pin down the exact cause.

◆ **General performance problems**—A common sign of a problem with the network's infrastructure is poor network performance. Of course, *poor performance* is a vague statement and can be attributed to everything from a misconfigured operating system or application to failed hardware. In the troubleshooting process, all these problems would likely be eliminated as causes before the network's infrastructure would become suspect. You are most likely going to encounter infrastructure problems when using new equipment or new applications on older networks. For example, perhaps the 10Mbps hubs and the Category 3 UTP cable just won't work. It is the network administrator's job to be aware of possible infrastructure problems before installing new network components or applications. You can save yourself a lot of legwork by fully exploring the impact that changes to the network will have on the existing infrastructure before modifying the network.

Baselines and Performance Monitoring

Often, the only way to know if the network is suffering from poor performance is to compare its current performance to its past performance, to see if it has changed. Such a comparison is done by using baselines. Baselines are used to measure network performance and provide a means of comparison when troubleshooting network performance.

Performing baselines on the network is not a one-time task. For baselines to be useful, they must be performed periodically. As a network expands, introducing new users and new applications, baselines can let you know if the network infrastructure can carry the load. As a rough estimate, you should consider the following guidelines in determining the frequency of network baselines:

◆ **Changes to network applications**—Some applications are more bandwidth hungry than others. Installing the latest and greatest application might be too much for the existing network infrastructure to handle. To determine whether this is the case, you should perform baselines before and after installing a new application.

◆ **Addition of users**—Network performance can slow down if too many users are on the system, using the same resources. If several new users are to be added to a network, a preemptive troubleshooting step would be to obtain baseline performance before and after the new clients are added.

◆ **Changes to the network hardware**—Changes such as installing a new NIC in the server or adding an additional hub can have an impact on the network's overall performance.

◆ **Software upgrade**—If you have to upgrade your network operating system, you should obtain a baseline. A network that is designed for and working with Linux might struggle if, for example, it were switched to Windows 2000.

TROUBLESHOOTING CHECKLISTS

In a real-world networking environment, you will be expected to be able to troubleshoot many different areas. You can expect to be tested on them on the CompTIA exam. The following sections provide some troubleshooting checklists that can help you review some of the various troubleshooting areas.

Troubleshooting Cable Problems

Cable accounts for a great many of the problems on a network. There are many places to look when you suspect a cable-related problem. If you suspect that cable is at the bottom of your network troubles, consider the following areas:

◆ **Loose connections**—You need to verify that cables are securely attached and that they are attached to the correct ports.

◆ **Poorly crimped or bent cable**—Sometimes a chair running over a cable or a cable that has a poor crimp can cause problems.

EXAM TIP

Baseline Strategy To get an accurate and comparable measurement, you should perform baselines during both peak and nonpeak times.

NOTE

Troubleshooting Scenario Users on your network have been complaining that network performance has been slow, and many of their everyday tasks are taking longer than they used to. What should you do?

Troubleshooting Solution Take a baseline and compare it with information from your baseline history. Interpret the information to see if there is actually a problem or if users are just perceiving a problem that does not actually exist. If you determine that there is a problem, you need to find out if there have been any changes to the network that might account for the slow network performance, such as changes to the hardware or software configurations.

◆ **Incorrect cable length**—Recall from Chapter 2 that cables cannot exceed a specified maximum length.

◆ **Cable placement**—Care must be taken when cables are run too closely to strong electrical devices. If cables are run too closely to electrical devices, you need to ensure that they are designed for the task.

◆ **Termination**—If you are using a bus topology, you need to ensure that the correct termination is being used.

Troubleshooting Network Connectivity

As a network administrator, you can expect to troubleshoot a number of connectivity issues. These might come in the form of local connectivity errors or remote connectivity errors. Either way, most of the troubleshooting techniques are the same. If you are struggling with connectivity issues, confirm the following:

◆ **Username/password**—Your first consideration when determining connectivity issues is to confirm that the correct username and password configuration is used. Often, this is as far as your troubleshooting needs to go.

◆ **Configuration**—It might be necessary to confirm that the network settings on the client computer have not changed.

◆ **Account activity**—You need to verify that the user has an active account on the network and that it has the correct permissions set. It is often a good idea to try to log on with a known working account.

◆ **Physical connections**—You should check to see if a cable has come unplugged. Correcting connectivity issues may be as simple as reconnecting a cable.

◆ **NIC**—From time to time, NICs fail. To confirm that a card is working, you might need to swap out the card with one that is known to be working.

Troubleshooting Network Printing

The time between a failed print job and a call to the network administrator is measured in milliseconds. Printing is one of the services that network users expect to be working, and it is the administrator's job to make sure it is available. When you find yourself on the hot seat, trying to get a printer back up and running, confirm the following:

◆ **Printer online status**—You should confirm that the printer is online and ready to go. If there is a problem with the printer itself, the printer might display error messages on an LCD panel or use LEDs to indicate a problem.

◆ **Printer functioning**—Nearly all printers have a test print feature. You can use it to make sure that the printer is functioning correctly.

◆ **Printer connectivity**—Verify that the printer is visible to the network. If the printer is using TCP/IP, for instance, you can ping the printer to test for connectivity.

◆ **Client configuration**—Ensure that the computers that are trying to access the printer are configured correctly to use that printer. Often, several printers are used in networks, and it might be necessary to confirm that the client is configured to send a print job to a particular printer.

◆ **Permissions**—On many operating systems, it is possible to set permissions to allow or deny users access to a printer. You need to verify that the correct permissions have been set.

◆ **Check logs**—Network operating systems log printer activity. Monitoring printer logs can often provide clues as to the source of a problem.

Troubleshooting Data Access

The inability to access data is not always a result of connectivity errors. Improperly set data security can prevent a user's access. If a user is unable to access data, there are a few key areas to verify:

◆ **Proper network login**—Sometimes people use a shortcut or try to access data without being properly logged on to the network. You should verify that users are correctly logged on to the network and that any necessary network drives are connected.

◆ **Permissions**—Access to data through the network is controlled by access permissions. When you are troubleshooting data access, ensure that the permissions are set correctly.

◆ **Connectivity**—You need to verify that the system that maintains the data is available. Many organizations use multiple servers to hold data. You need to confirm that the server is available.

◆ **Data integrity**—Sometimes data itself can be corrupt. This is the worst-case scenario, and it occurs rarely. This is when you need backups.

◆ **Viruses**—In some cases, viruses may be your problem. You can use a virus-checking program to determine if indeed this is the problem.

Troubleshooting NICs

When NICs are configured correctly and verified to be working, very little goes wrong with them. Despite their dependability, NICs can give you a little grief. When you are troubleshooting an NIC, you should consider the following:

◆ **Resource settings**—NICs require specific computer resources in order to operate. After you install a card or add new devices, you should check for input/output (I/O) address conflicts and interrupt request (IRQ) conflicts.

◆ **Speed settings**—If you are not getting the expected speed from the NIC, you should confirm the speed settings and, if applicable, the duplex settings.

◆ **Protocols**—In order for the NIC to work on the network, it must have a valid protocol assigned to it. Often, protocol information is provided via DHCP on TCP/IP networks.

A protocol issue is usually not a problem with the card itself, although a problem with the NIC can disguise itself as a protocol problem on occasion. If you are using multiple NICs in a system, each card needs at least one protocol assigned to it.

◆ **Faulty card**—Some NICs are faulty when they ship from the manufacturer, and some are damaged through poor handling. Whatever the case, the NIC you are troubleshooting might actually be faulty. To test for this, you can swap the card with one that is known to be working.

CHAPTER SUMMARY

Troubleshooting networks is an activity with which network administrators become very familiar. Successful troubleshooting does not happen by accident; rather, the troubleshooting process follows some defined procedures. These procedures include the following:

1. Establish what the symptoms are.

2. Identify the affected areas.

3. Establish what has changed.

4. Select the most probable cause.

5. Implement a solution.

6. Test the results.

7. Recognize the potential effects of the solution.

8. Document the solution.

You can use several strategies when troubleshooting different topologies, and each topology has unique troubleshooting considerations. When you are troubleshooting a network, it is necessary to identify the topology that is being used and think about the troubleshooting strategies associated with that particular topology.

KEY TERMS

- topology
- bus
- star
- ring
- mesh
- wireless
- ipconfig
- ifconfig
- protocol
- authentication
- permissions
- media
- interference
- attenuation
- EMI

CHAPTER SUMMARY

KEY TERMS

- baseline
- segment
- winipcfg
- NetBEUI
- AppleTalk
- TCP/IP
- IPX/SPX
- hub
- switch
- MSAU
- client software
- termination
- NIC
- log file
- virus

Troubleshooting client connectivity is a common task for network administrators. There are several areas to check when troubleshooting connectivity: You need to verify authentication, verify permissions, confirm physical connectivity, and confirm the protocols. Each of these areas may be at the root of a client connectivity issue, but the correct troubleshooting procedure requires starting with the most probable cause and working from there.

At times, you might find yourself troubleshooting wiring and infrastructure problems. Although they are less common than other troubleshooting areas, wiring and network devices should be considered possible causes of a problem. Tracking down infrastructure problems often requires using documentation and network maps or taking baselines to compare network performance.

APPLY YOUR KNOWLEDGE

Exercises

15.1 Using the Internet to Interpret Error Log Messages and Propose Possible Solutions

As a network administrator, you have been given the task of installing and configuring a new printer on a Windows 2000 computer system. You set up the printer, but each time you attempt to configure the printer, you receive the following error:

```
An application error has occurred and an
application error log is being generated.

SPOOLSS.EXE

Exception: access violation (0xc0000005),
Address: <Hex address>
```

To get the computer to print, you must access Internet resources to try to find a solution.

Estimated time: 10 minutes

1. Go to www.microsoft.com.

2. In the very top menu bar, choose Support, and then select the Knowledge Base option from the drop-down menu.

3. In the Search drop-down box on the left side of the screen, click the down arrow, and then select Windows 2000.

4. In the For Solutions Containing box, type the problem. In this case, you are looking for the spoolss.exe printing error. Type **spoolss.exe error** in the Solutions search box, and then click Search Now. You might have to scroll down the page to see the results.

5. The solutions search should produce numerous articles pertaining to your search. Find the article titled "Application Error in SPOOLSS.EXE When Printing" (Q147347).

6. Select the article to find a possible solution to the preceding error message.

Exam Questions

1. You have been contracted to isolate the cause of a client connectivity error on a network. Which of the following areas is likely to be your starting point in the troubleshooting process?

   a. Confirm that the cable distance does not exceed the specified maximum length to the client system.

   b. Replace the NIC in the client computer.

   c. Verify the authentication information.

   d. Verify the protocol configuration.

2. You are installing an NIC into a new computer system. After it is installed, the system does not recognize it. Which of the following should be confirmed? (Choose the two best answers.)

   a. Verify that the card has a unique IP address.

   b. Verify that the NIC has a unique IRQ.

   c. Verify that the NIC is Ethernet compatible.

   d. Verify that there are no I/O conflicts.

3. Joan, a worker in the payroll group, calls you and states that she is unable to print to a network printer. You confirm that other members of the payroll group can print and that Joan's account has permissions to the printer. Which of the following is a likely cause of her inability to print?

   a. The printer is in a different domain.

   b. The printer is offline.

APPLY YOUR KNOWLEDGE

c. Joan is not correctly logged on to the network.

d. There is a paper jam in the printer.

4. Marvin, a network user, calls you and is upset because he is unable to log on to the Windows 2000 server. Which of the following are valid troubleshooting steps that would help isolate the problem? (Choose the three best answers.)

    a. Try logging on with a different username and password combination.

    b. Verify Marvin's logon information.

    c. `ping` the logon server.

    d. Run `ifconfig` to verify that the IP address is valid.

5. A user calls you to say that he is unable to access a certain file on the server. You establish that the user has accessed the file before and that the user has the appropriate permissions, even though he is assigned permissions at the directory level rather than to the file itself. Which of the following are possible causes of the problem? (Choose the three best answers.)

    a. The user has become disconnected from the server.

    b. The file has been moved or deleted.

    c. The file has become infected with a virus.

    d. The file system on the server has become corrupted.

6. Which of the following should you consider when troubleshooting wiring problems? (Choose the three best answers.)

    a. The distance between devices

    b. Interference

    c. Atmospheric conditions

    d. Connectors

7. You get numerous calls from users who are unable to access an application. Upon investigation, you find that the application has crashed. You restart the application, and it appears to run okay. What is the next step in the troubleshooting process?

    a. Email the users and let them know that they can use the application again.

    b. Test the application to ensure that it is operating correctly.

    c. Document the problem and the solution.

    d. Reload the application executables from the CD and restart it.

8. A user calls to inform you that she is having a problem accessing her email. What is the next step in the troubleshooting process?

    a. Document the problem.

    b. Ensure that the user's email address is valid.

    c. Discuss the problem with the user.

    d. Visit the user's desk to reload the email client software.

9. You have successfully fixed a problem with a server and have tested the application and let the users back on the system. What is the next step in the troubleshooting process?

    a. Document the problem.

    b. Restart the server.

    c. Document the problem and the solution.

    d. Clear the error logs of any reference to the problem.

10. You are called in to troubleshoot a problem with the NIC on a server that has been running well for some time. The server reports a resource conflict. What would be the next step in the troubleshooting process?

    a. Change the NIC.

    b. Consult the documentation to determine whether there have been any changes to the server configuration.

    c. Download and install the latest drivers for the NIC.

    d. Reload the protocol drivers for the NIC and set them to use a different set of resources.

11. You are troubleshooting a network problem on a network that has a star topology. There are four segments on the network: sales, marketing, admin, and research. Three users from the admin department call you, reporting problems accessing the server. Where are you most likely to look for the source of the problem?

    a. The users' workstations

    b. The server

    c. The switch that services the admin segment

    d. The switch that services the sales segment

12. Which of the following need to be verified when you are troubleshooting client connectivity errors? (Choose the three best answers.)

    a. Protocol configurations

    b. Authentication

    c. Logon permissions

    d. File permissions

13. When you are troubleshooting connectivity on a wireless portion of a LAN, which of the following would you verify? (Choose the two best answers.)

    a. That there is a line of sight between the workstation and the wireless access point

    b. The distance between the workstations and the wireless access point

    c. Hardware resource conflicts on the workstation with the wireless NIC

    d. Cable termination

14. A user calls you to report that he is experiencing problems accessing a file on the server. Upon quizzing the user, you determine that he has not accessed the file before. Which of the following should be your next troubleshooting step?

    a. Set the file permission so that the user can access the file.

    b. Reset the user's password.

    c. Reboot the server to reinitialize the permissions set.

    d. Determine whether the user should have access to the file.

15. A user calls to inform you that she is unable to print. Upon questioning her, you determine that the user has just been moved from the second floor to the third floor. What is the most likely explanation for the problem?

    a. The user is still printing to the printer on the second floor.

    b. The printer is not working.

APPLY YOUR KNOWLEDGE

c. The printer drivers need to be reloaded on the workstation.

d. The print drivers have become corrupted.

16. You are troubleshooting a problem with a bus topology network. Users are reporting that they are sometimes unable to access the network, but it is fine at other times. Which of the following might you consider? (Choose the two best answers.)

    a. Faulty hubs or switch

    b. Improper or faulty termination

    c. Improper grounding

    d. Cable lengths in excess of 100 meters

17. You have been called in to troubleshoot a problem with a specific application on a server system. The client is unable to provide any information about the problem except that the application is not accessible. Which of the following troubleshooting steps should you perform first?

    a. Consult the documentation for the server.

    b. Consult the application error log on the server.

    c. Reboot the server.

    d. Reload the application from the original CD.

18. Users are occasionally experiencing problems accessing network resources. You suspect that the NIC on the server might not be able to keep up with the demands placed on it. Which of the following troubleshooting steps would you perform first?

    a. Replace the NIC with one that offers better levels of performance.

b. Check to see if updated drivers are available for the card.

c. Perform a baseline to determine whether the card is having a problem coping.

d. Swap the card with one that is known to be working, to see if there is a problem with the card.

19. A user calls to tell you that after a lunch break he cannot log on to the network. The user's workstation is a Windows 2000 system with a 10BaseT network connection. The user was able to log on before lunch, and then he logged off before he left. What should you ask the user to check first?

    a. Is the network cable securely plugged in to the back of the workstation?

    b. Are you using the right password?

    c. Is the Caps Lock key off?

    d. Are you using the right username?

20. A user is having problems logging on to the server. Each time she tries, she receives a "server not found" message. No other users have reported having this problem. Which of the following are possible explanations to the problem? (Choose the two best answers.)

    a. The protocol configuration on the workstation is incorrect.

    b. The Caps Lock key is on.

    c. The cable has become disconnected from the user's workstation.

    d. The server is down.

Answers to Exam Questions

1. **c.** Checking to make sure the authentication information is correct is the simplest of the steps listed and is also the most likely source of the problem. All the other options are valid troubleshooting steps, but you should check the authentication information first. For more information, see the section "Troubleshooting Client Connectivity Errors," in this chapter.

2. **b, d.** When installing a new device into a system, you must ensure that there are no resource conflicts. This includes verifying that there are no IRQ or I/O address conflicts. Answer a is not correct because a valid IP address would not affect whether the system is able to recognize the card. Answer c is not valid. For more information, see the section "Troubleshooting Checklists," in this chapter.

3. **c.** Of the answers provided, the most likely is that the user is not logged on to the network. Because you have confirmed that the other members of the payroll group are able to print, the problem lies with the user and not with some other aspect of the network or the printer. For more information, see the section "Troubleshooting Client Connectivity Errors," in this chapter.

4. **a, b, c.** Verifying that the user is using the correct logon information is the first troubleshooting step. Next, you should attempt to log on using another user account, which helps you verify that the workstation connectivity is correct. You can also ping the logon server, which enables you to ensure that it is up and running. Answer d is not a valid troubleshooting step because it is a Linux utility. For more information, see the section "Troubleshooting Client Connectivity Errors," in this chapter.

5. **a, b, c.** It could be that the user has been disconnected from the server or that the file has been moved or deleted. Less likely is that the file was infected by a virus, rendering it unusable. Answer d is not correct because if you have been able to certify the user's file permissions, there is not an apparent problem with the filesystem on the server. For more information, see the section "Troubleshooting Client Connectivity Errors," in this chapter.

6. **a, b, d.** When you're troubleshooting a wiring problem. you should consider the distance between devices, interference such as crosstalk and EMI, and the connection points. Answer c is not correct because bound media (that is, cables) are not affected by atmospheric conditions. For more information, see the section "Troubleshooting Wiring- and Infrastructure-Related Problems," in this chapter.

7. **b.** After you have fixed a problem, you should test it fully to ensure that the network is operating correctly before allowing users to log back on. The steps described in Answers a and c are valid, but only after the application has been tested. Answer d is not correct; you would reload the executable only as part of a systematic troubleshooting process, and because the application loads, it is unlikely that the executable has become corrupt. For more information, see the section "The Art of Troubleshooting," in this chapter.

8. **c.** There is not enough information provided to make any real decision about what the problem might be. In this case, the next troubleshooting step would be to talk to the user and gather more information about exactly what the problem might be. All the other answers are valid troubleshooting steps, but only after the information

APPLY YOUR KNOWLEDGE

gathering has been completed. For more information, see the section "The Art of Troubleshooting," in this chapter.

9. **c.** After you have fixed a problem, tested the fix, and let users back on to the system, you should create detailed documentation that describes the problem and the solution. Answer a is incorrect because you must document both the problem and the solution. It is not necessary to restart the server, so Answer b is incorrect and Answer d would be performed only after the documentation for the system has been created. For more information, see the section "The Art of Troubleshooting," in this chapter.

10. **b.** In a server that has been operating correctly, a resource conflict could indicate that a device has failed and is causing the conflict. More likely, a change has been made to the server, and that change has created a conflict. Although all the other answers represent valid troubleshooting steps, it is most likely that there has been a change to the configuration. For more information, see the section "The Art of Troubleshooting," in this chapter.

11. **c.** In this scenario, the common denominator is that all the users reporting a problem are connected to the same network switch. Therefore, this would be the first place to look for a problem. Because more than one user has a problem, looking at the users' workstations is not the best troubleshooting step. Because you have not received any other calls from other departments, it is unlikely that there is a problem with the server. Because no users from the sales department have reported problems, there is unlikely to be a problem with the sales section of the network. For more information, see sections "The

Art of Troubleshooting" and "Troubleshooting Client Connectivity Errors," in this chapter.

12. **a, b, c.** Client connectivity problems are normally due to authentication problems, but they can also be attributed to the protocol configuration on the workstation and logon permissions. File permissions do not represent a valid troubleshooting step when you're verifying client connectivity. For more information, see the section "Troubleshooting Client Connectivity Errors," in this chapter.

13. **b, c.** Wireless devices can operate only within a certain distance from the access point. Operating outside this distance can cause problems with the signal. Also, just as with wired NICs, you must take into account resources when you install wireless NICs in devices. Answer a is not correct because wireless devices do not need a line of sight between sending and receiving devices. Cable termination is not an issue for wireless devices, and so Answer d is not a valid answer. For more information, see the section "Troubleshooting Wiring- and Infrastructure-Related Problems," in this chapter.

14. **d.** Before you assign permissions in a case like this, it is important to verify that the user is supposed to have access to the file in the first place. Answer a is not valid because you must verify that the user should have access to the file before granting permissions. Because the user is able to log on to the server, resetting the password is not a valid troubleshooting step. Restarting the server is also not a valid troubleshooting step. For more information, see the section "Troubleshooting Client Connectivity Errors," in this chapter.

15. **a.** Sometimes the solution to a problem is not technical at all, and instead it just requires a little common sense. Answers b, c, and d are all possible problems, but they are less likely than Answer a. For more information, see the section "The Art of Troubleshooting," in this chapter.

16. **b, c.** A bus network must have a terminator at each physical end of the bus. It must also be grounded at one end. Improper grounding or faulty termination can lead to random network problems such as those described. Answer a is not correct because 10Base2 networks do not use hubs or switches. 10Base2 has a maximum cable length of 185 meters; therefore, Answer d is not valid either. For more information, see the section "Troubleshooting Topology Errors," in this chapter.

17. **a.** When you are working on an unfamiliar system, the first step should be to consult the documentation to gain as much information as you can about the server and the applications that run on it. All the other troubleshooting steps are valid, but they would be performed only after the information gathering process was complete. For more information, see the section "The Art of Troubleshooting," in this chapter.

18. **c.** By performing a baseline, it is possible to determine whether there is actually a problem with the NIC or whether the problem lies with another part of the server or network. All the answers are valid, but they would be performed only after the actual problem had been determined. For more information, see the section "Troubleshooting Wiring- and Infrastructure-Related Problems," in this chapter.

19. **c.** Windows 2000 systems use case-sensitive passwords. When a user enters a password, if the Caps Lock key is on and the user doesn't realize it, the password will be entered in the wrong case. All the other troubleshooting steps are valid, but you would perform Answer a first. For more information, see the section "Troubleshooting Client Connectivity Errors," in this chapter.

20. **a, c.** The information provided indicates that this user is the only one who is experiencing a problem. Therefore, it is likely that the configuration of the workstation or the physical connectivity is to blame. The "server not found" error message would appear before the user entered any user information. Or if he user had entered the wrong password and the server was able to be found, she would receive an "invalid password" message. Because only a single user has reported a problem, it is unlikely that the server is down. Therefore, it is unlikely that Answer d is correct. For more information, see the section "Troubleshooting Client Connectivity Errors," in this chapter.

APPLY YOUR KNOWLEDGE

Suggested Readings and Resources

1 Habraken, Joe. *Absolute Beginner's Guide to Networking,* third edition. Que Publishing, 2001.

2. Shinder, Debra Littlejohn. *Computer Networking Essentials.* Cisco Press, 2001.

3. Haugdahl, J. Scott. *Network Analysis and Troubleshooting.* Addison-Wesley, 2000.

4. Cisco Systems, Inc. *Internetworking Troubleshooting Handbook,* second edition. Cisco Press, 2001.

5. "Computer Networking Tutorials and Advice," `http://compnetworking.about.com`.

6. "TechEncyclopedia," `www.techencyclopedia.com`.

7. "Networking Technology Information from Cisco," `www.cisco.com/public/products_tech.shtml`.

8. "PC Hardware troubleshooting," `www.tomshardware.com`.

FINAL REVIEW

Fast Facts

Study and Exam Preparation Tips

Practice Exam

The fast facts listed in this chapter are designed as a refresher of key points and topics, knowledge of which is required to be successful on the Network+ certification exam. By using these summaries of key points, you can spend an hour prior to your exam to refresh your understanding of key topics and to ensure that you have a solid understanding of the objectives and the information you need in order to succeed in each major area of the exam.

This chapter is organized by test objective domains, highlighting the key points from each chapter. If you have a thorough understanding of the key points here, chances are good that you will pass the exam.

This chapter is designed as a quick study aid that you can use just prior to taking the exam. You should be able to review the fast facts here in less than an hour. This chapter cannot serve as a substitute for all the material supplied in this book. However, its key points should refresh your memory on critical topics. In addition to the information in this chapter, remember to review the glossary terms in Appendix A because they are intentionally not covered here.

CompTIA uses the following job domains, which are discussed in this book, to arrange the objectives for the Network+ exam:

▶ 1.0—Media and Topologies

▶ 2.0—Protocols and Standards

▶ 3.0—Network Implementation

▶ 4.0—Network Support

Fast Facts

NETWORK+

1.0—MEDIA AND TOPOLOGIES

Understanding media and topologies is important when designing and troubleshooting networks. Therefore, CompTIA has included several questions on the exam that are related to the different media types used with today's networks and their characteristics. In addition, the exam includes questions that test your knowledge of the various network topologies.

Network Types and Physical and Logical Topologies

The following are some of the important aspects of network types:

◆ There are two types of computer networks:

• **Peer-to-peer networks**—Peer-to-peer networks are useful for only relatively small networks. They are often used in small offices or home environments.

• **Client/server networks**—Client/server networks, also called server-centric networks, have clients and servers. Servers provide centralized administration, data storage, and security. The client system requests data from the server and displays the data to the end user.

The following are some of the important aspects of network topologies:

◆ Network topologies can be defined on a physical level or on a logical level.

◆ The bus network topology is also known as a *linear bus* because the computers in such a network are linked together using a single cable

called a *trunk,* or *backbone.* The following are important features of the bus topology:

• The computers can be connected to the backbone by a cable, known as a *drop cable*, or, more commonly, directly to the backbone, via T connectors.

• At each end of the cable, terminators prevent the signal from bouncing back down the cable.

• If a terminator is loose, data communications may be disrupted. Any other break in the cable will cause the entire network to fail.

Table 1 shows the advantages and disadvantages of the bus topology.

TABLE 1
BUS TOPOLOGY: FEATURES, ADVANTAGES, AND DISADVANTAGES

Features	Advantages	Disadvantages
It uses a single length of cable.	It is inexpensive and easy to implement.	It does not scale well; that is, it cannot be expanded easily.
Devices connect directly to the cable.	It doesn't require special equipment.	A break in the cable renders the entire segment unusable.
The cable must be terminated at both ends.	It requires less cable than other topologies.	It is difficult to troubleshoot.

◆ In a star topology, each device on the network connects to a centralized device via a single cable. The following are important features of the star topology:

• Computers in a star network can be connected and disconnected from the network without affecting any other systems.

- In a star configuration all devices on the network connect to a central device, and this central device creates a single point of failure on the network.

- The most common implementation of the physical star topology is the Ethernet 10BaseT standard.

Table 2 lists the features, advantages, and disadvantages of the star topology.

TABLE 2
STAR TOPOLOGY: FEATURES, ADVANTAGES, AND DISADVANTAGES

Features	Advantages	Disadvantages
Devices connect to a central point.	It can be easily expanded without disruption to existing systems.	It requires additional networking equipment to create the network layout.
Each system uses an individual cable to attach.	A cable failure affects only a single system.	It requires considerably more cable than other topologies, such as the linear bus.
Multiple stars can be combined to create a hierarchical star.	It is easy to troubleshoot.	Centralized devices create a single point of failure.

◆ In the ring topology, the network layout forms a complete ring. Computers connect to the network cable directly or, far more commonly, through a specialized network device. Breaking the loop of a ring network disrupts the entire network. Even if network devices are used to create the ring, the ring must still be broken if a fault occurs or the network needs to be expanded. Table 3 lists the features, advantages, and disadvantages of the ring topology.

TABLE 3
RING TOPOLOGY: FEATURES, ADVANTAGES, AND DISADVANTAGES

Features	Advantages	Disadvantages
Devices are connected in a closed loop or ring.	It is easy to troubleshoot.	A cable break can disrupt the entire network.
Dual-ring configuration can be used for fault tolerance.		Network expansion creates network disruption.

◆ The mesh topology requires each computer on the network to be individually connected to every other device. This configuration provides maximum reliability and redundancy for the network. Table 4 lists the features, advantages, and disadvantages of the mesh topology.

TABLE 4
MESH TOPOLOGY: FEATURES, ADVANTAGES, AND DISADVANTAGES

Features	Advantages	Disadvantages
A true mesh uses point-to-point connectivity between all devices.	Multiple links provide fault tolerance and redundancy.	It is difficult to implement.
A hybrid mesh uses point-to-point connectivity between certain devices, but not all of them.	The network can be expanded with minimal or no disruption.	It can be expensive because it requires specialized hardware and cable.

◆ Wireless networks use a centralized device known as a *wireless access point* (WAP) that transmits signals to devices with wireless network interface cards (NICs) installed in them. Table 5 lists the features, advantages, and disadvantages of wireless networks.

TABLE 5
WIRELESS NETWORKS: FEATURES, ADVANTAGES, AND DISADVANTAGES

Features	Advantages	Disadvantages
No physical connections are required.	It provides flexible network access.	It is still relatively new and expensive.
It can be used in local area network (LAN) or wide area network (WAN) environments.	It can be used in environments where physical access is not possible.	It has potential security issues. Speed is limited in certain implementations.

Standards and Access Methods

The following are descriptions of the Institute of Electrical and Electronics Engineers (IEEE) 802 standards:

◆ **802.1, internetworking**—Defines internetwork communications standards between devices and includes specifications for routing and bridging.

◆ **802.2, the LLC sublayer**—Defines specifications for the Logical Link Control (LLC) sublayer in the 802 standard series.

◆ **802.3, CSMA/CD**—Defines the carrier-sense multiple-access with collision detection (CSMA/CD) media access method used in Ethernet networks. This is the most popular networking standard used today.

◆ **802.4, a token passing bus (rarely used)**—Defines the use of a token-passing system on a linear bus topology.

◆ **802.5, Token Ring networks**—Defines Token Ring networking.

◆ **802.6, metropolitan area network (MAN)**—Defines a data transmission method called distributed queue dual bus (DQDB), which is designed to carry voice and data on a single link.

◆ **802.7, Broadband Technical Advisory Group**—Defines the standards and specifications of broadband communications methods.

◆ **802.8, Fiber-Optic Technical Advisory Group**—Provides assistance to other IEEE 802 committees on subjects related to the use of fiber-optics.

◆ **802.9, Integrated Voice and Data Networks Group**—Works on the advancement of integrated voice and data networks.

◆ **802.10, network security**—Defines security standards that make it possible to safely and securely transmit and exchange data.

◆ **802.11, wireless networks**—Defines standards for wireless LAN communication.

◆ **802.12, 100BaseVG-AnyLAN**—Defines standards for high-speed LAN technologies.

The Network+ exam focuses on the LAN standards 802.2, 802.3, 802.5, and 802.11.

Access methods govern the way in which systems access the network media and send data. Following are the key aspects of the CSMA/CD access method:

◆ CSMA/CD, which is defined in the IEEE 802.3 standard, is the most popular media access method because it is associated with Ethernet networking, which is by far the most popular networking system.

◆ CSMA/CD is known as a *contention media access method* because systems contend for access to the media. Table 6 shows the advantages and disadvantages of CSMA/CD.

TABLE 6
ADVANTAGES AND DISADVANTAGES OF CSMA/CD

Advantages	Disadvantages
It has low overhead.	Collisions degrade network performance.
It is able to utilize all available bandwidth when possible.	Priorities cannot be assigned to certain nodes.
	Performance degrades exponentially as devices are added.

Token passing is an access method that is specified in IEEE 802.5. Following are the important facts about token-passing networks:

◆ On a token-passing network, a packet called a *token* is passed among the systems on the network. The network has only one token, and a system can send data only when it has possession of the token.

◆ All cards in a token-passing network must operate at the same speed.

◆ Because a system can transmit only when it has the token, there is no contention, as with CSMA/CD.

◆ Ring networks are most commonly wired in a star configuration. In a Token Ring network, a multistation access unit (MSAU) is equivalent to a hub or switch on an Ethernet network.

◆ To connect MSAUs, the ring in (RI) and ring out (RO) configuration must be properly set.

Table 7 shows the advantages and disadvantages of token-passing networks.

TABLE 7
ADVANTAGES AND DISADVANTAGES OF TOKEN-PASSING NETWORKS

Advantages	Disadvantages
No collisions mean more consistent performance in high-load configurations.	The generation of a token creates network overhead.
Performance is consistently predictable, making token passing suitable for time-sensitive applications.	Network hardware is more complex and expensive than that used with other access methods.
	The maximum speed is limited due to the overhead of token passing and regeneration.

Media Considerations and Limitations

As a data signal travels through a specific media, it may be subjected to a type of interference known as *electromagnetic interference* (EMI). Following are important EMI facts:

◆ Many different factors cause EMI; common sources include computer monitors and fluorescent lighting fixtures.

◆ Copper-based media are prone to EMI, whereas fiber-optic cable is completely resistant to it.

Data signals may also be subjected to something commonly referred to as *crosstalk*, which occurs when signals from two cables in close proximity to one another interfere with each other.

Media has maximum lengths because a signal weakens as it travels farther from its point of origin. The weakening of data signals as they traverse the media is referred to as *attenuation*.

Two types of signaling methods are used to transmit information over network media:

◆ **Baseband**—Baseband transmissions typically use digital signaling over a single wire; the transmissions themselves take the form of either electrical pulses or light. Ethernet networks use baseband transmissions.

Using baseband transmissions, it is possible to transmit multiple signals on a single cable by using a process known as *multiplexing.*

◆ **Broadband**—Broadband signaling uses analog signals in the form of optical or electromagnetic waves over multiple transmission frequencies.

Dialog Modes

There are three main dialog modes:

◆ **Simplex**—The simplex mode allows only one-way communication through the media. A good example of simplex is a radio or television signal: There is only one transmitting device, and all other devices are receiving devices.

◆ **Half-duplex**—Half-duplex allows each device to both transmit and receive, but only one of these processes can occur at a time.

◆ **Full-duplex**—Full-duplex allows devices to receive and transmit simultaneously. A 100Mbps network card in full-duplex mode can operate at 200Mbps.

Network Media

Two types of coax are used in networking:

◆ **Thin coax**—Thin coax is only .25 inches in diameter and has a maximum cable length of 185 meters (that is, approximately 600 feet).

◆ **Thick coax**—Thick coax networks use a device called a *tap* to connect a smaller cable to the thick coax backbone. Thick coax has a 500-meter cable length.

There are two distinct types of twisted-pair cable: unshielded twisted-pair (UTP) and shielded twisted-pair (STP). STP has extra shielding within the casing, so it copes with interference and attenuation better than regular UTP.

The Electronic Industries Association/ Telecommunications Industry Association (EIA/TIA) has specified five categories of twisted-pair cable:

◆ **Category 1**—Voice-grade UTP telephone cable. Due to its susceptibility to interference and attenuation and its low bandwidth capability, Category 1 UTP is not practical for network applications.

◆ **Category 2**—Data-grade cable that is capable of transmitting data up to 4Mbps. Category 2 cable is, of course, too slow for networks. It is unlikely that you will encounter Category 2 used in any network today.

◆ **Category 3**—Data-grade cable that is capable of transmitting data up to 10Mbps. A few years ago, Category 3 was the cable of choice for twisted-pair networks. As network speeds pushed the 100Mbps speed limit, Category 3 became ineffective.

◆ **Category 4**—Data-grade cable that has potential bandwidth of 16Mbps. Category 4 cable was often implemented in the IBM Token Ring networks.

◆ **Category 5**—Data-grade cable that is capable of transmitting data at 100Mbps. Category 5 is the cable of choice on twisted-pair networks and is associated with Fast Ethernet technologies.

Fiber-optic cables are not susceptible to EMI or crosstalk, giving fiber-optic cable an obvious advantage over copper-based media. In addition, fiber-optic cable is highly resistant to attenuation.

Two types of optical fiber are available: single-mode and multimode.

Attachment unit interface (AUI) ports are network interface ports that are often associated with thick coax (that is, 10Base5) networks. The AUI port is a 15-pin socket to which a transceiver is connected.

SC and ST connectors are associated with fiber cabling, ST connectors offer a twist-type attachment, and SC connectors are push-on connectors.

RJ-45 connectors are used with UTP cable.

Table 8 summarizes the characteristics of the types of network cable.

TABLE 8
SUMMARY OF CABLE CHARACTERISTICS

Cable Type	Resistance to Attenuation	Resistance to EMI/Crosstalk	Cost of Implementation	Difficulty of Implementation
Thin coax	Moderate	Moderate	Low	Low
Thick coax	High	High	Moderate	Moderate
UTP	Low	Low	Low	Low
STP	Moderate	Moderate	Moderate	Low
Fiber-optic	Very high	Very high	Very high	Extremely difficult

10BaseX, 100BaseX, and 1000BaseX Standards

The following are important facts about the 10BaseX standards:

◆ 10Base2, sometimes called Thinnet or Thin Ethernet, is the 802.3 specification for a network that uses thin coaxial cable (that is, RG-58 cable).

◆ 10Base2 specifies a maximum speed of 10Mbps and uses BNC barrel and BNC T connectors to connect the cable and computers. At the physical ends of each cable segment, a 50-ohm terminator absorbs the signal, thus preventing signal reflection.

◆ Thinnet cable is prone to breaks, and a break anywhere in the cable renders the entire network unusable.

◆ The 10Base2 standard specifies a limit of 185 meters per segment (that is, approximately 600 feet).

◆ In a 10Base2 network, only 30 networked devices can be attached to a single segment. A maximum of 3 segments can have network devices connected.

◆ 10Base5 networks use thick coaxial cable (that is, RG-8 cable), also known as Thicknet or Thick Ethernet, and devices attach to it by using external transceivers and AUI ports.

◆ 10Base5 uses baseband transmission, has a maximum transfer rate of 10Mbps, and has a cable distance of 500 meters per segment.

Table 9 provides a summary of 100BaseX standards, and Table 10 provides a summary of 1000BaseX standards.

TABLE 9
SUMMARY OF 100BASEX STANDARDS

Characteristic	100BaseTX	100BaseT4	100BaseFX
Transmission Method	Baseband	Baseband	Baseband
Speed	100Mbps	100Mbps	100Mbps
Distance	100 meters	100 meters	412 meters (multi-mode, half-duplex)
			10,000 meters (single-mode, full-duplex)
Cable Type	Category 5 UTP, STP	Category 3, 4, 5	Fiber-optic
Connector Type	RJ-45	RJ-45	SC, ST, MIC

TABLE 10
SUMMARY OF 1000BASEX STANDARDS

Characteristic	1000BaseSX	1000BaseLX	1000BaseCX
Transmission Method	Baseband	Baseband	Baseband
Speed	1000Mbps	1000Mbps	1000Mbps
Distance	Half-duplex 275 (62.5 micron multimode fiber); half-duplex 316 (50 micron multimode fiber); full-duplex 275 (62.5 micron multimode fiber); full-duplex 550 (50 micron multimode fiber)	Half-duplex 316 (multimode and single-mode fiber); full-duplex 550 (multimode fiber); full-duplex 5000 (single-mode fiber)	25 meters for both full-duplex and half-duplex operations
Cable Type	62.5/125 and 50/125 multimode fiber	62.5/125 and 50/125 multimode fiber; two 10-micron single-mode optical fibers	Shielded copper cable
Connector Type	SC connector	SC connector	9-pin shielded connector, 8-pin Fibre Channel type 2 connector

Network Devices

Both hubs and switches are used in Ethernet networks. The following facts are relevant to hubs:

◆ Token Ring networks, which are few and far between, use special devices called multistation access units (MSAUs) to create the network.

◆ The function of a hub is to take data from one of the connected devices and forward it to all the other ports on the hub.

◆ Most hubs are referred to as *active* because they regenerate a signal before forwarding it to all the ports on the device. In order to do this, the hub needs a power supply.

◆ Passive hubs do not need power because they don't regenerate signals.

The following facts are relevant to switches:

◆ Rather than forward data to all the connected ports, a switch forwards data only to the port on which the destination system is connected.

◆ A switch makes forwarding decisions based on the Media Access Control (MAC) addresses of the devices connected to it in order to determine the correct port.

◆ In cut-through switching, the switch begins to forward the packet as soon as it is received.

◆ In store-and-forward switching, the switch waits to receive the entire packet before beginning to forward it.

◆ In fragment-free switching, the switch reads only the part of the packet that enables it to identify fragments of a transmission.

The following facts are relevant to both hubs and switches:

◆ Hubs and switches have two types of ports: medium-dependent interface (MDI) and medium-dependent interface crossed (MDI-X).

◆ A straight-through cable is used to connect systems to the switch or hub using the MDI-X ports.

◆ In a crossover cable, Wires 1 and 3 and Wires 2 and 6 are crossed.

◆ Both hubs and switches use light-emitting diodes (LEDs) to indicate certain connection conditions. At the very least, a link light on the hub indicates the existence of a live connection.

◆ Both hubs and switches are available in managed and unmanaged versions. A managed device has an interface through which it can be configured to perform certain special functions.

Bridges are used to divide up networks and thus reduce the amount of traffic on each network.

A bridge functions by blocking or forwarding data, based on the destination MAC address written into each frame of data.

Unlike bridges and switches, which use the hardware-configured MAC address to determine the destination of the data, routers use software-configured network addresses to make decisions.

With distance-vector routing protocols, each router communicates all the routes it knows about to all other routers to which it is directly attached.

Routing Information Protocol (RIP) is a distance-vector routing protocol for both Transmission Control Protocol (TCP) and Internetwork Packet Exchange (IPX).

Modems translate digital signals from a computer into analog signals that can travel across conventional phone lines.

Modems are controlled through a series of commands known as the Hayes AT command set:

Command	Result
ATA	Answers an incoming call
ATH	Hangs up the current connection
ATZ	Resets the modem
ATI3	Displays modem identification information

Following is a summary of UART chip speeds:

UART Chip	Speed (bps)
8250	9,600
16450	115,200
16550	115,200
16650	430,800

UART Chip	Speed (bps)
16750	921,600
16950	921,600

Table 11 summarizes the various devices used in networks.

TABLE 11
NETWORKING DEVICES SUMMARY

Device	Function/Purpose	Key Points
Hub	Connects devices on a twisted-pair network.	A hub does not perform any tasks besides signal regeneration.
Switch	Connects devices on a twisted-pair network.	A switch forwards data to its destination by using the MAC address embedded in each packet.
Bridge	Divides networks to reduce overall network traffic.	A bridge allows or prevents data from passing through it by reading the MAC address.
Router	Connects networks together.	A router uses the software-configured network address to make forwarding decisions.
Gateway	Translates from one data format to another.	Gateways can be hardware or software based. Any device that translates data formats is called a gateway.
CSU/DSU	Translates digital signals used on a LAN to those used on a WAN.	CSU/DSU functionality is sometimes incorporated into other devices, such as a router with a WAN connection.
Network card	Enables systems to connect to the network.	Network interfaces can be add-in expansion cards, PCMCIA cards, or built-in interfaces.
ISDN terminal	Connects devices to ISDN lines.	ISDN is a digital WAN adapter technology often used inplace of slower modem links. ISDN terminal adapters are required to reformat the data format for transmission on ISDN links.
System area network card	Used in server clusters to provide connectivity between nodes.	System area network cards are high-performance devices capable of coping with the demands of clustering applications.
WAP	Provides network capabilities to wireless network devices.	A WAP is often used to connect to a wired network, thereby acting as a link between wired and wireless portions of the network.
Modem	Provides serial communication capabilities across phone lines.	Modems modulate the digital signal into analog at the sending end and perform the reverse function at the receiving end.

2.0—PROTOCOLS AND STANDARDS

A MAC address is a 6-byte address that allows a NIC to be uniquely identified on the network. The first three bytes (00:D0:59) identify the manufacturer of the card; The last three bytes (09:07:51) are the Universal LAN MAC address, which makes the interface unique.

OSI Model

As data is passed up or down through the OSI model structure, headers are added (going down) or removed (going up) at each layer—a process called *encapsulation* (*added*) or *decapsulation* (*removed*).

Table 12 provides a summary of the OSI model layers, and Table 13 shows how each device maps to the OSI model.

TABLE 12
SUMMARY OF THE OSI MODEL

OSI Layer	Major Functions
Application	Provides access to the network for applications and certain end-user functions. Displays incoming information and prepares outgoing information for network access.
Presentation	Converts data from the application layer into a format that can be sent over the network. Converts data from the session layer into a format that can be understood by the application layer. Handles encryption and decryption of data. Provides compression and decompression functionality.
Session	Synchronizes the data exchange between applications on separate devices. Handles error detection and notification to the peer layer on the other device.
Transport	Establishes, maintains, and breaks connections between two devices. Determines the ordering and priorities of data. Performs error checking and verification and handles retransmissions, if necessary.
Network	Provides mechanisms for the routing of data between devices across single or multiple network segments. Handles the discovery of destination systems and addressing.
Data-link	Has two distinct sublayers: LLC and MAC. Performs error detection and handling for the transmitted signals. Defines the method by which the medium is accessed. Defines hardware addressing through the MAC sublayer.
Physical	Defines the physical structure of the network. Defines voltage/signal rates and the physical connection methods. Defines the physical topology.

TABLE 13
MAPPING DEVICE DRIVERS TO THE OSI MODEL

Device	OSI Layer at Which the Device Operates
Hub	Physical (Layer 1)
Switch	Data-link (Layer 2)
Bridge	Data-link (Layer 2)
Router	Network (Layer 3)
NIC	Data-link (Layer 2)

Application protocols map to the application, presentation, and session layers of the OSI model. Application protocols include AFT, FTP, TFTP, NCP, and SNMP.

Transport protocols map to the transport layer of the OSI model and are responsible for the transporting of data across the network. Transport protocols include ATP, NetBEUI, SPX, TCP, and UDP.

The NetBEUI protocol uses names as addresses.

Network protocols are responsible for providing the addressing and routing information. Network protocols include IP, IPX, and DDP.

RIP is responsible for the routing of packets on an IPX/SPX network.

Table 14 provides information on each protocol. Table 15 summarizes TCP/IP, including each protocol in the TCP/IP suite, Table 16 shows you the TCP/IP port assignments, and Table 17 describes the TCP/IP services.

TABLE 14
PROTOCOL SUMMARY

Protocol	Network Operating System	Routable?	Configuration	Primary Use
TCP/IP	Used by default with Unix, Linux, NetWare, and Windows systems; supported by Macintosh and just about every other computing platform available	Yes	Comparatively difficult to configure; has a number of different configuration requirements	Used on many networks of all shapes and sizes; is the protocol of the Internet
IPX/SPX	Used to be the default protocol for NetWare, but now TCP/IP is preferred; can also be used with Linux; Windows supports NWLink, a version of the IPX/SPX protocol suite that was created by Microsoft for cross-platform compatibility	Yes	Very easy to configure because most information is autoconfigured	Primarily used on legacy NetWare networks
AppleTalk	Used by Macintosh, with some support on other platforms	Yes	Minimal configuration difficulty; requires a node address (automatically assigned when systems boot) and a network address	Used on legacy Macintosh networks
NetBEUI	Used by Windows	No	Easy network configuration, requiring only the computer's NetBIOS name	Primarily used on small networks where routing is not required

TABLE 15
SUMMARY OF THE TCP/IP PROTOCOL SUITE

Protocol	Full Name	Description
IP	Internet Protocol	Connectionless protocol used for moving data around a network
TCP	Transmission Control Protocol	Connection-oriented protocol that offers flow control, sequencing, and retransmission of dropped packets
UDP	User Datagram Protocol	Connectionless alternative to TCP that is used for applications that do not require the functions offered by TCP
FTP	File Transfer Protocol	Protocol for uploading and downloading files to and from a remote host; also accommodates basic file management tasks

Protocol	Full Name	Description
TFTP	Trivial File Transfer Protocol	File transfer protocol that does not have the security or error-checking capabilities of FTP; uses UDP as a transport protocol and is therefore connectionless
SMTP	Simple Mail Transfer Protocol	Mechanism for transporting email across networks
HTTP	Hypertext Transfer Protocol	Protocol for retrieving files from a Web server
HTTPS	Hypertext Transfer Protocol Secure	Secure protocol for retrieving files from a Web server
POP/IMAP	Post Office Protocol/Internet Message Access Protocol	Used for retrieving email from a server on which the mail is stored
Telnet	Telnet	Allows sessions to be opened on a remote host
ICMP	Internet Control Message Protocol	Used for error reporting, flow control, and route testing
ARP	Address Resolution Protocol	Resolves IP addresses to MAC addresses, to enable communication between devices
NTP	Network Time Protocol	Used to communicate time synchronization information between devices

TABLE 16
SUMMARY OF TCP/IP PORT ASSIGNMENTS

Protocol	Port Assignment
FTP	21
SSH	22
Telnet	23
SMTP	25
DNS	53
TFTP	69
HTTP	80
POP3	110
NNTP	119
NTP	123
IMAP4	143
SNMP	161
HTTPS	443

TABLE 17
SUMMARY OF TCP/IP SERVICES

Service	Purpose/Function
DHCP/BOOTP	Automatically assigns IP addressing information
DNS	Resolves hostnames to IP addresses
NAT/ICS	Translates private network addresses into public network addresses
WINS	Resolves NetBIOS names to IP addresses
SNMP	Provides network management facilities on TCP/IP-based networks

TCP/IP

In a network that does not use DHCP, you need to watch for duplicate IP addresses that prevent a user from logging onto the network.

Following is a description of the classes of IP addresses:

◆ A Class A address uses only the first octet to represent the network portion, a Class B address uses two octets, and a Class C address uses three octets.

Class A addresses span from 1 to 126, with a default subnet mask of 255.0.0.0.

◆ Class B addresses span from 128 to 191, with a default subnet mask of 255.255.0.0.

◆ Class C addresses span from 192 to 223, with a default subnet mask of 255.255.255.0.

The 127 network ID is reserved for the local loopback.

An example of a valid IPv6 address is

42DE:7E55:63F2:21AA:CBD4:D773:CC21:554F

Public Versus Private Networks

A public network is a network to which anyone can connect, such as the Internet. Internet Assigned Numbers Authority (IANA) is responsible for assigning IP addresses to public networks.

A private network is any network to which access is restricted. Reserved IP addresses are 10.0.0.0, 172.16.0.0, and 192.168.0.0.

WAN Technologies

Table 18 summarizes the WAN technologies.

TABLE 18
WAN TECHNOLOGIES

WAN Technology	Speed	Supported Media	Switching Method Used	Key Characteristics
ISDN	BRI: 64Kbps to 128Kbps PRI: 64Kbps to 1.5Mbps	Copper/fiber-optic	Can be used for circuit-switching or packet-switching connections	ISDN can be used to transmit all types of traffic, including voice, video, and data. BRI uses 2B+D channels, PRI uses 23B+D channels. B channels are 64Kbps. ISDN uses the public network and requires dial-in access.
T-carrier (T1, T3)	T1: 1.544Mbps T3: 44.736Mbps	Copper/fiber-optic	Circuit switching	T-carrier is used to create point-to-point network connections for private networks.
FDDI	100Mbps	Fiber-optic	N/A	FDDI uses a dual-ring configuration for fault tolerance. FDDI uses a token-passing media-access method. FDDI uses beaconing for error detection.
ATM	1.544Mbps to 622Mbps	Copper/fiber-optic	Cell switching	ATM uses fixed cells that are 53 bytes long.

WAN Technology	Speed	Supported Media	Switching Method Used	Key Characteristics
X.25	56Kbps	Copper/fiber-optic	Packet switching	X.25 is limited to 56Kbps.

X.25 provides a packet-switching network over standard phone lines. |
| Frame Relay | 56Kbps to 1.544Mbps | Copper/fiber-optic | PVCs and SVCs | Frame Relay is a packet-oriented protocol, and it uses variable-length packets. |
| SONET | 51.8Mbps to 2.4Gbps | Fiber-optic | N/A | SONET defines synchronous data transfer over optical cable.

The European equivalent of SONET is SDH. |

Remote Access and Security Protocols

When a connection is made to the RAS server, the client is authenticated and the system that is dialing in becomes a part of the network.

RAS supports remote connectivity from all the major client operating systems.

Although the system is called RAS, the underlying technologies that enable the RAS process are dial-up protocols such as PPP and SLIP:

◆ SLIP also does not provide error checking or packet addressing, so it can be used only in serial communications.

◆ PPP provides a number of security enhancements compared to SLIP. The most important of these is the encryption of usernames and passwords during the authentication process.

Windows 2000 natively supports SLIP and PPP.

ICA protocol allows client systems to access and run applications on a server, using the resources of the server, with only the user interface, keystrokes, and mouse movement being transferred between the client and server computers.

IPSec is designed to encrypt data during communication between two computers. IPSec operates at the network layer of the OSI model and provides security for protocols that operate at higher layers of the OSI model.

L2F allows tunneling to be utilized as a connection method over insecure networks.

L2TP is a combination of PPTP and Cisco's L2F technology and uses tunneling to deliver data. L2TP operates at the data-link layer, making it protocol independent.

SSL is a security protocol that is used on the Internet. Secure Web site URLs begin with `https://` instead of `http://`. HTTPS connections require a browser to establish a secure connection. Secure SSL connections for Web pages are made through port 443 by default.

Kerberos provides a method to verify the identity of a computer system over an insecure network connection.

The security tokens used in Kerberos are known as *tickets*.

3.0—NETWORK IMPLEMENTATION

Fault tolerance involves ensuring that when network hardware or software fails, users on the network can still access the data and continue working with little or no disruption of service. One of the most common fault-tolerance solutions is RAID. Table 19 shows various RAID solutions.

TABLE 19
RAID SOLUTIONS

RAID Level	Description	Key Features	Minimum Disks Required
RAID 0	Disk striping	No fault tolerance; improved I/Operformance	2
RAID 1	Disk mirroring	Provides fault tolerance but at 50% disk overhead; can also be used with separate disk controllers, a strategy known as disk duplexing	2 (2 is also the maximum number of disks used for RAID 1.)
RAID 2	Disk striping with hamming code	Limited use	3
RAID 3	Disk striping with single-parity disk	Limited use	3
RAID 4	Disk striping with single-parity disk	Limited use	3
RAID 5	Disk striping with distributed parity	Widely used RAID solution; uses distributed parity	3
RAID 10	Striping with mirrored volumes	Increased performance with striping and offers mirrored fault tolerance	4

Backups

Table 20 describes various backup strategies.

TABLE 20
SUMMARY OF BACKUP STRATEGIES

Method	What Is Backed Up	Restore Procedure	Archive Bit
Full	All data	All data is restored from a single tape	Does not use the archive bit but clears it after files have been copied to tape
Incremental	All data changed since the last full or incremental backup	The restore procedure requires several tapes: the latest full backup and all incremental tapes since the last full backup.	Uses the archive bit and clears it after a file is saved to disk
Differential	All data changed since the last full backup	The restore procedure requires the latest full backup tape and the latest differential backup tape.	Uses the archive bit but does not clear it

You should use an off-site tape rotation scheme to store current copies of backups in a secure off-site location.

You should periodically introduce new tapes into the tape rotation and destroy the old tapes.

LANs and NAS

VLANs are used to segment networks. This is often done for organizational or security purposes.

NAS are used to offload data storage from traditional file servers. NAS devices are connected directly to the network and use the SMB and NFS application protocols.

Client Connectivity

At the very minimum, an IP address and a subnet mask are required to connect to a TCP/IP network. With just this minimum configuration, connectivity is limited to the local segment, and DNS and WINS resolution are not possible.

The Client for Microsoft Networks can be installed on a Windows 95, Windows 98, or Windows Me system to facilitate connection to a Windows Server platform such as Windows NT 4 Server or Windows 2000 Server.

To log onto a NetWare server, you might need a user-name, password, tree, and context.

Unix and Linux utilize the Network File System (NFS) protocol to provide file-sharing capabilities between computers.

Security: Physical, Logical, Passwords, and Firewalls

Physical security refers to the issues related to the physical security of the equipment that composes or is connected to the network.

Logical security is concerned with security of data while it is on the systems that are connected to the network.

Common password policies typically specify a minimum length for passwords, password expiration, prevention of password reuse, and prevention of easy-to-guess passwords.

A password that uses eight case-sensitive characters, with letters, numbers, and special characters, often makes a strong password.

User-level security offers greater security than share-level security.

Table 21 shows file permissions for a Windows 2000 server.

TABLE 21
FILE PERMISSIONS ON A WINDOWS 2000 SERVER

Right	Description
Full Control	Provides all rights
Modify	Allows files to be modified
Read & Execute	Allows files to be read and executed (that is, run)
List Folder Contents	Allows the files in a folder to be listed
Read	Allows a file to be read
Write	Allows a file to be written to

Valid file permissions on a Unix/Linux system include read, write, and execute.

When a user cannot access files that other users can access, you should verify that the correct permissions are set.

A firewall is a system or group of systems that controls the flow of traffic between two networks. A firewall often provides such services as NAT, proxy services, and packet filtering.

The TCP/IP protocol suite uses port numbers to identify what service a certain packet is destined for. By configuring the firewall to allow certain types of traffic, you can control the flow.

Proxy Servers

A proxy server acts as an intermediary between a user on the internal network and a service on the external network such as the Internet.

A proxy server enables a network to appear to external networks as a single IP address—the IP address of the external network interface of the proxy server.

A proxy server allows Internet access to be controlled. Having a centralized point of access allows for a great deal of control over the use of the Internet.

Port Blocking

Port blocking is one of the most widely used security methods on networks. Port blocking is associated with firewalls and proxy servers, although in fact it can be implemented on any system that provides a means to manage network data flow, according to data type.

4.0—Network Support

Network support includes utilities for monitoring and troubleshooting the network.

TCP/IP Utilities

ping is a command-line utility designed to test connectivity between systems on a TCP/IP-based network. Following are guidelines for using ping:

◆ You can ping the IP address of the local loopback adapter, by using the command ping 127.0.0.1. If this command is successful, you know that the TCP/IP protocol suite is installed correctly on your system and functioning.

◆ If you cannot ping other devices on your local network and you were able to ping your local NIC, you might not be connected to the network correctly, or there might be a cable problem on the computer. Trace route is a TCP/IP utility that is used to track the path a packet takes to reach a remote host and isolate where networks problems might be.

◆ Trace route reports the amount of time it takes to reach each host in the path. It is a useful tool for isolating bottlenecks in a network. ARP is the part of the TCP/IP suite whose function is to resolve IP addresses to MAC addresses.

◆ ARP operates at the network layer of the OSI model.

◆ netstat is used to view both inbound and outbound TCP/IP network connections.

◆ The netstat -r command can be used to display the routing table of the system.

◆ nbtstat is used to display protocol and statistical information for NetBIOS over TCP/IP connections.

◆ The ipconfig command shows the IP configuration information for all NICs installed within a system.

◆ The ipconfig /all command is used to display detailed TCP/IP configuration information.

◆ The `ipconfig /renew` command is used to refresh the system's DNS information.

◆ When looking for client connectivity problems using `ipconfig`, you should ensure that the gateway is correctly set.

◆ The `ifconfig` command is the Linux equivalent of the `ipconfig` command.

◆ `winipcfg` is the Windows 95, Windows 98, and Windows Me equivalent of the `ipconfig` command.

◆ The `nslookup` command is a TCP/IP diagnostic tool that is used to troubleshoot DNS problems.

DSL

Digital Subscriber Line (DSL) is an Internet access method that uses a standard phone line to provide high-speed Internet access.

A DSL modem connects to a system by using standard UTP and RJ-45 connectors.

Media Tools and LEDs

Following is a list of media tools and LED guidelines:

◆ A wire crimper is a tool that you use to attach media connectors to the ends of cables.

◆ Media testers, also called cable testers, are used to test whether a cable is working properly.

◆ An optical cable tester performs the same basic function as a wire media tester, but on optical media.

◆ The hardware loopback tests the outgoing signals of a device such as a network card.

◆ If a connection LED on a hub is not lit, all the physical connections are correct, and the connected system is powered on, you might have a faulty patch cable.

◆ If the LED on a network card is constantly lit, you might have a chattering network card.

Troubleshooting Steps

When presented with a troubleshooting scenario, consider the following procedures:

1. Establish what the symptoms are.

2. Identify the affected areas.

3. Establish what has changed.

4. Select the most probable cause.

5. Implement a solution.

6. Test the results.

7. Recognize the potential effects of the solution.

8. Document the solution.

These study and exam prep tips provide some general guidelines to help prepare for the Network+ exam. The information here is organized into three sections. The first section addresses pre-exam preparation activities and covers general study tips. Following this are some tips and hints for the actual test-taking situation. Before tackling those areas, however, you should think a little bit about how you learn.

LEARNING AS A PROCESS

To best understand the nature of preparation for the exams, it is important to understand learning as a process. You are probably aware of how you best learn new material. You might find that outlining works best for you, or you might be a visual learner who needs to "see" things. Whatever your learning style, test preparation takes place over time. Obviously, you cannot start studying for the Network+ exam the night before you take it; it is very important to understand that learning is a developmental process. And as part of that process, you need to focus on what you know and what you have yet to learn.

Learning takes place when we match new information to old. You have some previous experience with computers, and now you are preparing for the Network+ exam. Using this book, software, and supplementary materials will not just add incrementally to what you know; as you study, you will actually change the organization of your knowledge as you integrate this new information into your existing knowledge base. This will lead you to a more comprehensive understanding of the tasks and concepts outlined in the CompTIA objectives and of computing in general. Again, this happens as a repetitive process rather than as a singular event. If you keep this model of learning in mind as you prepare for the exam, you will make the best decisions concerning what to study and how much more studying you need to do.

Study and Exam Prep Tips

STUDY TIPS

There are many ways to approach studying, just as there are many different types of material to study. The following tips, however, should work well for the type of material covered on the Network+ exam.

Study Strategies

Although individuals vary in the ways they learn, some basic principles apply to everyone. You should adopt some study strategies that take advantage of these principles. One of these principles is that learning can be broken into various depths. Recognition (of terms, for example) exemplifies a surface level of learning in which you rely on a prompt of some sort to elicit recall. Comprehension or understanding (of the concepts behind the terms, for example) represents a deeper level of learning. The ability to analyze a concept and apply your understanding of it in a new way represents an even deeper level of learning.

Your learning strategy should enable you to know the material at a level or two deeper than mere recognition. This will help you do well on the exam. You will know the material so thoroughly that you can easily handle the recognition-level types of questions used in multiple-choice testing. You will also be able to apply your knowledge to solve new problems.

Macro and Micro Study Strategies

One strategy that can lead to this deeper learning includes preparing an outline that covers all the objectives for the exam. You should delve a bit further into the material and include a level or two of detail beyond the stated objectives for the exam. Then you should expand the outline by coming up with a statement of definition or a summary for each point in the outline.

An outline provides two approaches to studying. First, you can study the outline by focusing on the organization of the material. You can work your way through the points and subpoints of your outline, with the goal of learning how they relate to one another. You should be certain, for example, that you understand how each of the main objective areas is similar to and different from the others.

Next, you can work through the outline, focusing on learning the details. You should memorize and understand terms and their definitions, facts, rules and strategies, advantages and disadvantages, and so on. In this pass through the outline, you should attempt to learn detail rather than the big picture (the organizational information that you worked on in the first pass through the outline).

Research has shown that attempting to assimilate both overall and detail types of information at the same time can interfere with the overall learning process. To best perform on the exam, you should separate your studying into these two approaches.

Active Study Strategies

You should develop and actually exercise an active study strategy. You should write down and define objectives, terms, facts, and definitions. In human information-processing terms, writing forces you to engage in more active encoding of the information. Just reading over the information exemplifies more passive processing.

Next, you should determine whether you can apply the information you have learned by attempting to create examples and scenarios on your own: Think about how or where you could apply the concepts you are learning. Again, you should write down this information to process the facts and concepts in a more active fashion.

Common Sense Strategies

Finally, you should follow common sense practices when studying. You should study when you are alert, reduce or eliminate distractions, take breaks when you become fatigued, and so on.

Pretesting Yourself

Pretesting enables you to assess how well you are learning. One of the most important aspects of learning is meta-learning. *Meta-learning* has to do with realizing when you know something well or when you need to study some more. In other words, meta-learning is the ability to recognize how well or how poorly you have learned the material you are studying.

For most people, meta-learning can be difficult to assess objectively. Practice tests are useful in that they objectively reveal what you have learned and what you have not learned. You should practice test information to guide review and further study. Developmental learning takes place as you cycle through studying, assessing how well you have learned, reviewing, and assessing again until you think you are ready to take the exam.

You might have noticed the practice exam included in this book. You can use it as part of the learning process. The ExamGear software on the CD-ROM also provides a variety of ways to test yourself before you take the actual exam. By using the practice exam, you can take an entire timed, practice test quite similar in nature to the actual Network+ exam. You can use the ExamGear Adaptive Exam option to take the same test in an adaptive testing environment. This mode monitors your progress as you are taking the test, to offer you more difficult questions as you succeed. By using the Study Mode option, you can set your own time limit, focus only on a particular domain (for instance, configuration) and also receive instant feedback on your answers.

You should set a goal for your pretesting. A reasonable goal would be to score consistently in the 90% range.

See Appendix D, "Using the *ExamGear, Training Guide Edition*, Software," for a more detailed explanation of the test engine.

EXAM PREP TIPS

The Network+ certification exam is a standardized, computerized, fixed-form exam that reflects the knowledge domains established by CompTIA.

The original fixed-form, computerized exam is based on a fixed set of exam questions. The individual questions are presented in random order during a test session. If you take the same exam more than once, you will see the same number of questions, but you won't necessarily see the exact same questions. This is because two or three final forms are typically assembled for such exams. These are usually labeled Forms A, B, and C.

As suggested previously, the final forms of a fixed-form exam are identical in terms of content coverage, number of questions, and allotted time, but the questions differ. You might notice, however, that some of the same questions appear on, or are shared among, different final forms. When questions are shared among multiple final forms of an exam, the percentage of sharing is generally small. Many final forms share no questions, but some older exams might have a 10% to 15% duplication of exam questions on the final exam forms.

Fixed-form exams also have a fixed time limit in which you must complete the exam. The ExamGear test engine on the CD-ROM that accompanies this book provides fixed-form exams.

Finally, the score you achieve on a fixed-form exam is based on the number of questions you answer correctly. The exam's passing score is the same for all final forms of a given fixed-form exam.

Table 1 shows the format for the exam.

Exam	Time Limit in Minutes	Number of Questions	Passing %
Network+ exam	90	72	75

Remember that you should not dwell on any one question for too long. Your 90 minutes of exam time can be consumed very quickly.

Given all these different pieces of information, the task now is to assemble a set of tips that will help you successfully tackle the Network+ certification exam.

More Exam Prep Tips

Generic exam-preparation advice is always useful. Tips include the following:

◆ Become familiar with networking terms and concepts. Hands-on experience is one of the keys to success. Review the exercises throughout this book.

◆ Review the current exam preparation guide on the CompTIA Web site.

◆ Memorize foundational technical detail, but remember that you need to be able to think your way through questions as well.

◆ Take any of the available practice tests. We recommend the ones included in this book and the ones you can create by using the ExamGear software on the CD-ROM.

◆ Look at the CompTIA Web site for samples and demonstration items.

Tips for During the Exam Session

The following generic exam-taking advice that you have heard for years applies when taking the Network+ exam:

◆ Take a deep breath and try to relax when you first sit down for the exam session. It is very important to control the stress you might (naturally) feel when taking exams.

◆ You will be provided scratch paper. Take a moment to write down on this paper any factual information and technical detail that you committed to short-term memory.

◆ Carefully read all information and instruction screens. These displays have been put together to give you information relevant to the exam you are taking.

◆ Read the exam questions carefully. Reread each question to identify all relevant details.

◆ Tackle the questions in the order in which they are presented. Skipping around will not build your confidence; the clock is always counting down.

◆ Do not rush, but also do not linger on difficult questions. The questions vary in degree of difficulty. Don't let yourself be flustered by a particularly difficult or verbose question.

◆ Note the time allotted and the number of questions appearing on the exam you are taking. Make a rough calculation of how many minutes you can spend on each question, and use this to pace yourself through the exam.

◆ Take advantage of the fact that you can return to and review skipped or previously answered questions. Record the questions you cannot answer confidently, noting the relative difficulty of each question, on the scratch paper provided. After you have made it to the end of the exam, return to the troublesome questions.

◆ If session time remains after you have completed all questions (and if you aren't too fatigued!), review your answers. Pay particular attention to questions that seem to have a lot of detail or that involve graphics.

◆ As for changing your answers, the general rule of thumb is don't! If you read a question carefully and completely and you thought you knew the right answer, you probably did. Do not second-guess yourself. If as you check your answers, one clearly stands out as being incorrectly marked, of course you should change it. If you are at all unsure, however, go with your first impression.

If you have done your studying and follow the preceding suggestions, you should do well. Good luck!

This exam consists of 72 questions that reflect the material covered in this book. The questions are representative of the types of questions you should expect to see on the Network+ exam; however, they are not intended to match exactly what is on the exam.

Some of the questions require that you deduce the best possible answer. Often, you are asked to identify the best course of action to take in a given situation. You must read the questions carefully and thoroughly before you attempt to answer them. It is strongly recommended that you treat this exam as if it were the actual exam. When you take it, time yourself, read carefully, and answer all the questions to the best of your ability.

The answers to all the questions appear in the section following the exam. Check your letter answers against those in the answers section, and then read the explanations provided. You might also want to return to the chapters in the book to review the material associated with any incorrect answers.

Practice Exam

1. Which layer of the OSI model is responsible for placing the signal on the network media?

    a. Physical

    b. Data-link

    c. MAC

    d. LLC

2. As system administrator, you have been asked to install a NetWare 5.x server system on your network. You have 20 Windows 98 workstations and 4 Linux systems that are used as clients. Which of the following can you install on the Windows 98 systems to allow you to connect to the NetWare server? (Choose the two best answers.)

    a. Novell Client for Windows 95/98

    b. Microsoft Client for NetWare Networks

    c. Novell CAFS Client

    d. Nothing, as long as TCP/IP is the default protocol

3. You are a network administrator managing a midsized network that uses a NetWare print server, a Windows application server, and a Linux firewall server. One of your servers loses network connectivity; you type `ifconfig` at the command line to see if the server has a valid IP address. Which server has lost connectivity?

    a. The firewall server.

    b. The print server.

    c. The application server.

    d. `ifconfig` is not a valid command on any of these platforms.

4. You are managing a network that uses both a Unix server and a Windows 2000 server. Which of the following protocols can you use to transfer files between the two servers?

    a. Telnet

    b. PPP

    c. FTP

    d. PPTP

5. You have been called by a user who complains that access to a Web page is very slow. What utility can you use to find the bottleneck?

    a. `ping`

    b. Telnet

    c. `tracert`

    d. `nbtstat`

6. During a busy administrative week, you install a new virus suite in your network of 55 computers, a new RAID array in one of the servers, and a new office suite on 25 of the computer systems. After all the updates, you are experiencing system errors throughout the entire network. Which of the following would you do to help isolate the problem?

    a. Disable the RAID array

    b. Uninstall the office suite

    c. Check the virus suite vendor's Web site for system patches or service packs

    d. Reinstall the virus software

7. What utility do you use to check the IP configuration on a Windows 95 or Windows 98 workstation?

    a. `netstat`

    b. `winipcfg`

    c. `ping`

    d. `ipconfig`

8. When a system running TCP/IP receives a data packet, which of the following does it use to determine what service to forward the packet to?

   a. Port number

   b. Packet ID number

   c. Data IP number

   d. IP protocol service type

9. Which of the following backup methods clear the archive bit? (Choose the two best answers.)

   a. Differential

   b. Sequential

   c. Full

   d. Incremental

10. You are troubleshooting a server connectivity problem on your network—a Windows 95 system is having trouble connecting to a Windows 2000 Server. Which of the following commands would you use to display per-protocol statistics on the workstation system?

    a. arp -a

    b. arp -A

    c. nbtstat -s

    d. nbtstat -S

    e. netstat -s

11. You are working as a network administrator on a Unix system. The system uses dynamic name resolution. What is used to dynamically resolve a hostname on a Unix server?

    a. IPX

    b. ARP

    c. DNS

    d. LMHOSTS

12. During the night, one of your servers powers down. Upon reboot, print services do not load. Which of the following would be the first step in the troubleshooting process?

    a. Examine the server log files

    b. Reboot the server

    c. Reinstall the printer

    d. Reinstall the printer software

13. Which of the following technologies uses Category 5 cable?

    a. 100BaseTX

    b. Fiber-optic

    c. 10Base5

    d. 10Base2

14. Which of the following utilities can be used to view the current protocol connections on a system?

    a. ping

    b. netstat

    c. Telnet

    d. tracert

15. Which of the following protocols are part of the TCP/IP protocol suite? (Choose the three best answers.)

    a. AFP

    b. FTP

    c. DHCP

    d. HTTP

    e. NCP

16. Which of the following are connectionless protocols? (Choose the three best answers.)

   a. IP

   b. SPX

   c. IPX

   d. UDP

17. Which of the following networking standards specifies a maximum segment length of 100 meters?

   a. 10Base2

   b. 10Base5

   c. 10BaseYX

   d. 10BaseT

18. After several passwords have been compromised in your organization, you have been asked to implement a networkwide password policy. Which of the following represents the most practical and secure password policy?

   a. Daily password changes

   b. Weekly password changes

   c. Monthly password changes

   d. Password changes only after an account has been compromised

19. You are experiencing a problem with a workstation and want to ping the local host. Which of the following are valid ways to check your local TCP/IP connection? (Choose the two best answers.)

   a. `ping host`

   b. `ping localhost`

   c. `ping 127.0.0.1`

   d. `ping 127.0.0.0`

20. Which of the following network devices operates at the physical layer of the OSI model?

   a. Router

   b. Hub

   c. Bridge

   d. NIC

21. You have been asked to implement a RAID solution on one of your company's servers. You have two hard disks and two hard disk controllers. Which of the following RAID levels could you implement? (Choose the three best answers.)

   a. RAID 0

   b. RAID 1

   c. Disk duplexing

   d. RAID 10

   e. RAID 5

22. Which of the following represents a Class B IP address?

   a. 191.23.21.54

   b. 125.123.123.2

   c. 24.67.118.67

   d. 255.255.255.0

23. What utility would produce the following output?

```
Proto Local Address Foreign Address
State
TCP   laptop:1028   LAPTOP:0      LISTENING
TCP   laptop:1031   LAPTOP:0      LISTENING
TCP   laptop:1093   LAPTOP:0      LISTENING
TCP   laptop:50000  LAPTOP:0      LISTENING
TCP   laptop:5000   LAPTOP:       LISTENING
TCP   laptop:1031   n218.         ESTABLISHED
                    audiogalaxy.com:ftp
TCP   laptop:1319   h24-67-184-65.ok.
                    shawcable.net:nbsess
```

a. `netstat`

b. `nbtstat`

c. `ping`

d. `tracert -R`

24. You have been called in to troubleshoot a problem with a newly installed email application. Internal users are able to communicate with each other via email, but neither incoming nor outgoing Internet email is working. You suspect a problem with the port-blocking configuration of the firewall system that protects the Internet connection. Which of the following ports would you allow, to cure the problems with the email? (Choose the two best answers.)

a. 20

b. 25

c. 80

d. 110

e. 443

25. What is the default subnet mask for a Class B network?

a. 255.255.255.224

b. 255.255.255.0

c. 127.0.0.1

d. 255.255.0.0

26. At which OSI layer does TCP operate?

a. Network

b. Transport

c. Session

d. Presentation

27. What is the basic purpose of a firewall system?

a. It provides a single point of access to the Internet.

b. It caches commonly used Web pages, thereby reducing the bandwidth demands on an Internet connection.

c. It allows hostnames to be resolved to IP addresses.

d. It protects one network from another by acting as an intermediary system.

28. Email and FTP work at which layer of the OSI model?

a. Application

b. Session

c. Presentation

d. User

29. You have been tasked with installing five new Windows 98 client systems, including the Novell Client software. Which pieces of information will you need during the Novell Client install to configure the connection to the NetWare server? (Choose the two best answers.)

a. Target NDS replica name

b. NDS tree name

c. Username

d. The context in which the user resides

e. Password

f. Domain name

30. While reviewing the security logs for your server, you notice that a user on the Internet has attempted to access your internal mail server. Although it appears that the user's attempts were unsuccessful, you are very concerned about the

possibility that your systems may be compromised. Which of the following solutions are you most likely to implement?

a. A more secure password policy

b. A firewall system at the connection point to the Internet

c. File-level encryption

d. Kerberos authentication

31. Which of the following pieces of information is not likely to be supplied via DHCP?

a. IP address

b. NetBIOS computer name

c. Subnet mask

d. Default gateway

32. While troubleshooting a network connectivity problem, you notice that the network card in your system is operating at 10Mbps in half-duplex mode. At what speed is the network link operating?

a. 2.5Mbps

b. 5Mbps

c. 10Mbps

d. 11Mbps

33. Which of the following is a valid IPv6 address?

a. 42DE:7E55:63F2:21AA:CBD4:D773

b. 42CD:7E55:63F2:21GA:CBD4:D773:
   CC21:554F

c. 42DE:7E55:63F2:21AA

d. 42DE:7E55:63F2:21AA:CBD4:D773:
   CC21:554F

34. While troubleshooting a network connectivity problem on a Windows 2000 Server, you need to

view a list of the IP addresses that have been resolved to MAC addresses. Which of the following commands would you use to do this?

a. `arp -a`

b. `nbtstat -a`

c. `arp -d`

d. `arp -s`

35. Which of the following statements best describes RAID 5?

a. A RAID 5 array consists of at least two drives. Parity information is written across both drives to provide fault tolerance.

b. A RAID 5 array consists of at least three drives and distributes parity information across all the drives in the array.

c. A RAID 5 array consists of at least three drives and stores the parity information on a single drive.

d. A RAID 5 array consists of at least four drives. The first and last drives in the array are used to store parity information.

36. Which of the following IEEE specifications does CSMA/CD relate to?

a. 802.11b

b. 802.2

c. 802.5

d. 802.3

37. While you are troubleshooting a sporadic network connectivity problem on a Windows 2000 system, a fellow technician suggests that you run the `ping -t` command. What is the purpose of this command?

a. It shows the route taken by a packet to reach the destination host.

b. It shows the time, in seconds, that the packet takes to reach the destination.

c. It allows the number of ping messages to be specific.

d. It pings the remote host continually until it is stopped.

38. Which of the following statements best describes NAS?

   a. It provides address translation services to protect the identity of client systems.

   b. It refers to a storage device that is attached to a host system such as a server.

   c. It refers to a storage device that is attached directly to the network media.

   d. It refers to a small, dedicated network of storage devices.

   e. It is a directory services system used on NetWare networks.

   f. It provides a mechanism for users to access areas of a hard disk on a Linux system.

39. What type of physical topology is shown in the following diagram?

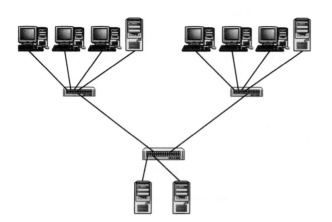

a. Hierarchical star

b. Ring

c. Star

d. Mesh

40. A remote user calls you to report a problem she is having connecting to the corporate network over her DSL connection. The user is able to connect to the Internet and browse Web pages, but she can't connect to the corporate remote access gateway. Which of the following troubleshooting steps would you perform first?

   a. Check the corporate remote access gateway to see if it is running and operating correctly

   b. Have the user reboot her system

   c. Have the user reconfigure the IP address on her system to one of the address ranges used on the internal corporate network, and then try again

   d. Have the user power cycle the DSL modem and try again

41. By using network monitoring tools, you determine that your 10Base2 network is suffering performance degradation from too many collisions. Which of the following devices could you use to divide up the network and so reduce the number of collisions?

   a. Ethernet switch

   b. Source-route bridge

   c. MSAU

   d. Transparent bridge

42. What command would generate the following output?

```
7    60 ms    30 ms    40 ms  home-
➥gw.st6wa.ip.att.net [192.205.32.249]
8    30 ms    40 ms    30 ms  gbr3-
➥p40.st6wa.ip.att.net [12.123.44.130]
9    50 ms    50 ms    60 ms  gbr4-
➥p10.sffca.ip.att.net [12.122.2.61]
10   60 ms    60 ms    60 ms  gbr3-
➥p10.la2ca.ip.att.net [12.122.2.169]
11   90 ms    60 ms    70 ms  gbr6-
➥p60.la2ca.ip.att.net [12.122.5.97]
```

a. ipconfig

b. netstat

c. ping

d. tracert

43. Your manager has asked you to implement security on your peer-to-peer network. Which of the following security models offers the highest level of security for this type of network?

a. Share level

b. User level

c. Password level

d. Layered

44. You are working on a Linux system and are having problems pinging a remote system by its hostname. DNS resolution is not configured for the system. What file might you look in to begin troubleshooting the resolution problem?

a. RESOLV

b. STATICDNS

c. PASSWD

d. HOSTS

45. You are tasked with specifying a way to connect two buildings across a parking lot. The distance between the two buildings is 78 meters. An underground wiring duct exists between the two buildings, although there are concerns about using it because it also houses high-voltage electrical cables. The budget for the project is very tight, but your manager still wants you to specify the most suitable solution. Which of the following cable types would you recommend?

a. Fiber-optic

b. UTP

c. Thin coax

d. STP

46. You are attempting to configure a client's email program. The user can receive mail but is unable to send any. In the mail server configuration screen of the mail application, you notice that the Type of Outgoing Mail Server field is blank. This explains why the client is unable to send mail. Which of the following protocols are you most likely to enter as a value in the Type of Outgoing Mail Server field?

a. NMP

b. POP3

c. SMTP

d. IMAP

47. A user calls to inform you that she can't access the Internet from her system. When you visit the user, you run the ipconfig /all utility and see the following information. What is the most likely reason the user is having problems accessing the Internet?

```
C:\>ipconfig /all

Windows 2000 IP Configuration
        Host Name . . . . . . . . . . .
        ➥: LAPTOP
        Primary DNS Suffix  . . . . . . . :
        Node Type . . . . . . . . . . .
        ➥ : Broadcast
```

```
        IP Routing Enabled. . . . . . . . :
        ➥No
        WINS Proxy Enabled. . . . . . . . :
        ➥No

Ethernet adapter Local Area Connection:
        Connection-specific DNS Suffix  . :
        Description . . . . . . . . . . . :
        ➥Intel 8255x-based PCI Ethernet
        Physical Address. . . . . . . . . :
        ➥00-D0-59-09-07-51
        DHCP Enabled. . . . . . . . . . . :
        ➥No
        IP Address. . . . . . . . . . . . :
        ➥192.168.2.1
        Subnet Mask . . . . . . . . . . . :
        ➥255.255.255.0
        Default Gateway . . . . . . . . . :
        DNS Servers . . . . . . . . . . . :
        ➥192.168.2.10
        ➥192.168.2.20
```

a. The system is on a different subnet than the DNS servers.

b. DHCP is not enabled.

c. The subnet mask is incorrect.

d. The default gateway setting is not configured.

48. Your ISP account manager suggests that it might be appropriate for you to install a DNS server internally. Which of the following functions does the DNS server provide?

   a. It performs network address translation services.

   b. It streamlines the resolution of NetBIOS names to IP addresses.

   c. It allows some hostname-to-IP address resolutions to occur internally.

   d. It allows users to retrieve Internet Web pages more quickly.

49. Which of the following is not one of the private address ranges?

   a. 192.168.x.x

   b. 10.x.x.x

   c. 172.16.x.x

   d. 224.181.x.x

50. Which of the following is a valid MAC address?

   a. 00:D0:59:09:07:51

   b. 00:D0:59

   c. 192.168.2.1

   d. 00FE:56FE:230F:CDA2:00EB:32EC

   e. 00:DG:59:09:07:51

51. If you contacted IANA, what would you most likely be trying to do?

   a. Get a new telephone number

   b. Get an IP address to connect a system to a public network

   c. Get an Internet domain name reassigned

   d. Get an IP address to connect a system to a private network

52. Which of the following technologies can be implemented on a switch to create multiple separate networks?

   a. Proxy

   b. Subnet masking

   c. NAS

   d. VLAN

53. Which of the following protocols are responsible for network addressing? (Choose the two best answers.)

    a. IP

    b. SPX

    c. IPX

    d. TCP

54. You are configuring a new NAS system. The configuration utility gives you the option to choose what application-level protocol you want to use with the system. Which of the following protocols are you likely to choose? (Choose the two best answers.)

    a. NCP

    b. SMB

    c. TCP

    d. NFS

55. For many years, the design department and the marketing department have operated separate networks. The design department uses AppleTalk, and the marketing department uses Token Ring. Now, the two departments have decided that they want to be able to access files from each other's servers. What network device or service would you implement to facilitate this?

    a. Gateway

    b. Source-route bridge

    c. Router

    d. Transparent bridge

56. Which of the following connectors would you use when working with fiber-optic cable? (Choose the two best answers.)

    a. RJ-11

    b. SC

    c. RJ-45

    d. ST

    e. BNC

    f. Vampire tap

57. Which of the following is not a commonly implemented feature of a firewall system?

    a. NAT

    b. Packet filtering

    c. Proxy

    d. NAS

58. You are the network administrator for a Token Ring network. An NIC in a system fails, and you replace it with a new one. However, the system is still unable to connect to the network. What is the most likely cause of the problem?

    a. The NIC is set to the wrong ring speed.

    b. The NIC is a 100Mbps card, and the ring is configured for only 10Mbps.

    c. The NIC is set to full-duplex, and the ring is running at only half-duplex.

    d. The NIC is faulty.

59. You have enabled HTTPS because of concerns about the security of your Web server application, which runs on a Web server system in the DMZ of your corporate network. However, remote users are now unable to connect to the application. Which of the following is the most likely reason for the problem?

    a. Port 80 is being blocked on the corporate firewall.

    b. Port 443 is being blocked on the corporate firewall.

    c. Remote users need to enable HTTPS support in their Web browsers.

d. Port 110 is being blocked on the corporate firewall.

60. Which of the following is a valid Class A IP address?

   a. 124.254.254.254

   b. 127.0.0.1

   c. 128.16.200.12

   d. 131.17.25.200

61. A user calls you from a hotel room. He has tried numerous times to dial in to the corporate RAS server, but the modem in his system is reporting a "no dial tone" error. When he plugs the hotel telephone back in to the phone socket, he gets a dial tone and is able to dial out successfully. What is the most likely cause of the problem?

   a. The phone line in the room is analog.

   b. The phone line in the room is faulty.

   c. The modem is faulty.

   d. The phone line in the room is digital.

62. Which of the following is not a valid file permission on a Windows 2000 system?

   a. Read

   b. Attribute

   c. Execute

   d. Write

63. What utility would you use to view the TCP connections that have been established between two systems?

   a. `netstat`

   b. `nbtstat`

   c. `tracert`

   d. `ipconfig`

64. Which of the following authentication systems uses tickets as part of the authentication process?

   a. HTTPS

   b. POP3

   c. Kerberos

   d. SSL

65. On an AppleTalk network, what is the function of AARP?

   a. It is a distance-vector routing protocol.

   b. It allows the resolution of AppleTalk addresses to MAC addresses.

   c. It allows the resolution of MAC addresses to AppleTalk addresses.

   d. It is a link-state routing protocol.

66. What term is used to describe the process of using parts of the node address range of an IP address as network IDs?

   a. Subnetting

   b. Supernetting

   c. Subnet masking

   d. Super routing

67. You are configuring a router. According to the manual, you will need a transceiver to connect to the LAN ports of the router. What kind of physical interface does the router have?

   a. AUI

   b. MSAU

   c. RJ-11

   d. BNC

68. In a hardware loopback plug, which wire numbers are connected? (Choose the two best answers.)

    a. 3 and 5

    b. 1 and 3

    c. 1 and 2

    d. 3 and 4

    e. 2 and 6

69. Which of the following network types is easiest to add new nodes to?

    a. Bus

    b. Ring

    c. Star

    d. Mesh

70. What kind of connector would you use to make a patch cable for a 10BaseT network?

    a. RJ-45

    b. RJ-11

    c. RJ-13

    d. BNC

71. Which TCP/IP port number is used by DNS?

    a. 21

    b. 25

    c. 53

    d. 110

72. What is the purpose of implementing fault tolerance?

    a. It reduces the amount of time the administrator spends performing backups.

    b. It promotes data availability by eliminating a single point of failure.

    c. It allows systems to be brought back online more quickly.

    d. It protects data from accidental deletion.

ANSWERS TO EXAM QUESTIONS

1. **a.** The physical layer of the OSI seven-layer model is responsible for placing the signal on the network media. The data-link layer (Answer b) is responsible for physical addressing and media access. MAC and LLC (Answers c and d) are sublayers of the data-link layer. For more information, see Chapter 4, "The OSI Model."

2. **a, b.** The Microsoft Client for NetWare Networks or the Novell Client for Windows 95/98 can be installed on the Windows 98 systems to facilitate connectivity. There is no such thing as the Novell CAFS client (Answer c). Although TCP/IP can be used to connect to certain versions of Novell NetWare, client software is needed unless NetWare 6 is being used (Answer d). For more information, see Chapter 11, "Configuring Network Connectivity."

3. **a.** The `ifconfig` command is used on a Linux system to determine the IP configuration of the system. With NetWare you use the `config` command to obtain information about network addresses. On a Windows 2000 system, the `ipconfig` command is used to view the networking configuration including the IP address. `ifconfig` can be used on Unix/Linux platforms to view the networking configuration. For more information, see Chapter 13, "Troubleshooting Connectivity."

4. **c.** FTP can be used to transfer files between Windows and Unix systems. FTP is part of the TCP/IP protocol suite and is platform independent. The Telnet utility is used to open a virtual terminal session on a remote host (Answer a). PPP is used to establish communications over a serial link; thus, Answer b is incorrect. PPTP is used to establish a secure link over a public network such as the Internet (Answer d). For more information, see Chapter 6, "Working with TCP/IP."

5. **c.** `tracert` is a Windows command that can be used to display the full path between two systems, including the number of hops between the systems. The `ping` utility (Answer a) can be used to test connectivity between two devices, but it only reports the time taken for the round trip; it does not give information about the time it takes to complete each hop in the route. The Telnet utility (Answer b) is used to open a virtual terminal session on a remote host. The `nbtstat` command (Answer d) is used to view statistical information about the NetBIOS status of a system. For more information, see Chapter 13.

6. **c.** Because the system errors are networkwide, it is likely that the cause of the problem in this scenario lies with the virus suite because it is installed on all computers. To troubleshoot such a problem, it would be a good idea to check for patches or updates on the vendor's Web site. A problem with a RAID array (Answer a) would affect only the server in which it is installed, not the entire network. Because the office suite (Answer b) was installed on only some of the systems, it can be eliminated as a problem because all the systems are affected. The virus software (Answer d) appears to be the cause of the problem, but re-installing it is unlikely to help. For more information, see Chapter 15, "Troubleshooting Procedures and Best Practices."

7. **b.** On Windows client-based systems such as Windows 95, Windows 98, and Windows Me, the `winipcfg` utility can be used to verify the TCP/IP configuration of the system. The same command does not work on Windows server systems. The `netstat` utility (Answer a) is used to view protocol statistics information. The `ping` utility (Answer c) is used to test the connectivity between two systems on a TCP/IP network. The `ipconfig` utility (Answer d) is used view the TCP/IP configuration on a Windows NT or Windows 2000 system. For more information, see Chapter 13.

8. **a.** The service to which a data packet is destined is determined by the port number to which it is sent. Answers b, c, and d are not valid. For more information, see Chapter 6.

9. **c, d.** Both the full and incremental backup methods clear the archive bit, to indicate which data does and does not need to be backed up. In a differential backup (Answer a), the archive bit is not cleared. Sequential (Answer b) is not a type of backup. For more information, see Chapter 10, "Fault Tolerance, Disaster Recovery, VLANs, and NAS."

10. **e.** The `netstat -s` command can be used to display per-protocol statistics. The `arp` command (Answers a and b) is used to view a list of the IP address-to-MAC address resolutions performed by the system. The `nbtstat` utility (Answers c and d) is used to view protocol statistics for the NetBIOS protocol. For more information, see Chapter 13.

11. **c.** DNS is used on Unix-based systems to resolve hostnames. IPX (Answer a) is a network-layer connectionless protocol. ARP (Answer b) resolves IP addresses to MAC addresses. The `LMHOSTS` file (Answer d) is used on Windows systems to resolve NetBIOS names to IP addresses. For more information, see Chapter 6.

12. **a.** In this scenario your first step is to gather information by examining the server log files. When you have that information, you can proceed with the rest of the troubleshooting process. Rebooting the server (Answer b) is unlikely to cure the problem. Before you reinstall the printer (Answer c), you should examine the log files to see if there are any problems reported in the server log files. Before you reinstall the printer software (Answer d), you should examine the log files to see if there are any problems reported in the server log files. For more information, see Chapter 15.

13. **a.** 100BaseTX uses Category 5 cable. Fiber-optic (Answer b) is a type of cable. 10Base5 (Answer c) is an Ethernet networking standard that uses thick coaxial cable. 10Base2 (Answer d) is an Ethernet networking standard that uses thin coaxial cable. For more information, see Chapter 2, "Cabling and Connectors."

14. **b.** The netstat -a command can be used to display the current connections and listening ports. The ping utility (Answer a) is used to test connectivity between two devices on a TCP/IP network. Telnet (Answer c) is an application-level protocol that allows a virtual terminal session on a remote host. The tracert utility (Answer d) allows a path to be traced between two hosts. For more information, see Chapter 13.

15. **b, c, d.** FTP, DHCP, and HTTP are all protocols in the TCP/IP protocol suite. AFP (Answer a) is part of the AppleTalk protocol suite. NCP (Answer e) is part of the IPX/SPX protocol suite. For more information, see Chapter 6.

16. **a, c, d.** UDP, IPX, and IP are all connectionless protocols. SPX (Answer b) is a connection-oriented protocol. For more information, see Chapter 5, "Overview of Network Protocols."

17. **d.** 10BaseT has a maximum segment length of 100 meters. The maximum length of a 10Base2 segment (Answer a) is 185 meters. The maxim length of a 10Base5 segment (Answer b) is 500 meters. Answer c is not a valid networking standard. For more information, see Chapter 2.

18. **c.** Changing passwords too frequently is not practical, and changing them too infrequently represents a security risk. Monthly password changing is adequate for most environments. Changing passwords too frequently (Answers a and b) can cause problems because users might have problems remembering passwords and so use passwords that are too similar to one another. Although passwords should be changed if they are compromised, they should also be changed periodically making Answer d incorrect. For more information, see Chapter 12, "Securing the Network."

19. **b, c.** To verify the IP configuration on a local computer system, you can either ping the localhost or the IP address 127.0.0.1. The default hostname for a system is localhost, not host which means Answer a is incorrect. Answer d is not correct as this is the network address for the Class A loopback address, not a valid node loopback address. For more information, see Chapter 13.

20. **b.** A network hub operates at the physical layer of the OSI model. A router (Answer a) operates at the network layer of the OSI model. A bridge (Answer c) operates at the data-link layer of the OSI model. An NIC (Answer d) operates at the data-link layer of the OSI model. For more information, see Chapter 4.

21. **a, b, c.** With two hard disks and two controllers, you can implement RAID 0, RAID 1, and disk duplexing. RAID 5 (disk striping with parity; Answer e) requires a minimum of three disks to

be implemented. RAID 10 (Answer d) is a combination of RAID 1 (disk mirroring) and RAID 0 (disk striping). RAID 10 requires a minimum of four disks. For more information, see Chapter 10.

22. **a.** The first octet of a Class B addresses must be in the range 128 to 191. Answers a and b represent Class A addresses. Class A addresses run from 1 to 126. Answer d is not a valid IP address. For more information, see Chapter 6.

23. **a.** The netstat utility can be used to display protocol statistic and TCP/IP network connections. The nbtstat utility (Answer b) shows statistical information about the NetBIOS over TCP/IP connections. The ping utility (Answer c) is used to test the connectivity between two devices on a TCP/IP network. The tracert utility (Answer d) traces the path between two hosts on a TCP/IP network. For more information, see Chapter 13.

24. **b, d.** TCP/IP port 25 is used by SMTP. TCP/IP port 110 is used by POP3. Because SMTP is used to send mail and POP3 is used to retrieve mail, port 25 and port 110 are the two ports that would need to be allowed for incoming and outgoing Internet email. TCP/IP port 21 (Answer a) is used by FTP. TCP/IP port 80 (Answer c) is used by HTTP. TCP/IP port 443 (Answer e) is used by HTTPS. For more information, see Chapter 6.

25. **d.** The default subnet mask for a Class B address is 255.255.0.0. Answer a is incorrect because it is not the default subnet mask for a Class B network. Answer b is the default subnet mask for a Class B network. Answer c is the local loopback address. For more information, see Chapter 6.

26. **b.** TCP operates at the transport layer of the OSI model. Answers a, c, and d are all incorrect; TCP does not operate at the network layer. For more information, see Chapter 5.

27. **d.** The purpose of the firewall system is to protect one network from another. One of the most common places to use a firewall is to protect a private network from a public one such as the Internet. Answer a is incorrect because although a firewall can provide a single point of access, that is not its primary purpose. Answer b more accurately describes the function of a proxy server. Answer c describes the function of a DNS server. For more information, see Chapter 12.

28. **a.** Both email and FTP work at the application layer of the OSI model. Email and FTP are application-layer protocols, not session-layer protocols. User (Answer d) is not a layer of the OSI model. For more information, see Chapter 4.

29. **b, d.** To configure the client software, you need to have the context and the NDS tree name. The username and password are not needed during the client configuration, but they are necessary to actually log on. Answer a is incorrect because you do not need to specify the target NDS replica to connect to a NetWare server. The username (Answer c) is needed only when the user actually wants to authenticate to the server. The password (Answer e) is needed only when the user actually wants to authenticate to the server. A domain name (Answer f) does not need to be specified in order to connect to a NetWare server. For more information, see Chapter 11.

30. **b.** To prevent unauthorized access to a private network from the Internet, you can use a firewall server to restrict outside access. Implementing a more secure password policy (Answer a) is a good idea, but it is not the best choice of those available. Implementing a file-level encryption system (Answer c) is a good idea, but it is not the best choice of those available. Kerberos (Answer d) is an authentication system, not a method to prevent unauthorized access to the system. For more information, see Chapter 12.

31. **b.** The NetBIOS computer name is not supplied to client systems by a DHCP server. The IP address (Answer a) is one of the pieces of information provided by DHCP. The subnet mask (Answer c) is one of the pieces of information provided by DHCP. The default gateway (Answer d) is one of the pieces of information supplied by DHCP. For more information, see Chapter 6.

32. **c.** Because the NIC is functioning at half-duplex 10Mbps, the transfer rate is 10Mbps. None of the other answers are correct. For more information, see Chapter 3, "Networking Components and Devices."

33. **d.** IPv6 uses a 128-bit address, which is expressed as eight octet pairs in hexadecimal format, separated by colons. Because it is hexadecimal, only numbers and the letters A through F can be used. An IPv6 address is composed of eight hexadecimal octets. Only numbers and the letters A through F can be used. For more information, see Chapter 6.

34. **a.** The arp -a command is used to display the IP addresses that have been resolved to MAC addresses. The nbtstat command (Answer b) is used to view protocol statistics for NetBIOS connections. arp -d (Answer c) is not a valid command. The arp -s command (Answer d) allows you to add static entries to the ARP cache. For more information, see Chapter 13.

35. **b.** A RAID 5 array consists of at least three hard disks and stripes parity information across all disks in the array. RAID 5 (disk striping with parity; Answer a) requires at least three drives. The parity information is stored in a stripe across all three drives in the array (Answer b). RAID 5 requires only three drives which makes Answer d incorrect. For more information, see Chapter 10.

36. **d.** CSMA/CD relates to the IEEE specification 802.3. The 802.11b (Answer a) standard describes wireless LAN networking. The 802.2 (Answer b) standard defines the media access methods for various networking standards. The 802.5 (Answer c) standard defines Token Ring networking. For more information, see Chapter 1, "Introduction to Networking."

37. **d.** The ping -t command is used to send continuous ping requests to a remote system. The ping request will continue until it is manually stopped. The trace route utility (Answer a) performs this task. The ping command (Answer b) shows the amount of time a packet takes to complete the round trip from the host to the destination. Answer c is incorrect because the ping command with the -n switch performs this task. For more information, see Chapter 13.

38. **c.** NAS is a storage device that attaches directly to the network media. DAS attaches to a server. Answer a describes NAT. Answer b describes DAS. Answer d describes a SAN, Answer e describes NDS and Answer f describes NFS. For more information, see Chapter 10.

39. **a.** The diagram in the question shows a hierarchical star topology. The difference between a hierarchical star and a regular star topology is that hierarchical is a layered architecture. Answers b, c, and d are all incorrect. The figure does not represent any of these network types. For more information, see Chapter 1.

40. **a.** In this scenario, you would first check the remote access gateway to see if it is running and operating correctly. Because the user can browse Web pages, this is not a connectivity problem. Answer b is incorrect because although rebooting the system might help, the system appears to be working correctly, and rebooting it is unlikely to cure the problem. The IP address configuration appears to be working because the user is able to access Web pages and so Answer c is incorrect.

The Internet connection appears to be working, so cycling the power on the DSL modem, as described in Answer d, is unlikely to help. For more information, see Chapter 15.

41. **d.** A transparent bridge is a device that can be used to divide up an Ethernet network to reduce collisions. Switches can also be used, but the network in the question is a 10Base2 network and uses coaxial cable rather than twisted-pair cable. Ethernet switches (Answer a) can be used only on networks that are created with twisted-pair cable. 10Base2 is a networking standard that uses thin coaxial cable. A source-route bridge (Answer b) is used on Token Ring networks. 10Base2 is an Ethernet networking standard. An MSAU (Answer c) is used on Token Ring networks. 10Base2 is an Ethernet networking standard. For more information, see Chapter 2.

42. **d.** The output displayed in this question is from the Windows tracert utility. Answers a, b and c are all incorrect. These utilities produce output that is different from the output shown. For more information, see Chapter 14, "Troubleshooting Tools and Utilities."

43. **b.** User-level security is more secure than share-level security and requires a user to provide a login ID, usually a username and password combination to access network resources. Answer a is incorrect because share-level security is not as secure as user-level security. Answers c and d are not accepted terms for describing levels of security. For more information, see Chapter 12.

44. **d.** The HOSTS file is used to manually configure hostname resolution, and if there is a problem with hostname resolution, entries in this file must be checked. Answers a and b are incorrect because files are not used on a Linux system. Answer c is incorrect because the PASSWD file is

used to store user account information. For more information, see Chapter 6.

45. **a.** Fiber-optic cable provides the most resistance to EMI and therefore is often used in environments where there is a risk of interference. Although it is inexpensive, UTP (Answer b) cable has very low resistance to EMI. Therefore, it should not be run near high-voltage electric cables. Thin coax (Answer c) has low resistance to EMI. Therefore, it should not be run near high-voltage electric cables. STP (Answer d) has a good level of resistance to EMI, but it is still not as resistant as fiber-optic. Not factoring in the cost, fiber optic is the most suitable solution. For more information, see Chapter 2.

46. **c.** SMTP is used for sending email. Answer a is not a valid answer. Answers b and d are incorrect because POP3 and IMAP are email retrieval protocols, not protocols for sending email. For more information, see Chapter 6.

47. **d.** The most likely cause of the problem is that the default gateway is not configured. Answer a is incorrect because from the output it appears that the DNS servers are on the same subnet as this system. Answer b does not apply because addressing is configured statically, so there is no DHCP service. This is not a problem, however. Answer c is incorrect because the subnet mask is the correct default subnet mask for a Class C network. For more information, see Chapter 13.

48. **c.** DNS allows hostname resolutions to occur internally. In most cases companies use a DNS server provided by the ISP. In some cases, however, it might be appropriate to have a DNS server on the internal network. Answer a is incorrect as NAT is normally a function of firewall or proxy servers. Answer b describes the purpose of a WINS server. Answer d describes the function of a proxy server. For more information, see Chapter 6.

49. **d.** Private address ranges are designed for use on private networks. The ranges are 192.168.X.X, 10.X.X.X, and 172.16.X.X–172.32.X.X. Answers a, b, and c are all valid private IP address ranges. For more information, see Chapter 6.

50. **a.** The MAC address is a 6-byte address expressed in six pairs of hexadecimal values. Because it is hexadecimal, only the letters A through F and numbers can be used. Answer b is incorrect because MAC addresses are expressed as six hexadecimal pairs. Answer c shows an example of an IPv4 address. Answer d shows an example of an IPv6 address. Answer e is incorrect because MAC addresses are expressed in hexadecimal; therefore, only the letters A through F and numbers can be used. For more information, see Chapter 3.

51. **b.** IANA is responsible for assigning IP addresses for systems on public networks—specifically, the Internet. Answer a is incorrect. IANA is responsible for assigning IP addresses for use on public networks (such as the Internet). Answer c is incorrect because Domain names are administered by domain registry organizations. Answer d is incorrect because you don't need to apply for a network address for use on a private network. For more information, see Chapter 6.

52. **d.** A VLAN is implemented on a switch to create multiple separate networks. A proxy server (Answer a) is used to control access to the Internet. Subnet masking (Answer b) is not a valid method of creating separate networks. NAS (Answer c) describes storage devices that are attached directly to the network media. For more information, see Chapter 10.

53. **a, c.** IP and IPX are responsible for network addressing. Answers b and d are incorrect because SPX and TCP are transport-layer protocols and so are not responsible for network addressing. For more information, see Chapter 5.

54. **b, d.** The protocols used by NAS are SMB and NFS. NCP (Answer a) is part of the IPX/SPX protocol suite. It is responsible for providing access to network services. TCP (Answer c) is a connection-oriented transport protocol. For more information, see Chapter 10.

55. **a.** A gateway is used to translate between networks that use dissimilar protocols. In this question, it is used to translate between an AppleTalk network and a Token Ring network. A source-route bridge (Answer b) is used on Token Ring networks. A router (Answer c) is use to connect two networks. Strictly speaking, a router does not perform translation tasks, although the gateway functionality can be implemented on some routers. A transparent bridge (Answer d) is used to segregate Ethernet networks. For more information, see Chapter 3.

56. **b, d.** Fiber-optic cable can use either SC or ST type connectors. RJ-11 connectors (Answer a) are associated with telephone cable, RJ-45 (Answer c) connectors are associated with UTP cable, and BNC connectors (Answer e) are associated with thin coaxial cable. For more information, see Chapter 2.

57. **d.** A firewall can provide several different services to the network, including NAT, proxy services, and packet filtering. NAS is not a function of a firewall server. Answers a, b, and c are all incorrect because NAT, packet filtering, and proxy functionality are all commonly implemented on firewall systems. For more information, see Chapter 12.

58. **a.** When a new NIC is installed on a Token Ring network, the speed of the card has to be set to match the speed used by the network. Answer b is incorrect because Token Ring networks operate at either 4Mbps or 16Mbps. Answer c is incorrect because full-duplex connections are not used on

Token Ring networks. Answer d is incorrect because, although it is possible, a faulty card is not the most likely answer. For more information, see Chapter 1.

59. **b.** The most likely explanation is that port 443, the HTTPS default port, is being blocked by a corporate firewall. Port 80 (Answer a) is used by HTTP. All modern Web browsers support HTTPS automatically, therefore Answer c is incorrect. Port 110 (Answer d) is used by POP3. For more information, see Chapter 6.

60. **a.** Class A subnets use the range 1 to 126 for the value of the first octet. Answer b is the loopback address, which allows the IP stack functionality to be tested. Answers c and d are both addresses in the Class B range (128–191). Class A addresses run from 1 through 126. For more information, see Chapter 6.

61. **d.** Most modern phone systems are digital, and therefore, regular analog modems that require analog lines will not work. Answer a is incorrect because, if the phone line in the room were analog, the modem would probably work. Answer b is incorrect because, the phone line in the room is not faulty because the user is able to use it to call you and report the problem. Answer c is incorrect because if the modem is able to get as far as reporting a "no dial tone" error, it is most likely working correctly. For more information, see Chapter 8, "Remote Access and Security Protocols."

62. **b.** The attribute file permission is not a valid NTFS file permission. Answers a, c, and d are all incorrect because they are all valid file permissions on a Windows 2000 system. For more information, see Chapter 12.

63. **a.** The netstat utility allows you to view the TCP/IP connections between two systems.

The nbtstat utility (Answer b) is used to see the status of NetBIOS over TCP/IP connections. The tracert utility (Answer c) is used to track the path that a packet of data takes between two hosts. The ipconfig utility (Answer d) is used to view the IP addressing configuration information on a system. For more information, see Chapter 14.

64. **c.** The Kerberos authentication system uses tickets as part of the authentication process. HTTPS (Answer a) is an implementation of SSL. It does not use tickets. POP3 (Answer b) is an email retrieval protocol. SSL (Answer c) does not use tickets. For more information, see Chapter 8, "Remote Access and Security Protocols."

65. **b.** AARP is used to map the AppleTalk addresses to both Ethernet and Token Ring physical addresses. The distance-vector routing protocol used on AppleTalk networks is RMTP which makes Answer a incorrect. Answer c is incorrect because AARP resolves AppleTalk addresses to MAC addresses—not the other way around. AARP is not a link-state routing protocol. For more information, see Chapter 5.

66. **a.** The term *subnetting* is used to refer to the process of using parts of the node address range for network addressing purposes. *Supernetting* (Answer b) refers to the process of borrowing parts of the network address portion of an assigned address to be used for node addressing. *Subnet masking* (Answer c) is the term used to describe the process of applying a subnet mask to an address. Answer d is not a valid term. For more informbion, see Chapter 6.

67. **a.** An AUI port is typically used to connect an external transceiver to a device such as a router. An MSAU (Answer b) is a type of network device used on Token Ring networks. RJ-11 (Answer c) is a connector type associated with telephone cable. BNC (Answer d) is a type of network

connector used on coaxial networks. For more information, see Chapter 2.

68. **b, e.** A hardware loopback plug connects the 2 and 6 wires and 1 and 3 wires to simulate a live network connection. Answers a, c, and d are all incorrect; these answers are not correct for the cable in a hardware loopback adapter. For more information, see Chapter 14.

69. **c.** Each node on a star network uses its own cable, which makes it easy to add users without disrupting current users. Adding a node to a bus network can sometimes involve breaking the segment, which makes it inaccessible to all other nodes on the network. This makes Answer a incorrect. Answer b is incorrect because a true ring network model would require that the ring be broken to add a new device. Answer d is incorrect because a mesh topology requires that every device be connected to every other device on the network. It is, therefore, quite difficult to expand a mesh network. For more information, see Chapter 1.

70. **a.** 10BaseT networks use twisted-pair cable and RJ-45 connectors. RJ-11 (Answer b) connectors are associated with telephone cable. RJ-T (Answer c) is not a valid type of connector. A BNC connector (Answer d) is associated with coaxial cable. The 10BaseT standard uses twisted-pair cable. For more information, see Chapter 2.

71. **c.** DNS uses TCP port 53. Port 21 (Answer a) is used by FTP. Port 25 (Answer b) is used by SMTP. Port 110 (Answer d) is used by POP3. For more information, see Chapter 6.

72. **b.** Fault tolerance promotes data availability by eliminating a single point of failure. Answer a is incorrect because, although fault tolerance may reduce the reliance on backups, they should still be performed. Answer c is incorrect because in the strict definition, being fault tolerant does not help a system get back online more quickly. Answer d is incorrect because being a fault tolerant system does not protect data from accidental deletion. For more information, see Chapter 10.

APPENDIXES

A Glossary

B Overview of the Certification Process

C What's on the CD-ROM

D Using the *ExamGear, Training Guide Edition* Software

Glossary

NUMBERS AND SYMBOLS

10Base2   The IEEE 802.3 specification for Ethernet at 10Mbps over thin coaxial cable. The maximum length of a 10Base2 segment is 185 meters (that is, 607 feet).

10Base5   The IEEE 802.3 specification for 10Mbps Ethernet using thick coaxial cable. The maximum length of a 10Base5 segment is 500 meters (that is, 1,640 feet).

10BaseT   The IEEE 802.3 specification for running Ethernet at 10Mbps over twisted-pair cabling. The maximum length of a 10BaseT segment is 100 meters (that is, 330 feet).

100BaseFX   The IEEE 802.3 specification for running Fast Ethernet at 100Mbps over fiber-optic cable. The maximum length of a 100BaseFX segment is 2000 meters (6,561 feet), in full duplex mode.

100BaseT   The IEEE 802.3 specification for running Ethernet at 100Mbps over twisted-pair cabling. The maximum length of a 100BaseT segment is 100 meters (that is, 330 feet).

100BaseT4   The IEEE specification that allows the use of Fast Ethernet (100Mbps) technology over existing Category 3 and Category 4 wiring, utilizing all four pairs of wires. The maximum length of a 100BaseT4 segment is 100 meters (that is, 330 feet).

100BaseTX   The IEEE 802.3u specification, also known as Fast Ethernet, for running Ethernet at 100Mbps over STP or UTP. The maximum length of a 100BaseTX segment is 100 meters (that is, 330 feet).

100BaseVG-AnyLAN   The IEEE 802.12 specification that allows data transmissions of 100Mbps over Category 3 cable, utilizing all sets of wires. *VG* in 100BaseVG-AnyLAN stands for *voice grade* because of its ability to be used over voice-grade cable. The maximum length of a 100BaseVG-AnyLAN segment is 100 meters (330 feet) on Category 3 cable, 150 meters (492 feet) on Category 5 cable, and 2000 meters (6,561 feet) on fiber-optic cable.

1000BaseX   The IEEE 802.3z specification, also known as Gigabit Ethernet, that defines standards for data transmissions of 1000Mbps (1Gbps).

A

ACK   The acknowledgment message sent between two hosts during a TCP session.

ACL (access control list)   The list of trustees assigned to a file or directory. A trustee can be any object that is available to the security subsystem.

Active Directory   An X.500-compliant directory services system created by Microsoft for use on Windows 2000 networks.

active hub   A hub that has power supplied to it for the purposes of regenerating the signals that pass through it.

active termination   A termination system used on a SCSI bus. Unlike passive termination, which uses voltage resistors, active termination uses voltage regulators to create the termination voltage.

address   A set of numbers, usually expressed in binary format, used to identify and locate a resource or device on a network.

administrator   A person who is responsible for the control and security of the user accounts, resources, and data on a network.

Administrator account   In a Windows NT system, the default account that has rights to access everything and to assign rights to other users on the network. Unlike other user accounts, the Administrator account cannot be deleted.

ADSL (Asymmetric Digital Subscriber Line)   A service that transmits digital voice and data over existing (analog) phone lines.

ANSI (American National Standards Institute)   An organization that publishes standards for communications, programming languages, and networking.

antivirus software   A type of software that detects and removes virus programs.

anycast address   An address that is used in ATM for shared multiple-end systems. An anycast address allows a frame to be sent to specific groups of hosts (rather than to all hosts, as with simple broadcasting).

application layer   Layer 7 of the OSI model, which provides support for end users and for application programs that are using network resources.

Application log   A log that is located in Windows NT/2000 Event Viewer and provides information on events that occur within an application.

archive bit   A flag that is set on a file after it has been created or altered. Some backup methods reset the flag to indicate that it has been backed up.

ARCnet (Attached Resource Computer Network)   A token-bus LAN technology used in the 1970s and 1980s.

ARP (Address Resolution Protocol)   A protocol in the TCP/IP protocol suite that is used to resolve IP addresses to MAC addresses.

ARP table   A table of entries used by ARP to store resolved ARP requests. Entries can also be stored manually.

array   A group of devices arranged in a fault-tolerant configuration. *See also* RAID.

ATM (Asynchronous Transfer Mode)   A high-speed WAN technology that uses fixed cells of 53 bytes each.

attenuation   The loss of signal that is experienced as data is transmitted across network media.

AUI (attachment unit interface)   An IEEE 802.3-specified interface that is used between a MAU and an NIC.

AUI connector   A 15-pin D-type connector that is sometimes used with Ethernet connections.

authentication   The process by which a user's identity is validated on a network. The most common authentication method is a username and password combination.

B

B (bearer) channel   In ISDN, the channel that carries the data. *See also* D channel.

backbone   A network segment that acts as a trunk between other network segments. Backbones are typically high-bandwidth implementations such as fiber-optic cable.

backup schedule   A document or another plan that defines the point at which backups are made, what backups are made, and what data is backed up.

bandwidth   The rated throughput capacity of a given network protocol or medium.

baseband   A term applied to any media that is capable of carrying only a single data signal at a time. *Compare with* broadband.

baseline   A measurement of performance of a device or system for the purposes of future comparison. Baselining is a common server administration task.

baud rate   The speed or rate of signal transfer. The word *baud* is derived from the name of French telegraphy expert J. M. Baudot.

BDC (backup domain controller)   A Windows NT server that provides a backup of the PDC's user, group, and security information. *See also* PDC.

binary   A base 2 numbering system that is used in digital signaling. It uses only the numbers 1 and 0.

Bindery   The name of the user account information database on NetWare servers up to and including NetWare 3.x

binding   The process of associating a protocol and an NIC.

biometrics   The science and technology of measuring and analyzing biological data. Biometrics is increasingly being used for security purposes, to analyze and compare characteristics such as voice patterns, retina patterns, and hand measurements.

BIOS (Basic Input/Output System)   A basic set of instructions that a device needs to operate.

bit   An electronic digit used in the binary numbering system. Bit is a contraction of the terms *binary* and *digit*.

blackout   A total loss of electrical power.

Blue Screen of Death   The term for the blue-screen STOP errors that occur and halt the system in Windows NT and Windows 2000.

BNC (British Naval Connector)   A T-shaped connector that is used to connect a device to a thin coaxial Ethernet network.

bound media   A term used to describe any media that have physical constraints, such as coaxial, fiber-optic, and twisted pair. *Compare with* unbound media.

boundless media   *See* unbound media.

BRI (Basic Rate Interface)   An ISDN digital communications line that consists of three independent channels: two B channels, each at 64Kbps, and one D channel, at 16Kbps. ISDN BRI is often referred to as 2B+D. *See also* ISDN, PRI.

bridge   A device that connects and passes packets between two network segments that use the same communications protocol. Bridges operate at the data-link layer of the OSI model. A bridge filters, forwards, or floods an incoming frame based on the MAC address of that frame.

bridging address table   A list of MAC addresses that a bridge keeps and uses when it receives packets. The bridge uses the bridging address table to determine which segment the destination address is on before it sends the packet to the next interface or drops the packet (if it is on the same segment as the sending node).

broadband   A communications strategy that uses analog signaling over multiple communications channels.

broadcast   A packet delivery system in which a copy of a packet is given to all hosts attached to the network.

broadcast storm   An undesirable condition in which broadcasts become so numerous as to bog down the flow of data across the network.

brouter   A device that can be used to combine the benefits of both routers and bridges. Its common usage is to route routable protocols at the network layer of the OSI model and to bridge nonroutable protocols at the data-link layer.

brownout   A short-term decrease in the voltage level, usually caused by the startup demands of other electrical devices.

buffer   An area of memory in a device that is used to store data before it is forwarded to another device or location.

bus   A path that is used by electrical signals to travel between the CPU and the attached hardware.

bus mastering   A bus accessing method in which the NIC takes control of the bus in order to send data through the bus directly to the system memory, bypassing the CPU.

bus topology   A linear LAN architecture in which all devices are connected to a common cable, referred to as a bus or backbone.

byte   A set of bits (usually 8 bits) that operate as a unit to signify a character.

C

cable modem   A device that provides Internet access over cable television lines.

cable tester   A device that is used to check for electrical continuity along a length of cable. *Cable tester* is a generic term that can be applied to devices such as volt/ohm meters and TDRs.

caching-only server   A type of DNS server that operates the same way as secondary servers except that a zone transfer does not take place when the caching-only server is started.

carrier   A signal that carries data. The carrier signal is modulated to create peaks and troughs, which represent binary bits.

CDDI (Copper Distributed Data Interface)   An implementation of the FDDI standard that uses copper cable rather than optical cable.

Centronics connector   A connector that uses teeth that snap into place to secure the connector.

change control   A process in which a detailed record of every change made to the network is documented.

channel   A communications path that is used for data transmission.

checksum   A basic method of error checking that involves calculating the sum of bits in a section of data and then embedding the result in the packet. When the packet reaches the destination, the calculation is performed again, to make sure the value is still the same.

CIDR (classless interdomain routing)   A technique that allows multiple addresses to be consolidated into a single entry.

circuit switching   A method of sending data between two parties, in which a dedicated circuit is created at the beginning of the conversation and broken at the end. All data transported during the session travels over the same path, or circuit.

Class A network   A TCP/IP network that uses addresses from 1 to 126 and supports up to 126 subnets with 16,777,214 unique hosts each.

Class B network   A TCP/IP network that uses addresses from 128 to 191 and supports up to 16,384 subnets with 65,534 unique hosts each.

Class C network   A TCP/IP network that uses addresses from 192 to 223 and supports up to 2,097,152 subnets with 254 unique hosts each.

client   A node that uses the services from another node on a network.

client/server networking A networking architecture in which front-end, or client, nodes request and process data stored by the back-end, or server, node.

clustering A technology that allows two or more computers to act as a single system to provide improved fault tolerance and load balancing.

coaxial cable A data cable, commonly referred to as *coax*, that is made of a solid copper core that is insulated and surrounded by braided metal and covered with a thick plastic or rubber covering. Coax is the standard cable used in cable television and in older bus topology networks.

CONFIG A command that is used on a NetWare server to see basic information such as the server name, NDS information, and the details of network interface configurations.

collision The result of two frames transmitting simultaneously on an Ethernet network and colliding, thereby destroying both frames.

collision domain A segment of an Ethernet network that is between managing nodes, where only one packet can be transmitted at any given time. Switches, bridges, and routers can be used to segment a network into separate collision domains.

collision light An LED on networking equipment that flashes to indicate a collision on the network. a collision light can be used to determine whether the network is experiencing a large number of collisions.

COM port (communication port) A connection through which serial devices and a computer's motherboard can communicate. A COM port requires standard configuration information, such as an IRQ, an I/O address, and a COM port number.

communication The transfer of information between nodes on a network.

concentrator Any device that acts as a connectivity point on a network.

connectionless communication Packet transfer in which delivery is not guaranteed.

connection-oriented communication Packet transfer in which delivery is guaranteed.

connectivity The linking of nodes on a network in order for communication to take place.

copy backup Normally, a backup of the entire hard drive. A copy backup is similar to a full backup, except the copy backup does not alter the state of the archive bits on files.

cost A value that is used to encourage or discourage the use of a certain route through a network. Routes that are to be discouraged are assigned a higher cost, and those that are to be encouraged are assigned a lower cost. *See also* metric.

cracker A person who attempts to break software code or gain access to a system to which he or she is not authorized. *See also* hacker.

cracking The process of attempting to break software code, normally to defeat copyright protection or alter the software's functioning. Also the process of attempting to gain unauthorized access to a computer system. *See also* hacking.

CRC (cyclical redundancy check) A method used to check for errors in packets that have been transferred across a network. A computation bit is added to the packet and recalculated at the destination, to determine whether the entire content of the packet has been transferred correctly.

crimper A tool that is used to join connectors to the ends of network cables.

crossover cable A UTP cable in which the 1 and 3 wires and the 2 and 6 wires are crossed for the purposes of placing the transmit line of one device on the receive line of the other. Crossover cables can be used to directly connect two devices—for example, two computer systems—or as a means to expand networks that use devices such as hubs or switches.

crosstalk Electronic interference that is caused when two wires are too close to each other.

CSMA/CA (carrier-sense multiple-access with collision avoidance) A contention media access method that uses collision-avoidance techniques.

CSMA/CD (carrier-sense multiple-access with collision detection) A contention media access method that uses collision-detection and retransmission techniques.

CSU (channel service unit) A network communications device that is used to connect to the digital equipment lines of the common carrier, usually over a dedicated line or Frame Relay. A CSU is used in conjunction with a DSU.

cut-through packet switching A switching method that does not copy the entire packet into the switch buffers. Instead, the destination address is captured into the switch, the route to the destination node is determined, and the packet is quickly sent out the corresponding port. Cut-through packet switching maintains a low latency.

D

D (delta) channel The channel used on ISDN to communicate signaling and other related information. Use of the D channel leaves the B channels free for data communication. *See also* B channel.

D-shell connector A connectors that is shaped like a letter D and uses pins and sockets to establish connections between peripheral devices, using serial or parallel ports. The number that follows *DB* in the name of a D connector is the number of pins used for connectivity; for example, a DB-9 connector has 9 pins and a DB-25 connector has 25 pins.

daemon A service or process that runs on a Unix or Linux server.

DAS (dual attached station) A device on an FDDI network that is connected to both rings. *Compare with* SAS.

DAT (digital audio tape) A tape recording technology that uses the helical scan recording method. This technology has been used in videotape recorders and VCRs since the 1950s.

Data field In a frame, the field or section that contains the data.

datagram An information grouping that is transmitted as a unit at the network layer. *See also* packet.

data-link layer Layer 2 of the OSI model, which is above the physical layer. Data comes off the cable, goes through the physical layer, and goes into the data-link layer. The data-link layer has two distinct sublayers: MAC and LLC.

DB-9 A 9-pin connector that is used for serial port or parallel port connection between PCs and peripheral devices.

DB-25 A 25-pin connector that is used for serial port or parallel port connection between PCs and peripheral devices.

DDNS (dynamic DNS) A form of DNS that allows systems to register and deregister themselves with the DNS system dynamically. This is in contrast with the conventional DNS system, in which entries must be made manually.

DDS (digital data storage) A format for storing computer data on a DAT. DDS-formatted tapes can be read by either a DDS or DAT drive. The original DDS standard specified a 4mm tape cartridge with a capacity of 1.3GB. Subsequent implementations of DDS have taken the capacity to 40GB with compression.

dedicated line A dedicated circuit that is used in WANs to provide a constant connection between two points.

default gateway   Normally a router or a multihomed computer to which packets are sent when they are destined for a host on a different network.

Delete or Erase   A right that is given to users, which allows them to delete a file or files in a directory or to delete a directory.

demarcation point   The point at which communication lines enter a customer's premises. Sometimes shortened to simply "demarc."

destination address   The network address to which the frame is being sent. In a packet, this address is encapsulated in a field of the packet so that all nodes know where the frame is being sent.

DHCP (Dynamic Host Configuration Protocol)   A protocol that provides dynamic IP addressing to workstations on the network.

dial-up networking   Refers to the connection of a remote node to a network using POTS.

differential backup   A backup of only the data that has been created or changed since the previous full backup. In a differential backup, the state of the archive bits is not altered.

directory services   The organization of the accounts and resources directory to help network devices locate service providers. Examples of directory services systems include Novell eDirectory and Microsoft Active Directory.

disaster recovery plan   A plan for implementing duplicate computer services in the event of a natural disaster, a human-made disaster, or another catastrophe. A disaster recovery plan includes offsite backups and procedures to activate information systems in alternative locations.

disk duplexing   A fault-tolerant standard that is based on RAID 1 that uses disk mirroring with dual disk controllers.

disk mirroring   A fault-tolerant standard that is defined as RAID 1 and mirrors data between two disks to create an exact copy.

disk striping   An implementation of RAID in which data is distributed across multiple disks in a stripe. Some striping implementations provide performance improvements (RAID 0), whereas others provide fault tolerance (RAID 5).

distance-vector routing   A type of routing in which a router uses broadcasts to inform neighboring routers on the network of the routes it knows about. *Compare with* link-state routing.

DIX (Digital, Intel, and Xerox)   A type of 15-pin connector that is used to connect to network media.

DLT (digital linear tape)   A high-performance and high-capacity tape backup system that offers capacities up to 220GB with compression.

DMA (direct memory access)   The process of transferring data directly into memory at high speeds, bypassing the CPU and incurring no processor overhead.

DNS (Domain Name Service)   A system that is used to translate domain names, such as www.quepublishing.com, into IP addresses, such as 165.193.123.44. DNS uses a hierarchical namespace that allows the database of hostname-to-IP address mappings to be distributed across multiple servers.

domain   A logical group of computers in a Windows NT/2000 network. Also, a section of the DNS namespace.

domain name server   A server that runs application software that allows the server to perform a role associated with the DNS service.

DoS (Denial of Service) attack   A type of hacking attack in which the target system is overwhelmed with requests for service, resulting in it not being able to service any requests—legitimate or otherwise.

downtime   A period of time during which a computer system or network is unavailable. This may be due to scheduled maintenance or to hardware or software failure.

drive mapping   A process through which an alias makes a network path appear as if it were a local drive.

DSL (Digital Subscriber Line)   A public network technology that delivers high bandwidth over conventional copper wiring over limited distances.

DSU (data service unit)   A network communications device that formats and controls data for transmission over digital lines. A DSU is used in conjunction with a CSU.

DTE (data terminal equipment)   A device used at the user end of a user network interface that serves as a data source, a destination, or both. DTE devices include computers, protocol translators, and multiplexers.

dumb terminal   A keyboard/monitor combination that allows access to a multiuser system but provides no processing or storage at the local level.

duplexing   In RAID, a RAID 1 mirror set in which each drive is connected to a separate controller to eliminate the single point of failure that the controller created.

dynamic routing   A routing system that allows routing information to be communicated between devices automatically and can recognize changes in the network topology and update routing tables accordingly. *Compare with* static routing.

dynamic window   A flow control mechanism that prevents the sender of data from overwhelming the receiver. The amount of data that can be buffered in a dynamic window varies in size, hence its name.

E

eDirectory   A standards-compliant directory services system created by Novell. eDirectory was originally implemented as NDS in versions of NetWare up to 5.0.

EIA (Electronic Industries Association)   A group that specifies electrical transmission standards.

EISA (Extended Industry Standard Architecture)   The successor to the ISA standard. EISA provides a 32-bit bus interface that is used in PCs.

EMI (electromagnetic interference)   External interference of electromagnetic signals that causes a reduction of data integrity and increased error rates in a transmission medium.

encapsulation   A technique that is used by layered protocols in which a layer adds header information to the protocol data unit from the layer above.

encryption   The modification of data for security purposes prior to transmission so that it is not comprehendable without the decoding method.

ERD (emergency repair disk)   A floppy disk that contains security files and resource configurations that are used for recovery when a Windows NT/2000 operating system becomes corrupt.

ESD (electrostatic discharge)   A condition that is created when two objects of dissimilar electrical charge come into contact with each other. The result is that a charge from the object with the higher electrical charge discharges itself into the object with the lower-level charge. This discharge can be extremely harmful to computer components and circuit boards.

Ethernet   The most common LAN technology. Ethernet can be implemented using coaxial, twisted-pair, or fiber-optic cable. Ethernet uses the CSMA/CD media access method and has various implementation standards.

Event Viewer   A troubleshooting tool that is available in both Windows NT and Windows 2000 systems. On Windows NT, the Event Viewer provides three logs that record system information: the System log, the Security log, and the Application log. More logs are included in the Windows 2000 version.

EXT2   The default file system used in Linux systems.

F

failover   The automatic switching from one device or system to another. Servers can be configured in a failover configuration so that if the primary server fails, the secondary server takes over automatically.

Fast Ethernet   The IEEE 802.3 specification for data transfers of up to 100Mbps over twisted-pair cable. *See also* 100BaseFX, 100BaseTX, 100BaseT, and 100BaseT4.

fault tolerance   The capability of a component or system to endure a failure.

FDDI (Fiber Distributed Data Interface)   A high-speed data transfer technology that is designed to extend the capabilities of existing LANs by using a dual-ring topology and a token-passing access method.

FDM (Frequency-Division Multiplexing)   A technology that divides the output channel into multiple smaller-bandwidth channels, each of which uses a different frequency range.

fiber-optic cable   Also known as fiber optics or optical fiber, a physical medium that is capable of conducting modulated light transmissions. Compared with other transmission media, fiber-optic cable is more expensive, but it is not susceptible to EMI or crosstalk, and it is capable of very high data rates.

fibre channel   A technology that defines full gigabit-per-second data transfer over fiber-optic cable.

firewall   A program, system, device, or group of devices that acts as a barrier between one network and another. Firewalls are configured to allow certain types of traffic to pass while blocking others.

FireWire   A high-speed serial bus technology that allows up to 63 devices to be connected to a system. FireWire provides sufficient bandwidth for multimedia operations and supports hot swapping and multiple speeds on the same bus.

fixed wireless   A technology that provides data communication capabilities between two fixed locations. Fixed wireless can be used as a private networking method but is also becoming increasingly common as an Internet access method.

flow control   A method of controlling the amount of data that is transmitted within a given period of time. There are different types of flow control. *See also* dynamic window, static window.

FQDN (fully qualified domain name)   The entire domain name that specifies the name of the computer as well as the domain in which it resides and the top-level DNS domain (for example, `www.quepublishing.com`).

fragment-free switching   A fast-packet-switching method that uses the first 64 bytes of a frame to determine whether the frame is corrupted. If this first part is intact, the frame is forwarded.

frame   A grouping of information that is transmitted as a unit across the network at the data-link layer of the OSI model.

FCS (Frame Check Sequence) field   A field of a packet that holds a CRC value to ensure that all of the frame's data arrives intact.

Frame Length field   In a data frame, the field that specifies the length of a frame.

Frame Relay   A high-speed data-link layer switching protocol that is used across multiple virtual circuits of a common carrier to give the end user the appearance of a dedicated line.

Frame Type field In a data frame, the field that names the protocol that is being sent in the frame.

frequency The number of cycles of an alternating current signal over a unit of time. Frequency is expressed in Hertz.

FTP (File Transfer Protocol) A protocol that provides for the transfer of files between two systems. FTP is part of the TCP/IP protocol suite.

full backup A backup in which files, regardless of whether they have been changed, are copied to the backup media. In a full backup, the archive bits of the files are reset.

full-duplex A system in which data is transmitted in two directions simultaneously. *Compare with* half-duplex.

G

gateway A hardware or software solution that enables communications between two dissimilar networking systems or protocols. A gateway can operate at any layer of the OSI model.

Gb (gigabit) 1 billion bits or 1000Mb.

Gbps (gigabits per second) The throughput of a given network medium in terms of 1 billion bps.

GFS (Grandfather-Father-Son) A backup strategy of maintaining backups on a daily, weekly, and monthly schedule. Backups are made on a five-day or seven-day schedule. A full backup is performed at least once a week. On all other days full, incremental, or differential backups (or no backups at all) are performed. The daily incremental, or differential, backups are known as the *son*. The *father* is the last full backup in the week (the weekly backup). The *grandfather* is the last full backup of the month (the monthly backup).

Gigabit Ethernet The IEEE 802.3z specification that defines standards for data transmissions of 1Gbps. *See also* 1000BaseX.

guaranteed flow control A method of flow control in which the sending and receiving hosts agree on a rate of data transmission. After the rate is determined, the communication takes place at the guaranteed rate until the sender is finished. No buffering takes place at the receiver.

H

hacker A person who carries out hacking on a computer software program. *See also* cracker.

hacking The process of deconstructing computer software in an effort to understand how it works and to improve it. *See also* cracking.

half-duplex A connection in which data is transmitted in both directions, but not simultaneously. *Compare with* full-duplex.

handshake The initial communication between two data communication devices, during which they agree on protocol and transfer rules for the session.

hardware address The hardware-encoded MAC address that is burned into every NIC.

hardware loopback A device that is plugged into an interface for the purposes of simulating a network connection and thus enabling the interface to be tested as if it is operating while connected.

High-Speed Token Ring A version of Token Ring that has a maximum speed of 100Mbps. This is in contrast with other Token Ring standards, which have maximum speeds of 4Mbps or 16Mbps.

hop The means by which routing protocols determine the shortest way to reach a given destination. Each router constitutes one hop; so if a router is four hops away from another router, there are three routers, or hops, between itself and the destination. In some cases, the final step is also counted as a hop.

host   Any computer system on a network. In the Unix world, any device that is assigned an IP address.

host ID   An identifier that is used to uniquely identify a client or resource on a network.

hostname   A name that is assigned to a system for the purposes of identifying it on the network in a more user-friendly manner than by the network address.

HOSTS file   A text file that contains hostname-to-IP address mappings. All commonly used platforms accommodate static name resolution using the HOSTS file.

hot site   A disaster-recovery term used to describe a site that can be immediately functional in the event of a disaster at the primary site.

hot spare   In a RAID configuration, a drive that sits idle until another drive in the RAID array fails, at which point the hot spare takes over the role of the failed drive.

hot swap   The removal and replacement of a component in a system while the power is still on and the system is functioning.

HSSI (High Speed Serial Interface)   The network standard for high-speed serial communications over WAN links. It includes Frame Relay, T1, T3, E1, and ISDN.

HTTP (Hypertext Transfer Protocol)   A protocol that is used by Web browsers to transfer pages and files from the remote node to the user's computer.

HTTPS (Hypertext Transfer Protocol Secure)   A protocol that performs the same function as HTTP but does so over an encrypted link, ensuring the confidentiality of any data that is uploaded or downloaded. Also referred to as S-HTTP.

hub   A hardware device that acts as a connection point on a network that uses twisted-pair cable. Also known as a concentrator or a multiport repeater.

HyperTerminal   A Windows-based communications program that allows users to establish host/shell access to a remote system.

I

IANA (Internet Assigned Numbers Authority)   An organization that is responsible for IP addresses, domain names, and protocol parameters. Some functions of IANA, such as domain name assignment, have been devolved into other organizations.

ICMP (Internet Control Message Protocol)   A network-layer Internet protocol documented in RFC 792 that reports errors and provides other information relevant to IP packet processing. Utilities such as ping and tracert use functionality provided by ICMP.

IDE (Integrated Drive Electronics)   The most common type of disk drive used in PCs today. In these devices, the controller is integrated into the device.

IEEE (Institute of Electrical and Electronics Engineers)   A professional organization that develops standards for networking and communications.

IEEE 802.1   A standard that defines the OSI model's physical and data-link layers. This standard allows two IEEE LAN stations to communicate over a LAN or WAN and is often referred to as the internetworking standard.

IEEE 802.2   A standard that defines the LLC sublayer of the data-link layer for the entire series of protocols covered by the 802.x standards. This standard specifies the adding of header fields, which tell the receiving host which upper layer sent the information.

IEEE 802.3   A standard that specifies physical-layer attributes, such as signaling types, data rates, and topologies, as well as the media access method used. It also defines specifications for the implementation of the physical layer and the MAC sublayer of the data-link layer, using CSMA/CD. This standard also includes the original specifications for Fast Ethernet.

IEEE 802.4   A standard that defines how production machines should communicate and establishes a common protocol for use in connecting these machines together. It also defines specifications for the implementation of the physical layer and the MAC sublayer of the data-link layer, using Token Ring access over a bus topology.

IEEE 802.5   A standard that is used to define Token Ring. However, it does not specify a particular topology or transmission medium. It provides specifications for the implementation of the physical layer and the MAC sublayer of the data-link layer, using a token-passing media-access method on a ring topology.

IEEE 802.6   A standard that defines the distributed queue dual bus technology to transfer high-speed data between nodes. It provides specifications for the implementation of MANs.

IEEE 802.7   A standard that defines the design, installation, and testing of broadband-based communications and related physical media connectivity.

IEEE 802.8   A standard that defines a group, called the Fiber Optic Technical Advisory Group, that advises the other 802 standard committees on various fiber-optic technologies and standards.

IEEE 802.9   A standard that defines the integration of voice and data transmissions using isochronous Ethernet.

IEEE 802.10   A standard that focuses on security issues by defining a standard method for protocols and services to exchange data securely by using encryption mechanisms.

IEEE 802.11   A standard that defines the implementation of wireless technologies, such as infrared and spread-spectrum radio.

IEEE 802.11b   An extension to the IEEE 802.11 standard that defines wireless access for local area networking.

IEEE 802.12   A standard that defines 100BaseVG-AnyLAN, which uses a 1Gbps signaling rate and a special media access method that allows 100Mbps data traffic over voice-grade cable.

IETF (Internet Engineering Task Force)   A group of research volunteers that is responsible for specifying the protocols used on the Internet and for specifying the architecture of the Internet.

IFCONFIG   A command used on Linux, Unix, and OS/2 systems to obtain configuration for and configure network interfaces.

IMAP (Internet Message Access Protocol)   A protocol that allows email to be retrieved from a remote server. It is part of the TCP/IP protocol suite, and it is similar in operation to POP but offers more functionality.

incremental backup   A backup of only files that have been created or changed since the last backup. In an incremental backup, the archive bit is cleared to indicate that a file has been backed up.

infrared   A wireless data communication method that uses light pulses in the infrared range as a carrier signal.

inherited rights   The file system or directory access rights that are valid at a given point as a result of those rights being assigned at a higher level in the directory structure.

intelligent hub/switch   A hub or switch that contains some management or monitoring capability.

intelligent UPS   A UPS that has associated software for monitoring and managing the power that is provided to the system. In order for information to be passed between the UPS and the system, the UPS and system must be connected, which is normally achieved through a serial or USB connection.

interface   A device, such as a card or a plug, that connects pieces of hardware with a computer so that information can be moved from place to place (for example, between computers and printers, hard disks, and other devices, or between two or more nodes on a network). Also, the part of an application or operating system that the user sees.

interference   Anything that can compromise the quality of a signal. On bound media, crosstalk and EMI are examples of interference. In wireless environments, atmospheric conditions that degrade the quality of a signal would be considered interference.

internal IPX address   A unique eight-digit hexadecimal number that is used to identify a server running IPX/SPX. It is usually generated at random when the server is installed.

internal loopback address   Functionality built into the TCP/IP protocol stack that allows one to verify the correct functioning of the stack by pinging any address in the 127.x.x.x range, except the network address (127.0.0.0) or the broadcast address (127.255.255.255). The address 127.0.0.1 is most commonly used.

Internet domain name   The name of an area of the DNS namespace The Internet domain name is normally expressed along with the high-level domain to which it belongs (for example, comptia.org).

Internet layer   In the TCP/IP architectural model, the layer that is responsible for addressing, packaging, and routing functions. Protocols that operate at this layer are responsible for encapsulating packets into Internet datagrams. All necessary routing algorithms are run here.

internetwork   A group of networks that are connected by routers or other connectivity devices so that the networks function as one network.

intrusion detection   The process or procedures that provide a warning of successful or failed unauthorized access to a system.

I/O (input/output)   An operation in which data is either entered into a computer or taken out of a computer.

IP (Internet Protocol)   A network-layer protocol, documented in RFC 791, that offers a connectionless internetwork service. IP provides features for addressing, packet fragmentation and reassembly, type-of-service specification, and security.

IP address   The unique address that is used to identify the network number and node address of a device that is connected to a TCP/IP network.

IPCONFIG   A Windows NT/2000 command that provides information about the configuration of the TCP/IP parameters, including the IP address.

IPSec (IP Security)   A protocol that is used to provide strong security standards for encryption and authentication on VPNs.

IPv6 (Internet Protocol version 6)   The new version of IP, which has a larger range of usable addresses than the current version of IP, IPv4, and enhanced security.

IPX (Internetwork Packet Exchange)   A network-layer protocol that is usually used by Novell's NetWare. IPX provides connectionless communication, supporting packet sizes up to 64KB.

IPX/SPX (Internetwork Packet Exchange/Sequenced Packet Exchange)   The default protocol used in NetWare networks. It is a combination of IPX, to provide addressing, and SPX, to provide guaranteed delivery for IPX. IPX/SPX is similar in nature to its counterpart, TCP/IP.

IPX address The unique address that used to identify a node in a network.

IRQ (interrupt request) A number assigned to a device in a computer that determines the priority and path in communications between a device and the CPU.

IRTF (Internet Research Task Force) The research arm of the Internet Architecture Board that performs research in the areas of Internet protocols, applications, architecture, and technology.

ISA (Industry Standard Architecture) The standard of the older, more common, 8-bit and 16-bit bus and card architectures.

ISDN (Integrated Services Digital Network) An internationally adopted standard for end-to-end digital communications over the PSTN that permits telephone networks to carry data, voice, and other source traffic.

ISDN terminal adapter A device that enables communication over an ISDN link.

ISO (International Organization for Standardization) A voluntary organization founded in 1946 that is responsible for creating international standards in many areas, including communications and computers.

ISP (Internet service provider) A company or an organization that provides facilities for clients to access the Internet.

J

jumpered (or jumpering) Refers to the physical placement of shorting connectors on a board or card.

jumperless A term used to describe devices that are configured via a software utility rather than by physical jumpers on the circuit board. Devices are increasingly

moving away from jumpered configuration and toward jumperless configuration.

K

Kb (kilobit) 1,000 bits.

KB (kilobyte) 1,000 bytes.

kernel The core of an operating system. The kernel provides basic functions and services for all other parts of the operating system, including the interface with which the user interacts.

L

L2F (Layer 2 Forwarding Protocol) A VPN protocol designed to work in conjunction with the PPP to support authentication standards, such as Terminal Access Controller Access Control System (TACACS+) and Remote Authentication Dial-In User Service RADIUS), for secure transmissions over the Internet.

L2TP (Layer 2 Tunneling Protocol) A dial-up VPN protocol that defines its own tunneling protocol and works with the advanced security methods of IPSec. L2TP allows PPP sessions to be tunneled across an arbitrary medium to a home gateway at an ISP or a corporation.

LAN (local area network) A group of connected computers located in a single geographic area—usually a building or campus—that share data and services.

laser printer A type of printer that uses electrophotography as the means of printing images on paper.

latency The delay induced by a piece of equipment or device that is used to transfer data.

learning bridge A bridge that builds its own bridging address table rather than requiring someone to enter information manually. Most modern bridges are learning bridges. Also called a smart bridge.

legacy   An older computer system or technology.

line conditioner   A device that is used to stabilize the flow of power to the connected component. Also known as a power conditioner or voltage regulator.

link light   An LED on a networking device such as a hub, switch, or NIC. The illumination of the link light indicates that, at a hardware level, the connection is complete and functioning.

link-state routing   A dynamic routing method in which routers tell neighboring routers of their existence through packets called link-state advertisements (LSAs). By interpreting the information in these packets, routers are able to create maps of the entire network. *Compare with* distance-vector routing.

Linux   A Unix-like operating system kernel that was created by Linus Torvalds. Linux is distributed under an open-source license agreement, as are many of the applications and services that run on it.

LLC (logical link control) layer   A sublayer of the data-link layer of the OSI model. The LLC layer provides an interface for the network-layer protocols and the MAC sublayer.

LMHOSTS file   A text file that contains a list of NetBIOS hostname-to-IP address mappings used in TCP/IP name resolution.

logical addressing scheme   The addressing method used in providing manually assigned node addressing.

logical topology   The appearance of the network to the devices that use it, even if in physical terms the layout of the network is different. *See also* physical topology.

loop   A continuous circle that a packet takes through a series of nodes in a network until it eventually times out.

loopback plug   A device that is used for loopback testing.

loopback testing   A troubleshooting method in which the output and input wires are crossed or shorted in a manner that allows all outgoing data to be routed back into the card.

LTO (Linear Tape Open)   An open standard that allows both high storage capacity and fast data access in tape backup systems. LTO is implemented in two forms: Ultrium and Accelis.

M

MAC (Media Access Control) address   A six-octet number that uniquely identifies a host on a network. It is a unique number that is burned into the network interface.

MAC layer   In the OSI model, the lower of the two sublayers of the data-link layer. It is defined by the IEEE as being responsible for interaction with the physical layer.

mainframe system   A large computer network in which the central computer handles all the data processing and storage; only the results that are requested are sent to the requesting nodes.

MAN (metropolitan area network)   A network that spans a defined geographical location such as a city or suburb.

master name server   The supplying name server that has authority in a DNS zone.

MAU (media access unit)   A transceiver that is specified in IEEE 802.3. Not to be confused with a Token Ring multistation access unit, which is abbreviated MSAU.

Mb (megabit)   1 million bits. Used to rate transmission transfer speeds.

MB (megabyte)   1 million bytes. Usually refers to file size.

Mbps (megabits per second)   The number of millions of bits that can travel across a given medium in a second. Used as a measurement for the bandwidth of network media.

MDI (medium-dependent interface)   A type of port found on Ethernet networking devices such as hubs and switches in which the wiring is straight through. MDI ports are sometimes referred to as uplink ports and are intended for use as connectivity points to other hubs and switches.

MDI-X (medium-dependent interface crossed)   A type of port found on Ethernet networking devices in which the wiring is crossed so that the transmit line of one device becomes the receive line of the other. MDI-X is used to connect hubs and switches to client computers.

memory address   The label assigned to define the location in memory where information is stored. Usually expressed in binary.

message   A portion of information that is sent from one node to another. Messages are created at the upper layers of the OSI model.

metric   A value that can be assigned to a route to encourage or discourage the use of the route. *See also* cost.

MIB (Management Information Base)   A data set that defines the criteria that can be retrieved and set on a device, using SNMP.

microsegmentation   The process of using switches to divide a network into smaller segments.

microwaves   Very short radio waves that are used to transmit data.

mirroring   A fault-tolerant technique in which an exact duplicate of data on one volume is created on another. Mirroring is defined as RAID 1. *See* RAID.

modem (modulator-demodulator)   A device used to modulate and demodulate the signals that pass through it. It converts the direct current pulses of the serial digital code from the controller into the analog signals that are compatible with the telephone network.

MSAU (multistation access unit)   A hub that is used in an IBM Token Ring network. It organizes the connected nodes into an internal ring and uses the RI and RO connectors to expand to other MSAUs on the network. Sometimes referred to as MAU.

MTBF (mean time between failure)   The amount of time, normally expressed in hours, that represents the average amount of time a component will function before it fails.

MTTF (mean time to fix)   The amount of time it normally takes to fix a problem or swap out a component.

multicast   A single-packet transmission from one sender to a specific group of destination nodes.

multihomed   A term used to refer to a device that has more than one network interface.

multiplatform   A term used to refer to a programming language, technology, or protocol that runs on different types of CPUs or operating systems.

multiplexing   A method of transmitting multiple logical signals across the same channel at the same time.

multiprocessor   A term that refers to the use of multiple processors in a single system.

multitasking   The running of several programs simultaneously. In actuality, during multitasking the processor is sharing its time between the programs, and it only appears as if they are running concurrently.

multithreading   A form of multitasking in which the different tasks that appear to be running concurrently are coming from the same application rather than from different applications.

N

name server   A server that contains a databases of name resolution information used to resolve network names to network addresses.

NAS (network attached storage)   A storage device, such as a disk drive or CD-ROM, that is connected directly to the network medium rather than to a server or another system.

NAT (Network Address Translation)   A standard that enables the translation of IP addresses used on one network to a different IP address that is acceptable for use on another network. This translation allows multiple systems to access an external network, such as the Internet, through a single IP address.

NBNS (NetBIOS name server)   A central server that provides name resolution for NetBIOS names to IP addresses.

NBTSTAT   A Windows operating system command-line utility that displays protocol statistics and current TCP/IP connections using NetBIOS over TCP/IP (NBT).

NCP (NetWare Core Protocol)   A protocol that provides a method for hosts to make calls to a NetWare server for services and network resources. NCP is part of the IPX/SPX protocol suite.

NDIS (Network Driver Interface Specification)   A specification for NIC drivers that allows multiple protocols to be bound to a single network interface.

NDS (Novell Directory Services)   A standards-compliant directory services system implemented by Novell in NetWare 4.x. NDS has since been renamed eDirectory.

NetBEUI (NetBIOS Extended User Interface)   A nonroutable, Microsoft-proprietary networking protocol that is designed for use in small networks.

NetBIOS (Network Basic Input/Output System)   A software application that allows different applications to communicate between computers on a LAN.

NETSTAT   A Windows operating system command-line utility that displays protocol statistics and current TCP/IP network connections.

NLM (NetWare loadable module)   A service or process that runs on a NetWare server.

NLSP (NetWare Link State Protocol)   A link-state routing protocol that is used on networks that use Novell's IPX/SPX protocol suite.

network card   *See* NIC.

network ID   The part of a TCP/IP address that specifies the network portion of the IP address. The network ID is determined by the class of the address, which in turn is determined by the subnet mask used.

network interface layer   The bottom layer of the TCP/IP architectural model, which is responsible for sending and receiving frames.

network layer   Layer 3 of the OSI model, which is where routing that is based on node addresses (that is, IP or IPX addresses) occurs.

network operating system   An operating system that runs on the servers on a network. Network operating systems include NetWare, Unix, Windows NT, and Windows 2000.

newsgroup   A discussion group that focuses on a specific topic and is made up of a collection of messages posted to an Internet site. Newsgroups are useful resources for support personnel.

NIC (network interface card)   A hardware component that serves as the interface, or connecting component, between a network and the node. It has a transceiver, a MAC address, and a physical connector for the network cable. Also known as a network adapter or a network card.

NIS (Network Information Services)   The user, group, and security information database that is utilized in a Unix internetwork.

NMS (Network Management System)   An application that acts as a central management point for network management. Most NMS systems use SNMP in order to communicate with network devices.

NMTP (Network News Transfer Protocol)   An Internet protocol that controls how news articles are to be queried, distributed, and posted.

noise   Another name for EMI. *See* EMI.

NTP (Network Time Protocol)   A protocol that is used to communicate time synchronization information between devices on the network. NTP is part of the TCP/IP protocol suite.

O

ODI (Open Data-Link Interface)   Heavily used drivers in both Novell and AppleTalk networks that allow multiple protocols to be bound to an NIC. This enables the card to be used by multiple operating systems. Similar to NDIS.

operating system   The main computer program that manages and integrates all the applications running on a computer.

OSI (Open Systems Interconnect) reference model
A seven-layer model that was created by the ISO to standardize and explain the interactions of networking protocols.

OSPF (Open Shortest Path First)   A link-state routing protocol that is used on TCP/IP networks. *Compare with* distance-vector routing.

P

packet filtering   A firewall method in which each packet that attempts to pass through the firewall is examined to determine its contents. The packet is then allowed to pass or it is blocked, as appropriate.

packet sniffer   A device or an application that allows data to be copied from the network and analyzed. In legitimate applications, it is a useful network troubleshooting tool.

passive hub   A hub that has no power and therefore does not regenerate the signals it receives. *Compare with* active hub.

passive termination   A SCSI bus terminator that uses a terminating resistor pack that is placed at the end of the bus. This resistor relies on the interface card to provide it with a consistent level of power.

password   A set of characters that is used with a username to authenticate a user on a network and to provide the user with rights and permissions to files and resources.

patch   A fix for a bug in a software application. Patches can be downloaded from the Internet to correct errors or security problems in software applications.

patch cable   A cable, normally twisted-pair, that is used to connect two devices together. Strictly speaking, a patch cable is the cable that connects a port on a hub or switch to the patch panel, but today people commonly use the term to refer to any cable connection.

patch panel   A device in which the cables used in coaxial or twisted-pair networks converge and are connected. The patch panel is usually in a central location.

PCAnywhere   A software program that allows users to gain control of a computer remotely.

PCI (Peripheral Component Interconnect)   A relatively new high-speed bus designed for Pentium systems.

PCMCIA (Personal Computer Memory Card International Association)   An industry group that was organized in 1989 to promote standards for credit card–sized devices such as memory cards, modems, and network cards. Almost all laptop computers today have multiple PCMCIA slots. PCMCIA cards are now generally referred to simply as PC cards.

PDC (primary domain controller)   In a Windows NT network, the server that acts as the main repository for the user, group, and security information of the domain. *See also* BDC.

peer-to-peer networking   A network environment that does not have dedicated servers, where communication occurs between similarly capable network nodes that act as both clients and servers.

permissions   Authorization provided to users that allows them to access objects on a network. The network administrators generally assign permissions. *Permissions* is slightly different from but often used with *rights*.

physical address   The MAC address on every NIC. The physical address cannot be changed.

physical layer   Layer 1 of the OSI model, where all physical connectivity is defined.

physical topology   The actual physical layout of the network. Common physical topologies include star, bus, and ring. *Compare with* logical topology.

PING   A TCP/IP protocol stack utility that works with ICMP and uses echo requests and replies to test connectivity to other systems.

plenum   The space between the structural ceiling and a drop-down ceiling that is commonly used for heating, ventilation, and air-conditioning systems as well as for running network cables. Network cables placed in this space must have a fire-retardant coating, which gives rise to the term "plenum rated."

plug and play   An architecture designed to allow hardware devices to be detected by the operating system and for the driver to be automatically loaded.

polling   The media-access method for transmitting data in which a controlling device is used to contact each node to determine whether it has data to send.

POP (point-of-presence)   The physical location where a long-distance carrier or a cellular provider interfaces with the network of the local exchange carrier or local telephone company.

POP (Post Office Protocol)   A protocol that is part of the TCP/IP protocol suite and is used for retrieving mail stored on a remote server. The most commonly used version of POP is POP3.

port   In physical networking terms, a socket on a networking device that allows other devices to be connected. In software terms, a port is the entry point into an application, a system, or a protocol stack.

port mirroring   A process by which two ports on a device, such as a switch, are configured to receive the same information. Port mirroring is useful in troubleshooting scenarios.

POTS (plain old telephone system)   The current analog public telephone system. *See also* PSTN.

PPP (Point-to-Point Protocol)   A common dial-up networking protocol that includes provisions for security and protocol negotiation and provides host-to-network and switch-to-switch connections for one or more user sessions. It is the common modem connection used for Internet dial-up.

PPTP (Point-to-Point Tunneling Protocol)   A protocol that encapsulates private network data in IP packets. These packets are transmitted over synchronous and asynchronous circuits to hide the underlying routing and switching infrastructure of the Internet from both senders and receivers.

presentation layer   Layer 6 of the OSI model, which prepares information to be used by the application layer.

PRI (Primary Rate Interface)   A high-level network interface standard for use with ISDN. PRI is defined as having a rate of 1.544Mbps, and it consists of a single 64Kbps D channel plus 23 T1 B channels for voice or data. *See also* BRI, ISDN.

primary name server   The DNS server that offers zone data from files that are stored locally on the machine.

private network   A network to which access is limited, restricted, or controlled. Most corporate networks are private networks. *Compare with* public network.

proprietary   A standard or specification that is created by a single manufacturer, vendor, or other private enterprise.

protocol   A set of rules or standards that control data transmission and other interactions between networks, computers, peripheral devices, and operating systems.

Protocol Identification field   In a frame, a 5-byte field that is used to identify to the destination node the protocol that is being used in the data transmission.

protocol suite   Two or more protocols that work together, such as TCP and IP or IPX and SPX. Also known as a protocol stack.

proxy   A device, an application, or a service that acts as an intermediary between two hosts on a network, eliminating the ability for direct communication.

proxy server   A server that acts as a go-between for a workstation and the Internet. A proxy server typically provides an increased level of security, caching, and administrative control.

PSTN (public switched telephone network)   A term that refers to all the telephone networks and services in the world. The same as POTS, PSTN refers to the world's collection of interconnected public telephone networks that are both commercial and government owned. All of the PSTN is digital, except the connection between local exchanges and customers (which is called the local loop or last mile), which remains analog.

public network   A network, such as the Internet, to which anyone can connect with the most minimal of restrictions. *Compare with* private network.

punchdown block   A set of ports that are connected to the network ports throughout a building. Connections to networking equipment such as hubs or switches are established at the punchdown block.

punchdown tool   A hand tool that enables the connection of twisted-pair wires to wiring equipment such as a patch panel.

PVC (permanent virtual circuit)   A logical path that is established between two locations in a packet-switching network. A PVC is similar to a dedicated line, and is known as a *permanent virtual connection* in ATM terminology. (Note that private virtual circuits are also called PVCs.)

PVC (private virtual circuit)   A circuit that provides a logical connection between locations through a Frame Relay/ATM cloud (for example, a company with three branch offices, where each location physically connects to the Frame Relay provider's network through a series of switches). To end users, the three branch offices appear to be directly connected to each other, and the PVC appears to be an unbroken circuit. (Note that permanent virtual circuits are also called PVCs.)

R

RAID (Redundant Arrays of Inexpensive Disks)   A method of storing data on multiple hard drives, allowing the overlapping of I/O operations. Depending on the level of RAID, there are either fault-tolerant or performance advantages.

RAID 0   A RAID configuration that employs data striping but lacks redundancy because there is no parity information recorded (*see* RAID 5). As a result, RAID 0 offers no fault tolerance, but it does offer increased performance.

RAID 1   A fault-tolerant method that uses disk mirroring to duplicate the information stored on a disk.

RAID 2   A fault-tolerant method that uses disk striping with error correction.

RAID 3   A fault-tolerant method that uses disk striping with a single disk for parity.

RAID 4   A fault-tolerant method that uses disk striping with a single disk for parity. Striping is done across the disks in blocks.

RAID 5   A fault-tolerant method that uses disk striping with distributed parity. Striping is done across the disks in blocks.

RAID 10   Also referred to as RAID 1/0, a RAID configuration in which stripe sets (RAID 0) are mirrored (RAID 1). This combination provides the fault-tolerant aspects of RAID 1 and the performance advantages of RAID 0.

RARP (Reverse Address Resolution Protocol)   A protocol, part of the TCP/IP protocol suite, that resolves MAC addresses to IP addresses. Its relative ARP resolves IP addresses to MAC addresses.

RAS (Remote Access Service)   A Windows NT/2000 service that allows access to the network through dial-up connections.

read-only   An assigned right that allows the user to open a file and look at the contents or to execute the file if it is an application. The user cannot change the file or delete it.

read-write   An assigned right that allows the user to open a file, to change a file, or to execute a file. The user cannot delete a read-write file in some network

operating systems, but can in others. The user can create new files in the directory if he or she is granted read-write permissions to a directory.

remote control   In networking, having physical control of a remote computer through software such as PCAnywhere or Microsoft Systems Management Server.

remote node   A node or a computer that is connected to a network through a dial-up connection. Dialing in to the Internet from home is an example of the remote node concept.

repeater   A device that regenerates and retransmits signals on a network. Repeaters are usually used to strengthen signals going long distances.

resolver   A system that is requesting the resolution of a name to an IP address. This term can be applied to both DNS and WINS clients.

resource conflict   A problem that occurs when multiple devices are using the same IRQ or I/O address at the same time, usually causing the devices to fail and the program to halt.

restore   To copy data from backup media to a server. The opposite of back up.

RFC (Request for Comments)   The process by which standards relating to the Internet, the TCP/IP protocol suite, and associated technologies are created, commented on, and approved.

RG-58   A designation for the coaxial cable used in thin coaxial networks that operate on the Ethernet standard.

RI (ring in)   A connector that is used in an IBM Token Ring network on an MSAU to expand to other MSAUs on the network. The counterpart to the RO, the RI on the MSAU connects to the medium to accept the token from the ring.

rights   An authorization provided to users that allows them to perform certain tasks. The network administrator generally assigns rights. Slightly different from but often used with the term *permissions.*

RIP (Routing Information Protocol)   A protocol that uses hop count as a routing metric to control the direction and flow of packets between routers on an internetwork. There are versions of RIP for use on both TCP/IP- and IPX/SPX-based networks.

RJ-11 connector   A connector that is used with telephone systems and can have either four or six conductors. A red/green pair of wires is used for voice and data; a black/white pair is used for low-voltage signals.

RJ-45 connector   An Ethernet cable connector that is used with twisted-pair cable and can support eight conductors for four pairs of wires.

RO (ring out)   A connector used in an IBM Token Ring network on an MSAU to expand to other MSAUs on the network. The counterpart to the RI, the RO on the MSAU connects to the medium to send the token out to the ring.

root   The top level of a file system or a directory services structure. Also, the name of the default administrative account on Unix and Linux systems.

route   The entire path between two nodes on a network.

router   A device that works at the network layer of the OSI model to control the flow of data between two or more network segments.

RS-232   A communications standard that defines the flow of serial communications and the particular functions assigned to the wires in a serial cable.

S

sag   A momentary drop in the voltage provided by a power source.

SAP (service access point)   A field in a frame that tells the receiving host which protocol the frame is intended for.

SAP (Service Advertising Protocol)   A NetWare protocol that is used on an IPX network. SAP maintains server information tables, listing each service that has been advertised to it, and provides this information to any nodes that attempt to locate a service.

SAP (Service Advertising Protocol) agent   A router or another node on an IPX network that maintains a server information table. This table lists each service that has been advertised to it and provides this information to any nodes that attempt to locate a service.

SAS (Single Attached Station)   In an FDDI system, a device that is attached to only one of the two rings. *Compare with* DAS.

SCSI (Small Computer System Interface)   A technology defined by a set of standards originally published by ANSI for use with devices on a bus known as a SCSI bus.

SCSI-1   The first set of ANSI standards for small computer systems that called for up to seven devices, known as targets, to be connected to a computer known as an initiator.

SCSI-2   The second set of ANSI standards for small computer systems, published in 1994. An upgrade to the SCSI-1 standard, SCSI-2 provides a synchronous data transfer rate of 2.5Mbps to 10Mbps for an 8-bit data bus and 5Mbps to 20Mbps for a 16-bit (or *wide*) bus.

SCSI-3   The SCSI standard most widely used today. SCSI-3 splits the 400-plus pages of documents used to describe SCSI-2 into a series of smaller documents.

SCSI-3 does not define any particular performance or transfer rate but rather is a set of documents that define the architecture of the updated SCSI specification.

SCSI bus   The high-speed channel between the SCSI devices on a chain. The SCSI bus architecture contains a multithreaded I/O interface that can process multiple I/O requests at the same time.

SCSI bus termination   The use of a set of electrical resistors called terminators at the extreme ends of the SCSI bus to reflect the electrical impulses being transmitted across the bus.

SCSI ID   A number ranging from 0 to 15 that is assigned to a SCSI device to identify the device and its priority when two or more devices are competing for the right to send data on the bus.

secondary name server   A type of DNS server that gets its zone data from another DNS name server that has authority in that zone.

Security log   A log located in the Windows NT 4/2000 Event Viewer that provides information on audit events that the administrator has determined to be security related. These events include logons, attempts to log on, attempts to access areas that are denied, and attempts to log on outside normal hours.

security policy   In general terms, a written policy that defines the rules and regulations pertaining to the security of company data and the use of computer systems. More specifically, the policy configuration on a server system or a firewall that defines the security parameters for a system.

segment   A physical section of a network. Also, a unit of data that is smaller than a packet.

server   A network node that fulfills service requests for clients. Usually referred to by the type of service it performs, such as file server, communications server, or print server.

server-based application   An application that is run from a network share rather than from a copy installed on a local computer.

server-based networking   A network operating system that is dedicated to providing services to workstations, or clients. *See also* client/server networking.

service pack   A software update that fixes multiple known problems and in some cases provides additional functionality to an application or operating system.

session   A dialog between two computers.

session layer   Layer 5 of the OSI model, which establishes, manages, and terminates sessions between applications on different nodes.

shared system   The infrastructure component that is routed directly into the backbone of an internetwork for optimal systems access. It provides connectivity to servers and other shared systems.

shell   An interface, graphical or otherwise, that enables the functionality of an operating system.

SLIP (Serial Line Internet Protocol)   A protocol that uses encapsulation to allow TCP/IP to be transmitted over asynchronous lines, such as standard telephone lines. Previously used for most Internet access, SLIP has been largely replaced by PPP because of SLIP's lack of error-checking capabilities.

SMDS (Switched Multimegabit Data Service)   The physical-layer implementation for data transmission over public lines at speeds between 1.544Mbps (T1) and 44.736Mbps, using cell relay and fixed-length cells. Defined in IEEE 802.6.

SMP (symmetrical multiprocessing)   The utilization of multiple processors on a single system.

SMTP (Simple Mail Transfer Protocol)   An Internet protocol that is used for the transfer of messages and attachments.

SNAP (Subnetwork Access Protocol)   An Internet protocol that specifies a standard method of encapsulating IP datagrams and ARP messages on a network.

SNMP (Simple Network Management Protocol)   A protocol that provides network devices with a method to monitor and control network devices; manage configurations, statistics collection, performance, and security; and report network management information to a management console. SNMP is part of the TCP/IP protocol suite.

SNMP agent   A software component that allows a device to communicate with, and be contacted by, an SNMP management system.

SNMP trap   An SNMP utility that sends an alarm to notify the administrator that something within the network activity differs from the established threshold, as defined by the administrator.

socket   A logical interprocess communications mechanism through which a program communicates with another program or with a network.

socket identifier   An 8-bit number that is used to identify the socket and is used by IPX when it needs to address a packet to a particular process running on a server. The developers and designers of services and protocols usually assign socket identifiers. A socket identifier is also known as a socket number.

SONET (Synchronous Optical Network)   A U.S. standard for data transmission that operates at speeds up to 2.4Gbps over optical networks referred to as OC-*x*, where *x* is the level.

source address   The address of the host that sent the frame. The source address is contained in the frame so the destination node knows who sent the data.

source-route bridge   A bridge that is used in source-route bridging to send a packet to the destination node through the route specified by the sending node.

spike   An instantaneous, dramatic increase in the voltage output to a device. Spikes are responsible for much of the damage that is done to network hardware components.

SPX (Sequenced Packet Exchange)   A protocol that is used in conjunction with IPX when guaranteed delivery is required. SPX is used mainly in NetWare network environments.

SSL (Secure Sockets Layer)   A method of securely transmitting information to and receiving information from a remote Web site. SSL is implemented through the HTTPS.

STA (Spanning Tree Algorithm)   A standard that is defined by IEEE 802.1 as part of STP to eliminate loops in an internetwork with multiple paths.

static IP address   An IP address that is assigned to a network device manually, as opposed to dynamically via DHCP.

static routing   A routing method in which all routes must be entered into a device manually and in which no route information is exchanged between routing devices on the network. *Compare with* dynamic routing.

static window   A mechanism used in flow control that prevents the sender of data from overwhelming the receiver. The amount of data that can be buffered in a static window is configured dynamically by the protocol.

station IPX address   A 12-digit number that is used to uniquely identify each device on an IPX network.

storage area network   A subnetwork of storage devices, usually found on high-speed networks and shared by all servers on a network.

store-and-forward   A fast-packet-switching method that produces a higher latency than other switching methods because the entire contents of the packet are copied into the onboard buffers of the switch. CRC calculations are performed before the packet can be passed on to the destination address.

STP (shielded twisted-pair) Twisted-pair network cable that has shielding to insulate the cable from EMI.

STP (Spanning Tree Protocol) A protocol that was developed to eliminate the loops caused by the multiple paths in an internetwork. STP is defined in IEEE 802.1.

subdomain A privately controlled segment of the DNS namespace that exists under other segments of the namespace as a division of the main domain.

subnet A logical division of a network, based on the address to which all the devices on the network are assigned.

subnet mask A 32-bit address that is used to mask, or screen, a portion of an IP address to differentiate the part of the address that designates the network and the part that designates the host from one another.

subnetting The process of dividing an assigned IP address range into smaller clusters of hosts.

supernetting The process of aggregating IP network addresses and using them as a single network address range.

Supervisor account In a NetWare network, a default account that has rights to access everything and to assign rights to other users on the network.

surge A voltage increase that is less dramatic than that of a spike but can last a lot longer. Sometimes referred to as a swell. The opposite of brownout.

surge protector An inexpensive and simple device that is placed between a power outlet and a network component to protect the component from spikes and surges. Also known as a surge suppresser.

SVC (switched virtual circuit) A virtual circuit that is established dynamically on demand to form a dedicated link and is then broken when transmission is

complete. Known as a switched virtual connection in ATM terminology.

switch A Layer 2 networking device that is used in twisted-pair networks. A switch forwards frames based on destination addresses.

SYN A message that is sent to initiate a TCP session between two devices.

synchronous transmission A digital signal transmission method that uses a precise clocking method and a predefined number of bits sent at a constant rate.

System log A log that is located in the Windows NT 4/2000 Event Viewer that provides information on events logged by Windows NT/2000 system components. These events include driver failures, device conflicts, read/write errors, timeouts, and bad block errors.

T

T-line A digital communication line used in WANs. Commonly used T designations are T1 and T3. It is also possible to use only part of a T1 line, which then becomes known as *fractional T1*.

TCP (Transmission Control Protocol) A connection-oriented, reliable data transmission communication service that operates at the transport layer of the OSI model. TCP is part of the TCP/IP protocol suite.

TCP/IP (Transmission Control Protocol/Internet Protocol) A suite of protocols that includes TCP and IP. TCP/IP was originally designed for use on large internetworks but has now become the de facto protocol for networks of all sizes.

TCP/IP socket A socket, or connection to an endpoint, that is used in TCP/IP communication transmissions.

TDI (Transport Driver Interface) A kernel-mode network interface that is exposed at the upper edge of all Windows NT transport protocol stacks. The highest-level protocol driver in every such stack supports the TDI interface for still higher-level kernel-mode network clients.

TDR (time-domain reflectometer)   A device that is used to test copper cables to determine whether and where a break is on the cable. For optical cables, an optical TDR is used.

Telnet   A standard terminal emulation protocol in the TCP/IP protocol stack. Telnet is used to perform terminal emulation over TCP/IP via remote terminal connections, enabling users to log in to remote systems and use resources as if they were connected to a local system.

Terminal Services   A service provided in Windows 2000 and as an add-on in Windows NT that allows clients to connect to the server as if it were a multiuser operating system. All the processing for the client session is performed on the server, with only screen updates and user input being transmitted across the network connection.

TFTP (Trivial File Transfer Protocol)   A simplified version of FTP that allows file transfers but does not offer any security or file management capabilities.

Thick Ethernet   The IEEE 802.3 standard 10Base5, which describes Ethernet networking using thick coaxial cabling.

thick coaxial   The thick cable most commonly used as the backbone of a coaxial network. It is approximately .375 inches in diameter.

thin client   An application that is run from a back-end server system such as Microsoft Terminal Services. The processing tasks are all performed at the terminal server rather than on the client.

Thin Ethernet   The 802.3 standard 10Base2, which describes Ethernet networking using thin coaxial cabling.

thin coaxial   Cable that is thinner than thick coaxial cable but still about .25 inches in diameter. It is commonly used in older bus topologies.

TIA (Telecommunications Industry Association)   An organization that, along with EIA, develops standards for telecommunications technologies.

token   A frame that provides controlling information. In a Token Ring network, the node that possesses the token is the one that is allowed to transmit next.

Token Ring   An IBM-proprietary token-passing LAN topology defined by IEEE standard 802.5. It operates at either 4Mbps or 16Mbps, in a star topology.

Token Ring adapter   Traditionally an ISA or a Microchannel device with 4Mbps or 16Mbps transfer capability that is used to connect nodes to a Token Ring network.

tone generator   A device that is used with a tone locator to locate and diagnose problems with twisted-pair cabling.

topology   The shape or layout of a physical network and the flow of data through the network. *See also* logical topology, physical topology.

trace route   A function of the TCP/IP protocol suite, implemented in utilities such as traceroute and tracert, that allows the entire path of a packet to be tracked between source and destination hosts. It is used as a troubleshooting tool.

transmit   To send data using light, electronic, or electric signals. In networking, this is usually done in the form of digital signals composed of bits.

transparent bridging   A situation in which the bridges on a network tell each other which ports on the bridge should be opened and closed, which ports should be forwarding packets, and which ports should be blocking packets—all without the assistance of any other device.

transport layer Layer 4 of the OSI model, which controls the flow of information.

TTL (time to live) A value that is assigned to a packet of data to prevent it from moving around the network indefinitely. The TTL value is decremented each time the packet crosses a router, until it reaches 0, at which point it is removed from the network.

twisted-pair A type of cable that uses multiple twisted pairs of copper wire.

U

UART (Universal Asynchronous Receiver/Transmitter) A chip that is responsible for communications carried over a serial port; it converts between data bits and serial bits.

UDP (User Datagram Protocol) A communications protocol that provides connectionless, unreliable communications services and operates at the transport layer of the OSI model. It requires a network-layer protocol such as IP to guide it to the destination host.

unbound media (or boundless media) A term used to describe any media that do not have physical constraints. Examples of unbound media include infrared, wireless, and microwave. *Compare with* bound media.

UNC (Universal Naming Convention) An industry naming standard for computers and resources that provides a common syntax that should work in most systems, including Windows, Unix, and NetWare. An example of a UNC name is \\servername\sharename.

unicast A network communication that is directed at a single network node. Unicast is the standard method of communication on a network.

UPS (uninterruptible power supply) A system that provides protection against power surges and power outages. During blackouts, a UPS gives you time to

shut down the network before the temporary power interruption becomes permanent. A UPS is also referred to as battery backup.

uptime The amount of time that a device has been on and operating.

URL (uniform resource locator) A name used to identify a site and subsequently a page on the Internet. An example of a URL is www.quepublishing.com/products.

USB (universal serial bus) A type of interface between a computer system and peripheral devices. The USB interface allows you to add or remove devices without shutting down the computer. USB supports up to 127 devices.

user account An account that an end user uses when logging in to a network. It contains the rights and permissions assigned to the user.

UTP (unshielded twisted-pair) A type of cable that uses multiple twisted pairs of copper wire in a casing that does not provide much protection from EMI. The most common network cable in Ethernet networks, UTP is rated in categories including Category 1 through Category 5, as well as Category 5e and Category 6.

V

virtual memory A process for paging or swapping from memory to disk that is used to increase the amount of RAM available to a system.

virus A software program that is designed specifically to affect a system or network adversely. A virus is usually designed to be passed on to other systems with which it comes in contact.

VLAN (virtual LAN) A group of devices that are located on one or more different LAN segments, whose configuration is based on logical instead of physical connections so that they can communicate as if they were attached to the same physical connection.

volume set   Multiple disks or partitions of disks that have been configured to read as one drive.

VPN (virtual private network)   A network that uses a public network such as the Internet as a backbone to connect two or more private networks. A VPN provides users with the equivalent of a private network in terms of security. VPNs can also be used as a means of establishing secure remote connectivity between a remote system and another network.

W

WAN (wide area network)   A data communications network that serves users across a broad geographical area. WANs often use transmission devices such as modems or CSUs/DSUs to carry signals over leased lines or over common carrier lines.

WAP (wireless access point)   A network device that offers connectivity between wireless clients and (usually) a wired portion of the network.

Web server   A server that runs an application and makes the contents of certain directories on that server, or other servers, available to clients for download via a protocol such as HTTP.

WiFi   A voluntary standard that manufacturers can adhere to, which aims to create compatibility between wireless (802.11b) devices.

window flow control   A flow control method in which the receiving host buffers the data it receives and holds it in the buffer until it can be processed. After the data is processed, an acknowledgment is sent to the sender. *See also* dynamic window, static window.

Windows NT Diagnostics   A troubleshooting tool that is provided in Windows NT and Windows 2000 that helps you diagnose hardware and driver problems. It provides a graphical database of system devices and resources that is similar to the Device Manager in Windows 95 and 98.

WINS (Windows Internet Name Service)   A NetBIOS name-to-IP address resolution program that is available in the Windows NT and Windows 2000 operating systems.

WINS database   A dynamically built database of NetBIOS names and IP addresses that is used by WINS.

wire crimper   A tool that is used to create networking cables. The type of wire crimping tool used depends on the cable being made.

wireless networking   Networking that uses any unbound media, such as infrared, microwave, or radio waves.

workstation   A client computer on a network that does not offer any services of its own but uses the services of the servers on the network.

Z

zone   A logical grouping of network devices in an AppleTalk network. Also, an area of the DNS namespace.

zone transfer   The passing of DNS information from one name server to a secondary name server.

Overview of the Certification Process

This appendix explains the CompTIA certification process and looks at what is involved in taking the Network+ Exam. At the time of writing, this information is accurate; however, CompTIA reserves the right to change exam and certification track information at any time, thus, it's worth checking their Web site at http://www.comptia.org to see whether there have been any changes to the program.

DESCRIPTION OF THE PATH TO CERTIFICATION

The Network+ exam is numbered N10-002. The closed-book exam provides a valid and reliable measure of your technical proficiency and expertise. Developed in consultation with computer industry professionals who have on-the-job experience with multivendor hardware and software server products in the workplace, the exams are conducted by Virtual University Enterprises (VUE), the electronic testing division of NCS Pearson. VUE has more than 2,500 authorized testing centers, serving more than 100 countries. Testing is also available from Sylvan Prometric.

The exam prices vary, depending on your CompTIA member status:

> CompTIA members: $149 each
>
> Non-CompTIA members: $199 each

ABOUT THE NETWORK+ CERTIFICATION PROGRAM

The Computing and Technology Industry Association (CompTIA) developed the Network+ certification to provide a vendor-neutral introductory-level networking certification. The exam is currently in its second revision. New exam objectives that take into account developments in networking technologies such as wireless networks and Gigabit Ethernet are being introduced in this revision of the exam.

CompTIA recommends that before you take the Network+ exam, you have hardware knowledge equivalent to what you need for ComTIA A+ certification and nine months' experience administering networks; however, these recommendations are certainly not set in stone. The concepts required to pass the Network+ exam provide a solid foundation for networking technologies and are a great place to start when you're considering a career in network management. In this way, prior networking experience would certainly be an asset, but it is not a requirement to pass the exam. We recommend that if you want to take the Network+ exam, you should have interest in computer networks and a desire to learn.

You might be asking why this exam is for you, and why now? Besides the fact that the certification brings certain obvious professional benefits to you, the Network+

program gives you access to the CompTIA organization and to the benefits that access affords. In addition, the Network+ exam is well recognized in the IT community and is used as an elective for such premier certifications as Microsoft's MSCE and MCSA certifications.

CompTIA's Web site (www.comptia.com) identifies further benefits for prospective CompTIA-certified individuals:

◆ **Recognized proof of professional achievement**—This is a level of competence that is commonly accepted and valued by the industry.

◆ **Enhanced job opportunities**—Many employers give preference in hiring to applicants who have certification. They view certification as proof that a new hire knows the procedures and technologies required.

◆ **Opportunity for advancement**—Certification can be a plus when an employer awards job advancements and promotions.

◆ **Training requirement**—Certification might be required as a prerequisite to attending a vendor's training course, so employers often offer advanced training to employees who are already certified.

◆ **Customer confidence**—As the general public learns about certification, customers will require that only certified technicians be assigned to their accounts.

For any additional information or clarification about the CompTIA Network+ certification path and its history and benefits, consult the CompTIA home page, at www.comptia.com. As discussed earlier, you can also check this site to see if there have been any recent changes in the Network+ certification program.

What's on the CD-ROM

This appendix is a brief rundown of what you'll find on the CD-ROM that comes with this book. For a more detailed description of the *PrepLogic Practice Tests, Preview Edition* exam simulation software, see Appendix D, "Using the *PrepLogic Practice Tests, Preview Edition* Software." In addition to the *PrepLogic Practice Tests, Preview Edition*, the CD-ROM includes the electronic version of the book in Portable Document Format (PDF), several utility and application programs, and a complete listing of test objectives and where they are covered in the book.

PREPLOGIC PRACTICE TESTS, PREVIEW EDITION

PrepLogic is a leading provider of certification training tools. Trusted by certification students worldwide, PrepLogic is, we believe, the best practice exam software available. In addition to providing a means of evaluating your knowledge of the Training Guide material, *PrepLogic Practice Tests, Preview Edition* features several innovations that help you to improve your mastery of the subject matter.

For example, the practice tests allow you to check your score by exam area or domain to determine which topics you need to study more. Another feature allows you to obtain immediate feedback on your responses in the form of explanations for the correct and incorrect answers.

PrepLogic Practice Tests, Preview Edition exhibits most of the full functionality of the *Premium Edition* but offers only a fraction of the total questions. To get the complete set of practice questions and exam functionality, visit PrepLogic.com and order the Premium Edition for this and other challenging exam titles.

Again for a more detailed description of the *PrepLogic Practice Tests, Preview Edition* features, see Appendix D.

Using the PrepLogic Practice Tests, Preview Edition Software

This Training Guide includes a special version of *PrepLogic Practice Tests*—a revolutionary test engine designed to give you the best in certification exam preparation. PrepLogic offers sample and practice exams for many of today's most in-demand and challenging technical certifications. This special Preview Edition is included with this book as a tool to use in assessing your knowledge of the Training Guide material while also providing you with the experience of taking an electronic exam.

This appendix describes in detail what *PrepLogic Practice Tests, Preview Edition* is, how it works, and what it can do to help you prepare for the exam. Note that although the Preview Edition includes all the test simulation functions of the complete, retail version, it contains only a single practice test. The Premium Edition, available at PrepLogic.com, contains the complete set of challenging practice exams designed to optimize your learning experience.

EXAM SIMULATION

One of the main functions of *PrepLogic Practice Tests, Preview Edition* is exam simulation. To prepare you to take the actual vendor certification exam, PrepLogic is designed to offer the most effective exam simulation available.

QUESTION QUALITY

The questions provided in the *PrepLogic Practice Tests, Preview Edition* are written to highest standards of technical accuracy. The questions tap the content of the Training Guide chapters and help you review and assess your knowledge before you take the actual exam.

INTERFACE DESIGN

The *PrepLogic Practice Tests, Preview Edition* exam simulation interface provides you with the experience of taking an electronic exam. This enables you to effectively prepare for taking the actual exam by making the test experience a familiar one. Using this test simulation can help eliminate the sense of surprise or anxiety you might experience in the testing center because you will already be acquainted with computerized testing.

EFFECTIVE LEARNING ENVIRONMENT

The *PrepLogic Practice Tests, Preview Edition* interface provides a learning environment that not only tests you through the computer, but also teaches the material you need to know to pass the certification exam.

Each question comes with a detailed explanation of the correct answer and often provides reasons the other options are incorrect. This information helps to reinforce the knowledge you already have and also provides practical information you can us on the job.

SOFTWARE REQUIREMENTS

PrepLogic Practice Tests requires a computer with the following:

◆ Microsoft Windows 98, Windows Me, Windows NT 4.0, Windows 2000, or Windows XP

◆ A 166MHz or faster processor is recommended

◆ A minimum of 32MB of RAM

◆ As with any Windows application, the more memory, the better your performance.

◆ 10MB of hard drive space

INSTALLING *PREPLOGIC PRACTICE TESTS, PREVIEW EDITION*

Install *PrepLogic Practice Tests, Preview Edition* by running the setup program on the *PrepLogic Practice Tests, Preview Edition* CD. Follow these instructions to install the software on your computer.

1. Insert the CD into your CD-ROM drive. The Autorun feature of Windows should launch the software. If you have Autorun disabled, click Start and select Run. Go to the root directory of the CD and select setup.exe. Click Open, and then click OK.

2. The Installation Wizard copies the *PrepLogic Practice Tests, Preview Edition* files to your hard drive; adds *PrepLogic Practice Tests, Preview Edition* to your Desktop and Program menu; and installs test engine components to the appropriate system folders.

Removing PrepLogic Practice Tests, Preview Edition from Your Computer

If you elect to remove the *PrepLogic Practice Tests, Preview Edition* product from your computer, an uninstall process has been included to ensure that it is removed from your system safely and completely. Follow these instructions to remove *PrepLogic Practice Tests, Preview Edition* from your computer:

1. Select Start, Settings, Control Panel.

2. Double-click the Add/Remove Programs icon.

3. You are presented with a list of software installed on your computer. Select the appropriate *PrepLogic Practice Tests, Preview Edition* title you want to remove. Click the Add/Remove button. The software is then removed from your computer.

USING PREPLOGIC PRACTICE TESTS, PREVIEW EDITION

PrepLogic is designed to be user friendly and intuitive. Because the software has a smooth learning curve, your time is maximized because you start practicing almost immediately. *PrepLogic Practice Tests, Preview Edition* has two major modes of study: Practice Test and Flash Review.

Using Practice Test mode, you can develop your test-taking abilities as well as your knowledge through the use of the Show Answer option. While you are taking the test, you can expose the answers along with a detailed explanation of why the given answers are right or wrong. This gives you the ability to better understand the material presented.

Flash Review is designed to reinforce exam topics rather than quiz you. In this mode, you will be shown a series of questions but no answer choices. Instead, you will be given a button that reveals the correct answer to the question and a full explanation for that answer.

Starting a Practice Test Mode Session

Practice Test mode enables you to control the exam experience in ways that actual certification exams do not allow:

◆ **Enable Show Answer Button**—Activates the Show Answer button allowing you to view the correct answer(s) and full explanation(s) for each question during the exam. When not enabled, you must wait until after your exam has been graded to view the correct answer(s) and explanation.

◆ **Enable Item Review Button**—Activates the Item Review button, allowing you to view your answer choices, marked questions, and to facilitate navigation between questions.

◆ **Randomize Choices**—Randomize answer choices from one exam session to the next. Makes memorizing question choices more difficult therefore keeping questions fresh and challenging longer.

To begin studying in Practice Test mode, click the Practice Test radio button from the main exam customization screen. This enables the options detailed in the preceding list.

To your left, you are presented with the option of selecting the preconfigured Practice Test or creating your own Custom Test. The preconfigured test has a fixed time limit and number of questions. Custom Tests allow you to configure the time limit and the number of questions in your exam.

The Preview Edition included with this book includes a single preconfigured Practice Test. Get the compete set of challenging PrepLogic Practice Tests at PrepLogic.com and make certain you're ready for the big exam.

Click the Begin Exam button to begin your exam.

Starting a Flash Review Mode Session

Flash Review mode provides you with an easy way to reinforce topics covered in the practice questions. To begin studying in Flash Review mode, click the Flash Review radio button from the main exam customization screen. Select either the preconfigured Practice Test or create your own Custom Test.

Click the Best Exam button to begin your Flash Review of the exam questions.

Standard PrepLogic Practice Tests, Preview Edition Options

The following list describes the function of each of the buttons you see. Depending on the options, some of the buttons will be grayed out and inaccessible or missing completely. Buttons that are appropriate are active. The buttons are as follows:

◆ **Exhibit**—This button is visible if an exhibit is provided to support the question. An exhibit is an image that provides supplemental information necessary to answer the question.

◆ **Item Review**—This button leaves the question window and opens the Item Review screen. From this screen you will see all questions, your answers, and your marked items. You will also see correct answers listed here when appropriate.

◆ **Show Answer**—This option displays the correct answer with an explanation of why it is correct. If you select this option, the current question is not scored.

◆ **Mark Item**—Check this box to tag a question you need to review further. You can view and navigate your Marked Items by clicking the Item Review button (if enabled). When grading your exam, you will be notified if you have marked items remaining.

◆ **Previous Item**—View the previous question.

◆ **Next Item**—View the next question.

◆ **Grade Exam**—When you have completed your exam, click to end your exam and view your detailed score report. If you have unanswered or marked items remaining you will be asked if you would like to continue taking your exam or view your exam report.

Time Remaining

If the test is timed, the time remaining is displayed on the upper-right corner of the application screen. It counts down minutes and seconds remaining to complete the test. If you run out of time, you will be asked if you want to continue taking the test or if you want to end your exam.

Your Examination Score Report

The Examination Score Report screen appears when the Practice Test mode ends—as the result of time expiration, completion of all questions, or your decision to terminate early.

This screen provides you with a graphical display of your test score with a breakdown of scores by topic domain. The graphical display at the top of the screen compares your overall score with the PrepLogic Exam Competency Score.

The PrepLogic Exam Competency Score reflects the level of subject competency required to pass this vendor's exam. Although this score does not directly translate to a passing score, consistently matching or exceeding this score does suggest you possess the knowledge to pass the actual vendor exam.

Review Your Exam

From Your Score Report screen, you can review the exam that you just completed by clicking on the View Items button. Navigate through the items, viewing the questions, your answers, the correct answers, and the explanations for those questions. You can return to your score report by clicking the View Items button.

GET MORE EXAMS

Each *PrepLogic Practice Tests, Preview Edition* that accompanies your training guide contains a single PrepLogic Practice Test. Certification students worldwide trust PrepLogic Practice Tests to help them pass their IT certification exams the first time. Purchase the Premium Edition of *PrepLogic Practice Tests* and get the entire set of all new challenging Practice Tests for this exam. PrepLogic Practice Tests—Because You Want to Pass the First Time.

Contacting PrepLogic

If you would like to contact PrepLogic for any reason including information about our extensive line of certification practice tests, we invite you to do so. Please contact us online at www.preplogic.com.

CUSTOMER SERVICE

If you have a damaged product and need a replacement or refund, please call the following phone number:

800-858-7674

Product Suggestions and Comments

We value your input! Please email your suggestions and comments to the following address:

feedback@preplogic.com

License Agreement

YOU MUST AGREE TO THE TERMS AND CONDITIONS OUTLINED IN THE END USER LICENSE AGREEMENT ("EULA") PRESENTED TO YOU DURING THE INSTALLATION PROCESS. IF YOU DO NOT AGREE TO THESE TERMS, DO NOT INSTALL THE SOFTWARE.

Index

NUMBERS

2B+D. *See* BRI

3DES, 486

5-4-3 rule
  Ethernet coaxial implementations, 87
  Ethernet twisted-pair implementations, 88

10Base2 standard, 84-86

10Base5 standard, 86-87

10BaseT standard, 87-88

100BaseFX standard, 89

100BaseT4 standard, 89

100BaseTX standard, 89-90

100VG-AnyLAN standard, 43-44

1000BaseT Gigabit Ethernet standard, 91-92

1000BaseX standards, 90-92

802 IEEE standards, 37-38, 45
  802.1q standard, 408
  802.3 IEEE standards, 84-92
  Ethernet (802.3), 45-46
  Fast Ethernet (802.3u), 46
  FDDI, 49-50
  Gigabit Ethernet (802.3z), 46-47
  LLC Sublayer (802.2), 45
  Token Ring (802.5), 47-48
  wireless networks (802.11b), 48-49

A

-a switch, 504, 507-508, 510

access methods, IEEE standards, 39
  CSMA/CD, 39-41
  demand priority, 43-44
  token passing, 41-43
  topologies, 44

accounts
  Administrator, 332
  user management, 331

Active Directory, 335-336, 444

activity lights, 132

adapters, ISDN, 135-137

add switch, 515

Add/Remove Programs dialog box, 451

Address Resolution Protocol. *See* ARP

addresses. *See* IP addresses; MAC addresses; network addresses

addressing
  AppleTalk, 189-190
  IPX, 186-187
  NetBEUI, 192
  network layer (OSI model), 156-157
  TCP/IP, 181

administration, client/server networks, 25

Administrator account (Windows NT 4), 332

ADSL (asymmetric DSL), 520

ADSP (AppleTalk Data Stream Protocol), 188

Advanced TCP/IP Settings dialog box, 441

AFP (AppleTalk File Protocol), 177, 188

agents, SNMP, 228

alerts, 339

/all switch, 512, 514

American Registry for Internet Numbers. *See* ARIN

APNIC (Asia Pacific Network Information Centre), 243

AppleShare, 188

AppleTalk, 119, 175, 188-189

    addressing, 189-190

    interoperability, 190

    LocalTalk, 189

    OSI model, 190

    routing, 191

AppleTalk Address Resolution Protocol. *See* ARP

AppleTalk Control Protocol. *See* ATCP

AppleTalk Data Stream Protocol. *See* ADSP

AppleTalk File Protocol. *See* AFP

AppleTalk Session Protocol. *See* ASP

AppleTalk Transaction Protocol. *See* ATP

application gateway firewalls, 477

application layer (OSI model), 160-161

applications

    Linux, 361-362, 371

    logs, 331, 338

    Macintoshes, 373

    new, 593

    Novell NetWare, 351-352

    operating systems, 322-324

    OSI model, 177

    permissions, 606

    protocols, 175, 412

    sharing, 20

    Windows 2000, 344

    Windows 2000 Professional, 369

    Windows 95, 368

    Windows 98, 368

    Windows ME, 368

    Windows NT 4, 334

    Windows NT Workstation, 369

    support for Windows XP Professional, 369

archive bits, clearing, 405

ARIN (American Registry for Internet Numbers), 243

ARP (Address Resolution Protocol), 188, 212-213, 506

    cache, 506-507

    switches, 507

arp utility, 539-540

arrays, 398

    RAID 0, 390

    RAID 1, 392

    RAID 5, 395

ascii command, 209

Asia Pacific Network Information Centre. See APNIC

ASP (AppleTalk Session Protocol), 188

asymmetric DSL, 520

Asynchronous Transfer Mode. *See* ATM

AT commands, 127, 533

ATCP (AppleTalk Control Protocol), 296

ATM (Asynchronous Transfer Mode), 277

    circuits, 277

    media, 278

ATP (AppleTalk Transaction Protocol), 178, 188

attachment unit interfaces. *See* AUI ports

attentuation (media), 64

auditing, 487-490

AUI (attachment unit interface) ports, D-shell connectors, 78-79

authentication, 604-605

    Linux, 360, 372

    logical security, 466-467

    Novell NetWare, 350

operating systems, 323

protocols, PPP, 295-296

    CHAP, 295

    EAP, 296

    MS-CHAP, 296

    PAP, 296

    SPAP, 296

remote access, troubleshooting, 534-535

user

    Linux, 363

    Novell NetWare, 352

    Windows NT 4, 334

Windows 2000, 342-343

Windows 2000 Professional, 370

Windows 95, 368

Windows 98, 368

Windows ME, 368

Windows NT 4, 333

Windows NT Workstation, 370

Windows XP Professional, 370

B

backbones, 29

backoff, 40

backup tapes. *See* tapes

backups, 403

    best practices, 407-408

    cartridges, 407

    client/server networks, 25

    comparison of methods, 405-406

    data, 20

    differential, 405

    full, 403-404, 416-417

    incremental, 404

    logs, 407

    peer-to-peer networks, 22

    rotating offsite, 407

    rotation schedules, 406

    testing, 407

bandwidth, media, 63-64

baseband signaling, 65-66

baselines

    infrastructure performance, 610-611

    system performance, 328

Basic Rate Interface. *See* BRI

baud rate, 128

BDC (Backup domain controller), 326

beaconing, 275

binary command, 209

bindery systems, 351

blackouts, 402

blocking port numbers, 483-484

BNCs (British Naval connectors), 69-70, 82, 550

BOOTP, 220

bound media, 68

bps rate, 128

BRI (Basic Rate Interface), 271-272

bridges, 114, 116

    data-link layer (OSI model), 163

    implementation considerations, 114-115

    manual configuration, 114

    primary, 115

    source-route, 116

    translational, 115

    transparent, 115

British Naval connectors. *See* BNCs

broadband signaling, 65-66

broadcases, DHCPDISCOVER, 219

broadcast addresses, 236

brouters, 123

brownouts, 402

budgets, operating systems, 323

buffering (flow control), 159

built-in NICs, 132, 135

buses

    compatibility, NICs, 129

    network errors, 598-599

    topologies, LANs, 29-30

bytes, netstat –e, 564

C

c switch, 510

cables, 68, 427

    backbones, 29

    basic characteristics, 73-74

    coaxial, 68-69

        10Base2 standard, 84-86

        10Base5 standard, 86-87

        5-4-3 rule, 87

        thick coax, 70

        thin coax, 69-70

    costs, 95

    crossover, 88, 111-112

    distances, 608

    DSL, 262

    EMI-resistant, 63

    fiber-optic, 72-73

    homemade versus manufactured, 550

    hubs, 111-112

    labeling, 551

    plenum, 65

    risers, 609

    segments, 67

    standards, 69

    straight-through, 111

    switches, 111-112

    testing, 609

    troubleshooting, 523-525

    trunks, 29

    twisted-pair, 70

        5-4-3 rule, 88

        EIA/TIA categories, 71

        STP (shielded), 70-71

        UTP (unshielded), 70-71, 87-88

    types, 608

cache, ARP, 506-507

Caching Array Routing Protocol. *See* CARP

caching proxy servers, 480-481

CANs (campus area networks), 28

Caps Lock, 335, 535

CARP (Caching Array Routing Protocol), 481

categories, EIA/TIA twisted-pair cable, 71

cd command, 208

CDDI (Copper Distributed Data Interface), 49, 274

centralized computing, 26

centronic connectors, 83-84

change switch, 515

CHAP (Challenge Handshake Authentication Protocol), 295

chips, 75

CIDR (Classless Interdomain Routing), 236-237

circuits

    ATM, 277

    firewalls, 477

    switching, 155, 267

Class A stations, 275

class=X switch, 514

classes, IP addresses, 235

Classless Interdomain Routing. *See* CIDR

clear text, 303

Client for Microsoft Networks, configuring, 444

Client Services for NetWare. *See* CSNW

client/server networks, 20, 23
  advantages, 24-25
  clients, 24
  disadvantages, 25
  servers, 23-24
clients
  configurations, 443
    Linux/Unix, 446
    Novell, 444-446
    obtaining IP information from DHCP servers, 451-452
    remote servers, 308-310
    TCP/IP, 439-441
    Windows, 443-444
  connectivity
    errors, 602-607
    Linux, 371
    Macintoshes, 373
    Novell, 444-446
    Windows 2000 Professional, 370
    Windows clients, 443-444
    Windows NT Workstation, 370
    Windows XP Professional, 370
  operating systems, 367
    Linux, 370-372
    Macintoshes, 372-373
    Windows, 367-370
  support, 365
    Linux, 366-367
    NetWare, 366
    RAS, 293-294
    Windows, 365-366
  VPNs, 305
clusters (server), 401
coaxial cable, 68-69
  5-4-3 rule, 87
  thick, 70, 86-87
  thin, 69-70, 84-86

coaxial networks, 435
code hamming, 392
combinations networks, 25
combo cards, 129
commands
  AT, 127, 533
  cConfig (NetWare), 349-350
  display servers (NetWare), 349
  FTP, 208-209
  HOSTS file, 221
  ifconfig, 360
  inetcfg (NetWare), 350
  ipconfig, 568-570
  ipconfig /all, 140, 511
  iptrace (NetWare), 350
  ipxping (NetWare), 350
  netstat, 508, 563
    netstat -a, 565-566
    netstat -e, 564-565
    netstat -r, 509, 566-567
    netstat -s, 567-568
  passwd, 359
  ping (NetWare), 350, 360, 557, 572
    Destination Host Unreachable error, 557-558
    Expired TTL error, 560
    Request Timed Out error, 558-559
    Unknown Host error, 559-560
  reset router (NetWare), 349
  tcpcon (NetWare), 350
  tping (NetWare), 350
  traceroute, 360, 504-505
  tracert, 560-563
    failure to get to remote host, 561-562
    identifying congested network, 562-563
    route names, 562
  version (NetWare), 349
  winipcfg, 570

communication networks, 19

communities, SNMP, 230

compatibility, NICs, 129

computers

    error messages, troubleshooting, 589-590

    policies, 590

config command (NetWare), 349-350

configurations

    bridges, 114

    client systems, 443

        Linux/Unix, 446

        Novell, 444-446

        remote servers, 308-310

        Windows, 443-444

    DHCP, fault tolerance, 219

    Network, Novell NetWare, 349-350

    NICs, 437-439

        client systems for TCP/IP, 439-441

        DNS servers, 441

        WINS servers, 441-442

    remote connectivity, 426-427

        dial-up access, 430-432

        physical connections, 427-428

        protocols, 428-429

        security, 432

        software, 429-430

    server, Novell NetWare, 348-349

connection-oriented protocols, 158

connectionless protocols, 158

connectivity, 426

    client systems, 443

        errors, 602-607

        Linux, 371

        Macintoshes, 373

        Novell, 444-446

        Windows 2000 Professional, 370

        Windows clients, 443-444

        Windows NT Workstation, 370

        Windows XP Professional, 370

    network services, 446-447

        adding, 447-449

        modifying, 447-449

        removing, 447-449

    NICs, 432

        configuration, 437-442

        connecting PCs, 435-436

        DHCP, 442-443

        installation, 433-434

        selecting, 433

        testing, 436-437

        troubleshooting, 436-437

    remote, 426-428

        dial-up access, 430-432

        physical connections, 427-428

        protocols, 428-429

        security, 432

        software, 429-430

    speeds (modems), 127-129

    VPNs, 306

connectors, 78

    BNCs, 69, 82

    centronic, 83-84

    D-shell, 78

        AUI ports, 78-79

        external SCSI, 79-80

        parallel, 81

        serial (RS-232), 80

    fiber, 82-83

    RJ, 81, 88

    selecting to add clients, 92-93

ConsoleOne, 347-348

contention media, 40

convergence, 120

cooling fans, 606

Copper Distributed Data Interface. *See* CDDI

costs

cables, 95

client/server networks, 25

NICs, 130

peer-to-peer networks, 22

count to infinity, 121

crackers, compared to hackers, 466

crossover cables, 88, 111-112

crosstalk, 63

CSMA/CD, IEEE standards, 39-41

CSNW (Client Services for NetWare), 364

CSU/DSUs, 125

cut-through switching, 108-109

D

d inet addr switch, 507

D-shell connectors, 78

AUI ports, 78-79

external SCSI, 79-80

parallel, 81

serial (RS-232), 80

daemons, 446

DASs (dual attached stations), 275

data availability. *See* disaster recovery; fault tolerance

data backups, 20

client/server networks, 25

peer-to-peer networks, 22

Data Encryption Standard. *See* DES

data files, 160

data sharing, 19

data-link layer (OSI model), 154-155, 161

bridges, 163

NICs, 163

switches, 162-163

Datagram Delivery Protocol. *See* DDP

datagram packet switching, 266

DDNS (dynamic DNS), 222

DDoS (Distributed Denial of Service), 478

DDP (Datagram Delivery Protocol), 178, 188

decapsulation, 152-153

decentralized networking, 21

decryption, 160

dedicated hardware routers, 123

default gateways, 124, 241-242, 440

configuration, 572-573

delete switch, 515

demand priority (IEEE standards), 43-44

demilitarized zones. *See* DMZs

density ports, 113

DES (Data Encryption Standard), 485-486

Destination Host Unreachable error, 557-558

devices, 104, 137

bridges, 114, 116

data-link layer (OSI model), 163

implementation considerations, 114-115

manual configuration, 114

primary, 115

source-route, 116

translational, 115

transparent, 115

CSU/DSUs, 125

ESD, 133

gateways, 124-125

default, 124

SNA (Systems Network Architecture), 124

hubs, 104-106, 109

cables, 111-112

indicator lights, 112

managed, 113

physical layer (OSI model), 162

ports, 110

rack mounts, 113
workgroup, 104-105
modems, 126-127
AT commands, 127
speed connections, 127-129
NICs, 129-130
built-in, 132, 135
bus compatibility, 129
combo cards, 129
configuration utilities, 133-134
costs, 130
data-link layer (OSI model), 163
drivers, 133
expansion, 131
hardware compatibility, 129
LEDs, 132-133
MAC addresses, 142
network compatibility, 129
PCMCIA cards, 131
port compatibility, 129
system area, 137
nodes, equal access, 40
repeaters, 104
routers, 116-118
brouters, 123
dedicated hardware, 123
network layer (OSI model), 163
routable protocols, 118-119
routing protocols, 119-122
server-based, 123
switches, 106-109
cables, 111-112
cut-through configurations, 108-109
data-link layer (OSI model), 162-163
dip, 133
fragment-free configurations, 109
full-duplex connections, 107-108

half-duplex connections, 107-108
indicator lights, 112
labels, 112
managed, 113
microsegmentation, 108
ports, 110
rack mounts, 113
store-and-forward configurations, 109
WAPs (wireless access points), 126
DFS (Distributed File System), 343
DHCP (Dynamic Host Configuration Protocol),
217-218, 220, 442-443, 594
fault tolerant configurations, 219
network services, 447-448
obtaining IP information from, 451-452
platforms, 218
process, 219
servers, 219-220, 247-250
DHCPACK packet, 219
DHCPDISCOVER broadcasts, 219
DHCPOFFER packet, 219
DHCPREQUEST packet, 219
diagnostic utilities, 437, 557
ipconfig command, 568-570
netstat command, 563
netstat -a, 565-566
netstat -e, 564-565
netstat -r, 566-567
netstat -s, 567-568
ping command, 557, 572
Destination Host Unreachable error, 557-558
Expired TTL error, 560
Request Timed Out error, 558-559
Unknown Host error, 559-560
tracert command, 560-563
failure to get to remote host, 561-562
identifying congested network, 562-563
winipcfg command, 570

dial-up access, remote connectivity, 430-432

dial-up modems, 270

dial-up remote access, 305

dial-up sequence, PPP, 296

dialog boxes

    Add/Remove Programs, 451

    Advanced TCP/IP Settings, 441

    Domain Security Policy, 490

    Internet Protocol (TCP/IP) Properties, 572

    IP Properties, 440

    Local Area Connection Properties, 452

    Local Security Settings, 489

    Microsoft authentication, 445

    Network, 444

    Networking Services, 451

    Novell Login, 445

    Properties, 437

    Routing and Remote Access Service, 430

    Security Policy Setting, 490

    TCP/IP Properties, 440

    Windows Components Wizard, 451

    Windows Security, 331

    winipcfg utility, 513

differential backups, 405

Digital Subscriber Line. *See* DSL

dip switches, 133

direct cable connections, 551

direct sequence modulation, 75

directories, security

    Linux, 363

    NetWare, 353

    Windows NT 4, 335

Dirty Cache Buffers indicator (NetWare Monitor), 346

disaster recovery, backup methods, 386, 403

    best practices, 407-408

    cartridges, 407

    comparison of, 405-406

    differential backups, 405

    full backups, 403-404, 416-417

    incremental backups, 404

    logs, 407

    rotating offsite, 407

    rotation schedules, 406

    testing, 407

discards, netstat –e, 564

disk drives, management

    Linux, 358-359

    Windows 2000, 341

disk duplexing, 391

disk mirroring, 390-391

    advantages, 391

    disadvantages, 391-392

    recovering from failed arrays, 392

disk queue length (Performance Monitor), 330

disk quotas, Windows 2000, 343

disk striping, RAID 0, 389

display servers command (NetWare), 349

distance-vector routing protocols, 119-122

distributed computing, 26

Distributed Denial of Service. *See* DDoS

DMZs (demilitarized zones), 478-479

DNS (Domain Name System), 220-221

    configuring, 441

    entries, 223-224

    implementations, 224

    namespace, 222-223

    network services, 449

    ping, 503

    resolution, 221

    reverse lookups, 223

    server addresses, 440

documentation, troubleshooting, 597

Domain Security Policy dialog box, 490

domain=NAME switch, 514

domains
    DNS namespace, 223
    Windows 2000, 335-336
    Windows NT 4, 325-326
drivers, NICs, 133
DSL (Digital Subscriber Line), 262, 291, 427
    asymmetric, 520
    cable, 262
    HDSL, 521
    ISDN, 520
    speeds, 521
    symmetric, 520
    troubleshooting, 520-522
    VHDSL, 520
dual attached stations (DASs), 275
dual rings, 33
duplexing, 66-67
dynamic DNS. *See* DDNS
Dynamic Host Configuration Protocol (DHCP), 594

E

-e switch, 509
E1 lines, 273
E3 lines, 273
EAP (Extensible Authentication Protocol), 296
eavesdropping, wireless media, 65
EFS (Encrypting File System), 343
EIA/TIA, twisted-pair cable categories, 71
ELAP (EtherTalk Link Access Protocol), 188
Electrical and Electronics Engineers. *See* IEEE
electromagnetic interference. *See* EMI
electrostatic discharge. *See* ESD
email
    SMTP, 209
    Web-based mail, 211

EMI (electromagnetic interference), 62-63
    cable resistant to, 63
    crosstalk, 63
encapsulation, 152-153
Encrypting File System. *See* EFS
encryption, 160, 484-485
    3DES, 486
    DES, 485-486
    IPSec, 485
    PGP, 486
entries, DNS, 223-224
equal access (nodes), 40
equipment, securing, 465
errors
    frequency, 590
    messages, 590
    netstat –e, 564
escalation procedures, development, 595
ESD (electrostatic discharge), 133
Ethernet
    5-4-3 rule, 87-88
    compared to Token Rings, 47
    Fast
        100BaseX standards, 89-90
        repeaters, 89
    Gigabit, 90-92
    IEEE standard (802.3 standard), 45-46
    standards, 30
EtherTalk Link Access Protocol. *See* ELAP
Event Viewer
    Windows 2000, 338
    Windows NT, 330-331
exam simulation, 707
Examination Score Report (PrepLogic practice tests), 710
exams, practice, 653-672, 707
    customized, 709
    displaying scores, 710

installing, 708

modes, 708

preconfigured, 709

reviewing the exam, 710

timed, 710

uninstalling, 708

exit switch, 514

expansion NICs, 131

Expired TTL error, 560

Extended AppleTalk Network, 189

Extensible Authentication Protocol. *See* EAP

external ISDN adapters, 136-137

external SCSI connectors, 79-80

F

-f switch, 504, 516

factional subnetting, 239

failures

client/server networks, 25

server hardware, 387

Fast Ethernet

repeaters, 89

standards, 100BaseX, 89-90

Fast Ethernet IEEE standard (802.3u standard), 46

FAT (File Allocation Table), 327-328, 337

FAT32, 327, 337

fault detection, 275

fault tolerance, 386-387, 398-399

DHCP configurations, 219

faulty power supplies, 399

memory, 399

mesh topologies, 34

NICs, 400

power threats, 402

processor failures, 399-400

RAID, 388-389

choosing levels, 396-397

hardware, 398

RAID 0, 389-390

RAID 1, 390-392

RAID 10, 395-396

RAID 2, 392

RAID 3, 393

RAID 4, 393

RAID 5, 393-395

software, 398

server clusters, 401

standby servers, 400

UPSs, 401-402

FCC (Federal Communications Commission), 75

FDDI (Fiber Distributed Data Interface), 49-50, 274

advantages/disadvantages, 275-276

compared to CDDI, 49

compared to IEEE 802.5, 274-275

fault detection, 275

implementing, 275

Fdisk, 358

Federal Communications Commission (FCC), 75

fiber connectors, 82-83

Fiber Distributed Data Interface. *See* FDDI

fiber-optic cable, 72-73

File Allocation Table. *See* FAT

file and print services

Linux, 360-361

Novell NetWare, 351

operating systems, 323

Windows 2000, 343

Windows NT 4, 333-334

File and Print Services for NetWare. *See* FPNW

file server storage, 411-412

file systems
  Linux, 355-356
  Novell NetWare, 345-346
  security, 471
    Linux, 472-473
    Novell NetWare, 471-472
    Unix, 472-473
    Windows 2000, 473-474
    Windows NT 4, 473-474
  Windows 2000, 337
  Windows NT 4, 327-328
File Transfer Protocol. *See* FTP
files
  data, 160
  graphic, 159
  HOSTS, 221
  permissions
    best practices, 474-475
    Linux, 473
    Novell NetWare, 472
    Unix, 473
    Windows 2000, 474
    Windows NT, 474
  security
    Linux, 363
    NetWare, 353
    Windows NT 4, 335
  sharing, enabling on Windows ME, 52
  sound, 160
  systems. *See* file systems
  text, 160
  video, 160
firewalls, 142, 475-476
  application gateway, 477
  circuit-level, 477
  DMZs (demilitarized zones), 478-479
  functions, 476
  packet filtering, 476-477
Flash Review mode (PrepLogic practice test), 708
  starting a session, 709
flooding, SYN, 206
flow control, transport layer (OSI model), 158-159
foreign addresses, netstat –a commands, 566
fox and hound (tone generator), 551
FPNW (File and Print Services for NetWare), 364
fractional T, 273
fragment-free switching, 109
Frame Relay, 278-279
frequency hopping, 75
FTP (File Transfer Protocol), 177, 207-208
  commands, 208-209
  OSI model, 207
full backups, 403-404, 416-417
full-duplex connections, 107-108
full-duplex duplexing, 67

G

Gateway Services for NetWare (GSNW), 364
gateways, 124-125
  default, 124, 241-242
  SNA (Systems Network Architecture), 124
get command, 208
GFS (Grandfather-Father-Son), 406
Gigabit Ethernet IEEE standard (802.3z standard), 46-47, 90-92
GNOME, 357
graphic files, 159
graphical utilities, 357-358
GSNW (Gateway Services for NetWare), 364

H

hackers, compared to crackers, 466
half-duplex connections, 107-108
half-duplex duplexing, 67
hamming code, 392
hard disk counters, 330
hardware
    changes, 593
    compatibility, NICs, 129, 322
    server, 387
    sharing, 19
hardware layer. *See* physical layer (OSI model)
hardware loopback connectors, 553
hardware RAID, 398
HDSL, 521
headers, IPv6 packets, 238
headless operations, 353
hierarchical star topologies, 31
hold-down timers, 120
home offices, troubleshooting, 516-519
    cable Internet access, 523-525
    DSL Internet access, 520-522
    POTS Internet access, 528-533
    satellite Internet access, 525-526
    technical support, 533-534
    wireless Internet access, 526-527
    xDSL Internet access, 520-521
homemade cables, 550
HOSTS file, 221
HTTP (Hypertext Transfer Protocol), 209-210
    proxy servers, 480
    UDP, 210
HTTPS (Hypertext Transfer Protocol Secure), 210
hub LEDs, 554-555

hubs, 104-106, 109
    cables, 111-112
    indicator lights, 112
    managed, 113
    physical layer (OSI model), 162
    ports, 110
    rack mounts, 113
    workgroup, 104-105
hybrid mesh topologies, 34
Hypertext Transfer Protocol Secure. *See* HTTPS
Hypertext Transfer Protocol. *See* HTTP

I

IANA (Internet Assigned Numbers Authority), 181
ICA (Independent Computing Architecture), 298-299
ICMP (Internet Control Message Protocol), 211-212, 501
ICP (Internet Cache Protocol), 481
ICS, 224, 226
IDC (insulation displacement connector), 551
identifiers, SNMP, 230
IDSL (ISDN DSL), 520
IEEE (Electrical and Electronics Engineers) standards, 30, 36
    802, 45-50
    802 standards, 37-38
    802.1q, 408
    802.3, 84-92
    access methods, 39-44
    cables, 69
    Ethernet, 30
    media, 44
    speed, 38-39
    topologies, 44

IEEE 802.5, 274-275

ifconfig command, 360

ifconfig utility, 511-512

incremental backups, 404

Independent Computing Architecture. *See* ICA

independent routing, 265

indicator lights (modems), 524

   hubs, 112

   switches, 112

inet addr switch, 507

inetcfg command (NetWare), 350

infrared wireless networking, 77-78

infrastructures, troubleshooting, 609-610

   baselines, 610-611

   nonspecific failures, 610

   poor performance, 610

   specific failures, 609

installations

   AppleTalk, 195

   DHCP server, 247-250

   media, 65

   NICs, 133-135, 433-434

   peer-to-peer networks, 22

   PrepLogic practice tests, 708

   TCP/IP, testing, 503

   Windows 2000 Advanced Server, 375-377

   WINS, 451

insulation displacement connector (IDC), 551

Integrated Services Digital Network. *See* ISDN

interactive logons, Windows 2000, 342

interface design, PrepLogic practice tests, 707-708

interference (EMI), 62-63

internal ISDN adapters, 136

International Organization for Standardization. *See* ISO

Internet, 262

   access. *See also* proxy servers

      cable, 523-525

      DSL, 520-522

      POTS, 528-533

      satellites, 525-526

      technical support, 533-534

      wireless, 526-527

      xDSL, 520-521

   as networks, 19

Internet Assigned Numbers Authority. *See* IANA

Internet Cache Protocol. *See* ICP

Internet Control Message Protocol. *See* ICMP

Internet Protocol (TCP/IP) Properties dialog box, 572

Internet Protocol. *See* IP

Internetwork Packet Exchange/Sequenced Packet Exchange. *See* IPX/SPX

internetworks, 27

interoperability

   AppleTalk, 190

   IPX/SPX, 187

   operating systems, 363-365

   TCP/IP, 182

interrupt request (IRQ), NICs, 134

interval switch, 509

IP (Internet Protocol) addresses, 178, 205, 233-234, 439

   broadcast addresses, 236

   CIDR, 236-237

   classes, 235

   IPv4, 234-235

   IPv6, 237-238

   network addresses, 233

   node addresses, 233

   packet filtering, 476

   private address ranges, 244-245

   public address ranges, 245

   single, 479

   subnet mask assignments, 236

IP Properties dialog box, 440

IP subnetting, 238-241

ipconfig /all command, 140, 511

ipconfig commands, 568-570

ipconfig utility, 511-512, 539

   switches, 512

   Windows NT 4, 332

IPSec, 300-301, 485

iptrace command (NetWare), 350

IPv4, 234-235

IPv6, 237-238

IPX, 158, 178, 184

   addressing, 186-187

   interoperability, 187

   naming, 187

IPX/SPX (Internetwork Packet Exchange/Sequenced Packet Exchange), 119, 175, 183-184, 429, 438-439

   OSI model, 187

   suite of protocols, 184

      IPX, 178, 184, 186-187

      NCP, 185

      NLSP, 185

      RIP, 185

      SAP, 185

      SPX, 178, 185

ipxping command (NetWare), 350

IRQ (interrupt request), NICs, 134

ISDN (Integrated Services Digital Network), 261, 270, 293, 427

   BRI (Basic Rate Interface), 271-272

   DSL, 520

   leased lines, 271

   PRI (Primary Rate Interface), 271-272

   RADSL, 520

   terminal adapters, 135-137

ISO (International Organization for Standardization), 151

-i TTL switch, 504

J-K

jumpers, 133-134

K Desktop Environment (KDE), 357

KDE (K Desktop Environment), 357

Kerberos, 303, 343

L

L2F, 301

L2TP (Layer Two Tunneling Protocol), 301-302

labeling cables, 551

LANs (local area networks), 26-27

   IEEE standards. *See* standards (IEEE)

   topologies, 28-29

      bus, 29-30

      logical, 29

      mesh, 33-34

      physical, 29

      ring, 32-33

      star, 31-32

      wireless, 34-36

latency, 109

Layer Two Tunneling Protocol. *See* L2TP

layers (OSI model), 152, 161, 166

   application, 160-161

   data-link, 154-155, 161

      bridges, 163

      NICs, 163

      switches, 162-163

   decapsulation, 152-153

   encapsulation, 152-153

   logical groups of bits, 153

   mnemonics, 152

network, 155
    addressing, 156-157
    routers, 163
    switching methods, 155-156
physical, 153-154, 161-162
presentation, 159-161
session, 159, 161
transport, 157, 161
    flow control, 158-159
    protocols, 157-158
lcd command, 208
leased lines, ISDN, 271
LEDs (light-emitting diodes), 132-133, 550
    hub, 554-555
    NIC, 555
    troubleshooting, 556
licensing, 77
light-emitting diodes (LEDs), 550
link lights, 132
link-state protocols, 122
Linux, 321, 353-354
    application support, 361-362
    authentication, 360
    client support, 366-367
    client system configurations, 446
    client systems, 370-372
    disk drive management, 358-359
    file and print services, 360-361
    file systems, 355-356
    interoperability with NetWare, 365
    interoperability with Windows, 364-365
    monitoring tools, 356
        disk drive management, 358
        graphical utilities, 357-358
        proc directory, 357
        Top utility, 356-357
        user management, 359

network settings verification, 360
performance tools, 356
    graphical utilities, 357-358
    proc directory, 357
    Top utility, 356-357
security, 362-363, 472-473
system requirements, 355
Telenet, 211
user management, 358-359
LLC sublayer (802.2 standard), 45
local addresses, netstat –a commands, 566
Local Area Connection Properties dialog box, 452
local area networks. See LANs
local security passwords
    policies, 490
    strength of, 490-491
Local Security Settings dialog box, 489
local users, administration, 342
LocalTalk, 189
log files, 589
logbooks, 597
logical groups of bits (OSI model), 153
logical LAN topologies, 29
logical security, 465-467
    authentication, 466-467
    file systems, 471
        Linux, 472-473
        Novell NetWare, 471-472
        Unix, 472-473
        Windows 2000, 473-474
        Windows NT 4, 473-474
    passwords, 466-467
        administrator, 469
        effectiveness, 470-471
        policies, 467-468
        strength of, 469
        user, 469-470

logically assigned addresses, 156

logs
 application, 331, 338
 performance, 339
 security, 330, 338
 system, 331, 338

Long Term Cache Hits indicator (NetWare Monitor), 347

loopback adapters, 502

loops (routing), 121-122

ls command, 208

-l size switch, 504

M

MAC (Media Access Control) addresses, 107, 138-139, 410, 570
 determining, 142
 packet filtering, 477
 viewing methods, 139-140
 VLANs, 410-411

MAC OS X, 373

Macintoshes, 372-373
 application support, 373
 client connectivity, 373
 operating systems, 321

managed hubs, 113

managed switches, 113

Management Information Bases. See MIBs

management systems, SNMP, 227

MANs (metropolitan area networks), 26, 28

mapped drives, connecting through Windows 2000, 52-53

MAUs, compared to MSAU, 42

maximum password age, 467

MDI ports (medium dependent interface), 110

MDIX ports (medium dependent interface crosses), 110

media, 62
 ATM, 278
 attenuation, 64
 bandwidth, 63-64
 baseband signaling, 65-66
 bound, 68
 broadband signaling, 65-66
 cables, 68
  basic characteristics, 73-74
  coaxial, 68-70, 84-87
  costs, 95
  crossover, 88
  fiber-optic, 72-73
  plenum, 65
  twisted-pair, 70-71, 87-88
 connectors, 78
  BNCs, 69, 82
  centronic, 83-84
  D-shell, 78-81
  fiber, 82-83
  RJ, 81, 88
  selecting to add clients, 92-93
 contention, 40
 duplexing, 66-67
 IEEE standards, 44
 installation, 65
 interference (EMI), 62-63
 length, 64
 repairs, 65
 security, 65
 unbound, 68
 wireless, 74
  eavesdropping, 65
  infrared, 77-78

microwave, 76-77

raido, 74-76

Media Access Control. *See* MAC (Media Access Control) addresses

media testers, 552

medium dependent interface crossed. *See* MDI-X

medium dependent interface. *See* MDI

member servers, Windows NT 4, 326

memberships, VLAN, 409

memory

addresses, NICs, 134

fault-tolerance, 399

memory available bytes (Performance Monitor), 329

memory pages/sec (Performance Monitor), 329

mesh network errors, 601-602

mesh topologies, 33-34

message switching, 156, 268

metrics, 120

metropolitan area networks. *See* MANs

mget command, 209

MIBs (Management Information Bases, 228-229

microsegmentation, 108

Microsoft Authentication dialog box, 445

Microsoft Challenge Handshake Authentication Protocol. *See* MS-CHAP

microwave frequencies, 76

satellite, 77

terrestrial, 76-77

mnemonics, OSI model layers, 152

modems, 126-127

AT commands, 127

connection speeds, 127-129

CSU/DSUs, 125

dial-up connections, 270

indicator lights, 524

troubleshooting, 531-533

monitoring tools

Linux, 356

graphical utilities, 357-358

proc directory, 357

Top utility, 356-357

Novell NetWare, 346-347

Windows 2000, 337-338

Event Viewer, 338

Performance console, 338-339

Recovery console, 340

System Information console, 340

Task Manager, 340

Windows NT 4, 328

Event Viewer, 330-331

Network Monitor, 330

Performance Monitor, 328-330

Task Manager, 330-331

mput command, 208

MS-CHAP, 296

MSAUs (multistation access unit), 42

Token Ring networks, 106

multimeters, 552

multiplexing, 66, 273

multiprotocol routing, 119, 122

multistation access units. *See* MSAUs

muxing, 273

N

N if addr switch, 507

n switch, 509-510

Name Binding Protocol. *See* NBP

name resolution, NetBIOs, 231

namespaces, DNS, 222-223

naming
    AppleTalk, 191
    IPX/SPX, 187
    TCP/IP, 182-183
NAS (network attached storage), 386, 411-413
NAT (Network Address Translation), 224-225, 479
    L2TP, 302
    proxy servers, 225
nbtstat utility, 509-510
-n count switch, 504
NCP (NetWare Core Protocol), 177, 185
NDPS (Novell Distributed Printing Services), 446
NDS (Novell Directory Services), 345, 351
NetBEUI, 178, 191, 439
    addressing, 192
    OSI model, 191-192
netstat –a commands, 565-566
    foreign address, 566
    local address, 566
    proto, 566
    state, 566
netstat –e commands, 564-565
    bytes, 564
    discards, 564
    errors, 564
    non-unicast packets, 564
    unicast packets, 564
    unknown protocols, 565
netstat –r commands, 509, 566-567
netstat –s commands, 567-568
netstat commands, 508, 563
    netstat -a, 565-566
    netstat -e, 564-565
    netstat -r, 566-567
    netstat -s, 567-568
netstat utility, 507-509

NetWare, 321, 344-345
    application support, 351-352
    authentication, 350
    client support, 366
    file and print services, 351
    file systems, 345-346
    interoperability with Linux, 365
    interoperability with Windows, 364
    monitoring tools, 346-347
    network configuration, 349-350
    performance tools, 346-347
    security, 352-353, 471-472
    server configuration, 348-349
    system requirements, 345
    user management, 347-348
NetWare Administrator, 347-348
NetWare Core Protocol. See NCP
NetWare Link State Protocol. See NLSP
NetWare Loadable Modules (NLMs), 352
NetWare Monitor, 346-347
Network Address Translation. See NAT
network attached storage. See NAS
network connectivity, 426
    client systems, 443
        Linux/Unix, 446
        Novell, 444-446
        Windows clients, 443-444
    network services, 446-447
        adding, 447-449
        modifying, 447-449
        removing, 447-449
    NICs, 432
        configuration, 437-442
        connecting PCs, 435-436
        DHCP, 442-443
        installation, 433-434
        selecting, 433

testing, 436-437

troubleshooting, 436-437

remote, 426-427

  dial-up access, 430-432

  physical connections, 427-428

  protocols, 428-429

  security, 432

  software, 429-430

Network dialog box, 444

Network File Systems, 412

network interface cards. *See* **NICs**

network layer (OSI model), 155

addressing, 156-157

routers, 163

switching methods, 155-156

network management systems. *See* **NMSs**

Network Monitor, 330

network services, 446-447

adding, 447

  DHCP, 447-448

  DNS, 449

  WINS, 448-449

modifying, 447

  DHCP, 447-448

  DNS, 449

  WINS, 448-449

removing, 447

  DHCP, 447-448

  DNS, 449

  WINS, 448-449

TCP/IP, 216-217, 232-233

  BOOTP, 220

  DDNS, 222

  DHCP, 217-220

  DNS, 220-224

  ICS, 224, 226

  NAT, 224-225

  SNMP, 226-230

  WINS, 230-232

Network Time Protocol. *See* **NTP**

networking, 18

networking operating systems. *See* **NOSs**

Networking Services dialog box, 451

networks, 19-20

administrators

  passwords, 469

  security responsibilities, 464-465

application sharing, 20

centralized computing, 26

client/server, 20, 23

  advantages, 24-25

  clients, 24

  disadvantages, 25

  servers, 23-24

coaxial, connecting to, 435

combination, 25

communication, 19

configuration, Novell NetWare, 349-350

connectivity. *See* network connectivity

data sharing, 19

decentralized networking, 21

definition, 18-19

distributed computing, 26

Ethernet. *See* Ethernet

Internet as, 19

LANs, IEEE standards. *See* standards (IEEE)

local area networks. *See* LANs

mesh, troubleshooting, 601-602

metropolitan area networks. *See* MANs

peer-to-peer, 20-22

  advantages, 22

  disadvantages, 22-23

  size, 22

private, 242-243
  address ranges, 244-245
  WANs, 263-264
protocols, 175-179
public, 242-243
  address ranges, 245
  WANs, 261-263
server-based networking, 23
services. *See* network services
settings, 594
  Linux, 360
  Windows NT 4, 332-333
size, troubleshooting, 587
star, troubleshooting, 599-600
Thinnet, 82
Token Ring
  compared to Ethernets, 47
    MSAU (multistation access unit), 42, 106
    token passing, 41-43
topologies. *See* topologies
virtual private networks. *See* VPNs
wide area networks. *See* WANs
wireless
    IEEE standard 802.11b, 48-49
    troubleshooting, 602
    war driving, 48
New Technology File System. *See* **NTFS**
NFS, 361, 446
NICs (network interface card), 129-130, 432, 549
  built-in, 132, 135
  bus compatibility, 129
  combo cards, 129
  configuration, 437-439
    client systems for TCP/IP, 439-441
    DNS servers, 441
    WINS servers, 441-442
  configuration utilities, 133-134

connecting PCs, 435-436
costs, 130
data-link layer (OSI model), 163
DHCP, 442-443
drivers, 133
ESD, 133
expansion, 131
fault tolerance, 400
hardware compatibility, 129
installation, 133-135, 433-434
LEDs, 132-133, 555
MAC addresses, 142
network compatibility, 129
PCMCIA cards, 131
port compatibility, 129
selecting, 433
system area, 137
testing, 436-437
troubleshooting, 108, 436-437
NLMs (NetWare Loadable Modules), 352
NLSP (NetWare Link State Protocol), 122, 185
NMSs (network management systems), 226
nodes, 39, 111
  addresses, 233
  equal access, 40
non-unicast packets, netstat -e, 564
NOSs, 319-320
  application support, 322-324
  authentication, 323
  choosing, 320-323
  client support, 365
    Linux, 366-367
    NetWare, 366
    Windows, 365-366
  file and print services, 323
  hardware compatibility lists, 322

interoperability, 363
  NetWare and Linux, 365
  Windows and Linux, 364-365
  Windows and NetWare, 364
Linux, 321, 353-354
  application support, 361-362
  authentication, 360
  disk drive management, 358-359
  file and print services, 360-361
  file systems, 355-356
  monitoring tools, 356-358
  network settings verification, 360
  performance tools, 356-358
  security, 362-363, 472-473
  system requirements, 355
  user management, 358-359
Macintosh, 321
Novell NetWare, 321, 344-345
  application support, 351-352
  authentication, 350
  file and print services, 351
  file systems, 345-346
  monitoring tools, 346-347
  network configuration, 349-350
  performance tools, 346-347
  security, 352-353, 471-472
  server configuration, 348-349
  system requirements, 345
  user management, 347-348
security, 324
third-party vendors, 323
Unix
  client system configurations, 446
  security, 472-473
  Telnet, 211
Windows, 320

Windows 2000, 335
  Active Directory, 335-336
  application support, 344
  authentication, 342-343
  disk drive management, 341
  file and print services, 343
  file systems, 337
  monitoring tools, 337-340
  performance tools, 337-340
  ping switches, 504
  security, 344, 473-474
  system requirements, 336-337
  user management, 342
Windows NT 4, 324-325
  application support, 334
  authentication, 333
  domains, 325-326
  file and print services, 333-334
  file systems, 327-328
  monitoring tools, 328-331
  performance tools, 328-331
  security, 334-335, 473-474
  system requirements, 327
  user management, 331-332
  verifying network settings, 332-333
  workgroups, 325-326
Novell Directory Services. *See* NDS
Novell Distributed Printing Services (NDPS), 446
Novell Login dialog box, 445
Novell NetWare, 321, 344-345
  application support, 351-352
  authentication, 350
  client support, 366
  client system configurations, 444-446
  file and print services, 351
  file systems, 345-346
  interoperability with Linux, 365

interoperability with Windows, 364

monitoring tools, 346-347

network configuration, 349-350

performance tools, 346-347

security, 352-353, 471-472

server configuration, 348-349

system requirements, 345

user management, 347-348

Novell Storage Services (NSS), 346

[no]d2 switch, 514

[no]debug switch, 514

[no]defname switch, 514

[no]msxfr switch, 514

[no]recurse switch, 514

[no]search switch, 514

[no]vc switch, 514

NPB (Name Binding Protocol), 189

nslookup utility, 513-514

NSS (Novell Storage Services), 346

NT LAN Manager (NTLM), 343

NTFS (New Technology File System), 327-328, 337

partitions, 328

NTLM (NT LAN Manager), 343

NTP (Network Time Protocol), 213

numbering (OSI), 154

NWLink, 184, 438-439

O

object-based security, 334

OC levels (SONET), 279

Open Shortest Path First (OSPF), 122

Open Systems Interconnect. *See* OSI

operating systems, 319-320, 367

application support, 322-324

authentication, 323

choosing, 320-323

client support, 365

Linux, 366-367

NetWare, 366

Windows, 365-366

file and print services, 323

hardware compatibility lists, 322

interoperability, 363

Linux and NetWare, 365

Windows and Linux, 364-365

Windows and NetWare, 364

Linux, 321, 353-354, 370

application support, 361-362, 371

authentication, 360, 372

client connectivity, 371

client support, 366-367

disk drive management, 358-359

file and print services, 360-361

file systems, 355-356

interoperability with NetWare, 365

interoperability with Windows, 364-365

monitoring tools, 356-358

network settings verification, 360

performance tools, 356-358

security, 362-363, 372, 472-473

system requirements, 355

user management, 358-359

log files, 589

Macintosh, 321

Macintoshes, 372-373

Novell NetWare, 321, 344-345

application support, 351-352

authentication, 350

client support, 366

file and print services, 351

file systems, 345-346

interoperability with Linux, 365

interoperability with Windows, 364
monitoring tools, 346-347
network configuration, 349-350
performance tools, 346-347
security, 352-353, 471-472
server configuration, 348-349
system requirements, 345
user management, 347-348
security, 324
third-party vendors, 323
Unix, 321, 472-473
Windows, 320, 367, 369-370
application support, 368
authentication, 368
client support, 365-366
interoperability with Linux, 364-365
interoperability with NetWare, 364
security, 368
Windows 2000, 335
Active Directory, 335-336
application support, 344
authentication, 342-343
disk drive management, 341
file and print services, 343
file systems, 337
monitoring tools, 337-340
performance tools, 337-340
ping switches, 504
security, 344, 473-474
system requirements, 336-337
user management, 342
Windows NT 4, 324-325
application support, 334
authentication, 333
domains, 325-326
file and print services, 333-334
file systems, 327-328

monitoring tools, 328-331
performance tools, 328-331
security, 334-335, 473-474
system requirements, 327
user management, 331-332
verifying network settings, 332-333
workgroups, 325-326
optical cable testers, 552
optical time-domain reflectometer (OTDR), 552
option switch, 514
organizationally unique identifiers (OUIs), 139
OSI (Open Systems Interconnect), 151
FTP site, 207
layers, 152, 161, 166
application, 160-161
data-link, 154-155, 161-163
decapsulation, 152-153
encapsulation, 152-153
logical groups of bits, 153
mnemonics, 152
network, 155-157, 163
network layer (OSI model), 161
physical, 153-154, 161-162
presentation, 159-161
session, 159, 161
transport, 157-159, 161
numbering, 154
protocols, 177
AppleTalk, 190
application protocols, 177
IPX/SPX, 187
NetBEUI, 191-192
network protocols, 178-179
TCP/IP, 183
transport protocols, 178
TCP, 206
UDP, 207

OSPF (Open Shortest Path First), 122
OTDR (optical time-domain reflectometer), 552
OUIs (organizationally unique identifier), 139

P

p proto switch, 509
p switch, 516
packet assemblers/disassemblers. *See* PADs
packets, 153
   DHCPACK, 219
   DHCPOFFER, 219
   DHCPREQUEST, 219
   Filtering,
   IPv6, 238
   sniffing, 476-477, 484
   switching, 156, 265-266
      datagram, 266
      virtual-circuit, 266
PADs (packet assemblers/disassemblers), 278
PAP (Password Authentication Protocol), 296
PAP (Printer Access Protocol), 189
parallel connectors, 81
partitions, NTFS, 328
passphrases, 467
passwd command, 359
Password Authentication Protocol (PAP), 296
passwords, 466-467
   administrator, 469
   backups, 407
   caps locks, 335
   effectiveness, 470-471
   enforcing policies, 468
   length, 467
   maximum password age, 467
   Novell NetWare, 350

   passphrases, 467
   policies, 467-468, 490
   shadowing, 359
   strength of, 469, 490-491
   user, 469-470
patches, 593
   cables, 554
   panels, 550
PCMCIA cards (NICs), 131
PCs, connecting to networks, 435-436
PDC (primary domain controller), 325
peer-to-peer networks, 20-22
   advantages, 22
   disadvantages, 22-23
   size, 22
percent disk time (Performance Monitor), 329
percent processor time (Performance Monitor), 329
Performance Console (Windows 2000), 338-339
Performance Monitor (Windows NT), 328-330
performance
   baselines, 328
   Linux, 356
      proc directory, 357
      Top utility, 356-357
   logs, 339
   Novell NetWare, 346-347
   Windows 2000, 337-338
      Event Viewer, 338
      Performance console, 338-339
      Recovery console, 340
      System Information console, 340
      Task Manager, 340
   Windows NT 4, 328
      Event Viewer, 330-331
      Network Monitor, 330
      Performance Monitor, 328-330
      Task Manager, 330-331

permanent virtual circuits. *See* PVCs

permissions

best practices, 474-475

changes, 593

errors, 605-606

Linux, 473

Novell NetWare, 472

Unix, 473

Windows 2000, 474

Windows NT, 474

PGP (Pretty Good Privacy), 486

physical connections

errors, 606-607

remote, 427-428, 535-536

physical LAN topologies, 29

physical layer (OSI model), 153-154, 161-162

physical security, 465-466

physical slots, NICs, 134

ping command (NetWare), 350, 360, 501-503, 539, 557, 572

Destination Host Unreachable error, 557-558

DNS, 503

Expired TTL error, 560

Request Timed Out error, 558-559

simulating bad connections, 572

simulating communication problems, 572

switches, 503-504

Unknown Host error, 559-560

Windows NT 4, 332

ping test, 556

plain old telephone system. *See* POTs

plain old telephone system. *See* PSTN

platforms, DHCP, 218

plenum cables, 65

Point-to-Point Protocol over Ethernet. *See* PPPoE

Point-to-Point Protocol. *See* PPP

poison reverses, 121

policies, computer usage, 590

POP/IMAP (Post Office Protocol/Internet Message Access Protocol), 210

port-based VLANs, 410

ports

AUI (attachment unit interface), 78-79

compatibility, 129

density, 113

MDI (medium dependent interface), 110

MDIX (medium dependent interface crosses), 110

numbers

blocking, 483-484

packet filtering, 476

RI, 42

RO, 42

TCP, 214-216

UDP, 214-216

uplink, 110

Post Office Protocol/Internet Message Access Protocol. *See* POP/IMAP

POTs (plain old telephone system), 427

troubleshooting Internet access, 528-529

connection speeds, 531

modems, 532-533

procedures, 529-531

power supplies

fault tolerance, 402

faulty, 399

PPP (Point-to-Point Protocol), 295, 428

authentication protocols, 295-296

CHAP, 295

EAP, 296

MS-CHAP, 296

PAP, 296

SPAP, 296

dial-up sequence, 296

PPPoE (Point-to-Point Protocol over Ethernet), 428-429

PPTP, 297-298, 301-302

practice exam, 653-672

Practice Test mode (PrepLogic practice test), 708

  buttons, 709

  starting a session, 709

PrepLogic, contacting, 711

PrepLogic Exam Competency (PrepLogic practice tests), 710

PrepLogic practice tests

  buttons, 709

  customized tests, 709

  Examination Score Report, 710

  Flash Review mode

  starting a session, 709

  installing, 708

  interface design, 707-708

  modes, 708

  options, 709

  Practice Test mode, starting a session, 709

  preconfigured tests, 709

  PrepLogic Exam Competency Score, 710

  reviewing the test, 710

  software requirements, 708

  timed tests, 710

  uninstalling, 708

presentation layer (OSI model), 159-161

pressures, troubleshooting, 585

Pretty Good Privacy (PGP), 486

PRI (Primary Rate Interface), 271-272

primary bridges, 115

Primary Rate Interface. See PRI

print sharing, enabling on Windows ME, 52

print switch, 516

Printer Access Protocol. See PAP

printer settings, 594

private networks, 242-243

  address ranges, 244-245

  WANs, 263-264

problem determination, troubleshooting, 586

proc directory (Linux), 357

Process Utilization indicator (NetWare Monitor), 346

processors, failures, 399-400

production environments, 109

Properties dialog box, 437

PROSet, 134

proto, netstat –a commands, 566

protocols, 174-175, 192-193

  ADSP, 188

  AFP (AppleTalk File Protocol), 177, 188

  AppleShare, 188

  AppleTalk, 175, 188-189

    addressing, 189-190

    installing on Windows 2000 Server, 195

    interoperability, 190

    LocalTalk, 189

    naming, 191

    OSI model, 190

    routing, 191

  application, 175, 177, 412

  ARP (Address Resolution Protocol), 188, 212-213, 506

    cache, 506-507

    switches, 507

  ASP, 188

  ATP (AppleTalk Transaction Protocol), 178, 188

  BOOTP, 220

  CARP (Caching Array Routing Protocol), 481

  CHAP (Challenge Handshake Authentication Protocol), 295

  DDP (Datagram Delivery Protocol), 178, 188

  DHCP (Dynamic Host Configuration Protocol), 217-218, 220, 442-443

    fault tolerant configurations, 219

    network services, 447-448

    platforms, 218

    process, 219

    servers, 219-220

ELAP, 188

errors, 603-604

FTP (File Transfer Protocol), 177, 207-208
    commands, 208-209
    OSI model, 207

functions, 175-176

HTTP, (Hypertext Transfer Protocol), 209-210
    proxy servers, 480
    UDP, 210

HTTPS (Hypertext Transfer Protocol Secure), 210

ICMP (Internet Control Message Protocol), 211-212, 501

IDs, packet filtering, 477

IP (Internet Protocol), 205

IPSec, 300-301, 485

IPX, 158, 178, 184
    addressing, 186-187
    interoperability, 187
    naming, 187

IPX/SPX, 175, 183-184, 438-439
    (Internetwork Packet Exchange/Sequenced Packet Exchange), 429
    interoperability, 187
    naming, 187
    OSI model, 187
    suite of protocols, 178, 184-187

Kerberos, 303

L2F, 301

L2TP, 301-302

NBP, 189

NCP (NetWare Core Protocol), 177, 185

NetBEUI, 178, 191, 439
    addressing, 192
    OSI model, 191-192

network, 175, 178-179

NLSP (NetWare Link State Protocol), 185

NTP (Network Time Protocol), 213

NWLink, 184, 439

OSI model, 177
    AppleTalk, 190
    application protocols, 177
    IPX/SPX, 187
    NetBEUI, 191-192
    network protocols, 178-179
    TCP/IP, 183
    transport protocols, 178

PAP, 189

POP/IMAP (Post Office Protocol/Internet Message Access Protocol), 210

PPP (Point-to-Point Protocol), 295, 428
    authentication protocols, 295-296
    dial-up sequence, 296

PPPoE (Point-to-Point Protocol over Ethernet), 428-429

remote access, 292
    ICA, 298-299
    PPP, 295-296
    PPTP, 297-298, 301-302
    SLIP, 294
    troubleshooting, 536-537

remote connectivity, 428-429

RIP (Routing Information Protocol), 185

routable, 118-119

routing, 119-120
    AppleTalk, 191
    distance-vector, 119-122
    link-state, 122
    TCP/IP, 183

RTMP, 189

SAP, 185

security, 299-300
    IPSec, 300-301
    Kerberos, 303
    L2F, 301

L2TP, 301-302
SSL, 302
SLIP (Serial Line Internet Protocol), 294, 428
SMTP (Simple Mail Transfer Protocol), 177, 209
SNMP (Simple Network Management Protocol), 177, 226
    agents, 228
    communities, 230
    components, 226-227
    identifiers, 230
    management systems, 227
    MIBs, 228-229
    versions, 228
SPX, 158, 178, 185
SSL, 302
STP (Spanning Tree Protocol), 115
TCP (Transmission Control Protocol), 157, 178, 206
TCP/IP, 175, 179, 205, 213-214, 429, 437
    addressing, 181
    ARP, 212-213
    configuring client systems, 439-441
    Dynamic Host Configuration Protocol. See DHCP
    FTP, 207-209
    history, 179
    HTTP, 209-210
    HTTPS, 210
    ICMP, 211-212
    interoperability, 182
    IP, 205
    IP addressing, 233-238, 244-245
    IPSec, 301
    naming, 182-183
    network services, 216-233
    NTP, 213
    OSI model, 183

POP/IMAP, 210
ports, 214-216
routing protocols, 183
SMTP, 209
standards, 180-181
suite of protocols, 180
TCP, 206
Telnet, 211
TFTP, 209
UDP, 206-207
Telnet, 211
TFTP (Trivial File Transfer Protocol), 209
transport, 175, 178
transport layer (OSI model), 157-158
UDP (User Datagram Protocol), 157, 178, 206-207
    HTTP, 210
    OSI model, 207
VPN, 306
ZIP, 189
proxies, WINS, 442
proxy servers, 479-480, 482
    caching, 480-481
    HTTP, 480
    NAT, 225
PSTN (plain old telephone system), 261, 427
public networks, 242-243
    address ranges, 245
    WANs, 261
        advantages/disadvantages, 262-263
        Internet, 262
        PSTN, 261
Public switched telephone network. See PSTN
punchdown tools, 550-551
put command, 208
PVCs (permanent virtual circuits), 277

Q-R

querytype=X switch, 514

r switch, 509-510
rack mounts
    hubs, 113
    switches, 113
RADIUS (Remote Authentication Dial-In User Service),
    304
RADSL (ISDN DSL), 520
RAID (Redundant Arrays of Inexpensive Disks), 341,
    388-389
    choosing levels, 396-397
    hardware, 398
    software, 398
RAID 0, 389
    advantages, 389
    disadvantages, 390
    disk striping, 389
    recovering from failed arrays, 390
RAID 1, 390-391
    advantages, 391
    disadvantages, 391-392
    recovering from failed arrays, 392
RAID 10, 395-396
RAID 2, 392
RAID 3, 393
RAID 4, 393
RAID 5, 393
    advantages, 394
    disadvantages, 394-395
    recovering from array failures, 395
raido frequency (RF), 74-76
RAS, 292-293, 430
receiving devices, protocol functions, 176

-r count switch, 504
Recovery console (Windows 2000), 340
Redundant Arrays of Inexpensive Disks. *See* RAID
registered addresses, 243
/release switch, 512
remote access, 291-292, 304
    client configuration for remote servers, 308-310
    dial-up, 305
    enabling on Windows 2000, 307-308
    protocols, 292
        ICA, 298-299
        PPP, 295-296
        PPTP, 297-298, 301-302
        SLIP, 294
    RADIUS, 304
    RAS, 292-294
    services, 292
        RADIUS, 304
        RAS, 292-294
        SSH, 303
    SSH, 303
    troubleshooting connectivity errors, 534
        authentication failures, 534-535
        physical connectivity, 535-536
        protocol configuration problems, 536-537
    VPNs (virtual private networks), 305-306
remote access service. *See* RAS
Remote Authentication Dial-In User Service. *See*
    RADIUS
remote connectivity, 426-427
    dial-up access, 430-432
    physical connections, 427-428
    protocols, 428-429
    security, 432
    software, 429-430
removing
    network services, 447-449

/renew switch, 512

repairs, media, 65

repeaters, 89, 104

replication, Windows NT 4, 326

Request Timed Out error, 558-559

reset router command (NetWare), 349

resolution

DNS, 221

HOSTS file, 221

resolvers, 221

resources, peer-to-peer networks, 22

retry=X switch, 514

reverse lookups, DNS, 223

RF (radio frequency), 74-76

RI ports, 42

Ring In. *See* RI ports

ring network errors, 601

Ring Out. *See* RO ports

ring topologies

dual rings, 33

LANs, 32-33

RIP, 185

risers, 609

RJ connectors, 81, 88

RJ-11 connectors, 81

RJ-45 connectors, 81-82

RJ-45 network cables, 88

RO ports, 42

root=NAME switch, 514

routable protocols

AppleTalk, 119

IPX/SPX, 119

TCP/IP, 118

route commands, interpreting, 563

route print commands, 566

route utility, 515-516

routers, 116-118

brouters, 123

dedicated hardware, 123

network layer (OSI model), 163

routable protocols, 118-119

routing protocols, 119-120

distance-vector, 119-122

link-state, 122

server-based, 123

routing

AppleTalk, 191

loops, 121-122

metrics, 120

multiprotocol, 119, 122

protocols, 183

static, 119

Routing and Remote Access Service dialog box, 430

Routing and Remote Access Service. *See* RRAS

Routing Information Protocol. *See* RIP

routing loops, 120

Routing Table Maintenance Protocol. *See* RTMP

RRAS (Routing and Remote Access Service), 293

RTMP (Routing Table Maintenance Protocol), 189

S

s inet addr eth addr switch, 507

s switch, 509-510

sags, 402

Samba, 361, 365, 446

SANs (storage area networks), 411, 413-414

SAP, 185

SASs (single attached stations), 275

satellites, 428

microwave transmissions, 77

troubleshooting, 525-526

scalability, client/server networks, 25

screwdrivers, 549

SDH (Synchronous Digital Hierarchy), 279

SDSL (symmetric DSL), 520

Secure Sockets Layer. *See* SSL

security, 462, 482

   auditing, 487-490

   authentication

      Linux, 360

      Novell NetWare, 350

      troubleshooting remote access connectivity, 534-535

      user, 334, 352, 363

      Windows 2000, 342-343

      Windows NT 4, 333

   blocking port numbers, 483-484

   client/server networks, 24

   encryption, 160, 484-485

      3DES, 486

      DES, 485-486

      IPSec, 485

      PGP, 486

   firewalls, 142, 475-476

      application gateway, 477

      circuit-level, 477

      DMZs (demilitarized zones), 478-479

      functions, 476

      packet filtering, 476-477

   Linux, 362-363, 372

   logical, 465-466

      authentication, 466-467

      file systems, 471-474

      passwords, 466-471, 490-491

   logs, 330, 338

   media, 65

   network administrator responsibilities, 464-465

   Novell NetWare, 352-353

   operating systems, 323-324

   passwords

      backups, 407

      caps lock, 335

      shadowing, 359

   peer-to-peer networks, 22

   physical, 465-466

   protocols, 299-300

      IPSec, 300-301

      Kerberos, 303

      L2F, 301

      L2TP, 301-302

      SSL, 302

   remote connectivity, 432

   threats, 462-463

   Windows 2000, 344

   Windows 2000 Professional, 370

   Windows 95, 368

   Windows 98, 368

   Windows ME, 368

   Windows NT 4, 334-335

   Windows NT Workstation, 370

   Windows XP Professional, 370

security identifier (SID), 333

Security Policy Setting dialog box, 490

segments, 67, 75

sending devices, protocol functions, 176

serial (RS-232) connectors, 80

Serial Line Internet Protocol. *See* SLIP

server NAME switch, 514

server-based networking, 23

server-based routers, 123

servers

   addresses, WINS, 440

   callbacks, RAS, 293

   client/server networks, 23-24

   clusters, 137

   configuration, Novell NetWare, 348-349

DHCP, 219-220
    installation, 247-250
    obtaining IP information from, 451-452
DNS
    addresses, 440
    configuring, 441
    network services, 449
fault tolerance, 400-401
file storage, 411-412
hardware, failure rates, 387
member, Windows NT 4, 326
NetWare, 353
PDC (primary domain controller), 325
proxy, 479-480, 482
    caching, 480-481
    HTTP, 480
    NAT, 225
security, Windows NT 4, 334
troubleshooting, 585-593
    hardware changes, 593
    new applications, 593
    patches and updates, 593
    permissions, 593
    user accounts, 593
VPNs, 306
WINS
    addresses, 440
    configuring, 441-442
    installation, 451
    network services, 448-449
Service Advertising Protocol. *See* SAP
session layer (OSI model), 159, 161
shadowing (password), 359
share-level security, 324
shielded twisted-pair cable. *See* STP
Shiva Password Authentication Protocol. *See* SPAP
SID (security identifier), 333

signal regeneration, 64
Simple Mail Transfer Protocol. *See* SMTP
Simple Network Management Protocol. *See* SNMP
simplex duplexing, 67
simplex transmissions, 67
single attached stations (SASs), 275
single IP addresses, 479
single sign-on, 334
single-frequency RF transmissions, 75
size, peer-to-peer networks, 22
slash value, 237
SLIP (Serial Line Internet Protocol), 294, 428
small office businesses, troubleshooting networks, 516-519
    cable Internet access, 523-525
    DSL Internet access, 520-522
    POTS Internet access, 528-533
    satellite Internet access, 525-526
    technical support, 533-534
    wireless Internet access, 526-527
    xDSL Internet access, 520-521
SMTP (Simple Mail Transfer Protocol), 177, 209
SNA (Systems Network Architecture), 124
SNMP (Simple Network Management Protocol), 177, 226
    agents, 228
    communities, 230
    components, 226-227
    idenitifers, 230
    management systems, 227
    MIBs, 228-229
    versions, 228
software
    loopback tests, 553
    new, 594
    RAID, 398
    remote connectivity, 429-430
    requirements, PrepLogic practice tests, 708

solutions, implementation, 595

SONET, 279

sound file, 160

source-route bridges, 116

Spanning Tree Algorithm. *See* STA

Spanning Tree Protocol. *See* STP

SPAP (Shiva Password Authentication Protocol), 296

speed

    DSL, 521

    IEEE standards, 38-39

    modem connections, 127-129

    POTS, troubleshooting, 531

    UART chips, 128-129

speed lights, 132

spikes, 402

split horizon algorithm, 121

spread-spectrum communication, 75-76

SPX, 158, 178, 185

srchlist=N1[/N2/.../N6] switch, 514

SSH, 303

SSL (Secure Sockets Layer), 302

SSL/TLS, 343

STA (Spanning Tree Algorithm), 115

standards (IEEE), 36

    802, 37-38, 45

        Ethernet (802.3), 45-46

        Fast Ethernet (802.3u), 46

        FDDI, 49-50

        Gigabit Ethernet (802.3z), 46-47

        LLC sublayer (802.2), 45

        Token Ring (802.5), 47-48

        wireless networks (802.11b), 48-49

    802.3, 84

        1000BaseX, 90-92

        100BaseFX, 89

        100BaseT4, 89

        100BaseTX, 89

        100BaseX, 89-90

        10Base2, 84-86

        10Base5, 86-87

        10BaseT, 87-88

    access methods, 39

        CSMA/CD, 39-41

        demand priority, 43-44

        token passing, 41-43

        topologies, 44

    cables, 69

    Ethernet, 30

    media, 44

    speed, 38-39

standby servers, 400

star network errors, 599-600

star topologies

    hierarchical, 31

    LANs, 31-32

static routing, 119

storage area networks. *See* SANs

store-and-forward method, 156

    message switching, 109, 268

STP (Spanning Tree Protocol), 70-71, 115

straight-through cables, 111

subnets, 156

    masks, 236, 439

subnetting, 238-239, 240-241

surges, 402

SVCs (switched virtual circuits), 277

switches, 106-109

    ARP, 507

    cables, 111-112

    cut-through configurations, 108-109

    data-link layer (OSI model), 162-164

    dip, 133

    fragment-free configurations, 109

    full-duplex connections, 107-108

half-duplex connections, 107-108

indicator lights, 112

ipconfig utility, 512

labels, 112

managed, 113

microsegmentation, 108

nbtstat utility, 509-510

netstat utility, 508-509

nslookup utility, 514

ping, 503-504

ports, 110

rack mounts, 113

route utility, 515-516

store-and-forward configurations, 109

switching methods, 155-156

circuit switching, 155

message switching, 156

packet switching, 156

WANs, 264, 268-269

circuit switching, 267

message switching, 268

packet switching, 265-266

symmetric DSL, 520

SYN flooding, 206

Synchronous Digital Hierarchy. *See* SDH

System Information console (Windows 2000), 340

system logs, 331, 338

System Monitor (Windows 2000), 339

system requirements

Linux, 355

Novell NetWare, 345

Windows 2000, 336-337

Windows NT 4, 327

system resources, NICs, 134

Systems Network Architecture. *See* SNA

T

T-carrier lines, 272-273

tapes (backup), 470

cleaning tips, 403

security, 470

write protection, 407

Task Manager (Windows NT 4), 330-331, 340

TCP (Transmission Control Protocol), 157, 178, 206

OCI model, 206

ports, 214-216

TCP/IP, 118, 175, 179, 205, 213-214, 429, 437

addressing, 181

ARP, 212-213

configuring client systems, 439-441

DHCP, 218-220

FTP (File Transfer Protocol), 207-208

commands, 208-209

OSI model, 207

history, 179

HTTP, 209-210

HTTPS, 210

ICMP, 211-212

installation, 503

interoperability, 182

IP (Internet Protocol), 205

IP addressing, 233-234

broadcast addresses, 236

CIDR, 236-237

classes, 235

IPv4, 234-235

IPv6, 237-238

network addresses, 233

node addresses, 233

private address ranges, 244-245

public address ranges, 245

subnet mask assignments, 236

IPSec, 301
naming, 182-183
network services, 216-217, 232-233
    BOOTP, 220
    DDNS, 222
    DHCP, 217-220
    DNS, 220-224
    ICS, 224, 226
    NAT, 224-225
    SNMP, 226-230
    WINS, 230-232
NTP, 213
OSI model, 183
POP/IMAP, 210
routing protocols, 183
SMTP, 209
standards, 180-181
suite of protocols, 180
TCP (Transmission Control Protocol), 206, 214-216
Telnet, 211
TFTP, 209
UDP (User Datagram Protocol), 206-207
    HTTP, 210
    ports, 214-216
TCP/IP Properties dialog box, 440
tcpcon command (NetWare), 350
TDM (Time-Division Multiplexing), 66
technical support
    operating systems, 323
    troubleshooting Internet access, 533-534
technologies, troubleshooting, 587
Telnet, 211
terminal adapters, ISDN, 135-137
terrestrial microwave transmissions, 76-77
testing
    backups, 407
    NICs, 436-437

results of troubleshooting, 596
    TCP/IP installations, 503
tests, practice, 707
    customized, 709
    displaying scores, 710
    installing, 708
    modes, 708
    preconfigured, 709
    reviewing the test, 710
    timed, 710
    uninstalling, 708
text files, 160
TFTP (Trivial File Transfer Protocol), 209
thick coax, 70, 86-87
thin client technology, 298
thin coax, 69-70, 84-86
Thin Ethernet, 84
Thinnet, 84
    BNCs, 82
third-party vendors, 323
ticks, 120
time, troubleshooting, 586-587
Time to Live (TTL), 560
Time-Division Multiplexing (TDM), 66
timeout=X switch, 514
TLAP (TokenTalk Link Access Protocol), 189
token passing, IEEE standards, 41-43
Token Ring networks
    compared to Ethernets, 47
    IEEE standard (802.5 standard), 47-48
    MSAUs (multistation access unit), 42, 106
    token passing, 41-43
TokenTalk Link Access Protocol. See TLAP
tone generators, 551
tools, 500-501
    ARP utility, 506, 539-540
        cache, 506-507
        switches, 507

ifconfig utility, 511-512, 539

nbtstat utility, 509-510

netstat utility, 507-509

nslookup utility, 513-514

ping, 501-503

    DNS, 503

    switches, 503-504

ping utility, 539

route utility, 515-516

trace route, 504-506

trace route utility, 540

winipcfg utility, 512-513

wiring, 549

    hardware loopback connector, 553

    media tester, 552

    punchdown, 550-551

    screwdriver, 549

    tone generator, 551

    wire crimper, 550

Top utility (Linux), 356-357

topologies

IEEE standards, 44

LAN, 28-29

    bus, 29-30

    logical, 29

    mesh, 33-34

    physical, 29

    ring, 32-33

    star, 31-32

    wireless, 34-36

troubleshooting, 598

    bus network errors, 598-599

    mesh network errors, 601-602

    ring network errors, 601

    star network errors, 599-600

    wireless network errors, 602

Total Cache Buffers indicator (NetWare Monitor), 346

tping command (NetWare), 350

trace route utility, 504-506, 540

traceroute command, 360

tracert commands, 560-563

failure to get to remote host, 561-562

identifying congested network, 562-563

route names, 562

viewing paths to Internet destinations, 142

Windows NT 4, 332

translational bridges, 115

Transmission Control Protocol. *See* TCP

Transmission Control Protocol/Internet Protocol. *See* TCP/IP

transmission rates

microwave

    satellite, 77

    terrestrial, 76-77

RF (radio frequency), 75-76

transparent bridges, 115

transport layer (OSI model), 157, 161

flow control, 158-159

protocols, 157-158

transport protocols, 175, 178

trap managers, 227

triggered updates, 120

Trivial File Transfer Protocol. *See* TFTP

troubleshooting, 500-501, 584-585

ARP utility, 506-507, 539-540

checklists, 611

    cable problems, 611-612

    data access, 613-614

    network connectivity, 612

    network printing, 613

    NICs, 614-615

client connectivity errors, 602-603

    authentication, 604-605

    permissions, 605-606

physical connectivity, 606-607

protocol, 603-604

considerations, 586-588

development of escalation procedures, 595

diagnostic utilities, 557

ipconfig command, 568-570

netstat command, 563-568

ping command, 557-560, 572

tracert command, 560-563

winipcfg command, 570

dial-up connectivity, 431-432

ifconfig utility, 511-512

infrastructure, 609-611

ipconfig utility, 511-512, 539

media repairs, 65

nbtstat utility, 509-510

netstat utility, 507-509

networks, 588-589

changes, 592-594

documentation, 597

effects of solutions, 596-597

identifying affected area, 592

implementation of solution, 595

probable cause, 594-595

symptoms, 589-591

testing results, 596

NICs, 108, 436-437

nslookup utility, 513-514

ping utility, 501-504, 539

remote connectivity errors, 534

authentication failures, 534-535

physical connectivity, 535-536

protocol configuration problems, 536-537

route utility, 515-516

servers, 585-586

small/home offices, 516-519

cable Internet access, 523-525

DSL Internet access, 520-522

POTS Internet access, 528-533

satellite Internet access, 525-526

technical support, 533-534

wireless Internet access, 526-527

xDSL Internet access, 520-521

topology, 598

bus network errors, 598-599

mesh network errors, 601-602

ring network errors, 601

star network errors, 599-600

wireless network errors, 602

trace route, 504-506

commands, 504-505

isolating bottlenecks, 505

trace route utility, 540

virus, 596

visual indicators, 553-554

hub LEDs, 554-555

LEDs, 556

NIC LEDs, 555

winipcfg utility, 512-513

wiring, 608-609

wiring tools, 549

hardware loopback connector, 553

media tester, 552

punchdown, 550-551

screwdriver, 549

tone generator, 551

wire crimper, 550

workstations, 585-586

trunks, 29

-t switch, 504

TTL (Time to Live), 560

tunneling, 305

twisted-pair cable, 70

    5-4-3 rule, 88

    crossover, 112

    EIA/TIA categories, 71

    STP (shielded), 70-71

    straight-through, 111

    UTP (unshielded), 70-71, 87-88

twisted-pair networks

    connecting to, 435

    ports, 553

type=X switch, 514

U

UART chips (Universal Asynchronous Receiver/Transmitter), 128-129

UDP (User Datagram Protocol), 157, 178, 206-207

    HTTP, 210

    OSI model, 207

    ports, 214-216

unbound media, 68

unicast packets, netstat –e, 564

uninterruptable power supplies. *See* UPSs

Universal Asynchronous Receiver/Transmitter, 128-129

Unix, 321

    client system configurations, 446

    security, 472-473

    Telnet, 211

Unknown Host error, 559-560

unknown protocols, netstat –e, 565

unshielded twisted-pair (UTP), 70, 550

updates, 593

uplink ports, 110

UPSs (uninterruptable power supplies), 401-402

user accounts, management, 331

User Datagram Protocol. *See* UDP

user-level security, 324

users

    authentication

        Linux, 363

        Novell NetWare, 352

        Windows NT 4, 334

    changes to accounts, 593

    management

        Linux, 358-359

        Novell NetWare, 347-348

        Windows 2000, 342

        Windows NT 4, 331-332

    passwords, 469-470

    troubleshooting information, 590

UTP (unshielded twisted-pair), 70-71, 87-88, 550

V

vendors, operating systems, 323

version command (NetWare), 349

VHDSL (Very High Bit Rate DSL), 520

video files, 160

virtual local area networks. *See* VLANs

virtual private networks (VPNs), 262, 305-306

virtual-circuit packet switching, 266

virtual private networks. *See* VPNs

viruses, troubleshooting, 596

visitors, security, 466

visual indicators, 553-554

    hub LEDs, 554-555

    LEDs, troubleshooting, 556

    NIC LEDs, 555

VLANs (virtual local area networks), 386, 408

    advantages, 408-409

    MAC addresses, 410-411

    membership, 409

How can we make this index more useful? Email us at indexes@quepublishing.com

port-based, 410

protocol-based, 409

volumes, 398

VPNs (virtual private networks), 262, 305-306

-v TOS switch, 504

W

WANs (wide area networks), 26-27, 260-261, 269, 280, 282

ATM, 277

dial-up modem connections, 270

FDDI, 274

advantages/disadvantages, 275-276

compared to IEEE 802.5, 274-275

fault detection, 275

implementing, 275

Frame Relay, 278-279

internetworks, 27

ISDN, 270

BRI (Basic Rate Interface), 271-272

leased lines, 271

PRI (Primary Rate Interface), 271-272

private networks, 263-264

public networks, 261

advantages/disadvantages, 262-263

Internet, 262

PSTN, 261

SONET, 279

switching methods, 264, 268-269

circuit switching, 267

message switching, 268

packet switching, 265-266

T-carrier lines, 272-273

X.25, 278

WAPs (wireless access points), 126

war driving, 48

warm swaps, 400

Web-based mail, 211

wide area networks. *See* WANs

WiFi (Wireless Fidelity certification), 49

windowing (flow control), 159

Windows, 320

client operating systems, 367-370

client support, 365-366

client system configurations, 443-444

interoperability with Linux, 364-365

interoperability with NetWare, 364

Windows 2000, 335

Active Directory, 335-336, 444

application support, 344

authentication, 342-343

Client for Microsoft Networks, 444

connecting mapped drives, 52-53

disk drive management, 341

enabling remote access, 307-308

file and print services, 343

file systems, 337

installing AppleTalk, 195

monitoring tools, 337-338

Event Viewer, 338

Performance console, 338-339

Recovery console, 340

System Information console, 340

Task Manager, 340

performance tools, 337-338

Event Viewer, 338

Performance console, 338-339

Recovery console, 340

System Information console, 340

Task Manager, 340

ping switches, 504

security, 344, 473-474
system requirements, 336-337
user management, 342
Windows 2000 Advanced Server, 375-377
Windows 2000 Professional, 369-370
Windows 2000 Server, 489-490
Windows 95, 367
application support, 368
authentication, 368
Client for Microsoft Networks, 444
security, 368
Windows 98, 367
application support, 368
authentication, 368
Client for Microsoft Networks, 444
security, 368
Windows Components Wizard dialog box, 451
Windows Internet Name Service. *See* WINS
Windows ME, 367
application support, 368
authentication, 368
Client for Microsoft Networks, 444
enabling file sharing, 52
enabling print sharing, 52
security, 368
Windows NT 4, 324-325
application support, 334
authentication, 333
Client for Microsoft Networks, 444
domains, 325-326
file and print services, 333-334
file systems, 327-328
monitoring tools, 328
    Event Viewer, 330-331
    Network Monitor, 330
    Performance Monitor, 328-330
    Task Manager, 330-331

performance tools, 328
    Event Viewer, 330-331
    Network Monitor, 330
    Performance Monitor, 328-330
    Task Manager, 330-331
security, 334-335, 473-474
system requirements, 327
user management, 331-332
verifying network settings, 332-333
workgroups, 325-326
Windows NT Workstation, 369-370
Windows RAS, 430
Windows Security dialog box, 331
Windows XP Professional, 369-370
winipcfg commands, 570
winipcfg utility, 512-513
winipcfg utility dialog box, 513
WINS (Windows Internet Name Service), 230, 232, 511
configuring, 441-442
installation, 451
NetBIOS name resolution, 231
network services, 448-449
proxies, 442
server addresses, 440
SNMP, 230
wire crimpers, 550
wireless access points. *See* WAPs
Wireless Fidelity (WiFi) certification, 49
wireless media, 74
eavesdropping, 65
microwave, 76-78
raido, 74-76
wireless networks
errors, 602
IEEE standard 802.11b, 48-49
troubleshooting Internet access, 526-527
war driving, 48

wireless topologies, LANs, 34-36
wiring
    tools, 549
        hardware loopback connector, 553
        media tester, 552
        punchdown, 550-551
        screwdriver, 549
        tone generator, 551
        wire crimper, 550
    troubleshooting, 608
        identifying characteristics, 608
        identifying use, 608-609
workgroups (Windows NT 4), 325-326
    hubs, 104-105
workstations
    changes, 594
        network settings, 594
        new software, 594
        printer settings, 594
    troubleshooting, 585-586
wrapping (FDDI), 275
write protection, 407
-w timeout switch, 504

X-Z

X Window System, 298
X.25, 278
ZIP (Zone Information Protocol), 189
zones, AppleTalk, 190

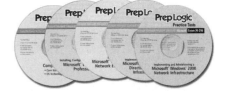